Multicultural Students with Special Language Needs

Practical Strategies for Assessment and Intervention

✦ *Third Edition*

Celeste Roseberry-McKibbin, Ph.D., C.C.C.
Department of Speech Pathology
California State University, Sacramento

Academic
Communication
Associates, Inc.

P. O. Box 4279
Oceanside, CA 92052-4279

Dedicated to Mike
for always being there

About the Author

Dr. Celeste Roseberry-McKibbin is currently a Professor in the Department of Speech Pathology at California State University, Sacramento. In addition to teaching at the university level, she continues to work on a part-time basis as a speech-language pathologist in the public schools.

Dr. Roseberry-McKibbin lived in the Philippines for much of her childhood and came to live in the United States permanently at 17 years of age. She has lectured and given workshops nationwide on issues relating to multicultural assessment and intervention. Her previous publications include textbooks, assessment instruments, and professional journal articles. She is a Fellow of the American Speech-Language-Hearing Association and is a recipient of the Upton Sinclair Outstanding Educator Award.

Academic Communication Associates, Inc.

P. O. Box 4279
Oceanside, CA 92052-4279

WEB: **http://www.acadcom.com**
E-Mail: acom@acadcom.com
Telephone Order Line: (888) 758-9558
Fax: (760) 722-1625
Printed in the United States of America
International Standard Book Number: 978-1-57503-139-2

Table of Contents

Preface to the Third Edition

The previous edition of this book, published in 2002, was written to provide special education professionals with information and strategies for working with the increasing population of culturally and linguistically diverse (CLD) students with special needs. Since that time, many changes have occurred within our schools in efforts to improve the academic performance of all students. Strategies for meeting the needs of multicultural student populations are evolving as educational professionals learn more about other cultures and their languages. Indeed, issues relating to the education of children from CLD backgrounds have become the focus of many workshops and training programs throughout the country.

Although changes are occurring, we still have a long way to go. Many CLD students continue to flounder in the classroom, and it is often difficult to determine whether or not a "disability" is the cause of their academic failure. Students continue to progress slowly in many classrooms because the instruction is not culturally and/or linguistically appropriate for their needs. School professionals must provide culturally and linguistically appropriate programs to promote academic development, language development, and ultimately the empowerment that will prepare students to function as successful citizens in society. These professionals also, however, must develop strategies that make it possible to serve CLD students who are truly in need of special education programs.

The third edition of *Multicultural Students with Special Language Needs* is written to provide school professionals with information and strategies so that they can work effectively with the growing number of CLD students who require various types of special education services. The book is based on research from a number of disciplines, including anthropology, linguistics, second language acquisition, health care, sociology, speech-language pathology, bilingual/multicultural education, and special education. The goal is to provide a multidisciplinary, well-rounded, and comprehensive view of CLD students.

A special challenge faced by educators in the schools is the appropriate, accurate identification of CLD students with special education needs. When a CLD student struggles academically, there are many questions that an educator needs to consider:

❑ Is the student a "typical" second language learner who is struggling because of limited proficiency in the language of instruction?

❑ What linguistic and/or sociocultural variables are playing a role in the student's performance?

❑ Is the student's performance in the first language similar to that observed among other students who have had similar cultural and linguistic experiences?

❑ Does the student have a disability that affects his/her ability to acquire language skills?

❑ What service delivery model is most appropriate for the needs of the student?

These questions are of great importance, for they determine the focus of assessment and ultimately the direction of the services provided to the student.

The current edition of this book includes an updated discussion of current practices in serving special needs students who come from CLD backgrounds, research information from recent studies, and updated references. Practical information is included about response to intervention (RtI) as well as best practices in nonbiased assessment. Chapter 16, a completely new chapter, addresses service delivery to CLD students who have language impairments associated with exceptional needs such as hearing impairment and autism spectrum disorder. Chapter 16 also addresses the issue of service delivery to internationally adopted children.

Literally hundreds of researchers and professionals in the field helped provide me with information and guidance during the writing of the first, second, and third editions of this book. To each of them, I owe much gratitude. I want to acknowledge Dr. Larry Mattes, Patty Schuchardt, and the staff at Academic Communication Associates, for all their help in making the third edition possible. My students at California State University, Sacramento, were instrumental in helping me revise and improve chapters from the previous edition of this book. Gretchen Hess and Sonya Musso were especially hepful. Finally, a project like this could never have been completed without the love and support of my husband, Mike McKibbin, and my son, Mark McKibbin.

The updated third edition of this book includes much new information and suggestions based on recent research and the experiences of practicing professionals. In fact, more than 600 new references are included, many of which are research studies supporting the information presented. It is my hope that this book will provide speech-language pathologists, special-education specialists, and other educational professionals with practical strategies that will enable them to develop high-quality, culturally relevant programs to meet the diverse needs of CLD students experiencing various types of learning challenges in our nation's schools.

Introduction

The ever-increasing presence of culturally and linguistically diverse (CLD) students in our schools is creating exciting challenges for professionals. Both general and special education personnel and administrators are being given opportunities to think creatively and strategically about best practices for meeting the needs of these students. Educators are evaluating their instructional programs and asking how these programs can be adapted to best serve the interests of CLD students. In addition to adapting instructional programs to meet the needs of CLD students, professionals are realizing that they must teach all students to appreciate cultural differences so that they can interact effectively with others who have different customs, values, and beliefs (Centeno, 2007). However, issues such as those described in the Preface can present substantial hurdles for professionals.

Providing appropriate services for CLD students can be quite challenging when these students have disabilities that affect learning. According to one estimate, approximately 10% of the members of all racial/ethnic minority groups have speech, language, or hearing disorders—the same percentage as in the United States population in general (Deal-Williams, 2002). However, at present the materials that are available for special education students who speak a language other than English are limited. Moreover, there are few special education professionals who are able to speak a second language fluently (Roseberry-McKibbin, Brice & O'Hanlon, 2005). Approximately 6% of speech-language pathologists are from linguistically and culturally diverse groups (for example, only 1.7% of the American Speech-Language-Hearing Association's members are Hispanic; [ASHA, 2006]).

What should a school do if a child who speaks only Vietnamese needs special education services? How does one determine if a child's learning problems can be attributed to limited proficiency in English or to a "disorder" that is affecting his or her ability to acquire language skills? Placement in a speech and language program is appropriate only for students who have been identified as having a "disability." Students with language difficulties resulting from limited exposure to English can be helped within the general education program and do not need the direct services of a speech-language pathologist. Distinguishing between language differences and language disorders is often difficult (Mattes & García-Easterly, 2007; Mattes & Saldaña-Illingworth, 2008).

The demand for special education services designed to meet the needs of students from diverse cultural and linguistic backgrounds has been increasing every year. The U.S. Bureau of the Census (2000) reported that racial and ethnic minorities accounted for up to 80% of the nation's population growth in the 1990s. In the year 2000, there were nearly 87 million persons from minority backgrounds living in the U.S., up 43% from 1990 (in the 1980s, the growth rate was 33%). Over the past 20 years, this population has grown by over 90%, whereas, the non-Hispanic White population has grown by 7.6%. Population growth among specific segments of the U.S. population during the 1990s was as follows:

1. The Hispanic population increased by 58%.
2. The Asian population increased by 48%.
3. The Native American and Alaska Native[1] population increased by 26%.
4. The African American population increased by 16%.
5. The Pacific Islander and Alaska Native population increased by 9%.

---

[1]The "Alaska Native" category is often reported in combination with both the "Native American" and "Pacific Islander" categories.

Researchers have projected that the percentage of residents of the U.S. who are White will drop from 75.7% to 52.8% between 1990 and 2050. It has also been projected that the percentage of residents who are Black will increase from 12.3% to 15.4%, the percentage of residents from the Asian and Pacific Islander group will increase from 3.0% to 8.7%, and that the percentage of residents who are Hispanic (of any race) will increase from 9.0% to 24.5% (Spencer & Hollmann, 1998). If trends continue, White non-Hispanics will be the largest minority group in the country by 2080.

From the 1992-1993 school year through the 2002-2003 school year, the number of limited English proficient students in public schools increased by 85%, whereas total enrollment increased by only 11% (National Clearinghouse for English Language Acquisition, 2005). In 18 states, LEP enrollment grew more than 200% between 1992-1993 and 2002-2003. The 2000 U.S. census reported that one in five school-age children is a non-native English speaker. As of the 2002-2003 school year, there were more than 5 million LEP students in schools from pre-K through 12th grade across the nation, representing 10% of the total enrollment (National Clearinghouse for English Language Acquisition, 2005).

Although experts acknowledge the great potential resource that multilingual, multicultural students represent for United States society, these students have often become academic underachievers with limited vocational and economic opportunities (Obama, 2006; Sue & Sue, 2008). In 1990, Sobol described the situation as follows:

> We are not always dealing well with this diversity. In our schools, the rate of failure is higher among people of color than among whites. In our economy, we are developing a seemingly permanent underclass, skewed by race. . . A society dedicated to liberty and justice for all its people cannot deny justice to some without betraying its ideals. Nor can our economy thrive with a permanently alienated underclass: we must help all young people to acquire the skills and knowledge they need to function effectively in the workplace. (p. 28)

Unfortunately, the problems described by Sobol in 1990 have not been alleviated. Many researchers and experts in the 21st century have described the achievement gap in American schools that exists between White children and children of color. Eschevarria & Short (2006) reported that the level of academic achievement for English Language Learners (ELLs) has lagged significantly behind that of their majority-language peers. For example, in California in 2002, only 11% of 7th grade ELLs who took the reading portion of the state test scored at or above the 50th percentile *as* compared to 57% of English-proficient language minority students and 48% of all students who took the tests.

When professionals consider this "big picture," it is clear that CLD students need culturally and linguistically fair, appropriate, and success-promoting materials, pedagogy, and placement options.

One major barrier to achieving this goal is that many professionals who work with these students lack the academic and experiential preparation to provide culturally and linguistically appropriate instruction (Eschevarria & Powers, 2006; Rosa-Lugo & Fradd, 2000; Roseberry-McKibbin et al., 2005). Although college and university courses are beginning to include subject matter relevant to serving these students, many practicing professionals have not received such training. This situation is improving, but there is still much progress to be made.

In a national survey of 1,145 speech-language pathologists, for example, Roseberry-McKibbin & Eicholtz (1994) found that 90% of them did not speak a second language fluently enough to provide services in that language, and 76% of them had completed no coursework addressing the needs of multicultural children. When this study was replicated in 2001 (Roseberry-McKibbin, Brice, & O'Hanlon, 2005), the percentage of respondents who had completed no coursework addressing the needs of multicultural children decreased to 27%, indicating that a greater number of students are learning about multicultural issues.

In yet another study assessing multicultural competencies, more than 85% of classroom teachers reported that they were not prepared to assess or instruct students who were learning English as a second language (National Center for Education Statistics, 1999). Clearly, universities and school districts must place a greater emphasis on educating professionals to meet the needs of these students.

A second major barrier to providing appropriate services is the limited availability of bilingual-bicultural professionals in the schools. In Los Angeles County, for example, over 90 different languages are spoken by school children. Other regions of the United States are experiencing a great influx of students from many language backgrounds. Often, there are no professionals who are of the same ethnic-linguistic background as these students. As one of its focused initiatives, the American Speech-Language-Hearing Association (see ASHA, 2001) is working to increase the numbers of racial/ethnic minority members of ASHA as well as giving all ASHA members access to resources developed to facilitate the acquisition of cultural competency. It is hoped that these efforts will increase and improve service delivery to members of multicultural populations. This is important because only a small percentage of certified speech-language pathologists are from racial minority groups (ASHA, 2003).

A third barrier to providing appropriate services is the limited availability of the empirical research necessary to develop appropriate assessment and treatment services. There is much research in the fields of second language acquisition and bilingualism, but this research generally focuses on individuals who do not have disabilities. In the fields of speech-language pathology and special education, few empirical studies provide scientifically sound information on which to base nonbiased assessment and treatment practices.

Empirical studies are badly needed, because a growing emphasis in many professions, especially speech-language pathology, is that of evidence-based practice (Kamhi, 2006). When providing services for CLD students, professionals must operate from the framework of evidence-based practice as much as possible. The American Speech-Language-Hearing Association (ASHA, 2005) stated that the goal of evidence-based practice is to integrate best current evidence, clinical expertise, and client values to provide the highest possible quality services to those whom we serve. Roseberry-McKibbin and Hegde (2006) (p. 615) described the importance of evidence-based practice:

> Evidence-based practice ensures that the clients receive services that are known to be based on reliable and valid research and sound clinical judgment....Most experts consider efficacy for treatment procedures to be a significant part of evidence-based practice. It is unethical to use treatment procedures that have not been supported by experimental research...Evidence-based practice requires an integration of best research evidence for clinical methods with clinical expertise and sound judgment. Evidence-based practice is always client-centered...In selecting assessment and treatment procedures, the clinician takes into consideration not only the research evidence, but also what is best for an individual patient and his or her preference.

A fourth barrier to providing appropriate services to CLD students is the time frame typically allotted for assessments. Many practitioners have found that the assessment of CLD students takes much longer than the assessment of monolingual, English-speaking students. Langdon (1992) estimated that assessment of a monolingual child, on the average, takes 3.5 hours. Assessment of a bilingual child, however, takes approximately six hours. In my clinical experience, assessment may take longer than six hours, especially when the child has a complex case history.

The final barrier to provision of appropriate services is the limited availability of appropriate materials (Roseberry-McKibbin, 2001b). Although there is an abundance of materials for working with ESL children, there are few published materials for special education professionals to use when assessing and treating CLD children. The lack of appropriate assessment materials and methods is particularly acute (Mattes & Saldaña-Illingworth, 2008; Roseberry-McKibbin et al., 2005).

Because these barriers operate together, professionals face serious challenges in trying to provide appropriate services to CLD students. With these issues in mind, each section in this book begins with an explanatory narrative of the topics to be covered. The goal of each narrative is to provide a theoretical context and rationale for the practical suggestions that follow. Readers will find many references for further reading and research of the topics covered. Practical "Monday morning" strategies for working with CLD students are emphasized.

The third edition of this book differs in numerous respects from the first and second editions. When the first edition of this book was written in the early 1990s, actual research regarding service delivery to CLD students was scarce. Thankfully, in the 21st century, more research has been conducted to support recommendations for assessment and intervention "best practices" with CLD students. Although the third edition of this book retains its practical, "how to" emphasis, it places more emphasis on actual research to support its recommendations and statements—especially with regard to service delivery.

Among the other changes contained in the third edition are the following:

1. The chapters relating to intervention have been expanded to include a wider range of topics relating to the development of language and literacy skills that are critical for academic success. Strategies are described, for example, that can be used to promote phonological awareness in CLD students with language-learning disabilities. Strategies are also presented to foster emergent literacy skills in preschoolers and literacy skills in school-age students.

2. Response to Intervention (RtI) strategies are described as they relate to the needs of CLD students.

3. An expanded description of simultaneous and sequential bilingual language acquisition is included to reflect recent research findings.

4. A totally new chapter has been added in this edition to address the needs of special populations. The chapter includes information pertaining to service delivery to internationally adopted children, whose unique needs are a growing challenge for general and special educators throughout the United States. The chapter also includes information on service delivery to CLD students who have disabilities stemming from conditions such as mental retardation and autism spectrum disorder. Recent research on the use of AAC devices with CLD students is also presented.

GOALS FOR THE READER

This book was written to help readers achieve the following specific academic and practical goals.

❏ The student will provide a basic definition of culture.

❏ The student will demonstrate cultural competence and awareness of factors that often affect communication between students, families, and professionals.

❏ The student will demonstrate awareness of general cultural and linguistic characteristics, including cross-cultural differences in communication styles.

❏ The student will describe normal second language acquisition and bilingual development in children.

❑ The student will demonstrate familiarity with laws and public policies that affect service to students from multicultural backgrounds.

❑ The student will demonstrate an understanding of the information that needs to be obtained to differentiate between communication differences and communication disorders in linguistically and culturally diverse populations.

❑ The student will demonstrate an understanding of the potential limitations of standardized testing and issues related to the use of alternative, nonstandardized methods for non-biased assessment.

❑ The student will demonstrate familiarity with procedures for using a team-oriented, multi-disciplinary approach to identification, assessment, and intervention.

❑ The student will demonstrate familiarity with educational program planning and the various options that are available for serving multicultural students.

❑ The student will demonstrate familiarity with effective intervention techniques/strategies and the materials available for use with multicultural students.

❑ The student will demonstrate the ability to write instructional goals that reflect a collaborative, holistic, communicative competence approach to language learning.

❑ The student will acquire knowledge that will facilitate effective interactions with families of students from diverse backgrounds.

❑ The student will describe the unique needs of special populations of CLD children, such as those who are internationally adopted and those who are on the autism spectrum, and will recommend practical service delivery strategies for these populations.

Again, this book was written to provide students and professionals with valuable, practical information that will increase their overall cultural competence and give them many research-based, hands-on, "Monday-morning" strategies for increasing and improving service delivery to the many CLD students in our schools.

Study questions are included at the end of each chapter to facilitate learning of the material. The appendices at the end of this book include information and reproducible forms that should prove to be useful in program planning.

There are no easy answers to many of the problems speech-language pathologists, special education teachers, and other specialists encounter in their efforts to identify and provide appropriate services for CLD students with communication disorders and other special learning needs. It is my hope that readers will be able to use the information in this book to maximize learning, to promote effective social interactions, and to help students become more accepting of others who have different customs, beliefs, and values.

Part 1

Cultural and Linguistic Variables Affecting Service Delivery

Chapter 1

LEARNING ABOUT CULTURAL DIVERSITY

Outline

Professionals who provide instructional services to students from culturally and linguistically diverse (CLD) populations must have an understanding of cultural characteristics and the impact that these characteristics have on students' performance in the classroom learning environment. Cultural behaviors affect how students interact with one another and how they respond to the learning experiences made available to them. An awareness of cultural differences is essential to ensure that students from CLD backgrounds are provided with appropriate educational programs. It is also important for professionals to be aware of the impact that an immigrant/refugee status can have on students and their families.

This book includes information about a variety of cultural groups to show the diversity that exists in our schools and to help professionals understand general trends within various cultural groups. The references cited can be used by professionals who need additional information about specific cultural groups. Learning about other cultures helps professionals to develop a better understanding of behaviors observed in the school setting. By becoming "culturally competent," professionals will be able to adapt their instructional programs to meet the needs of students from CLD backgrounds.

The understanding of basic issues relating to culture, race, and ethnicity is critical in the discussion of cultural competence. These terms are defined below.

KEY TERMS

- **Culture** (defined in more detail later) is the shared beliefs, traditions, and values of a group of people.

- **Race** is a classification that distinguishes groups of people from one another based on physical characteristics such as skin color. It is a statement about a person's biological attributes (Long, 2006).

- **Ethnicity,** a term sometimes confused with race, is the social definition of groups of people based on shared ancestry and culture (Murphy & Dillon, 2008). Ethnicity includes race and also factors such as customs, nationality, language, and heritage (Coleman & McCabe-Smith, 2000).

Professionals frequently use the term "minority group" when making reference to persons of various races and ethnic backgrounds who live in the United States. This term can be misleading and inaccurate. For example, California has large populations of African Americans, Hispanics, and Asians which, when combined, make Whites the minority group. Also, the term "minority" can denote a numerically smaller or politically powerless group in relation to a larger, dominant, and controlling majority (Murphy & Dillion, 2008). Thus, the term "culturally and linguistically diverse" (CLD) is more appropriate and will be used throughout this book.

LEGAL CONSIDERATIONS

The development of appropriate educational programs for students is challenging when students come from diverse cultural and linguistic backgrounds. Students from these backgrounds have often been misdiagnosed as having disabilities when they fail to achieve in the classroom (Hardman, Drew, & Egan, 2006; Oller, Oller, & Badon, 2006). Children with communication differences resulting from limited exposure to English may be misdiagnosed as having communication disorders if educational decisions are made based solely on the results of norm-referenced tests (Mattes & Saldaña-Illingworth, 2008). The law requires that all students be assessed using measures that are culturally and linguistically appropriate.

The Individuals with Disabilities Education Improvement Act of 2004 includes provisions relating specifically to the assessment of CLD students. Several aspects of the original IDEA (1997) were modified in the reauthorization. The need to reverse the trend of overrepresentation of non-native English speaking and CLD children in special education was one of the concerns that motivated policy makers to reauthorize the IDEA. The IDEA (2004) mandates that procedures and materials used to evaluate a child be provided and administered in that child's native language or mode of communication unless it is clearly not feasible to do so. It is hoped that administering assessments in a child's native language will help differentiate communication differences from communication disorders and reduce the likelihood that students are inappropriately diagnosed as having learning disabilities.

In order to understand what constitutes a communication disorder, one must understand basic typical, developmental features of the student's primary language. One must also be able to identify "errors" commonly produced in English that result from the influence of the primary language. These "errors" are not signs of a disorder, but of language differences. Students are not eligible for remediation in a special education program if their "problems" can be attributed to limited experience in using the English language; the students must demonstrate disabilities that impact performance in any language they speak.

In addition, professionals must recognize cultural influences that impact students' communication behaviors (Brice, 2002). Professionals who do not recognize the effect of cultural influences on students' communication are in danger of violating legal mandates that require schools to provide all students with culturally and linguistically appropriate assessment and instruction (Rojas, 2006). Therefore, before making decisions regarding a student's need for special education services, professionals must know what "typical" behavior is for the student's community and culture.

UNDERSTANDING CULTURAL DIVERSITY

Culture has been described by Cheng (1991) as a dynamic, multi-faceted phenomenon:

> Culture is dynamic, never fixed or static; it is learned and shared by a people; it is creative and meaningful to the lives of individuals . . . it has value and belief systems that guide people in their thinking, feeling, and acting . . . in short, culture is the total way of life of people in a society. (p. 4)

Culture can be viewed as a framework through which actions are filtered as individuals go about the business of daily living. Values are at the heart of culture; thus, when we study other cultures, it is important to examine their basic values.

One of the dangers inherent in the study of any cultural group and its values is that stereotyping and overgeneralizing may occur. Stereotypes can be viewed as a means of categorizing others based on perceptions that are incomplete.

Payne (1986) described stereotyping as follows:

> Stereotyping exists when an uncritical judgment is made about an entire group based on the actions of a few members. Sometimes stereotyping is the result of a misinterpretation or an exaggeration of an actual cultural behavior, either intentionally or unintentionally . . . generalizations about cultures or ethnic groups are valid only when influences of class and personality can be factored out or when historical evidence is unquestionable. (p. 24)

Galanti (2004) and Murphy and Dillon (2008) described the differences between stereotypes and generalizations. A *stereotype* is an oversimplified, fixed image we have of members of a group. A stereotype is an ending point. No effort is made to find out whether the individual in question fits the statement (e.g., "Hispanics have large families.").

Part of being a culturally competent professional is recognizing that each person in any cultural group must be viewed first and foremost as an individual. If we view people in some sense as "representative" of a culture, then we presume a homogeneous and fixed presence that can be adequately represented by those whom we serve. When learning about other cultures, it is important to understand that not all members of a culture have the same beliefs, values, or customs; much variation occurs within any cultural group. Professionals should keep in mind the great heterogeneity that exists within cultural groups. Although cultural norms tend to influence behavior, each individual and each family has unique experiences that influence beliefs, attitudes, and behavior.

A student who comes from a specific cultural group can be viewed through various "lenses." Professionals sometimes view students solely through the lens of their personal knowledge, experience, and biases. Many people have selective perception—what they look for, they find. This practice often leads to subjective and incorrect decisions regarding service delivery to students from CLD backgrounds. Professionals need to take a transactional and situational approach wherein individual students and their families are recognized as having unique needs, characteristics, and strengths.

It is my profound hope that readers will not be led to form stereotypes of other cultures as they read about cultural "tendencies" in this book. The values, behaviors, and customs described for a specific culture are not necessarily observed among the majority of people within that culture. It is also hoped that readers will have a sense of cultural relativism, not ethnocentrism.

Galanti (2004) discussed the concepts of ethnocentrism and cultural relativism. **Ethnocentrism** is the view that members of one's own culture do things the right way. All other ways of doing something are unnatural, inferior, maybe even barbaric. Proponents of **cultural relativism** hold the attitude that other ways of doing things are different yet equally valid; the goal is to understand other people's behavior in its cultural context.

The statement that "Americans watch a lot of baseball," for example, does not mean that most Americans enjoy baseball or that they spend a considerable amount of time watching the game. Americans do, however, have a tendency to enjoy baseball, although some have no interest in the sport. Much diversity exists within the "American culture" and within virtually every other cultural group. It is important for professionals to realize that individuals adapt to cultural expectations in different ways. By increasing their understanding of tendencies within various cultural groups, it will be easier for professionals to view students as individuals within the general framework of their community and culture (Roseberry-McKibbin, 2007).

Strategies that can be helpful in developing cultural competence are listed in Table 1.1. Increasing our cultural competence *must* result in more effective service delivery to CLD children. As Hegde and Maul (2006, pp. 332-333) stated,

> ...the quest for cultural competency should go beyond merely enhancing clinicians' intrapersonal qualities. We need evidence to show that cultural competence, once developed, will result in more efficacious therapy. In other words, it is not enough to ask clinicians to become culturally compe-

Table 1.1

Suggestions for Increasing Cultural Competence

1 **Team up with persons from the local cultural community who can act as interpreters.** Utilizing the knowledge and skills of these individuals is generally the best way to obtain the information necessary to serve multicultural students and their families.

2. **Read as much as possible about the family's culture and language.** Such information may be gathered from local community libraries, university libraries, and individuals in the community who are from that cultural group. In addition, references cited in this text (e.g., Battle, 2002; Brice, 2002; Goldstein, 2000; Lynch & Hanson, 2004) include excellent information about specific cultural groups.

3. **Visit students' homes.** Ascertain first that the family is willing to be visited, and choose times that are convenient for these visits.

4. **Evaluate your own assumptions and values.** Consider how your own assumptions and values influence your way of communicating information about students' achievements, instructional needs, and goals for school success.

5. **Consider the student's needs in the larger context of the family and community.** If you want the student to receive additional services above and beyond those available in the regular classroom, examine the student's needs within the context of the family as a whole. Be sure to include family members in the decision-making process.

6. **Consider the value system of the family when setting goals.** For example, educational professionals often stress the importance of helping physically disabled students become as independent as possible. However, in a particular child's culture, independence may not be emphasized or considered important; instead, family members may be expected to care for all of the student's needs. Intervention plans will not likely succeed unless the family's values and style of living are taken into account.

7. **Be aware that both verbal and nonverbal communication can affect a family's attitudes toward the school and the professionals working with the student.** Professionals need to show that they are truly interested in helping the family.

8. **Talk with individuals from a variety of cultural backgrounds.** Participate in social interactions with people whose cultural, ethnic, and linguistic origins are different from yours. This can be accomplished by attending holiday celebrations, community functions, etc.

9. **Ask students to share important aspects of their culture with you and other students.** Some students may not be comfortable talking about their cultural/language background. However, when students are willing to share, everyone benefits from this exchange.

10. **Learn some basic communication skills (e.g., vocabulary, simple phrases) in the student's language.** Many American professionals are monolingual English speakers. When these professionals begin learning a second language, their empathy for ESL students may increase greatly! In addition, multicultural families appreciate professionals' efforts to relate to them, even if they speak only a few simple phrases of the family's home language.

11. **Be aware that students from different cultural backgrounds may begin school with different cultural assumptions about human relations and about the world.** These assumptions may cause conflict for the student initially. Professionals need to be sensitive to this possibility, especially for students who enter the country as immigrants or refugees.

12. **Learn to pronounce and use students' actual names rather than just "Americanized" versions of these names.** Show an interest in learning how to pronounce the student's name correctly.

tent by learning about other cultures and linguistic differences. . .What is needed is to establish that such efforts will result in better treatment outcomes for children of all linguistic backgrounds . . . Ultimately, experimental research should demonstrate that specific clinical skills that presumably show cultural competence indeed result in effective services to children (and adults) with communication disorders.

Historically, the United States was viewed as a "melting pot"– people from around the world came to the United States, brought their cultures, and threw them into the American pot. The mixture was stirred and heated until the various cultures melted together. Today, it is common to describe the United States as a tapestry or mosaic. Differences are accepted and celebrated. Each thread of the tapestry is distinct and adds to the overall beauty of the object. Differences in ethnicity, religion, gender, and other personal characteristics are acceptable, worthy of being celebrated, and need not be abandoned in order for individuals to have equal opportunities to achieve their life goals (Dillon & Murphy, 2008; Weaver, 2006).

✐REFLECTION✐

Define *culture*. Why is it important to understand cultural tendencies of various groups with whom we work as professionals?

_____

_____

_____

_____

_____

CULTURAL VARIABLES INFLUENCING BEHAVIOR

Many variables influence the behavior of individuals within a culture. The manner in which services are provided may be influenced by general cultural practices in combination with variables unique to the individual. Thus, professionals must understand not only general characteristics of various cultural groups, but also the variables that interact to make each student and family unique within that cultural group. An understanding of these variables can be enhanced by interacting with family members and asking questions. Many families appreciate the opportunity to share their stories and appreciate being viewed as unique. The following variables are important to consider:

❏ Educational background of family members

❏ Languages spoken

❏ Length of residence in an area

❏ Country of birth (immigrant vs. native born)

❏ Reasons for immigration to the United States

❏ Urban vs. rural background

❏ Individual choice within the intrapersonal realm (e.g., idiosyncratic behavior)

❏ Socioeconomic status/upward class mobility in the United States as well as country of origin

❏ Age and gender

❏ Religious beliefs and their impact on daily life activities

❏ Neighborhood of residence and peer group

❏ Degree of acculturation into mainstream American life

❏ Generational membership (first, second, third generation)

❏ Beliefs about health care and disabilities

❏ Possible presence of post-traumatic stress syndrome

If the family immigrated to the United States, reasons for this immigration should be considered. It is also important to find out about generational patterns of immigration. To what extent are other relatives living in close proximity? To what extent are members of a cultural group marrying those from different ethnic backgrounds? These questions and all the above factors need to be considered when professionals provide services to students and families from various cultural backgrounds.

WORKING WITH IMMIGRANTS AND REFUGEES

Many professionals in the schools work with large numbers of students who are immigrants or refugees. The term **immigrant** is used to describe an individual who enters a country with the intention of becoming a permanent resident. The term **refugee** is used to describe an individual who flees to another country because of fear of persecution. Religion, nationality, race, political opinion, or an affiliation with a particular social group may account for the individual's departure from the homeland. An awareness of the effects that immigrant/refugee status have on students, their families, and the delivery of instructional services is a critical component in cultural competence.

For the purposes of efficiency in this section, immigrants and refugees are often referred to as "immigrants/refugees." It is important to remember that not all immigrants are refugees, and not all refugees are immigrants. Professionals should keep the above definitions and distinctions in mind when reading this section.

GENERAL BACKGROUND INFORMATION

The statistics below are integrated from the following sources: Holliday, 2001; U.S. Center for Immigration Studies (as summarized by Camarota, 2001; 2003); National Center for Children in Poverty, 2006; The Urban Institute, 2005.

❏ In 1900, there were 10.3 million immigrants to the United States. In 2000, there were 28.4 million immigrants to this country. The growth rate of the foreign-born population since 1970 is higher than at any previous time in history.

❏ On November 29, 1990, President George H. W. Bush signed the Immigration Act of 1990. This reform increased annual immigration in the United States to 700,000.

❑ The 11.2 million legal immigrants who arrived in the United States in the 1990s represented 43.8% of the country's population growth in that decade.

❑ The United States adds a new immigrant approximately every 31 seconds. More than 1.2 million legal and illegal immigrants combined now settle in the United States each year.

❑ The number of immigrants living in the United States has more than tripled, from 9.6 million in 1970 to 28.4 million in 2000. In terms of percentage of the U.S. population, the number of immigrants has more than doubled, increasing from 4.7% in 1970 to 10.4% in 2000. As of March, 2003, there were 3.5 million foreign-born persons living in the United States—the largest number ever recorded in American history.

❑ It is projected that 800,000 legal and illegal immigrants will enter the United States annually throughout the rest of the 21st century.

❑ Within the last 20 years, 80% of legal immigrants to the United States were from Latin America and Asia. Mexico has the highest rate of immigration and accounts for 27.7% of all immigrants worldwide, with 7.9 million of these immigrants living in the United States.

❑ There is enormous diversity among immigrants/refugees. They represent every echelon of society from wealth, privilege, and education to poverty and illiteracy; they speak varying degrees of English.

Profile

Thuy, a 12-year-old Vietnamese boy, was referred for a speech-language evaluation. He was making poor academic progress in comparison to other Vietnamese students, and an underlying language-learning disability was suspected. Thuy was the youngest of eight children and had spent the great majority of his life in Southeast Asian refugee camps. Apparently he had been placed in school at one point, but the family moved so frequently that he received a very fragmented education. He had minimal literacy in Vietnamese. The speech-language pathologist's challenge was to determine the extent to which Thuy's limited formal education was contributing to his lack of academic progress. Was Thuy truly language-learning disabled, or was he struggling because of lack of educational opportunities in his home country?

❑ Over 70% of immigrants to the United States live in only five states. The percentage of immigrants that settle in each of these states is shown below:

1. California (8.8 million, or 30.9% of the nation's total immigrant population)
2. New York (12.8%)
3. Florida (9.8%)
4. Texas (8.6%)
5. Illinois (4.1%)

❑ In the year 2000, there were 8.6 million school-aged children from immigrant families in the United States. Immigration accounted for most of the increase in public school enrollment over the past decades.

GENERAL CHARACTERISTICS OF IMMIGRANTS AND REFUGEES

Due to the great diversity among immigrants/refugees, it is impossible to construct a paradigm into which they will all neatly fit. The following characteristics are true of *SOME, but not all* immigrants/refugees. Students and families must be evaluated and served based on an understanding of their unique characteristics, backgrounds, and needs. They should not be stereotyped.

❏ Persons who wish to immigrate legally to the United States must meet the requirements of United States immigration laws. Medical screenings, for example, are required of *all* immigrants.

❏ Many immigrants/refugees are educated, financially successful individuals who come to the United States because of a desire for greater freedom and increased economic opportunity.

❏ Some immigrant/refugee students come to the United States with strong literacy skills in their native languages; others are illiterate and have had minimal education.

❏ Students from immigrant homes in which parents have a strong focus on education tend to perform better in school than those from homes in which education is not a focus (National Literacy Trust, 2006).

❏ Many refugees have spent time in camps in "countries of second asylum," during a period of transition while preparing for resettlement. Some refugees have even lived in countries of third asylum. For example, refugees from Vietnam might have lived in Cambodia and then in the Philippines before finally coming to the United States to settle permanently. Consequently, children may have had little or no formal education before coming to the United States.

❏ Historically, immigrants/refugees were encouraged to adopt American values and to speak English rather than their native language. However, the importance of respecting and celebrating linguistic and cultural differences is now recognized.

❏ Because of rapid recent immigration, children with immigrant parents make up a rising share of the nation's young child population. Immigrants comprise 12% of the U.S. population, but children of immigrants make up 22% of the 23.4 million American children under 6 years of age. By the year 2020, nearly 30% of all American children will have at least one foreign-born parent (The Urban Institute, 2006).

❏ There are some common ways in which refugees/immigrants adapt to United States culture. Locke (1998) proposed a model of acculturation that is based on attitude as well as involvement with one's culture of origin and also the society in which one is currently living. Locke delineated four levels of acculturation that professionals should be aware of as they work with refugee/immigrant families:

1. **Traditional**: Individuals do not adapt to the new culture and continue to adhere solely to the practices and values of their culture of origin.

2. **Marginal**: Individuals adapt minimally to the new culture.

3. **Acculturated**: Individuals adapt to the new culture but lose some parameters of their culture of origin.

4. **Bicultural**: Individuals retain strong ties with their culture of origin while successfully adapting to the new culture.

Profile

I held a parent conference with the mother of José F., a Filipino kindergartner. José had never been to preschool and was cared for at home by his grandparents while his parents worked. During his preschool years, *at* home with his grandparents, he had been allowed to watch approximately 10 hours of TV a day. Mrs. F. spoke Tagalog; her husband spoke Visayan; the grandparents spoke Pampango. José came to kindergarten at 4:9 years of age speaking no English.

José was referred by his teacher for a speech-language screening because he was struggling in class and she thought he might have a language-learning disability. The teacher said that José could not pay attention, follow instructions, or complete his work in a timely fashion. The Filipino interpreter said that José spoke so little of any of his Filipino languages that she could not validly assess him in any of the languages spoken. At the parent conference, Mrs. F. (a bright woman with excellent English) ruefully shared that she and her husband had virtually no time to spend with José. The mother had read a lot to José's older sister, who was doing well in school, but she was just too tired at night to do the same with José. I empathized with her situation and asked if she and/or her husband could read for just 5 minutes in the evening. She said that this might be possible. We did not place José into any type of special education program because we wanted to give him time to develop and adjust to the routine of school. José was provided with a peer "buddy" to help him with class routines and work.

ACCULTURATION

The term **acculturation** refers to the degree to which people from a particular cultural group behave in a manner that is similar to that which is pervasive within the culture. It is important for professionals to determine the degree of acculturation experienced by students and their families. Generally, immigrants/refugees who experience a high level of acculturation tend to have smoother transitions and experience greater success in the mainstream society. Factors that may result in a higher level of acculturation include:

❏ a relatively high level of formal education

❏ middle to high socioeconomic status

❏ being born into a family that has lived in the United States for at least a few years

❏ immigration to the United States at an early age

❏ limited migration back and forth to the country of origin

❏ previous residence in an urban environment

❏ extensive contact with people outside the family and/or ethnic network

Ideally, when immigrants/refugees acculturate to the U.S. way of life, they do not weaken connections with their families, communities, or cultural traditions.

DIFFICULTIES COMMONLY EXPERIENCED BY IMMIGRANTS/REFUGEES

The statistics and facts reported below are from the U.S. Center for Immigration Studies, as summarized by Camarota (2001, 2003) as well as The Urban Institute (2006), Han (2005), Huang, Yu, & Ledsky (2006), the National Center for Children in Poverty (2006), the National Literacy Trust (2006), and Van Hook, Brown, & Kwenda, (2003).

❏ Refugees leave their homeland for a variety of reasons. There are two types of refugee movements: *acute* and *anticipatory*.

    1. Refugees who anticipate leaving their country sense danger and leave early; they resemble voluntary migrants.

    2. Refugees in an acute movement situation, however, have not planned to leave their country and are not prepared for it. Most Southeast Asian refugees who came to the United States in the 1970s were in an acute situation; some made their decision to flee their homeland one to two days—or even hours—before their departure. As a result, they experienced many traumas and sometimes even abuses during their flight and were ill-prepared to adjust to their receiving country.

❏ Undocumented immigrants/refugees may be quite fearful of forced repatriation. If they must return to the homeland, consequences can be quite severe. For example, some Chinese repatriated refugees have been sentenced to forced labor camps.

❏ Undocumented immigrants/refugee workers may be treated poorly by their employers and paid less than the minimum wage.

❏ Many refugees have witnessed and/or endured oppressive and traumatic experiences such as disease, persecution, death, atrocities, forced labor, separation from family members, starvation, and forced dislocation. Such experiences can result in post-traumatic stress disorders, health problems, and many other negative consequences.

❏ Many refugee children have spent years in camps and have had little to no educational background (Hwa-Froelich & Westby, 2003; Vang, 2005).

❏ Many refugees/immigrants have been separated from their families due, in part, to situations in which some family members come to the United States while others remain in their homeland. It may be years before family members are reunited.

❏ Students may experience problems adjusting to schools in the United States with rules and expectations different from those in the homeland.

❏ Some immigrants/refugees from rural areas may have experienced difficulty adjusting to the technological emphasis in the urban work environment.

❏ Many immigrants/refugees experience substantial poverty in the United States, even if they are from middle-upper class socioeconomic backgrounds.

❏ In the United States, 28.8% of the native population live at or near the poverty level, whereas 41.4% of immigrants live at or near the poverty level. Among children of immigrants (those under age 21), 65% are from low-income families. Sixty-two percent of children of low-income, recent immigrants have a parent who is employed full-time, year-round, as compared to 51% of children of low-income native-born parents.

❏ Seventy-one percent of children of low-income, recent immigrants live with married parents, as compared to 42% of children of low-income, native-born parents. Forty-five percent of children of low-income, recent immigrants live with parents who do not hold a high school degree, as compared to 18% of children of low-income, native-born parents.

❏ The annual median income of immigrants is approximately 76% of that of U.S. natives; for the most recent immigrants, their median income is only 58% of that earned by U.S. natives.

❏ The proportion of immigrant households that receive welfare benefits is 30% to 50% higher than that of native households.

❏ One third of immigrants have no health insurance. Recent immigrants and their U.S.-born children account for much of the increasing population of uninsured U.S. residents.

❏ Of the many health issues faced by immigrants, the most challenging are those related to insurance and access to health care. Families' lack of access to health care is related to several key variables, including lack of knowledge of available resources, language barriers, and cultural barriers. Low-income immigrants are twice as likely to be uninsured as low-income U.S. citizens.

❏ Older immigrants who have moderate or heavy accents in English may encounter vocational and social barriers because of these accents.

❏ The United States has experienced a macro-economic shift from a manufacturing- and agricultural-based economy to an information-based economy. This shift has made circumstances more challenging for immigrants who are not educated and do not speak English; these immigrants are especially vulnerable to poverty (Vang, 2005).

✐*REFLECTION*✐

Describe two difficulties commonly experienced by immigrant/refugee students and their families. How might we as professionals help these students and their families to deal with these difficulties?

_____

_____

_____

_____

_____

POSSIBLE FAMILY CONCERNS

Many researchers have documented the existence of intergenerational tensions in families as they immigrate to the United States and experience changes in almost every area of life (Chan & Lee, 2004; Chen, 2006; Fontes, 2005; Han, 2005; Sharifzadeh, 2004; Sue & Sue, 2008; Westby, 2007). Some of the sources of tension are as follows:

❏ Young people often want to become Americanized, but they are expected by their elders to maintain traditional customs. For example, in many Hmong families, parents have strict curfews and expect girls to marry early and spend their lives bearing and raising children (Vang, 2005). This can produce conflicts when girls want to obtain a higher education.

❏ Children often learn English more quickly than their elders and thus become spokespersons for their families; this may usurp the elders' traditional role as authority figures. As Chen (2006, p. 581) stated:

> ...not only do children of immigrants learn to take care of themselves, but they also learn to take care of their parents. The tables are now turned in the United States, where immigrant parents must often depend on their children's help for English translation and various other tasks. What were once clear lines of authority are now muddled.

❏ Some family members (e.g., parents) must work long hours in order to survive financially and may not be available to their children for much of the day.

❏ Children may want to marry Americans instead of persons from their home culture; elders may greatly disapprove of this practice.

❏ The harmonious nature of marital relationships may be disrupted if women who have previously stayed at home and obeyed their husbands *must now* begin working outside the home to earn income for the family.

❏ Many families have traditionally been interdependent; the American social emphasis on independence may cause upheaval in families with members who rely on one another.

❏ Immigrants who received specialized training in their own country often encounter occupational barriers in the United States because their professional training is viewed as inadequate. They may need to "jump through the hoops" by completing additional schooling, obtaining additional credentials, etc. For example, an individual who was a heart surgeon in his homeland may end up working as a dishwasher in this country. Thus, families from middle-upper class socioeconomic backgrounds in their home country may experience new-found poverty in the United States.

❏ These families may be accustomed to having servants to care for their children and may be shocked to learn that in the United States, they are expected to do things such as transporting their children to therapy or helping them complete homework assignments.

❏ Many immigrants/refugees have suffered from great trauma in their home countries; often, their children may suffer from mental health consequences through the intergenerational transmission of trauma. Parent-child bonding and attachment may be negatively affected.

❏ Statistically, children in immigrant families may be at somewhat greater risk for abuse than children from non-immigrant families. The stresses described above may lead parents to abuse their children; in addition to the above-described stresses, many immigrant parents find themselves isolated and miss the help that was provided previously in their home countries by their extended families.

❑ Some immigrant parents may also discipline their children in public when they perceive the children to be acting disrespectfully or disobediently. This action can bring the parents to the attention of protection and advocacy services.

❑ Some cultures engage in disciplinary practices that would be considered abusive by U.S. standards. For example, in some Central American cultures, children may be given potions containing mercury to ward off "mal ojo" (evil eye). When children in Jamaica misbehave, parents may flog them. Many parents from Singapore believe that caning their children on the buttocks and limbs is the best method of punishment.

❑ Many immigrant parents, especially those from Asian countries, believe that in the U.S., their children have too much freedom and too many choices and consequently are disrespectful, "wild," disobedient, and difficult to control.

PUBLIC PERCEPTIONS ABOUT IMMIGRANTS/REFUGEES

As the number of immigrants/refugees to the United States increases, it is important to look not only at the facts and numbers, but also at the attitudes of Americans toward immigrants/refugees. Beliefs about immigrants/refugees help determine public policy, including educational and financial provisions and services. These provisions and services affect the availability of school resources that serve immigrant students. The attitudes of professionals toward immigrants/refugees also impact service delivery to these students and their families.

The United States is a nation of immigrants and descendants of immigrants. Some came voluntarily, others involuntarily. Immigrants/refugees bring many positive qualities to the United States. Many immigrants/refugees are diverse, young, and dynamic persons who have great potential to contribute positively to American society.

Many people living in the United States have negative feelings about individuals who immigrate to this country. These perceptions are reflected in increased legislation to stem the flow of immigrants into the United States. Many believe that these immigrants cause social and economic problems. Professionals who work directly with immigrants/refugees must make certain that they personally do not hold biases that could negatively impact the effectiveness of service delivery.

IMPLICATIONS FOR PROFESSIONALS

❑ The degree of acculturation and education of immigrant/refugee students and their families may affect how they view the general education curriculum and special education services. A highly-educated immigrant/refugee family might be more responsive to special education, for example, than a family with limited educational experiences.

❑ Students from undocumented immigrant/refugee families may suddenly "disappear" from school, possibly because of forced repatriation.

❑ Emotional problems that affect school performance may be experienced by students who have encountered great trauma. Help may need to be provided for these problems. Professionals can help students express feelings through art and writing. For example, there are art therapy classes that allow students to express their grief over loss of family members.

❏ When professionals collect case histories from members of immigrant/refugee families, they should remember that revisiting past experiences may be painful for some families.

❏ Professionals can facilitate mutual enrichment for both immigrant/refugee and their main-stream peers by asking immigrant/refugee students to share information about their home language, culture, and experiences.

❏ Professionals can also encourage parents to share their culture at their children's schools. Research shows that both immigrant students and their peers in schools are enriched when immigrant parents share their culture and life experiences with others (Carreon, Drake, & Barton, 2005).

❏ One of the best ways to assist immigrant/refugee families is to connect them with local support networks, especially those consisting of persons from their own culture who can provide needed information and resources (Roseberry-McKibbin, 2007, 2008). In Sacramento, California, for example, Russian immigrants have been assisted by Russian churches in a variety of ways.

❏ Pregnant female refugees who are malnourished may deliver babies with health problems or specific disabilities. In addition, many refugee children in our schools have poor health and/or medical conditions that may affect their ability to learn.

❏ Some families do not know the exact birth dates of their children; for example, refugees who are fleeing for their lives may not attach great importance to birth certificates and other records.

❏ Professionals should stress that their concern is to help the family. Some families suffer the daily torment of never knowing when and how they may be discovered and subjected to deportation (Zuniga, 2004).

❏ Some families may have difficulty planning for the future because they have put so much effort into trying to survive from one day to the next. Thus it may be hard for them to understand or appreciate the concept of long-term goals often emphasized in special education programs.

❏ Lum (2004) found that many of his clients who felt despair or anger because of hardship masked their feelings with flat affects. However, as they began to feel comfortable with and respected by professionals, they were able to relax. Professionals, therefore, should not take it personally if clients seem angry or "hard" initially.

❏ Many immigrant/refugee students need to acquire the practical, functional skills necessary to read bus schedules, use telephone directories, etc.

❏ In the United States, school is compulsory for all immigrant students, even those who arrive in their teens. However, in some cultures, adolescents are not required to attend school, which may result in a conflict between family traditions and values and American law. (In one dramatic instance in California, the mother of a teenage Vietnamese boy wanted her son to drop out of school so that he could help run her beauty parlor. After dropping out against his wishes, the boy ended up participating in criminal activities with his peers.)

❏ Because some immigrants/refugees may have had family servants in their native country, the children may be unaccustomed to caring for themselves and functioning independently and may therefore be viewed as "too dependent" by teachers and other school professionals.

❑ As previously stated, some parents may be unaccustomed to actually participating in their children's activities because they had servants to do this in their countries of origin. Professionals can sensitively share with the families that in U.S. culture, parents are regularly expected to engage in activities at home such as helping their children with homework.

❑ Because immigrant families tend to suffer from poverty in disproportionate numbers compared to native-born Americans, these families can greatly benefit from programs that would help them increase their English language proficiency so that they might obtain jobs that pay a living wage (National Center for Children in Poverty, 2006).

❑ Children of immigrants are less likely than children of natives to be in preschool programs or center-based child care; they are much more likely to be in the care of their parents. However, evaluations of Head Start and pre-kindergarten programs show that high-quality early education can benefit children's language and socialization skills as well as increase parental access to the community and its benefits (The Urban Institute, 2006).

❑ High-quality early-childhood education programs are especially beneficial to students from low-income homes. Research has found that availability and access are important factors; when pre-kindergarten programs are offered through public schools, Asian and Hispanic American children are more likely to participate (Takanishi, 2006).

❑ Professionals must constructively deal with parents who punish and discipline their children in ways that are considered unacceptable and illegal in the United States. Professionals need to ensure that parents understand U.S. laws regarding what exactly constitutes child abuse. Parents also need to be advised that if they break these laws, their children may be removed from their custody.

❑ Fontes (2005) suggested that professionals discuss child-raising goals with parents who use physical discipline. For example, all parents want their children to grow up to be successful, secure, and happy. Immigrant parents want their children to get good jobs and make their parents proud. Fontes explains to parents that their children are more likely to get good grades and good jobs, and be successful, if they are not hit or otherwise harshly physically disciplined.

❑ It is important for professionals to provide immigrant parents with appropriate, alternative methods of discipline and behavior management. For instance, professionals can help parents receive training and information about such methods as time-out, consequences (e.g., withdrawal of privileges), and others that respect the child's integrity, establish the parents' authority, and are culturally respectful to the family as a whole (Westby, 2007).

❑ In some countries, schools emphasize a specific set of morals or religious beliefs. Some immigrant parents may believe that American schools do not do this. In these cases, professionals can work with cultural mediators who may, if appropriate, encourage the parents to seek moral training for their children from local churches.

In her study of immigrant Taiwanese families, Chen (2006) showed that many families benefited from attending a local Chinese church. She stated that cultivating Christian virtues in one's children is consistent with traditional Taiwanese values of filial piety. In addition, Chen (2006) found that the local church also served as a support network where immigrant parents could disseminate information on family life. At Grace Church (attended by Taiwanese immigrants in this study), parents exchanged tips about a wide range of topics such as how to fill out college applications, teenage dating, the acceptability of children's wearing baggy pants, and others.

The church also offered a supportive environment to the children of the Taiwanese immigrant families who struggled with family issues. At one family night, an American-trained Chinese psychologist talked about how children may feel overwhelmed by parental pressure for academic achievement and how children may feel neglected by their parents' lack of emotional expressiveness. He also talked about parents becoming friends with their children. In Chen's words (2006, p. 593), "Although the idea of becoming friends with one's children is admittedly foreign to most Taiwanese immigrants, accepting this proposal is far more palatable under the aegis of a Chinese Christian church than an American secular institution."

Profile

Jose was a 13-year-old, monolingual Spanish-speaking student from Mexico. He experienced a head injury after being struck by a car and received language and cognitive rehabilitation at the local facility. Jose's family was very supportive of the services offered by the speech-language pathologist and often expressed gratitude for the services that were being provided.

After 34 weeks of treatment, Jose suddenly stopped coming to therapy. A somewhat incomprehensible phone message was left on the facility's answering machine. After numerous phone calls, it was learned that Jose's family returned to Mexico after being identified as "illegal aliens." The family left the country without any written documentation about the intervention program that had been provided.

CONCLUSION

American society has been enriched by immigration. Providing services to students and families from immigrant/refugee backgrounds can be both challenging and rewarding. As professionals work with culturally and linguistically diverse student groups, they expand their knowledge, become more flexible, and expand their expertise in service delivery.

STUDY QUESTIONS

1. Professionals are likely to encounter families who discipline their children in ways that are considered abusive in the U.S. How can professionals respectfully support these families as they transition into U.S. cultural expectations of appropriate child-raising?

2. Describe three ways in which professionals can increase their cultural competence.

3. Describe four specific ways that professionals can help immigrant/refugee students and their families.

TRUE-FALSE

Circle the number beside each statement that is true.

4. Multicultural students in public schools are eligible for special education if their primary problem is limited proficiency in the English language.

5. A good way to increase one's cultural competence is to attend social events sponsored by various cultural groups.

6. Immigrant families from middle- and upper-class backgrounds in their home countries generally experience a similar or higher level of success in the U.S.

7. In immigrant/refugee families, older persons who do not speak English are very grateful that their children speak English and are able to take care of tasks such as paying the utility bills.

8. Highly trained immigrants generally are able to find jobs in the U.S. that are comparable to jobs they had in their home countries.

9. Some families may find it painful to discuss the past when efforts are made to obtain case histories.

10. Families experiencing the **bicultural** level of acculturation retain strong ties with the culture of origin and successfully adapt to the new culture as well.

MULTIPLE CHOICE

11. Which one of these factors does ***not*** tend to impact a family's acculturation into U.S. life?
    A. Urban vs. rural background
    B. Educational level
    C. Neighborhood of residence and peer group
    D. Length of residence in an area
    E. Number of times church is attended each week

12. You are working with the Fa family from Beijing, China. They immigrated to the U.S. two years ago, and their sixth-grade daughter, Meuy, is experiencing some difficulties in the classroom. The classroom teacher tells you he thinks that Meuy feels as though she is "losing" some aspects of her Chinese culture as her parents work hard to adapt and fit into U.S. culture. Meuy and her family are probably experiencing which level of acculturation?
    A. Acculturated
    B. Traditional
    C. Marginal
    D. Bicultural
    E. Compensatorily cultural

13. Difficulties commonly experienced by immigrants and refugees include the following:
    A. Forced repatriation is feared.
    B. Students who have had servants in their native countries are often considered "immature" and "dependent" by American teachers.
    C. Separation from family members may make it difficult for them to function in society.
    D. Choices B and C
    E. Choices A, B, and C

14. When working with immigrant/refugee students and families, it is helpful for professionals to do which of the following?
    A. Ask immigrant/refugee students to provide information about their home language, culture, and experiences living in various countries and situations.
    B. Help families connect with local support networks consisting of persons from their own culture who can provide needed information and resources.
    C. Assure families that even though professionals may report their illegal status to the INS, services will still be continued if the families remain in the U.S.
    D. Encourage use of English in all social situations.
    E. Choices A and B

15. Which one of the following statements is FALSE?
    A. The 11.2 million immigrants who arrived in the U.S. in the 1990s account for 43.8% of the U.S. population growth during that decade.
    B. On November 29, 1990, President H. W. George Bush signed the Immigration Act of 1990. This reform restricted annual immigration in the United States to 500,000.
    C. More than 1.2 million legal and illegal immigrants combined now settle in the U.S. each year.
    D. California has 8.8 million immigrants or 30.9% of the nation's total immigrant population.
    E. It is projected that 800,000 legal and illegal immigrants will enter the U.S. annually throughout the rest of the 21st century.

ANSWERS TO STUDY QUESTIONS

    4. False
    5. True
    6. False
    7. False
    8. False
    9. True
    10. True
    11. E
    12. A
    13. E
    14. E
    15. B

Chapter 2

THE IMPACT OF RELIGIOUS DIFFERENCES

Outline

Islam
Buddhism
Confucianism
Implications for Professionals
Conclusion

As cultural and linguistic diversity increases in the United States, religious diversity also increases. It is important for the professional who works with CLD students and their families to understand their religious beliefs. These beliefs influence behavior and attitudes towards disabilities, assessment, and intervention for those disabilities (Dillon & Murphy, 2008; Roseberry-McKibbin & Hegde, 2006; Yamey & Greenwood, 2004).

Three of the major religions now represented in the United States are described briefly here. It is impossible to provide an in-depth description and analysis of each religion; the purpose of this section is to give the professional a general overview of each religion's basic tenets. These ideas and tendencies are described as generalities, not absolutes. Each religion has great variety within it and, therefore, each family and student must be considered individually. The information presented should help professionals to better understand how various beliefs impact service delivery. Moreover, the information should help professionals to become more sensitive to family dynamics that might be influenced by religion.

ISLAM

KEY TERMS

- **Islam** is a monotheistic (one god) faith. *Islam* means surrender or obedience to the will of God (Ott, Al-Khadhuri & Al-Janaibi, 2003). Islam, not Muslim, is the name of the religion.

- A **Muslim**, also spelled *Moslem*, is a follower of Islam.

- **Allah** (Arabic) is the term used for "God."

- **Muhammed**, also spelled *Mohammed* is the prophet and founder of Islam. He was born in 570 A.D. in Mecca, and began to spread his teachings around 612 A.D.

- The **Quran** (also spelled *Koran*) is the sacred book of Islam. It has 30 parts, contained in 114 chapters. A central message of the Koran is that submission to one god results in peace. The primary act of faith is to perform/obey the will of Allah in both public and private life (Haleem, 2004; Pridmore & Pasha, 2004).

- **Mecca** is the principal holy city for Muslims. Most Muslims try, at least once in their lives, to complete the *Hajj*, or pilgrimage to Mecca.

❏ Islam has existed for over 13 centuries. Today it is practiced in at least 180 countries around the world, with more than 1.2 billion followers worldwide (Mahmood, 2004). Muslims represent the majority of the population in 56 countries (Pridmore & Pasha, 2004).

❏ Islam is one of the fastest growing religions in the U.S. By 2010, the U.S. Muslim population is expected to surpass the Jewish population; this will make Islam the country's second-largest faith after Christianity.

❏ Most Muslims in the U.S. (77.7%) are immigrants; most of these (approximately 51%) have immigrated from the Middle East and South Asia. Approximately 32.2% of American Muslims live on the East Coast, 25.3% live in the South, 24.3% live in the Central/Great Lakes region, and 18.2% live in the West (U.S. State Department, 2007).

❏ Muslims believe that Allah revealed through the Angel Gabriel to the Prophet Muhammed the rules that govern society and that Allah gave mores for the conduct of the members of society. These mores are presented in the Koran, which is viewed as the literal word of Allah (Hall & Livingston, 2006).

❏ Muslims are not a homogeneous group; they represent a variety of ethnic and cultural backgrounds. Two major Muslim sects are the Sunnis (Majority) and the Shi'ites (Minority) (Afsaruddin, 2006). Approximately 90% of Muslims worldwide are Sunnis. Shi'ites comprise the remaining 10% and can be found primarily in Iran and Iraq (Hodge, 2005).

❏ Islam is a comprehensive way of life (Geaves, 2005; Karamustafa, 2003). Unlike mainstream Americans, who separate church and state, Muslims believe that religion cannot be separated from political and social life. Many passages in the Koran support a strong relationship between Islam, the society, and the state (Pridmore & Pasha, 2004; Stodolska & Livengood, 2006).

❏ In Islam, there are five basic *pillars,* or principles, that are commonly accepted by all Muslims (Ali, Liu, & Humedian, 2004; Shaikh, 2005).

1. The first pillar of Islam is the belief in one god and the belief that the prophet Muhammed was his last and final prophet.

2. The second pillar of Islam is prayer (*salat*). Muslims pray at five specific times during the day, turning toward Mecca and reciting a prescribed prayer.

3. The third pillar of Islam is *zakat,* or the alms tax. Most Muslims donate a percentage of their wages to help and support the poor and needy.

4. The fourth pillar of Islam is fasting (*sawm*), which is completed during the month of Ramadan (no food or drink from sunrise to sundown). Ramadan is the ninth month of the lunar calendar. In some areas, patriarchal hierarchies allow the father/senior male of the household almost complete authority over the rest of the family (Kobeisy, 2004). Family members believe that women should obey their husbands in all matters.

5. The fifth pillar of Ramadan is the Hajj, or pilgrimage to Mecca, to be performed once in a Muslim's lifetime. When they arrive in Mecca, located in southwestern Saudi Arabia, pilgrims are required to perform a complex set of rituals to commemorate the lessons learned by Abraham. Muslims believe that in Mecca, Abraham and his son Ishmael built the first house of worship on earth.

❑ Muslims are not supposed to drink alcohol or use drugs (Ahmad, 2004). Pridmore and Pasha (2004) stated that drug and alcohol use can result in severe punishment; the Koran prescribes 80 lashes, and local authorities may impose additional penalties.

❑ Muslims do not eat pork (Rasheed, Ming, & Humedian, 2004). Many Muslims eat only *hallal* foods, or those foods that come from an animal slaughtered in the name of God. The purpose of the slaughter is for all the blood to be drained, thus making the food cleaner and healthier.

❑ In some families, there is a traditional division of labor in the household; the woman takes care of the house, cooking, and children (even if she has a paying job outside the home). The man is the provider and makes the important decisions. He always has the final word (Hodge, 2005; Stodolska & Livengood, 2006).

❑ Some Muslim marriages are arranged; the bride and groom may not meet until the wedding day. Many Muslim parents prefer that their children marry other Muslims. I have personally spoken with young Muslim women in California who believe that arranged marriages are very beneficial. One 21-year old Pakistani student said, "My parents are older, and they love me. They know what is best for me and will make a much better choice for me than I would for myself. Why wouldn't I trust them?"

❑ Among Muslim Arabs, especially in nomadic and rural communities, families prefer that first and second cousins marry each other. This within-family marriage helps ensure that people marry a "known quantity" and also that money and possessions remain in the family (Omar Nydell, 2006).

❑ Many Muslims greatly frown upon divorce.

❑ Muslims are permitted to practice polygamy in some countries (Kobeisy, 2004). For example, polygamy is outlawed in Iraq and Tunisia, but the practice is allowed in Yemen, Jordan, Syria, and Iran. In some cases, court approval is required for such marriages to occur.

❑ In some Muslim societies and Muslim-American communities, polygamy is a religiously sanctioned practice. The Koran originally sanctioned polygamy in response to times of war, where widows and orphans were left without husbands and fathers. These widows and orphans were allowed to be integrated into previously-existing families. According to the Koran, a man may marry up to four women if he is able to treat them equally in all aspects (Ali et al., 2004).

❑ Women are valued as mothers and guardians of the family, and modest dress for women is regarded as symbolic of this value. Theoretically, dressing modestly preserves women's respect, dignity, and virginity and protects them from abuse and harassment by men. Modesty requirements may range from a simple *hijab* (scarf) to a full body and face covering (*burqa*).

❑ The wearing of coverings may be determined by individual preferences and cultural norms for each country, not just religious norms (Kopp, 2002; Ott et al., 2003).

❑ Kopp (2002) interviewed a number of immigrant Muslim women about their views on dress. She found that many preferred to dress modestly, viewing this as protective and as reflective of their level of spiritual development. They also viewed it as symbolic of their communal solidarity with other Muslims.

❏ Among some Muslim groups, sexual activity outside of marriage is considered to be so wrong that for a woman, it is punishable by flagellation, imprisonment, or even death. Forms of punishment, however, vary greatly from area to area.

❏ Islam encourages mothers to breastfeed their babies; breastfeeding may continue until the child is two to three years old (Hedayat & Pirzadeh, 2001). Generally, Muslim women do not breastfeed in public and only do so discreetly in front of family members (Ott et al., 2003).

✐REFLECTION✐

List and describe three Muslim values/practices that differ from those of mainstream Americans. Why is it important for professionals to be aware of these values/practices?

_____

_____

_____

_____

Profile

Nadiah M., a 17-year-old Muslim high-school girl on a speech-language pathologist's caseload, came to therapy one day feeling very unhappy. She related that next year, after her senior year of high school, she wanted to move to a different state and go to college to become a physician. Her father had become extremely unhappy with her, saying that she needed to get married and start a family after she graduated from high school.

A husband had already been selected for her. Nadiah explained that she wanted some independence and freedom. She wanted a career, she said, so she could support herself eventually if she needed to. The speech-language pathologist, who had several Muslim friends, talked this situation over with them (maintaining total confidentiality, of course). Upon their recommendation, the speech-language pathologist (who was female) approached a male Muslim teacher, Mr. Mojibi, at the high school and asked for his assistance and support.

Mr. Mojibi contacted Nadiah's father and an Imam (religious leader) from a local mosque. The three men had a conference. Mr. Mojibi and the Imam communicated to Nadiah's father in a sensitive and kind way that in Nadiah's family's country of origin, early marriage and motherhood were indeed very appropriate. However, they stressed that in the U.S., women are encouraged to be independent and prepare for careers to help them not only achieve financial independence but also support their elderly parents in their later years. The Imam spoke of several Muslim mothers, members of his mosque, who worked part-time outside the home and successfully balanced the demands of career and family. After some discussion, Nadiah's father agreed to allow her to consider pursuing her dream of attending medical school in a different state.

BUDDHISM

KEY TERMS

- The title **Buddha** means "Enlightened One," literally, a supremely enlightened person. The present Buddha is Siddhartha Gautama, a former Indian prince, who lived from approximately 584-563 B.C. Buddha is not considered to be a god; he made no claims to divinity. Rather, he is considered a great man and teacher, an ideal guide for those seeking enlightenment.

- **Karma** means that a person's fate or destiny in this life is determined by what happened in a previous life. Karma also embodies the principle that those who do good receive good and those who do evil receive evil.

- **Reincarnation** is the repeated cycle of being born into the world as we know it, until enlightenment is achieved.

- **Nirvana** is a divine state that liberates one from the cycle of reincarnation. It represents separation from pain and escape from misery and trouble. It is the highest state of spiritual bliss that one can achieve.

❏ Many Asians practice Buddhism. It is the primary religion in Laos, Vietnam, and Cambodia. Shintoism, a religion based on the worship of ancestors and ancient heroes, is practiced widely in Japan.

❏ There are various forms of Buddhism. The two primary types are *Theravada* Buddhism (found predominantly in Sri Lanka, Burma, Laos, Thailand, and Cambodia) and Mahayana Buddhism, commonly practiced in Vietnam, China, Korea, Japan, Mongolia, and Tibet (Topmiller, 2000).

❏ In the U.S., there has been a great deal of public interest in Buddhism, especially within the last two decades. Between 1987 and 1997, the number of Buddhist meditation centers in the United States doubled (Cadge, 2005).

❏ One's chance of a better life in the next rebirth is determined largely by the number of good deeds accomplished in the present lifetime. Buddhists are encouraged to avoid evil and to achieve merit. Buddhism emphasizes supreme human effort.

❏ Most Buddhists believe that meaningful life events such as marriage, birth circumstances, or serious illnesses can be affected by unknown past actions (Visscher, 2006).

❏ Four principles have been described that are emphasized in Buddhism (see Arond, 2006; Hanna & Green, 2004):

1. All of life is suffering and is inevitably sorrowful.

2. People suffer because they experience craving, are attached to the world, and are not content with what they have.

3. One must eliminate desire to extinguish suffering and attachment.

4. One can eliminate desire by living a virtuous life of carefully disciplined and moral conduct. This involves the eight-fold path of enlightenment, which stresses the right view, intent, speech, conduct, means of livelihood, endeavor, mindfulness, and meditation.

❏ To live a virtuous life requires the avoidance of lying, theft, immoral sexual conduct, excessive alcohol consumption, and various "frivolous" activities such as dancing.

❏ In Buddhism, there is an emphasis on accepting things as they are. Most Buddhists believe that suffering comes from our mind and heart. How we interpret and respond to what we encounter in life is responsible for our experience of suffering (Arond, 2006).

❏ Buddha believed that it is important to live in the present moment and to be mindful, or aware, of the present. Ultimately, Buddha emphasized that when we live in the present moment, it is possible to know true happiness.

❏ Quiet reflection is one of the most important practices among Buddhists. They may chant, or quietly repeat specific mantras or prayers many times. Meditation is a central practice for many Buddhists (Smith-Stoner, 2003).

❏ The individual's responsibility for actions taken is an important value among many practitioners of Buddhism.

❏ Some forms of Buddhism emphasize asceticism.

❏ Buddhists may visit a Buddhist temple when ill in order to facilitate the healing process.

❏ Some Buddhists may regard illness as a personal failure; there may be an assumption that if we are living truly spiritual lives, we will not be subject to illness (Rosenberg, 2000).

❏ Thus, if a Buddhist family is informed that a child has a communication disorder, the family may think that the problem is the fault of family members; if they were truly spiritual, the communication disorder would not have occurred.

❏ Buddhists regard a child's third, fifth, and seventh birthdays as extremely important. Families go to shrines on these birthdays and pray for the child's development (Nellum-Davis, Gentry & Hubbard-Wiley, 2002).

❏ Many Zen Buddhist temples hang prayer flags and lanterns on specific days of the year. Monks and members of a temple celebrate Buddha's birthday once a year by parading down the streets carrying images and flags of Buddha (Holden, 2004).

❏ Most Buddhists are vegetarians. Many practice acupuncture and believe in herbal therapy.

Profile

A speech-language pathologist worked at San Quentin prison with Phuong, an 18-year-old Laotian Buddhist. Phuong was in prison because he had shot and killed eight people in a drive-by shooting. The speech-language pathologist tried to help Phuong with his spoken and written English skills, as these skills were extremely low. Phuong said that he did not expect to improve because he had a "bad spirit." Efforts to improve his language skills were unsuccessful at first.

The speech-language pathologist talked to some Buddhist members of the community and, based on their recommendations, implemented a novel strategy to help Phuong. She tied a new white string around his left wrist. Many Buddhists believe that a white string represents "salvation." After Phuong started wearing this string, he told the speech-language pathologist that the bad spirit had left him and a good spirit had entered him. Phuong suddenly began to make progress in developing oral and written language skills.

CONFUCIANISM

❑ Confucianism was established by Confucius, a Chinese philosopher who lived from 551-479 B.C.

❑ The Confucian religion has approximately 6 million followers worldwide, primarily in China and throughout various Asian countries (Ontario Consultants on Religious Tolerance, 2004). The teachings of Confucius had a profound impact on China's history. The religion has been especially influential in Japanese, Chinese, and Vietnamese cultures.

❑ In pure Confucian philosophy, the terms "God" and "Heaven" are synonymous and imply a supreme spiritual state or being.

❑ Confucius did not discuss the question of life after death. The goal of Confucius was not religious salvation but, rather, full realization in the present life of human potential for virtue and wisdom. Pursuit of salvation in the next life is not the ultimate concern; rather, people should strive to bring vitality and prosperity to their families (Lu, 2002).

❑ According to Confucius, Heaven's will cannot be changed by human prayers. People need to follow their fate to seek harmony with nature rather than always attempting to change it (Hsin & Macer, 2006).

❑ Education is extremely important to followers of Confucianism. School is considered to be of utmost importance, and a formal education is highly valued (Dragga, 1999).

❑ Confucius' teachings of *jen, li*, and *yi* are the most basic fundamentals in Confucianism. Jen refers to ideal relationships between persons. These relationships should be characterized by benevolence, love, perfect virtue, and humaneness.

❑ *Li* indicates sociopolitical order. This involves ceremony, rites, courtesy, decorum, and etiquette. *Yi* means appropriateness, obligation, righteousness, and justice (Tsai, 2006).

❏ Followers of Confucianism believe that the universe is characterized by order, regularity, and harmonious integration of its parts; a person's highest calling is to devote himself to the accumulation of knowledge of this order. Hard work is prized. *Dao* refers to the law of the moral world, the path by which people travel. It is a living way that people need to follow in their daily moral relationships with other people (Chung, 2006).

❏ Confucianism strongly emphasizes harmony in human society (Herr, 2003). This harmony is achieved by each person accepting a social role and contributing to social order through proper behavior.

❏ Followers of Confucianism believe that hierarchy is natural. Almost all social interaction is defined by relative status differences. Common distinctions that guide interaction are gender, age/seniority, educational attainment, and place of employment. Each person is to act in accordance with his status to create a harmoniously-functioning society and to ensure loyalty to the state (Tsai, 2006). It is important to act in accordance with tradition and ancient wisdom (Nuyen, 2007).

❏ *Wulun* refers to the five cardinal relationships in Confucianism that emphasize acceptance of authority: subordination of subject to ruler, son to father, wife to husband, younger brother to elder brother, and mutual respect between friends (Doan, 2005; Liu & Regehr, 2006).

❏ Doan (2005, p. 460) states that "Confucian values also emphasize the superior role of male over female in the contexts of family, community and society. . .mothers and grandparents have important roles in shaping children's personalities and helping them develop morally through family education."

❏ Individualism is de-emphasized in Confucianism. The individual's needs and desires may need to be suppressed for the greater good of the group, especially the family. Individuals do not necessarily have inalienable rights and liberty; self-realization is not important. An individual is viewed in relationship to others, and "hence bears an unremitting burden of responsibilities and obligations" (Zhao, 2007, p. 79).

❏ In the view of Confucians, the life of each individual is only a link in that person's family lineage. An individual is a continuation of her ancestors (Lu, 2002). Ancestor veneration is very important (Visscher, 2006).

❏ Thus, the family's welfare and continuity are more important than the individual interests of any family member. Individuals are considered members not only of the living family but of a long line of ancestors and future descendants. Filial piety is a central principle that guides behavior. Central to filial piety is the concept of obligation and indebtedness to one's mother and father (Chen, 2006).

❏ Children are expected to revere ancestors and give parents unquestioning obedience and loyalty. Filial piety is so important to Confucians that if a child is very successful, the whole family shares in his achievement. However, if the child shows aberrant behavior or fails, the entire family loses face (Chen, 2006).

❏ Monarchical absolutism, filial piety, the subordinate role of women, and the family system are viewed as integral to the functioning of society.

❑ It is important for wives to produce male heirs to carry on the family line. If there is no male heir, a husband may divorce his wife to marry someone else.

❑ Confucius did not treat women as individuals in their own right; rather, he stated that they should be respected only through their maternal roles. Women are primarily defined through their husbands.

❑ Confucius stated explicitly that wives should be subordinate, and husbands should be dominant. Girls may be socialized to be able workers, obedient wives, and submissive daughters-in-law. In return, girls expect to rely upon their husbands and sons for their future security (Liu & Regehr, 2006).

✐REFLECTION✐

You provide special education programs for students in a school district that has just had an influx of families that practice Confucianism. When you provide service delivery to children from these families, what are two important things that you will keep in mind?

_____

_____

_____

_____

_____

_____

IMPLICATIONS FOR PROFESSIONALS

When professionals are aware of a family's religious background and basic beliefs, they can relate to the family in ways that are more sensitive and culturally appropriate. Some of the following implications may apply in various situations when working with families from diverse religious backgrounds:

❑ In some families (especially those from Muslim and Confucian backgrounds), a specific family member such as the father may be the spokesperson. It is considered inappropriate for professionals to address questions to the wrong family member during meetings relating to the needs of a student.

❑ If the family believes in seniority and authority based on age, the grandparents might have the final say in any decisions that are made relating to assessment and intervention.

❑ If there is a possibility of miscommunication between a professional and a Muslim family, it can be helpful to consult with an Imam, or Muslim religious leader. An Imam can help the professional understand legitimate religious variables that may be impacting a family's receptiveness to services and can also inform the professional if the family's negative reaction to services is outside the expected norm (Hodge, 2005).

❏ It might be considered inappropriate for a female professional to make any kind of physical contact with a male in the family (e.g., shaking hands).

❏ Many Buddhist and Muslim families prefer that professionals not work with family members who are of the opposite sex (Ott et al., 2003). Therefore, they believe that female professionals should not be allowed to work with male clients and vice versa.

❏ Muslims often have negative views of female professionals who wear "immodest" clothing. These female professionals should consider dressing conservatively when interacting with traditional Muslim families.

❏ Families of Muslim children may not want home-based services because they view the home as a private place (Campbell, 2001).

❏ Many Muslim immigrants find a great deal of support from other members of their mosque (Kopp, 2002). Support groups for families who are struggling to meet the needs of a child with a disability might be found in a mosque, and families may feel comfortable attending those groups.

❏ Students from Muslim backgrounds, after age 8 or 9, might not be allowed to eat during the day in the month of Ramadan. Professionals should try to avoid serving snacks during this period or offering food or drink to family members during meetings.

❏ Some Muslims discourage anthropomorphism. Thus, stories with talking animals would be viewed as inappropriate if used in the instructional curriculum (Nellum-Davis et al., 2002).

❏ Many Muslims are discouraged from disclosing familial or personal affairs outside the family. Self-disclosure and focus on the self (not the group) are discouraged (Ali et al., 2004). Because of this, professionals may have to take time to build trust and to not pry into "personal" matters too soon.

❏ Another important reason for professionals to take time to build trust with Muslims is that in the U.S., they may have been targets of hatred and discrimination, especially after the events of September 11, 2001 (Hodge, 2005).

❏ Bililci (2005, p. 55) stated that "The consequences of 9/11 on Muslims in the United States have been dramatic. First and foremost, the decades-old media habit of associating Islam with terrorism found its justification in the 9/11 attacks. Islam is perceived to be an inherently violent religion...."

❏ Most American professionals highly value direct, honest communication. However, among some Muslims, this directness may be viewed as selfish and insensitive to the need to maintain group harmony.

❏ If Muslims are led to engage in the behaviors of direct communication and confrontation, they may be considered selfish and insulting to their community. Muslims may be especially open to ecological, holistic interventions that incorporate family members and members of the broader community (Daneshpour, 1998).

❏ Families from various religious backgrounds may believe that disabilities (e.g., stuttering, cleft palate, etc.) are caused by the actions of God, fate, or a person's actions in a previous life. They may view a child's disability as part of some divine plan that was not meant to be altered (Shipley & Roseberry-McKibbin, 2006; Yamey & Greenwood, 2004).

❏ Some families may view a disabled child as a gift from God, sent to test the goodness of their character and their ability to take truly excellent care of this special child (Hedayat & Pirzadeh, 2001; Hegde & Maul, 2006).

❏ If the family believes that a child was born with a disability because of fate or because of actions that God has taken, intervention may be viewed as inappropriate or undesirable.

❏ Some professionals may view Muslims as not desiring intervention for children who have communication disorders. However, Khan, Roseberry-McKibbin, O'Hanlon, Roberts, Weger, & Roy, (2005) found that Sunni Muslim immigrants from Afghanistan and Pakistan in two California cities strongly supported rehabilitation/intervention for children with disabilities.

❏ In some Buddhist families, parents may feel that a child's disability is a result of their actions in a previous lifetime. Thus families may be willing to accept their "karmic fate" and may not support intervention or efforts at rehabilitation (Yamey & Greenwood, 2004).

❏ A family's belief that a disability is from God may conflict with the goals of special education. For example, a well-meaning school team may construct a detailed individualized education plan for a child with a disability, only to find that the family expects to care personally for the child throughout his life. Promoting independent functioning in that child is not a goal because the child will be well cared for within the family unit (Hegde & Maul, 2006).

❏ Parents may feel personally responsible for a child's disabling condition. In some religious belief systems, the actions of the parents are viewed as the cause of the child's disabilities. Professionals must be especially sensitive to emotional issues surrounding the student's disability and must work in a supportive manner with families who hold these beliefs.

❏ Some families may resist intervention efforts that are in conflict with their belief systems about life and death. Buddhist families, for example, often believe that disabled children will be reincarnated into a more whole form. The traditionalist Buddhist parents of a child with a disability may believe that the child's disability is part of his suffering in this life, and thus intervention to alleviate the suffering is not welcome (Heine & Prebish, 2003).

❏ The family may balk at medical practices suggested by professionals (e.g., pressure equalizing tubes to drain middle ear fluid, braces, surgery to correct a physical defect) if the treatment procedures differ from those used within the culture.

❏ Most Buddhist families believe that suffering is part of life and is to be accepted calmly. Thus they may not be willing to use medication in treatment. For example, family members may choose not to use medication to treat a child who has been identified as having attention deficit hyperactivity disorder (ADHD).

❏ Smith-Stoner (2003) recommended that in such cases, professionals might point out that medication could help the child focus better on religious rituals such as meditation.

❏ In some religions and cultures, girls are expected to marry at a young age (Vang, 2004). Their primary duties after marriage are to raise children and to be faithful wives. Education for girls may be viewed as less important than education for boys. Professionals might become frustrated if a female student has poor school attendance or drops out of school early to get married.

Profile

Nadia, a 10-year-old child, was from a religiously conservative Eastern European family with 13 children. She was absent from school frequently and experienced repeated academic failure. Her poor school attendance was an important factor to consider in determining her need for special education services.

Nadia's parents believed that a girl's role in life is to grow up, marry, and raise children. Nadia and the other girls in her family were expected to take care of their younger siblings. If her younger siblings were ill, Nadia was expected to stay home and care for them. The family believed that education was unimportant for Nadia because she would not need a formal education for her future role as a mother.

❏ Professionals should try to avoid scheduling major events on religious holidays if these events would be viewed as inappropriate. For example, planning a school party on the last day of Ramadan will be viewed as insensitive by some Muslims.

❏ Students may come from religious backgrounds that do not permit the celebration of holidays commonly commemorated in U.S. schools. For example, the majority of Muslims do not celebrate Halloween.

❏ Parents may pull their children out of school in order to celebrate or observe religious holidays or activities.

❏ Many public schools offer family life (sex education) activities for students. Some religious groups may object to this type of education.

❏ Some Muslim immigrants to the U.S. do not approve certain aspects of American life such as premarital sex, abortion, and the display of violence on television. They may protect their children, keeping them segregated from their American peers for fear of bad influences (Kopp, 2002).

❏ Some students who are fasting for religious reasons may not be able to participate in school activities relating to meals or food consumption (e.g., snacks given during therapy, bake sales, etc.).

❏ Among families with Confucian beliefs, conformity is very important. Most children are not taught to directly express their thoughts and feelings and may even be punished if they do. Zhao (2007, p. 85) stated that:

In societies endorsing Confucianism...the direction of the effort is always mostly toward the interests of the group/family/society. Little effort is made to nurture the child's nature for the sake of its own growth. When the original nature of the child seems likely to disrupt the social good, it is targeted, controlled, and oppressed. Children living in these societies are likely to experience suffocation and limited space for self-expression, self-fulfillment, and self-realization.

This belief in limiting a child's self-expression is in direct conflict with United States mainstream culture, which strongly encourages children to express themselves freely. Professionals must be sensitive to children from Confucian homes; professionals may need to encourage these children to be "bicultural" so that they feel comfortable expressing themselves freely in the classroom, but continue to show verbal restraint in the expected manner at home.

❏ For Confucians, it is important to defer to authority figures. Confucians generally do not disagree with the opinions of those in positions of authority and power (Liu & Regehr, 2006). Thus they may say what they think professionals want to hear but not follow through with actions that were "mutually agreed upon."

❏ If a child from a Confucian home requires special education services, the family may resist because they fear losing face. The child's "problem" may be a disgrace to the entire family. Thus, instead of writing an individualized education plan for the child and providing direct special education services to her, professionals may attempt to support that child through non-special education interventions, which will be discussed in subsequent chapters.

❏ Among Confucians, the family (not the individual) is the primary source of authority in decisions regarding intervention options (Fan, 2002; Tsai, 2006). Thus, professionals may find that a child's entire family wants to be present at meetings in which intervention plans are discussed.

❏ In addition, Confucians believe that family members should be interdependent. If a family member is suffering, he is supposed to relax and be cared for by other family members (Fan & Li, 2004). Thus, a family might view intervention from a professional as shameful; after all, they—the family—are supposed to be meeting the needs of the person who is suffering. Professionals should encourage families to share information and should be supportive.

❏ Because Confucian families emphasize group relationships so much, some children might feel uncomfortable if treatment is provided individually. Grouping these students with peers may be helpful.

❏ Professionals can take advantage of the high value that Confucian families place on education. If a child has special needs, professionals can discuss how a special education program might help the child become more successful in school and ultimately more successful in obtaining a good job.

Profile

Pablo, an 11-year-old male, generally participated actively in instructional activities in the classroom. When crossword puzzles relating to the Easter holiday were presented, however, he showed signs of disinterest. When asked to explain what was the matter, he said that his father disapproved of activities relating to the celebration of Easter. Pablo felt that doing the crossword puzzle activity was a violation of his father's wishes.

Profile

D.S., a southeast Asian girl from a Buddhist family, was referred to me for speech-language assessment. She was being considered for a self-contained special day class placement. I found out that D.S. had a unique medical history. She and her family were refugees who had spent time in Laos and Thailand. When they came to the U.S. and settled in Washington, it was discovered that D.S. had profound difficulties with her kidneys and needed a transplant. The family did not want to follow the Washington doctors' recommendations for the transplant or any type of "surgery." In addition, they believed that if they allowed her to pass away, she would be reincarnated into a more whole form where she would not experience the pain and suffering that would naturally be engendered by a kidney transplant. Finally the Washington doctors prevailed, and D.S. had the transplant. She had missed a great deal of school, however, and was far behind the other southeast Asian students academically. The team decided to place D.S. into a special classroom under the category of "Other Health Impaired." She worked with a primary language interpreter, and made excellent progress in all areas

CONCLUSION

It is critical for professionals working with CLD students to be sensitive to the religious beliefs of their families. Not every family will fit neatly into a religious category. Many people practice a combination of religions. When religious beliefs impact service delivery, professionals must be sensitive to the concerns of the family.

Often a professional can achieve the best results by working with an interpreter or religious leader from the family's culture who understands both the family's religious viewpoint and the value of intervention. If this cultural go-between can build trust and rapport with the family, chances of providing appropriate treatment to students will be greatly increased.

STUDY QUESTIONS

1. Describe the major tenets of Buddhism.

2. List six values that are important to Muslims.

3. How might some Buddhist families regard suggestions for intervention? What might their attitude be when a professional recommends placement in a special education program?

TRUE-FALSE

Circle the number beside each statement that is true.

4. Followers of Confucius believe that a child's third, fifth, and seventh birthdays are extremely important.

5. The religious group that often discourages anthropomorphism is the Muslims.

6. When professionals meet with Muslim families, questions should be addressed primarily to the mother because she is the family caretaker.

7. Confucianism has been especially influential in Japanese, Chinese, and Vietnamese cultures.

8. Buddhist families may resist intervention efforts because they believe that a child with a disability will be reincarnated into a whole form in the next life.

9. Many Confucians may, out of respect for authority, say what the professional wants to hear without any intention of following through on the professional's recommendations.

10. Followers of Confucianism believe that hierarchy is natural, and that it is very important in governing human relationships.

MULTIPLE CHOICE

Unless otherwise indicated, circle the letter beside each choice that is correct.

11. The philosophy underlying the belief that a person's fate or destiny in this life is determined by what happened in a previous life is called:
    A. Nirvana
    B. Ramadan
    C. Karma
    D. Hajj
    E. Asceticism

12. Shintoism is a religion that is practiced widely in:
    A. Vietnam
    B. Japan
    C. China
    D. Laos
    E. Cambodia

13. When working with Muslim families, it is important to remember the following:
    A. Women dress modestly because, theoretically, this modest dress symbolizes their role as mothers and guardians of the family.
    B. Most Muslims are eager for home-based services because they appreciate the convenience of having a professional come to them.
    C. Family ties are extremely important, and extended families are common.
    D. Female teachers are likely to be trusted more than male teachers.
    E. Choices A and C

14. Which one of the following is FALSE regarding general principles professionals should remember when serving students from various religious groups?
    A. Girls are encouraged to get an education, to have good attendance, and to participate in intervention if special learning needs are identified.
    B. Family members may believe that disabilities are caused by the actions of the child's parents.
    C. Female professionals may not be allowed to work with male clients and vice versa.
    D. Celebration of traditional U.S. holidays may be viewed as offensive.
    E. Parents may pull their children out of school to celebrate religious holidays.

15. Yousef, a Muslim 12-year-old male, has been diagnosed as having a language-learning disability. Which of the following may NOT be appropriate in his situation?
    A. Addressing primarily his father during the meeting.
    B. Shaking the father's hand warmly upon meeting him.
    C. Believing that Yousef's family will view intervention as the will of Allah.
    D. Telling the family that Yousef will receive intervention from a female speech-language pathologist in a one-to-one situation.
    E. Showing the family potential therapy materials that include books with interesting animal characters such as Donald Duck.

ANSWERS TO STUDY QUESTIONS

    4. False
    5. True
    6. False
    7. True
    8. True
    9. True
   10. True
   11. C
   12. B
   13. E
   14. A
   15. B, C, D, E

Chapter 3

FAMILIES FROM ANGLO EUROPEAN BACKGROUNDS

Outline

Anglo European English-speaking Americans continue to be the dominant cultural group in the United States. Many Anglo European Americans raised in traditional, middle-class, mainstream, monolingual English-speaking households have not had the opportunity to view their culture through the eyes of people from different cultures and/or other countries. Lynch (2004) stated that mainstream Anglo European Americans often have a limited awareness of the influence that their cultural background has on their behavior and interactions. The "melting pot" theory heavily influenced how the dominant culture expected immigrants to interact and behave during the early waves of immigration. Persons from "other" cultural backgrounds were encouraged to disavow their cultural and linguistic roots so that they could take on American customs and values, as described by Chamberlain (2005, p. 197):

> Mainstream, or dominant, U.S. culture reflects the European American values of the people who established the major institutions in this country. Although these value systems have taken on certain values of the myriad cultural groups that comprise the U.S. population, the mainstream culture's way of seeing and doing has been prominently maintained over many generations....

Thus, the purpose of this chapter is to help professionals from mainstream Anglo European American backgrounds develop a heightened awareness of unconsciously-held assumptions and values that influence their interactions with others. This knowledge will help professionals become more sensitive to cultural differences and how they might affect service delivery to students and families from various cultural groups. Most people tend to be less judgmental and more open-minded when they realize what assumptions they themselves hold (Roseberry-McKibbin, 2000a).

Galanti (2004) discussed the concepts of ethnocentrism and cultural relativism. *Ethnocentrism* is the view that members of one's own culture do things the right way. All other ways of doing something are unnatural, inferior, maybe even barbaric. Proponents of *cultural relativism* hold the attitude that other ways of doing things are different yet equally valid; the goal is to understand other people's behavior in its cultural context. It is hoped that this chapter will help the reader to adopt an attitude of cultural relativism.

GENERAL BACKGROUND INFORMATION

❏ The United States is the third largest country in the world (following China and India), with a population exceeding 280 million.

❏ The United States is slightly over 200 years old, making it one of the youngest countries in the world.

❏ The original inhabitants were indigenous peoples, primarily Native American Indians, who were displaced by European settlers beginning in the 17th century. The Europeans slaughtered Native Americans, spread diseases among them, and attempted to annihilate them in order to take over their land.

❏ Since that time, the United States, which has been composed primarily of people of Anglo European descent, has been rapidly changing in ethnic composition.

❏ In the 2000 census, Americans were given the option of selecting more than one racial category. In response, 97.6% of Americans chose one race category, and 2.4% chose two or more race categories.

❏ Racial and ethnic minorities accounted for approximately 80% of the U.S. population growth in the 1990s. In 1990, 43 million residents of the U.S. were minorities; in 2000, nearly 87 million residents were minorities (U.S. Bureau of the Census, 2000).

❏ Racial minorities and Hispanics now comprise approximately one-third of the U.S. population, and in the past 20 years have increased by more than 90%. In contrast, the White non-Hispanic population has increased by 7.6%. The growth rate was found to be at least 48% among Asians, 26% among Native Americans and Alaska Natives, 16% among African Americans, and 9% among Native Hawaiians and Pacific Islanders (U.S. Bureau of the Census, 2000).

❏ The United States was founded on Judeo-Christian principles and values. Most Anglo European Americans are Protestants or Catholics. Approximately 90% of Americans identify with a religion.

❏ The United States has prided itself on guaranteeing freedom and equal rights for all. White male Americans, however, have traditionally had greater access to these liberties than women and persons of color. White male Americans also have the highest median income of any group (Sleeter, 1994).

❏ White males make up 35% of the adult population in the United States. They comprise 80% of tenured professors, 80% of the House of Representatives, 90% of the U.S. Senate, 92% of the Fortune 500, 97% of school superintendents, 65% of physicians, and 71% of lawyers (James, 1999).

❏ White Americans still have the lowest poverty rate of any group in the U.S. Twenty seven percent of White children and 30% of Asian children are from low-income families. In contrast, 61% of African American children and 63% of Hispanic children live in poverty (National Center for Children in Poverty, 2006).

ANGLO EUROPEAN AMERICAN FAMILY LIFE

❏ Although the American family has been considered the basic unit of society, it has undergone substantial changes in the past few decades.

❏ Many American homes have been comprised of "nuclear families" that include the father, mother, and children. There has been a shift toward other family structures.

❏ Today, more American women are living without a husband than with one. In 2005, married couples became a minority of all American households for the first time. Overall, a larger share of men (53%) than women (49%) are married and living with their spouses (U.S. Bureau of the Census, 2005).

❑ In 1970, 81% of all U.S. households were comprised of "traditional," nuclear families with a mother and father present in the home. In the year 2000, 69% of households were comprised of families of this type (U.S. Bureau of the Census, 2004).

❑ Persons living with unmarried partners increased from 3.2 million households in 1990 to 5.5 million in 2000 (U.S. Census Bureau, 2004). The increase in cohabitation among unmarried persons was one of the most significant changes in family life in the latter part of the 20th century (Bianchi & Casper, 2005).

❑ In 1970, 90% of White children, 58% of Black children, and 78% of Hispanic children lived in households with both their mother and father. In 1998, those numbers had decreased to 74% of White children, 36% of Black children, and 64% of Hispanic children living in two-parent households (U.S. Bureau of the Census, 2000).

❑ The decline in married-couple families with children fell from 40% in 1970 to 24% in 2000. The number of persons living alone increased from 17% in 1970 to 26% in 2000 (Bureau of the Census, 2004). Today, one third of all births occur outside of marriage.

❑ An issue for children in single-parent homes is poverty. In 2004, American children living in single-parent homes with no husband present experienced a higher poverty rate (42%) than children living in married-couple families (9%) (Forum on Family and Child Statistics, 2006).

❑ Families are becoming more mobile; family members no longer live in close proximity to one another. The use of e-mail, cell phones, and other electronic means of communication are on the rise, but the amount of actual family face-face interaction has diminished (Darling, 2005).

❑ A major and pressing need for many modern American families is accessibility to high quality, affordable child care. Many American children are placed in child care programs and spend most of the day with caregivers other than their parents.

❑ American adults often feel uncomfortable living under the same roof as their parents. Elderly parents also often desire their own dwellings, preferring not to live with their children and grandchildren.

❑ Care for elderly Americans has become a more pressing issue. In 1900, the average life expectancy was 45 years old. In 2000, it had risen to 75 years of age. Many elderly need care and support from their families.

❑ However, with more fragmented homes and less multigenerational help, creative solutions for elder care are being sought. Family policy makers are facing the problem that there are fewer women in the role of unpaid caregiver for the elderly and also for children (Darling, 2005). This is true both for the elderly and for children.

It is common for Anglo European Americans to hold these beliefs about family members:

1. Children should be encouraged to be independent as soon as possible (Beane, 2006; Hwa-Forelich & Vigil, 2004). Families have high expectations for children to develop self-help and self-reliance skills. For example, approximately one third of American mothers breast-feed children who have reached six months of age; at that age, most American children are expected to drink from a cup. However, in many countries, children are routinely nursed until they are between 3 and 4 years old. Many mainstream American parents and pro-

fessionals consider it inappropriate for children to sleep in the same bed as their parents. However, many cultures view the practice of having infants and young children sleep alone in their own beds and rooms as neglectful (Westby, 2007).

2. It is natural for families to be mobile and to move from place to place. Adult children do not necessarily feel obligated to live near their parents.

3. After marriage, the husband and wife should no longer live with other family members. They should seek a home of their own.

4. There are specific places and personnel outside of the home to care for children and the elderly (e.g., day care centers, skilled nursing facilities).

✐REFLECTION✐

Matthew, a 3-year-old male, was brought to a speech-language pathologist by his parents. Both parents had doctorates. The father, who was born and raised in the Midwestern U.S., had concerns that his son might be "slow" because of several factors in the child's history. First, it was difficult to wean him from breast-feeding prior to 2 years of age. At age 3, Matthew was still not dressing himself and had only recently been potty-trained. The father was concerned because Matthew did not want to attend preschool and preferred to stay home with his mother. In addition, he was very quiet around other children, although he reportedly talked freely and in complete sentences at home. Matthew's mother was raised in the Philippines as the daughter of Baptist missionaries. She was not concerned about Matthew's development because his behavior seemed typical of that observed among many Filipino children. The father, however, insisted that the child be evaluated and, if necessary, seen for intervention.

What would you as a professional say to these parents? Does Matthew have a delay, or is the concern a by-product of the father's cultural values as an American born and raised in the U.S?

_____

_____

_____

_____

_____

EDUCATION AND LITERACY

❏ Education in the United States is compulsory for students from 5 to 16 years of age.

❏ Americans view education as a major determinant of professional and social opportunity.

❏ In American schools, the freedom allowed to students is greater than that allowed in many other countries. Parents educated in other countries may be shocked when they learn about the degree of freedom and informality available to American students. For example, in Hong Kong, it would be unthinkable for students not to rise and bow when a teacher enters the classroom.

❏ Many American children are expected to attend college, regardless of their innate capacity to succeed in the academic curriculum. Parents, especially those from middle- and upper-socio-economic backgrounds, generally expect that their children will complete college with at least a Bachelor's degree.

❏ White students from privileged neighborhoods tend to have higher educational and occupational expectations than most of their CLD counterparts, especially if those CLD counterparts are from low-income homes (Barnett & Camilli, 2002).

CULTURAL CUSTOMS, COURTESIES, AND BELIEFS

❏ Beliefs commonly held by Anglo European Americans have been reported widely in the literature (Beane, 2006; Ingram, 2005; Galanti, 2004; Hanson, 2004b; Hwa-Froelich & Vigil, 2004; Leipzig, 2006; Roseberry-McKibbin, 2008; Sue & Sue, 2008; Weaver, 2006) and are summarized below (see Table 3.1 for a summary of mainstream Anglo European American beliefs as contrasted with those of persons from other cultural backgrounds):

❏ Independence is extremely important; each individual's goal is to be as independent as possible.

❏ Individualism and autonomy are to be encouraged (as opposed to conformity). Many Americans believe in the importance of "looking out for number one." Group effort is not as important as individual effort and performance.

❏ Hard work is a virtue. The harder people work, the more industrious and valuable they are to their employers and to society in general. The desirable pace of life is driving, busy, and fast. Sitting quietly and doing nothing is considered a waste of time.

❏ Time is of utmost importance. Promptness and punctuality are necessary in social and work settings.

❏ Financial independence and material prosperity are hallmarks of success and of "making it" in life.

❏ Privacy for individuals is highly valued. Many Americans enjoy spending time alone.

❏ Youth and beauty are highly desirable. Growing old is often viewed negatively because physical attractiveness, strength, and ability supposedly diminish with age.

❏ It is each individual's right to challenge authority when injustice is experienced.

❏ Individuals have a great deal of control over their own destinies. It is believed that "God helps those who help themselves."

❏ It is appropriate for members of the opposite sex to show physical affection in public.

❏ If someone does a good job on a task, offering praise through public accolades is one of the most effective ways of rewarding them.

Table 3.1
Anglo European Beliefs and Values: Contrasting Practices

Anglo European "Mainstream"	Other Cultures
Materialism; more money and possessions equal success ("She who dies with the most toys wins.")	Detachment from money and possessions; spirituality
"Dress for success" ideal; wide range of accepted dress	Dress is a sign of prestige, wealth, position; often signifies religious beliefs
Eating is a necessity; often done as quickly as possible; "fast food"	Eating is a social experience; no rush to finish eating
Focus on nuclear family; child-oriented; youth respected and valued; status diminishes with old age	Focus on extended family; loyalty and responsibility to family; age revered; children may have much responsibility for well-being of entire family
Individualism; privacy; "looking out for number one"	Group orientation
Competition	Cooperation
Personal control over circumstances; self-help; internal locus of control: "God helps those who help themselves."	Fate; will of God or other higher *Being*; external locus of control
Work/goal/action orientation; rewards based on individual achievement; work has intrinsic value	"Being" orientation; enjoying life; emphasis on relationships; rewards based on relationships, seniority; work is a necessity of life
Efficiency, speed, punctuality; clock dominates ("the early bird gets the worm")	Relationships with other people dominate; time is secondary; quality of life important
Change highly valued ("That's so 5 minutes ago.")	Tradition; living in the past
Future orientation	Past orientation
Directness, honesty, openness; words carry bulk of meaning; conflict dealt with by confrontation	"Saving face;" indirectness; emphasis placed on context, or meaning surrounding words
Informality	Formality; use of titles important, especially for older and/or highly educated people
Human equality ("All men are created equal."); status and power ideally dependent on one's personal qualities (not sex, age, family)	Hierarchy, rank, status; importance of *family;* Status based on variables such as gender, occupation, family heritage

Compiled based on information reported in the following sources: Beane, M. (2006); Galanti, G. (2004); Gardenswartz, L., & Rowe, A. (1994); Hanson, M. (2004b); Hegde, M.N., & Maul, C. (2006); Hwa-Froelich, D.A. & Vigil, D.C. (2004); Ingram, L. (2005); Leipzig, C. (2006); Roseberry-McKibbin, C. (2008); Sue, D., & Sue, D. (2008); Weaver, G. (2006); Westby, C. (2007)

❑ All people are created equal and have the same rights. Women are equal to men; people from various ethnic groups are equal to each other. State and federal laws mandate equality of treatment for workers regardless of gender, ethnic background, age, and lifestyle orientation.

❑ Ideally, women should be allowed to have the same work opportunities as men and should be given equal pay for their work. However, this idea is not practiced in many work settings. American women tend to earn less than American men who hold similar jobs.

❑ Speed and efficiency are extremely important when completing any task. The rapid completion of tasks is valued. "Time is money."

❑ People must plan for the future. Progress and change are high priorities. The present must take second place to the needs of the future. The past is not as important.

❑ Change is equated with progress. Holding onto traditions may seem outdated and old-fashioned.

❑ Competition is a way of life, and it is healthy for children to learn to compete at an early age.

❑ Cleanliness is of utmost importance; natural odors should be covered by using perfume or deodorant.

Profile

Meghan K. was a 16-year-old girl from an Anglo English-speaking home. Her father was a high school physical education instructor, and her mother had full-time employment inside the home caring for Meghan and her younger brother. The family came from a middle-class neighborhood. Meghan was born with the umbilical cord wrapped tightly around her neck, resulting in fetal anoxia. Meghan was slow in reaching developmental milestones, and she had been in special education settings since kindergarten. The speech-language pathologist at Meghan's high school was asked to carry out a comprehensive speech and language assessment so that Meghan could be placed in the most appropriate setting. The results indicated that Meghan was functioning approximately seven years below her chronological age. Assessment data obtained by the school psychologist indicated that she had a full-scale IQ of 70, a score that is considerably below normal.

The assessment team recommended that Meghan continue in special education and that she participate in a vocational training program designed specifically for students with special learning needs. Meghan's parents were incensed, and the meeting lasted for 3 hours. The parents felt outraged that a "vocational track" was recommended for their daughter. They shared that she was going to go to college, and they were determined to see that she attended the best college available. The parents were not interested in special education for their child in her high school years.

HEALTH CARE AND DISABLING CONDITIONS

❑ Traditional American health care has focused on cures for illness rather than prevention, although this may be changing in some areas. Many insurance companies cover few, if any, costs for preventative care.

❏ American medical practitioners tend to separate illnesses of the body and mind, in contrast to other cultures in which the body and mind are seen holistically as being inseparable.

❏ American medicine relies greatly on technology. American medical technology has made it possible for many disabled and elderly individuals to maintain "life" that relies almost exclusively on expensive, highly technological mechanical support.

❏ In recent decades, the American legal system has mandated that persons with disabilities be given equal access to education and jobs.

❏ Most Americans believe that disabilities can be caused by variables such as genetics, trauma, disease, and teratogens (e.g., toxins).

❏ Most Americans, believing in mastery over nature, expect that someone who has an illness or disability will struggle against these circumstances and overcome them (Yamey & Greenwood, 2004).

❏ HIV/AIDS is a growing problem in the United States. Another increasing problem is obesity in both children and adults. Obesity in children has become of particular concern (Darling, 2005).

❏ Health and fitness are popular trends, especially on the West Coast. Many people try to exercise regularly. Hundreds of products are labeled "low cholesterol" and "low fat" (Galanti, 2004).

Profile

A Hmong child was hospitalized after undergoing surgery for a cleft palate. The American speech-language pathologist smelled smoke one afternoon when walking past the child's room. After calling for fire extinguishers, she entered the room to discover that the family had made a small fire under the child's hospital bed. The family believed that the smoke from the fire would drive out the evil spirits that had caused the cleft palate. The speech-language pathologist made an appointment with the hospital's Hmong interpreter to discuss how they might best approach the family to discuss their perspective regarding communication disorders, medical issues, and their treatment.

ANGLO EUROPEAN AMERICAN COMMUNICATION STYLES

❏ It is generally considered impolite to ask personal questions of others. For instance, asking people to reveal information about their salary is considered inappropriate in most contexts. It is also considered rude to ask people to reveal their age.

❏ Americans tend to be friendly and to make informality a goal in interactions. For example, many Americans will call others by their first names only, not using titles even if the other person is older and/or more highly educated. This may seem discourteous and "uncultured" to people from other cultural groups.

❏ When two Americans converse, they generally stand about two feet apart.

❏ Americans tend to be outspoken and frank; they appreciate these same qualities in others. Cultural value is attached to the person who is forthright, does not beat around the bush, and is not "two-faced" (Zhao, 2007).

❏ In professional situations such as meetings, most Americans get to the point immediately with little preamble or small talk.

❏ Most Americans rely more on verbal than nonverbal messages; this can be termed "low-context" communication.

❏ When talking to others, Americans generally consider it important to make direct eye contact and to maintain an open yet assertive physical stance.

❏ Americans believe that directness and assertiveness are critical in interactions with other people. For example, if one is angry at another person, this feeling may be expressed directly. Candidness is valued.

❏ In the United States, people believe that good listeners make eye contact, ask questions, indicate when they do not understand something, nod occasionally, and make facial expressions that indicate empathy with and interest in their conversational partners.

❏ American children from mainstream homes are generally encouraged to express their opinions, thoughts, needs, and wishes freely. In most mainstream American school classrooms, highly verbal students are rewarded in various ways.

ANGLO EUROPEAN AMERICAN LANGUAGE CONSIDERATIONS

❏ Many citizens of the United States speak Mainstream American English (MAE), also referred to as Standard American English. The historical, financial, legal, scientific, and educational foundations of the United States are recorded in Mainstream American English (McLaughlin, 2006).

❏ Americans from different areas of the United States speak different dialects but are still able to understand one another. There are at least 10 regional dialects in the United States. These include Eastern New England, New York City, Western Pennsylvania, Middle Atlantic, Appalachian, Southern, Central Midland, North Central, Southwest, and Northwest (Owens, 2005).

✐REFLECTION✐

List four qualities of "good" communicators from an Anglo European American perspective. How might these qualities conflict with the communication expectations and practices of students and families from other cultural backgrounds?

_____

_____

_____

_____

_____

IMPLICATIONS FOR PROFESSIONALS

It is important to remember that people from different backgrounds often have cultural assumptions that differ from those of "mainstream" Americans. Again, it is crucial not to make judgments about which cultural attitudes are right or wrong. Much can be learned by interacting with others who have beliefs, ideas, and styles of living different from one's own. As previously stated, adapting a position of cultural relativism is encouraged.

The following guidelines should help professionals to reduce the negative impact of mainstream U.S. assumptions during interactions with individuals from other cultural groups.

❑ Professionals should use titles when addressing adults from other cultures. Addressing others by their first names, a common practice among American professionals, may be viewed as offensively over-familiar to some families. It is probably best to err on the side of being too formal when working with persons from different cultures.

❑ Persons from some cultures (e.g., Filipino) may ask personal questions such as "Are you married?" or "Why don't you have any children?" (Roseberry-McKibbin, 1997b). Professionals need to be aware that questions such as these are considered appropriate within some cultural groups.

❑ Professionals need to be patient and open. Because many Americans believe in their personal ability to shape and control their own future, they may be less tolerant of those who believe in fate or outside forces that they cannot control. Professionals should not label these persons as being "passive" (Yamey & Greenwood, 2004).

❑ Professionals should take time to engage in preliminary courtesies. American professionals must remember that it is considered rude in some cultures (e.g., Hispanic, Arab) to delve immediately into business without small talk and some conversational preamble (Brice, 2002; Shipley & Roseberry-McKibbin, 2006).

❑ American professionals must remember that most cultures value the family unit highly. Professionals must work with students and their families, rather than working only with students.

❑ Older immigrant parents often expect their adult children to provide for them in old age. For example, one Filipino mother-in-law lived with her adult daughter and her husband for seven years.

❑ In some cultures, working adult children are expected to give some of their earnings to the family. It is not viewed as appropriate for unmarried adult children to get their own apartments (Ingram, 2005). Professionals may encounter families who are enduring conflict over the value systems of older vs. younger family members.

❑ In many cultures (e.g., Asian, Middle Eastern), elderly family members are highly valued and respected; their opinions carry more weight than those of younger family members. Thus, professionals should defer to the oldest family members present in an interaction.

❑ Upon conducting home visits, American professionals may be shocked to find large numbers of people sharing a single apartment. However, this is the norm in many countries. For example, in the Arab culture, there is no word for *privacy;* individuals long for and expect a great degree of closeness and physical proximity to one another (Omar Nydell, 2006).

❏ Some American professionals may experience frustration when they discover that nontraditional forms of healing are being used by the family to help a child. Although school professionals may not feel that these treatment practices are appropriate, the beliefs of the family should be respected.

❏ School professionals should work in tandem with health practitioners that the family trusts. For example, some Hispanic families might be more open to accepting educational recommendations made by a priest than to accepting recommendations made by a special education teacher.

❏ For many families from diverse cultural backgrounds, the past may be viewed as more important than the future. Spending money on a monument to an ancestor, for example, may be viewed as more important than using this money to meet the needs of children who require special education services (Ingram, 2005).

❏ Most traditional Americans view birth defects as a mistake in the transcription of DNA during the process of meiosis. However, someone who believes in reincarnation might see the birth defect as resulting from a family member's improper behavior in a past life and thus, the birth defect is a punishment for sins. This type of client might not be open to genetic counseling or to rehabilitation, believing that a child with a birth defect is the "cross they have to bear" (Galanti, 2004; Shipley & Roseberry-McKibbin, 2006).

❏ Professionals must exercise caution in using terms such as "dependent," "immature," etc. because early independence may not be considered an important goal within the child's family. American parents foster independence in children at an early age. Other cultures, however, have different beliefs about early independence (Hwa-Froelich & Vigil, 2004; Roseberry-McKibbin, 2000a).

❏ In the American culture, it is considered acceptable for females to ask direct questions of males. In some cultures, many consider this practice to be highly offensive. For example, in some Muslim countries, only males ask direct questions of one another.

❏ Because Americans are generally accustomed to equality between men and women, female professionals may be shocked and chagrined to discover that because of their gender, men from some cultural groups do not respect them and will not listen to their opinions and statements (Roseberry-McKibbin, 2000a). It is important to be willing to allow a male professional to speak with these men, remembering that the most important goal of any interaction is ultimately the welfare of the child.

❏ American professionals may discover that certain adolescent immigrant students do not regularly use deodorant or bathe daily. It is important to gently and sensitively advise these students and their families about mainstream U.S. expectations, and to diplomatically discuss the social consequences of allowing one's natural body odors to remain uncovered.

❏ American professionals may find CLD students and their families to be quite "slow" in completing tasks or responding to messages. Although speed and efficiency are highly valued in the United States, American professionals need to realize that "speed" and "deadlines" are less important in other cultures. Families should not be made to feel inadequate if they are not as quick in meeting deadlines as might be expected.

❑ Professionals who work with Anglo American families can expect that some of these families may be angered when informed that a child with special needs may not have the skills required to attend or graduate from college. Families may remain in denial until their children graduate from high school.

❑ Professionals need to remember that children from many cultures are not encouraged to freely express their thoughts, opinions, needs, and emotions; for these children, conformity and respect for adults are key (Zhao, 2007). Professionals must not misjudge these children as being insecure or as having language delays simply because they display little verbal communication, especially in the classroom.

✎*REFLECTION*✎

You are a female speech-language pathologist or special education teacher in a school where a 5th-grade boy from the Middle East has been identified as needing special education services. The father has indicated that he will not speak with you about the child's needs because you are a woman. The custodian at the school is from the Middle East, and he has volunteered to serve as a "cultural broker" or go-between in this situation. What will you do? Will you work with the custodian, or will you expect the father to listen to what you have to say? Why?

_____

_____

_____

_____

_____

ASSUMPTIONS ABOUT AMERICANS

Commonly held beliefs about Americans have been described by a number of authors (see Beane, 2006; Chen, 2006; Darling, 2005; Ingram, 2005; Omar Nydell, 2006. I also encountered many of these beliefs while growing up in the Philippines. For the last five years, I have had my university students interview immigrants from all over the world to obtain information about how immigrants feel about Americans. Commonly held beliefs about Americans include the following:

❑ Americans have the freedom to do whatever they want to do.

❑ Americans are talkative and friendly.

❑ Americans are honest and frank.

❑ Americans are loud and shout a lot.

❑ Americans are materialistic and think only about money.

❑ Americans are rich.

❑ Americans do not have the ability to enjoy the present; they are always rushing toward the future.

❑ Americans do not frown upon premarital sex and are highly immoral.

❑ Americans are rude. They always rush into business without engaging in any preliminary social amenities.

❑ Americans have superficial relationships.

❑ Americans do not value their families. They are more concerned about success and "getting ahead" than about the happiness of family members.

❑ Americans are much too permissive with their children and do not demand that they respect and obey their elders.

❑ When Americans travel to other countries, they drink a lot of alcohol.

❑ Americans eat hot dogs and wear cowboy boots.

❑ Americans are very aggressive.

❑ Americans want to control the world.

❑ Americans experience so many family problems (e.g., high divorce rates, runaway children) because they are too individualistic (Chen, 2006; Darling, 2005).

Some readers may find these assumptions and stereotypes offensive because no one wants to be "categorized" and "stereotyped" without consideration of individual differences. Most Americans would not want to be described in this way. Yet some people from other cultures hold these stereotypes about Americans as a group.

Whenever members of a cultural group hold stereotypes about members of other cultural groups, the potential for misunderstanding and conflict is great. By realizing how Americans are stereotyped by members of other cultures, one can better understand how members of other cultural groups feel when they are stereotyped. It is important to look inward at one's own cultural beliefs and assumptions. Professionals must be honest with themselves if they are to develop the sensitivity necessary to serve others without bias. As previously stated, a major part of cultural competence is contained in the statement "know thyself."

STUDY QUESTIONS

1. Choose three mainstream U.S. values that you consider important to maintain (e.g., the belief that men and women should have equal rights). Why are these values important to you?

2. Describe three stereotypes about mainstream Americans that you find particularly offensive. Why do these stereotypes offend you?

3. Describe four mainstream Anglo American communication behaviors that might be viewed as inappropriate by individuals from other cultural backgrounds. Why might these behaviors be viewed negatively?

TRUE-FALSE

Circle the number beside each statement that is true.

4. Members of most cultural groups appreciate the fact that Americans are informal and address others using their first names.

5. Ethnocentrism is the view that members of one's own culture do things the right way. All other ways of doing something are unnatural, inferior, maybe even barbaric.

6. Anglo European Americans generally believe that the extended family should care for children and elderly parents; they would be dismayed at the thought of sending family members to day care settings or convalescent homes.

7. Anglo European Americans tend to value being indirect, diplomatic, and subtle in interactions with others.

8. Americans are often stereotyped as having weak family values.

9. Anglo European American professionals appreciate the fact that multicultural clients usually carry out intervention recommendations with speed and efficiency.

10. American females who work as professionals might be angered if not accepted as professionals by men from other cultural groups.

MULTIPLE CHOICE

Circle the letter beside each of the choices that is correct.

11. Which one of the following statements about Anglo European Americans is FALSE?
    A. Most are Protestants or Catholics.
    B. They believe that "children should be children" and allowed to develop at a relaxed pace.
    C. They value directness and assertiveness in communication.
    D. They value change and plan for the future.
    E. They believe in privacy for the individual.

12. Which statements about health care are TRUE?
    A. Anglo European American medical practitioners tend to separate illnesses of the body and mind.
    B. American medicine relies greatly on technology.
    C. Most Anglo European Americans believe that factors such as genetics, trauma, disease, and terato-gens (e.g., toxins) can cause disabilities.
    D. Most disabilities affecting learning can be treated using medication.

13. Which of the following statements is/are often made to "stereotype" Americans?
    A. Americans are rich.
    B. Americans are morally decadent.
    C. Americans are too strict with their children and need to allow their children much more freedom.
    D. Americans are superficial.
    E. Americans love soccer.

14. Which of the following communication behaviors do most Anglo Europeans view as being acceptable?
    A. Asking others personal questions about their age, salary, and marital status
    B. Standing approximately two feet apart during conversations
    C. Maintaining a manner of openness, friendliness, and informality during interactions
    D. Beginning a meeting or business interaction with lengthy, personal chit-chat to help all parties feel comfortable before business is addressed
    E. Making eye contact and asking questions to indicate interest during interactions

15. An Anglo European American mother has brought her 26-month-old son to you for an assessment. She stays at home and cares for him, and he is her only child. He does not go to preschool. Her son says no words yet, and he appears not to comprehend even simple requests and questions. Which of the following would be APPROPRIATE in your interaction with this mother?
    A. Being quite indirect and suggesting that time might automatically take care of the problem
    B. Telling her that the communication problem may persist into adulthood and that, in the future, the child should be trained for a vocation that does not require a college education
    C. Recommending a preschool for several hours a day to increase his speech and language skills
    D. Telling her to spend several hours a day drilling him on new vocabulary words

ANSWERS TO STUDY QUESTIONS

4. False
5. True
6. False
7. False
8. True
9. False
10. True
11. B
12. A, B, and C
13. A, B, and D
14. B, C, and E
15. C

Chapter 4

FAMILIES FROM AFRICAN AMERICAN BACKGROUNDS

Outline

African Americans in the United States have had a profound influence on the American way of life. In contrast to other immigrant populations, most African Americans did not come to the United States by choice. Rather than coming to America in search of a better life, they were transported here involuntarily and forced into slavery. Although conditions for African Americans have improved, many continue to experience discrimination in a variety of social contexts.

GENERAL BACKGROUND INFORMATION

❏ African Americans are unique in their history of immigration (Willis, 2004). Historically, some chose to enter the United States. However, most were forcibly taken from African villages (either by White slave traders or by Africans from other villages) and sold into slavery in the southern United States. Today, Black immigrants enter the United States each year from such areas as South and Central America, Africa, and the Caribbean.

❏ In 1990, there were 29,986,060 Blacks or African Americans in the U.S. (12.1% of the total U.S. population). In 2000, there were 34,658,190 Blacks or African Americans (race alone) in the U.S. (U.S. Bureau of the Census, 2000).

❏ When the figures were obtained for race alone and race in combination (e.g., a person indicated that he was from both African American and Hispanic backgrounds), there were 36,419,434 Blacks or African Americans in the United States (U.S. Bureau of the Census, 2000). Blacks or African Americans experienced a much slower growth rate than Hispanics and Asians.

❏ As of July 1, 2005, the estimated population of Black residents in the U.S. (race alone or in combination) was 39.7 million, comprising 13.4% of the total U.S. population. It is projected that as of July 1, 2050, 61.4 million single-race Blacks will comprise 15% of the U.S. population (U.S. Census Bureau, 2006).

❏ In early African religions, ancestors and spirits of nature were worshiped. Religion has traditionally played an important role in African American communities in the United States and it is integral to the lives of many African Americans today. They often come from traditional Christian backgrounds, including Baptist, Methodist, and Episcopal denominations (Willis, 2004).

❏ At the time of the Civil War, the vast majority of the country's African Americans lived in the south.

❏ The Emancipation Proclamation (1863) resulted in freedom from slavery. Many African Americans moved to the northern United States to find better opportunities. Prejudice, however, was widespread. In recent years, there has been a "reverse migration" of African Americans back to southern states . In the mid-1970s, African Americans began returning to the south.

❏ "By 1901, laws dealing with 'Jim Crow,' a term that had become synonymous with African Americans, had become the fabric of how the races would relate to one another based on skin color and myths of genetic superiority for whites and inferiority for African Americans" (Willis, 2004).

❏ Historically there was much discrimination against African Americans, including widespread segregation and the absence of voting rights. Such deprivation denied them true assimilation into mainstream society.

❏ Historical turning points for African Americans included:

1. the 1954 Brown v. Board of Education decision, and its effect in eliminating segregated schools;
2. the Civil Rights Movement with its leader, Dr. Martin Luther King;
3. the implementation of the Economic Opportunity Act and the Civil Rights Act of 1964;
4. the implementation of the Voting Rights Act of 1965.

❏ Unfortunately, even today, "African Americans remain only partially assimilated. . . .Their path to full assimilation appears to be blocked by the lack of opportunities for mobility upward and out of the predominantly Black enclaves where African American language flourishes" (van Keulen, Weddington, & DeBose, 1998, p. xxii).

❏ There is a measurable gap in the average wages of Black and White males in the United States. Some authors estimate that this gap may be as high as 58% (Western & Pettit, 2005).

❏ The experiences of slavery, institutional racism, and continued economic oppression in the United States have caused many African Americans to experience distrust and anger toward Anglo European Americans (Obama, 2006; Terrell, Battle, & Grantham, 1998; van Keulen et al., 1998).

❏ Middle class African Americans may feel more anger than low income African Americans because they work hard, are educated, and have been exposed to the rewards the system offers. Yet because of their skin color, they have not had equal access to these rewards and have not been equally remunerated (Terrell & Terrell, 1996).

❏ Discrimination against African Americans continues in the United States to this day. Illinois senator Barack Obama, who is the son of a Black African father and White mother, gives examples of incidences such as being followed by police (without just cause) or standing in front of a hotel waiting for his limousine and having a White couple throw him their car keys, thinking he was the valet (2006).

❏ Poverty is widespread for African Americans as a group (Ispa, Thornburg, & Fine, 2006). Sixty-one percent of African American children live in low-income families (National Center for Children in Poverty, 2006).

❏ In Black high-poverty counties in the southern states, one third of poor children under 18 live in female-headed households with no husband present (United States Department of Agriculture, 2007).

❏ Fortunately, there has been a slight reversal in this economic trend, with African Americans in the U.S. gaining increased financial stability and equity. In 2005, the annual median income of African American households was $30,858, up from $25,642 in 1985. In 1985, 31.3% of "Black only" Americans lived in poverty; in 2005, 24.9% of "Black only" Americans lived in poverty (U.S. Census Bureau, 2006).

Obama (2006) wrote eloquently about the following economic reality: (pp. 242-243)

> ...[progress of African Americans] is a testament to that generation of African American mothers and fathers...who worked all their lives in jobs that were too small for them, without complaint...parents who pushed their children to achieve and fortified them with a love that could withstand whatever the larger society might throw at them...the black middle class has grown fourfold in a generation...the black poverty rate cut in half....these black workers...make our economy run and our democracy flourish... And yet, for all the progress that's been made in the last four decades, a stubborn gap remains between the living standards of black, Latino, and white workers. The average black wage is 75 percent of the average white wage...more minorities may be living the American dream, but their hold on that dream remains tenuous.

✐REFLECTION✐

Takesha, an 8-year-old African American girl on your caseload, tells you that she has not been receiving invitations to any of her classmates' birthday parties. Also, despite the fact that there are eight Girl Scout troops represented at the school, none of them has a space for Takesha. She seems depressed because of this. How will you handle this situation? Will you talk with Takesha about it? How can you assist her in this situation?

_____

_____

_____

_____

_____

AFRICAN AMERICAN FAMILY LIFE

❏ Families from African American backgrounds may include blood relatives and others who are not blood relatives but have special caring relationships.

❏ Many African Americans place high value on developing children's knowledge of who their immediate and extended family members are. These families emphasize knowledge of African American heritage, a sense of pride, and knowledge of cultural uniqueness (Obama, 2006; Willis, 2004).

❏ Nationally, approximately 44% of African American families are married-couple families. Although many African American households are designated "female single head of household" status, this designation does not take into account extended relationships and support systems available to many families (Ispa et al, 2006; Willis, 2004). Many African Americans have extended family networks that provide economic and emotional support (Sue & Sue, 2008).

❏ Rather than emphasizing the importance of individual effort and gain, many African American families emphasize group effort for the common interest and expect that those who succeed will share with the larger community. These families view collective responsibility, interdependence, and cooperation as important values (Obama, 2006).

❑ Most African American families value obedience to parents, older siblings, and other older persons. They place great emphasis on respect for elders, who are seen as having hindsight and wisdom. Most families expect young children to treat others well, to obey family rules, and to work hard in school.

❑ African American families tend to use an approach to child-rearing that is more authoritative than in some other groups (Tannen, 1994). Many families believe strongly in discipline to teach children appropriate behavior (Ispa et al., 2006). Mothers may be firm and physical in their discipline (Bagli, 2002).

❑ Many African Americans believe that children must be loved, guided, protected, and disciplined; all responsible adults in many communities partake in the discipline and training of children.

❑ In many African American families, infants are nurtured warmly and affectionately; young children are given the opportunity to "be children" and to enjoy play (Willis, 2004).

❑ African American families tend to be flexible about family roles (Sue & Sue, 2008). Fathers and mothers share child-care responsibilities, and older siblings carry out household chores and help care for younger siblings.

❑ Sue and Sue (2008) stated that African American men are often more accepting of "women's work" and are more willing to share responsibilities traditionally assigned to women (such as picking up children from school).

❑ "African Americans are not as concerned about sex role identities as European Americans...they are more concerned with overcoming obstacles based on racial membership than with gender affiliation" (van Keulen et al., 1998, p. 218).

❑ In some African American families, the family unit is built around a matriarch or grandmother figure who will raise more than one generation of children. This matriarch has a strong influence on the actions of her family members .

EDUCATION AND LITERACY

❑ Among African Americans 25 years and older, 80% were reported in 2005 to have earned at least a high school diploma. Seventeen percent had a Bachelor's degree or higher. In 2005, 1.1 million African Americans 25 years and older had advanced degrees (e.g., M.D., Ph.D., J.D.), whereas 10 years earlier, in 1995, only 677,000 African Americans possessed this level of education (U.S. Census Bureau, 2006).

❑ Education is viewed as an important and desirable achievement by many African Americans. Children in African American families are often taught that an education is something that no one can take away from them. However, despite this view, the school dropout rate for African Americans is approximately 13% for African American students (Banks, 2002). This compares with just over 7% for Whites in the same age range. Poverty is the most significant sociocultural cause of the academic achievement gap between African American and White children (Talbert-Johnson, 2004).

❏ Unfortunately, African American students often experience barriers in the educational setting (Hale, 2004; Holt & Smith, 2005). For example, conflicts may occur because of differences between school values and peer group values (Ogbu, 1992).

❏ Ogbu (1995) stated that members of involuntary minority groups (e.g., African Americans) who have a history of discrimination and suppression may be less likely to buy into majority group values and practices that uphold educational attainment as the surest route to personal and professional success.

❏ Researchers (e.g., Ladson-Billings, 1994; Sue & Sue, 2008) frequently cite the fact that young African American males are at risk for disengaging from the educational process, especially during middle school and high school.

❏ They may view academic success as a barrier to good peer relationships, i.e., that working hard academically might be viewed by their peers as "acting White." They may, therefore, believe that their only option is to refuse to do well in school (Ladson-Billings, 1994).

❏ Sue and Sue (2008) pointed out that some African American students communicate in a style that is persuasive, animated, and confrontational. Schools (where many teachers are White women) expect quietness, conformity, and the ability to sit still for long periods of time as well as engage in teacher-focused and individualized, competitive activities.

❏ Mainstream professionals may see the communication style of African American students as aggressive or even as unacceptable conduct and may inappropriately penalize the students. For example, some African American students refer to individuals close to them as "dawg." Teachers may misinterpret the use of this term as inappropriate and punish the students for using it (Salend & Duhaney, 2005).

❏ Some African American students have difficulty in school because the language used in instruction and in books differs from the spoken language as it is used in their community. These children may use African American English (AAE) in their community and home, although school teachers conduct classes in Mainstream American English (MAE) and often expect students to use "standard English" at school.

❏ Van Keulen et al. (1998) likened AAE-speaking students to second language learners in that these students have conversational language proficiency, but struggle with the academic English used in textbooks.

❏ Children who speak MAE at home have congruence in the home language and the language in which books at school are written. AAE-speaking children who come from print-rich environments where parents model and reinforce emergent literacy skills will likely enter first grade equal to their MAE counterparts who have had similar experiences. However, for children who speak AAE and have not been taught emergent literacy skills, their spoken home language is not represented in conventional storybooks or textbooks. This lack of congruence can cause AAE-speaking children to have challenges with reading, and professionals must be careful not to misdiagnose them as having reading disabilities (van Keulen et al., 1998).

❏ Students who speak AAE may struggle with reading, writing, and spelling especially (Harris & Moran, 2006; Kohler, Bahr, Silliman, Bryant, Apel, & Wilkinson, 2007). This can put them at a disadvantage academically and may be a factor contributing to the overrepresentation of African American students in special education.

❑ The overrepresentation of African American students in special education is well documented (Hardman, Drew, & Egan, 2006; van Keulen et al., 1998). Talbert-Johnson (2004) discussed the fact that the disproportionate placement of African American males into special education classes has created a "ghetto within a ghetto," where these students have little chance of eventual academic success.

❑ African American boys are overrepresented in terms of their classification as students with three types of disabilities: emotional disturbance, mental retardation, and learning disabilities. This misidentification raises serious concerns, because these students often end up having limited access to the general education curriculum (Salend & Duhaney, 2005).

❑ Unfortunately, many of the schools attended by low-income African American students are very dilapidated and segregated. One third of all African American students attend schools that have minority enrollments of 90% or more. Low-income students and students of color are also more likely to have poorly trained teachers (Talbert-Johnson, 2004).

❑ Gifted and talented African American students may be under-identified in schools because of assessment procedures that do not adequately reflect the strengths of individuals from African American backgrounds. Traditional intelligence tests are notoriously biased against African Americans.

❑ Craig and Washington (2004b) discussed in detail the effects of poverty on the academic and language performance of African American students. They stated that African American children are more than three times as likely as their White peers to live in poverty; these children are also more likely to live in families in which parental education levels are low.

❑ According to Craig and Washington (2004b), poverty is a variable that is implicated in school reading failure for African American students. They stated that "...although poverty and its co-variables can have profound adverse effects on a child's well-being, recent research indicates that formal public preschool experience may mitigate some of these effects for literacy learning" (p. 234).

❑ Washington (2001) discussed the poor reading achievement of African American children in urban schools and stated that intervention efforts have traditionally focused on children in kindergarten through 5th grade. She suggested that prevention efforts must begin prior to kindergarten.

❑ Hale (2004) recommended that linkages be created between preschools and kindergartens attended by African American children, with expanded training given to preschool teachers. In this way, young African American children could be better prepared for kindergarten.

HEALTH CARE AND DISABLING CONDITIONS

❑ Many African Americans lack access to adequate health care and do not have medical insurance (Ispa et al., 2006; Terrell & Jackson, 2002). In 2005, 19.6% of African Americans lacked health insurance (U.S. Census Bureau, 2006).

❏ The African American population tends to have a higher infant mortality rate than that of other groups in some communities (Chen, Martin, & Matthews, 2006). Lower income, less frequent prenatal care, poorer maternal nutrition, and other factors make it more difficult for many African Americans to raise healthy children.

❏ Approximately 17.9% of African American mothers give birth to pre-term infants; 16.84% give birth to low-birthweight (less than 5 lbs.) or very low-birthweight (less than 3 lbs.) infants (National Center for Health Statistics, 2004). African American mothers are less likely to receive prenatal care than White mothers (Chen et al., 2006).

❏ Jaundice may not be noticed in African American infants because the typical symptom is yellow skin; as a result, some infants go untreated and experience varying degrees of brain damage.

❏ Death from nutritional deficiency in infancy is 10 times more likely among African American children than among White children (Willis, 2004).

❏ Sickle cell disease, a hereditary disease of the red blood cells affecting Blacks worldwide, has been associated with sensorineural hearing loss (Scott, 1998).

❏ Approaches to health care vary depending on the income and/or educational level of individual families. Some African Americans, especially in the rural south, rely on home remedies or holistic health approaches in which herbs, roots, teas, and natural foods are used (Willis, 2004).

❏ Some low-income families may not understand or have access to the traditional health care system. Thus they may only receive care when they are seriously ill. Preventative health care may not be available or utilized.

❏ Health care may differ in quantity and quality more for African Americans than for other groups. For example, when compared to Whites, some African Americans experience longer waiting periods in doctors' offices and slower transfer times from emergency rooms to critical care units in hospitals (Ghali, Cooper, Kowatly, & Liao, 1993).

❏ Major inner city areas of the United States are comprised primarily of African Americans. These areas have limited services, poor housing, unemployment, crime, poverty, overcrowding, and illegal drug activities (Willis, 2004). All of these phenomena have negative implications for health.

❏ African American children from low-income families are often exposed to harmful environmental pollutants such as lead, air pollution, and ambient noise (Dilworth-Bart & Moore, 2006). These exposures can negatively impact their health and, in turn, their academic performance in school.

❏ Many African American children under 6 years of age have an elevated level of lead in the blood, partly caused by high lead-levels in low-income housing. High lead levels in the blood have been linked to many learning problems and health risks (Roseberry-McKibbin, 2008).

❏ African American children who live in low-income housing may also be susceptible to asthma (Ispa et al., 2006). If they experience frequent episodes of asthma, this can negatively impact their attendance at school.

❏ Some African Americans believe that disabling conditions are due to evil spirits, the work of the devil, punishment for disobeying God, and/or bad luck (Willis, 2004).

❏ African American families are often able to accept children who have disabilities. This acceptance may result, in part, from support within the extended family and strong ties with their churches.

AFRICAN AMERICAN COMMUNICATION STYLES

❏ Approval and agreement between participants in a conversation may be expressed through touching or physical contact. African Americans, during interactions, touch each other more than they touch Anglo Americans (Long, 2006). This is especially true of African Americans from lower socioeconomic backgrounds (van Keulen et al., 1998).

❏ Eye contact is used as a form of nonverbal communication. However, rolling of the eyes during conversation may be viewed as offensive (Willis, 2004).

❏ Some African American students make little eye contact with adults, who may view such behavior as disrespectful.

❏ African Americans can be intense, emotional, and demonstrative with each other in public; other groups may view this behavior as unrestrained (Long, 2006; Owens, 2005; Willis, 2004).

❏ African American students often speak in a manner that is animated, interpersonal, and confrontational. This manner of speaking contrasts with that of Anglo students, who often speak in a manner that is dispassionate, non-challenging, and impersonal (van Keulen et al., 1998).

❏ African Americans may not observe traditional turn-taking rules during conversations. It is acceptable to interrupt if a participant feels a need to add valuable information. Abruptly changing the topic is also acceptable.

❏ Individuals are expected to participate verbally in conversations and to not remain silent. Conversations may be quite competitive, with the most assertive participants doing most of the talking. Mainstream professionals must be careful not to label this behavior as "rude" or "lacking in pragmatic skills."

❏ Among many African Americans, charismatic speech with distinctive intonational patterns and rhythm is rewarded and valued. African Americans frequently speak with emotional vitality.

❏ Because of the relatively continuous presence of music or words among African Americans, some people might characterize them as "loud" or "shallow." To use these pejorative terms would demonstrate a lack of understanding of African American values, which are as legitimate as mainstream values (Willis, 2004).

❏ African American culture encourages many communication rituals and distinctive styles that affirm cultural identity and allegiance to the group. One example is "call and response," in which the listeners echo part of the speaker's previous utterance. For example, in a church setting, the preacher might *say*, "And the Lord told Noah to build an ark." The congregation might respond "Build an ark." (see van Keulen et al., 1998, for more details regarding communication rituals).

❏ African American students' narrative styles often differ from those of mainstream Anglo students who speak MAE. These differences can lead to incorrect judgments about the students' behavior (Gutiérrez-Clellen & Quinn, 1993; Terrell & Jackson, 2002; van Keulen et al., 1998).

1. African American students often rely on gestures to accompany verbalizations or narratives.
2. When African American students tell stories, they may include personal judgments and evaluations about the characters.
3. In mainstream school programs, students are expected to tell stories in a topic-centered style, characterized by topic elaboration, structured discourse on a single topic, and lack of presupposed shared knowledge. African American students often use a topic-associating style, characterized by presupposition of shared knowledge between the speaker and listener(s), structured discourse on several linked topics, and lack of consideration for detail. Unfortunately, examiners who expect students to use the topic-centered style may incorrectly view African American children as disorganized and perhaps even language-learning disabled.

In a recent study, Price, Roberts, and Jackson (2006) examined the structural development of the fictional narratives of typically-developing African American preschoolers. The children's narrative skills were examined by identifying their use of story grammar elements when retelling a fictional story called "The Bus Story" (Renfrew, 1991).

In this study, 65 African American children were asked to tell the story when they were 4 years old and again at kindergarten entry. At age 4 years, most children's narrations included at least one main character, at least one of the bus' attempts to run away, and at least one component of the end of the story. By the second testing session, which occurred right before kindergarten entry, more story grammar elements were included. Right before kindergarten, the children's scores were significantly higher than they were at 4 years of age. Price et al. (2006) concluded that 1) at kindergarten entry, children had higher total narrative scores and included more of almost every type of story element than they did at 4 years of age; and 2) *"The Bus Story,"* which uses colorful pictures and has a brief administration time, appeared to be a useful clinical tool for examining the growth of African American preschoolers' narrative skills.

AFRICAN AMERICAN ENGLISH CONSIDERATIONS

African American English (AAE), the language spoken by some residents of the United States, has undergone many changes in nomenclature. AAE has been referred to as Black Dialect, Black English, Black English Vernacular, African American Vernacular, African American Language, and Ebonics (Bland-Stewart, 2005; Craig, Washington, & Thompson-Porter, 1998; Long, 2006). The changes in nomenclature have been due, in part, to an increasingly sophisticated understanding of AAE and to changes in sociolinguistic theory. Because it contains much similarity to MAE, AAE is considered by most experts today to be a dialect of MAE, not a separate language (McLaughlin, 2006; Owens, 2005; Terrell et al., 1998).

The extent to which African American English is used is influenced by a number of factors:

❏ Use of AAE is influenced by geographic region, socioeconomic status, education, gender, and age.

❏ Middle-class African Americans generally use AAE less than working class African Americans, especially in formal settings. African Americans from low-socioeconomic status backgrounds are more likely to use a higher percentage of AAE features (Long, 2006).

❏ African American children from low-income homes use more "dialectal forms" than their peers from middle class homes. The discourse of boys shows more evidence of use of these forms than that of girls (Craig et al., 1998).

❏ Syntax is the area in which differences between AAE and MAE are most apparent (Willis, 2004).

❏ There are a number of West African languages that have impacted modern-day African American English: Bambara, Ewe, Fanta, Fon, Fula, Ga, Ibo, Ibibio, Kimbundu, Longo, Mandinka, Mende, Twi, Imbundu, Wolof, and Yoruba.

❏ Before they are three years of age, it is difficult to detect differences in the language development of children who speak MAE and children who speak AAE. Prior to age three, the morphosyntactic development of children who speak AAE differs very little from that of children who speak MAE. However, between 3 and 5 years of age, children who are acquiring AAE begin to use a greater number of "nonstandard" grammatical forms (Wyatt, 1998).

❏ As many as 39% of the utterances of African American preschoolers from low-income, urban homes include morphosyntactic forms that are characteristic of African American English (Washington & Craig, 1994).

❏ Craig, Thompson, Washington, and Potter (2003) stated that preschool and kindergarten African American students produce up to sixteen different morphosyntactic types of AAE.

MISCONCEPTIONS ABOUT AFRICAN AMERICAN ENGLISH

There are numerous possible misconceptions about AAE that professionals must be aware of if they are to interact effectively with AAE speakers:

Misconception #1. All African Americans speak AAE.

Some African Americans speak AAE and some do not. Some codeswitch back and forth between MAE and AAE depending on context (van Keulen et al., 1998).

Profile

Dr. Ndidi Johnson is Chair of the Nursing Department in a university setting. She shared with this author that she codeswitches between MAE and AAE, depending upon the situation. In Dr. Johnson's words, "When I'm at work, I speak White English because that's what I need to do. When I get home, I switch to Black English. [Linguistically], it's like wearing high heels all day—when I get home, I kick them off and put on a pair of comfortable tennis shoes."

Misconception #2. AAE is only spoken by African Americans.

AAE can be spoken by people of any ethnic and linguistic background. Non-African Americans may speak AAE if their primary peer group is composed of African Americans. For example, some Puerto Rican students in New York City speak AAE as do some Anglo students in Oakland, California. In contrast, African Americans who are socialized primarily with Anglos will generally speak MAE.

Misconception #3. AAE is a substandard form of Mainstream American English.

Historically, the language patterns of African Americans have been viewed as "deficient." A major premise of this view was that African Americans were cognitively unable to learn MAE. Currently, AAE is viewed as a fully developed system with rules governing its structure and use (McLaughlin, 2006).

Misconception #4. AAE needs to be eradicated so that children can learn the language as it is used in school.

It is possible to learn Mainstream American English without eradicating African American English. Some experts believe that speakers of AAE should become "bilingual" or "bidialectal" so that they can speak both AAE and MAE fluently (van Keulen et al., 1998). In this optimal situation, students can preserve their culture, heritage, and community dialect while at the same time they learn the style of speaking required in school and in various types of social interactions.

Misconception #5. Speakers of AAE can be adequately assessed with standardized tests of intelligence, language, etc. if a representative sample is included in the norming population.

Many published assessment instruments used in schools were developed and standardized on student populations consisting primarily of Anglo, middle class, monolingual English speakers. These tests, especially those designed to assess aspects of grammar and sentence production, have been criticized by numerous experts as being inappropriate for use with African American children and other cultural groups (Smith, Lee, & McDade, 2001; Thompson, Craig, & Washington, 2004; Thomas-Tate et al., 2004; Wyatt, 1997). Including a small sample of AAE speakers in the norming population does little to make the test appropriate for these students.

BIAS IN ASSESSMENT MEASURES

When AAE speakers are tested, it is critical to differentiate which aspects of their speech and language are reflective of AAE rules and which aspects are indicative of a disorder (Johnson, 2005; Thomas-Tate et al., 2004). It is illegal for speech-language pathologists in the public schools to enroll AAE speakers for "remediation" of speech-language "disorders" if the goal of intervention is to teach standard English grammar. An understanding of AAE and how it differs from MAE is critical if speech-language pathologists are to distinguish between a language difference and a language disorder in an AAE-speaking student. Important morphosyntactic and articulatory-phonological characteristics of AAE are presented in Tables 4.1 and 4.2 respectively. Additional examples of bias are as follows:

❏ Bias in articulation and phonological tasks

Most tests of articulation and phonology are normed on Anglo children. The unique characteristics of AAE must be considered when assessing articulation and phonology. For example, on most articulation tests, the substitution of /f/ for the initial sound in *thumb*, would be con-

Table 4.1

Characteristics Of African American English Morphology and Syntax

AAL Feature/Characteristic	Mainstream American English	Sample AAE Utterance
Omission of noun possessive	That's the woman's car. It's John's pencil.	That *the woman* car. It *John* pencil.
Omission of noun plural	He has 2 boxes of apples. She gives me 5 cents.	He got 2 *box* of *apple*. She give me 5 *cent*.
Omission of third person singular present tense marker	She walks to school. The man works in his yard.	She *walk* to school. The man *work* in his yard.
Omission of "to be" forms such as "is, are"	She is a nice lady. They are going to a movie.	*She a* nice lady. *They going* to a movie.
Present tense "is" may be used regardless of person/number.	They are having fun. You are a smart man.	*They is* having fun. *You is* a smart man.
Utterances with "to be" may not show person number agreement with past and present forms.	You are playing ball. They are having a picnic.	You *is* playing ball. They *is* having a picnic.
Present tense forms of auxiliary "have" are omitted.	I have been here for 2 hours. He has done it again.	I been here for 2 hours. He done it again.
Past tense endings may be omitted.	He lived in California. She cracked the nut.	He *live* in California. She *crack* the nut.
Past "was" may be used regardless of number and person.	They were shopping. You were helping me.	They *was* shopping. You *was* helping me.

AAE Feature/Characteristic	Mainstream American English	Sample AAE Utterance
Multiple negatives (each additional negative form adds emphasis to the negative meaning.)	We don't have any more. I don't want any cake. I don't like broccoli.	We **don't** have **no** more. I **don't never** want **no** cake. I **don't never** like broccoli.
"None" may be substituted for "any."	She doesn't want any.	She don't want **none.**
Perfective construction; "been" may be used to indicate that an action took place in the distant past.	I had the mumps last year I have known her for years.	I **been had** the mumps last year. I **been known** her.
"Done" may be combined with a past tense form to indicate that an action was started and completed.	He fixed the stove. She tried to paint it.	He **done fixed** the stove. She **done tried** to paint it.
The form "be" may be used as the main verb.	Today she is working. We are singing.	Today **she be** working. **We be** singing.
Distributive "be" may be used to indicate actions and events over time.	He is often cheerful. She's kind sometimes.	**He be** cheerful. **She be** kind.
A pronoun may be used to restate the subject.	My brother surprised me. My dog has fleas.	My brother, **he** surprise me. My dog, **he** got fleas.
"Them" may be substituted for "those."	Those cars are antiques. Where'd you get those books?	**Them cars**, they be antique. Where you get **them books**?
Future tense "is, are" may be replaced by "gonna."	She is going to help us. They are going to be there.	She **gonna** help us. They **gonna** be there.
"At" is used at the end of "where" questions.	Where is the house? Where is the store?	Where is the house **at**? Where is the store **at**?
Additional auxiliaries are often used.	I might have done it.	I **might could have** done it.
"Does" is replaced by "do."	She does funny things. It does make sense.	**She do** funny things. **It do** make sense.

Table 4.2

Characteristics of African American English Articulation and Phonology

AAE Feature/Characteristic English	Mainstream American English	African American English
/l/ phoneme lessened or omitted	tool always	too' a'ways
/r/ phoneme lessened or omitted	door mother protect	doah mudah p'otek
f/voiceless "th" substitution at end or middle of word	teeth both nothing	teef bof nufin'
t/voiceless "th" substitution in beginning of a word	think thin	tink tin
d/voiced "th" substitution at the beginning, middle of words	this brother	dis broder
v/voiced "th" substitution at the end of words	breathe smooth	breave smoov
Consonant cluster reduction	desk rest left wasp	des' res' lef was'
Differing syllable stress patterns	guitar police July	**gui** tar **po** lice **Ju** ly

AAE Feature/Characteristic	Mainstream American English	African American English
Final consonant in verb may change when past tense ending is added	liked walked	li-tid wah-tid
Metathesis occurs	ask	aks ("axe")
Devoicing of final voiced consonants	bed rug cab	bet ruk cap
Final consonants may be deleted	bad good	ba' goo'
High front vowel substituted for mid-front vowel ("i" replaces "e")	pen ten	pin tin
b/v substitution	valentine vest	balentine bes'
Diphthong reduction	find oil pound	fahnd ol pond
n/ng substitution	walking thing	walkin' thin'

Note: Characteristics may vary depending on variables such as geographic region.

sidered an error. However, for AAE-speakers, this substitution is a dialectical difference, not a speech error.

❏ **Bias in sentence repetition tasks**

Examiner: "Repeat these sentences after me. Remember to say them EXACTLY like I say them!"

1. Neither child is using the swings.

2. They had been hungry.

3. She looks at the big, brown dog.

❏ **Bias in grammatical closure tasks**

Examiner: "I am going to say some sentences. I want you to fill in the word that is missing."

Demonstration item: A rose is a flower and a daisy is a flower.
Daisies and roses are both _____. (flowers)

1. Today I play the marimba; yesterday I _____ the marimba.

2. I have a cat, and you have a cat; we have two _____.

3. Today Sue is going to the store; yesterday she _____ going to the store.

❏ **Bias in receptive grammatical tasks**

Examiner: "We are going to look at some pictures. Each page has three pictures. When I say a sentence, you point to the picture that goes with the sentence I say. Here's the first picture."

1. Show me, "The cats are playing in the garden."

2. Show me, "He played baseball."

3. Point to, "They have been painting the fence."

❏ **Bias in grammatical judgment tasks**

Examiner: "Tell me whether the following sentences are correct or incorrect."

1. Them girls is having a good time.

2. The boys is going to the party.

3. We don't have no time to talk to you.

Although the sentence examples above are "incorrect" according to the rules of MAE, they might not sound incorrect to speakers of AAE. Additional examples of language differences affecting sentence production are presented in Table 4.3.

✐ REFLECTION ✐

Ms. Smith had a number of African American students in her class. One day she was overheard talking with an African American child who was leaving her room to go back to the school library.

"Bye, Ms. Smith," he said cheerfully. "We be goin' back to the library now."

"DeJon!" she exclaimed. "That's the <u>bad</u> grammar! We are learning to use the good grammar. Say, 'We ARE going back to class now.'"

Why was the comment made by Ms. Smith inappropriate? What might she have said instead?

_____

_____

_____

_____

_____

FACTORS TO CONSIDER IN ASSESSMENT

❏ There are many considerations to keep in mind when assessing the speech and language of African American students. Professionals must be nonjudgmental, open, and knowledgeable about linguistic and cultural issues that can impact the evaluation of African American students.

❏ It is sometimes necessary to avoid asking personal and direct questions during the first meeting with African American students. Questions of this type may be viewed as offensive and intrusive. The question, "Can you tell me about your family?" may be too personal and therefore insulting to an African American student who does not know the interviewer.

❏ If an African American student feels intimidated by a school professional's questions, his responses may provide limited information, possibly causing the professional to conclude, inappropriately, that the student has poor expressive language skills.

❏ Children who speak AAE demonstrate morphological patterns that differ from those of MAE (Bland-Stewart, 2005; Johnson, 2005; Thompson, et al., 2004). Coles-White (2004) cautioned that use of morphology to identify specific language impairment in AAE-speaking children is a problem and recommended that other more valid diagnostic measures be used instead.

❏ Researchers have recommended alternative forms of assessment (nonstandardized measures) that can be used to assess the presence of communication disorders in African American students. These include contrastive analysis (McGregor, Williams, Hearst, & Johnson, 1997), a

Table 4.3

Examples of Acceptable Utterances by Speakers of African American Language

Mainstream American English	African American Language
That boy looks like me.	That boy, he look like me.
If he kicks it, he'll be in trouble.	If he kick it, he be in trouble.
When the lights are off, it's dark.	When the lights be off, it dark.
It could be somebody's pet.	It could be somebody pet.
Her feet are too big.	Her feet is too big.
I'll get something to eat.	I will get me something to eat.
She is dancing and the music's on.	She be dancin' an' the music on.
What kind of cheese do you want?	What kind of cheese you want?
My brother's name is Joe.	My brother name is Joe.
I raked the leaves outside.	I rakted the leaves outside.
After the recital, they shook my hand.	After the recital, they shaketed my hand.
They are standing around.	They is just standing around.
He is a basketball star.	He a basketball star.
They are in cages.	They be in cages.
It's not like a tree or anything.	It not like a tree or nothin'.
He does like to fish.	He do like to fish.
They are going to swim.	They gonna swim.
Mom already repaired the car.	Mom done repair the car.

description of the child's functional communication skills, and language sample analysis (Bliss, 2002; Seymour, Bland-Stewart, & Green, 1998; Stockman, 1996).

❑ Culturally fair, dialectically nonbiased methods for analyzing information obtained from language samples have been described (Craig & Washington, 2000; Smith, Lee, & McDade, 2001). The measurement of C-unit length has been found to be more useful than traditional measures such as mean length of utterance. C-units consist of independent clauses plus their modifiers (see Craig et al., 1998 for information about measuring C-unit length).

❑ Craig and Washington (2004) devised a language screening protocol that was found to be useful for preschool- and kindergarten-aged African American children living in urban settings. The protocol used, among other tasks, non-word repetition tasks and the Nonverbal Scale of the Kaufman Assessment Battery for Children (KABC; Kaufman & Kaufman, 1983). Craig and Washington concluded that this screening protocol, when used in conjunction with parent report, had strong potential for helping to differentiate language differences from true language impairments in young African American children.

❑ Professionals can use a new test created specifically for use with four- to nine-year-old African American children. The Diagnostic Evaluation of Language Variation (DELV) is designed to be dialectically neutral with respect to AAE (Seymour, Roeper, & de Villiers, 2004). The DELV assesses a variety of areas, and yields information that can be helpful in determining whether a child is at risk for a language impairment. By using this instrument, a child who speaks AAE can be identified as being at risk for a language impairment without being penalized for using features of AAE.

❑ Jackson and Roberts (2001) examined changes in the complex syntax production of 85 three- and four-year old African American children and looked at the role of child and family factors in the children's production of complex syntax. Child factors included gender, age, and use of AAE. Family factors included home environment factors such as responsiveness and stimulation. They found that children from more communicatively responsive homes used more complex syntax forms. In other words, the amount of complex syntax that children use was related to home responsiveness, apart from the use of AAE. Jackson and Roberts concluded that home environment especially affected the complex syntax development of their subjects and suggested that "the finding that complex syntax use was not affected by dialect use suggests the usefulness of examining this area of language development across different cultural groups" (p. 1094).

❑ Washington, Craig, and Kushmaul (1998) compared two language sampling situations for young African American children entering school. They found that African American English language production was more diverse and frequent during a picture description activity than it was in a free play situation. Picture description was also found to be more efficient than free play for language sampling. They recommended that for young African American children entering school, picture description is an excellent way to obtain a "more ecologically valid picture of the African American child as a classroom dialect user. Picture description more closely resembles the kinds of tasks that might be encountered in an MAE classroom environment than free play." (p. 112)

❑ In many African American families, the development of social interaction skills may be viewed as having greater importance than the development of a large vocabulary. Students who have had limited experience with activities in which they are asked to "name" objects may do poorly on vocabulary assessment measures, giving the false impression that they have language-learning disabilities. Thus, professionals should use vocabulary tests with caution when they are assessing the language skills of African American students.

❑ When assessing speech sound production, it must be remembered that misdiagnosis is likely to occur if the determination of an articulation disorder is based entirely on the results of formal articulation tests. These tests are often biased against African American children (Stockman, 2006). It is important to examine the child's speech in everyday situations and to consider how others in the local community react to the child's speech.

❑ African American boys often demonstrate a high level of physical activity and may be mislabeled as having ADHD (attention deficit hyperactivity disorder). In one study, it was shown that African American boys were rated by teachers as having the most severe ADHD symptoms; White girls were rated with the least severe symptoms (Reid, Riccio, Kessler, DuPaul, Power, Anastopolous, Rogers-Adkinson, & Noll, 2000).

❑ African American girls were found to be 3.5 times more likely to screen positive for ADHD than Anglo American girls, and African American boys were 2.5 times more likely to screen positive for ADHD than Anglo American boys (Reid, Casat, Norton, Anastopolous, & Temple, 2001). Behaviors that are viewed by Anglo American teachers as "hyperactivity" in African American students may not be perceived in this way by teachers who are African American.

The extent to which norm-referenced tests commonly used in the assessment of Anglo children are appropriate for use with African American students has been a topic of debate for years. One of the most commonly used receptive vocabulary measures is the Peabody Picture Vocabulary Test, Third Edition (PPVT-III; Dunn & Dunn, 1997). Washington and Craig (1999) found that this test was more culturally fair than the earlier edition (PPVT-R) and that the changes in the PPVT-III made it possible to obtain unbiased outcomes for at-risk African American subjects as a group. They did caution, however, that the overall high group scores masked lower scores that were common among subjects from homes in which the mother had limited educational experiences. In addition, a possible limitation of the study was that all the children were from metropolitan Detroit.

Champion, Hyter, McCabe, and Bland-Stewart (2003) examined the PPVT-III for use with 49 typically-developing preschool-aged African American children from low-income families in the Tampa Bay area. These children's scores were disproportionately lower than the normative sample, and were negatively skewed. The PPVT-III disproportionately assigned low scores to young African American children from low-income backgrounds.

Champion and colleagues proposed that the differences in their results and those of Washington and Craig (1999) might have been due to income differences between the two samples; Washington and Craig's subjects were not exclusively from low-income families. It appeared that young African American children's performance on standardized vocabulary tests may be strongly related to their socioeconomic status. More research, however, is needed to test this hypothesis.

Despite the fact that the PPVT-III appears to be one of the better tests available for nonbiased assessment of the receptive vocabulary skills of African American students, Stockman (2000) cautioned that more research is needed and that the PPVT-III should be used in conjunction with other measures of vocabulary knowledge and use.

Thomas-Tate, Washington, Craig, and Packard (2006) examined the validity of the *Expressive Vocabulary Test* (*EVT*; Williams, 1997) for assessing the expressive vocabulary skills of Midwestern preschool and kindergarten African American students. The researchers administered the *Expressive Vocabulary Test* to these students; some were typical language learners, and others were atypical learners. The researchers concluded that the *Expressive Vocabulary Test* was valid for assessing the vocabulary skills of their subjects, but cautioned that more research must be done to see if these findings generalize to African American children in other geographic regions.

Profile

Recently, I was asked to evaluate the language skills of Poppy M., a second grade African American girl. Poppy was born two months prematurely and had a history of many special needs (e.g., delays in language, gross motor skills, fine motor skills, and cognition). Poppy's file indicated that she also had ADHD, combined with behavioral issues. When my colleague and I attempted to assess Poppy, she spit on my colleague, bit her, and kicked her. When I assessed Poppy, she hit me and tried to pull my hair. She told me repeatedly that I was nasty. Despite my colleague's and my best efforts, we were not able to obtain a valid assessment of Poppy's language skills through formal or informal testing. Miss M., Poppy's full time aide in the classroom, gathered a language sample of Poppy's utterances over a 4-day period. My colleague and I supplemented this sample with one of our own so that we could get a somewhat representative sample of Poppy's expressive language skills and ability to interact in a variety of situations with different interlocutors (teacher, peers, Miss M., and others). At the IEP meeting, it was concluded that before Poppy could benefit from intervention, she needed to work with a trained behaviorist who could help her focus and behave appropriately.

IMPLICATIONS FOR PROFESSIONALS

❑ Professionals should always address family members formally, using titles and surnames, unless specifically invited to do otherwise.

❑ Professionals should address students' needs with a family-focused approach to intervention. Families may be experiencing stress because of health and safety hazards, poverty, lack of access to medical care, etc. It is best to utilize the strong family support systems that exist within many African American families when helping them to achieve specific goals.

❑ Local religious organizations, supported by the family, can often be used as allies in intervention. Their assistance may be of greater value than that provided by agencies that the family has never used. Church personnel usually have an understanding of a family's dynamics and living conditions. For many African Americans, churches are places of religious, social, and even practical support.

❑ In order to help families follow intervention suggestions appropriately, Willis (2004) maintained that professionals may need to do the following:

1. Make sure that at least two family members understand the recommendations.
2. Design easy-to-use take-home materials and treatment plans.
3. Follow up on the family's progress and make appropriate adjustments.
4. Make sure the family can obtain the materials and equipment necessary to carry out instructions.

❑ When working with families, remember that poverty is not necessarily an indicator of dysfunction; many low-income families provide stable, loving environments for their children.

❑ Professionals should also remember, however, that because disproportionate numbers of African American families in the United States experience poverty, the need for educational services and rehabilitation often are viewed as less important than the need for food, clothing, shelter, and medical care (Terrell et al., 1998). Professionals should not judge these families as being uncaring or indifferent.

❑ When working with families of African American children, it is important to consider the family's socioeconomic status (SES) as an important variable impacting communication patterns in the home. For example, Wallace, Roberts, and Lodder (1998) showed that mothers from low-income families scored lower on measures related to care-giving than did mothers who were not experiencing financial hardship.

❑ Hammer and Weiss (1999), in their study of low- and mid-SES African American mother-child dyads, showed that mid-SES mothers tended to include significantly more language goals (e.g., labeling objects) in their interactions than did low-SES mothers. They speculated that as the children in the low-SES group grew older, they might be at risk for lower language gains as measured by standardized tests. When home interaction styles differ from what is expected at school, children may not develop the skills needed to perform well on the tests administered in the school setting.

❑ Additionally, it was seen that low-SES African American mothers initiated play interactions to teach their children less frequently than did mid-SES African American mothers; instead, low-SES children often initiated play interactions with their mothers (Hammer & Weiss, 2000). Hammer and Weiss recommended that these parents be provided with strategies to help them facilitate play within child-initiated interactions.

❑ African American parents often interact with their children through story-telling. They should be encouraged to stimulate their children's interaction with print by reading to them frequently (van Keulen et al., 1998).

❑ Britto, Brooks-Gunn, and Griffin (2006) studied African American children and their mothers, who were young and poor. Britto et al. hypothesized that differences they observed in maternal teaching and reading patterns would be associated with their children's school readiness outcomes. They found that the children's vocabularies appeared to be positively associated with a more interactive, maternal book-reading style that included behaviors such as encouraging children to participate, asking questions, and extending children's knowledge beyond the pages of the book.

❑ When parents provided high levels of guided participation and support during reading activities, Britto et al. found that children demonstrated greater expressive language use and school readiness than did children who received low levels of maternal engagement during reading activities. Thus, professionals can work with parents, especially mothers, to help them learn behaviors that will facilitate school readiness in their children.

❑ One longitudinal research study with low-SES African American mothers found that home visitors could be most supportive and helpful by gaining the mothers' trust gradually, being indirect (e.g., not giving commands or prescriptions), and modeling appropriate parenting and language stimulation strategies (Ispa et al., 2006). It was more useful to make home visits over a period of time rather than just at one point in time.

❏ Some researchers have found that African American infants are more advanced in their motor development than infants from other ethnic groups; this is an important consideration when looking at case history information relating to motor development (Carter et al., 2005).

❏ Educators in regular and special education programs should be flexible in identifying the special talents of their African American students. Identification of students' strengths and limitations should be based, to a greater degree, on observations made by teachers and parents than on scores obtained from standardized tests.

❏ Among African Americans, the cultural emphasis on verbal expectations can lead some parents to perceive a language or articulation problem as a fluency problem. They hear a disruption in their child's speech and attribute it to abnormalities in the speech flow. Thus, it is important in these cases to carefully elicit parents' or clients' perception of the presenting communication problem in order to ascertain the precise nature of that problem (Robinson & Crowe, 1998).

❏ Because of the strong emphasis African Americans place on oral communication, they may feel the need to speak fluently, rapidly, and without struggle. This can cause some African Americans, especially males, to do everything possible to conceal their stuttering (van Keulen et al., 1998).

❏ If African American students qualify for intervention, professionals should work to ensure that service delivery is culturally sensitive to and appropriate for these students.

❏ Professionals should remember that some young African American children learn best when the teaching strategies emphasize interpersonal interaction rather than independence. Child-rearing practices in African American culture have been described as "people oriented."(Terrell & Hale, 1992).

❏ Teaching styles that emphasize open affection, encouragement, and praise are highly effective with many African American children. These children may do their best work if they feel like they are in a community of learners that is like an extended family (Love & Krueger, 2005).

❏ African American students often possess a relational cognitive style in which gestalt learning, opportunities for muscular movement, and variation in learning activities positively affect performance (Robinson & Crowe, 1998; van Keulen et al., 1998).

❏ When teaching African American students, professionals should remember that learning may be enhanced through the use of auditory and kinesthetic techniques in a high-energy, fast-paced atmosphere with a varied format (Terrell et al., 1998).

❏ Because African American culture emphasizes cooperation and sharing rather than competition, cooperative learning activities benefit many African American students (Salend & Duhaney, 2005). Effective educators studied by Ladson-Billings (1994) gave students numerous opportunities to learn cooperatively and collectively.

❏ African American students tend to be more responsive in educational situations in which the professional (e.g., teacher, speech-language pathologist) is charismatic and encourages sharing, team work, and open discussions. These students tend to be least responsive in situations in which they are expected to sit still, be passive, and refrain from interaction (van Keulen et al., 1998).

❑ Experts recommend that professionals be culturally responsive to their students, spending time to build relationships with them. When relationships are established, students will usually respond more favorably (Talbert-Johnson, 2004). Students of color who have caring relationships with professionals are more motivated and perform better academically than students who do not.

❑ Because African American students often prefer a field-dependent learning style, peer interaction and aspects in the surrounding environment should facilitate learning. A student might experience feelings of low self-esteem and mistrust if he or she is isolated from peers and not given opportunities to interact with others during instruction (Terrell et al., 1998).

❑ Professionals should incorporate African American music, literature, art, and history into learning activities. Experiences of this type have been shown to enhance pride and to enhance learning (Love & Krueger, 2005). King (1993) recommended the use of rap music and African American proverbs to cultivate students' sense of history and culture.

❑ African American students who are accustomed to "call and response" may respond verbally in class to the teacher's question without first raising their hands. These students may be viewed as disrespectful, rude, and aggressive (van Keulen et al., 1998). Although "school rules" may need to be explained to these students, school professionals should be understanding when such behaviors do occur.

❑ Phrases such as "raise your hand," "take a seat," or "line up" are not necessarily familiar to African American students when they enter school if they have not attended preschool. Professionals can help these children adjust to the school setting by teaching the language of the classroom.

❑ If professionals feel that African American students are misbehaving when they are communicating in a style that is confrontational and emotional, these professionals can help the students learn that there is a "home way" and a "school way" of communicating.

❑ Professionals can teach the differences between "home talk" and "school talk" in a nonperjorative manner that helps African American students become bidialectal in both oral and written language (Campbell, 1993). Specific instructional strategies have been described by van Keulen et al. (1998).

❑ It is important for students' home/preferred communication style to be supported and affirmed; however, most future employers are not seeking employees who are emotional and confrontational in their communication styles. African American students must be given two sets of behaviors/communication styles to choose from, depending upon the situations in which they find themselves.

❑ Within the African American culture, the name given to a child is considered extremely important (Terrell & Jackson, 2002). Professionals should always ask students the name that they prefer to be called. If the pronunciation of the name appears unique to mainstream professionals, these professionals should make every attempt to memorize this unique pronunciation and use it appropriately.

❏ Most experts agree that it is not the province of school-based speech-language pathologists or special education teachers to provide services for "remediation" of AAE. It is important to remember that use of AAE is not a "disorder" and that students may not be enrolled in any type of special education program without evidence of a disorder or disability. It is recommended that classroom teachers help these students learn MAE (van Keulen et al., 1998).

❏ Connor and Craig (2006) suggested that for African American children who are not sensitive to subtle and implicit cues that contribute to strong literacy development, professionals might help to increase their conscious awareness of code shifting by providing "explicit instruction in dialect awareness" (p. 782). This instruction could take place in the classroom setting.

❏ Teachers and other professionals should not overtly correct or criticize the oral language of students who speak AAE. However, professionals can model MAE. For instance, if a student says, "Hey, he cool," the professional might reply, "Yes, he is cool. I think he is cool, too."

❏ Speech-language pathologists can provide in-service programs to enhance teachers' knowledge of specific ways to differentiate between a language difference and a language disorder in speakers of AAE. In this in-service, strategies for teaching MAE in the classroom can also be shared. Such in-service programs are likely to result in fewer inappropriate referrals, as illustrated in the school situation below:

> The student population at Apple Elementary School in California consisted primarily of Anglo speakers of MAE. Recently, there had been a large influx of African American students. Several dozen speakers of African American English were referred inappropriately to the speech-language pathologist for testing. One teacher told the speech-language pathologist that "someone has to teach these kids how to talk right!"
>
> In an effort to reduce the number of inappropriate referrals, the speech-language pathologist held an hour-long in-service for the teachers. She explained that it is legal to enroll students for speech and language services only if a disorder has been identified. She provided the teachers with a detailed handout to help them distinguish communication differences from disorders in speakers of AAE. The next year, inappropriate referrals of AAE-speaking students decreased substantially, and teachers became more accepting of individual differences within their classrooms.

STUDY QUESTIONS

1. Briefly describe factors in the history of African Americans in the United States that have led to feelings of anger and mistrust toward Anglo Americans.

2. List characteristics that are common to many African American families. What values do many of them hold regarding child-rearing?

3. Describe educational barriers that African American students may experience when they attend traditional U.S. schools. In what ways has African American English been described as a barrier to achievement? Do you agree or disagree that AAE is a barrier?

4. Describe some alternatives to using traditional standardized tests with African American students who have potential language impairments.

TRUE-FALSE

Circle the number beside each statement that is true.

5. African American English (AAE) is a substandard form of the English language characterized primarily by limited use of grammatical rules.
6. African American students who interrupt others during conversations typically have significant pragmatic language difficulties or internalized feelings of anger.
7. African American mothers from low socioeconomic backgrounds tend to interact with their infants and small children differently than African American mothers from middle income backgrounds.
8. When collecting case history information, one must remember that African American infants are often slower to develop gross motor skills than infants from other ethnic groups.
9. A speaker of AAE who said "He do like to play with the other kid" is showing signs of a difference, not a disorder.
10. Sickle cell disease in African Americans has been associated with sensorineural hearing loss.
11. When speakers of AAE tell stories, they tend to use a topic-associating style characterized by structured discourse on a single topic.

MULTIPLE CHOICE

Circle the letter beside each of the choices that is correct.

12. Many African American students respond best to intervention methods that:
    A. Require that they sit still and demonstrate "good" behavior.
    B. Incorporate many kinesthetic and auditory cues.
    C. Include African American music, history, and cultural materials.
    D. Allow students to receive individual therapy so they get one-to-one attention from an adult.
    E. Are fast-paced and varied.

13. Which of the following are recommended as nonbiased, valid assessments of the communication skills of speakers of AAE?
    A. Language samples
    B. Analysis of C-units
    C. Mean length of utterance
    D. Norm-referenced tests standardized on a national sample
    E. Sentence repetition tasks

14. Ganesha T., a 6-year-old speaker of AAE in first grade, is referred by her classroom teacher for testing. The referral form says that "Ganesha is disruptive in class. I'm wondering if she needs therapy for her social communication skills." Which of the following indicate that Ganesha is manifesting a communication difference (not disorder) based on her cultural background?

A. When the teacher asks a question in class, Ganesha answers without raising her hand first.
B. When Ganesha tells a story, she assumes that the listener has enough background information to understand what she is talking about.
C. Ganesha looks down when she is talking with teachers and administrators (e.g., the principal).
D. Ganesha has difficulty sitting still and listening to the teacher lecture to a group of students.
E. Ganesha tends to talk loudly with her peers and (to the Anglo teacher) appears to be "in your face."

15. On this same form, the teacher states that "Ganesha also has poor grammar. I'm concerned that this will interfere with her reading and writing." He gives several examples. Which one of the following utterances would NOT be typical for a speaker of AAE?

A. My daddy done buy the groceries.
B. They ain't no be gonna havin' a good time.
C. That might be my friend pencil.
D. We be readin' our book in class.
E. Those mice is gettin' chased by the cat.

16. Which of the following would be considered inappropriate in service delivery to African American students and their families?

A. Giving students nicknames to help them feel special (e.g., calling Ganesha "Nesha")
B. Calling family members by their first names to establish a cordial, comfortable relationship
C. Helping families develop strategies for reading and telling stories to their children
D. Asking for the parent's consent to conduct an assessment
E. Expecting the student to answer questions that can be answered by the parent

ANSWERS TO STUDY QUESTIONS

5. False
6. False
7. True
8. False
9. True
10. True
11. False
12. B, C, and E
13. A and B
14. A, B, C, D, and E
15. B
16. A and B

Chapter 5

FAMILIES FROM HISPANIC BACKGROUNDS

Outline

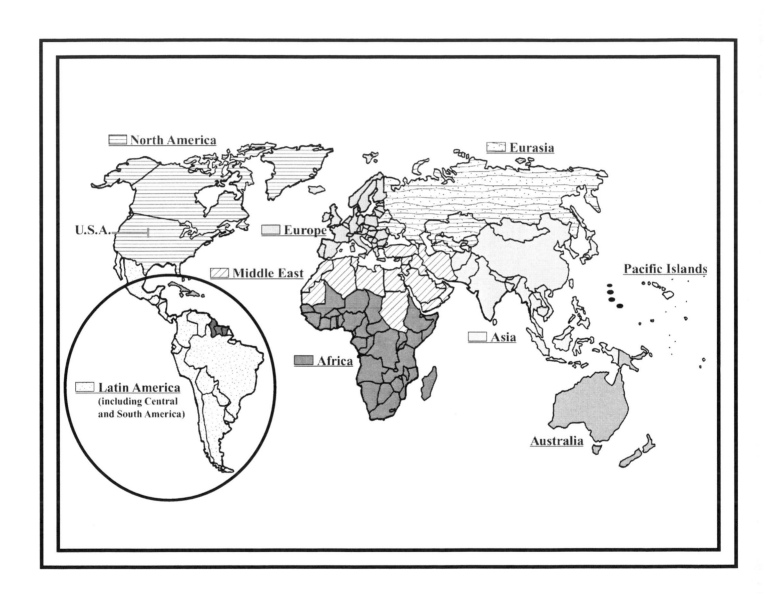

The Hispanic population in the United States is growing rapidly. Many Hispanic students come to school speaking only Spanish. Although bilingual education programs are available in many school districts, few programs are available to meet the needs of the growing population of Spanish speakers with special learning needs (Centeno, 2007).

The term **Hispanic** is used to refer to individuals who were born in or trace the background of their families to one of the Spanish-speaking Latin American nations or to Spain (Jordan Institute for Families, 2002). Hispanics may also come from Caribbean countries such as Puerto Rico and Cuba. The largest portion of the Hispanic population in the United States is Mexican.

Spanish is the language most often spoken in Mexico and throughout most countries in Central and South America (see Figure 5.1).

Figure 5.1

GENERAL BACKGROUND INFORMATION

❑ The term "Hispanic" is used as an ethnic label by the U.S. Bureau of the Census; it does not denote a race, because most Hispanics are racially mixed. Hispanics have diverse ancestral roots (e.g., African, Native Indian, and European). Hispanics descending from each of these heritages differ in terms of phenotype (skin color), immigration history, socioeconomic status, and other parameters.

❏ Senices (2005) emphasized that the process of racialization has masked the heterogeneity of the Hispanic people's characteristics. He emphasized that professionals should not treat Hispanics as a monolithic entity, but rather as individuals with many diverse characteristics and values. Moore, Giesen, and Cavenaugh (2005) echoed this, stressing that the Hispanic population of the U.S. is highly diverse and cannot be easily categorized.

❏ Some individuals from Spanish language backgrounds do not like the term "Hispanic." Many prefer to be called "Latino." (Iglesias, 2002). Others prefer a reference to their family's country of origin. For example, some Hispanics like to be called Cuban Americans, Mexican Americans, etc.

❏ Many Hispanics are born in the United States; others immigrate for reasons such as family re-unification and economic opportunity. Many individuals from Central and South America have come to the United States to escape from politically unstable situations in their native countries.

❏ Immigrants tend to settle in parts of the United States where others from their country have established residence. Most Mexican Hispanics live in the Southwestern states. The majority of Puerto Rican Hispanics live in New York and New Jersey. Many Cubans live in Florida. Although most Hispanics in California are of Mexican descent, other groups are also represented in large numbers. Many Central Americans, for example, reside in San Francisco.

❏ Hispanics comprise one of the fastest-growing segments of the population. The U.S. Hispanic population grew to 35 million people, a 58% increase, in 10 years. Hispanic immigrants come primarily from Mexico, Central America, Puerto Rico, Cuba, and South America. Today, the Hispanic population constitutes the largest minority in the United States (U.S. Bureau of the Census, 2000).

❏ Approximately 31 million U.S. residents speak Spanish at home, making Spanish the second-most spoken language in the country (Kent & Lalasz, 2006).

❏ Hispanics comprise 12.1% of the U.S. population. Thirty-five percent of this population is under 18 years of age (U.S. Bureau of the Census, 2000). The average age of Hispanic Americans is almost 9 years younger than that of the general population.

❏ The importance of Hispanics in the United States work force is increasing because of their youth and numbers relative to the aging Anglo European American population. For example, in the future, Hispanics are expected to comprise 40% of California's work force (U.S. Bureau of the Census, 2000).

❏ Many Hispanics are blue collar workers, hold unskilled or semiskilled occupations, and live at the poverty level. Sixty-three percent of Hispanic children live in low-income families (National Center for Children in Poverty, 2006).

❏ Consequences of poverty include poor housing conditions, educational and employment barri-ers, and health problems (Brice, 2002). Stresses caused by poverty can have a highly negative impact on the family life of many Hispanics (Delgado & Canabal, 2004).

❏ The following states contain counties with high concentrations of Hispanics who are living in poverty: Texas, New Mexico, Florida, Georgia, Missouri, and Washington (United States Department of Agriculture, 2007).

❏ Despite numerous social and economic disadvantages, many Hispanics have benefited from improved educational opportunities, a strong work ethic, strong families, high labor force participation, and low reliance on welfare (Jordan Institute for Families, 2002; Iglesias, 2002).

❏ Many Hispanics are Catholic. The church often plays an important role in their lives. Participating in church gives many Hispanics a sense of belonging to a community. It often offers them a sense of direction in their lives, and helps guide them in raising and educating their children successfully (Jordan Institute for Families, 2002).

HISPANIC FAMILY LIFE

❏ Family life is a high priority among most Hispanics. **Familialism** is a cultural value in which individuals have a strong identification with and attachment to their nuclear and extended families and greatly value solidarity, loyalty, and reciprocity among family members (UIpdegraff, McHale, Whiteman, Thayer, & Delgado, 2005).

❏ Most Hispanic homes are maintained by married couples.

❏ In some families, bearing children is viewed as the purpose of marriage. Children may be expected shortly after marriage (Zuniga, 2004).

❏ Large and extended families are common. Divorce is relatively uncommon due, in part, to the influence of Catholicism.

❏ The father is generally the authority figure. The welfare of the family is the responsibility of the father (Zuniga, 2004). The husband may make decisions without consulting his wife.

❏ In many families, the man is the breadwinner and the woman cares for the family. This situation is becoming increasingly less common, however, because many Hispanic women now need to obtain jobs outside the home. Nevertheless, **familismo** is very important for most Hispanic mothers, who are the family's primary caretakers and nurturers (Jordan Institute for Families, 2002).

❏ Many Hispanic children are taught to listen, obey, and not challenge authority. In many families, girls have restricted freedom and are taught that they need to be protected (Zuniga, 2004).

❏ Families may travel frequently from the United States to the home country to be with family members.

❏ Experiences associated with age are held in high regard, and children are expected to show respect for their elders, regardless of status or formal education (Zuniga, 2004). The advice of elderly grandparents, for example, is often solicited and followed because grandparents are integral and important family members.

❏ Parents may be indulgent and permissive with young children, especially infants, and often do not push them towards achievement to the extent that Anglo families do. For example, Hispanic preschool-age children may drink from baby bottles and pre-teens may sit on their mothers' laps. Direct physical closeness is the norm for many Hispanic families (Zuniga, 2004).

Profile ━━

Carlos G. was born to parents who came to Texas as refugees from El Salvador. Carlos was born with the umbilical wrapped around his neck, and he suffered from severe fetal anoxia. He experienced hydrocephalus and was eventually diagnosed with severe mental retardation. Doctors told his parents that Carlos would never walk or talk, much less learn to read or write. His mother sought as many early intervention services for Carlos as possible, and Carlos did learn to walk and talk, albeit very slowly. However, his father did not participate in meetings or in carrying out the recommendations made by professionals. The mother felt that she carried the entire burden of Carlos' rehabilitation. Eventually, the parents divorced.

As Carlos grew older, he received special education services in school and eventually learned to read and write at a basic level. However, his mother would not allow him to participate in events such as field trips or to socialize with other students. She felt that social interactions caused too much stress for the child. No effort was made in the home to help Carlos develop independent living skills. The child was not taught how to catch a bus, order food in a restaurant, etc. In fact, his mother did everything for him.

When Carlos was in 10th grade, he began manifesting symptoms of serious depression and mentioned suicide several times. He told the psychologist, "It would be better for me to die than for all these people to be working so hard for me." At his IEP meeting, 15 people were in attendance, including his mother. The meeting lasted for several hours. The team managed to persuade his mother to allow Carlos more social freedom and to allow school district personnel to teach the "basic life skills" he would need to support himself in a sheltered vocational setting.

━━

❏ Communication styles in many Spanish-speaking families differ somewhat from styles in mainstream Anglo families. For example, when Anglo mothers go shopping, they often talk constantly with their children about what they are doing. They, for example, may name the foods that they are buying, what they are used for, and may ask the child questions about these foods. Hispanic parents often do not comment or verbalize about ongoing events.

❏ Many parents do not participate in their children's play activities and may view play as a distraction from household chores, etc. Children are often expected to work toward goals that are viewed as critical for the family's survival (Zuniga, 2004).

❏ In some homes, children may be expected to be seen and not heard (Jordan Institute for Families, 2002).

❏ Many children are raised to value cooperation within the family unit more than individual achievement (Brice, 2002). Family members help one another and work as a team to achieve common goals.

HISPANIC EDUCATION AND LITERACY

❑ Many families hold teachers in high regard. Teachers and other educational professionals are viewed with great respect.

❑ Education is very important to families and is often viewed as the route to upward mobility (Brice, 2002)

❑ More than 70% of all migrant farm workers in the U.S. speak Spanish; they move frequently due to the nature of their jobs. If the family moves frequently, educational opportunities for the children may be sporadic and limited. These children often have gaps in content knowledge (Rubenstein-Avila, 2006). Fifty percent of U.S. migrant farm children leave school before ninth grade (Bennett, 2003).

❑ A "field-sensitive" cognitive style is common among Hispanic children (Nellum-Davis et al., 1998). These children are sensitive to nonverbal indicators of feelings and learn best when interacting in situations where they experience warmth, responsiveness, and frequent attention (Zuniga, 2004). They often respond well to physical touch and affection.

❑ Some girls are not encouraged to complete school or to train for a career. They are expected to marry and bear children. Hispanic girls who grow up to attend college and train for careers may find that their educational level is a barrier to their less-educated relatives. In fact, Hispanic female students have shared with me that relatives are dismayed that they are obtaining an education rather than marrying and bearing children at a young age.

❑ Students who immigrate to the United States may vary considerably in their school experiences and literacy skills. Many Hispanics in the United States have not had educational opportunities commensurate with those of Anglo European Americans. Their educational attainments, therefore, have been limited.

❑ National tests of reading and writing showed that at the three grade levels tested (grades 4, 8, 12), many more Hispanic students than Asian/Pacific and White students performed at the below-basic level. (Eschevarria, Short, & Powers, 2006; National Center for Education Statistics, 2002).

❑ Dropping out of school is common among Hispanic adolescents. In the early 1990s, in the 25-34 year age group, 58% of Hispanics had attained a high school education, compared to 89% of non-Hispanics (Riquelme, 1994). In the early 21st century, over one third of Hispanic students dropped out before completing high school. This is nearly double the drop-out rate for African Americans and almost four times higher than the rate for White students (Moore, 2001).

❑ The high drop-out rate of Hispanic students is a major national concern and, as Rubenstein-Avila (2006) stated, is "a ticking social and economic time bomb" (p. 39).

❑ In the year 2000, only 10% of Hispanics nationwide had earned a college degree as compared to 18% of African Americans and 34% of Anglo European Americans (National Center for Education Statistics, 2001).

❑ The 23rd Annual Report to Congress on the Implementation of IDEA indicated that a significant number of students with limited English proficiency have accompanying disabilities, and these students are at great risk for negative educational outcomes. This report also revealed that

12.7% of students with language and speech impairments were Latinos (U.S. Department of Education, 2001).

❑ Possible reasons for the less-than-optimal educational attainment of Hispanics in the U.S. include: 1) culture shock and the differences between home and school expectations; 2) sporadic school attendance due to high family mobility; 3) poverty; and 4) fluctuating funding for programs designed to assist students learning English as a second language.

❑ In Texas, Mexican Americans were found to be overrepresented by 300% in special education programs under the classification of "learning disabled" (Sue & Sue, 2008). Moreover, over 55% of Spanish-speaking children in the U.S. come from families with annual incomes of $20,000 or lower (Hammer & Miccio, 2001).

❑ Gandara (2004) pointed out that Hispanic families often lack the social capital to help their children succeed. They do not know how school bureaucracies operate and do not have easy access to key people in decision-making positions (e.g., principals). In addition, Hispanic children are likely to attend underfunded, overcrowded schools where few teachers are well qualified to teach.

❑ Hispanic students may be under-represented in gifted programs in schools because of cultural and/or linguistic bias in the assessment procedures used to determine giftedness.

❑ Young Mexican American children are far less likely to be placed in center-based child care programs than are Asian American, White, or African American children. Children from Hispanic families do not participate in preschool programs in proportion to their representation in the child population (Takanishi, 2006).

❑ Hammer, Miccio, and Wagstaff (2003) studied the developing bilingual skills of preschool Spanish-speaking children in a U.S. community and found two types of bilingual learners: sequential and simultaneous. The **sequential learners**, i.e., those who learned Spanish first and English later, had been exposed to English through activities of daily living (e.g., grocery shopping), but they had not been required to interact in English until they attended preschool at three years of age. The **simultaneous learners**, however, had been systematically exposed to both Spanish and English from birth; that is, they had been required to interact in both languages. Hammer and her colleagues pointed out that simultaneous learners may find it easier to interact and fit in, initially, in environments where only English is spoken. Because young sequential learners will probably take longer to actually interact in English than their counterparts who learned English and Spanish simultaneously, professionals should be careful not to misdiagnose them as having language impairments.

❑ Kummerer, López-Reyna, & Hughes (2007) studied Mexican immigrant mothers' perceptions of their children's communication disabilities, emergent literacy development, and speech-language therapy programs. These researchers found that the mothers in their study seemed more focused on their children's expressive language and/or speech intelligibility than their emergent literacy abilities. It was recommended that professionals help Mexican immigrant families incorporate specific activities to support their children's emergent literacy development.

✐ *REFLECTION* ✐

    Describe two characteristics relating to family life and two characteristics relating to the educational experiences of many Hispanic students in the U.S.

CULTURAL CUSTOMS, COURTESIES, AND BELIEFS

❑ Allocentrism (collectivism) is a fundamental Hispanic value that emphasizes the objectives and needs of an in-group rather than emphasizing competition and individualism.

❑ Families strive to be friendly, to welcome guests to their homes, and to offer refreshments.

❑ Many Hispanics have a flexible attitude about time and the importance of maintaining schedules. Thus, appointments are often not kept with the precision expected by school professionals. Hispanics tend to place greater value on interpersonal relations than on factors related to time.

❑ Girls are often encouraged to be modest and feminine. The sexual behaviors of adolescent females are often severely restricted, whereas male adolescents are afforded greater freedom (Sue & Sue, 2008).

❑ A strong Hispanic value is **personalismo,** or an emphasis on interpersonal relationships. Behaviors that convey personalismo include loyalty, honesty, generosity, hospitality, and willingness to help others.

❑ From the perspective of personalismo, many Hispanics will not engage in confrontations with others. They might say what they think the person wants to hear rather than being the bearers of bad news; they also might give ambiguous responses to avoid upsetting others.

❑ Hispanics also value **respecto** (respect), believing that all people, especially elders, deserve to be treated with courtesy and dignity.

❑ **Dignidad** (dignity) is important to Hispanics, who strive to present themselves with dignity, especially in public. Dignidad entails having a sense of pride and self-respect, which are often demonstrated through hard work and responsibility. It is shameful and humiliating to have one's dignity violated by another person.

HEALTH CARE AND DISABLING CONDITIONS

❑ Many Hispanic families have limited access to health care (McHatton & Correa, 2005; Riquelme, 1994)). For example, Roseberry-McKibbin, Peña, Hall, and Smith-Stubblefield (1996) found that of 254 migrant Hispanic families surveyed, 90% had no health insurance. These families were the "working poor" who had no work-related health benefits and who could not afford private health insurance. Sue & Sue (2003) reported that thirty percent of Hispanic American children are not covered by health insurance as compared to 20% of African Americans and 4% of Whites.

❑ Various types of acute, chronic, communicable, and traumatic diseases are more common in the Hispanic population than in most other groups. Hispanic Americans have disproportionately high rates of obesity, type 2 diabetes, asthma, AIDS, and tuberculosis (McHatton & Correa, 2005; Sue & Sue, 2008).

❑ Poverty and poor prenatal care lead to disproportionate numbers of Hispanic children who are sick or undernourished from birth. Mexican American mothers experience maternal risk factors and inadequate prenatal care more frequently than non-Hispanic white mothers (National Center for Health Statistics, 2004).

❑ Hispanics are least likely of any ethnic group in the U.S. to have adequate insurance coverage (Riquelme, 1994; Sue & Sue, 2008).

❑ Families may believe in "**curanderismo**," a healing process believed to occur when folk medicine practices are used. Often these practices are more prevalent in groups with less access to modern health care (e.g., individuals who live in rural areas).

❑ Among some Hispanics, there may be resistance to institutionalization. Rather, individuals with illnesses or disabilities are likely to be cared for within the family (Madding, 2002).

❑ Families differ in their reactions to disabilities. In some families, a visible disability (e.g., cleft palate, cerebral palsy) is often attributed to an external, non-medical cause such as witchcraft. Some parents may believe that a child's disabilities are punishment for their own wrong-doing (Zuniga, 2004). Many Catholic parents accept disabilities stoically, as part of a larger divine plan that is not comprehensible to humans (Maestas & Erickson, 1992).

❑ In some families with special needs children, fathers may discriminate against and reject the children, even leaving the family. This results in economic hardship for mothers, who become single and are forced to rely upon public assistance (McHatton & Correa, 2005).

❑ Families may have more difficulty accepting invisible disabling conditions such as learning disabilities or reading disorders than visible disabling conditions.

❑ Families that greatly prize vitality and health may hide a disabled child, thereby depriving that child of treatment. At the same time, family and friends may indulge these children, often not expecting them to participate actively in their own treatment and care.

❑ The roles of health agencies may cause confusion for family members. Families may prefer small clinics to large medical centers.

❑ Some families turn to spiritualists to seek healing and dispel evil spirits (Zuniga, 2004).

Salas-Provance, Erickson, and Reed (2002) studied forty persons from four generations of one Hispanic family. They found that beliefs in folk causes of and cures for disabilities varied according to family members' income, education, age, and gender.

The older, less-educated family members in their study tended to believe strongly in folk remedies for problems. They placed much importance on religion and religious rites (e.g., praying a novena) as related to health and illness. In contrast, younger and more educated family members used traditional medical care more frequently for curing illnesses. More than half the younger family members were unfamiliar with the important cultural ritual of praying a novena. Thus, Salas-Provance et al. (2002) showed that Hispanic family members' beliefs about disabilities may vary along several parameters (e.g., age, educational level).

Rodríguez and Olswang (2003) investigated the cross-cultural and intracultural diversity of Hispanic mothers' beliefs and values regarding child rearing, education, and the causes of language impairment. Two groups of mothers were compared: Mexican American and Anglo American. A major finding from this study was that 80% of the Mexican American mothers attributed their children's language problems to extrinsic factors such as God's will, the lack of a stimulating home environment, and mismatches between the home and school. In contrast, only 40% of Anglo American mothers attributed their children's language problems to extrinsic factors.

Profile

Juan Jaramillo, a handsome, courteous 10-year-old Hispanic fourth grader, was referred for assessment by his classroom teacher because he was struggling academically. Psychoeducational testing in both Spanish and English revealed that Juan had a learning disability. His mother came to the IEP meeting and was informed in Spanish that special education services appeared to be necessary. During the meeting she said, "Juan is just lazy—I know he can do the work. Look at him—he's a normal boy."

The IEP team explained that although Juan was normal in appearance, he had a clinically significant learning disability that was hampering his academic progress. Mrs. Jaramillo was visibly dubious about this conclusion but signed the IEP and agreed to special education services for her son.

HISPANIC COMMUNICATION STYLES

❏ Many Hispanics utilize the social script of **simpatica**, which emphasizes positive personal interactions that convey empathy for others, emphasize harmony in interpersonal relations, and de-emphasize negative behaviors in circumstances of conflict. It is considered important to initiate conversations on a personal note before proceeding with business.

❏ Embraces are common between friends. Members of the same sex may have physical contact in public.

❏ Standing close and touching during conversations is acceptable. Hispanics tend to stand closer during conversation than Anglos and other groups (Long, 2006). Many Hispanics feel insulted when someone steps away from them during conversation.

❑ Due to differences in cultural norms for physical distance or space (proxemics), some Hispanics view Anglos as being uninterested, aloof, or cold. In contrast, Anglos may view Hispanics as being too pushy or getting too close.

❑ One may beckon another person by producing a "psssst" sound; this is not considered rude.

❑ Hispanic children may look away or lower their heads when talking to adults because avoiding eye contact is considered a sign of respect and deference; furthermore, sustained eye contact may be seen as a challenge to authority.

❑ Children often learn through observation and hands-on participation rather than through verbal interactions with adults.

❑ When adults are talking, children are not to interrupt. They are not expected to participate in adult conversations, and they show respect for adults by considering themselves as "non-equals" during interactions. Parent-child conversation is not usually collaborative; rather, it tends to be more directive (Long, 2006).

❑ Children interact verbally more often with siblings or peers than with adults. Peers are considered equal partners in conversation (Kayser, 1998).

❑ In many Hispanic homes, parents do not verbalize about ongoing events; they don't relate actions to words.

❑ Often, adults do not ask children to voice their preferences or to give their personal evaluations of situations. Adults usually do not ask children to foretell what they will do or to repeat facts.

❑ When Hispanic children converse with adults, they may show a reluctance to provide more information than is requested. Extending topics in this manner may be viewed as disrespectful to the listener (Pajewski & Enriquez, 1996).

❑ Some Hispanic parents do not consider the learning of colors, shapes, or letters to be a high priority for their children. Instead, respect and politeness are emphasized. Many Mexican mothers regard themselves as "mothers" rather than "teachers" (García, Mendez Pérez, & Ortiz, 2000; Madding, 2000).

❑ Some Spanish-speaking children, especially those from the Caribbean or Central America, come from homes where narratives are frequently characterized by a de-emphasis on actions and event sequencing (Bliss, McCabe, & Mahecha, 2001).

SPANISH LANGUAGE CHARACTERISTICS AND CONSIDERATIONS

Numerous dialects/varieties of Spanish are spoken in the United States (McLaughlin, 2006). The two major Spanish dialects in the U.S. are the Caribbean (e.g., Cuban and Puerto Rican) and southwestern (Mexican/Mexican American) dialects. However, many other dialects exist, and it is imperative to remember that the diversity among Spanish speakers is great (Mahecha, 1991). Although Spanish is spoken in Spain and most of Central and South America, there are variations from country to country that are reflected in pragmatics, syntax, morphology, and phonology (Goldstein, 2000; Mattes & García-Easterly, 2007). The word *gordo* (fat), for example, is pronounced "goldo" by many Spanish speakers in Puerto Rico. In Argentina, the word *pollo* may be pronounced "po-sho."

Mattes & García-Easterly (2007) emphasized that contact between cultures, economic variables, technology, and various other factors are influencing the Spanish language as it is used in the United States and around the world. Some words commonly used by Spanish-speaking populations in the U.S. have been "borrowed" from English. Words such as *rufo* (roof), *marqueta* (market), and *trábol* (trouble) are examples of words used by some Spanish speakers that would not be recognized as "good Spanish" by many Spanish speakers living outside of the United States.

Mattes & Saldaña-Illingworth (2008) created a variety of informal Spanish language assessment tasks, protocols, questionnaires and other resources that can be adapted quite easily for use with different Spanish dialects. Specific guidelines are described for implementing assessment strategies based on an analysis of the student's language usage history and family background.

Thus, professionals must consider the individual student's background when evaluating language performance. Normative information has been reported for Spanish articulation and phonological development (Acevedo, 1991; Goldstein & Iglesias, 1996; Jiménez, 1987; Merino, 1992). The accent commonly heard among students learning English as a second language is to be expected and should not be viewed as evidence of a disorder. It is important for professionals who work with Spanish-speaking students to understand the language differences commonly observed when these students learn English.

Information about articulation and language differences commonly observed when Spanish speakers speak English is presented in Table 5.1 and Table 5.2. Additional information about Spanish articulation and language differences, dialectal differences in Spanish vocabulary, idiomatic uses of language, and other factors that affect language production in English have been described by Mattes & García-Easterly, 2007).

Profile

Rosa S., an 8-year-old girl from a migrant Mexican family, was being tested by the school psychologist. He noticed that she seemed to be unusually quiet, and he tried unsuccessfully for 15 minutes to encourage her to speak to him. Finally he asked her if anything was wrong. She responded by telling the psychologist that a snake had been found in her house and that snakes in the home are viewed in Mexico as a sign of bad luck. The psychologist sympathized with Rosa and said that luckily, in California, finding a snake was considered to be good luck. After several minutes of conversation about California's "good luck snakes," Rosa brightened considerably and was much more verbal in the testing situation.

IMPLICATIONS FOR PROFESSIONALS

❏ Professionals need to include the entire family in any meetings or procedures involving an individual student and should encourage active family participation (Brice & Roseberry-McKibbin, 1999a).

Table 5.1

Language Differences Commonly Observed Among Spanish Speakers

Language Characteristics	Sample English Utterances
1. Adjective comes after noun.	The house green is big.
2. 's is often omitted in plurals, possessives, and regular third person present tense.	We have five plate here. The girl book is brown. The baby cry.
3. Past tense -ed is often omitted.	We walk yesterday.
4. Double negatives are used.	I don't have no more.
5. Negative imperatives may be used; no is used instead of don't.	No touch the hot stove.
6. "No" may be used before a verb to signify negation.	The kid no cross the street.
7. Superiority is demonstrated by using more before an adjective in a similar manner to the use of mas in Spanish).	This cake is more big.
8. The adverb often follows the verb.	He drives very fast his motorcycle.
9. Postnoun modifiers are used.	This is the book of my sister.
10. Articles may be used with body parts.	I bruised the knee.
11. "Have" may be used in place of the copula when talking about age.	I have 12 years (Instead of I am 12 years old.)
12. Articles are often omitted.	Papa is going to store.
13. When the subject has been identified in the previous sentence, it may be omitted in the next sentence.	Mama is sad. Lost her purse.
14. There may not be noun-verb inversion in questions.	What this is? (instead of What is this?)

Table 5.2

**Articulation Differences Commonly Observed
Among Spanish Speakers**

Articulation Characteristics	Sample English Patterns
1. /t, d, n/ may be dentalized (tip of tongue is placed against the back of the upper central incisors).	
2. Final consonants are often devoiced.	dose/doze
3. b/v substitution	berry/very
4. Deaspirated stops (sounds like speaker is omitting the sound because it is said with little air release).	
5. ch/sh substitution	chew/shoe
6. d/voiced th, or z/voiced th (voiced "th" does not exist as a distinct phoneme in Spanish).	dis/this, zat/that
7. t/voiceless th (voiceless "th" does not exist as a distinct phoneme in Spanish).	tink/think
8. Schwa sound is inserted before word initial consonant clusters.	eskate/skate espend/spend
9. *In Spanish* words can end in 10 different sounds: a, e, i, o, u, l, r, n, s, d	may omit *other* sounds at the ends of words
10. When words start with /h/, the /h/ is silent.	'old/hold, 'it/hit
11. /r/ is tapped or trilled (tap /r/ might sound like the tap in the English word "butter").	
12. There is no /j/ (e.g., judge) sound in Spanish; speakers may substitute "y."	Yulie/Julie yoke/joke
13. Spanish /s/ is produced more frontally than English /s/.	Some speakers may sound like they have frontal lisps.
14. The ñ is pronounced like a "y" (e.g. "baño is pronounced "bahnyo").	

Spanish has 5 vowels: a, e, i, o, u (ah, eh, ee, long o, oo) and few diphthongs.
Thus, Spanish speakers may produce the following vowel substitutions:

15. ee/ih substitution	peeg/pig, leetle/little
16. eh/ae, ah/ae substitutions	pet/pat, Stahn/Stan

❑ Professionals should use formal titles to show respect when interacting with Hispanic adults. Adults should be addressed with the formal *you* (*Usted*) rather than the less formal *you* (*tu*). It is acceptable to use *tu* with children.

❑ Professionals should attempt to communicate with both parents in meetings. However, it is important to understand that in many families, the father is the spokesperson and the primary decision maker (Zuniga, 2004).

❑ Professionals will more readily gain the trust of family members if they have a humanistic orientation during meetings rather than a task orientation. Informal, friendly chatting can set the stage for work to be done. Discussing business immediately or appearing hurried may be considered rude. For this reason, professionals may need to allow extra time for the meeting to accommodate Hispanic families (Brice, 2002).

❑ Relationships are very important to Hispanic families; they may care more about the professional's personal qualities (e.g., approachability, interest in and respect for the family) than about the professional's technical qualifications (Kayser, 1998).

❑ Some Hispanic families may be uncomfortable collaborating with professionals because they do not see parent participation as necessary. They may prefer to leave decisions to school personnel. Thus, professionals should make sure that families truly understand their role in assessment and treatment plans. Family participation should always be strongly encouraged (Johnson & Viramontez Anguiano, 2004; Saldaña-Illingworth, 2006).

❑ Because of their respect for professionals, parents may not openly disagree with them or question them during meetings. At the same time, they may not follow suggestions that they have agreed to follow. Professionals should always follow up when suggestions have been given.

❑ Professionals should define terms such as "language disorder" and "learning disability" to ensure that parents understand their meanings. Otherwise, the parents may think professionals are talking about mental retardation or mental illness. As one Colombian immigrant told me, "In my country, children are normal, lazy, crazy, or retarded."

❑ Families may appear passive about accepting treatment for a child's condition if they believe that the condition is the result of external forces, as discussed previously. Professionals must work within the framework of the family's culture to foster confidence and trust.

❑ Professionals should openly state their expectations and explain the importance of maintaining schedules. Otherwise, families may be late for or miss appointments because they have a different perspective about time and/or lack of understanding about the importance of schedules.

❑ Professionals need to remember that there may be child-rearing norms among some Hispanic families that do not fit the Anglo mainstream time line for developmental milestones. For example, some Puerto Rican children are not weaned off the bottle until age 3 years, and some Mexican American preschool-age children may still use pacifiers or bottles.

❑ Because of the relaxed attitude toward child rearing, some parents may be resistant to the concept of early intervention, believing that children will eventually "catch up" to their peers.

Professionals can sensitively emphasize that early intervention will enhance performance in elementary school and beyond.

❏ Because of the primary importance of the family, children may be kept home from school to tend to sick family members, help meet the family's financial needs, attend a family function, etc. Professionals must help these families to understand U.S. laws about school attendance and the high value that is placed on attendance in American schools.

❏ If families are grieving about a child's disability, they may find comfort at a local church. Professionals can consider presenting this option when appropriate.

❏ Professionals may need to assist families so that they can be assertive in obtaining needed services (e.g., educational, medical).

❏ Be mindful of the child's and family's privacy when choosing other family members or friends to act as interpreters.

❏ Professionals who are offered gifts, food, or drink by the family should—within ethical boundaries—accept them because some Hispanic families may be insulted if professionals refuse these gifts.

❏ Clients may sit or stand close to the professionals with whom they are interacting. It is important not to move away.

❏ Parents may believe that an all-English program is superior to bilingual programs that enhance Spanish skills. It is therefore important to emphasize to parents that initial literacy instruction in Spanish often enhances future academic success.

❏ Professionals should do what they can to promote bilingual education opportunities for Hispanic students. Ideally, Hispanic students, especially those with language-learning disabilities, should receive bilingual instruction that maintains and promotes their Spanish skills while helping them learn to learn English (Gutiérrez-Clellen, 1999a; Restrepo & Kruth, 2000).

❏ Unfortunately, many Hispanic students are placed into all-English classrooms with no support in Spanish; this can be detrimental to their learning and progress. Language loss in Spanish is a major issue for these students, especially as they get older. Students who have limited opportunities for continued use of Spanish are likely to become less proficient in the language over time. (Kohnert, Bates, & Hernández, 1999; Mattes & García-Easterly, 2007).

❏ When interacting with students at home, parents who don't speak English well should continue to use Spanish. Parents should be encouraged to speak the language in which they feel most comfortable (Gutiérrez-Clellen, 1999a). Reproducible handouts developed by Saldaña-Illingworth (2006) in English and Spanish include practical suggestions for interacting with young children.

❏ It is better for children to hear fluent Spanish than "broken" English. Interacting in Spanish in the home reduces the likelihood of language loss and consequent negative cognitive and linguistic effects (Guiberson, Barrett, Jancosek, & Yoshinaga-Itano, 2006; Madding, 2002).

❏ Patterson (1999) and Brice (2000a) stated that parents should be reassured that modeling the behavior of codeswitching (alternating languages over phrases or sentences) is not detrimental to their children's language development in English or Spanish.

❏ A study by Gonzales, Ezell, and Randolph (1999) found that migrant Mexican-American families provided literacy experiences for their children in the home. However, these families generally engaged in story-telling or book-reading no more than a few times each week. It was recommended that parents be encouraged to provide literacy experiences daily and to make efforts to enhance their children's awareness of print.

❏ Madding (1999) found that Mexican Hispanic mothers were not highly verbal or directive in interactions with their children. When asked whose job it was to teach their children concepts such as colors or shapes, the mothers indicated that instruction of this type was the responsibility of teachers. In addition, the mothers believed that it was not appropriate to begin reading to their children prior to kindergarten. Thus, professionals may need to encourage mothers to read to their children prior to kindergarten and to stimulate the development of basic language concepts.

❏ Professionals can help parents carry out other home activities that will promote their children's cognitive and linguistic development. Parents can engage children in songs, rhymes, riddles, oral history, proverbs, and folklore in Spanish.

❏ Saldaña-Illingworth (2006) stressed that parents are "key players" in the learning process, emphasizing their importance in fostering the learning of vocabulary and basic listening skills. She described a variety of culturally appropriate listening and speaking activities for young Hispanic children that can be implemented by Spanish-speaking parents in the home environment. The activities are presented in English and Spanish and target language skills that are critical for success in the early school curriculum.

❏ Bliss et al. (2001) recommended that professionals help parents understand that talking with children about past experiences is an important foundational skill for literacy achievement. Parents should be taught to elicit narratives from their children.

❏ It is important for professionals to give families books that are enjoyable to read and relevant to children's daily living experiences. By doing this, families read to their children more often (Kayser, 2006).

❏ In addition, professionals should suggest language development activities for the home that are concrete and relevant to the interests and communication needs of children (Kummerer & López-Reyna, 2006).

❏ Professionals need to be sensitive to the cultural values, beliefs, and practices of parents when making recommendations that will affect their interactions with the child at home. However, as Zuniga (2004) emphasized, many Hispanic parents come to the U.S. specifically to obtain better educational opportunities for their children, and it would therefore be a disservice to withhold information that could facilitate language development and learning. Professionals should therefore present parents with a range of options so that they can make appropriate choices.

❏ Professionals must consider a variety of options other than standardized tests when attempting to identify gifted and talented Hispanic students.

❏ Many standardized tests require children to name pictures; however, many Spanish-speaking children will provide functions for objects rather than names. Clinicians may need to rephrase questions or present prompts to elicit appropriate responses.

✐ *REFLECTION* ✐

Describe two language interaction patterns commonly observed between parents and children in Spanish-speaking homes that differ from interaction patterns commonly observed in mainstream English-speaking families. How might these differences impact the performance of Spanish-speaking children in our schools?

_____

_____

_____

_____

_____

❏ Because some Hispanic children feel that it is rude to extend a topic when talking to an adult, clinicians need to be careful that they do not judge these children as having limited expressive language skills. Many standardized tests have tasks that require verbal elaboration (e.g., "Tell me all you can about a horse.") These types of tasks may be biased against Hispanic children, who have been taught that this type of verbal elaboration is rude.

❏ Professionals need to be extremely careful when using standardized tests with Hispanic children because of the bias inherent in these measures. Dialectal variations and individual differences in the amount of exposure that children have had to English and Spanish make it difficult to make educational decisions based on test norms (Mattes & García-Easterly, 2007; Mattes & Saldaña-Illingworth, 2008).

❏ Peña and Quinn (1997) assessed the language skills of preschool Spanish-speaking children. They found that a task requiring descriptive responses (e.g., "What are stoves used for?") was more sensitive than a labeling task (e.g., "Tell me what's in this picture") in differentiating preschoolers who were developing typically from those who had low language skills.

❏ Professionals must also remember that many Hispanic students have stronger vocabulary skills in English in some areas and stronger vocabulary skills in Spanish in others. The students, for example, may know school vocabulary in English and home vocabulary in Spanish (Gutiérrez-Clellen, Restrepo, Bedore, Peña, & Anderson, 2000; Mattes & García-Easterly, 2007). Professionals can dual-score vocabulary tests, using both Spanish and English responses to achieve a total score for the test (Mattes & Saldaña-Illingworth, 2008).

❏ Some Hispanic children may not perform well on tasks that require repeating facts or foretelling what they will do in the future. They may have little experience with these activities in the home.

❏ In addition, Hispanic children may remain silent when interacting with unfamiliar adult professionals who are attempting to assess and/or treat them. It is important not to misinterpret the children's silence as indicative of a language-learning disability.

❏ Experts recommend the use of information from parent interviews and language samples when assessing Spanish-speaking children for possible communication disorders (Gutiérrez-Clellen et al., 2000; Mattes & Saldaña-Illingworth, 2008; Patterson, 2000; Restrepo, 1998). Specific techniques for collecting language samples have been described (see Gutiérrez-Clellen et al., 2000; Mattes & Saldaña-Illingworth, 2008).

❏ When conducting parent interviews to ascertain the language skills of young children, professionals may consider utilizing the Fundación MacArthur Inventario del Desarrollo de Habilidades Comunicativas: Palabras Enunciadoes (IDHC: PE; Jackson-Maldonado, Bates, & Thal, 1992). However, research has only shown this instrument to be valid with monolingual, Spanish-speaking children living in Mexico in educated, middle- and upper-class families (Thal, Jackson-Maldonado, & Acosta, 2000). Professionals should be cautious when using this instrument with children from families that do not fit that profile.

❏ Gutiérrez-Clellen, Restrepo, and Simon-Cereijido (2006) evaluated the discriminant accuracy of a grammatical measure to identify language impairment in Latino Spanish-speaking children. They found that this measure was appropriate for identifying language impairment in either Spanish-dominant or Spanish-only speakers between 4 and 6 years of age. However, for older children, supplemental testing was recommended.

❏ When Hispanic students are served in educational settings, professionals should remember to be sensitive to cultural and linguistic phenomena that impact service delivery to these students.

❏ Hispanic students may be more comfortable with cooperative, group learning than with individualistic, competitive learning situations. Many perform best in cooperative learning situations in which they experience warmth and enthusiasm.

❏ Brice & Montgomery (1996) found that older Hispanic students with and without language-learning disabilities needed to learn how to ask questions, interact with teachers, and participate actively in classroom settings.

❏ Westby, Dezale, Fradd, & Lee (1999) found that in classrooms taught by Hispanic teachers, students were encouraged to engage in overlapping discourse to co-construct their understanding of tasks. In these classrooms, the teachers used social communication to relate personal experiences to academic context. Humor was used to create a positive atmosphere that encouraged students to participate. Use of these strategies may be effective in fostering learning among Hispanic students.

❏ Restrepo (1998) found that Spanish-speaking children with language impairments used fewer complex sentences than Spanish-speaking children who were developing according to expectations. Thus it was recommended that Spanish-speaking students with language impairments be encouraged to use complex sentences more frequently.

❏ Hispanic students with language-learning disabilities may also need direct assistance in learning to figure out word definitions during literacy activities in the classroom. Professionals can utilize dictionaries for this purpose (Gutiérrez-Clellen & DeCurtis, 1999).

❏ Several researchers have studied the narrative skills of Spanish-speaking children with language impairments. Brito, Pérez, Bliss, and McCabe (1999) found that the narratives of these children contained fewer evaluative statements. They suggested that professionals elicit evaluative statements more frequently so that communication becomes more personal and emotionally expressive.

❏ Gutiérrez-Clellen (1998) studied Mexican Spanish-speaking children with language impairments and found that the task of re-telling a story based on a short, silent movie elicited more complex language than story-retelling based on a wordless book. She therefore suggested that professionals use movies to promote the development of narrative skills in language-impaired Spanish-speaking children.

❏ Bedore and Leonard (2000) suggested that professionals overlay new information onto what is already known when teaching Hispanic students. For example, if a professional is teaching a new inflectional form to a Spanish-speaking child, this form should be introduced in a context in which familiar vocabulary is used. In this way, the professional maximizes the resources available and makes learning relevant to the student's previous learning experiences.

❏ Rubenstein-Ávila (2006) recommended that in instruction for older Hispanic students, professionals employ content-area cognates. For example, a geometry teacher can point out the similarities in terms such as *angle (angulo)*, *sphere (esfera)*, and *parallel lines (lineas paralelas)*. A geography teacher can highlight such cognates as *gulf (golfo)*. In this way, students can consciously apply their knowledge of Spanish vocabulary when reading and learning in English.

❏ As mentioned previously, Hispanic families tend to utilize preschool programs less than families from other groups. Professionals should encourage these families to send their children to preschool to help them acquire the basic skills necessary for school success (Takanishi, 2006).

❏ Some parents are fearful about having their young children away from them and, therefore, may not wish to have their children in preschool programs. Encourage these parents to make observations in the classroom or to volunteer as helpers. Such participation is likely to reduce their reluctance to send their children to preschool.

❏ A study by Mendez Pérez (2000) examined the attitudes and beliefs of Spanish-speaking Mexican American mothers whose young children had disabilities. Mendez Pérez found that the mothers in her study did not expect their children to talk until the age of three years. Thus, they were not concerned about their young children's limited verbal skills, believing that their children would eventually "catch up."

❏ Hispanic mothers of children with disabilities often experience discrimination. The discrimination occurs most often when parents are raising the child alone and need public assistance (McHatton & Correa, 2005). Documents needed by parents, for example, have often been provided in English rather than Spanish.

❏ Professionals need to make sure that any relevant paperwork is translated into Spanish. If caregivers are nonliterate, interpreters can be utilized to explain the purpose of the paperwork and what needs to be done.

❏ Mainstream professionals tend to emphasize independence and self-sufficiency in students with disabilities. However, this may conflict with the beliefs and goals of some Hispanic parents. Rueda, Monzo, Blancher, Shapiro, and González (2005, p. 412) found that "Where the system repeatedly tried to view the young adult child as an autonomous individual, mothers found this approach a disturbing violation of their view of the child as embedded in the family." Thus, professionals must always remember that some Hispanic parents may view their role as "forever caregivers" who anticipate taking care of their "disabled children" for a lifetime, not just for 18 years.

❑ Hispanic high school students have been found to perform better academically when Hispanic literature is used in the instructional program; students respond well to books written by Hispanic authors. In addition, these students benefit from interactions with older Hispanic mentors and friendships with other Hispanic students who have high academic ideals (Gandara, 2004).

By incorporating the Hispanic student's language and culture into the educational curriculum, school professionals are better able to provide the comprehensible input necessary for these students to succeed in the classroom. Our efforts to meet the needs of the rapidly growing Hispanic student population will require collaborative efforts between parents, school professionals, and members of the Hispanic community. Progress is being made, but much more needs to be done to ensure that students from Hispanic backgrounds receive appropriate instructional services.

Profile

Jorge, a 17-year-old high school sophomore, had a documented bilateral 50 dB sensorineural hearing loss. His family moved to California from rural Mexico when Jorge was 16 years old. In Mexico, Jorge had not learned sign language or lipreading, and he had never had hearing aids. The school district tested Jorge's hearing and informed his parents that he would need hearing aids to function effectively in school and in a vocation.

Jorge and his family were angry because of the school district's "interference," and denied that the hearing loss existed. Thus, Jorge received no additional assistance and was performing poorly in high school. The speech-language pathologist contacted Jose R., a Mexican professional from the State Department of Vocational Rehabilitation, who himself had come from a migrant Mexican family. Mr. R. met with Jorge and his parents, and found that they actually knew about Jorge's hearing loss but denied it, believing that the hearing loss meant that they (the parents) had sinned against God. The parents felt that Jorge's "defect" was punishment for their sins. They had accepted their fate and believed that no intervention was appropriate.

Mr. R. arranged a meeting with Jorge's family and the local priest to discuss the situation. After this meeting, the priest assured the parents that Jorge's hearing loss was not an indication of sin on their part. The parents then informed the school district that they would permit the use of hearing aids. Jorge was subsequently fitted with aids and his academic performance improved markedly.

STUDY QUESTIONS

1. Describe three ways in which cultural expectations within the Hispanic culture differ from cultural expectations within the mainstream Anglo culture in the United States (e.g., degree to which punctuality is important). How might these differences impact service delivery to Hispanic students and their families?

2. Traditional language assessment measures are often biased in favor of mainstream Anglo students. Describe two nondiscriminatory strategies, recommended by researchers, that can be used to conduct language assessments with Hispanic students.

3. Describe health considerations that are relevant to many Hispanic families in the U.S.

TRUE-FALSE

Circle the number beside each true statement below.

4. Puerto Ricans are the largest Hispanic group in the U.S.

5. When assessing vocabulary proficiency levels in Spanish-speaking students, tasks that require the description of the function of objects are more helpful than tasks that require the naming of objects.

6. At the beginning of a meeting, most Hispanic families prefer that professionals "cut to the chase" and not waste time on social preliminaries or chit-chat.

7. Researchers have found that Mexican mothers have their children practice using basic concepts such as colors, shapes, and numbers in the home so that they will be prepared for kindergarten.

8. The utterance, "This cake chocolate is more big than that cake" would suggest a language difference rather than a disorder, in a Spanish-speaking child learning English.

9. Young Hispanic children often respond better in educational situations that promote feelings of warmth, physical closeness, and cooperative learning than in situations that encourage competitive, individualistic learning.

10. Hispanic families may oppose recommendations for early intervention when informed that their children have not mastered specific preschool-level skills.

MULTIPLE CHOICE

11. Unfortunately, Hispanic students often experience academic difficulties and fail to complete high school. Possible reasons for this failure are:
    A. Fluctuating funding for programs designed to assist students in learning English as a second language
    B. Sporadic school attendance due to high family mobility
    C. Culture shock and other differences in home and school expectations
    D. Negative affective on learning that have resulted from bilingualism

12. Which of the following recommendations reflect "best practice" for professionals who work with Hispanic children and their families?
    A. Tell parents to speak only English in the home so that children can learn faster and experience greater academic success.
    B. Encourage parents to teach their young children basic concepts and to read to them in the early years (e.g., before kindergarten).
    C. Rely on nationally normed language tests to ensure that language skills are measured precisely when differentiating language differences from disorders in Spanish-speaking children.
    D. Encourage Hispanic students to be assertive in the classroom (e.g., raise their hands, interact with teachers).
    E. State expectations and let families know about the importance of keeping to a schedule (e.g., for meetings).

13. A teacher has referred a Spanish-speaking child to you for assessment. In the teacher's words, "This child has trouble pronouncing his sounds in English. I think he may need speech therapy." Which of the following English productions are indicative of an articulation difference rather than an articulation disorder?
    A. My tum (thumb) got cut when I was eskating wit (with) my friends in de (the) park.
    B. The pawk (park) had a bun (bunch) of dwied (dried) gwass.
    C. Dere (there) was a leetle peeg (little pig) in de (the) park and I wanted to as' (ask) if I could pet it.
    D. Lat (that) TV tow (show) is not bunny (funny).

14. Which one of the following general statements is NOT true about Hispanics in the U.S.?
    A. Most Hispanics have strong family values.
    B. Most Hispanics receive welfare services because poverty impacts so many of them.
    C. Most Hispanics are Catholic.
    D. Young Hispanic children tend to interact more often with other children at home than with adults.
    E. Hispanics may experience inadequate medical care because they frequently do not have health insurance.

15. Many Hispanic families do not:
    A. Emphasize education for girls
    B. Respect and listen to older family members
    C. Emphasize cooperation and the welfare of the whole family
    D. Question professionals out of respect
    E. Eat food that is not kosher

ANSWERS TO STUDY QUESTIONS

    4. False
    5. True
    6. False
    7. False
    8. True
    9. True
    10. True
    11. A, B, and C
    12. B, D, and E
    13. A and C
    14. B
    15. A and D

Chapter 6

FAMILIES FROM ASIAN BACKGROUNDS

Outline

Many families from Asian countries have come to live in the United States in recent years. Students who are classified as "Asian" come from three primary geographic regions:

East Asia:	Japan, Korea, China
Southeast Asia:	Philippines, Laos, Cambodia, Thailand, Indonesia, Singapore, Myanmar (Burma), Vietnam, Malaysia
South Asia:	Sri Lanka, Pakistan, India

A large number of Asians originate from countries in the Pacific Rim, which includes all nations and regions touching the Pacific Ocean. As shown in Figure 6.1, China is the largest country in Asia. Although most countries in Asia are small in physical size, some (e.g., Japan) have large populations.

Figure 6.1

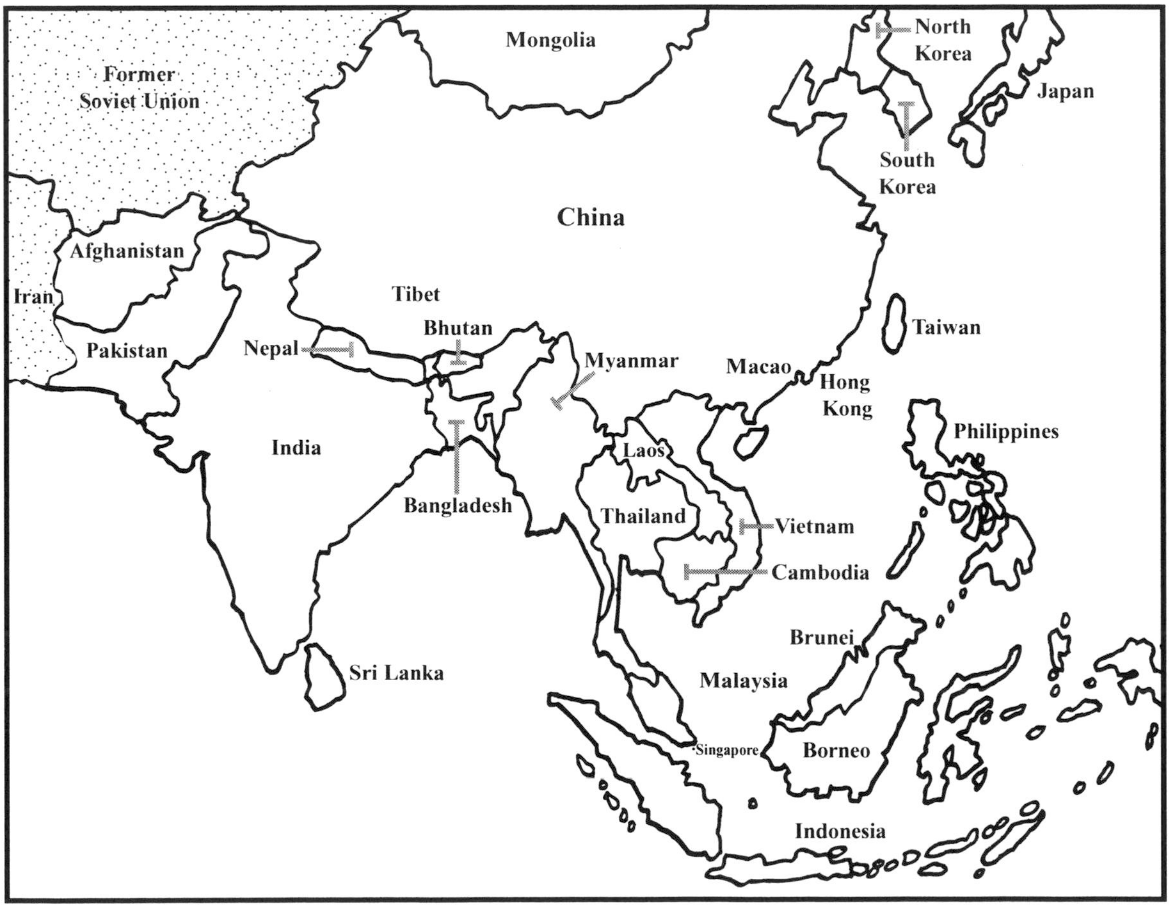

GENERAL BACKGROUND INFORMATION

❏ Some Asian cultures (Korean, Chinese, Vietnamese) are rooted in civilizations that are over 4,000 years old (Chan & Lee, 2004).

❏ Common religions in Asia are Buddhism, Taoism, and Confucianism (Chung, 2006). Confucianism is especially prevalent in China. Other religions include animism (all forms of spirit worship, including the spirits of nature), Hinduism, Islam, and Shintoism.

❏ Many Southeast Asians are Buddhist, and some groups believe in fortune-telling, astrology, shamanism, and ancestor worship.

❏ Residents of the Philippines are primarily Roman Catholic (Schmit, 2005). However, some Filipinos are Protestant. In the Philippines, as in other Asian countries, religion is intertwined with everyday life. Suico (2005, p. 195) stated that "...the interrelationships between culture and religion in Philippine society have had great impact in almost every facet of community life."

❏ The majority of Indians are Hindus. The caste system is a unique feature of Hindu life. There are four castes, with Brahmins being the highest caste and Sudras being the lowest caste or "menials." The traditional caste system is not promoted today, but individuals from different castes commonly do not maintain contact (Cheng, 2002).

❏ Indian Hindus regard the cow as sacred and pure because it gives milk, one of the purest substances. Most Hindus, therefore, do not eat beef.

❏ Between 1990 and 2000, using the category of "race alone," the number of Asians in the U.S. increased by 48.3%. If one uses the figures from the category of "race alone or in combination," the number of Asians in the United States grew by 72.2% between 1990 and 2000, reaching a total of 11,898,828 persons in the U.S. in 2000 (U.S. Bureau of the Census, 2000).

❏ In July, 2005, an estimated 14.4 million U.S. residents said that they were Asian or Asian in combination with one or more other races. This group comprised approximately 5% of the total U.S. population, with 4.9 million of these residents living in California (U.S. Census Bureau, 2007).

❏ Between the years 2004 and 2005, the number of Asians in the U.S. grew by 3%, the highest of any race group during that time period. Chinese Americans are the largest detailed group currently, followed by Filipinos, Asian Indians, Vietnamese, Koreans, and Japanese (American Community Survey, 2005).

❏ Thirty percent of Asian children live in low-income families, compared with 61% of African American children and 63% of Hispanic children (National Center for Children in Poverty, 2006).

❏ In 2005, the median income for single-race Asians was $61,094, the highest among all racial groups in the U.S. There were some differences among Asian groups; for example, the median income for Vietnamese Americans was $50,925; for Asian Indians, it was $73,575 (American Community Survey, 2007).

❏ Asians in the United States are often referred to as the "model minority." For example, Steinberg (1996; cited in Johnston, 2001) stated, "It is more advantageous to be Asian than to be wealthy, to have nondivorced parents, or to have a mother who is able to stay home full time." The "model minority" belief can cause many problems such as the following:

1. Asians may be targets of resentment because they are put into an uncomfortable comparative position with other ethnic groups (Sue & Sue, 2008).
2. Social problems such as gang membership among Asian youth, poverty, substance abuse, domestic violence, and mental illness may be ignored, making it difficult for Asians to receive help in dealing with these problems.

3. The needs of Asian students often go unrecognized and, consequently, unmet by the educational system. This can contribute to a higher dropout rate (Chan & Lee, 2004). Whereas Asian students are typically underrepresented in special education programs, they are overrepresented in programs for the gifted (Poon-McBrayer & García, 2000). In 1998-1999, Asian Americans accounted for 8% of California's K-12 enrollment, but represented 40% of the student body at University of California at Berkeley. However, numerous researchers point out that not all Asian students perform equally well in the educational system (Johnston, 2001; Sue & Sue, 2008; Vang, 2005; Wong & Halgin, 2006). Groups such as Cambodians, Hmong, and Laotians tend to have less money and perform more poorly in school than Japanese and Korean students. Among the Hmong, only 31% typically complete high school. Thus, when all Asian students are viewed as a monolithic group, the needs of the lower-achieving students often are not met (Wong & Halgin, 2006).

ASIAN FAMILY LIFE

❏ The family is the basic societal unit and the central focus of an individual's life (Doan, 2005). Extended families, with several generations living under the same roof, are quite common. Filial piety is a strong value for most Asian families (Hsin & Macer, 2006).

❏ Most, but not all, Asian cultures are patriarchal; the family structure in the Philippines, for example, is matriarchal (Roseberry-McKibbin, 1997b). Mothers often play equal roles in the family and are the primary decision makers regarding finances, children, and health care (de Jesus, 2005).

❏ In most Asian families, there is a high emphasis on family interdependence and conformity. Family support and maintenance of social harmony are seen as lifelong obligations (Vansteenkiste, Zhou, Lens, & Soenens, 2005).

❏ As stated earlier, role relationships within hierarchies are often considered important, especially in Confucian families. Individuals within the family are expected to fill their roles according to gender, age, and position. For example, wives may submit to husbands, younger male children may submit to older male children, and female children may submit to everyone.

❏ In Confucian Asian families, each individual child is a developing part of a continuing family lineage. Lai (2006, p. 688) describes this as a "we-self" in contrast to the Western "I-self."

❏ Fathers may hold the highest authority in the family. Eldest sons also frequently have high positions of respect.

❏ Children are encouraged to defer to adults and other authority figures. Respect for elders is expected.

❏ Some families may value boys more than girls and stress education more for boys (Yunus, 2005).

❏ Differences between parenting styles in Asian families have been found. In one study, Filipino American and Japanese families tended to have the most egalitarian relationships with their children, whereas Chinese, Korean, and Southeast Asian American families were more authoritarian (Blair & Qian, 1998).

❑ Many Asian mothers treat their infants in a way that Americans would consider "spoiling." For example, infants are carried frequently; if they are away from a caregiver and begin crying, they are attended to immediately. Most are breast-fed on demand around the clock. Children may sleep with their parents for the first several years of their lives. Parents often believe that this is the best way to create a confident, secure individual (Yunus, 2005).

❑ In many Asian families the children learn to rely heavily on nonverbal cues from their caregivers. Adults may model or demonstrate a particular action as a child watches, and there may be little emphasis on verbal communication (Yunus, 2005).

❑ Some Asian parents hand feed their children in order to ensure that their children will get enough to eat. When these children come to preschool, they may not know how to feed themselves and may need to be shown (Hwa-Froelich & Westby, 2003).

❑ Many Asian adults do not create learning situations for their children; rather, children are responsible for learning culturally valued behaviors through observing and being with adults during the course of a day (Zhao, 2007).

❑ Hwa-Froelich and Westby (2003) emphasized that in their study, caregivers did not show love for children by playing with them but rather by taking care of their needs (e.g., dressing, feeding, bathing children).

❑ Some families believe that learning through exploration is unnatural. If children express curiosity and engage in active exploration, they are viewed as ill-mannered. Children should be self-restrained and quiet, not spontaneous and exuberant (Yunus, 2005; Zhao, 2002).

❑ The viewpoint that children "should be seen and not heard" is common. Talking at the family dinner table is generally viewed as impolite. Many Asians believe that "a quiet child is a good child" (Van Kleeck, 1994, p. 70).

❑ Parents often control the direction of a conversation, the length of time children can talk, and the topics discussed.

❑ The child's individual growth and development is not viewed as a priority in many families; Neither self-realization nor self-expression are viewed as priorities (Zhao, 2007).

❑ Parents tend to initiate conversation with children, verbally explain tasks, verbally monitor children's activities, and ask children factual questions.

❑ If a child behaves badly, the entire family may lose face. Children are expected to work toward family goals and not engage in behaviors that would bring dishonor to the family (Sue & Sue, 2008).

❑ Children may be strictly controlled and punished physically (Fung & Roseberry-McKibbin, 1999; Pelczarski & Kemp, 2006). They may be beaten with belts (Yunus, 2005).

❑ Children may stay in the home as long as they are unmarried, even if they have reached adulthood. These individuals may help care for nieces and nephews.

❑ Older siblings commonly care for younger siblings.

❏ Among some groups such as the Hmong, it is common for girls to marry between 13 and 16 years of age (Vang, 2005).

❏ Marriage may be a concern of the entire family rather than a private matter between the two people involved.

❏ In some groups, the whole family's reputation may be in danger if a young woman has a boyfriend before she is married.

❏ Among some Asian groups, women bring honor to themselves and their families by bearing sons. Sons are more highly valued than daughters.

❏ Divorce is often viewed as being unacceptable.

❏ Many Asian students come from two-parent homes. In the U.S., single-parent Asian families are rare (Shekar & Hegde, 1995).

Profile

Ameet Singh (not his real name) was referred to me by his kindergarten teacher, who was worried about his behavior, language, and overall lack of engagement in classroom activities. Ameet came from a Hindi-speaking home, so I engaged the services of a Hindi-speaking interpreter to screen his language and cognitive skills. Ameet would not look at the interpreter or talk to her; he showed her the same hostile behavior he had directed at other adults at the school site. I met with Mrs. Singh and spoke with her extensively. Mrs. Singh revealed that Ameet had never been to preschool, and that he only went to temple when accompanied by his family. He had never been in the care of anyone other than family members. Mrs. Singh indicated that she wanted Ameet to spend his time with family members and that he should never be alone with strangers (e.g., day care providers or preschool teachers). Not wanting to mislabel Ameet as "special ed," my colleagues and I decided to give him time to develop and acclimate to being away from his family and to being in a school environment. Ameet struggled with kindergarten, but ended up performing quite well in subsequent grades. He did not have a language-learning disability or cognitive problem. He merely needed time to adjust to a formal school setting.

EDUCATION AND LITERACY

As a student who attended Asian schools, I learned much about the Asian educational system. Additional information for this section was obtained from interviews with individuals from Asian cultures and a review of the research cited below.

❏ Educational levels vary widely among Asian immigrants. For example, only 3% of persons arriving from India lack a high school education, and 75% of working Indians are college graduates (United States Center for Immigration Studies, 2001).

❏ Asian Indians and Filipinos in the U.S. have the highest educational attainment of all ethnic groups (Chan & Lee, 2004; Shekar & Hegde, 1995). Conversely, many refugees from other countries are preliterate (Cheng, 1999). For example, many Hmong students in the U.S. are among the poorest students in the American educational system. Many enter school preliterate and without any school experience (Vang, 2005).

❏ Forty-nine percent of single-race Asians 25 years of age or older have a Bachelor's degree or higher level of education. Only 27% of the general population aged 25 or older have attained this same level of education. Ten percent of all people in the U.S. who are 25 or older have graduate or professional degrees (e.g., Master's, doctorate). Approximately 20% of Asians, however, have these advanced degrees (American Community Survey, 2005).

❏ Many Asians have great respect for learning. Education is viewed as a means of advancement for the individual and represents honor for the family. Many immigrant Asian parents view education for their children as a way out of poverty (F. Tolentino, personal communication, 2/26/07).

❏ Asians have high expectations for their children's educational attainment. Okagaki and Frensch (1998) studied educational expectations of parents from Asian, Hispanic, and European American groups and found that the Asian parents set higher expectations for their children and had higher standards for achievement. Asian parents also expected their children to complete more years of schooling than they themselves had.

❏ Abboud and Kim (2007, pp. 1-2) stated that "The role of Asian children in the family is clear-cut and two-fold: Respect your elders and obey your parents. Study hard and do well in school to secure a bright future." Asian children in the U.S. may perform better academically than their non-Asian counterparts because non-Asian children often divide their time between many activities, while Asian children focus more on their school work.

❏ Abboud and Kim (2007) also pointed out that many American non-Asian parents try hard to boost their children's self esteem, while Asian parents praise their children less frequently. Asian parents may show that they are proud of their children's efforts yet unsatisfied with their performance.

❏ Asian parents encourage their children to work hard to boost their grades. Children are constantly exhorted to "do better."

❏ In some groups, the greatest honor children can bestow on their parents is academic achievement. Children are under constant pressure to succeed academically and have a good career (particularly in the technical fields or hard sciences). Such success is evidence of a good family upbringing (Sue & Sue, 2008).

❏ Many Asian parents see themselves as active agents in their children's learning and work diligently at home with their children (Abboud & Kim, 2007). However, other parents may see school work as the "school's job" and therefore be reluctant to participate (Lai & Ishiyama, 2004; Vang, 2005).

❏ In many schools (e.g., those in Vietnam), proper manners in human relations are the most important value that students are taught; knowledge is secondary. Moral education occupies a significant part of the curriculum (Doan, 2005).

❏ Hwa-Froelich and Westby (2003) found that the goals viewed as important by Head Start teachers are not necessarily viewed by parents as being important. The Southeast Asian parents' goals for their children were not oriented toward developing self-esteem and independence. Rather, a primary goal for the Southeast Asian parents was that their children develop respect for and obedience to authority figures. They believed that both respect and listening were more important than learning. In fact, some parents believed that the teachers were like royalty.

❏ Some Asian parents may not attend school events such as a family fun night, a pancake breakfast, or PTA meetings because they do not see a direct relationship between these events and academics (Pearce & Lin, 2005).

❏ For some Asian families, if children perform poorly at school, it is preferable for the children to stay home than to go to school, struggle, and cause the entire family to lose face (Hwa-Froelich & Westby, 2003).

❏ In some Asian countries, boys are separated from girls during instruction.

❏ Students and their families accord teachers great respect. In some countries, teachers are revered as much as doctors.

❏ In some schools students are expected to stand up and bow when the teacher enters the room. Students sit down only when given permission to do so.

❏ Some Asian schools rely heavily on rote learning and memorization. Conformity may be considered more important than creativity.

❏ In some Asian schools, corporal punishment is acceptable. Teachers may physically discipline children whose behavior, performance, or both do not conform to expected norms.

❏ Many Asian students are accustomed to authoritarian teachers. Asian students are expected to maintain a proper social distance from their teachers (Yunus, 2005).

❏ Teachers often lecture to students without offering opportunities for discussion of the information presented.

❏ Many Asians consider it rude for students to volunteer or to ask questions in class.

❏ Asian students are unlikely to correct a teacher or to hear a teacher admit that an error was made.

❏ Students tend to avoid eye contact with teachers because direct eye contact is considered rude.

❏ In U.S. schools, Asian students may take fewer risks, participate less, and hesitate in response to questions (Yeh, Chen, Kwong, Chiang, Wang, & Pu-Folkes, 2002).

❏ Some Asian schools do not provide textbooks to individual students. Students are expected to copy information from the blackboard or to take oral dictation.

❏ In some Asian schools, teachers have complete responsibility for the care of their students. They may even take students to the doctor if medical care is needed.

❑ Some Asian schools require students to wear uniforms. Schools are generally not considered places to display the latest fashions.

❑ In many countries, students go home for lunch because food is not served at school.

Profile

A former college student of mine was from a Chinese immigrant family. The student, "Rica," was very bright and hardworking; she was clearly going to be an excellent speech-language pathologist. Once, in class, she shared that her family had originally expected her to be a pharmacist. Her decision to major in speech-language pathology led to a considerable amount of family conflict. Her mother was especially disappointed, cried a great deal, and continually pressured Rica to change her mind and major in pharmacy. Rica shared that her mother "backed off" when she told her that speech-language pathologists' salaries had risen and, although not commensurate with those of pharmacists, would provide Rica with a good living.

CULTURAL CUSTOMS AND COURTESIES

❑ Hospitality is highly valued.

❑ Many Asians bow slightly when greeting others.

❑ In some homes, guests are expected to remove their shoes.

❑ Public hand holding or touching between same-sex members may be acceptable. In some countries, same-sex friends commonly walk arm-in-arm.

❑ Public displays of affection between members of the opposite sex may be frowned upon and seen as distasteful. Holding hands in public may be considered daring.

❑ Among some groups, dating is not permitted and premarital sex is frowned upon.

❑ Modesty in dress and appearance is highly valued; some American clothing may be considered immodest and revealing.

❑ Modesty and humility are highly valued; "blowing your own horn," on the other hand, may be viewed as arrogant and unseemly. In Japan, it is said that "the nail that sticks its head up gets hammered down."

❑ Other important personal qualities for many Asians include self-restraint, self-sacrifice, inner strength, perseverance, and patience.

❑ Authority figures of any kind generally should not be questioned.

❑ Hierarchical relationships tend to be viewed as important, especially for Chinese who are from Confucian backgrounds (Tsai, 2006). Conventions can be based on age, gender, social status, etc.

❏ Many Asian groups show reverence for the elderly. Asians therefore approach old age with self-respect, dignity, and pride. In addition, the number of grandchildren one has may be viewed as a measure of one's success in life.

❏ Some students (e.g., Vietnamese) may wear a Buddhist symbol that is shaped like a swastika. They may be aware only of the Buddhist meaning of this symbol.

HEALTH CARE AND DISABLING CONDITIONS

❏ In the U.S., lack of health insurance is a significant problem for many Asian immigrants and refugees. This is particularly true for those from China and Korea (United States Center for Immigration Studies, 2001).

❏ Many Asians only consider physical disabilities to be worthy of treatment.

❏ Many Asian parents believe that children who are "disabled" will show physical evidence of that disability. Conditions that are not visible (e.g., stuttering, learning disability) are believed to result from "not trying hard enough." Because of these beliefs, parents may not see any need for therapy or rehabilitation (Bebout & Arthur, 1992).

❏ Hwa-Froelich and Westby (2003) found that Southeast Asian parents in their study believed that learning problems were associated with fate, stubbornness, or laziness. When students did not perform as expected in school, strict discipline was used to force these students to study longer and work harder. Some parents referred to learning problems as the child's "fate" or as the result of being born under "bad stars." All of the Southeast Asian parents preferred administering physical punishment to their children over losing face; none of them wanted their children to repeat a grade.

❏ Hwa-Froelich and Westby (2003) found that Asian parents viewed students with severe physical conditions such as blindness or deafness as a potentially shameful burden on the family. These children were not viewed as capable of doing anything useful.

❏ Among many Asians, there is a tendency to define the causes of health-related problems and disabilities in spiritual terms. For example, problems may be attributed to spoiled foods, demons or spirits, or a bad wind (Cheng, 1999). Many Filipinos believe that illnesses are a result of God's ultimate plan (Schmit, 2005).

❏ Fadiman (1997) told the story of a Hmong girl with epilepsy who lived in central California. Doctors wanted to treat the epilepsy with traditional Western medical methods. Her family, however, believed that her condition was caused by spiritual forces, stating that "the spirit catches you and you fall down." The family disagreed with the doctors about using recommended medical treatment.

❏ Some Asians feel that disabling conditions occur because of one's "fate" and that nothing can or should be done to interfere (Yamey & Greenwood, 2004).

❏ Other families believe that birth defects and disabilities result from sins committed by parents and even remote ancestors. As a result, the child may be looked upon as an object of shame for the entire family and consequently isolated from society.

❑ To "save face" some families hesitate to seek medical or other care for children with disabilities.

❑ Many Asian groups believe that caring for the disabled child is the responsibility of the family rather than the school.

❑ Health practices may involve acupuncture, herbs, massage, and baths in hot springs. People may visit religious shrines or temples to seek healing.

❑ Some Western practices such as collecting blood, surgery, performing biopsies, etc., may be alien to the Asian families.

❑ Attitudes about disabilities and their rehabilitation are often influenced by the degree of acculturation. First generation immigrants may feel more "hopeless" than Asians born and raised in the United States (Huer, Saenz, & Doan, 2001).

Profile

Melanie, an 8-year-old Filipino girl, was born with a cleft palate. She had undergone several surgical operations, but her speech continued to be affected by hypernasality and poor articulation. The surgeon had recommended pharyngeal flap surgery for Melanie to resolve the velopharyngeal incompetence that was causing Melanie's hypernasality, but the family refused the surgery. At the triennial IEP meeting, the speech-language pathologist informed Melanie's parents that the student's speech had become more intelligible as a result of treatment, although she still exhibited hypernasality.

The speech-language pathologist expressed the concern that further therapy to modify Melanie's resonance would not be effective unless she had pharyngeal flap surgery. The father was very angry and refused to allow Melanie to come back for more speech therapy. He smiled as he left, however, and thanked the speech-language pathologist for the work she had done with Melanie over the last 3 years.

ASIAN COMMUNICATION STYLES

❑ Many Asian languages have formal rules of communication propriety based on the relative status of each of the participants in the interaction. Personal questions Americans might find offensive (e.g., "How old are you?" or "Are you married?") are considered appropriate as a means of ascertaining each participant's status.

❑ Smooth and harmonious interpersonal relationships are a high priority. Asians may therefore avoid public confrontations and open competition.

❑ Many Asians are indirect in their communication, giving the impression that they are evasive and noncommittal (Chan & Lee, 2004). Much information is conveyed nonverbally through subtle gestures, postures, positioning, facial expressions, eye contact, and silence (Fung & Roseberry-McKibbin, 1999).

❑ Direct eye contact may be considered an open show of rudeness or challenge between individuals who are conversing. Interrupting a conversation may also be considered impolite.

❏ Many Asians believe that it is inappropriate and offensive to display anger publicly or to contradict others (Roseberry-McKibbin, 1997b). Rather, it is considered proper to keep one's outward composure, no matter how one may feel inside.

❏ Cheng (2007) emphasized that a polite smile, nod, or response of "yes" may simply be an acknowledgement that the client has heard a message. It may not indicate agreement with the comments. When asked to do something, Asians often give a positive response in an effort to be polite. However, they may not follow through (Chan & Lee, 2004).

❏ Smiling does not necessarily imply happiness or pleasure; it can connote many positive or even negative emotions. Some Asians smile or laugh in situations when they are embarrassed. "Saving face" or avoiding public embarrassment is very important.

❏ Many groups (e.g., the Japanese and Indians) value silence and think that Westerners are verbose. Silence may be used to avoid expressing disagreement.

❏ Among some groups, it is considered unacceptable to touch others on the head.

❏ Some groups, such as the Japanese, may be accustomed to more personal space than that commonly experienced during interactions with Anglo Americans. It is important not to violate space boundaries.

❏ Among many traditional Japanese, honorifics and formalities are the norm. Such formalities might seem excessive to Americans.

ASIAN LANGUAGE CONSIDERATIONS

❏ Some of the most widely spoken Asian languages in the United States are Chinese, Filipino, Vietnamese, Japanese, Khmer, and Korean (Cheng, 2002).

❏ Many Asian languages have numerous dialects that may or may not be mutually intelligible; for example, there are over 87 dialects in China and the Philippines (Cheng, 1991). Most Philippine dialects spoken in the Philippines are mutually unintelligible (Roseberry-McKibbin, 1997b).

❏ The Indian constitution recognizes 15 major languages, but India has over 700 dialects. Hindi is recognized as the national language, although many Indians do not speak it.

❏ Kannada is another major language of India. English is the official language of education and the government (see Shekar & Hegde, 1995, for a complete description of the phonetics, phonology, and grammar of Hindi and Kannada).

❏ Students from countries such as Vietnam and Cambodia may speak French in addition to their primary language.

❏ Some groups have politeness conventions that dictate the use of certain word forms depending upon the relative status of the participants in the interaction. For example, Japanese has more than 100 words for "I" and "me" that are selected based on one's social status (Cheng, 1991).

❑ Vietnamese, Chinese, and Laotian are tonal languages. Each tone change is phonemic in nature and represents a meaning change. For example, in Mandarin, the word "ma" can mean *mother, horse, scold, flax,* or *curse* depending on the tone used.

❑ Mandarin has four types of tones that affect meaning. These are referred to as tonemes. Cantonese has seven tonemes; Northern Vietnamese has six tonemes; Central and Southern Vietnamese each have five tonemes.

❑ Japanese, Khmer, and Korean are not tonal languages.

❑ Written Asian language systems vary widely. The Vietnamese, for example, use a modified Roman alphabet whereas the Chinese use symbols to represent concepts.

❑ When stating their names in writing, the last name precedes the first name in most Asian cultures (see Table 6.1).

❑ Chinese, Vietnamese, and Laotian languages are basically monosyllabic.

❑ The Hmong language has only recently developed written forms. Very few people have received formal Hmong literacy instruction (Kan & Kohnert, 2005; Vang, 2005).

❑ Some languages (e.g., Indonesian, Japanese, Tagalog) do not have specific gender pronouns such as "he" or "she."

❑ The prosody or intonation of an Asian-born speaker of English may sound very "choppy" and monotonous to the ears of those born in the U.S. Some speakers sound nasal when speaking English.

It is difficult to provide generalities about Asian speakers' English language patterns because of the variety of languages and dialects spoken by this population. However, some of the commonly observed characteristics of the English of Asian speakers are listed in Table 6.2 and Table 6.3 based on information reported in the literature (Chan & Lee, 2004; Cheng, 1991, 1994, 2002; Fang & Ping-An, 1992; Peña-Brooks & Hegde, 2007; Yoshinaga-Itano, 1990).

✐REFLECTION✐

A classroom teacher has referred a Chinese 5-year-old kindergarten student to you. She stated that the child "sounds nasal and choppy." He also leaves the ending sounds off of his words and can't pronounce long words very well. Pronouncing the /r/ and /l/ sounds is very difficult for him. What will you share with this teacher? Does this student have a communication difference or a communication disorder?

Table 6.1
Information About Asian Family Names

Characteristics of names most often given to members of various Asian populations are summarized below.

Cambodian: Names consist of two parts. Family name precedes personal name. Middle names are rare.

Chinese: Names consist of two parts. Family name precedes personal name. Most Chinese names consist of only one syllable. Common Chinese names Chan, Chang, Chiang, Chin, Chow, Chung, Lee, Louie, Lum, Wong, Woo.

Hmong: Most names consist of two parts. Family name precedes personal name. Common Hmong family names: Chang, Chue, Fang, Her, Khang, Kue, Lor, Lee, Moua, Thao, Vang, Vue, Xiong, Yang.

Indonesians: Names consist of two parts. Many are polysyllabic and thus quite lengthy by American standards (e.g., "Pranawahadi"). Many Indonesians have Muslim names.

Japanese: Most names consist of two parts. Family name precedes personal name. To be polite when interacting with an authority figure, "san" is added to the end of the individual's last name. Japanese names often consist of more than one syllable. Common Japanese surnames: Kawaguchi, Nakamura, Tanaka, Watanabe, Yamamoto.

Koreans: Most names consist of a family name that precedes a two-part personal name. Common Korean surnames are: Kim, Park, Lee.

Laotians: Family name precedes personal name. Names may consist of more than one syllable, and some are quite lengthy by American standards (e.g., Souphanouvong).

Thais: Personal name precedes the surname. Some names are quite long (e.g., Suvarnarami).

Vietnamese: Names consist of three components: family, middle, and given names. The family name is followed by the middle name and personal name respectively. The name, Nguyen Van Thieu, for example, begins with the family name "Nguyen" and ends with "Thieu," the name that the individual is called by family members and friends. Approximately 52% of Vietnamese individuals have the family name "Nguyen"; 31% have the family name "Tran." Other common family names are Pham, Le, Ngo, Do, Dao, Vu, Hoang, Dang, Dinh, and Duong.

Table 6.2

Language Differences Commonly Observed Among Asian Speakers

Language Characteristics	*Sample English Utterances*
Omission of plurals	Here are 2 piece of toast. I got 5 finger on each hand.
Omission of copula	He going home now. They eating.
Omission of possessive	I have Phuong pencil. Mom food is cold.
Omission of past tense morpheme	We cook dinner yesterday. Last night she walk home.
Past tense double marking	He didn't went by himself.
Double negative	They don't have no books.
Subject-verb-object relationship differences/omissions	I messed up it. He like.
Misordering of interrogatives	You are going now?
Misuse or omission of prepositions	She is in home. He goes to school 8:00.
Misuse of pronouns	She husband is coming. She said her wife is here.
Omission and/or overgeneralization of articles	Boy is sick. He went the home.
Incorrect use of comparatives	This book is gooder than that book.
Omission of conjunctions	You _____ I going to the beach.
Omission, lack of inflection on auxiliary "do"	She _____ not take it. He do not have enough.
Omission, lack of inflection on forms of "have"	She have no money. We_____ been the store.

Table 6.3

Articulation Differences Observed Commonly Among Asian Speakers

Articulation Characteristics	*Sample English Utterances*	
In many Asian languages, words end in vowels only or in just a few consonants; speakers may delete many final consonants in English.	ste/step ro/robe	li/lid do/dog
Some languages are monosyllabic; speakers may truncate polysyllabic words or emphasize the wrong syllable.	efunt/elephant **di**versity/diversity (emphasis on first syllable)	
Possible devoicing of voiced cognates	beece/bees luff/love	pick/pig crip/crib
r/l confusion	lize/rise	clown/crown
/r/ may be omitted entirely.	gull/girl	tone/torn
Reduction of vowel length in words	Words sound choppy to Americans.	
No voiced or voiceless "th"	dose/those zose/those	tin/thin sin/thin
Epenthesis (addition of "uh" sound in blends, ends of words).	bulack/black	wooduh/wood
Confusion of "ch" and "sh"	sheep/cheap	beesh/beach
/ae/ does not exist in many Asian languages	block/black	shock/shack
b/v substitutions	base/vase	Beberly/Beverly
v/w substitutions	vork/work	vall/wall

IMPLICATIONS FOR PROFESSIONALS

Much diversity exists among Asian populations. Among the cultural variables that may be important to consider are the following:

❑ Asians generally prefer to be referred to as "Asians" rather than "Orientals."

❑ Shaking hands with someone of the opposite sex may be considered unacceptable.

❑ Use of one's left hand to touch someone or to hand something to someone may be frowned upon. Some Asians consider the left hand to be unclean.

❑ The older members of the family should be addressed first, as a sign of respect.

❑ Because of the great value Asians place on education, they greatly respect educated professionals. They may even revere the professional as an "expert" and therefore hesitate to volunteer opinions or responses. Also, Asian individuals may agree to carry out recommendations yet have no intention of actually doing so (Liam & Abdullah, 2001).

❑ As stated, when family members say "yes," they may mean "I hear you" rather than "I agree." Professionals need to encourage open communication as much as possible (Roseberry-McKibbin, 1999b).

❑ It is best if professionals establish rapport before venturing into frank discussions of specific problem areas.

❑ Many American professionals treat a child's mother as the family expert and decision maker. However, in some Asian families, especially those who are Confucians, it is believed that husbands are dominant and wives are subordinate (Liu & Regehr, 2006; Yunus, 2005). Thus, professionals may need to defer to husbands when decisions regarding a child (e.g., placing that child into special education) are to be made.

❑ Because most Asians are very family oriented, the whole family may need to be a primary source of authority in decisions (Fan, 2002). This includes decisions about whether or not a child will receive intervention.

❑ It may be considered disloyal or disgraceful to the family for parents to openly discuss a child or family-related problem such as a disability. For many Asians, public discussion of family problems is considered to be a source of embarrassment and an indication of the family's failure (Sue & Sue, 2008). Professionals need to be sensitive when asking personal questions and may need to be indirect when discussing areas of concern.

❑ Because not all Asian homes emphasize verbal skills in infants and young children, families may be very surprised at recommendations for early intervention for a child who is not speaking. As stated previously, infants and young children are often taught through nonverbal cues and demonstrations (Yunus, 2005). Thus, professionals may find that recommendations for early language intervention are not greeted with enthusiasm.

❑ Early intervention professionals often utilize play therapy with children, emphasizing exploration and independence. This may run directly counter to an Asian family's cultural practices, which emphasize quietness, conformity, and respect. Many Asian parents do not play with their children (Hwa-Froelich & Westby, 2003).

❏ Because Asian children are often quiet and respectful, learning problems are sometimes overlooked or may be inappropriately attributed to limited proficiency in English.

❏ It was emphasized by Hwa-Froelich and Westby (2003) that for American professionals, children's independence is the paramount goal. However, because of the interdependence of its members, many Asian families do not share the goal of helping a child to be as independent as possible.

❏ As stated previously, in Confucian Asian families, each individual child is a developing part of a continuing family lineage; he is a continuation of his ancestors (Lai, 2006; Lu, 2002). Thus, a family may reject a diagnosis of any type of disability because the entire family lineage would be disgraced. They might, therefore, refuse special education services for a child.

❏ In these cases, children with special needs might be served through other models, which will be described in later chapters (e.g., classroom modifications, non-special education supports). In this way, the family can save face and the child's needs can still be met.

❏ In some Asian countries, there is limited tolerance for children with disabilities. Professionals should reassure families that in the U.S., disabilities are not considered shameful and that there are laws, agencies, and services to support children with disabilities and their families (Cho, Singer, & Brenner, 2003).

❏ In some Asian countries (e.g., Malaysia), it is considered rude to say "yes" when first offered an item or service; to be polite, one should first say "no." The person who made the offer then tries to persuade the other person to accept it. Thus professionals may need to offer services many times before these services are accepted (Liam & Abdullah, 2001).

❏ Families may offer gifts in exchange for professional services and may feel offended if professionals do not accept these gifts.

❏ Professionals should dress formally, even when making home visits, because informal dress may be seen as a sign of disrespect.

❏ Some parents may believe that ESL or bilingual classes are inferior to monolingual English classrooms. Professionals should provide parents with information about bilingual programs of instruction and emphasize that bilingualism is a great asset in today's increasingly global economy.

❏ Parents may feel uncomfortable about sex education programs offered in schools. Many families do not openly discuss sex at home (Chan & Lee, 2004; Yunus, 2005).

❏ Many Asian immigrant parents believe that children in the U.S. have too much freedom and are consequently disobedient, disrespectful, and uncontrollable. Some parents fear that their own children will become this way (Chen, 2006). Thus, professionals should not teach social skills to Asian students that will be viewed as unacceptable by their parents.

❏ Students can be taught "home talk rules" and "school talk rules." For example, a professional can say "At school, adults expect you to raise your hand, speak out in class, and look them in the eye. At home, it is important to be silent and not look adults in the eye." In this way, Asian students will be given two sets of behaviors from which to choose depending on the circumstances.

❏ Many Asian children are urged to control their feelings, especially if the feelings are negative (e.g., anger). They are not to verbalize these feelings, or punishment may ensue. This clashes directly with the American value of "letting it all hang out"; professionals need to be sensitive to this difference (Yunus, 2005).

❏ Professionals should understand that some immigrant Asian students may be unaccustomed to participating in groups of mixed gender.

❏ Professionals can help immigrant students (especially in junior high and high school) to become accustomed to moving from classroom to classroom for different subjects, as they may have only had one "home room" in their countries.

❏ The informal atmosphere in American schools may be disconcerting to some Asian students and parents. Professionals can offer guidance to help students feel more comfortable in the classroom.

❏ Parents often expect students to bring home large amounts of homework. Professionals may be asked to account for "too little" homework.

❏ Students may need help in learning how to use libraries.

❏ Some immigrant Asian students may not be accustomed to being called upon in class and may feel uncomfortable speaking up or even reading in front of the group.

❏ Zhao (2007, p. 85) stated that in some Asian families, "Children...are likely to experience suffocation and limited space for self-expression..." Thus, some students may not "take initiative" in the classroom. Many Asian students have grown accustomed to being told what to do by authoritarian parents and may seem "passive" in the classroom.

❏ Students may appear to have "expressive language problems" because they have been taught to be quiet and respectful.

❏ In some Asian families, girls are socialized to grow up to become willing workers, submissive daughters-in-law, and obedient wives. Wives expect to count on their husbands and sons for their future security (Liu & Regehr, 2006).

❏ Thus, some Asian girls may appear to be especially "passive" to American professionals. It is important to not misjudge these girls as having language-learning disabilities or other special education needs.

❏ Professionals should gently ease students into tasks requiring them to express opinions, form judgments, and solve problems. Such activities may be a new experience for students who had been taught to sit quietly in class and to defer to adults in all settings.

❏ Yeh et al. (2002) recommended that due to the group orientation of many Asian cultures, cooperative learning activities are culturally congruent for these students and may be their most comfortable way of learning new information.

❏ Yeh et al. (2002) also recommended that because many Asian students are so quiet in the classroom, written homework assignments and portfolio assessment (described in a later chapter) might be a more valid means of evaluating their academic progress than analyzing expressive language skills.

❏ The concept of winning a game may be unfamiliar to some students (Cheng, 2002). Professionals can help students for whom this is the case.

❏ When working with Hindu Indian students, professionals must be sensitive about pictures depicting beef or about offering beef as part of a snack or general eating activity.

❏ Wong, Au, and Stokes (2004) found the use of story retelling tasks based on custom-designed stories to be an efficient method for evaluating the language skills of Cantonese-speaking children. The procedure took less than 10 minutes to complete.

❏ As stated earlier, many Asian children omit language structures in English (e.g., articles, plurals, and other bound morphemes) that do not occur in their first language. (Fletcher, Leonard, Stokes, & Wong, 2005).

Jia (2003) studied English plural morpheme acquisition by children who spoke Mandarin Chinese. Ten native Mandarin-speaking typically-developing children (5-16 years of age) who had immigrated to the U.S. were followed for 5 years. Jia found that whereas typically-developing children whose first language is English master the plural morpheme by around 3 years of age, only 7 out of her 10 Mandarin-speaking subjects did so after five years of exposure to English. The younger children, however, learned the English plural morpheme faster than the older children.

Jia suggested that older second language learners who are still dominant in their first language (such as Mandarin) may make morphosyntactic errors in the second language even after years of exposure to it. This, however, should not be taken as a sign of a language impairment in these older learners.

Johnston and Wong (2002) surveyed English-speaking North American and Chinese mothers regarding the discourse practices used with their children. The Chinese mothers in this study were much less likely to report that they (1) allowed their children to converse with adults who were non-family members, (2) often talked with their children about nonshared events of the day, and (3) prompted their children for personal narratives. Johnston and Wong (2002) also found that only 30% of Chinese mothers reported that they frequently read books with their young children.

Based on the results of their research, Johnston and Wong (2002) made several practical recommendations for professionals who work with Chinese families. First, many Western professionals recommend embedding language stimulation activities into games. Chinese parents may be more comfortable if they carry out these activities in the form of explicit lessons. Second, when a currently-recommended Western practice such as reading with children is not prioritized by families, professionals can recommend "functional equivalents" such as oral story telling, looking at family photo albums, and other activities that are culturally congruent.

Profile

A teacher in Stockton, California, was teaching in a classroom that had many Vietnamese students. The teacher spelled the name of one of the boys incorrectly numerous times in the first half of the school year. The boy saw his name spelled incorrectly on his name card, and proceeded to misspell his name on all his papers from then on. Some months later, the teacher became aware of her error and asked the boy why he didn't tell her she had spelled his name incorrectly. He said, "I thought that was the way you wanted me to spell it." The boy did not dare challenge his teacher!

STUDY QUESTIONS

1. Why are Asians often called the "model minority?" Describe problems that this label creates for them.

2. Compare and contrast mainstream U.S. beliefs about causation of disabilities and the need for intervention with the beliefs commonly held within Asian countries.

3. You will be meeting with the family of a 3-year old Southeast Asian girl who is well-behaved but is not talking at all. You find through testing that she has a language-learning disability. Describe what you will need to remember as you prepare to talk with her family about this in a culturally sensitive manner.

TRUE-FALSE

Unless indicated otherwise, circle the number beside each statement that is true.

4. Among Asians, laughter and smiling generally indicate happiness and pleasure.

5. Asian Indians in the U.S. have the highest median income.

6. Many Asians attribute the causes of disabilities to spiritual etiologies (e.g., a bad wind).

7. When working with Asian students, professionals must remember that because modesty and humility are not highly valued by them, it is important to help Asian students realize the importance of these qualities.

8. Some of the most widely spoken Asian languages in the United States are Chinese, Filipino, Vietnamese, Japanese, Khmer, and Korean.

9. The family structure in Asian countries is always patriarchal.

10. Asian parents often feel relieved by the informal structure of American schools because it allows opportunities for a high level of participation and interaction with the teacher.

11. Which one of the following is FALSE?
    A. Japan, Korea, and China are in East Asia.
    B. Sri Lanka, Pakistan, India, and Saudi Arabia are in South Asia.
    C. The Philippines, Laos, Cambodia, Thailand, Indonesia, Singapore, Burma, Vietnam, and Malaysia are in Southeast Asia.
    D. Most Indians are Hindus.
    E. The Asian American population in the U.S. is now over 10 million.

12. The following statements describe communication styles observed frequently among Asian cultures:
    A. Personal questions (e.g., asking one's age) are considered highly inappropriate.
    B. Direct eye contact may be considered an open display of rudeness or challenge between individuals who are conversing.
    C. Periods of silence during a conversation are considered awkward and should be avoided if at all possible.
    D. Many Asians avoid open competition and public confrontation.
    E. To maintain harmony, many Asians, when they disagree with others, will not outwardly express their feelings of disagreement.

13. A teacher refers a child to you for assessment. This student recently moved to this country from China. Which of the following would indicate a communication difference, not a disorder?
    A. Omission of articles (e.g., "Little dog is playing in water.")
    B. Difficulty with consonant clusters
    C. An a/ae substitution (e.g., substituting "block" for "black" by saying, "The sky gets <u>block</u> at night.")
    D. Substitution of /r/ for /n/
    E. Substitution of /t/ for /k/ (e.g., *tat* for *cat*)

14. Which statements about Asian education are true?
    A. In Asia, teachers are often formal and tend to maintain a distance from students.
    B. Teachers are not highly respected.
    C. Some Asian parents see themselves as active agents in their children's learning and work diligently at home with their children.
    D. Teachers in Asian schools tend to discourage rote learning and memorization so that divergent thinking and creativity can be promoted.
    E. Many Asians believe that the greatest honor children can bestow on their parents is academic achievement.

15. Which of the following beliefs or actions would suggest a professional's lack of "cultural awareness" during interactions with the parents of an Asian child?
    A. The professional is aware that Asians often agree to recommendations out of respect, although they have no intention of following through on these recommendations.
    B. The professional assures parents that to prevent stress in the home environment little homework will be given.
    C. The professional is direct and forthright when informing the family that the student has a communication disorder.
    D. When making recommendations, the professional speaks in a stern voice to earn the respect of the parents.

ANSWERS TO STUDY QUESTIONS
    4. False
    5. True
    6. True
    7. False
    8. True
    9. False
    10. False
    11. B
    12. B, D, and E
    13. A, B, and C
    14. A, C, and E
    15. B, C, and D

Chapter 7

FAMILIES FROM NATIVE AMERICAN BACKGROUNDS

Outline

There are approximately 650-700 separate and distinct Native American tribal entities with distinct languages and cultures in the United States. Thus there is considerable heterogeneity within and across tribes; they may differ in terms of cultural, sociological, linguistic, and demographic variables. When reading this chapter, it is important for readers to remember that not all Native American groups have the same customs, beliefs, and values.

GENERAL BACKGROUND INFORMATION

❑ In 1990, approximately 1.9 million people identified themselves as Aleuts, Native Americans, or Eskimos (U.S. Bureau of the Census, 1992).

❑ Between 1990 and 2000, the population of Native American and Alaska Natives in the U.S. grew 26% based on the 2,474,956 identified during the census as Native American by "race alone." Those who identified themselves as Native American by "race alone or in combination" totaled 4,119,301. If one uses the latter figure, there was a 110.3% rate of growth among Native Americans between 1990 and 2000 (U.S. Bureau of the Census, 2000).

❑ As of July 1, 2004, there were 4.4 million Native Americans and Alaska Natives (race alone or in combination), making up 1.5% of the U.S. population (U.S. Census Bureau, 2005). California had the largest Native American population, followed by Oklahoma and then New Mexico.

❑ Today, the Navajo Nation is the largest Native American population in the U.S. It has the largest number of native speakers whose native language is their first language. The geographic home of the Navajo Nation includes some of the most remote regions in the U.S. (Robinson, Sandoval, Baldwin, & Sanderson, 2005).

❑ There are various names for Native Americans (e.g., First People). Some prefer to be called American Indians. Others believe that this term is an unhappy legacy of Christopher Columbus' "discovery" and may prefer to be called Native Americans (Fleming, 2006).

❑ Historically, most Native Americans lived in nations that were made up of tribes and clans.

❑ When Europeans came to North America, millions of Native Americans were slaughtered or died of disease and/or starvation.

❑ Some Europeans deliberately gave Native Americans blankets that would spread small pox. Buffalo were exterminated so that Plains Indians would starve to death. Native Americans were constantly forced to move (Dapice, 2006). They also were given rum.

❑ To early Whites in North America, extermination of Native Americans and racial genocide were perceived as the easiest way to deal with the Indian "problem"—that is, Native Americans stood in the way of Whites' free reign over the land and its resources (including gold) (Garrett & Pichette, 2000). For example, the Iroquois occupied very fertile land in Canada and the U.S.

American and British invaders took over and regulated the Iroquois' trade, demanded land cessions, and enforced criminal jurisdiction (Tsai & Alanis, 2004).

❏ It is estimated that by the end of the 18th century, the population of Native Americans decreased to 10% of its original number (Sue & Sue, 2008).

❏ Many Native American children were, in the past, removed from their families and forced to attend government-run boarding schools, where a major goal was to eliminate the children's language and culture (Poupart, 2003; Rivera & Tharp, 2006; Szlemko, Wood, & Thurman, 2006).

❏ These children were often punished severely for speaking their native languages. In addition, they were forbidden to dress in traditional clothing and forced to wear school uniforms instead (Dapice, 2006; Starnes, 2006).

❏ These practices, viewed by many Native Americans as cultural genocide, have led to renewed efforts to preserve Native American culture and family unity. On some reservations, elders are working to teach Indian languages to children and youth (Bowen, 2005).

❏ After the enactment of the Indian Child Welfare Act in 1974, most boarding schools began to close. Children were allowed to return home.

❏ The Indian Relocation Act resulted in efforts to assimilate Indians into White society by moving them into cities for jobs or job training. Unfortunately, the years of relocation substantially increased the probability that many Indian families would spend part or all of their lives in "ghettoized" urban poverty.

❏ The Native American population is young; a greater number are under 20 years of age than in most other ethnic groups.

❏ Despite their history of oppression and disenfranchisement, Native Americans serve in the U.S. military at a higher rate than any other ethnic group (Hayden, 2004).

❏ Poverty is endemic among Native Americans. "Native American groups are ranked at the bottom of virtually every social status indicator with regard to health, income, and education. Twice as many Indian families live in poverty and are headed by women than in the general U.S. population" (Harris, 1998, p. 138).

❏ Native American reservations have a 31% poverty rate, the highest in the U.S. The unemployment rate for Native Americans has been reported to be around 46% (Murphy, 2001). Many reservations are located in remote, geographically barren parts of the U.S. Employment opportunities are virtually nonexistent.

❏ Most Native American religious traditions emphasize a universal spirituality that is integral to all of life. Native Americans believe that all things, supernatural and natural, are interconnected. (Rybak, Eastin, & Robbins, 2004). For example, the Lakota Indians use the term *mitakuye oyas'in*, which means that everything that has ever been or will be created is related. This includes Father Sky, Mother Earth, and all persons, animals, plants, and minerals (Bowen, 2005).

❏ Members of many tribes believe in one Creator or Great Spirit. They have great respect for Mother Earth (Chamberlain & Roseberry-McKibbin, 2008).

❑ Whereas Anglo European Americans have been most concerned with harnessing and controlling nature, Native Americans have attempted to live in harmony with nature. For example, they look to the land to provide treatment for diseases (e.g., using herbal remedies) (Galanti, 2004).

❑ Historically, Native Americans did not believe in private or individual ownership of land, but rather viewed (and continue to view) themselves as caretakers of it.

❑ Today, most tribes teach respect for the land and forbid destruction of their ancestral lands.

❑ Long hair has spiritual significance for some Native American males.

❑ Many Native Americans hold dual citizenship status with their own tribal nations and the U.S. (Clark & Mendoza, 2002).

❑ Garrett and Pichette (2000) delineated five levels of acculturation experienced by Native Americans. These levels provide a helpful framework for professionals who work with these children and their families (see Table 7.1).

Table 7.1
Level of Acculturation Experienced by Native Americans

Level of Acculturation Between Tribal Tradition and Mainstream/White Society	Description
Traditional	Generally think or speak in native language; may or may not speak English; practice only traditional tribal customs and methods of worship; hold traditional values
Bicultural	Generally accepted by tribe/nation as well as by dominant society; able to simultaneously accept and practice both traditional and maistream beliefs and values
Marginal	May speak both tribal language and English; may not fully identify with mainstream society or fully accept cultural heritage
Assimilated	Accepted by mainstream society; embrace only mainstream culture's values, expectations, and beliefs
Pantraditional	Fully assimilated but have chosen to go back to "old ways"; accepted by mainstream society but seek to embrace lost cultural values and practices of their tribal heritage; may speak both English and tribal language

Adapted from Garret and Pichette (2000)

NATIVE AMERICAN FAMILY LIFE

❑ Close-knit, extended families are common. Members of the extended family often care for children and provide long-term nursing care for elderly family members (University of Michigan Health System, 2007). Many families are headed by a single adult female (Sue & Sue, 2008).

❑ For many Native Americans, family ties are more important than anything else, including money, school, and prestige.

❑ Each family member is expected to support others in the family. Working members of the family may be expected to care for needy brothers and sisters, elderly parents, and even more distant kin.

❑ Often, the grandparents and other elders are in positions of authority and assume more responsibility for the training of children than either the mother or father.

❑ Because the family is so close-knit, many Native Americans do not leave their children in the care of people outside the family or tribe. Baby-sitters and day-care workers are never used by some families.

❑ Native Americans tend to be affectionate with their children. Touching and closeness are integral in parent-child relationships (Joe & Malach, 2004).

❑ Children are often accorded great respect and given individual responsibility. They may even be allowed to make decisions for themselves about matters that other cultural groups might consider too important to be left to a child or young adult. There is tolerance for mistakes, and little censure or punishment. Professionals from the majority culture, who value "taking charge," may see this as permissive and even neglectful (Sue & Sue, 2008).

❑ Native American children are encouraged to become independent and master self-care skills at an early age; children who help around the house are praised.

❑ Many Native Americans do not shower babies with compliments because such behavior draws attention that is believed to be harmful (Joe & Malach, 2004).

❑ In many tribes, there is a high fertility rate and a large percentage of out-of-wedlock births (Sue & Sue, 2008). Professionals must be careful when they describe the birth of a baby as "out of wedlock." In many tribes, men and women are married in tribal ceremonies that are not officially recognized by the United States government. Thus, the marriage "exists" by tribal standards but not by technical legal standards as mandated by mainstream society.

❑ Before Europeans came to North America, Native Americans valued all members of their families and communities as gifts from the spirit world. Violence was virtually nonexistent within families (Poupart, 2003).

❑ Unfortunately, a number of Native American families today experience family violence, incest, homicide, and suicide. Child abuse has become more prominent (Westby, 2007). These are manifestations of racism, internalized oppression, and other problems (Poupart, 2003).

REFLECTION

Describe three characteristics of Native American family life that are important for professionals to remember as they work with these families.

_____

_____

_____

_____

_____

NATIVE AMERICAN EDUCATION AND LITERACY

❏ Native American schools are the most poorly funded in the U.S. (McCarty, 2003). Students from these schools may have difficulty obtaining a higher education.

❏ Many Native American children begin school at an academic disadvantage when compared to other children (Demmert, 2005). They may have difficulties in school resulting from cultural and linguistic differences between the home and school. They have the highest dropout rate of any group in the U.S. (Allison & Vining, 1999; Dapice, 2006).

❏ Many Native American students work at expected levels until they reach the fourth grade, where a pattern of decline and dropping out begins to develop.

❏ Around seventh grade, achievement may dramatically decline because students who work hard in school are accused of "acting White" by their peers (Sue & Sue, 2008). By 10th grade, many Native American students are, on average, three years behind their peers (Powers, 2005).

❏ Sixty-six percent of Native Americans graduate from high school, while 75% of the general population graduates from high school (Sue & Sue, 2008).

❏ Few Native Americans who pursue higher education actually graduate (Juntunen, Barraclough, Broneck, Seibel, Winrow, & Morin, 2001; Wiseman, 2000).

❏ Only 8% of Native Americans have finished four or more years of college, as compared to 16% of the general U.S. population (Harris, 1998). Some Native American young people can find jobs on the reservation, so they see no need for "White man's education."

❏ In addition, children who are used to having large extended families around them may feel isolated when they "break out" and go to college. Relatives may view them as trying to break away from their culture. These factors make it even more challenging for young people to obtain a higher education. For example, one of my son's teachers, a Native American, wanted to get her Ph.D. in art. She shared with me that she tried to go to college to obtain this degree, but she was so homesick that she dropped out and went back to the reservation to be with her family.

❏ Students may miss school because of traditional family obligations. Some also move on and off of reservations regularly (Demmert, 2005). Poor attendance can cause them to fall behind academically and can create a conflict between family loyalties and school expectations.

❏ Native American students represent less than 1% of the school-age population; however, they make up 1.3% of the special education population (U.S. Department of Education, 2001). A disproportionate number of Native American students are identified as requiring special education services (Sparks, 2000).

❏ These students are typically identified as having speech-language disorders, emotional disturbances, intellectual disabilities, or learning disabilities. Early intervention can help prevent later failure (Diken & Rutherford, 2005).

❏ Many Native Americans value patience and the ability to wait quietly. Native American students are often thought to have a reflective rather than impulsive learning style. Thus, in school, the continuous flurry of activities according to a rigid schedule can cause confusion for these students.

❏ In many Native American tribes, such as the Chippewa tribe, it is stressed that children should learn through observation and display knowledge later (Kay-Raining Bird & Vetter, 1994).

❏ Native American students may be viewed as unmotivated because they are often reluctant to compete with peers in the classroom. To compete would be seen as an unacceptable expression of individuality that suggests that the student is better than the tribe (Sue & Sue, 2008).

❏ Information is often passed down from one generation to the next by story-telling. Some Native American groups had no system for writing down information until recently. Reading, therefore, is often not culturally reinforced (Kay-Raining Bird & Vetter, 1994).

❏ White-Kaulaity (2007), who grew up on a Navajo reservation, stated that no one ever read to her as a child; she emphasized that many literate Native Americans "...are masters of oral literacy. Unless there is a specific purpose, they choose not to bother with print literacy" (p. 560). She stated that to her grandmother, reading was a sign of laziness because unlike household chores, reading does not require any overt physical activity.

❏ According to White Kaulaity (2007), Native American culture demands that people be involved with activities that produce practical, visible, and tangible results. Reading and writing are not considered to be such activities. In addition, some Indians consider reading and writing to be "White man's" activities. In Indian communities, the oral tradition is far more valued.

❏ Genesee, Paradis, and Crago (2004) described language practices among the Inuit families of Canada. Inuit mothers do not converse with their babies. Children's needs are met silently, and children are expected to look, listen, and observe. Children interact primarily with their peers.

❏ Parents don't often read books with their children, and book-reading by older children may be frowned upon because the child is just sitting around instead of developing physical strength and prowess. Activities that strengthen the body and teach the child about the physical world are much more valued than literacy activities.

CULTURAL CUSTOMS, COURTESIES, AND BELIEFS

❑ It is considered culturally unacceptable in some tribes to seek outside assistance when a family is in need; the extended family is supposed to provide everything that is needed.

❑ Many Native Americans are taught not to interfere in the affairs of others (Joe & Malach, 2004). Thus, they may not give advice or information unless it is specifically asked of them.

❑ Most groups teach their younger members to show respect for authority and for the elderly, who are regarded as valuable sources of knowledge and experience (Westby & Vining, 2002).

❑ Anglo American society emphasizes competition and winning. Native Americans believe in doing their best, but they do not want to stand out as being "superior" to others. As previously stated, Native Americans strive to avoid competing with peers.

❑ Native Americans are often reluctant to exalt themselves above others in their community; high achievers may downplay or even mask their talents in order to be accepted. Bragging about oneself and one's abilities is considered rude.

❑ Happiness and harmony between individuals, society, and nature is emphasized Chamberlain & Roseberry-McKibbin, 2008).

❑ A core value among many Native Americans involves The Circle of Life, which is believed to consist of the basic elements of life (earth, wind, fire, water).

❑ Spiritual practices are such an integral part of everyday life that in many Native American languages, there is no word for "religion." Some Native Americans may practice a combination of Christianity and tribal ceremonies (Tsai & Alanis, 2004).

❑ Many tribes emphasize generosity in the sharing of resources, possessions, and self. Honor and respect are obtained through sharing and giving rather than through accumulating material goods (Bridges & Midgette, 2000; Sue & Sue, 2008).

❑ Many young Native Americans experience conflict between the old and new ways of doing things. They may feel that they are on a "bridge between two worlds." Parents and grandparents often hold certain beliefs that are rejected by the "younger generation" because of their desire to assimilate into White culture. This can lead to pain, frustration, and conflict within families.

❑ Ceremonies and traditional activities have an important place in the lives of many Native Americans. Some activities are highly religious, while others are social and recreational. Activities might include Pow Wows, giveaways, rodeos, and competitive dance contests.

❑ The establishment of human relationships is considered to be far more important than adherence to schedules. Punctuality and planning may be de-emphasized and even viewed negatively (Bridges & Midgette, 2000).

❑ Native Americans believe in being flexible, having a sense of humor, and accepting changes calmly and gracefully. James (2007) shared that the Native American concept of balance in life includes the famous saying "If you are riding a horse and it dies, get off the horse."

HEALTH CARE AND DISABLING CONDITIONS

❑ In some tribes, medicine people serve a dual role as religious leaders and doctors for physical illnesses. Many medicine people believe in treating the whole person, not just the affected part of the body.

❑ There is a lack of effective, comprehensive health and prevention programs for Native Americans, although the Indian Health Service (IHS) has attempted to provide as many health services as possible (Lillie-Blanton & Ruobideaux, 2005).

❑ Most Native American health facilities are difficult to staff. They are located in isolated rural areas on or near reservations (Warne, 2006).

❑ However, more than half of the Native American population does not permanently reside on a reservation and thus has limited or no access to IHS services (Office of Minority Health, 2007).

❑ A major variable contributing to health problems among Native Americans is the housing on reservations. Many families live in government housing that is poorly insulated. Other families live in mobile homes or tar-paper shacks. Often, three generations live together under one roof (Bowen, 2005).

❑ Some of the top health problems experienced by Native Americans are obesity and diabetes, stroke, heart disease, cancer, and cirrhosis of the liver (Mohammed, 2006; Office of Minority Health, 2007). Other health problems common among Native Americans include gastrointestinal disease, malignant neoplasms, and tuberculosis (Hayden, 2004).

❑ Native Americans have among the shortest life expectancies of any group in the U.S. (Warne, 2006). For example, the average lifespan of all groups in the U.S. is 72.2 years, but in Arizona the average lifespan of Native Americans is 54.7 years (Indian Health Services, 2000).

❑ Native Americans, as a group, also have the highest infant mortality rate in the United States. Children on Arizona reservations are one of the groups at the highest risk for developing type 2 diabetes in the world (Warne, 2006).

❑ From very early in U.S. history, alcohol has played a prominent and destructive role in the lives of Native Americans (Szlemko et al., 2006). Benjamin Franklin is reported to have said:

> If it be the design of Providence to extirpate these savages in order to make room for the cultivators of the earth, it seems not improbable that rum may be the appointed means. It has already annihilated all the tribes who formerly inhabited the seacoast (Franklin, n.d.).

❑ A high incidence of alcoholism among Native Americans is a well-documented phenomenon (Evans, Spear, Huang, & Hser, 2006; Koss et al., 2003; Libby et al., 2006; Savin, Garry, Zuccaro, & Novins, 2006). Alcohol use often starts when Native Americans are young teenagers.

❑ Almost half of Native American deaths are due to cirrhosis of the liver. In fact, the number of alcohol-related deaths among Native Americans is five times greater than among Americans as a whole.

❑ The incidence of Native American babies born with Fetal Alcohol Syndrome (FAS) is six times higher than the incidence within the general population; approximately 20% of Native American babies are born with FAS.

❑ Among many Native Americans, alcoholism is related to poverty, lack of education, unemployment, poor living conditions on reservations, and a general lack of purpose in life (Bowen, 2005).

❑ Higher than average prevalences of certain health conditions associated with communication disorders are reported for the Native American population. Otitis media, bacterial meningitis, fetal alcohol syndrome, and cleft lip and palate, for example, are all more prevalent among Native Americans than among other groups.

❑ Research data indicate that 22% of Native American and Alaska Natives have one or more disabilities. This is the highest rate of disability in the U.S. when compared with all other races. Of interest to speech-language pathologists in particular, deafness and learning disabilities are among the most frequently reported (National Council on Disability, 2003).

❑ Many Native American children have otitis media and related hearing problems. Studies indicate that the prevalence of otitis media among Native American children ranges from 17% to 76% (Pang-Ching, Robb, Heath, & Takumi, 1995). The high incidence of otitis media is due, in part, to the limited availability of appropriate health care services as well as other variables.

❑ In one study of Minnesota Native Americans, Daly, Pirie, Rhodes, Hunter, & Davey (2007) reported that 63% of infants had experienced an episode of otitis media by 6 months of age. Factors related to this early onset of otitis media were maternal otitis media history, infant history of upper respiratory infection, and maternal attitudes and behaviors. Prepartum interviews with mothers showed that more than 90% knew the signs and symptoms of otitis media, but continued with such behaviors as smoking and feeding their children formula (breast-feeding tends to diminish the possibility of otitis media).

❑ Daly et al. (2007) concluded that maternal knowledge alone was not enough to prevent otitis media; they recommended that interventions to reduce otitis media risk factors should focus on barriers to change as well as better health insurance coverage.

❑ Native Americans who qualify for health care may only receive services while residing on the reservation; if they live in urban areas, they do not qualify for "reservation health care" and sometimes their health needs go unattended.

❑ Most tribal lands are located in remote rural areas of the U.S.; they lack public transportation systems, making it difficult for persons with disabilities to function independently (National Council on Disability, 2003).

❑ Healing and purification ceremonies are quite common among many tribes (Joe & Malach, 2004). Many of the herbs used by Native American medicine men have been shown to have true healing properties (Westby, 2007).

❑ Some Native Americans accept a disabled child as the Great Spirit's gift; others may believe that the handicapping condition resulted from witchcraft or moral transgressions.

❑ Many Native Americans believe that thoughts, words, and actions have the power to bring about misfortunes such as disabilities, serious illnesses, or even death. Allison and Vining (1999, p. 198) stated that "Out of this basic belief comes the assumption that parents and family members have a clear and ever-present responsibility for causing and preventing serious illness and disability in children."

❏ Marshall and Hawk Largo (1999) stated that the individual who has the disability may be the one who has violated one or more natural laws; however, more often than not, it's the individual's parents or grandparents who are scrutinized as the ones responsible for the disability.

❏ Some Native American groups are able to accept disabled individuals because of a strong belief that these individuals still have a viable role to play in the community. Many Native American parents, therefore, do not share professionals' beliefs that early intervention is desirable for children with disabilities (Allison & Vining, 1999).

❏ Some Native Americans believe that a child is born with a disability because that child has made a choice prenatally to be disabled. Other beliefs about what causes disabilities, as cited by Vining (1999), include:

1. Events and experiences encountered by the Holy People

2. Traditional teachings not being honored

3. Curses placed on the child

4. Taboos violated by parents (e.g., the mother viewed a solar or lunar eclipse during pregnancy)

❏ Many Native Americans are unaware of services provided by speech-language pathologists. Some, such as the Navajo, believe that certain types of communication disorders can be treated by performing such rituals as breaking a pot over a child's head, having a child eat roasted corn with straight kernels, holding a purification ceremony, and others (Vining, 1999).

A recent research project (Nichols & Keltner, 2005) was carried out with Native American families in the Great Plains and the Southeastern parts of the U.S. The purpose of the study was to explore how Native American families respond and adapt to having school-age children with disabilities. The researchers found that there were two general ways that families reacted to having a disabled child. In the group experiencing "constructive adjustment," families believed that the child with the disability was given to them for a reason; there was a purpose to the child's being a part of that family.

In these families, the disabled children were included in everyday family activities and special events such as pow wows. The families were able to adjust family life to meet the children's needs. They were also able to utilize community supports, obtain services needed by the children, and show love to the children.

In families experiencing "limited adjustment," life felt strained and out of balance. To them, there was no clear purpose to having a disabled child. They were not sure how to cope with their disabled children and felt isolated. Sometimes the disabled children in these families were ignored and even mistreated. Some families used drugs and alcohol to cope with their situations. Nichols and Keltner recommended that professionals be sensitive to the problems experienced by families with children who have disabilities and that they promote community and tribal support for these families.

Profile

An early intervention team was made aware of a Cherokee girl who had been born with cerebral palsy and had been recently enrolled in the local preschool. The team head arranged to visit the family at home to talk about services for the child (speech, occupational, and physical therapy). Upon visiting the home, the team leader found that the family expressed gratitude for the child's cerebral palsy. The mother shared that this condition was a gift from the Great Spirit to help her become a more patient person. She added that she had also been given the opportunity to appreciate every minor development her child made. The family stated that they would like to postpone rehabilitative efforts until their daughter was in school.

NATIVE AMERICAN COMMUNICATION STYLES

❏ Respect is highly valued; one way of signifying respect for another person is to avoid eye contact by looking down.

❏ Children's communication with adults is respectful and discrete, with little eye contact. A child who makes eye contact is considered defiant, disrespectful, or rude.

❏ Native American mothers, especially those in the Navajo population, may be silent during interactions with their infants. As mentioned previously, Inuit mothers in Canada are also silent with their infants, expecting them to learn by listening, watching, and observing (Genesee et al., 2004).

❏ In many families, adults either do not carry out verbal exchanges with infants or they respond to infants' vocalizations as if these vocalizations carry no meaning.

❏ Most children are taught that one learns more by listening and observing than by speaking.

❏ Parents often feel that their children's auditory comprehension skills are more advanced than their expressive language skills.

❏ Children are generally discouraged from speaking the tribal language before they are capable of correct articulation. Opportunities for oral practice in the language may be limited.

❏ Among Apache Native Americans, silence is valued (Owens, 2005). Silence is also valued among the Navajo, who are comfortable with long periods of silence (University of Michigan Health System, 2007). Among some Western Apache Indians, children may be rebuked for "talking like a White man" if they speak English or talk too much in the village.

❏ Native American etiquette requires a lapse of time between the asking and answering of a question. Some Native Americans believe that an immediate answer to a question implies that the question was not worth thinking about. A person may be considered immature who answers too quickly or interrupts someone else (University of Michigan Health System, 2007).

❏ Children often do not answer a question unless they are confident that their answer is correct.

❏ Children do not express opinions on certain subjects because they first need to earn the right to express such opinions.

❏ In many groups, it is considered inappropriate for a person to express strong feelings publicly. Adults usually express grief around outsiders only during official mourning ceremonies.

❏ It is important to avoid stereotypes about the communication styles of Native Americans. In a somewhat humorous vein, Garrett, Garrett, Torres-Rivera, Wilbur, and Roberts-Wilbur (2005, p. 195) wrote:

> That Native people have been cast as uncommunicative, distant, or mysterious by people from mainstream America says little about the true essence of an entire nation of many nations of Native people. It says more about a history of stereotyping Native people as either faithful sidekicks who are barely able to speak a complete sentence or as strangely mystical beings who seem to transcend the world of physical reality.

NATIVE AMERICAN LANGUAGE CONSIDERATIONS

❏ There are over 200 Native American languages spoken in the United States, and dialectal variations exist within each of these languages.

❏ Six general "families" of Native American languages are Eskimo-Aleut, Algonquin, Penutian, Na-Dane', Macro-Siouan, and Aztec-Tanoan (Goldstein, 2000). Some of the most commonly spoken Native American languages are Navajo, Teton Sioux, Cherokee, and Dinneh.

❏ Native American languages may be in jeopardy; 71.8% of all Native Americans and Alaska Natives speak only English at home (U.S. Census Bureau, 2006).

❏ The number of Native American children who speak English only is increasing. Many speak a form of pidgin English. Native American languages are often spoken only by elders (McCarty, 2003).

❏ Indian tribes are making attempts to revitalize their languages. For example, in the Cherokee Nation in northeastern Oklahoma, the Cherokee Immersion Preschool was opened in 2001. In this program, teachers use only Cherokee throughout the day. There have been many positive benefits of this program (Peter & Hirata-Edds, 2006). Since the 1990s, both Acoma and Cochiti Indians have been actively involved in community-based language-renewal planning.

❏ Many Indian languages have no word for time, contain no future-tense verbs, and are based almost entirely on the present tense.

❏ Many Native American languages contain fewer vowel sounds than English. The English sound system is often difficult for students to master.

❏ Native American languages contain some sounds that do not occur in English. For example, there may be voiceless stops in combination with velar fricatives, ejectives (sounds made with a glottalic egressive airstream), and implosives (sounds made with an ingressive glottalic airstream).

❏ Navajo belongs to the Athabaskan language family, one of the most widespread indigenous language families on the North American continent. Navajo itself is spoken primarily in the

Four Corners region of the U.S. Southwest, where the Navajo Nation encompasses parts of New Mexico, Utah, and Arizona. North of Mexico, there are more speakers of Navajo than any other indigenous language. Peña-Brooks & Hegde (2007) reported that among the consonants, the glottal stop is one of the few sounds that is common to most Native American languages. In addition, many vowels are nasalized (Goldstein, 2000).

❏ There are other differences between Native American languages and Standard American English (SAE) that make SAE difficult to master. For example, word order may change, even in the same language, depending on the speaker's intended meaning. Pronoun deletion is also common (Robinson-Zañartu, 1996).

❏ Harris (1998), in her extensive description of the Navajo language, details other differences, such as the language's absence of gender and its intricate verb system. Professionals should be aware that Native American students learning English may struggle in school because Native American languages are so different from English.

It is beyond the scope of this book to describe the characteristics of all the Native American languages spoken in the United States. Consultation with native speakers is important in situations where a problem is suspected. For more specific information about Native American languages, see Westby & Vining (2002).

✑ REFLECTION ✑

Communication styles differ between many Native Americans and Anglo Americans. Describe two common characteristics of Native American communication styles that professionals might interpret inaccurately as signs of a communication disorder.

_____

_____

_____

_____

_____

IMPLICATIONS FOR PROFESSIONALS

❏ Professionals need to learn by asking questions of Native American faculty, staff, and community members. Professionals should work closely with Indian community mentors and attend appropriate cultural events. It may be especially helpful to work with elders (Starnes, 2006).

❏ Many Native Americans believe in taking life as it comes and accepting all circumstances; professionals should not interpret this as passivity and as resistance to change.

❏ If a member of an urban-dwelling family needs health care that can only be obtained on a reservation, the entire family must relocate, sometimes resulting in a situation in which children miss school for a period of time.

❏ Pow wows are sacred and often honor elders and ancestors. Thus parents may remove their children from school to take them to pow-wows, ceremonies, and events considered important within the culture.

❏ Some tribal groups are forced to constantly choose between White people's modern medicine and traditional Native American approaches. This can cause uncertainty and guilt for some tribal members.

❏ It is often appropriate to consult with an Indian medicine person before recommending a therapeutic intervention or medical procedure.

❏ Professionals should not be surprised if grandparents show up for conferences instead of parents.

❏ To maintain pride, some families may be reluctant to take advantage of aid and services that are available, such as health care, welfare, legal aid, and counseling. Well-founded mistrust of the "establishment," including government agencies, may also contribute to their reluctance to accept assistance. Part of this mistrust stems from the aforementioned placement of children into boarding schools (Rayle, Chee, & Sand, 2006).

❏ Because of their history of being forced into boarding schools, some Native Americans may be especially distrustful of the educational system or the professionals who work within it. Professionals will need to work hard to gain their trust, as many have had bad educational experiences within mainstream schools.

❏ In a similar vein, when families do seek health care or services such as speech-language remediation, they may be slow to open up to professionals. It is important to take time to build trust. (Sue & Sue, 2008).

❏ Some Native Americans may be unwilling to discuss family affairs freely. They may believe that words have power to hurt as well as heal, so they feel that if they even discuss a disabling condition, the discussion itself can bring greater problems to the person or the family as a whole.

❏ It is critical to reach out to the families, both immediate and extended (especially the grandparents), of Native American students. One should not attempt to treat the student in isolation. Many Native American families view rehabilitation as a family-centered rather than client-centered affair (Westby & Vining, 2002).

❏ Professionals should be flexible when scheduling meetings. It is also important for Native Americans to understand that schools within the United States are "time-oriented" institutions with schedules that professionals need to maintain. Developing an understanding of our time-dominated mainstream social system is critical.

❏ Professionals should address all family members during meetings, rather than addressing only the parents.

❏ At the beginning of meetings and visits with families, it is important for professionals to engage in small talk to establish rapport with family members (Rivera & Tharp, 2006).

❏ If families feel that personnel are hurried, they may not discuss their true concerns. Allow plenty of time for meetings so that families will not feel rushed.

❑ Malach, Segel, and Thomas (1989) found that the families of the Pueblo Indian children in their study valued the professional's emotional support and respect for them much more than they valued the professional's title or the agency's status. Thus, professionals must be especially careful to take time to build rapport.

❑ Family members may feel that it is a sign of respect to avoid eye contact with school professionals and to refrain from asking them direct questions (Joe & Malach, 2004).

❑ Professionals should always ask families to share concerns that they have regarding the use of interpreters; families may be uncomfortable with interpreters selected by school professionals.

❑ Professionals should help families to coordinate services through various agencies; this process may seem overwhelming to families.

❑ Parents of Native American children with disabilities may not be aware of the support and services their children are entitled to receive. They may need help in advocating effectively for their children (National Council on Disability, 2003).

❑ Support groups should be provided when possible. The traditional group approach to problem-solving in some tribes fits ideally with the support group concept, and professionals can take advantage of this.

❑ Some families (e.g., Navajo) do not attach great importance to developmental milestones. They feel that children will develop individually at their own pace. Thus, during the gathering of the case history, professionals may find that parents/caretakers are unable to provide details about children's acquisition of specific skills.

❑ Research has found that Native American infants may achieve gross motor developmental milestones (e.g., walking) later than infants from other ethnic groups (Harris, 1998). Professionals must keep this in mind and avoid labeling these children inappropriately as "delayed."

❑ Efforts should be made to preserve students' traditions as much as possible. For example, native styles of dress should be accepted as much as possible within the school setting.

❑ Students may experience religious conflict in educational situations in which they are asked to complete culturally inappropriate activities (e.g., dissecting animals in traditional biology classes). Professionals should give Native American students alternate assignments in these situations.

❑ School professionals need to be aware that certain markings or objects (e.g., amulets) may be placed on Native American students during sacred ceremonies. It is important to learn about these customs so that students are not criticized or punished for culturally appropriate behavior.

❑ When professionals arrive at the home for a previously scheduled meeting, they should make sure that the family is ready for their visit. If family members are involved in a religious ceremony or some other activity, they may not wish to be interrupted (Joe & Malach, 2004).

❑ During home visits, professionals should not assume that they can sit anywhere. They should ask the family if there is a place to sit.

❑ In the home, it is customary to address all who are present.

❑ Professionals may be offered food or coffee in the home. If the professional chooses to refuse these offerings, an explanation should be provided (e.g., "I have just finished eating.").

❑ Children with special needs may not be disciplined because the family feels that they have suffered a great deal already. Professionals need to clearly delineate their own role and the roles of family members in providing discipline (Joe & Malach, 2004).

❑ Some studies have shown that Native American students tend to do better on tests of spatial ability and visual skills than on tests of verbal and/or auditory skills (Harris, 1985; Harris, 1998; McAvoy & Sidles, 1991). Professionals should be aware of this in assessment situations.

❑ Certain pictures, toys, dolls, and animals may be viewed as causes of evil or bad luck within certain tribes. The family should be consulted to make certain that the materials used in assessment and intervention are appropriate.

❑ As stated, it is culturally appropriate within many Native American groups for children to avoid eye contact with adults. Professionals may misinterpret this as evidence of shyness, immaturity, rudeness, or a deficit in interpersonal language skills (Powers, 2005).

❑ Native American students often respond well when professionals attempt to strengthen interpersonal relationships with them. Strong relationships between students and professionals promote a feeling of belonging and may help students negotiate cultural discontinuities between home and school (Powers, 2005). Personal warmth may be especially effective (Fleming, 2006).

❑ Native American students may be incorrectly diagnosed as having language-learning disabilities if they do not interact with adult examiners or if they give limited responses. These behaviors, however, are often culturally appropriate for situations in which children are asked to respond to questions from an adult authority figure (Neha, 2003; Hardman et al., 2006).

❑ During assessment and intervention, silence is often a culturally appropriate response. Remember, students are taught to reflect before answering a question. Students should not be penalized when they fail to respond immediately to questions directed toward them. It might be best to start off with closed questions that are easy for children to answer, and then progress to more open-ended questions as the students become more comfortable.

❑ In many tribes, children observe while elders tell stories. Thus when asked to perform narrative tasks in an assessment, young Native American students may not respond in the desired manner. Kay-Raining Bird and Vetter (1994) emphasized that traditional Chippewa-Cree children —those who have had limited interaction with mainstream culture—produced longer, more complex stories with increasing age.

❑ Scores on formal tests may fall "below the norm" because of a variety of factors. Low parental education, poverty, nonstandard English usage, lack of facility with English, poor health and nutrition, limited experience in taking formal tests, and other factors are likely to influence the test performance of Native American students . This is especially true when taking tests that emphasize auditory and verbal skills (Robinson-Zañartu, 1996).

❑ Many Native American children will not respond to a question if the answer is something that the person asking the question already knows. The child, for example, might not respond to the test question, "What color is a banana?" Thus, in testing situations, they may be nonresponsive (Harris, 1998).

❏ Ukrainetz, Harpell, Walsh, and Coyle (2000) conducted a preliminary investigation of the use of dynamic assessment in evaluating Native American kindergartners. They found that dynamic assessment was less biased in evaluating children's language-learning ability than traditional, knowledge-based assessment.

❏ To assess Native American students in a nonbiased manner, dynamic assessment strategies are recommended. Language samples, portfolios, and questionnaires are also helpful in collecting non-biased assessment data (Allison & Vining,1999; Demmert, 2005).

❏ In terms of intervention, Native American students tend to have strengths in the visual modality and often learn quickly by observing the behavior of others (Carter et al., 2005). Professionals can make use of these strengths to enhance learning. For example, colorful visual aids can be used to complement material delivered auditorily (Sparks, 2000).

❏ Many Native American children are "whole-to-parts learners" (Sparks, 2000; Starnes, 2006). They perform best if they see the whole, or "big picture" first; then they can begin to understand individual and discrete parts of the whole, using simultaneous rather than sequential processing.

❏ In addition, most Native American students are "hands-on" learners. They benefit best from experiential teaching (Rivera & Tharp, 2006; Starnes, 2006).

❏ Many Native American students perform more readily when learning activities are presented in a group situation. Individual instruction may, therefore, be less effective than group instruction. Cooperative learning situations are ideal for many Indian students (Starnes, 2006).

❏ As previously mentioned, many Native American students feel uncomfortable in competitive situations—they believe they should not stand out from the group (Rivera & Tharp, 2006).

❏ Because Native American students often do not wish to be singled out from the group, they should be praised for special accomplishments in situations where others are not present. In some traditional cultures, it is taught that children should not attempt to outshine their peers (Fleming, 2006).

❏ Some children may give less feedback than Anglo children during interactions (e.g., nodding, smiling, looking at the speaker). It is important not to judge these children as having clinically significant pragmatic language problems.

❏ Many Native American students will observe an activity repeatedly before attempting to do it themselves (Harris, 1998). In the European-American culture, children are encouraged to use the trial-and-error method of learning; for some Native American children, however, the cultural norm is that competence should truly precede performance. Thus, professionals should allow Native American students to watch activities several times before asking them to do the activities.

❏ In addition, Native American students may respond more often if they are allowed longer "wait times" (Harris, 1998). Because of the cultural emphasis on silence, these students often do not answer a question immediately—but they will respond eventually if professionals are willing to wait.

❑ Because of the cultural emphasis on cooperation rather than competition, Native American students may feel uncomfortable defending themselves verbally or openly disagreeing with others. Thus, Native American students may need extra support in these kinds of situations.

❑ Because of cultural differences in the importance of time and punctuality, some Native American students may not understand why homework assignments are due on a specific date. This should not be interpreted as laziness or irresponsible behavior (Robinson-Zañartu, 1996).

❑ Professionals should use materials in assessment and intervention that are culturally relevant. Native American children and children from other cultural backgrounds may enjoy learning about local Indian history and traditions.

❑ Using Native American folktales for intervention activities is recommended. However, Reese (2007), a Pueblo Indian expert, stressed that these folktales not just represent Indians as "a vanquished people of the past" (p. 247). Current, modern-day Indians should also be pictured. Reese also recommended that stories depicting families should include extended families, not just nuclear ones.

❑ Inglebret, Bear Eagle, and Chixapkaid (2007) stated that, reflecting a view that all things in life are interconnected, many stories are told through the elements of the natural environment—plants, animals, and the forces of fire, wind, water, and earth. These stories frequently carry a message about the importance of caring for Mother Earth.

❑ Stories and intervention activities can emphasize the Native American concept of the Medicine Wheel, symbolizing the cyclical nature of the self and of the world. The Medicine Wheel depicts four directions, each of which represents an aspect of life that is necessary for harmony: mind, body, natural environment, and spirit (Dapice, 2006; Rybak et al., 2004). These directions or inner dimensions are connected dimensions flowing from one another. This interrelatedness of all living beings is symbolized by the Circle of Life, which is expressed in Native American art and tradition (Hunter & Sawyer, 2006).

❑ Relevant activities that utilize these principles can involve the use of nature and pets in therapy. For example, children may plant gardens or care for animals (Hunter & Sawyer, 2006). Connecting with nature can be very successful (Dapice, 2006).

❑ Starnes (2006) described in detail how the federal law "No Child Left Behind" (NCLB, 2002) is mismatched to the learning styles and preferences of Native American students. Table 7.2 is a listing of ways that NCLB programs are mismatched with research on Native American students' learning styles.

❑ Celebrations of holidays such as Thanksgiving and Columbus Day may be perceived as "prejudiced" by Native Americans. For many of them, Columbus Day is a day of mourning. The arrival of Columbus in North America is viewed as the beginning of cultural genocide among many Native American communities.

❑ Feathers are sacred to Native Americans and, therefore, their use in instructional activities may be viewed as offensive and disrespectful.

❑ Some Native Americans believe that owls are bad luck. Before using owls (or stories about them) in any activity, professionals should check with children to ensure that they will not be afraid.

Table 7.2
The Mismatch Between Research on Native American Learning and No Child Left Behind Programs

No Child Left Behind Programs	Research-based Best Practices or Native Americans
Drill and kill, abstract	Experience-based, hands-on
Culturally generic	Use of culturally relevant materials
Extreme inflexibility, high structure	Flexible, informal learning environment
Isolating, highly individualistic	Cooperative learning, teamwork
Top-down, teacher centered	Teacher as coach or facilitator
Part-to-whole, fragmented learning	Whole-to-part, holistic approach
Memorization, rote learning	Reflective meaning making
Heavy emphasis on print	Visual learning mode, involving illustrations and pictures
Emphasis on dominant culture's values	Based in children's tribal values
Failure-focused	High warmth, low criticism style of interaction
Test-driven, emphasizes conformity	Group focused, emphasizes creativity

- Adapted from Starnes, 2006

❑ Professionals should avoid using materials and terms that portray Native Americans in ways that promote negative stereotypes, e.g., using terms such as "injun," "squaw," "savage," "papoose," or "brave", singing songs such as "Ten Little Indians", collecting "scalps", or making a whooping war cry.

❑ To reduce prejudice, professionals can discuss the stereotypes of Native Americans and other minorities as portrayed through the popular media.

❑ Professionals can devote bulletin board space for mini-language lessons using local Native American words and phrases (Sparks, 2000).

❑ To support Native American students with expressive language delays, professionals can utilize the Talking Circle, a group activity which emphasizes respect for self and others (Rybak et al., 2004; Szlemko et al., 2006). The purpose of the Talking Circle is to bring people together and have them share. Everyone learns to speak and also to listen respectfully using the following activity:

1. In the Talking Circle, an instrument is introduced. It can be an item such as a totem or deco-rated stick that is called the Talking Stick. After an individual speaks, she hands the Talking Stick to another group member.

2. Individuals in the group who are handed the Talking Stick are not required to speak; they may hand the Talking Stick to someone else (Hunter & Sawyer, 2006). The Talking Circle, again, can be used to encourage verbal expression, improve listening comprehension, and develop conversational turn-taking skills in students.

❏ Some Native Americans rename a child with an animal name to denote the values of strength and courage as well as to demonstrate respect for the child. In Indian folklore, certain animals stand for certain virtues. For example, dogs stand for loyalty, turtles for perseverance, hawks for watchfulness, ants or bees for cooperation, and squirrels for thriftiness. Children can be asked which animal they admire most and why. They can assign the name trait to themselves, design a mask, and write an essay or poem that describes the animal's qualities and how they relate to this animal. They can then wear the mask while sharing the essay or poem with the group (Hunter & Sawyer, 2006).

❏ An activity called "Earth's gift" is also relevant for building self esteem and encouraging the de-velopment of receptive and expressive language skills. The professional can get a large stick and take a group of children on a nature walk. Each child is to find something special to contribute to the decoration of the stick. When each child finds a special object, he brings it to the group, talks about it, tells why it has special qualities, and then attaches it to the stick. All children are reminded to thank Mother Earth for sharing this special gift with them and to remember the im-portance of protecting the gifts that nature freely provides. The stick can then be presented to a special adult in the children's lives (Hunter & Sawyer, 2006).

❏ Story-telling is important within Native American families and can be used as a tool for teaching vocabulary. Stories should be accompanied by clear, non-biased, realistic illustrations. Some stu-dents may prefer to hear a story in its entirety before discussing it or answering questions about it.

❏ As previously mentioned, White-Kaulaity (2007) emphasized that oral traditions are far more important to many Native Americans than written traditions, and that for Native American people, reading has not traditionally been a way to attain knowledge. White-Kaulaity suggested specific strategies that professionals can use to help Native American children increase their lit-eracy skills:

1. Use wordless books so that children can turn the pages and make up stories about pictures as they go.

2. Encourage children, especially young ones, to learn tribal songs.

3. Remember that many Native Americans especially value stories that include animals and that feature content of a sacred or religious nature.

4. Choose books that contain a considerable amount of dialogue. Rather than reading long descriptions of events, Native American students often prefer to "listen to people talking" in the pages of a book.

5. Remember that some students may struggle with reading. Provide extra support for them, especially in the form of one-on-one assistance. This support can also be provided by older peer tutors or even adult volunteers.

6. Older Native American students may especially enjoy stories with Indian protagonists to whom they can relate.

7. It is helpful to read stories aloud and talk with the students before, during, and after presenting the stories. This helps students connect oral words to printed words.

Profile

Luis, a five-year-old Native American child from the Shoshone tribe, was referred to the special education team by his kindergarten teacher for assessment. She stated that Luis was "non-participatory, extremely shy, and lacking in social skills." In addition, he seemed to "catch on very slowly to new information" and was "slow to process directions."

The special education team contacted a member of the Shoshone tribe for a consultation. Joy Buffalo Earthwoman, the tribal member, observed Luis in class on several different occasions. When she reported back to the team, she indicated that Luis was behaving in a manner consistent with what he had learned growing up on the reservation. She cautioned that his parents had told him that he shouldn't talk too much or he will "sound like a White person." Thus, the team concluded that it was unnecessary to carry out an evaluation of Luis' cognitive and linguistic skills.

A Shoshone tutor was hired to work with Luis for 30 minutes each day in the classroom. At the end of the year, Luis was performing at grade level and had learned to be "bicultural" by speaking more in the classroom, although he still remained quiet, as was culturally appropriate, when in the presence of adults on the reservation. Luis said, "At school, I talk like White people. At home, I'm an Indian."

STUDY QUESTIONS

1. Describe health issues that tend to impact members of the Native American community. What impact might these issues have on communication skills?

2. Briefly outline the history of Native Americans in the U.S. Why might some of them experience feelings of fear and mistrust toward Anglo professionals and Anglos in general?

3. You are giving an in-service to some student interns who are going to begin working in a Head Start program attended by many Native American children. List and describe five recommendations to help them provide services in a culturally sensitive and appropriate manner.

TRUE-FALSE

Circle the number beside each statement that is true.

4. Native American infants tend to be somewhat slower in their gross motor development than infants from other ethnic groups.

5. Native Americans emphasize spirituality and the interconnectedness of all living things.

6. Native American mothers encourage their children to speak as much as possible from early on because this will help the children perform better in school.

7. In many Native American languages, vowels are nasalized.

8. Fetal Alcohol Syndrome is a common problem within the Native American population.

9. Historically, the mainstream American establishment (e.g., government, schools) has strongly encouraged Native American families to retain their linguistic and cultural roots.

10. When working with Native American children, professionals should encourage competitive games to help them feel more comfortable.

MULTIPLE CHOICE
Unless indicated otherwise, circle the number beside each choice that is correct.

11. Which one of the following is NOT considered characteristic of Native American communication styles?
    A. There is a great deal of nodding, smiling, and interjecting during conversations.
    B. Children look down or away to show respect for elders.
    C. In many families, adults do not carry out verbal exchanges with infants.
    D. It is polite to hesitate for a period of time before answering a question.
    E. Children may be rebuked for talking too much.

12. With regard to health care and longevity, the following statements are true:
    A. Native Americans have a high incidence of otitis media.
    B. Diseases common among Native Americans include diabetes, gastrointestinal disease, malignant neoplasms, and tuberculosis.
    C. The average life span within the Native American population is 82 years.
    D. Alcohol consumption is viewed as sinful and occurs rarely in Native American populations.

13. Native American students often experience challenges with the education system for the following reasons:
    A. There are many differences between Native American languages and mainstream English.
    B. Impulsivity is a common characteristic of their behavior.
    C. Confusion may result from a rigid classroom schedule packed with activities.
    D. Their competitive nature often results in disruptions within the classroom.
    E. They may not respond to a question if they are confident that the adult already knows the answer.

14. Culturally sensitive service delivery to Native American students and their families would include keeping the following facts in mind:
    A. Story-telling is not important and should be avoided because it is not culturally congruent for students.
    B. It is important to engage students in non-competitive, cooperative learning activities.
    C. Teachers should single out children so that they can be praised in front of their peers.
    D. The professional should ask a wide range of personal questions to demonstrate a sincere interest in what family members know.

15. Which one of the following is NOT commonly observed among Native Americans?
    A. They may be very reluctant to discuss personal affairs.
    B. They try not to interfere in the affairs of others.
    C. Some believe that a child's disability is a gift.
    D. Happiness and harmony are valued highly.
    E. They greatly value the accumulation of material possessions.

ANSWERS TO STUDY QUESTIONS

4. True	11. A
5. True	12. A and B
6. False	13. A, C, and E
7. True	14. B
8. True	15. E
9. False	
10. False	

Chapter 8

FAMILIES FROM PACIFIC ISLAND BACKGROUNDS

Outline

General Background information
Pacific Island Family Life
Pacific Island Education
Cultural Customs and Courtesies
Health Care and Disabling Conditions
Pacific Island Communication Styles
Pacific Island Language Considerations

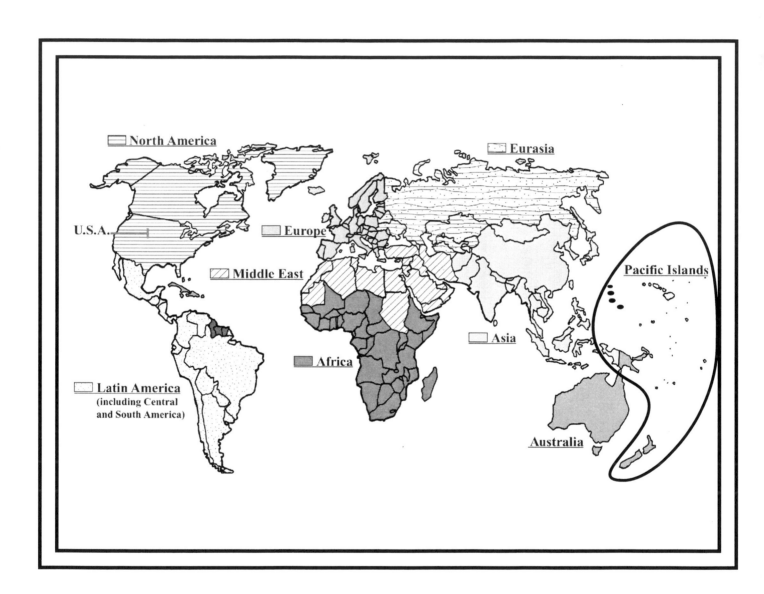

The Pacific Islands include three major geographic areas: Melanesia, Micronesia, and Polynesia, as shown in Figure 8.1. Within each of these areas are several island groups. Each island nation has a unique history that has influenced the customs and way of life of its inhabitants.

Figure 8.1

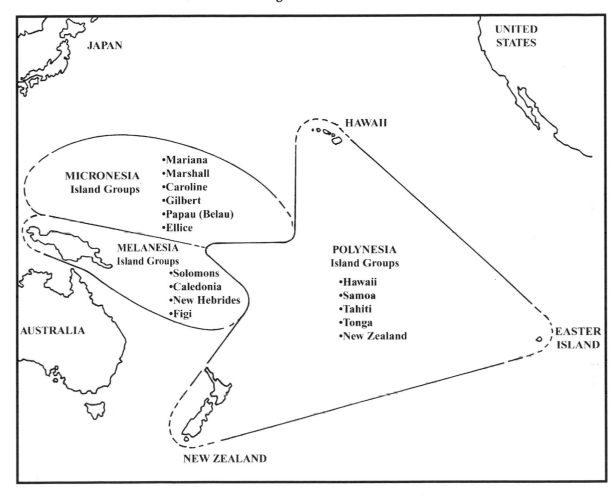

Melanesia

1. The island groups included in Melanesia are New Guinea, the Bismarck and Louisiade archipelagos, the Admiralty Islands, Bougainville Island, Solomon Islands, New Caledonia and Loyalty Islands, Vanuatu, Fiji, and Norfolk Island.

2. The natives on these island groups are heterogeneous in culture and language.

Micronesia

1. The island groups included in Micronesia are Kiribati, Nauru, the Republic of the Marshall Islands, Palau (Belau), and the Federated States of Micronesia.

2. Guam of the Marianas is the most populous island in all of Micronesia and has over 95,000 inhabitants.

3. Micronesia has considerable diversity, especially between the societies of the low coral atolls and those of the high islands (NOAA Pacific Services Center, 2006).

Polynesia

1. The island groups included in Polynesia are Hawaii, New Zealand, Easter Island, Samoa, Cook, Tonga, French Polynesia, Nuie Island, Tokelau and Tuvalu, Wallis and Futuna, and Pitcairn Island.

2. Polynesia encompasses the Hawaiian Islands, areas that have been influenced in a variety of ways by Filipino, Chinese, Korean, and Japanese cultures.

GENERAL BACKGROUND INFORMATION

❑ The largest populations in the Pacific Islands are the Hawaiians, Samoans, and Chamorros (Cheng, 2002).

❑ The Pacific Islands have been influenced by cultural groups from many countries, including France, the United States, Spain, Portugal, Germany, and Japan. Many areas in the Pacific Islands have a history of colonialism.

❑ Many religions are practiced in the Pacific Islands. Christianity is widespread, and many Pacific Islanders consider the Bible a major source of inspiration (Cheng, 2002).

❑ Forms of Christianity (e.g., Catholicism, Protestantism) may be combined with folk medicine, which may include faith healing, herbs, etc. Magic and sorcery are practiced in some places, particularly in Melanesia.

❑ Most Samoans have strong religious beliefs; Samoa's motto is "Samoa is founded upon God."

❑ Most Pacific Islanders have expertise in fishing and farming. They prize resource management and conservation of land (NOAA Pacific Services Center, 2006).

❑ In the U.S., the "Native Hawaiian and Other Pacific Islander" group increased considerably between 1990 and 2000. Based on "race alone," census data indicate that this population has grown 9.3% over this 10-year period. Based on "race alone or in combination," this population grew 139.5% between 1990 and 2000 (U.S. Bureau of the Census, 2000).

❑ The census data indicate that Asian Americans in combination with Pacific Islanders in the U.S. (AAPI) comprise 4% of the total U.S. population.

❑ AAPIs are the fastest-growing racial/ethnic group in the United States and are expected to represent 10% of the U.S. population by the year 2050 (U.S. Bureau of the Census, 2000).

❑ Some Pacific Islanders in the U.S. experience abject poverty. For example, 20.2% of Samoans live below the poverty threshold as compared to 12.4% of the total population (Asian and Pacific Islander American Health Forum; APIAHF, 2006)

PACIFIC ISLAND FAMILY LIFE

❏ Children are often viewed as gifts of God (Mokuau & Tauili'ili, 2004).

❏ Extended families of several generations are quite common. Families may be quite large, with 12 or more children (Faumuina, 2001).

❏ Childcare is frequently provided by multiple caretakers, including siblings. Children may be raised by members of the extended family or even friends (Cox, 2006).

❏ The Chamorro and Carolinian societies are matriarchal, with clearly defined roles for members of the nuclear family. "Fathers are responsible for making financial decisions, and mothers hold the responsibility for raising the children and housekeeping" (Hammer, 1994, p. 6).

❏ In some Chamorro families, daughters live at home until they are married. Living alone can have negative sexual connotations for a single woman.

❏ When a couple is married in the Northern Marianas, they will usually live with the groom's parents and conceive their first child within the first few years of the marriage (Hammer, 1994).

❏ Villagers often have close ties and help one another in many situations.

❏ Reciprocity, interdependence, and cooperation are inherent values of many groups.

❏ Islanders place a strong emphasis on authority and respect. Children and subordinates must comply with the wishes of elders.

❏ Islanders are more concerned about the well-being of the family than about the rights of individuals. In Samoa, for example, a person is expected to help other members of the family, regardless of the cost.

❏ Although Samoans may appear to be poor in the eyes of outsiders, there is no "homelessness" in Samoa. Extended families and family networks freely share food, material goods, and shelter (Faumuina, 2001). The Samoan language has no word for "person" because individual people are considered to be part of the whole group (Cheng, Nakasato, & Wallace, 1995).

❏ The welfare of the family is considered a much higher priority than the welfare of individual children; children are often preoccupied with pleasing their parents. Everyone is expected to work together for the benefit of the community.

❏ Many Hawaiian families are quite physically affectionate with their children. In some places such as Bali, a baby may be carried so much that he does not have contact with the floor for the first several months of his life.

❏ Mothers may not leave the home for at least one week after a child is born; in some groups, babies do not leave the house for the first month of life (Mokuau & Tauili'ili, 2004).

❏ In some homes, women may be physically abused by their husbands; violence against women is a concern in some Islander cultures.

❑ One survey found that during a 12-month period, Native Hawaiians had experienced sexual abuse or domestic violence at twice the rate of Whites (Anderson, Crengle, Kamak, Chen, Palafox, & Jackson-Pulver, 2006). Various associations are beginning to address this problem (The Asia Foundation, 2007).

❑ Physical punishment is quite common among Samoans and some other groups in the Pacific Islands (Australian Centre for International and Tropical Health, 2003). Rulers, belts, and other implements may be used regularly to discipline children. In many of these families, physical discipline begins at about 3 years of age and continues through mid-adolescence.

❑ Among Samoans, loving and expressive parenting typically coexists with wide acceptance of physical punishment. Physical discipline ensures proper behavior from children (Pelczarski & Kemp, 2006). Many Samoans use corporal punishment to ingrain respect into their children so that, as adults, the children will fit into society's hierarchical structure.

✎REFLECTION✎

Describe four patterns of behavior commonly observed within Pacific Islander families that occur much less frequently within mainstream U.S. families.

_____

_____

_____

_____

_____

PACIFIC ISLAND EDUCATION

❑ Twenty-seven percent of the total U.S. population 25 years of age and older has at least a Bachelor's degree, whereas only 15% of single-race Hawaiians and Other Pacific Islanders have reached this educational level. Ten percent of the total U.S. population has received a graduate or professional degree, but only 4% of Pacific Islanders have received this type of degree (American Community Survey, 2005).

❑ The educational style in the Islands is generally relaxed; absenteeism among both teachers and students is common.

❑ Some classes are quite unstructured and informal; teachers may come to school without lesson plans.

❑ Books and other educational resources are often in short supply because many areas are remote.

❑ The educational tradition emphasizes oral learning (Sileo & Prater, 1999).

❏ Hawaiian public school students generally perform below their counterparts on the U.S. mainland on many measures of academic achievement (Deering, 2005).

❏ Western Samoa, however, has a 98% literacy rate. In traditional villages, education is received at a minister's school, where children learn to read. Later they attend both elementary and secondary schools (Cox, 2006).

❏ Some schools provide bilingual education in the native language and English.

❏ For many students, it is a major adjustment to go from Island schools to mainland schools in the United States; Island students often experience "...persistent disproportionate school failure" (Ogbu & Matute-Bianchi, 1990, p. 73).

❏ Rote memorization is a common learning strategy in many Islander schools (Cox, 2006).

❏ It is quite difficult for Pacific Islander students to go from relaxed schools in which orally-based learning and rote memorization are stressed to U.S. schools in which individual excellence and creativity are emphasized (Cheng, 2002).

❏ Educators in the United States have been concerned about the high percentage of Islander students who fail in school and/or drop out (Andrade, Hishinuma, McDermott et al., 2006). For example, approximately 12.6% of Native Hawaiians complete college, but only 3.2% have a graduate or professional degree (Anderson et al., 2006).

❏ A concern for American educators is that some Islander parents do not feel that it is important for children to attend school on a regular basis.

❏ Some Islander families want their children to go to work as soon as possible, feeling that children who continue in school selfishly drain the family's resources instead of contributing to the family's well-being. Many families encourage their children to enter the job market before completing high school.

❏ Samoans in the United States want very much for their children to be educated; however, values emphasized in school often conflict with those of the home.

CULTURAL CUSTOMS AND COURTESIES

❏ Many Islanders have a "collective rights" attitude in which generosity and sharing are valued (Australian Centre for International and Tropical Health, 2003). Collectivism and cooperation are important, whereas individualism and privacy are usually not priorities.

❏ In Samoa, many homes are comprised of one large, communal room. Adjusting to American homes with many rooms can be difficult and very divisive to Samoan families.

❏ Hospitality is important among many groups (Chadwick, 2000).

❏ Festive occasions and celebrations in which food is served are very common.

❏ It is considered inappropriate, by some Samoans, to drink or eat while walking or standing (Mokuau & Tauili'ili, 2004).

❏ Compared to U.S. standards, the pace in the Northern Marianas is slow. "There is a tacit belief that if something is not done today, it will be done tomorrow, and if it is not done tomorrow, it is very possible that it does not have to be done at all. This notion is observed in all aspects of life, including work settings, the government, and access to speech and language services" (Hammer, 1994, p. 7).

HEALTH CARE AND DISABLING CONDITIONS

❏ When people are sick, families may call upon faith healers or practitioners of folk medicine.

❏ Among some groups, massage and the use of fruits, roots, and leaves in treatment are common (Cox, 2006).

❏ Some Islanders have poor access to health care (Frisbie, Cho, & Hummer, 2006). They may lack access to insurance.

❏ Infant mortality rates in the U.S.-associated Pacific Island jurisdictions exceed the U.S. rate, and may be twice as high (Singh, 2001).

❏ Diabetes, hypertension, lung cancer, heart disease, and obesity are prevalent (Cheng at al., 1995). In some groups there is a belief that the more one eats, the higher his status (Australian Centre for International and Tropical Health, 2003).

❏ Samoans especially have a high rate of obesity (APIAHF, 2006). In Tonga, type II diabetes is very common, even in children; it is primarily due to obesity (Fukuyama, Inaoka, Matsumura, Yamauchi, Natsuhara, Kimura, & Ohtsuka, 2005).

❏ Unfortunately, as in many regions of the world, Pacific Island residents are contracting AIDS in greater numbers. For example, it is estimated that in Papua, New Guinea, 100,000 people have HIV (Cullen, 2006).

❏ Hearing problems due to factors such as impacted wax and otitis media are common among some groups. High rates of otitis media are common among Samoan and Hawaiian children (Pang-Ching et al., 1995).

❏ Islanders are at increased risk for ingesting high levels of mercury because of the amount of seafood in their diets (Hightower, O'Hare, & Hernández, 2006). Children who are prenatally exposed to mercury are at risk for problems such as developmental delays, lowered IQs, and impaired hearing and vision (Health and Environment Alliance, 2006).

❏ Some families protect disabled children and do not expect them to be independent.

❏ Some Hawaiian families attribute physical disabilities to spiritual causes; the disabilities may be viewed as beyond the control of human beings.

❏ Some members of the Carolinian and Chamarro cultures believe that spirits can cause disabilities in children (Hammer, 1994).

❏ Some cultures (e.g., the Chamorro culture) view a disability as God's gift, and believe that the individual should be cared for and protected.

❏ Parents may acquiesce to their children's desires, particularly if the children have experienced a number of medical difficulties.

❏ Among the Samoans and some other groups, there is a tendency toward intolerance for disabilities. Families may try to conceal the disability.

❏ Some Samoans believe that the birth of a handicapped child is a sign of God's displeasure with the family (Mokuau & Tauili'ili, 2004).

❏ In many regions of the Pacific Islands, special education programs are scarce. Efforts are being made to provide programs for children with special needs and to integrate them into regular education programs (United Nations Economic and Social Commission for Asia and the Pacific, 2002).

Profile

Lee T., a 16-year-old Chamorro, was diving off a cliff into the ocean with his friends. He struck his head on the rocks below and experienced a profound head injury. He was flown by helicopter to Hawaii, where doctors were able to save his life. However, after awakening from a coma two months later, Lee experienced major cognitive and linguistic deficits and had difficulty walking and dressing himself. The hospital staff offered the family both in- and out-patient rehabilitative services that included occupational, physical, and speech therapy. The family thanked the staff and declined to accept any services, saying that they would take care of Lee from that point on. The family did not feel that it was appropriate to try to "force" Lee to become independent again. They felt that he had suffered enough already, and they believed it was their job to protect him from now on.

PACIFIC ISLAND COMMUNICATION STYLES

❏ To avoid offending others, some Islanders may say what they think the listener wants to hear.

❏ Some groups (e.g., Hawaiians) tend to favor interpersonal communication styles that emphasize cooperation rather than competition.

❏ Children may be unaccustomed to interacting with adults on a one-to-one basis because their primary communication experiences are with other children, not adults.

❏ It may be considered inappropriate to touch a child on the top of the head because this area is considered sacred.

❏ Oral language proficiency and story-telling are often highly prized.

❏ Nonverbal cues in interactions are important to most Islanders.

❏ Some Islanders may view prolonged eye contact as a sign of disrespect.

❏ Persons from the Carolinian and Chamorro cultures use their eyebrows extensively to communicate meaning.

❏ Among many Samoans, it is inappropriate to walk past a person of status or authority without a display of deference such as downcast eyes.

❏ In some Samoan families, children, as a sign of respect, are to sit down when addressing an older person.

❏ In the Samoan culture, movement of the shoulders often indicates ambivalence or confusion (Mokuau & Tauili'ili, 2004).

❏ In the Samoan household, the mother has power and authority as chief caregiver. Since Samoan children are expected to accommodate adults, most Samoan mothers don't simplify their vocabulary or sentence structure when interacting with their children. If a child says something unintelligible, the Samoan mother may call attention to the problem and might even ignore the utterance (Tannen, 1994).

❏ Many Samoan mothers play with their infants and cuddle them but do not respond to their vocalizations as intentional or social. Thus, in some homes there may be little emphasis on early language development (Cheng et al., 1995).

PACIFIC ISLAND LANGUAGE CONSIDERATIONS

❏ The Pacific Island languages fall within the Austronesian language family.

❏ Over 1,200 indigenous languages are spoken in the Pacific Islands (Campbell, 1989). Major languages include Fijian, Hawaiian, Samoan, Tahitian, Chamorro, Carolinian, Korean, Palauan, Marshallese, Papua New Guinean, Yapese, Trukese, and Pompean. Most Pacific Island languages are mutually unintelligible.

❏ The linguistic variety is great in some areas. For example, more than 800 languages are spoken on Papua, New Guinea.

❏ The languages of Polynesia have more homogeneity than the languages of Melanesia.

❏ Languages spoken in Hawaii include Mandarin, Tagalog, Samoan, Ilocano, Korean, Cantonese, Japanese, and Hawaiian. English is spoken by almost all Hawaiians.

❏ Some Hawaiians speak a fluent dominant language (e.g., English, Japanese) as well as pidgin.

❏ Many children of Hawaiian descent speak pidgin English, also known as Hawaiian Creole (Genesee et al., 2004). These children often need assistance in acquiring formal written and oral English skills (Deering, 2005).

❏ The three major languages spoken in many areas of Micronesia are English, Chamorro, and Carolinian.

❏ Language use and vocabulary are influenced by culture. In the Carolinian language, for example, there are more than 10 words that depict the various stages of a coconut's growth.

❑ Samoa's schools are bilingual (Samoan and English).

❑ Some cultures (e.g., Samoan and Hawaiian) place a strong emphasis on oral traditions.

❑ Many Pacific Islanders understand English but speak a pidgin form of the language.

❑ In the writing systems of languages spoken in the Pacific Islands, letters for vowels represent one sound only.

❑ The apostrophe within a word (e.g., ali'i) is pronounced as a glottal stop (momentary stopping of the breath in the throat).

❑ In general, consonants are identical or close approximations to their English equivalents. The "g" in English is usually hard; however, in Samoan, g is always pronounced as "*ng*" (e.g., Pago Pago is pronounced Pango Pango) (Cox, 2006).

❑ Characteristics of several languages spoken in the Pacific Islands are described below.

Hawaiian language

1. The language is alphabetical and polysyllabic, with stress being placed on the next to last syllable.
2. Five vowels are used: *a, e, i, o, u.*
3. Eight consonants are used: *w, p, n, m, h, l, k* and the glottal stop.
4. The language has no consonant clusters.
5. The language is characterized by words that always end in vowels.
6. *w* is pronounced as *v* when it follows an *e* or *i.*

Tahitian language

1. The alphabet has only 13 letters.
2. Five vowels are used:

   a (as in father)

   e (as in *May*; may also be pronounced as in *egg*)

   i (pronounced "ee" as in *tree*)

   o (pronounced "o" as in *goat*)

   u (pronounced "u" as in *flute*)
3. Eight consonants are used: *f, h, m, n, p, r, t, v*; these are pronounced like their English equivalents, but they are never used at the end of syllables.
4. Syllables end in vowels.
5. Vowels are often grouped together; each should be pronounced separately (e.g., Faaa is pronounced "Fa-ah-ah").
6. Most words are accented on the next to last syllable, except when an apostrophe separates the final vowel from the vowel preceding it; in this case, both vowels are given equal emphasis (e.g., *mataura'a* [custom] is pronounced "mah-tah-oo-ra-ah").

Fijian language

1. *b* is pronounced as if it is preceded by *m* (e.g., "ba" is pronounced as "mba").

2. *c* is pronounced as "th" (e.g., "Yanuca" becomes "Yanu tha").

3. *d* is pronounced as "nd" (e.g., "Nadee" becomes "Nan dee").

4. *g* is pronounced as "ng" (e.g., "Sigatoka" becomes "Singatokaî").

5. *q* is pronounced as "ngg" (e.g., "Beqa" becomes "Mbeng-ga").

Chamorro language

1. The language has six vowels and 11 allophonic variations of these vowels. Vowel sounds in Chamorro include *i, e, ae, a, o,* and *u.*

2. The language has 18 consonants and the glide *w.*

3. Most consonants are pronounced as they are in English with some exceptions.

4. *ch* is pronounced "ts" as in "tsar."

5. *y* is pronounced "ds" as in "goods."

6. *ñ* is pronounced "ny" as in "Bunyan."

7. *w* is pronounced "gw" as in "Gwendolyn."

Samoan language

1. This is an Austronesian language spoken in Western and American Samoa.

2. Vowels can be long or short.

3. Syllables consist of a vowel or a consonant plus a vowel.

4. The language uses the glottal stop frequently.

5. Consonants never appear together or in syllable-final position.

6. Consonants are *p, t, m, n, g, f, v, s, l.*

Profile

I received a request to assess the language and articulation skills of Fa'aola T., a friendly 5th-grade Samoan girl who had transferred into the school. According to Fa'aola's school records, she was being raised by her mother; however, another set of records indicated that her aunt and uncle were her primary caregivers.

Fa'aola had developmental delays and had received special education services since kindergarten (in the previous school district). There were notations that Fa'aola had continuous allergies and appeared sleepy in class much of the time. According to her records, school personnel had asked her caregivers to take her to a doctor; there was no indication that this had occurred. Apparently, school personnel also had concerns about Fa'aola's hearing and vision; there was no home follow-through in these areas either.

When I assessed Fa'aola, I found her language skills to be commensurate with those of a kindergartner. When I evaluated her articulation, it became apparent that major dental and orthodontal deviations were having a strong impact on her intelligibility. I wrote a lengthy diagnostic report, with very specific recommendations for supporting Fa'aola in all areas tested. When I checked on Fa'aola a few months later, I discovered that she and her family had moved.

REFLECTION

List two verbal and two nonverbal characteristics commonly observed in the communication of Pacific Islanders. Why is it important to be aware of these characteristics?

_____

_____

_____

_____

_____

IMPLICATIONS FOR PROFESSIONALS

❑ Professionals should remember that families may be late for meetings or may not come at all if a family matter arises; family needs are generally a higher priority than meetings.

❑ Professionals should not automatically assume that the biological parents are in charge of a student because care-taking may rotate between relatives (e.g., aunts, uncles, grandparents, older siblings). Thus, when contacting the home, professionals may need to find out who is currently in charge of the student.

❑ It is imperative to involve the entire family in any processes and decisions, not just the student. Some parents may even want elders to be present during decision-making.

❑ Professionals should be formal when addressing authority figures within the family.

❑ In the matriarchal Carolinian and Chamorro societies, an elder female such as the paternal grandmother may have the final say in some family matters. Professionals should relate positively with this person because the opinions expressed may determine whether or not a child receives services (Hammer, 1994).

❑ Professionals may observe bruises on students or hear reports of physical punishment. It is critical for parents to be informed about American laws regarding child abuse. In addition, professionals should be aware that physical punishment may occur at home if the parents learn that the child was disciplined at school. In cases such as these, professionals will want to work with the local community and local churches in order to intervene in culturally appropriate ways in matters relating to discipline.

❑ During interactions with parents, professionals may need to emphasize the importance of keeping students in school until graduation. By remaining in school, students will be better equipped to find jobs in the work force.

❑ Some students (e.g., Carolinian) may come from an environment in which several languages are spoken. Thus the identification of a "primary" language may prove to be a challenge. When assessing these students, professionals must rely heavily on information from parents and teachers and on natural, informal, environmental assessment methods.

❏ It is considered culturally appropriate for professionals to show their concern and interest in the welfare of the entire family (Deering, 2005). However, professionals should not venture immediately into frank discussions about personal problems or difficulties.

❏ Among some groups, it is considered rude for people to converse when they are standing.

❏ Professionals must remember that although families may say "yes" to indicate that they acknowledge receiving information, a "yes" response does not necessarily indicate agreement with what has been said. For this reason it is better to ask open-ended questions than yes-no questions.

❏ Professionals should respect the family's spiritual values and beliefs about healing. Western professionals can work in collaboration with traditional folk healers.

❏ Islanders tend to take a holistic approach to problems. Professionals can utilize the services and support of the family, community, and church to support families (Pacifica Mental Health, 2006).

❏ Professionals must fully explain forms that require signatures. Many parents are accustomed to signing only documents relating to major life events such as births and deaths. They may not understand why signatures are needed on school forms.

❏ When parents are asked to come to school for a meeting, they may feel that their child is being criticized. The purpose of the meeting should be explained clearly.

Important considerations for professionals working with Islander students include the following:

1. Remember that students who are proficient in basic conversational English do not necessarily have the language skills necessary to perform effectively in classroom reading and writing activities.

2. Remember that students may come from low socioeconomic backgrounds in which there have been few opportunities for language stimulation.

3. Encourage a "buddy system" in which students are paired with peers from the same background (Deering, 2005).

4. Increase knowledge of the home language (e.g., learning basic vocabulary).

5. Become familiar with the sociolinguistic/pragmatic rules of discourse within the child's language (e.g., leave-taking, greeting, complimenting, etc.).

6. Remember that at home, students are often taught to be quiet, observant, and not to challenge authority. The classroom learning environment, however, may require the child to criticize, evaluate, speculate, and render judgments. Such behaviors conflict with behavioral expectations in the home environment.

7. Teach students how to interact with adults if they are not accustomed to such interactions at home.

8. Use a collective rather than individual story-telling method. A number of students should be included.

9. Teach students story-telling skills. Professionals can build listening and story-telling skills with folktales that are congruent with children's cultural backgrounds (Education World, 2007). *Talk-story*, a give-and-take conversational structure in Hawaii, can be used with children who are familiar with this method of communication.

10. Teach students problem-solving skills.

11. Provide opportunities for contextualized learning. Use literature and symbols from students' cultures.

12. Provide summer orientation programs for students who are unfamiliar with conventional school routines (Deering, 2005). These programs familiarize the student with the structure of the classroom so that they will be ready for school.

13. Remember that the traditional American educational system, which relies on competition and individualized learning, encourages students to interact in ways that they may not have experienced within their culture. These students may learn more efficiently if opportunities for cooperative learning are provided. (Sileo & Prater, 1999).

Profile

Alisi, a Samoan 7-year-old, recently moved to the U.S. with her family. She was quiet in class, and struggled academically, so the speech-language pathologist collaborated with the teacher to help Alisi increase linguistic and cognitive skills in English. Alisi was learning to raise her hand, give opinions, ask questions of the teacher, and engage in verbal problem-solving.

One day Alisi came to school with bruises on her face, arms, and back. The teacher noticed the bruises immediately, and the case was referred to Child Protective Services (CPS). When the CPS worker came to the school and spoke with Alisi, she told him that her parents had beaten her for asking too many questions and challenging their authority.

Alisi's parents were called to court for breaking U.S. child abuse laws. They defended their actions, saying that Alisi has been showing a lack of respect for her elders. They stated that she was becoming too "mouthy" and Americanized.

After this incident, the teacher and speech-language pathologist arranged a meeting with the pastor of the local Samoan church that Alisi's family attended. The pastor explained U.S. child abuse laws in further detail to Alisi's parents. The need for the child to be verbally assertive in the classroom was also stressed. The parents did not agree with this recommendation but indicated that they would find other ways to discipline the child. They also indicated that they would make an effort to be more understanding of differences in how the school expected children to interact with others.

STUDY QUESTIONS

1. List the three major geographic areas of the Pacific Islands. Which area is the most homogeneous?

2. Discuss health concerns that are typical for many Pacific Islanders. How might these concerns impact communication skills, if at all?

3. Describe educational practices of schools in the Pacific Islands. How do these practices impact the adjustment of students who move to the U.S. and enroll in school?

TRUE-FALSE

Circle the number beside all statements that are true.

4. Persons from the Samoan culture use their eyebrows extensively to communicate meaning.

5. When professionals discuss personal problems or difficult areas with families, it is best to address these issues immediately or the families will think professionals are "beating around the bush."

6. The apostrophe within a word (e.g., ali'i) is pronounced as a glottal stop (momentary stopping of the breath in the throat).

7. Samoans tend to be very lenient with their children, using verbal reprimands as a last resort to punish undesirable behaviors.

8. Middle ear infections are more common among Samoan and Hawaiian children than among children from most other cultures.

9. Professionals can help students in school by encouraging a "buddy system" in which these students work with peers who come from a similar cultural background.

10. Most families are very comfortable signing forms because, in the Pacific Islands, placing a signature on a document is a way of showing one's status.

MULTIPLE CHOICE

Circle the letter beside each of the choices that is correct.

11. The following may be observed in the Pacific Islands:

    A. Some Hawaiian families attribute physical disabilities to spiritual causes; the disabilities may be viewed as beyond the control of human beings.

    B. Some Samoans feel that the birth of a disabled child is a sign of God's displeasure with the family.

    C. Some cultures (e.g., the Chamorro culture) view a disability as a gift from God, and hence the individual is to be protected and sheltered.

    D. Most Pacific Islanders believe that a disabled individual should be given as many rehabilitative services as possible.

    E. Healers or folk medicine practitioners may be called upon by some groups.

12. When professionals work with Pacific Islander students, they can be most helpful by thinking about and doing the following:

    A. They should remember that students who are proficient in basic conversation do not necessarily have the language skills necessary to perform effectively in classroom reading and writing activities.

    B. They should understand that many of these students come from middle class socioeconomic backgrounds that have supported learning experiences in schools.

    C. They should focus on critical thinking and evaluation tasks because students are encouraged to give opinions and render judgments at home.

    D. They should use collective story-telling methods.

    E. They should teach problem-solving skills.

13. Which of the following are TRUE?

    A. The Pacific Island languages fall within the Austronesian language family.

    B. Hawaiian is alphabetical and polysyllabic, with stress being placed on the next to last syllable.

    C. Vowels are often grouped together in the Tahitian language, but each should be pronounced separately.

    D. Samoan is the most widely used language in the Philippines.

14. Aspects of communication that are important to remember when working with families from the Pacific Islands include the following:

    A. Oral language proficiency and story-telling are often highly prized.

    B. Nonverbal cues are relatively unimportant; verbal cues carry most of the meaning.

    C. Samoan mothers often cuddle and physically care for their babies but do not respond to the infants' vocalizations as meaningful attempts to communicate.

    D. The frequent asking of questions is encouraged in the classroom in all cultural groups within the Pacific Islands.

15. A Chamorro child has been found to have a communication disorder, and you need to discuss the assessment with his family. What should you be aware of in planning your meeting?

   A. The family will arrive promptly to avoid experiencing feelings of shame that are often associated with tardiness.

   B. The grandmother may be the primary decision maker.

   C. The biological parents are in charge of the child, so questions should be directed to them first.

   D. It is best to ask *yes-no* questions (rather than open-ended questions) to reduce feelings of anxiety that family members might experience.

   E. If family members agree to have the child placed in a special education program, it is highly likely that they will make sure that all homework assignments are completed.

ANSWERS TO STUDY QUESTIONS

   4. False
   5. False
   6. True
   7. False
   8. True
   9. True
   10. False
   11. A, B, C, E
   12. A, D, E
   13. A, B, C
   14. A, C
   15. B

Chapter 9

FAMILIES FROM MIDDLE EASTERN BACKGROUNDS

Outline

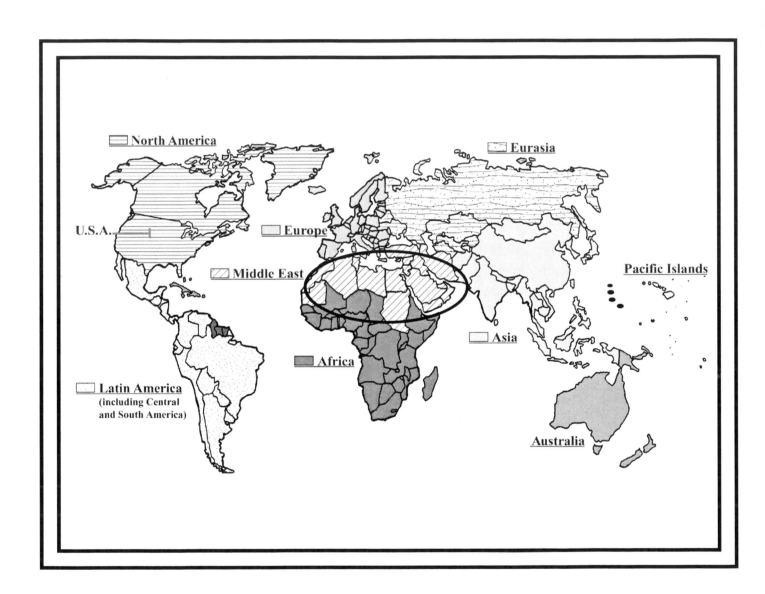

North America

Eurasia

U.S.A.

Europe

Pacific Islands

Middle East

Asia

Africa

Latin America
(including Central
and South America)

Australia

The Middle East is often called the cradle of civilization. Countries included in this area are Israel, Syria, Lebanon, the Occupied Territories, Iraq, Iran, Jordan, Saudi Arabia, Bahrain, Kuwait, Qatar, Oman, Yemen, the United Arab Emirates, Egypt, Turkey, and Sudan, as shown in Figure 9.1.

Figure 9.1

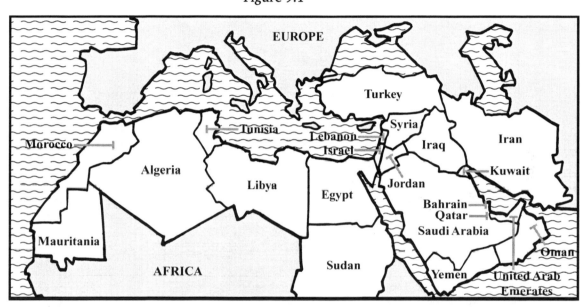

GENERAL BACKGROUND INFORMATION

❏ A large number of Middle Eastern immigrants have come to the United States since the 1980s. According to the U.S. Census (2000), 1.2 million residents of the U.S. reported Arab ancestry. During the decade of the 1990s, the Egyptian population had increased numerically more than any other group.

❏ States with the highest concentrations of Arabs are New York, Michigan, California, Florida, and New Jersey. In 2000, New York City had the highest number of any city in the U.S. (U.S. Census Bureau, 2000).

❏ The Middle East stretches over a large area, approximately the size of the United States, where the continents of Africa, Asia, and Europe come together.

❏ Most of the Middle East is comprised of deserts.

❏ The largest city in the Middle East is Cairo, Egypt.

❑ The largest country in the Middle East is Saudi Arabia. It is one million square miles in size, roughly one-third the size of the United States. Saudi Arabia is often considered a bridge between Asia and the Western world.

❑ The Muslim holy cities of Mecca and Medina are located in Saudi Arabia. Thousands of Muslims journey to these cities annually (especially Mecca) to pray and worship.

❑ The Arab population in the Middle East is larger than that of any other group. Thus, the majority (but not all) of Middle Easterners are Arabs. More than 75% of the people in the Middle East identify themselves as Arabs.

❑ The Arab countries include Morroco, Mauritania, Algeria, Tunisia, Libya, Chad, Sudan, Egypt, Syria, Iraq, Jordan, Lebanon, Kuwait, Saudi Arabia, Bahrain, Qatar, United Arab Emirates, Yemen, and Oman.

❑ The Arabic language provides a linguistic bond among the Arab countries. Anyone who speaks Arabic as a native is considered to be an Arab, no matter what country he or she is from. The term "Arab" is not based on race; Arabs have widely varied physical features (Ahmad, 2004).

❑ Wilson (1998, pp. 197-198) stated that "...the term *Arab* itself is not strictly definable. In a purely semantic sense, no people can be classified as *Arab* because the word connotes a mixed population with widely varying ethnologic and racial origins. . . . Hence, *Arab* is best used within a cultural context. Arab countries are those countries in which the primary language is Arabic and the primary religion is Islam." (*Note: In this chapter, the terms "Arab" and "Middle Easterner" are used interchangeably although readers need to be aware of the distinctions between the two groups.)

❑ Approximately 92% of Arabs in the Middle East are Muslim (Ahmad, 2004). Most belong to the Sunni branch of Islam. In Lebanon, however, approximately half of the population is Christian. Most residents of Israel are Jewish.

❑ Other religious groups include the Bahais, Zoroastrians, and Armenian Christians.

❑ The Bahai faith is derived from Islam, but Bahais take Bahaullah as their prophet and they emphasize modernization and equality. Bahais in Iran have been persecuted by Shi'ite Muslims, and many Iranian Bahais have fled to other countries (Mohtasham-Nouri, 1994).

❑ Key values for many Middle Easterners include family and religion. Religion is an integral part of everyday life and activity.

❑ For Arabs, religious affiliation is essential; it is not acceptable to be an agnostic or atheist. Because Arabs respect religious people, they may lose respect for people who have no religious affiliation or who do not believe in God (Omar Nydell, 2006).

❑ Many Middle Easterners live in small villages; over 30% live in cities or large towns. There are small numbers of semi-nomadic or nomadic people who live in sparsely populated areas.

❑ Some nomads in Saudi Arabia are called "Bedouins" (Arabic for "people who live in the open country"); many of them are shepherds who live in clans and tribes.

❏ Middle Easterners in the U.S. are often stereotyped in negative ways (Al-Hazza & Lucking, 2005; Arida, 2006; Hall & Livingston, 2006). These stereotypes are caused by several phenomena, which include actions in the U.S. and in Middle Eastern countries by extremist Muslim groups (Bozorgmehr, 2001).

❏ In a survey of Americans by Kamalipour (2001), it was found that the terms associated most with Middle Easterners were "oil," "mean people," "dark skin," and "terrorism." Clark (2003) wrote that for centuries the Arab has played the role of the hustler, thief, seducer of women— the barbarian lurking at the gates of civilization.

❏ The negative stereotypes that many Americans have of Iranians have caused many Middle Easterners to identify themselves according to their "specific ethno-religiosity" (e.g., Armenian, Bahai, Jewish) rather than by their Iranian ethnicity (Bozorgmehr, 2001).

✐*REFLECTION*✐

Describe four general characteristics that are commonly observed among individuals from the Middle East.

MIDDLE EASTERN FAMILY LIFE

❏ In Arab families where Islam is the spiritual tradition, family members live out their roles as prescribed in the Koran. For example, the Koran values wealth and preeminence of male children and subordination of women to men (Hall & Livingston, 2006).

❏ The family is the primary focus of loyalty for many Middle Easterners; families are usually considered the pillars of society. Children are loved and cherished.

❏ Extended, multigenerational families are quite common. The achievements of any individual in the family affect how the family is perceived by others in the community.

❏ In many marriages, procreation is a higher priority than marital love and intimacy. Children are greatly valued, and not having children may be a cause for unhappiness (Sharifzadeh, 2004).

❏ For many Middle Eastern parents, a major life goal is that their children get married. Children's marriages mark the success and self-actualization of the parents.

❑ If a daughter does not get married, she is negatively judged by society and, as a result, her family will probably feel personally hurt. Thus, families often make their daughters available for marriage at young ages (Abu Baker, 2003).

❑ Parents may continue to provide for children even after the children have married (Abu Baker, 2003).

❑ Younger members of the family respect and care for the elderly. Many children support their parents in old age.

❑ In Saudi Arabia and some other areas, marriages are often arranged by the parents of the bride and groom. Sometimes the bride and groom meet one another before the wedding, but not always.

❑ Among Muslim Arabs, especially in nomadic and rural communities, people prefer to marry first or second cousins. In 1996, 58% of Iraqis married their cousins, followed by 55% of Saudi Arabians, 54% of Kuwaitis, and 50% of Jordanians. Intermarriage ensures that the spouse is a "known quantity" and that money and possessions stay within the family (Omar Nydell, 2006).

❑ Marriage among blood relatives may increase the incidence of genetic disorders such as Down Syndrome, sickle cell anemia, and severe sensorineural hearing loss (Aarts, 2001: Ott et al., 2003).

❑ Polygamy is practiced in some areas. In Iran, for example, men are often allowed to have up to four wives as long as they can provide for them. Each wife is supposed to be treated equally in all respects.

❑ Generally, the father is the head of the household; most Middle Eastern societies are patriarchal.

❑ Husbands often take little responsibility for the care of very young children and infants (Ahmad, 2004; Hedayat & Pirzadeh, 2001). However, when boys reach the age of 4 or 5, fathers often assume a more active role (Sharifzadeh, 2004).

❑ Arab boys may be expected to be decisive and aggressive, and girls may be expected to play a passive role.

❑ Arab adults generally do not reason with young children. They tell them to do things because "that is how it is done" or teach their children to avoid certain actions because of the fear of what others might think or say. Children are taught that it is important to conform to an expected social image (Omar Nydell, 2006).

❑ Children are not to interrupt when adults are talking and may not question rules relating to obedience and authority.

❑ Among Arabs, the most important aspect of acceptable conduct among children is respectful behavior in front of adults.

❏ In some areas, arranged marriages are common. Though this may be shocking to mainstream Americans, many families view arranged marriages as the parents' responsibility to help their adult children find happiness (Ingram, 2005).

❏ Traditionally, girls stay at home until they are married. In some groups, women may not be allowed to speak to strangers until after marriage.

❏ Divorce is rare and, in some groups, brings shame upon the woman and her family. A divorced woman may not be permitted to marry again.

❏ Cultural norms for the behavior of men are quite different from those for women in many (though not all) Arab homes (Gandhi, 2003). Men can come and go at will without anyone knowing where they are. They can spend money on themselves without explaining their purchases to anyone. If a woman behaves in this manner, the result might be an immediate divorce, and all the woman's rights as a wife and mother can be withheld (Abu Baker, 2003).

❏ There is a direct relationship between the number of children in a family (especially boys) and the amount of prestige experienced by the father and his family. A large family is a sign of prestige.

❏ Male children are often preferred over female children, in part, because boys carry on the family tradition and name. In agricultural societies, the male's potential for economic contribution is greater than that of the female.

❏ Many mothers in the Middle East emphasize attachment and parent-child bonding rather than individualism and independence (Sharifzadeh, 2004).

❏ Children are encouraged at early ages to take on family and household responsibilities. Girls are expected to take on household chores at about 5 years of age, but boys are generally exempt from these chores (Sharifzadeh, 2004).

❏ Many young Arabs admire and prefer Western entertainment, dress, and liberal thought. This is distressing to older, traditional Arabs, and has created an increasing generation gap in the Arab world (Omar Nydell, 2006).

❏ Historically, family relationships and gender roles in Middle Eastern cultures have been based on Islam and have been influenced little by changes in other parts of the world. Middle Eastern countries, however, are becoming more Westernized, resulting in changed attitudes toward marriage and family life (Schvaneveldt, Kerpelman, & Schvaneveldt, 2005).

❏ Schvaneveldt, et al. (2005) found that both mothers and daughters in the United Arab Emirates considered their Islamic religious beliefs to be important. However, the daughters (all of whom were university students with a mean age of 20 years) wanted to marry later than their mothers had and did not necessarily want to have big families. They also wanted husband-wife roles in their own marriages that were more egalitarian than those of their parents. In addition, 93% of the daughters reported a desire for a career, in contrast to 7% of the mothers.

Profile

Omar Y., a 4-year-old Middle Eastern boy, was brought to the local preschool by his mother. She wanted him to learn English (his primary language was Yemeni) and socialize with other children. Her husband traveled much of the time on business, and she was concerned that Omar was exposed primarily to her at home and was not receiving enough outside stimulation. The American preschool teachers noticed that Omar expected them to help him complete tasks such as putting on his sweater and throwing out leftovers from his snacks. They also noticed that Omar was so extremely respectful that he never asked questions or interacted with the teachers at all, even when he started learning some English.

One of the teachers, who had lived in the Middle East for several years as a Peace Corps volunteer, asked Omar's mother to meet with her after preschool for tea and snacks while Omar played nearby. The teacher related her challenging experience of raising American children in the Middle East, with its different cultural mores, and discussed the changes that had to be made in her parenting while the family lived in Saudi Arabia. The teacher also discussed U.S. expectations for children's independence as well as the American school system's expectation that children initiate interactions with teachers.

Omar's mother was open and receptive to the teacher's suggestions, so the teacher invited her to observe classroom instruction. Mrs. Y. observed for 20 minutes each day, and the teachers began to see an increase in Omar's social interaction skills and independent activity in the classroom.

EDUCATION AND LITERACY

❑ Educational opportunities and teaching styles vary greatly from country to country as does literacy. In Israel, for example, schools are well attended and the literacy rate is quite high. Most residents of Yemen, however, are not literate.

❑ Classes are often quite large and may have as many as 60 students (elementary level).

❑ Formal Arabic is taught in many schools.

❑ Many Arabs in the U.S. are well educated and possess advanced degrees (Al-Hazza & Lucking, 2005).

❑ The education of children is a high priority in many families. Parents see education as a means of professional and financial advancement.

❑ Some girls do not continue their education beyond elementary school because of the fear that they will be exposed to and left unprotected in inappropriate social situations within the school environment (Sharifzadeh, 2004).

❑ Traditionally, females were not encouraged to attend college. Higher education for women, however, is viewed more positively than in previous years and is becoming more common (Sharifzadeh, 2004).

❑ Co-educational schools are not an option for children in many Middle Eastern countries.

❏ Compulsory education usually begins at around 6 or 7 years of age.

❏ Story-telling is very common in schools in the Middle East.

❏ Children from middle-class, educated families often learn poems and share storybook reading activities with their parents.

CULTURAL CUSTOMS, COURTESIES, AND BELIEFS

❏ Some of the character traits most important to Middle Easterners are generosity, bravery, friendship, and hospitality.

❏ Guests generally are treated with kindness; food is available in abundance.

❏ Some groups (e.g., Saudi Arabians) generally do not talk much during meals; these groups prefer to talk after meals.

❏ Women in some cultures may be expected to eat in separate rooms from men.

❏ Some groups (e.g., Saudi Arabians) consider the left hand to be unclean. It is to be used for lavatory purposes only. Some people may be offended if the left hand is used when greeting others.

❏ Among Arabs, there is no concept of privacy. When translated, the Arabic word that most closely resembles the concept of privacy is "loneliness" (Omar Nydell, 2006).

❏ Arabs tend to have a relaxed attitude about time and are not expected to apologize when they arrive late for meetings or events.

❏ In some countries (e.g., Kuwait), birthdays have traditionally not been celebrated (Micek, 1992). Birthdays, however, are now celebrated in some families.

❏ Arab society is conservative and demands conformity from its members. Arabs have a high regard for tradition, and they are not as mobile as Westerners (Omar Nyell, 2006).

❏ It is acceptable in most places for friends of the same sex to show public affection (e.g., holding hands). Members of the opposite sex, however, generally do not show affection in public.

❏ In some areas, women are not to talk to strangers and may not leave the home without permission from the husband. In some parts of the Middle East, males are not supposed to approach women.

❏ There is a great emphasis on premarital chastity, especially for girls. Some immigrant Middle Eastern families may leave the United States because of a fear that their daughters will engage in premarital sexual activity (Sharifzadeh, 2004).

❏ Premarital sex for males, although not condoned, is secretly tolerated; however, it is considered "totally shameful for the female and it can carry grave consequences for the individual female and her extended family" (Ahmad, 2004, p. 8).

❏ In some areas, women cover themselves in clothing from head to toe before going out in public. Many women wear modest clothes and do not show their faces. Dress varies from country to country.

❑ Traditional Arabs view clothing restrictions for women as a means of providing protection from the competition, stress, temptations, and indignities found in outside society. Many Arab women themselves feel that the present social system gives them protection, security, and respect (Omar Nydell, 2006).

❑ Many Middle Easterners do not wear bright colors.

❑ In the Arabian Gulf states, Yemen, and Saudi Arabia, few women work outside the home. The few with employment outside the home work in all-female environments or in the medical professions.

❑ Some Middle Eastern women in the United States work outside the home. This has led to a reversal of roles for many women who did not work outside the home in their countries of origin. Some Middle Eastern men have difficulty accepting the greater freedom that women are afforded in the U.S. (Mohtasham-Nouri, 1994).

HEALTH CARE AND DISABLING CONDITIONS

❑ Health conditions and the availability of health care vary from country to country.

❑ In some war-torn countries (e.g., Iraq), thousands of children have died because of inadequate health care, embargoes on food, and other war-related problems.

❑ In many traditional Muslim families, it is considered unacceptable for women to be examined by male doctors. Experienced older women often provide health care to female patients. Most Middle Easterners, in fact, prefer to be treated by a professional of the same gender (Ahmad, 2004).

❑ Minor health problems experienced by children may be treated using nutritional remedies. For example, pediatricians in Iran may put children with chicken pox or small pox on a strict watermelon diet.

❑ Many Middle Eastern parents, especially those who come from cold climates, have their children cover themselves in warm attire to ward off illnesses.

❑ If a child is born with a disability, it is common for the mother to feel shame and guilt; the father may view the child's disability as a personal defeat and a blemish on the family's pride.

❑ Reactions to a child with disabilities may include denial, isolation, overprotection, or in some cases total abandonment.

❑ Many Middle Eastern families have strong beliefs about the causes of serious mental disabilities. Families with children who have these disabilities may become isolated from everyone except other family members (Sharifzadeh, 2004).

MIDDLE EASTERN COMMUNICATION STYLES

Middle Eastern communication styles have been described by a number of authors (Battle, 2002, Omar Nydell, 2006; Sharifzadeh, 2004; Wilson, 1998).

❏ It is generally acceptable to speak loudly in conversation. Loudness in the Arab culture connotes sincerity and strength; speaking softly implies that one is frail. Observers, however, may think that conversational partners are angry because of the loudness of the communication.

❏ Arabs tend to speak rapidly. Americans may view their speaking rate as "too fast."

❏ Gestures, intonation, and facial expressions are important factors in communication.

❏ In the Arab world, a good personal relationship is the most important factor in successfully conducting business. A few minutes at the beginning of a meeting may be devoted to developing such a relationship by discussing recent activities and matters relating to the well-being of others (Omar Nydell, 2006).

❏ Arabs look directly into the eyes of the person with whom they are communicating and may do so for an extended period of time. Eye contact is an indication that one is using words truthfully and also conveys an interest in what is being said. In many Arab cultures, however, it is taboo for a woman to look a man in the eye.

❏ Among Arabs, verbal eloquence is highly prized. Common rhetorical patterns include repetition, overassertion, and exaggeration. Emphatic assertions are common.

❏ In communication, Arabs highly value displays of emotion that Westerners may regard as immature. Westerners may label Arabs as too emotional while Arabs may find Westerners inscrutable and cold (Omar Nydell, 2006).

❏ Poets are held in very high esteem in Arabic societies; many educated Arabs, at some point in their careers, will attempt to write poetry.

❏ Arab writers look to the Koran as the ultimate book of grammar and style, in much the same way that writers in English once relied on the King James version of the Bible.

❏ It is often difficult to obtain a direct answer from an Arab; a common answer is *inshalla* (God willing).

❏ Usually it is considered discourteous to say "no." Words such as "perhaps" or "maybe" are often used in place of the word "no."

❏ An alveolar click (*"tsk, tsk"*) can mean "no" to an Arab.

❏ Communication is often indirect and, therefore, listeners must be sensitive to the underlying meaning of the speaker's message.

❏ It may be unacceptable, in some groups, to cross one's legs or stretch one's legs in a group setting.

❏ Among some groups, it is acceptable during conversations to retreat into silence and internal reflection. "Tuning out" is accepted and valued.

❏ During conversations, many Middle Easterners stand or sit close to other persons. Americans tend to maintain a distance of approximately five feet between themselves and their conversational partners, but for Middle Easterners a distance of two feet is typical. Touching during conversations is common.

❏ It is generally expected that people will show proper respect to others. Titles and last names are used in greetings.

❑ Lack of eye contact between men and women during conversation is common to maintain respect and proper distance between genders.

REFLECTION

Compare and contrast two communication style differences between Americans and Middle Easterners. Why is it important to be aware of these differences?

_____

_____

_____

_____

_____

MIDDLE EASTERN LANGUAGE CONSIDERATIONS

❑ Middle Eastern languages are divided into three different language families: Altic, Hamito-Semitic, and Indo-European.

❑ Arabic, the language spoken most widely in the Middle East, is the world's sixth most common language and is spoken by over 160 million people worldwide.

❑ Arabic falls under the Semitic subdivision of the Hamito-Semitic language family.

❑ Other common Middle Eastern languages are Kurdish, Farsi (Persian), and Turkish. Hebrew is the official language of Israel.

❑ Farsi is the official language of Iran. Farsi shares 28 of its 32 letters with Arabic and is written from right to left.

❑ Arabic, as it is used during conversation, differs in important ways from the written form of the language. Written, classic, formal Arabic is unchangeable and is used everywhere. Written Arabic is more grammatically complex and includes a richer vocabulary than spoken Arabic. There are many spoken dialects of Arabic, some of which are mutually unintelligible (Ahmad, 2004).

❑ Most educated Arabs are bilingual. They speak Modern Standard Arabic as well as their local Arabic dialect.

❑ There are 29 letters in the Arabic alphabet. All but one of the letters is a consonant. The Arabic language is written from right to left.

❑ The most common word order in Arabic is *verb + subject + object*.

❑ Some consonants in the Arabic language are not used in English. Among these consonants are glottal stops, voiceless and voiced uvular fricatives, and voiced and voiceless pharyngeal fricatives (Goldstein, 2000).

Characteristics of the Arabic speaker's articulation and language are presented in Table 9.1.

Table 9.1
Articulation and Language Differences Commonly Observed Among Arabic Speakers
(see Battle, 2002; Omar Nydell, 1996).

Articulation Characteristics	*Possible English Errors*
n/ng substitution	son/song, nothin'/nothing
sh/ch substitution	mush/much, shoe/chew
w/v substitution or f/v substitution	west/vest, Walerie/Valerie fife/five, abofe/above
t/voiceless "th" substitution or s/voiceless "th" substitution	bat/bath, noting/nothing sing/thing, somesing/something
z/voiced "th" substitution	brozer/brother, zese/these zhoke/joke, fuzh/fudge
retroflex /r/ doesn't exist;	speakers of Arabic will use a tap or trilled /r/
There are no triple consonant clusters in Arabic, so epenthesis may occur	kinduhly/kindly, harduhly/hardly
o/a substitutions	hole/hall, bowl/ball
o/oi substitutions	bowl/boil, foble/foible
uh/a substitutions	snuck/snack, ruck/rack
ee/i substitutions	cheep/chip, sheep/ship

Language Characteristics	*Possible English Errors*
Omission of possessives 's and "of"	That Kathy book. The title the story is...
Omission of plurals	She has 5 horse in her stable. He has 3 pen in his pocket.
Omission of prepositions	Put your shoes.
Omission of form "to be"	She ___ my friend.
Inversion of noun constructs	Let's go to the station gas.

IMPLICATIONS FOR PROFESSIONALS

❏ As stated in a previous chapter, it is ideal if professionals can cultivate relationships with Islamic clergy. These relationships can provide professionals with a deeper understanding of Arab values, cultural customs, and worldviews (Hall & Livingston, 2006). Many clergy are very happy to share their expertise with professionals, as they are usually strong pillars of support for immigrant families especially.

❏ Because of the many negative stereotypes that Americans hold of Arabs, professionals should make sure that families feel comfortable and understood (Barrow, 2004).

❏ Professionals should begin meetings with inquiries about the family and informal, light conversation. Most Arabs regard people who discuss business immediately as being brusque. Arabs mistrust people who do not appear to take an interest in them personally. If Arabs do not like or trust someone, they will often not listen to that person.

❏ Professionals may be more successful in communicating with families if they are informal and perceived as "family friends" rather than authority figures. It may be difficult for some families to trust those outside the extended family circle (Sharifzadeh, 2004). Many Arabs do not feel comfortable going to strangers for help with problems (Abu Baker, 2003).

❏ Some families may be offended if professionals offer their left hand in greeting, as the left hand is often considered unclean.

❏ It may not be considered appropriate for female professionals to shake hands with male family members.

❏ Most Arabs accept Western female professionals and especially admire those who are well educated. Thus, female professionals may want to find a comfortable, non-threatening way to reveal their professional education and credentials with families.

❏ Professionals should sit with good posture and dress formally to indicate respect for the family. It is considered disrespectful to talk when slouching, leaning against a wall, or holding one's hands in one's pockets.

❏ Families may be late for appointments or may not keep appointments at all. Professionals should emphasize the need for promptness so that families can receive the time and support that they need within the professional's schedule.

❏ Many professionals speak to the student's mother first. In some Middle Eastern families, the father is the official liaison between the family and any "strangers." Thus, professionals may need to consult with the father first.

❏ It is important to find out family members' titles and use them—omission of a title is an insult.

❏ Arab families may communicate emotionally during interactions with professionals, a pattern of behavior that is viewed as acceptable within their culture.

❏ Arabs are quite aware of social class, and upper-class Arabs may not socialize with those from lower socio-economic backgrounds. If an interpreter is from a social class different from that of the family, feelings of alienation may affect their interactions.

❏ Arabs are often uncomfortable during discussions that focus directly on death, illness, or disasters; they use euphemisms or avoid these topics altogether.

❏ Disabilities are often associated with feelings of denial, shame, and guilt that impede communication in a formal interview situation. Thus, professionals should approach discussions of disabilities with tact and diplomacy.

❏ Honor (*sharaf*) is highly valued in Arab families (Ahmad, 2004). Arabs may deny the existence of conditions that threaten their personal dignity (e.g., a child's disability) because honor is more important than facts.

❏ However, an aforementioned survey of ethnic Pashtuns from Pakistan and Afghanistan found that those surveyed believed in intervention for disabilities and supported the idea that intervention was appropriate for children and adults with communication disorders (Khan et al., 2005). Professionals should not automatically assume that Middle Easterners will reject recommendations for intervention.

❏ Professionals should not be shocked if Middle Easterners ask such personal questions as "What is your salary?" or "Why do you have no children?"

❏ Professionals who are used to keeping physical distance when interacting with others may feel uncomfortable when Arabs stand close to them or touch them during conversations. It is important not to move away or appear to be disturbed by these communication patterns.

❏ The limited knowledge that many Arabs have about speech, language, and hearing services can affect their willingness to accept and participate in service delivery. They may feel uncomfortable utilizing services provided by a non-Arab.

❏ Many Arab countries provide free universal health care; private care costs much less than it does in the U.S. Thus, new Arab immigrants may have difficulty understanding aspects of the complex U.S. health care system (e.g., third-party insurance), and professionals may need to help them negotiate the system (Ahmad, 2004).

❏ Many American professionals emphasize that both parents need to work together to help their children. Some Middle Eastern men may resist child-rearing activities because they do not see child-rearing as their responsibility. Child care is generally the province of women, especially in the early years (Hedayat & Pirzadeh, 2001).

❏ The mastery of self-help skills at an early age is often not considered critical in Middle Eastern families. Professionals should not label children as "delayed" based on developmental expectations for American-born, Anglo children.

❏ The emphasis on interdependence within the family may conflict with the professional's goal of independence for a student with a disability.

❏ Some families indicate agreement with the recommendations of professionals because the expression of disagreement is considered rude. A "yes" response may be an expression of good will rather than an indication that recommendations will be followed.

❏ Rather than saying "no" directly, most Arabs will give a noncommittal answer.

❑ Professionals need to have frequent contacts with families to make sure that appropriate action is being taken to meet the needs of children.

❑ Because families are expected to take care of the needs of family members, problems may be encountered when outside agencies intervene to provide assistance. Professionals need to help families understand how these agencies can help them.

❑ Because of the frequent use of exaggeration, assertion, and repetition among Arabs, professionals should use repetition and emphasis to convey to families that what is said is truly meant to be taken seriously. "If you speak softly and make your statements only once, Arabs may wonder if you really mean what you are saying" (Omar Nydell, 2006, p. 118).

❑ Some Middle Easterners view the term "Middle East" as ethnocentric. Thus, professionals may wish to avoid this term when communicating with families. It is best to base any statements on the family's actual country of origin. For example, in a report, a professional can refer to a student as a "Pakistani American" rather than a "Middle Easterner."

❑ Arabs who are Muslim often rely on religiously-based rather than medically-based explanations about the cause of a disability (Langdon & Cheng, 2002).

❑ Professionals should carefully review the content of materials used in assessment and intervention with children from Arab families. Because some books portray negative stereotypes and images of Arabs, it is important not to use these books (Al-Hazza & Lucking, 2005).

Profile ▬▬▬▬▬▬▬▬▬▬▬▬▬▬▬▬▬▬▬▬▬▬▬▬▬▬▬▬▬▬▬▬▬▬

Mahbohbah K., a 9-year-old girl, came to the U.S. from Kuwait with her parents. In Kuwait, Mahbohbah had been diagnosed with cerebral palsy. She had been kept at home and cared for by her mother. Mahbohbah had never attended school, and her family ensured that her needs were met.

In the Colorado city where the family settled, school personnel became aware of Mahbohbah and told her parents that school attendance was mandatory in the U.S. The parents objected strongly. The school met with the parents, discussed all the special education options that were available to Mahbohbah, and recommended placement in a special education program. The family refused to sign the program enrollment forms.

Finally the speech-language pathologist was able to obtain assistance from Abdullah S., a respected member of the local Muslim mosque. After much discussion in Arabic between the family and Abdullah, the family agreed to allow Mahbohbah to attend school and to receive special education services. Abdullah later told the speech-language pathologist privately that Mahbohbah's father felt that it was the duty of the family to care for this child's needs. The father didn't view education as being important for girls. Abdullah had worked hard to convince the family of the importance in America of educating both boys and girls. The family was informed that Mahbohbah would be at a severe disadvantage without the services offered by the school district.

STUDY QUESTIONS

1. Describe the traditional roles of men and women in the Middle East. How might these roles impact the relationship and communication between a female professional and a Middle Eastern man?

2. Discuss views of disabilities that are common in the Middle East.

3. List three practical suggestions that will help professionals communicate more effectively with Middle Eastern families.

TRUE-FALSE

Circle the number beside all statements that are true.

4. There are few differences between spoken Arabic and written Arabic.

5. Most Middle Eastern women work in jobs outside the home.

6. Muslim Arabs, especially in the big cities, prefer to marry first and second cousins.

7. Many Arabs communicate in an emotional manner, and professionals should be prepared for this style.

8. Families may experience feelings of guilt, shame, and denial if a family member has a disability.

9. Among Middle Eastern countries, Yemen has one of the highest literacy rates.

10. Arab society tends to be conservative and emphasizes conformity among its members.

MULTIPLE CHOICE

Circle the letter beside all choices that are correct.

11. Which country is not referred to as either a Middle Eastern or Arab country?

   A. Jordan
   B. Iran
   C. Bahrain
   D. Kuwait
   E. China

12. A five-year-old Middle Eastern child, Farrah, has been referred to you. Her teacher suspects a developmental delay. You realize that you will need to meet with the special education team and the child's family to discuss the need for a full psychoeducational assessment. What are some important things you will keep in mind before and during this meeting?
    A. Most Middle Eastern parents strongly encourage early independence in their children.
    B. It will be best to direct the questions to Farrah's father during the meeting.
    C. To help family members relax so that they will not feel intimidated, you should dress informally and slouch slightly during the meeting.
    D. The family may deny the existence of any disability because it is a discredit to their honor.
    E. You need to repeat yourself and emphasize important points several times.

13. Which of the following is/are true about Farsi?
    A. Farsi is the official language of Iraq.
    B. Farsi shares 28 of its 32 letters with Arabic.
    C. Farsi is written from right to left.
    D. Farsi is the smallest country in the Middle East.
    E. Farsi is a city that separates two very different cultures.

14. Consonants that occur in Arabic but not in English include
    A. Voiceless and voiced uvular fricatives
    B. Glottal stops
    C. Alveolar laterals
    D. Voiced and voiceless pharyngeal fricatives
    E. Voiced bilabial fricatives

15. Which of the following are TRUE statements about education in the Middle East?
    A. Schools are often co-educational.
    B. Formal Arabic is taught in many schools.
    C. Traditionally, most females were not encouraged to attend college.
    D. The education of boys is a high priority in many families.
    E. Compulsory education usually begins at around 5 years of age.

ANSWERS TO STUDY QUESTIONS

    4. False
    5. False
    6. False
    7. True
    8. True
    9. False
    10. True
    11. E
    12. B, D, and E
    13. B and C
    14. A, B, and D
    15. B, C, and D

Chapter 10

FAMILIES FROM RUSSIAN BACKGROUNDS

Outline

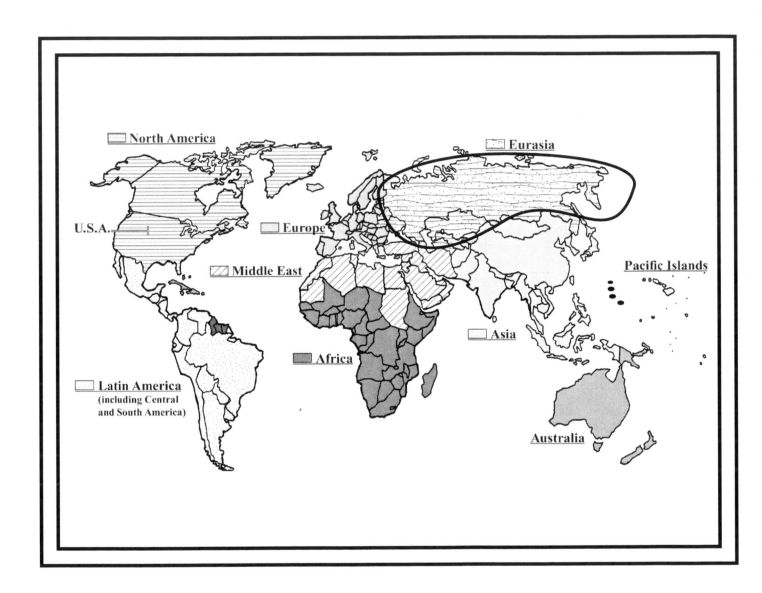

The increasing number of immigrants from the former Union of Soviet Socialist Republics (USSR) has resulted in a need for many professionals in special education to learn about the language and cultural background of this population. In 1989, the U.S. Lautenberg Amendment broadened the definition of refugees to include "a presumption of persecution." Thus Soviet citizens could obtain refugee status by stating that they feared religious persecution in the Soviet Union. Since that time, 350,000 religious refugees from the former USSR (80% Jews, 20% Christians) have settled in the United States.

The information in this chapter refers primarily to immigrants and refugees from Russia itself. The former USSR consisted of 15 different republics (Russia was one), so it is important to remember that much diversity continues to exist within the individual republics that were once part of the Soviet Union (see Figure 10.1). Thus, to increase the accuracy of the information presented in this chapter, the vast majority of the research cited is based on studies of Russians.[1]

Figure 10.1

[1] I wish to thank several of my university students from the former USSR for their helpful comments and editorial suggestions for this chapter. Lisa Domyancic helped immensely with the version of this chapter that appeared in the previous edition of this book. Irina Krivoruchko from Uzbekistan, Elizabeth Panansenko from Ukraine, and Tatyana Oselskaya from Siberia generously gave of their time and expertise to help me update the information in the current version.

GENERAL BACKGROUND INFORMATION

❏ According to the U.S. Immigration and Naturalization Service, approximately 62,800 immigrants from the former USSR entered the U.S. in 1996. Of these immigrants, 4,300 were from Belarus; 1,800 were from Moldova; 19,700 were from Russia; and 21,100 were from Ukraine (U.S. Bureau of the Census, 1999).

❏ According to the U.S. Census Bureau (2000), there are currently 2.9 million Russians living in the U.S. The 10 states with the largest population of Russian speakers are (in order) New York, California, New Jersey, Illinois, Massachusetts, Pennsylvania, Washington, Florida, Maryland, and Oregon.

❏ Of the 20 non-English languages spoken most frequently in U.S. homes, the largest proportional increase was for Russian speakers. The Russian-speaking population nearly tripled from 242,000 in 1990 to 706,000 in 2000 (Kent & Lalasz, 2006).

❏ Most Russians have come to the U.S. because of religious persecution, economic hardship, and limited educational and vocational opportunities for themselves and their children (Katz-Stone, 2000; Leipzig, 2006).

❏ Church congregations of Adventist, Pentecostal, and Baptist Christians often sponsor entire congregations of refugees from the Russian Federation. This large-scale migration to parts of the U.S. encourages the maintenance of language, values, and beliefs brought from home (Hume & Hardwick, 2005).

❏ The general area of the Russian Federation is 17,075,000 square kilometers, extending across 11 time zones between the Pacific and the Baltic. The capital of the Russian Federation is Moscow.

❏ Russia, the largest of the former Soviet republics, is nearly twice the size of the U.S. and is the largest country in the world.

❏ The Russian Federation has 89 administrative units, of which 31 are autonomous entities where most of the non-Russians live (Richmond, 2003). In 1990, the former USSR had a population of 290 million people. Population shifts, however, have occurred in recent years.

❏ During World War I, Czar Nicholas II abdicated due to popular unrest among the people. The 1917 revolt was led by Vladimir Lenin, head of the Bolshevik party, and the Communists came to power in 1922. At that time, they formed the USSR and forcibly incorporated Belarus, Azerbaijan, Georgia, Ukraine, and Armenia. Many Russians died when Lenin reorganized Russian geographical and political boundaries.

❏ Trotsky became the ruler after Lenin's death in 1924. However, in 1925, Joseph Stalin assumed power as a dictator and forced the people into a lifestyle of industrialization and collective agriculture.

❏ In the mid-1930's, Stalin initiated the Great Purge, a program of terror designed to crush opposition by Soviet citizens who disagreed with his policies. It is estimated that 20 million Russians *were* killed during the Great Purge.

❏ Russians lived in great fear of the KGB (secret police) under Stalin and his successors, especially under Kruschev and Brezhnev.

❏ Mikhail Gorbachev, who became president of the USSR in 1985, was generally viewed as the first of a new generation of leaders. He instituted the policy of *perestroika* (restructuring) to improve economic conditions and performance. Unfortunately, this policy failed; inflation grew worse and shortages increased.

❏ *Glasnost*, a policy of openness that resulted in increased, widespread freedom to express opinions and critically discuss issues of concern (even if these issues differed from those of the Communist leaders) was introduced by Gorbachev.

❏ The USSR was formally dissolved on December 25, 1991 when Gorbachev resigned as Soviet president. In September 1991, the three Baltic republics were recognized as independent by Moscow.

❏ Powerful leaders announced the formation of a new, loose confederation, headed by Boris Yeltsin, that was called the Commonwealth of Independent States (CIS).

❏ The CIS consisted of independent republics: Armenia, Azerbaijan, Belarus, Kazakhstan, Kyrgyzstan, Moldova, Russia, Tajikistan, Turkmenistan, Ukraine, and Uzbekistan. President Vladimir Putin was elected on March 27, 2000.

❏ Approximately 70% of Russians belong to Slavic ethnic groups. The second and third largest Slavic ethnic groups are the Ukrainians and the Belarussians respectively.

❏ Turkic peoples comprise a large ethnic group in the Russian Federation. The largest Turkic groups include the Uzbeks, the Kazakhs, the Kyrgyz, and the Turkmens. In Russia today, people are very proud of their distinct ethnic heritages.

❏ Russians have a history of invasion, persecution, and suffering. During the past thousand years, Russia has been repeatedly invaded and occupied by different ethnic groups such as the Mongols, Germans, Turks, and others. Entire Russian villages have been slaughtered or, at least, brutally occupied and ruled.

❏ From 1917-1991, under Soviet Communism, as many as 61 million people were purged as "enemies of the state." This included Christians, Jews, Muslims, and followers of other faiths.

❏ Communist control resulted in restrictions in every aspect of life until 1991. Before 1991, it was considered a great honor to be accepted into the Communist party.

❏ Career advancement was most likely to occur among individuals who were members of the Communist party; in fact, people in high positions were expected to be members of this party. Conversely, people who refused to belong to the Communist party often remained low on the career ladder, with little or no opportunity for advancement.

❏ To survive within a country that had a long history of totalitarianism, many Russians developed a fatalistic attitude toward life. Prior to 1991, Russians were under such oppressive rule that they had few opportunities to make their own decisions.

❏ For Russians raised in previous eras, the state suppressed personal initiative, personal responsibility, and the desire to work independently. Citizens had to conform to the government's opinions and dictates.

❏ Although Russia has great potential wealth, the long-term effects of a Marxist centralized command economy have been devastating. The collectivization and industrialization of farms were achieved with great cruelty and oppression.

❏ In the last few decades, the Russian government's efforts to reduce state ownership and liberalize the economy have had variable success because of the resistance of the vast bureaucracy and entrenched leadership structures that are threatened by change. Economic decline and hyper-inflation have resulted. There has also been a rise in crime (Romanovich, 2005).

❏ Poverty is rampant in Russia. The annual per capita annual income was reported to be $2,320.00 (U.S. Department of State, 2004). Approximately 25% of the Russian population were reported to live below the poverty line, and 8.4% of the population was unemployed (U.S. Central Intelligence Agency, 2004).

❏ In 1991, the USSR was among the most developed nations in the world. On the Human Development Index (an objective measure of quality of life) at that time, the USSR was ranked 31st among the countries of the world.

❏ By the year 2003, however, Russia's ranking had fallen to 63rd, with Ukraine falling to 75th. Both nations were placed in the "medium-developed nations" category (World Bank, 2003).

❏ Abbott and Sapsford (2006) conducted a large survey of citizens of Russia and Ukraine to ascertain their feelings of general satisfaction and happiness with life, especially after the fall of Communism. The sample consisted of 4,000 residents of Russia and 2,500 residents of Ukraine. The survey was carried out using face to face interviews by organizations with experience in survey research. The primary findings were the following:

1. Overall, survey respondents stated that post-1991 changes had a negative impact on their society overall and on their individual lives. For example, 78% of Russians and 83% of Ukrainians said that the disintegration of the USSR had a negative impact on the country's economy.

2. Over 75% of respondents thought the post-1991 changes had negative effects on the health of citizens; only slightly over one third of respondents from both countries were definitely opposed to a return to communism.

3. Less than one third of all survey respondents said they could afford major items such as cars; 67% of Ukrainians and 47.5% of Russians said they had to do without basic food sometimes, and many respondents could not afford medical treatment. The results were summarized by Abbot and Sapsford (2006, p. 261) as follows:

> We can conclude that Ukraine and Russia are societies that have undergone significant change that has had a negative impact on the welfare of the population. A majority of citizens in both countries view the social, political, and economic situation as having deteriorated, a majority experience material hardship, there is a lack of social cohesion and integration into wider society....there are low levels of perceived control over life, and the physical and psychosocial health status of the populations are poor.

❏ On a less formal note, Martz (2005), an American professor who specializes in Russian culture and has traveled to Russia, said that "I talked with people who described the current situation in Russia as much worse than during the communist times, due to the rising prices and economic pressures" (p. 119).

❏ However, some research shows that young people, in contrast to their middle-aged and older counterparts, have a higher degree of satisfaction with their lives. They are more confident in their ability and power to change their lives for the better (Zorkaia & Diuk, 2005).

❏ Russian Orthodoxy has been the state religion in Russia for almost 1,000 years. Before 1990, however, the Communists had greatly restricted religious practices in the former USSR.

❏ Officially, the Communists were atheists and viewed religion as an anti-Communist force, in fact, as a form of mental enslavement from which people must be liberated. For over 75 years, Russians were told that religion was the "opiate of the people" by Marxist-Leninist leaders.

❏ After the revolution in 1917, the Communists instituted separation of church and state; later, during the Lenin and Stalin eras, many churches were forced to close. Gorbachev was the first Soviet leader to change official policy and tolerate religion.

❏ In the 1990s, the Russian Orthodox Church began to attain increased visibility and freedom. Today, the Russian Orthodox church is viewed by most Russians as the state religion.

❏ Many Russians are Orthodox. Other religions in Russia include Islam, Buddhism, Judaism, and various sects/cults.

❏ With the demise of the Soviet Union in 1991 and the discrediting of the Communist philosophy, there emerged a moral and spiritual vacuum in the former USSR. Many religions attempted to fill this vacuum and began proselytizing in Russia (Kornblatt, 1999).

❏ As stated, a number of Russians have come to the U.S. because of religious persecution in their country. Jews experienced persecution in Russia before 1991 as a result of the Soviet Union's policy of state-sponsored anti-Semitism (Minochin, 1999).

❏ Evangelical Christians in the former USSR have historically been killed, put into prison, tortured, harassed, exiled, and denied an education for themselves and their children because of their faith in God (Johnstone, 1993; A. Soldatenkov, personal communication, May 3, 2000; E. Panansenko, personal communication, October 8, 2007). Pentecostal Christians have especially been persecuted and many have attempted to emigrate to the U.S. This situation has improved since the USSR formally dissolved.

✐REFLECTION✐

What impact does the history of the former USSR have on the life of people living there today?

_____

_____

_____

_____

_____

RUSSIAN FAMILY LIFE

❑ Russian culture is based on collectivism (Lebedko, 2003). Russians value their families greatly (Lapin, 2004).

❑ Historically, Russians have married at an early age. This was especially prevalent among peasants in earlier centuries, when extended families were common and much intergenerational help was given.

❑ Early marriage is still prevalent today. For young Russian women, marriage at 17 or 18 years of age is common. If a Russian woman is not married by age 22 or so, she may be considered an "old maid."

❑ Marriage is a primary concern for young women (E. Panansenko, personal communication, October 8, 2007). By the time they turn 40, only 4% of Russian women have never been married, compared with 15% for all women in that age group elsewhere (Bellafante, 2004). Society dictates that they marry and raise children to help increase the population.

❑ Russian women tend to start families at younger ages than American women. Most urban couples have only one or two children whereas rural families are larger.

❑ Pentecostal Christians often have very large families, consisting of 10 or more children (I. Krivoruchko, personal communication, 4/26/07).

❑ Extended families are quite common in Russia even today, with several generations living under one roof. Most families are strongly united and mutually interdependent; they tend to rely on each other a great deal.

❑ Most Russians in cities and towns live in tall apartment buildings. Some families live in their own apartments. Others live in communal housing, with as many as 18 families sharing a building. In communal housing, everyone shares one or two bathrooms, and food is prepared in one big kitchen.

❑ Historically in Russia, the people found it difficult to trust anyone outside their families (especially during the Stalin years), and so to this day, many people only feel safe with and close to their families, distrusting outsiders.

❑ Although Russians value their families greatly, the divorce rate in Russia is unfortunately high (over 30 percent) and is rising. Reasons associated with the high divorce rate include alcoholism, adultery, personality and cultural differences, and lack of privacy due to the housing shortage.

❑ Because it is hard to obtain housing, young couples often live with their parents for some time, even up to several years (Leipzig, 2006). Urban apartments are small by American standards, and a family of three people or more may live in one room.

❑ In many Russian families, both parents work outside the home. Nearly 40% of parents work nine or more hours a day and face lengthy commutes on crowded public transportation. Few families can afford to own cars.

❏ A great hardship for many Russian families is that one or both parents may work several jobs, yet still be unable to adequately provide for their children. Children naturally feel disconnected from their parents, who have no time for them, so these children may end up on the streets.

❏ By the year 2015, in fact, there could be up to 2 million homeless or neglected children in Russian cities. In addition, at present, approximately one million children exhibit antisocial behavior, including narcotics abuse, crime, and alcoholism (Rimashevskaia, 2007). There are higher levels of conduct problems among Russian adolescents than there are among American adolescents. In one study, parents were found to relate with detachment and low communication to their preadolescents with conduct problems.(Drabick, Beauchaine, Gadow, Carolson, & Bromet, 2006).

❏ As a result of multiple sources of stress in daily life, domestic violence is on the rise in Russia. Men in particular are susceptible to problems such as poverty, unemployment, alcoholism, and constant tension. Domestic violence is frequently the result (Rimashevskaia, 2007).

❏ For decades there has been economic discrimination against Russian women (Kolchevska, 2005). Many studies of the Russian labor market since the early 1990's document significant gender differences in wages and employment. Women are generally paid less; they are also more vulnerable to layoffs than men (Linz, 2003).

❏ The roles of men and women in Russia tend to be more distinct and specifically defined than the roles of men and women in the U.S. For example, Sperling (1999) cited the Russian Orthodox Church as stating that "A man is more aggressive, more active, more curious, more risk-taking... Women create continuity, peace, reliability. Man creates, woman reproduces" (p. 77).

❏ However, attitudes toward women vary from region to region. For example, in Russia, authority in the home is shared by husband and wife. In Ukraine, the husband may wield more authority. The wife may be expected to stay home, bear children, and perform traditional household duties (E. Panansenko, personal communication, October 8, 2007).

❏ During the Soviet period, most women worked outside the home, and many continue to work outside the home today. As in the past, many women in Russia take on the "double burden" of working full time outside the home for a salary and also taking the primary responsibility for maintaining the household and raising the children (Goehner, 2005; Kolchevska, 2005; Leipzig, 2006; Richmond, 2003).

❏ Fathers may spend much less time with children than mothers, and many Russian men are minimally involved in household maintenance activities. Changes in the roles of men within the family unit, however, are beginning to occur.

❏ Some Russian men prefer that their wives work inside the home managing the household and caring for children (Panansenko, personal communication, April, 2001). Generally, women in Russia carry much responsibility and wield little authority.

❏ At 18 years of age, Russians obtain full citizenship rights, including the rights to vote, marry, and obtain a driver's license. Although Russians must be 18 to marry, girls may marry younger if special permission is granted.

❏ One issue affecting many Russians is birth control. Abortion is free in Russia while birth control is expensive and often ineffective. It is estimated that the average Russian woman has between three and eight abortions in her lifetime due to these circumstances. Abortions among girls during the teen-age years are increasing in Russia, a country in which permission from parents is not required.

❑ Sometimes families that do not have the financial resources to support their children place them in orphanages. In the year 2002, it was estimated that 700,851 Russian children lived in institutions (Rimashevskaia, 2007).

❑ Child care in Russian orphanages ranges in quality. In some orphanages, children are fed primarily oatmeal. They may spend 3 hours in the morning and 3 hours in the afternoon in a crib. Sometimes abuse occurs.

❑ In Russia today, there has been a steep decline in the number of births. Between 1991 and 2003, the number of children from birth to age 18 fell by 9 million—from 39.5 million in 1991 to 30.5 million in 2003.

❑ According to some forecasts, in the year 2015, the number of children may fall to as low as 22.5 million (Rimashevskaia, 2007). Causes of this decline include high rates of infant and child mortality and an increasing desire to keep families small.

❑ In some areas of the former USSR, families are offered great benefits if they have more children. For example, in Belarus, families who have between 5-10 children may receive free housing, discounts on food and other necessary items, medals, and early retirement benefits for parents (A. Kerez, personal communication, 6/3/06).

❑ Russian parents do not encourage independence at an early age as strongly as do parents in the U.S. What mainstream Americans might consider as "babying" a child might be viewed as a demonstration of love by many Russian parents, especially mothers (Leipzig, 2006).

Profile

Alexi D., an Uzbeki 6-year-old male, was being evaluated by both a speech-language pathologist and a psychologist. The teacher had referred Alexi for attention and behavior problems, saying that "he is immature and he can't sit still." Attention Deficit Hyperactivity Disorder (ADHD) was suspected. The speech-language pathologist was supervising a student intern from Uzbekistan, who observed Alexi during the evaluation. She also spoke with Alexi in Uzbeki, taking and later analyzing a language sample. The speech-language pathologist and psychologist felt that Alexi had symptoms of ADHD, although no language problems in Uzbeki were noted.

The team discussed referring Alexi to a physician for a medical evaluation. The intern shared with the team that in Uzbekistan Alexi's behavior would be viewed as quite normal and that for his cultural background she did not think he had a clinically significant attention problem. It was recommended that the classroom teacher pair Alexi with a peer tutor and increase the level of structure in his program. Under the supervision of the speech-language pathologist, the intern made suggestions to the parents designed to help Alexi improve his attention skills.

❏ Discipline may be quite lax by American standards (Barker, 1999). Boys are permitted a considerable amount of behavioral freedom, although the level of permissiveness varies from republic to republic (A. Borodovsky, personal communication, May, 2001).

❏ In Russia, many children—some as young as 6 years of age—have a key to let themselves into the house until an adult comes home from work. No one views this practice as neglectful or improper (Leipzig, 2006).

EDUCATION AND LITERACY

❏ Russia has a very high literacy rate. In fact, 99.6% of individuals over the age of 15 are able to read and write (U.S. Central Intelligence Agency, 2004). Many Russians read frequently.

❏ During the Stalin era, the importance of education was stressed, and even today many Russian men and women hold college degrees.

❏ According to a survey conducted in Russia in 2000, 45% of the people considered the spread of literacy and of secondary and higher education to be the greatest accomplishments of the Soviet Union. Almost two thirds of Russians said a good education was the most important factor in the upbringing of their children (Andreev, 2003).

❏ Most Russians believe that a good education is essential for children, although some parents who experience poverty tend to be in "survival mode" and do not encourage their children to go on for a higher education (Kliucharev & Kofanova, 2005).

❏ As previously stated, traditionally, Christians in Russia were denied access to higher institutions of learning because of their faith.

❏ School generally starts on September 1 and lasts until mid-June. Children begin first grade at 6 years of age and most attend school until they have completed the 11th grade. Only nine grades are compulsory. Elementary, junior high, and senior high students usually study together in one building with multiple stories.

❏ Educational reform in Russia is progressing slowly. There are still many obstacles to this reform such as low salaries for teachers and lack of basic necessities (in some schools), such as heat, indoor plumbing, sewer systems, and textbooks (Richmond, 2003). Despite this, many students continue on to universities.

❏ When students are admitted to universities, they have already chosen their specialties. Most of the courses taken are required; few elective courses are available. Students study between four and six years, and must write and defend a thesis in the final year.

❏ The final degree earned is somewhat higher than a Bachelor's degree in the U.S. After students graduate, they are expected to work in a government-assigned position for two or three years. Tuition in universities is free, and most students receive stipends.

❏ Russia's top universities have very competitive entry requirements; special entry examinations are held annually. Many Russian universities are beginning to offer distance education.

❏ Russian schools have traditionally been responsible for moral education or *vospitaniye* (upbringing) (Richmond, 2003). Values that are considered important in the school setting include discipline, the needs of the collective (as opposed to the individual), and the need to show great respect for teachers and elders in general.

❏ Discipline is strict, and there may be little discussion allowed (Richmond, 2003). Even in universities, students are often taught to accept only one answer as correct and not to express their individual viewpoints (Richmond, 1995). Instruction in universities is theoretical; students rarely challenge their professors (Richmond, 2003).

❏ Statistics indicate that Russian children are often between two and three years ahead of American children in math and science; they are also more advanced than American children in literature and history (Richmond, 2003). Russian students attending school in California have told me how "easy" American schools are in comparison to those they attended in Russia.

❏ A problem in Russia today is that thousands of children are unable to obtain a standard education because of poor health; it is estimated that 10% of children enrolled in school are unable to master the curriculum (Rimashevskaia, 2007).

❏ Education of Russian children may be adversely affected by lack of access to and knowledge of technology. This is improving slowly, however. In 1994, 68.1% of the Russian population had not mastered computer skills. In 2003, that figure was down to 62.9% (Kliucharev & Kofanova, 2005).

CULTURAL CUSTOMS, COURTESIES, AND BELIEFS

❏ Russians try to avoid *nyekulturno* (bad manners). Bad manners can include behaviors such as standing with one's hands in one's pocket, displaying affection in public, crossing one's arms behind one's head, and others (Goehner, 2005).

❏ When people enter Russian homes, they immediately remove their shoes and put on special slippers to wear inside.

❏ If a guest eats dinner in a Russian home, it is customary for the guest to bring a gift such as alcohol, candy, or flowers. There should never be an even number of flowers in a bouquet; even numbers are reserved for funeral arrangements.

❏ Russians eat breakfast in the morning and a "dinner" around one o'clock that is the main meal of the day. This main meal includes appetizers, a main course, potatoes/noodles/rice, vegetables, and dessert.

❏ A popular feature of many Russian meals is the many appetizers (*zakuski*) that are served. Many Russians eat an afternoon snack at around four o'clock. A light meal is consumed in the evening.

❏ Russians are famous for their *gostepriimstvo* (hospitality). Because they often expect that guests will eat several helpings of everything put in front of them, they may be offended if guests turn down offers of food.

❏ Russian cuisine is internationally considered to be varied and of high quality. Regular mainstays in the Russian diet include bread, meat, potatoes, soups, and pickled fish. Due to food shortages in Russia, it is almost impossible to obtain vegetables and fruits in winter. Russians on limited incomes (such as the elderly) eat mainly potatoes.

❑ Scientists consider approximately one-fourth of Russia's water to be unsafe, and ice is not served in cold drinks. Tea, the most popular nonalcoholic drink in Russia, is consumed after meals and during mid-afternoon breaks. In some families, it is considered inappropriate to drink tea with a meal.

❑ When Russians arrive for a meeting or appointment, they may engage in a number of rituals before getting down to business. Discussions relating to family and personal issues, small talk, and refreshments (e.g., something to drink) may precede a business meeting.

❑ For many Russian parents, when dealing with professionals, the professional comes first; the parents' ideas are secondary to those of the professional.

❑ Relationships are all-important to Russians, and good personal relationships take priority over business concerns. Thus, Russians may be late for appointments because they place a higher premium on conversation than punctuality (Lebedko, 2003).

❑ Many Russians welcome inquiries about their families and are genuinely interested in hearing about the families of others.

❑ In Russia, important holidays include:

January 7 　*Russian Orthodox Christmas*

February 23 　*Soviet Army Day (All young men are still required to give some military service; on the 23rd of February, it is customary for women to give men small gifts.)*

March 8 　*International Women's Day (Men phone female friends to wish them well and give flowers to their special friends.)*

April/May 　*Russian Orthodox Easter* (Orthodox Russians are not supposed to do any menial labor on Easter Sunday nor on the two days that follow.)

May 1 　*International Workers' Solidarity Day*

May 9 　*Victory Day*

May 27 　*St. Petersburg's Birthday*

June 12 　*Independence Day*

September 1 　*Day of Knowledge (This is the first day of school, so children bring gifts to teachers.)*

December 12 　*Russian Federation Constitution Day*

December 31 　*January 1- New Year*

Note: If a person is having a birthday, she will stay at home in the evening while friends and relatives drop by with congratulations. The person having the birthday provides the food for the guests.

◈REFLECTION◈

Describe three communication practices commonly observed among Russians that are important for professionals in the U.S. to understand. Why should professionals be especially aware of these practices?

_____

_____

_____

_____

HEALTH CARE AND DISABLING CONDITIONS

❑ At present, the Russian health-care system is in a fluctuating and uncertain state. The state medical system predominated until 1987, and all medical care (except for prescription drugs purchased at pharmacies) was free.

❑ Unfortunately, the scarcity of prescription drugs and the inadequacy *of* medical equipment have made providing medical care difficult.

❑ There continues to be a shortage of necessary medicine and equipment. Also, unfortunately, maternal mortality rates are rising in Russia, and increasing numbers of children are born with medical problems.

❑ The 1986 explosion in Ukraine's Chernobyl nuclear power plant caused three immediate fatalities. However, in 2000, there were three million children who continued to require medical treatment for radiation exposure as a result of the Chernobyl explosion.

❑ Smoking in Russia is widespread. It is estimated that 70% of Russian adults smoke. One Russian cartoon portrays a restaurant with two sections: Smoking and Chain Smoking.

❑ Alcoholism, which is rampant in Russia, is often associated with social and health problems. Many Russians, especially males, start drinking as early as 12 years of age. The average life expectancy for Russian men has fallen to 58.5 years—the lowest in the developed world (World Health Organization, 2004).

❑ The short life expectancy of Russian men may be a result, in part, of their copious vodka consumption. Vodka is the most common alcoholic beverage consumed in Russia. Vodka, which is distilled by using water, is typically, 40% grain alcohol with 80 proof strength.

❑ What might be considered alcoholism in the U.S. is often tolerated in Russia. Leipzig (2006) stated that it is acceptable to drink to excess as long as one is relaxing with friends. People may stop at a kiosk during the day and have a drink or two; having a shot of vodka on the way to work would not provoke disapproval among many Russians. However, in general, Russian Christians do not drink alcohol (I. Krivoruchko, personal communication, 4/26/07).

❏ Children may experience Fetal Alcohol Syndrome or Fetal Alcohol Effects. There are no public health programs that educate women about the deleterious effects of drinking alcohol during pregnancy. In extreme cases of alcoholism in the home, children may be placed in orphanages because parental rights have been terminated (Aronson, 2007; Landry, 2007).

❏ Due to economic circumstances and other variables, poor health among Russian citizens has increased. The most common illnesses among Russians are the flu and the common cold. Other prevalent diseases in Russia include cholera, typhoid fever, tuberculosis, measles, and whooping cough.

❏ Though Russians believe that colds are spread by viruses, both patients and doctors think that cold drinks, drafts, or sitting on cold surfaces are also significant causes of colds (Dabars, 1995). Thus if a Russian with a cold is offered a cold drink, he or she will probably decline it.

❏ The incidence of venereal disease has increased since the end of the Soviet era. Incidences of HIV and AIDS are also on the rise. Growth rates of new HIV infections in the Russian Federation are among the world's highest, and currently an estimated one million Russians are HIV-positive (World Health Organization, 2004).

❏ Russia has no nationwide sex education program; the Russian Orthodox Church has vocally opposed such programs. The Orthodox Church encourages abstinence, but young people are often sexually active.

❏ The Center for International Rehabilitation's report on Russia (2004) stated that there are approximately 11 million people in Russia who have disabilities.

❏ It is currently estimated that in Russia today, 4.8 million children suffer from chronic diseases. In the past ten years, the rate of childhood disability rose by 4.5 times. Some of these children with disabilities are placed into boarding schools (Rimashevskaia, 2007).

❏ Unless children's health improves, it is estimated that by the year 2015, 3.6 million Russian children will suffer from chronic diseases and one million will have disabilities (Rimashevskaia, 2007).

❏ Among some communities, there may be negative attitudes toward children with disabilities. Korkunov, Nigayev, Reynolds, and Lerner (1998) indicated that in the former Soviet Union, the administration developed a policy of "defectology." Under this policy, any child with anomalies was labeled "defective"; the discipline of special education was called "defectology" (Martz, 2005). It was not until recently that one university in Urals changed its program name from the Department of Defectology to the Department of Special Education (Korkunov et al., 1998).

❏ Historically, children in Russia with "defects" were isolated and often sent to boarding schools. During summer vacations, "defective" children were not allowed to play with typically-developing children. Even today, many exceptional children in Russia continue to be placed in boarding institutions at an early age.

❏ The Russian educational system segregates individuals with disabilities; others may pity them, and believe that they should be passive recipients of charity (Martz, 2005; E. Panansenko, personal communication, October 8, 2007).

❑ Fortunately, however, students with mild disabilities are now being educated in regular schools and being given opportunities to interact with typically-developing peers (Martz, 2005). These schools are the exception rather than the rule, however, and many agencies see their primary job as placing children in existing special education facilities (Korkunov et al., 1998).

❑ In the late 1990s, children with disabilities in Russia were categorized under one of the following labels: speech defects, delay in psychological development, mental defects, hearing defects, sight defects, defects of movement, and other anomalies. There were no categories involving learning disabilities or behavior disorders (Korkunov et al., 1998).

❑ Moskovina, Pakhomova, and Abramova (2001) studied teachers' and parents' attitudes towards children with mental retardation. These researchers found that both teachers and parents had negative stereotypes of children with mental retardation. Moskovina et al. stated that this could be indicative of a reluctance to interact with these children.

❑ Today in Russia, disability is defined primarily from a medical perspective. An individual with a disability must be assigned to a category by the Bureau of Medical and Social Experts before government assistance or services can be provided (Center for International Rehabilitation, 2004).

COMMUNICATION STYLES

❑ People in Russia usually shake hands when being introduced. However, if a new person joins a group, introductions are not considered necessary. The person who just joined the group usually takes the initiative and introduces himself.

❑ Age is respected in Russia, and some older Russians might not want to take advice or directions from younger people.

❑ Russians generally stand quite close to others during conversations. A distance of 12 inches from the other person is common.

❑ Russians have more physical contact with one another in their daily lives than do Americans. Females may walk arm-in-arm on the street and may stand physically close during conversations.

❑ Some older Russian men will embrace and kiss (on the cheek) an acquaintance they have not seen for a while. Russians frequently touch others when speaking to them; some Americans would consider this intrusive (Dabars, 1995).

❑ The Russian language does not have a word for "privacy." In contrast to individualistic Americans, Russians live by the philosophy of "sobornost" (togetherness, communal spirit) and believe that the needs of the group or collective are paramount (Richmond, 2003).

❑ Touching others and sharing space are considered positive values.

❑ Russians often enjoy group activities. The individual's business is everyone's business, and some Russians are blunt in giving their personal opinions about other lifestyles and activities.

❏ Russians are often straightforward. They are not prone to mince words when they speak their minds. Also, some Russians may inform others of wrongdoing in an openly emotional manner; maintaining a harmonious atmosphere is not as high a priority in Russia as it is in the United States (Richmond, 2003).

LANGUAGE CONSIDERATIONS

❏ The official language in Russia is Russian, which was also the official language of the former USSR. Russian is the first language of approximately 170 million people. It is used as a second language by at least an additional 10 million people in the Commonwealth of Independent States and Eastern Europe.

❏ Russian, Ukrainian, and Belarusian are Slavic languages. Russian uses the Cyrillic alphabet, which consists of 33 letters. Many of these letters are unlike any in the Roman (Latin) alphabet.

❏ Russian is one of the chief languages of the world because of its wide use and its prestige in the former USSR. It is used officially by the United Nations.

❏ There are many languages indigenous to specific geographic locations. For example, the residents of Ukraine speak Ukrainian, Tartars speak Tartar, and Chuvashes speak Chuvash.

❏ Speakers of these languages are often bilingual, speaking Russian as well as their native language. Individual languages such as Ukrainian are taught at schools in each individual republic in which the majority of people use the language.

❏ It takes about 10% longer to say something in Russian than in English. Experienced interpreters often say they need two or three Russian words to interpret a single English word.

❏ Words are inflected for number, gender, case, tense, mood, and person. Many negatives are used; for example, a small object will be described as "not big"; something that is good will be described as "not bad."

❏ A double negative does not create a positive, as in English, but rather increases the overall negativity of the utterance (Richmond, 2003).

❏ It can be difficult to master Russian because there are no set rules for stress in words; any syllable can be accented. Syllable stress needs to be learned separately for each word.

❏ Some words that are spelled alike are only distinguished by different spoken syllable stress. There is no significant differentiation between long and short vowels.

IMPLICATIONS FOR PROFESSIONALS

❏ Professionals should be cautious when referring to families as "Russian." It is important to ask the families for information about their country of origin. Families from Ukraine, for example, may be offended if referred to as "Russians." As one Ukrainian said to me, "We have fought wars and died in order to be called according to our individual nationalities" (Dubya, personal communication, March 2001).

❏ Even among Russian young people, national and ethnic identity remain very important (Zorkaia & Diuk , 2005).

❑ Because Russians in previous decades have been accustomed to obeying the government without question or argument, it is a great change for them to learn to discuss issues, compromise, be creative, and take risks. Thus, if professionals are working with older Russian parents, these parents might appear to have a "fatalistic" attitude and tend not to question the professional's recommendations.

❑ The parents might accept everything the professional says without question, relying almost completely on the professional for their child's special needs. These parents should be encouraged to be contributing partners in the clinical relationship.

❑ Zorkaia and Diuk (2005) emphasized that younger Russians may be more proactive and individualistic than their middle-aged and older counterparts. Thus, professionals need to take parents' ages into account when working with them.

❑ Many Russians, even today, have a great distrust of the police, government, and military. Professionals should remember that some Russians may not feel comfortable responding to personal questions; under Communist rule, providing answers to these questions could lead to imprisonment or even death. It is ideal to work with a Russian interpreter or cultural mediator in these situations. English-speaking family members can also be helpful.

❑ Female professionals who work with traditional Russian fathers may need to expend extra effort to be taken seriously. Helpful strategies include informing the father and family that the professional possesses an advanced degree; an expensive-looking business card also increases credibility (Richmond, 2003).

❑ Although many Russian immigrants are grateful to be in the U.S., they encounter challenges that may leave them discouraged (Hume & Hardwick, 2005). Professionals need to be sensitive to these challenges.

❑ Limited proficiency in English is an obvious barrier for many Russian immigrants (Domyancic, 2000). A related problem for many Russian immigrants is that their skills and educational background are not acknowledged in the U.S. (Hubenthal, 2004; Leipzig, 2006). For example, Russian doctors and architects may work as custodians in the U.S. because of differing laws for licensing and professional practice. It is critical for professionals to be sensitive to such reversals of fortune; the mother who is washing dishes at a restaurant in the U.S. might have been a heart surgeon in Russia. Professionals may find it helpful to ask parents what jobs they held in Russia.

❑ Some researchers have found that although older Russian immigrants are often well educated and intelligent, they are quite self conscious about their limited English skills and may even be ashamed to communicate with Americans (Hubenthal, 2004; Leipzig, 2006). Professionals, then, may need to have interpreters readily available to help these immigrants feel more comfortable during interactions.

❑ Domyancic (2000) found that approximately half of families that she studied from the former USSR did not have health insurance. Thus some Russian students may not be receiving adequate health care. Professionals can help Russian families by having on hand a list of affordable or free local resources.

❑ A major challenge for some families is accepting the egalitarian views of the roles of men and women that exist in the U.S. The balance of power in the marriage is shifting as women become more actively involved in the work force (Leipzig, 2006).

❑ Because Russians care so much about personal relationships, professionals should spend the first few minutes of any meeting in "small talk" to avoid appearing rude or uncaring.

❑ By sharing a limited amount of personal information about their own families, professionals can create an environment in which families feel at ease when talking about their child. In the U.S., this small talk is considered inappropriate and unprofessional; however, families from other cultures often relate better to the professional when a small, appropriate amount of personal information is shared (Shipley & Roseberry-McKibbin, 2006). When interacting with family members, I usually mention briefly that I have a son in elementary school and share some of my own experiences. Families seem to become more open to sharing information when they realize that the "professional" understands what parenting is like and empathizes with their concerns.

❑ Gift-giving is important to Russians, and they may bring a small gift to break the ice with the professional at the beginning of a relationship. It is important to be culturally sensitive when gifts are offered, and to accept the gift if ethically possible.

❑ Professionals who work with older Russian parents and grandparents may be expected to dress conservatively.

❑ As mentioned, Russian immigrant families who are evangelical Christians may have been denied a formal education in Russia because of their faith. Thus, the language skills and conceptual knowledge of these students may be below that of their Russian peers.

❑ Russian Christians who refused to join the Communist party because of religious beliefs were generally denied opportunities for career advancement and remained at a low socio-economic level. Professionals need to be sensitive to situations in which immigrants have experienced job discrimination and financial hardship because of their refusal to give up their religious beliefs.

❑ Because individuals from Russian backgrounds often stand close to and touch one another during interactions, professionals should be careful not to shy away from them or judge them to be rude or intrusive when they display such behaviors.

❑ As previously mentioned, over half the population of Russia had not mastered basic computer skills (Kliucharev & Kofanova, 2005). Russian families from more provincial areas may have limited experience with modes of communication commonly used in the U.S. (e.g., fax machines, e-mail). Thus, it is often best to meet with family members in person when information needs to be exchanged.

❑ Russians may promise more than they can deliver because they want to please the professional. "Da" or "yes" might mean "maybe" or even "no." It is critical for professionals to follow through with families and clients to be sure that they are doing what they said they would do.

❑ When working with interpreters, professionals need to understand that more words are generally required to communicate an idea in Russian than in English.

❑ Russian mothers read to their children more often than do fathers. Professionals should encourage both parents to read to their children (Domyancic, 2000).

❏ Due to the stresses they frequently encounter in the U.S., Russians often benefit greatly from support groups (Susan & Susan, 2005). Participation in these groups may decrease the sense of isolation often felt by parents.

❏ As mentioned earlier, some church congregations in the U.S. sponsor Russian Christians when they move to this country. These churches are often excellent sources of support for immigrants who are struggling to adjust to life in the U.S. (Hume & Hardwick, 2005).

❏ Professionals should provide information to help parents overcome negative stereotypes about children with mental retardation and other disabilities (Korkunov et al., 1998; Moskovkina et al., 2001).

❏ Professionals should draw attention to the positive qualities of the child who has special needs.

❏ The field of speech-language pathology is "new" to many Russians. For this reason, it is often necessary to provide information about the role of the speech-language pathologist in supporting children who have communication disorders.

Profile

Janey and Mike T., an American couple, adopted Viktor from a Russian orphanage when he was 8 years old. Viktor spoke little English and was extremely shy with his adoptive parents. A doctor diagnosed him as having problems related to his mother's alcohol consumption during pregnancy. He was put into a third-grade classroom in the U.S. but showed little progress during the course of the year. Viktor also had frequent nightmares and showed signs of angry, aggressive behavior. Mike and Janey, being quite concerned, sought an evaluation of Viktor's emotional as well as cognitive and linguistic skills.

The speech-language pathologist found a Russian interpreter, who spoke extensively with Viktor about his past life in Russia. Viktor related that he spent much of his time alone in the orphanage and that, in that setting, he was hit quite hard in the face by the orphanage caretakers for even a slight infraction. Viktor told the interpreter that once he was hit so hard on the side of the head that he could not hear anything for a while (subsequent audiological testing revealed a 30 db sensorineural hearing loss in the left ear). There was little to eat at the orphanage, and Viktor was afraid to ask for more food. There were no toys or books for the children, so they spent much of the day watching television. Viktor indicated that he was happy in the U.S., although he did not understand much of what went on in the classroom. He also talked about having nightmares about his experience in the orphanage.

After the interpreter shared this conversation with the school team, counseling services were set up for Viktor with the help of the Russian interpreter. In addition, Viktor was enrolled in the after-school Homework Club and was placed in the school's daily Reading Clinic to help him develop English literacy skills. A Russian-speaking family from the local Russian church agreed to spend time with Viktor each week, taking him on outings and talking with him about his previous experiences in the homeland.

STUDY QUESTIONS

1. Discuss ways in which the former Soviet Union's history of Communist rule continues to influence the lives of Russians today.

2. Summarize health matters that are of concern to Russians today. Describe one health problem that might have a major impact on the communication skills of children.

3. Although many Russians are highly educated, several educational practices can make it difficult for Russian immigrant students to adjust to American educational expectations. What are these practices?

TRUE-FALSE

Circle the number beside each statement that is true.

4. The vast majority of Russians are opposed to Communism because of the instability that resulted from Communist rule.

5. Alcohol consumption, a problem that begins at around age 12 for many males, is a major health concern in Russia.

6. The literacy rate in Russia is above 99%; Russians read quite a bit.

7. Because of the deplorable condition of Russian schools, most students do not go on to attend universities.

8. When interacting with family members, professionals may refer to the household as a Russian family but should not refer to it as a Soviet family.

9. Historically in Russia, discrimination has been shown towards persons with disabilities (for example, children with disabilities might not be allowed to play with typically-developing children).

10. Most Russians strongly encourage early independence so that children will be able to cope with the problems of daily life at an early age.

MULTIPLE CHOICE

Unless otherwise specified, circle the number beside each choice that is correct.

11. Features of the Russian language include the following:
    A. A double negative is used to produce an affirmative statement.
    B. Russian is a tonal language.
    C. Russian uses the Cyrillic alphabet, a symbol system that consists of 33 letters.
    D. It can be difficult to master Russian because there are no set rules for stress in words; any syllable can be accented. Syllable stress needs to be learned separately for each word.
    E. There is a significant differentiation between long and short vowels.

12. Which statements below are correct representations of how Russian students with disabilities are viewed and treated in their homeland?
    A. Independence for those with disabilities is highly emphasized.
    B. A term like "defect" would never be used because it is so perjorative.
    C. In many communities, those with disabilities are viewed positively because they are believed to still be able to contribute to society.
    D. Individuals with disabilities may be pitied.
    E. There are currently no categories for children with learning disabilities and behavior problems.

13. Which one of the following is NOT a true statement about Russian communication styles?
    A. Many Russians stand quite close and often make physical contact when conversing.
    B. Privacy is critical, and people like to do things individually rather than in groups.
    C. Russians tend to be blunt in giving their personal opinions about other people's lifestyles and activities.
    D. Russians often become quite emotional when informing others that they are "wrong" about something.
    E. During conversation it is considered discourteous for one to fold arms across the chest or to keep hands in pockets, especially when speaking to an older person.

14. Health issues for many Russians include the following:
    A. Cholera, typhoid fever, tuberculosis, measles, and whooping cough are prevalent among Russians.
    B. Increasing numbers of children are being born with medical problems.
    C. There are very high numbers of new HIV cases in Russia.
    D. Walking pneumonia is the leading cause of death among adolescents and has become a major epidemic in recent years.
    E. Women are educated about the consequences of drinking during pregnancy, but they drink anyway.

15. Professionals who work with Russian students and their families should remember the following:
    A. Evangelical Christian families have had especially good opportunities to receive an education, and their children's linguistic and cognitive skills tend to be highly developed.
    B. Parents, especially older ones, will often question the professional's decisions.
    C. Many Russians will promise more than they intend to deliver because of their desire to please the professional.
    D. Most Russians prefer face-to-face conversations rather than communication through the use of e-mail.
    E. An effort should be made to encourage fathers to spend time reading with their children.

ANSWERS TO STUDY QUESTIONS

4. False	12. D and E
5. True	13. B
6. True	14. A, B, and C
7. False	15. C, D, and E
8. False	
9. True	
10. False	
11. C and D	

Part 2

Assessment of Linguistically and Culturally Diverse Students

Chapter 11

BILINGUALISM AND SECOND LANGUAGE LEARNING

Outline

When a child is assessed because of a possible language-learning disability, it is necessary to determine how the behavior observed differs from that of children who acquire communication skills without difficulties (Roseberry-McKibbin, 2003, 2008). A major challenge confronting professionals is that "typical behavior" varies widely even among monolingual children. When working with culturally and linguistically diverse (CLD) student populations, the picture becomes far more complex.

In spite of the complexity of the situation confronting professionals who work with CLD students, there are certain general facts about second language acquisition and bilingualism that can be outlined and then used as a foundation for distinguishing language differences from language-learning disabilities. In this chapter, these facts will be discussed.

TYPICAL PROCESSES OF SECOND LANGUAGE ACQUISITION

The processes of second language acquisition must be understood if one is to differentiate between a language difference and a language-learning disability (Goldstein, 2004; González, 2007; Restrepo & Kruth, 2000). Typical second language acquisition processes often result in differences that can impact communication. These differences need to be recognized as normal, typical behaviors for students who are not yet proficient in English. Some of the most commonly observed processes are described in this section.

1. Interference (Transfer)

Interference or **transfer** refers to a process in which a communicative behavior from the first language is carried over into the second language. Transfer can occur in all areas: syntax, morphology, phonology, pragmatics, and semantics. Although there is disagreement among researchers about the extent to which transfer occurs in second language acquisition, educators need to be aware that some speech and language characteristics from the first language may be carried over into the second language (Brice, 2002). Of particular note is that grammatical morphemes in the second language (L2) may be particularly challenging for children to acquire, resulting in omission of these morphemes (Jacobson & Schwartz, 2005; Paradis, 2005, 2007; Rowe & Levine, 2006). For example, a child might say, "We had three ball[s], but one lost behind the swing[s]." Jia (2003) studied the English development of nine Mandarin-speaking children, noting that it took an average of 20 months of exposure to English for these children to master the plural –s in English (their L2).

Language patterns from the first language may influence how one phrases a particular message in the second language. In German, for example, "Ich habe Hunger" means "I'm hungry." A literal translation of the German, however, would be "I have hunger." Thus, a German-speaking student who says "I have hunger" would be manifesting interference from German. In Visayan (a dialect spoken in the Philippines), "Ambot sa iya" translates to "I don't know to you." But a Filipino would use this expression to mean "I don't know—it's completely up to you." A Filipino student who says, "I don't know to you" could easily be diagnosed as having a language impairment if assessment personnel do not consider the influences of the first language on the learning of a new language.

When the second language is not the language of the student's social milieu, transfer is greater. Thus, when second language learners produce errors in English, it is important to consider the possibility that these errors result from language transfer or from the student's limited experience in using English.

Information about the student's first language can sometimes be obtained from a local library or possibly from a local university with a foreign language program. In addition, there are now many Internet web sites that provide specific information about various languages. Bilingual paraprofessionals can be of great assistance in helping the professional determine the presence of first language interference. One must be certain, however, that the paraprofessional is familiar with the dialect spoken by the student.

2. Fossilization

Fossilization occurs when specific second language "errors" remain firmly entrenched despite good proficiency in the second language (Pica, 1994; Rowe & Levine, 2006). For example, an individual from Cuba was heard to say, "the news are that...." This same individual, however, had flawless grammar most of the time. Fossilized items can be idiosyncratic to a child, or can be common within a linguistic community. Fossilized items may occur because of the inconsistencies of the English language (Hedge & Maul, 2006). For example, irregular past tense and plural forms may be fossilized (e.g., "My foots are sore") because they are inconsistent. It is important to conduct a comprehensive evaluation of the student's communicative capabilities rather than focusing on isolated aspects of language that have little effect on the communication of meaning.

3. Silent Period

Some students, when learning a second language, go through a **silent period** in which there is much listening/comprehension and little output (Brice, 2002). It is believed that students are learning the rules of the language during this silent period; they may be covertly rehearsing what they are hearing (Hegde & Maul, 2006). The silent period can last anywhere from three to six months, although estimates vary (Paradis, 2007). Practitioners might be led to believe that a student has an expressive language delay, when in reality the student's attention is focused on learning the language. Tabors (1997) stated that generally, the younger the child is when exposure to the second language occurs, the longer the silent period lasts. Tabors gave the example of a child who came to the U.S. from Greece when he was 2 years old. His silent period lasted almost 1.6 years. The silent period for elementary school children who began learning a second language at 5 or 6 years old, however, lasted between six and eight weeks.

Profile

Arisbel R., a 3-year-old Spanish-speaking girl, was brought to a local preschool where only English was spoken. According to Arisbel's mother, Arisbel had no problems acquiring Spanish, and her Spanish acquisition skills were commensurate with those of her siblings. However, the preschool teachers contacted the local speech-language pathologist after two months because Arisbel "isn't talking and we think she might have a language delay."

After assessing Arisbel in Spanish in both the home and preschool settings, and gathering an extensive case history from Arisbel's parents, the speech-language pathologist concluded that Arisbel was a typically-developing language learner who needed more exposure to English before she began speaking it. The speech-language pathologist explained to the preschool teachers that because Arisbel was so young when she was exposed to a second language, an extended silent period was normal and could be expected. Ten months later, Arisbel was making functional use of the second language and interacting effectively with the other children in the preschool setting.

4. Interlanguage

Genesee et al. (2004), defined **interlanguage** as the period in second language development when the learner starts to use language productively until he attains competence that is similar to that of a native speaker. Paradis (2007, p. 2) described interlanguage as "...a dynamic system balancing L1 transfer processes with target language developmental processes that gradually moves closer to the target language system." When learning a second language, the learner tests hypotheses about how language works and forms a personal set of rules for using language. The individual's production changes over time as language is experienced in different contexts. Inconsistent errors reflect the progress that the student is making in learning a new language and should not be viewed as evidence of an abnormality.

5. Language Loss

If use of the first language decreases, it is common for the learner to lose skills in that language as proficiency is acquired in the second language (Brice, 2002; Coltrane, 2003; Guiberson et al., 2006; Mattes & García-Easterly, 2007). This process is referred to as **language loss**. Many CLD children hear and speak only English in the school environment; bilingual education is often nonexistent, especially for students who speak languages that are not spoken by any of the teachers. Since English is the dominant language of society in the United States, children often experience language loss in the first language and a gradual replacement of that language by English (González, 2007; Paradis, 2007). As discussed later in the chapter, this is particularly true for children whose languages have minority status (e.g., those of working class immigrants) or are spoken by people who have limited access to the political and economic institutions of the dominant group (Anderson, 1999).

If a student has experienced language loss and is still acquiring English, the student may appear to be low-functioning in both languages (see Figure 11.1). Based on language test scores, one might be led to conclude that the student has a language-learning disability. Differentiating between language differences and language-learning disabilities in a situation where language loss has occurred is challenging.

Figure 11.1
English-Language Learners at Risk

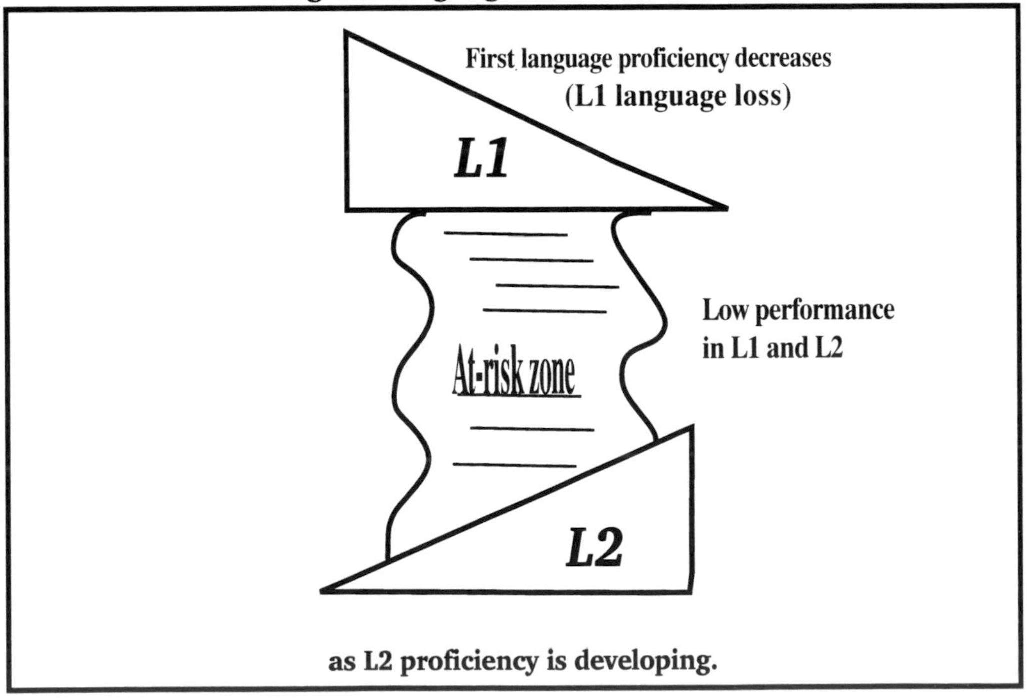

First language proficiency decreases
(L1 language loss)

L1

At-risk zone

Low performance
in L1 and L2

L2

as L2 proficiency is developing.

6. Code-switching

Alternating between two languages in discourse is commonly observed among bilingual speakers and is not necessarily an indicator of a problem (Anderson, 2004). **Code-switching** is the alternation between two languages within a single constituent, sentence, or discourse. Language alternation within a sentence is also called **code-mixing**. Code-switching/mixing behavior is used by typical, proficient bilingual speakers throughout the world (Centeno, 2007; Genesee et al., 2004; Langdon, 2008; Mattes & García-Easterly, 2007). During the early stages of second language learning, the learner may substitute structures, forms, or lexical items from the first language for forms in the second language that have not yet been learned. Bilingual children commonly use code-switching as a strategy, and the use of code-mixing seems to help bridge the two languages that a child is learning (Brice & Anderson, 1999). Children may code-switch in some situations more than others; the context of the interaction is a variable (Oller et al., 2006). Although code-switching is a normal communicative behavior, it may occur excessively in situations in which an individual lacks competence in one language.

AFFECTIVE VARIABLES IN SECOND LANGUAGE ACQUISITION

The influence of affective variables in second language acquisition has been documented by many researchers (Centeno, 2007; Cummins, 2000; Dickinson & Tabors, 2001; González, 2007). In this section, these variables are described in terms of their effect on the academic and linguistic performance of culturally diverse students.

1. Motivation

Motivation impacts a student's success in acquiring L2 (Klingner, Artiles, & Barletta, 2006; Paradis, 2007). When attempting to determine a student's level of motivation, the following questions can be asked:

A. *Is the student becoming acculturated into the English language environment?*
   Acculturation refers to psychological integration with speakers of the second language. Often second language learners acquire the second language to the degree that they acculturate. Thus, if a student is not integrated into situations with English-speaking peers, he or she may not be highly motivated to learn English. Some parents of CLD students discourage them from playing and interacting with American English-speaking students. In these cases, motivation to learn English may be quite low. In other situations, peers may discourage a student from learning English.

B. *How much enclosure exists between the student's culture and the American culture?*
   Enclosure refers to the degree to which ethnic groups share the same things in life: schools, churches, recreational facilities, professions, leisure activities, etc. If a student comes from an ethnic-linguistic community that has little enclosure, or little in common with the dominant English-speaking community, the acquisition of English will usually not take place as rapidly.

C. *Is there congruence between the student's cultural group and the dominant group?*
   The more congruent, or similar two cultures are, the greater the likelihood that one will experience the social contact necessary for success in learning the second language.

D. *What are the attitudes of the CLD student group and the dominant group toward one another?* If the feelings toward one another are positive, second language learning is usually facilitated.

E. *How long does the CLD student's family intend to stay in the United States?* Will the family be going back to the home country? In families that plan to remain in the United States, motivation to learn English is often higher than in families that plan to return to their homeland.

F. *Does the student feel that learning a second language will threaten his or her identity?* If a student is rejected by family and/or peers for speaking English, motivation will be affected.

G. *Have the student and her family experienced trauma in the home country?* Genesee et al. (2004), pointed out that immigrant and refugee students who have experienced trauma in their home countries may have challenges that affect their willingness to adapt to a new culture and learn a second language.

2. Personality

Personality characteristics may also affect second language acquisition (Paradis, 2007). It is important for professionals to keep these in mind, as they can impact a student's developing English skills.

A. **Self-esteem**. The student's feelings and judgments relating to his/her own abilities and worthiness have an effect on second language acquisition. To maximize learning, students need to have a positive self-concept and a positive attitude. The more positive that students feel about themselves, the more rapidly and completely second language acquisition is likely to take place. Students whose first language and culture are rejected may have low self-esteem and consequently learn English more slowly than children whose backgrounds are accepted (Cummins, 2000).

B. **Extroversion**. There is some evidence that extroverted students learn English conversational skills faster than introverted students (Wong Fillmore, 1976; Ventriglia, 1982). Shy students may take longer to develop conversational competence than outgoing students.

C. **Assertiveness**. Being assertive can be helpful in facilitating second language learning, as assertive learners avail themselves of increased opportunities for second language practice. If a student is non-assertive, there may be fewer opportunities to practice English skills with native speakers.

3. Anxiety Level

Motivated individuals with a low anxiety level are more readily able to benefit from language input in the second language. Krashen (1992) described such students as having a low affective filter. These students learn better because they are in an environment that is relatively stress-free and accepting. If students have a high level of anxiety, there can be a resulting "mental block" that prevents optimal learning.

4. Socioeconomic Status

CLD students who come from a socioeconomic background different from that of most other students in their school may experience difficulty developing friendships with native English speakers and may not interact with them frequently enough to learn a second language.

SECOND LANGUAGE LEARNING STYLES AND STRATEGIES

Students bring a variety of language learning styles and strategies to the second language learning situation. This section delineates learning styles and strategies that might influence students' oral communication.

1. Modeling

A student may exhibit language patterns similar to those used by parents and other family members. When conducting assessments, it is important for professionals to familiarize themselves with the student's daily speech and language models. Many professionals have had the experience of assessing a student and subsequently talking with a parent about the child's performance. It is often discovered that the parents' speech and language patterns sound very similar to those of the child! In addition to considering the impact of parents as language models, it is important to consider the influence of siblings, peers, grandparents, baby-sitters, and others in the student's environment. Some students come from extended families in which they spend much time with grandparents or baby-sitters who are not native speakers of English.

Profile

L. M. was referred for speech-language screening by his first-grade teacher. The speech-language pathologist assessed L. M. informally in the classroom setting. The student conversed readily and confided that he wanted to be a pediatrician in the future. Language comprehension appeared to be good. Some morphosyntactic errors were noted during conversation. In addition, L. M. was slightly difficult to understand due to misarticulated speech sounds. The speech-language pathologist reviewed the Home Language Survey in the student's school file. The survey, filled out by his mother, indicated that English was the language used most often by the student and other family members. Because this was the case, the speech-language pathologist felt that L. M. should be formally tested to determine if he was eligible for speech and language intervention.

After receiving information about the proposed assessment, the student's father came to the school and informed the speech-language pathologist that the child's mother spoke several Filipino dialects in the home, although use of these languages was not indicated on the Home Language Survey. The mother was not a proficient English speaker, but she tutored her child in English on a daily basis. The father was from Cuba, spoke rapidly, was difficult to understand, and made frequent grammatical errors in English.

It appeared that L. M.'s speech and language patterns were influenced by the language models available to him in the home. L. M.'s parents did not feel that the child was having difficulty learning language. The student did not appear to be self-conscious about his speech, and his classmates did not make fun of him. Although the student made some expressive errors in English, it was felt that his needs could be met within the classroom language curriculum. The problems did not appear to stem from a disorder and, therefore, placement in special education would not be appropriate.

2. Avoidance

A student may avoid communicating in the second language to avoid ridicule from others. This strategy could result in the student's language performance appearing to be inadequate even though he is learning the language appropriately. Students don't want to be laughed at when they speak. This may be particularly true of older students who speak English with a pronounced accent.

3. Practice Opportunities

Much of a student's progress in second language acquisition depends on the availability of functional opportunities for second language practice (Centeno, 2007; Gibbons, 2002; Jia & Aronson, 2003). Some students speak English in the classroom but not in any other contexts. The learning of a second language is likely to be slow if the student makes little use of that language with family and friends outside of the classroom.

Profile

P. B. is a Laotian kindergarten student who came to school speaking only Laotian. The Home Language Survey in her school file indicated that only Laotian was spoken in the home. P. B.'s refugee family came to the United States when P. B. was one year old. When P. B. came to school, she was evaluated with an oral language proficiency test and classified as "non-English speaking." A language dominance test, administered one month later, showed the student to be a "Limited Bilingual," with limited skills in English and Laotian. Laotian was found to be the dominant language.

P. B. was retained in kindergarten. At the end of her second year in kindergarten, she showed little progress in acquiring English skills although she apparently got along quite well in class. Her teachers were not concerned at this point because P. B. was a cooperative child who followed the daily curriculum and was good at art. The teachers did not feel that P. B. was a child with special education needs. Nevertheless, the speech-language pathologist was concerned because P. B.'s basic English conversational skills continued to be quite limited. Pre- and post-testing during the second year of kindergarten revealed little progress in learning English.

P. B. interacted almost exclusively with Laotian-speaking students at school and in her neighborhood. She received no instruction in English. Her parents, monolingual speakers of Laotian, were illiterate and gave her no help with homework.

Is P. B. a potential special education child? Should she undergo special education testing because of her limited progress in acquiring English? This would be an easy conclusion to reach; however, P. B.'s limited opportunities for practice in English must be considered. Since she rarely spoke English inside or outside of the classroom, her opportunities for acquiring English were limited indeed. Should special education testing occur anyway?

The speech-language pathologist felt that P. B.'s limited progress in acquiring English may have resulted from limited experiences in using the English language. The clinician recommended tutoring to develop Laotian language skills and skills in using English. It was also recommended that her oral language proficiency be tested again, following a period of instruction, to assess progress in learning English. Finally, the speech-language pathologist spoke with the site ESL specialist and asked him to monitor P. B. for problems that might be indicative of a disability. Although the possibility of a language-learning disability was not ruled out, it was felt that classroom language instruction should be attempted before implementing any type of special education assessment.

4. Use of Routines

Routines are phrases such as "Have a good day" that are learned as a whole. These can be described as telegraphic or formulaic. They are memorized phrases that children rely on heavily when they are in the early stages of learning English (Paradis, 2007). Second language learners may use these phrases appropriately, although they may not know the meaning or grammatical function of individual words within the phrases. Students who use these memorized phrases are often able to initiate and sustain simple conversation and, therefore, give the false impression that they are fluent speakers of the language.

5. High- vs. Low-Input Generators

Students who are **high-input generators** avail themselves of many opportunities for language practice. These students are often extroverted and initiate conversations with speakers of the second language. This initiation, in turn, generates an interchange that gives the students increased opportunities to practice communication. **Low-input generators**, on the other hand, are usually not assertive, generate few opportunities for language practice, and acquire language skills more slowly than high-input generators.

TYPES OF LANGUAGE PROFICIENCY

Language proficiency is a complex phenomenon that has been defined in a variety of ways. In this section, several models of language proficiency are described. When differentiating between a language difference and a language-learning disability, knowledge of what constitutes language proficiency in the two languages is critical.

Separate Underlying Proficiency versus Common Underlying Proficiency

Cummins (1992c, 2000) described two models of language proficiency. In the **Separate Underlying Proficiency** (SUP) model, language proficiency in the first language is viewed as entirely separate from proficiency in the second language and, therefore, skills learned in the first language will not transfer to the second language. One implication of this model is that people believe that language development activities in the first language will not enhance learning of a second language.

Supporters of this viewpoint have often tried to eradicate languages other than English by encouraging students and their families to speak English only. Children who learn English from models who lack proficiency in the language will speak the language as they hear it used in their environment. Supporters of the SUP model believe that exposure to poor language models in English will be more beneficial to the child in developing English language skills than exposure to fluent, rich L1 models.

Unfortunately, many professionals tell parents of CLD children to discontinue use of the primary language at home and "just speak English." This practice has been reported in the United States and other parts of the world. For example, in Flanders, speech-language pathologists have told parents to stop speaking their first language (English) in the home and to speak only Dutch (Houwer, 1999). In a workshop described by Cummins (2000), several participants who worked in the Los Angeles area shared that in their schools, teachers were being told to discourage parents from speaking to their children in Spanish. Teachers were also being instructed that they should NOT send Spanish books home for parents and children to read together. Again, this deleterious advice is given by professionals who believe that the SUP model is accurate.

There is no evidence to support the SUP model (Cummins, 1992b, 2000). As children learn their first language, they acquire concepts and strategies that will facilitate the learning of a second language. Concepts are acquired through interaction with the environment. High quality exposure enhances the learning of concepts that are important for cognitive and linguistic development. As children hear and use their native language in a variety of contexts, they develop the conceptual knowledge and cognitive strategies necessary for success in acquiring new information and linguistic skills.

Cummins (1992c, 2000) described the **Common Underlying Proficiency** (CUP) model as an alternative to the SUP model (see Figure 11.2). In describing the CUP model, Cummins stated that "...the literacy-related aspects of a bilingual's proficiency in L1 and L2 are seen as common or interdependent across languages...experience with either language can promote development of the proficiency underlying both languages, given adequate motivation and exposure to both either in school or in the wider environment" (Cummins, 1992c, pp. 23-25). This underlying proficiency is that which is involved in cognitively demanding communicative tasks, and it is interdependent across languages (Cummins, Chow, & Schecter, 2006).

As children hear and use their first languages in a variety of contexts, they develop the cognitive strategies and conceptual knowledge necessary to acquire new skills in L2. This is true for both oral and literate language (Chamberlain, 2005; Kayser, 2004; Lipka, Siegel, & Vukovic, 2005; Miller, Heilmann, Nockerts, Iglesias, Fabiano, & Francis, 2006). Cummins (2000) and Zecker (2004) reported that there is a strong correlation between reading skills in the first and second language; the better the reading skills in the first language, the better will be the reading skills in the second language. Also, the student who does not read in the first language at all is likely to have a more difficult time reading in English than the student who reads fluently in the first language (Ramírez, Yuen, & Ramey, 1991).

The CUP model has major implications for professionals working with CLD children. If a student has had limited exposure and experience in the first language, the conceptual foundation necessary for success in the classroom will be underdeveloped. Researchers recommend strengthening the foundation in the first language before instruction is attempted in the second language (Baker, 2000; Cummins, 2000; Coltrane, 2003; Gibbons, 2002). Negative cognitive consequences may result if efforts are made to switch the child to English before the first language is fully developed.

Using the second language for instruction when the first language has not yet been fully developed is like building a house on an unstable foundation (see Figure 11.3). By building a solid foundation in the first language, the child acquires concepts and strategies that will facilitate learning another language. By suddenly switching the child to a new language, school professionals deprive students of opportunities to make use of their previously acquired knowledge when confronted with learning situations in the classroom. When children have difficulty relating new experiences to what they already know, learning is a slow process.

Rather than eradicating the first language, efforts should be made to help students become fluent bilingual speakers. By helping students to develop high levels of proficiency in the first and second languages, students may experience growth in various cognitive skills that have been associated with success in school. Children who speak two or more languages fluently have been found to outperform monolingual children in various cognitive and linguistic tasks (Cummins et al., 2006; Thomas & Collier, 1998; Tannenbaum, 2005). Individuals who are bilingual can also make greater contributions to society. Being a fluent bilingual individual has many advantages (Brice, 2000; Paradis, 2007).

The ramifications for CLD students are clear. If a student is struggling academically or not learning English as rapidly as would be expected, one is likely to suspect that the student needs special education services. However, it can be seen from the above discussion that limited progress in school is often due, at least in part, to limited skills in the first language and lack of opportunities for continued development of skills in that language.

Thomas and Collier (1998) stated that the average English speaker generally gains 10 months of academic growth in a 10-month school year. Second language learners must show more growth than native speakers by making one and one-half years' progress on academic tests in English for

Figure 11.2

Two Models of Language Proficiency

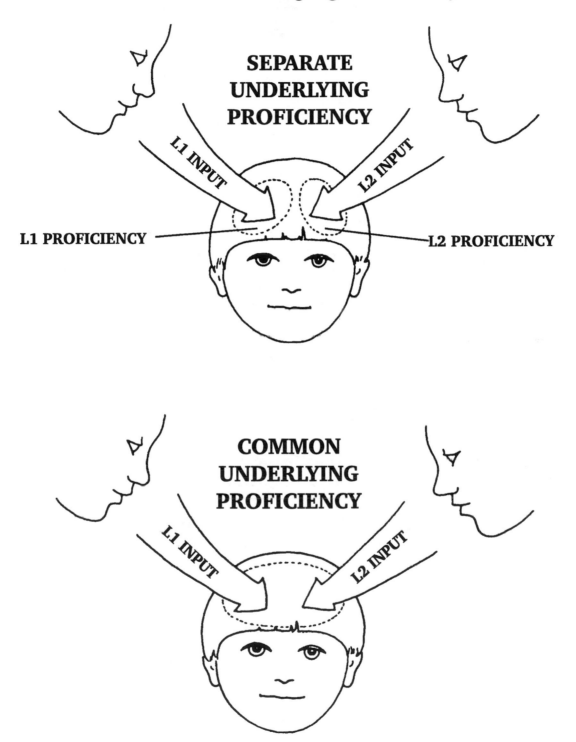

Source: Adapted from Cummins, J. (1992). The role of primary language development in promoting educational success of language minority students. In California State Department of Education, *Schooling and language minority students: A theoretical framework.*

Figure 11.3
Thresholds of Bilingual Development

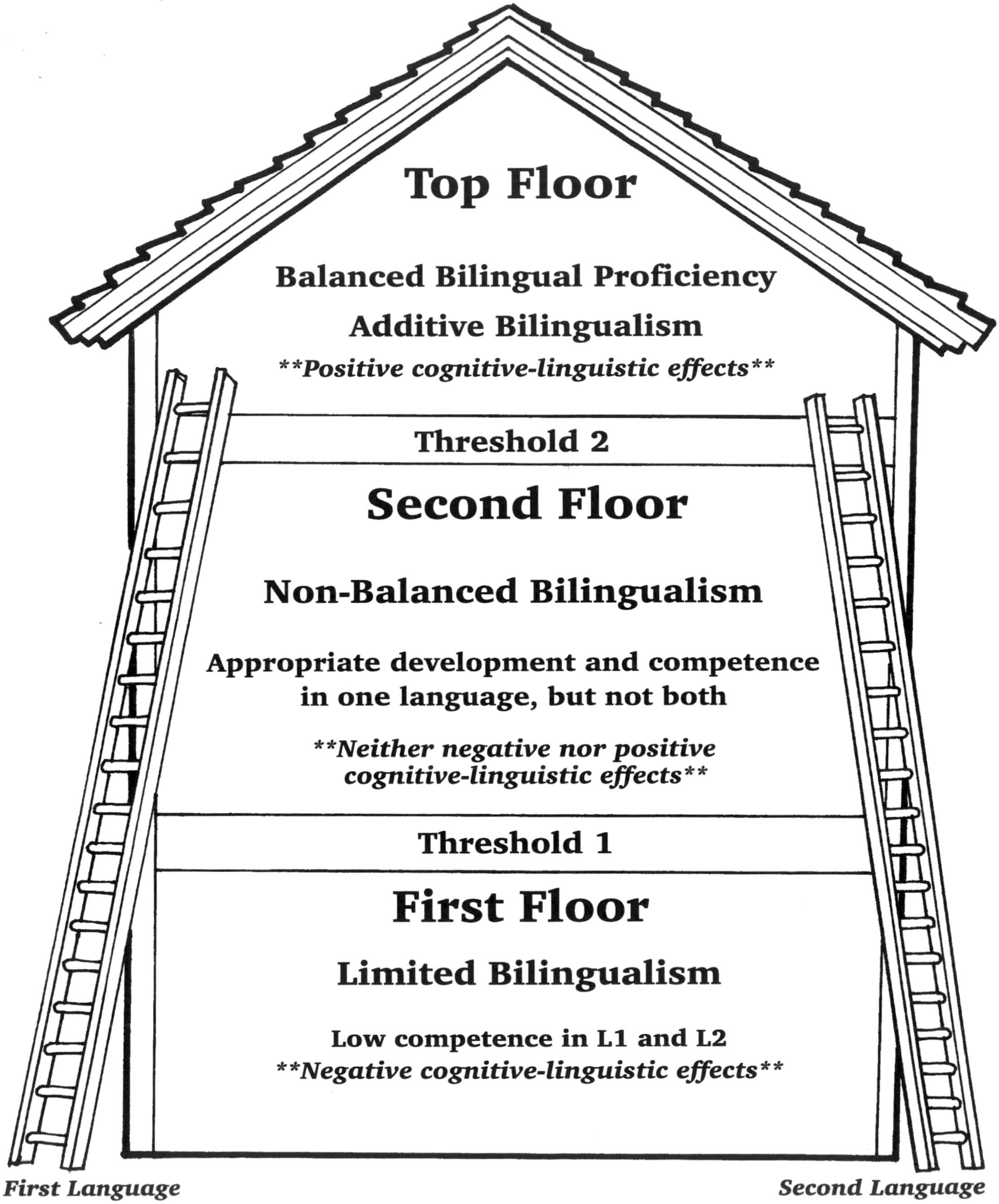

Top Floor

Balanced Bilingual Proficiency
Additive Bilingualism
Positive cognitive-linguistic effects

Threshold 2

Second Floor

Non-Balanced Bilingualism

Appropriate development and competence in one language, but not both

Neither negative nor positive cognitive-linguistic effects

Threshold 1

First Floor

Limited Bilingualism

Low competence in L1 and L2
Negative cognitive-linguistic effects

First Language   *Second Language*

six successive school years. Thus, in order to perform at a level commensurate with that of native speakers, ESL learners must make nine years' progress in six years. It is no wonder that schools create deficits in students that are not related to language-learning disabilities, but rather to an educational system that does not even begin to adequately meet the needs of students who are learning English as a second language.

BICS and CALP

When assessing language proficiency, it is important to distinguish between **Basic Interpersonal Communication Skills** (BICS) from **Cognitive Academic Language Proficiency** (CALP) (see Figure 11.4). (*Note: Some experts describe BICS and CALP as being on a continuum rather than being discrete and separate entities [Cummins, 2000; Genesee et al., 2004]. However, for verbal brevity and ease, the terms BICS and CALP are used here.)

According to Cummins (1992c; 2003), BICS take approximately two to three years (in an ideal situation) to develop to a level commensurate with that of native speakers of the language. It should be noted that other researchers have estimated longer times for the development of oral L2 skills (e.g., Hakuta, Butler, & Wiitt, 2000). The length of time that it takes CLD children to develop oral language skills that are commensurate with those of native speakers depends greatly upon how oral language skills are measured (Paradis, 2007). In addition, the socioeconomic status of CLD students plays a role, with low-income CLD students often taking longer to acquire oral skills in L2 (Roseberry-McKibbin, 2008).

CALP takes between five and seven years to develop to a native-like level (Cummins et al., 2006; Freeman, 2004; Torres-Guzman, 2002). This five- to seven-year time frame is common for students from enriched backgrounds. Some researchers are even maintaining that it can take between seven and ten years for CALP to develop to a native-like level under less than optimal conditions (Cummins, 2002; Eschevarria, Short, & Powers 2006; Peregoy & Boyle, 1997). Shohamy (1999) reported ongoing research being conducted in Israel, where it is being found that immigrant students take seven to nine years to arrive at the level of native Hebrew students in literacy, and slightly less time for mathematics.

Basic Interpersonal Communication Skills involve cognitively undemanding, context-embedded forms of communication. Cognitive Academic Language Proficiency refers to cognitively demanding, context-reduced forms of communication, or expertise in understanding and using literacy-related aspects of language *(see* Figure 11.5). In **context-embedded communication**, participants have a shared reality and can actively negotiate meaning. Context-embedded communication is typical of that found in the everyday world outside the classroom, where language is supported by a wide range of meaningful situational cues and paralinguistic gestures.

For example, in a discussion about a field trip, there is a shared reality and participants can negotiate meaning with one another. Gestures and facial expressions facilitate the communication of meaning in this context-embedded situation. In another example of context-embedded communication, some students on a playground may want to play tether ball; others want to use the monkey bars. A discussion of these choices has a shared reality, a concrete and visible situation, and nonverbal cues to support the interaction (Roseberry-McKibbin, 2003).

Context-reduced communication, on the other hand, does not assume a shared reality. It may rely exclusively on linguistic cues for meaning. Proficiency in context-reduced communication involves the ability to make complex meanings clear by means of language itself rather than by use of contextual support or paralinguistic cues (Cummins, 2000). Context-reduced communication is very typical of many U.S. classroom settings today, even beginning in kindergarten (Roseberry-McKibbin, 2008).

Figure 11.4

**Length of Time Required to Achieve Age-appropriate Levels of
Context-Embedded and Context-Reduced Communicative Proficiency**

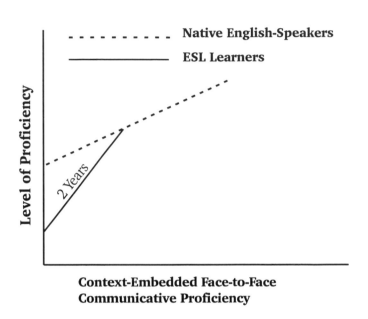

Context-Embedded Face-to-Face
Communicative Proficiency

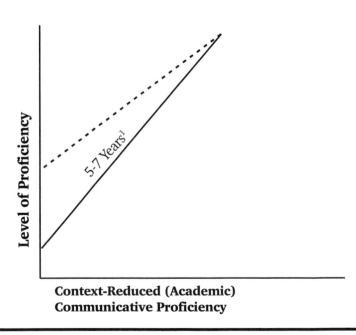

Context-Reduced (Academic)
Communicative Proficiency

Source: Cummins, J. (1992). The role of primary language development in promoting educational success of language minority students. In California State Department of Education, *Schooling and language minority students: A theoretical framework.* Reprinted with permission.

[1]Although Context-Reduced (Academic) Comunicative Proficiency is typically acquired in 5-7 years, it may take up to 10 years in some cases. Comtext-Embedded Face-to-Face Communication Proficieny is most often acquired in 2-3 years.

Figure 11.5
Illustration of Cummins' Grid of Cognitive Demands

Cognitively Undemanding

A

Asking permission to go to the
restroom

Following directions to line up for
recess

Participating in various art, physical
education, and music activities

Discussing a class field trip

BICS

B

Talking on the phone

Following written
instructions without an
illustration

Listing categorical items
(e.g., "Name all of the fruits
that you can think of.")

CALP

C
Context-Embedded

Projects and hands-on activities

Basic math computations

Lab experiments and demonstrations

Lessons using visuals (e.g., charts,
overheads)

BICS

D
Context Reduced

Algebra

Teacher lectures

Most textbooks

Standardized tests
(Special education)

Statewide achievement tests

CALP

Cognitively Demanding

Cognitive involvement refers to the amount of information that needs to be processed simultaneously or in close succession by a student in order to do an activity (Cummins, 1992c). **Cognitively undemanding** tasks are those that are generally automatized and require little active cognitive involvement for adequate performance. For instance, a cognitively undemanding task for most people is to state their name, address, and phone number when asked for this information. **Cognitively demanding** tasks, however, involve situations in which knowledge is not automatized and the person must make use of various cognitive strategies to perform the task. For example, writing an essay in a foreign language is cognitively demanding for a student who has not yet mastered that language. For many readers of this book, studying subjects like advanced math and physics are highly cognitively demanding activities.

Thus, when professionals are assessing a student because of a suspected language-learning disability, it is important to examine the school environment. Is the student in a classroom situation where cognitively demanding tasks are presented regularly? How much contextual information is available to facilitate comprehension? If the student has not yet had opportunities to develop the cognitive strategies necessary to perform context-reduced classroom activities, educational professionals need to be aware of this fact. Students will struggle if they have not yet acquired the cognitive academic skills necessary to complete classroom assignments.

Professionals in the United States who work with CLD students in public schools know that these students are often placed into submersion or sink-or-swim classrooms where only English is spoken. Moreover, often no special provisions are made to help these students learn the English they need for school. Students who speak no English are often expected to learn English in the classroom setting where the linguistic input is often context-reduced and cognitively demanding.

Because a student's initial exposure to English is often of this nature, many students fail to acquire a solid conceptual foundation and end up struggling academically. The acquisition of CALP is difficult if the student's primary exposure to the language occurs within situations in which contextual cues are limited. Helping students to develop a basic conceptual foundation is critical if students are to acquire the strategies necessary for academic success (Cummins, 2002; Eschevarria et al., 2006). Often, students' development of a basic conceptual foundation is measured by English language proficiency tests.

Many English proficiency tests administered in school evaluate only BICS. The student may be asked to respond to simple questions such as, "What do you like to watch on TV?" or "What is your favorite food?" A problem occurs when professionals use the test results to determine whether or not the student has the language skills necessary to function appropriately in an English-only program of academic instruction (Cummins, 2000).

Another related problem is that when a student is labeled "Fully English Proficient" on BICS-type proficiency measures like those described above, many professionals breathe a sigh of relief. Clearly, they may now use norm-referenced English language and academic assessment measures with these students; after all, aren't the students fully English proficient? These professionals believe that a label of "English Proficient" based on English proficiency tests means that the students have the CALP skills necessary to perform adequately on tests standardized on monolingual, English-speaking children. A student who is identified as Fully English Proficient based on BICS-type language proficiency measures can easily be misdiagnosed as having a language-learning disability if CALP has not been fully developed. When assessing language proficiency, it is important to assess performance on the types of language tasks that are used in the classroom setting.

When professionals make judgments about overall proficiency in English based on a student's performance in face-to-face communication situations, they risk the possibility of creating academic deficits in these students (Chamberlain, 2005; Johnstone, 2002) (see Figure 11.6). Again, it is important to keep in mind that BICS is acquired in two or three years, but CALP takes much longer.

Figure 11.6

LANGUAGE PROFICIENCY MISDIAGNOSIS MODEL

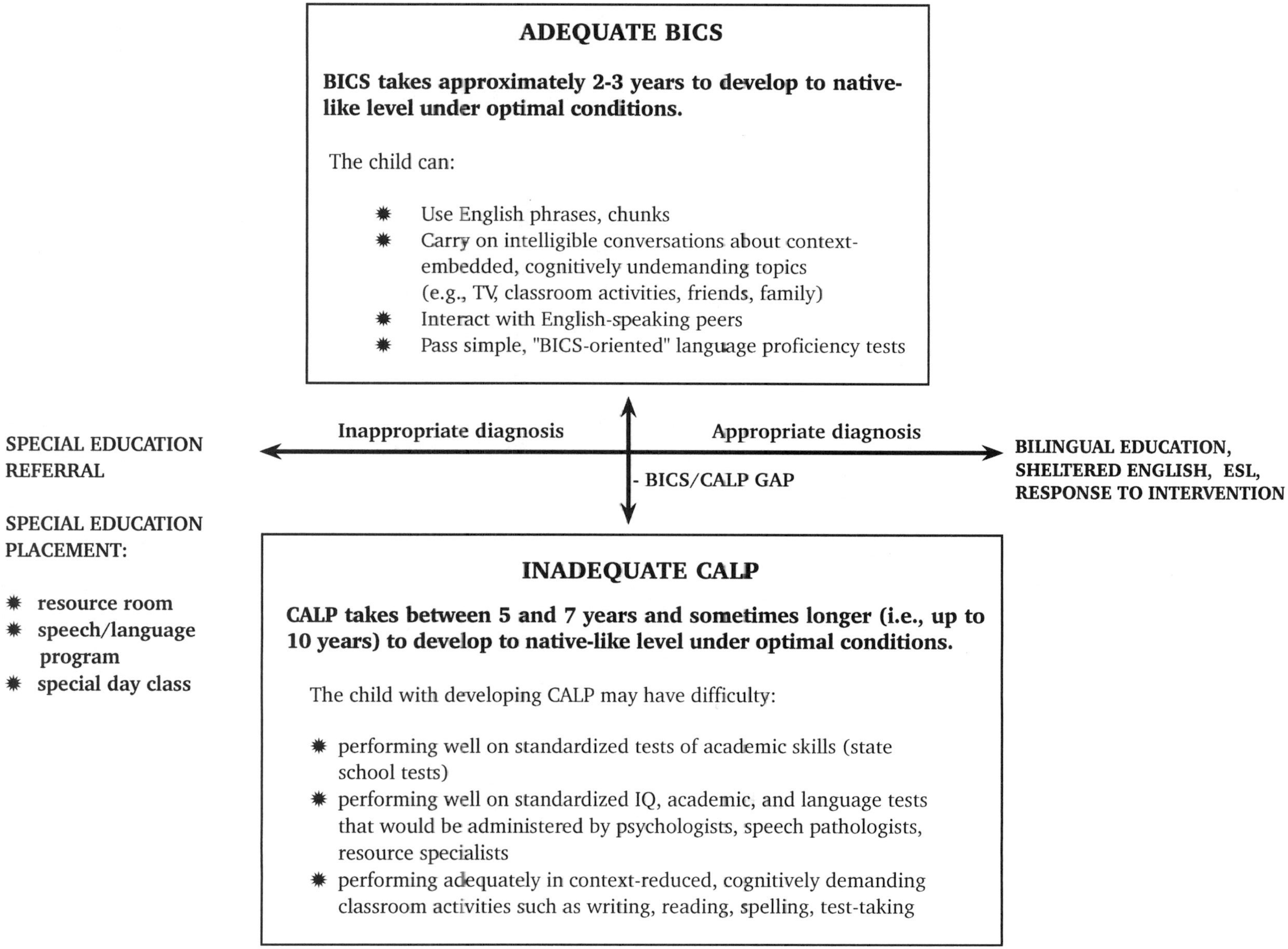

ADEQUATE BICS

BICS takes approximately 2-3 years to develop to native-like level under optimal conditions.

The child can:

* Use English phrases, chunks
* Carry on intelligible conversations about context-embedded, cognitively undemanding topics (e.g., TV, classroom activities, friends, family)
* Interact with English-speaking peers
* Pass simple, "BICS-oriented" language proficiency tests

Appropriate diagnosis

- BICS/CALP GAP

Inappropriate diagnosis

BILINGUAL EDUCATION, SHELTERED ENGLISH, ESL, RESPONSE TO INTERVENTION

INADEQUATE CALP

CALP takes between 5 and 7 years and sometimes longer (i.e., up to 10 years) to develop to native-like level under optimal conditions.

The child with developing CALP may have difficulty:

* performing well on standardized tests of academic skills (state school tests)
* performing well on standardized IQ, academic, and language tests that would be administered by psychologists, speech pathologists, resource specialists
* performing adequately in context-reduced, cognitively demanding classroom activities such as writing, reading, spelling, test-taking

SPECIAL EDUCATION REFERRAL

SPECIAL EDUCATION PLACEMENT:

* resource room
* speech/language program
* special day class

Profile

P. S., a male student from India, was referred to the Student Study Team by his teacher because of problems in reading and math. The teacher reported that the child had good receptive and expressive language skills. P. S. was described as cooperative, courteous, and helpful, and he frequently asked questions when he did not understand classroom assignments. Areas of concern included sight word vocabulary, knowledge of phonics, basic word attack skills, sentence structure, written expression, spelling, and math concepts. P. S. was able to do well in math when manipulatives were used and was ahead of some of his classmates in math manipulative skills. When I asked about the student's language background, no one on the team was able to provide this information. I left the meeting briefly to check the student's school records. A review of the Home Language Survey revealed that Hindu was the primary language of the home and the language used most often by P. S. He had been exposed to English for 2.5 years, but spoke only his native language when he entered kindergarten. I brought this information back to the Student Study Team.

I told the classroom teacher about the CALP versus BICS distinction. She had never heard about this distinction and realized that P. S. had BICS that were quite good. He would need more time to acquire the CALP necessary for success in academic subjects. Thus, rather than testing P. S. for special education, the team concluded that he should receive increased tutoring in the first language and increased ESL support.

In looking at the student's profile, it was clear that he had mastered the basic interpersonal communication skills. He was, however, having difficulty with the context-reduced, cognitively demanding aspects of English academics. This is very typical of children who enter kindergarten speaking only their first language. This case illustrates the importance of utilizing language proficiency models when attempting to determine the cause of a child's difficulties in the classroom. The case of P. S. also underscores the great importance of taking the time to gather information about children's language backgrounds. I was able to obtain this information in less than five minutes. If those few minutes had not been spent, P. S. might have been inappropriately placed into special education.

ISSUES IN BILINGUALISM AND BILINGUAL EDUCATION

Additive and Subtractive Bilingualism

Additive bilingualism occurs when both languages spoken by the student are reinforced, resulting in high levels of proficiency in the two languages. The student's first language continues to be nurtured and encouraged as the child learns the second language. The goal is to help the student become a fluent and balanced bilingual speaker (Education Week Research Center, 2007; Whitmore & Crowell, 2006). As stated previously, there are advantages to additive bilingualism. By becoming fully bilingual, individuals develop high-level metalinguistic skills, enhance their employability, and increase their potential for making valuable contributions to society (Cummins et al., 2006; Genesee et al., 2004; King & Fogle, 2006; McLaughlin, 2006).

Research shows that bilingual children younger than six years of age tend to outperform monolingual children on tasks of metalinguistic awareness and other language skills (García, 1999;

García, Jiminez, & Pearson, 1998; Sheng, McGregor, & Marian, 2006). Bialystok (1997) found that four- and five-year-old bilingual preschoolers in Canada (Mandarin-English and French-English speakers) outperformed monolingual English-speaking preschoolers on a metalinguistic task related to beginning reading. Bialystok (2001) showed that bilingual children had an advantage in performing a variety of cognitive tasks when selective attention was required during information processing; misleading information was inhibited in favor of relevant information.

In today's global economy, bilingualism is a great asset. Being bilingual is considered much more advantageous than being monolingual (Freeman, 2004). In many parts of the world, multilingual individuals are considered educated and cosmopolitan. Takanishi (2006, p. 71) stated that "The competitive demands of a global economy place bi- and multilingual individuals at a competitive advantage in 'the race' for economic security."

Children who experience additive bilingualism also are able to continue to speak with their families in L1. This is extremely important, because many parents and especially grandparents communicate best (with the most possible intimacy and naturalness of expression) in L1 (Baker, 2000; Dickinson & Tabors, 2001; Yan, 2003). For children, being bilingual provides a bridge across generations. When children can no longer speak L1, relationships with immediate and extended family members suffer (Restrepo & Gutiérrez-Clellen, 2004; Wong Fillmore, 2000). Unfortunately, this is common in the U.S.

In **subtractive bilingualism**, a phenomenon in which the student's first language is replaced by the second language, language loss in the first language occurs, and the student gradually becomes a monolingual speaker of English or the majority language (Genesee et al., 2004; González, 2007). However, if English skills continue to be considerably below those of their monolingual peers, the student's cognitive and linguistic growth is likely to be negatively affected (Brice, 2002).

Children who are sequential language learners (described later) and belong to a minority ethnolinguistic community may be especially vulnerable to subtractive bilingualism (Genesee et al., 2004). A **minority ethnolinguistic community** is one in which the language has lower social status, is less widely valued and spoken, and receives little to no institutional support (Centeno, 2007). Genesee et al. gave the examples of Turkish-speaking children in Germany, Spanish-speaking children in the U.S., and speakers of Cantonese in Canada as belonging to minority ethnolinguistic communities. Basically, members of these communities lack cultural, social, and linguistic power. As an example, Hammer, Miccio, and Rodríguez (2004) emphasized that for Spanish-speaking children in the U.S., it can be a struggle for parents to maintain the children's Spanish skills because schools provide little to no support for this. As stated elsewhere in this chapter, parents may even be discouraged from using Spanish in the home.

Children who belong to **majority ethnolinguistic communities** are much less vulnerable to experiencing subtractive bilingualism and often experience additive bilingualism when they are exposed to a second language. In this situation, their first language (English in this discussion) is widely used and has high social status. It is the language of business and enjoys widespread institutional support. These children's parents often place them into language programs where they learn an L2 for enrichment purposes.

For example, in California's Silicon Valley, there is a private school called the French-American School of Silicon Valley. Parents are urged to give their children the benefit and gift of bilingual education. At West Portal Elementary School in San Francisco, there are elementary Cantonese immersion classes for English-speaking children whose parents want them to learn Cantonese. In some high schools, Chinese has been included in the Advanced Placement program, and parents want their children to partake of this opportunity to broaden their linguistic skills and enhance their desirability to future employers (Posnick-Goodwin, 2006). These types of programs stand in sharp contrast to those attended by low-income Spanish-speaking children in Los Angeles (mentioned earlier), where their parents are discouraged from using Spanish and are encouraged to speak only

English with their children. As Cummins (2000, p. 16) summed it up, "Bilingualism is good for the rich but bad for the poor."

CLD students who struggle academically and linguistically from year to year are often those who have experienced subtractive bilingualism. Subtractive bilingualism often creates negative cognitive effects; children are left with a reduced conceptual foundation on which to build academic and linguistic skills. These students do not have "disabilities" and, therefore, are not appropriate candidates for special education. Instructional activities that build conceptual knowledge in the first language can help students with limited proficiency in English acquire cognitive strategies that will facilitate learning English and functioning effectively in the classroom learning environment.

✐REFLECTION✐

Compare and contrast the SUP and CUP theories. What effects might widespread implementation of programs based on the SUP theory have within school districts? How can professionals help school districts subscribe to and implement the CUP theory instead?

_____

_____

_____

_____

Bilingual Education and Academic Success

As stated, additive bilingualism is the ideal for all students. To promote additive bilingualism, optimally, students should participate in bilingual education throughout the elementary years and beyond if possible (Cummins, 2000; Walqui, 2006). Such instruction provides students with culturally appropriate learning experiences, opportunities for continued use of the first language, and experiences designed to promote the learning and effective use of a second language. Programs of bilingual education appear to promote the greatest linguistic, cultural, and cognitive benefits when there is active parent and community involvement.

In many places around the world, the ability to speak several languages is viewed as a valuable asset. For example, Armenians believe that the more languages a person speaks, the more well-educated and well-rounded she is. Armenians take pride in speaking as many as six languages. Most Swiss are trilingual, speaking German, French, and Italian. In Luxembourg, citizens commonly switch back and forth between Flemish, English, Dutch, German, and French (Rowe & Levine, 2006). When I was being raised in the Philippines, standard English was spoken at home. Odionganon was spoken in the town of Odiongan, Tagalog was learned in school, and Hiligaynon was spoken in church.

Unfortunately, negative attitudes toward bilingualism are prevalent in the U.S. today, and thus programs of bilingual education have suffered. Historically, the U.S. has been isolationist; the emphasis on monolingualism reflects this attitude. In the early 20th century, when there was a huge wave of non-English-speaking immigrants from Europe, families were advised to "assimilate" by giving up the languages of their home countries. Parents were told that being bilingual would confuse their children. In the early 1920s, researchers concluded that bilingualism caused children to perform poorly in school (Rowe & Levine, 2006).

Skutnabb-Kangas (2000) summarized the beliefs and practices of teaching English in colonial and post-colonial educational settings:

1. English is best when taught monolingually.
2. The ideal teacher of English is a native speaker.
3. The earlier English is introduced, the better the results.
4. The more English is taught, the better the results.
5. If other languages are used very much, English standards will drop.

Even today, 100 years later, many U.S. citizens cling to the outmoded, inaccurate belief that being bilingual has negative cognitive and social effects on children (Education Week Research Center, 2007; Freeman, 2004). Early in 1998, Newt Gingrich, former Speaker of the House, summarized the views of many conservative policy makers: "When we allow children to stay trapped in bilingual programs where they do not learn English, we are destroying their economic future" (Hornblower, 1998, p. 44). Hornblower (p. 44) also stated that "He [Gingrich] and other Republicans call for a return to the traditional expectation that immigrants will quickly learn English as the price of admission to America."

In another example, on January 8, 2002, Title VII (the Bilingual Education Act) was eliminated as part of the No Child Left Behind Act (NCLB, 2002). As of 2002, Title III, the new law, had a new name: "Language Instruction for Limited English Proficient and Immigrant Students." Cahnmann and Varghese (2005, p. 59) summarized the current state of affairs by stating that "after 34 years, the word 'bilingual' has been deleted from all government offices and legislation—a not so subtle message concerning the assimilationist, English-only orientation of the Bush Administration."

Under the guise of "flexibility," NCLB turns most federal funding for English language learner programs into block grants administered by the states. Yet, in the name of "accountability," it mandates high-stakes English testing that is likely to discourage districts from supporting first language instruction (Crawford, 2003). Clearly, in the U.S., there is a widespread lack of financial and political support for bilingual education. Indeed, there is vocal opposition to it.

Several states have passed measures that are clearly anti-bilingual education. In 1998, California passed Proposition 227, an initiative that almost entirely eliminated bilingual education in public schools. Today in California, most English language learners are placed in English-immersion programs. Following California's lead, Arizona passed Proposition 203, a proposition similar to Proposition 227. In 2002, Massachusetts approved a ballot initiative that did away with the oldest bilingual education law in the nation.

Cummins et al. (2006), discussed three views that are held by most educators regarding the languages children bring to school with them: (1) language-as-resource, (2) language-as-right, and (3) language-as-problem. Unfortunately, many U.S. educators subscribe to the language-as-problem view (Cashman, 2006; Crawford, 2003). This is based on long-held assumptions based on the traditional, negative beliefs about bilingualism that were explained earlier.

Malakoff & Hakuta (1991, p. 141) described the **monolingual-norm assumption**—the belief that monolingualism is the cognitive-linguistic norm and that the child's cognitive system is fragile and only designed to cope with one language. Genesee et al. (2004), described this belief as the **limited capacity hypothesis**: the belief that acquiring more than one language is problematic because the language faculty has a limited capacity.

Genesee et al. (2004), described this further as the belief that a child's underlying mental language-learning capacity is like a balloon that can only contain so much air; when the balloon inflates as a result of acquiring one language, there is limited space for acquisition of another language. The monolingual-norm assumption/limited capacity hypothesis gave rise to the negative myths surrounding bilingualism—bilingualism has been blamed for cognitive, social, and emotional damage to children.

As stated earlier, Cummins (2000) pointed out the irony of bilingualism being good for the rich and bad for the poor. He stated (p. 23):

> The very positive media picture of bilingual education for affluent children in countries around the world is similar to the way French immersion programs have typically been depicted in the Canadian context. These programs serve the interest of dominant middle-class majority language children. By contrast, when bilingual education aims to serve the interests of marginalized children from minority groups, the media appear to have extreme difficulty understanding the rationale for these programs.

Cashman (2006) also commented on this topic, stating that in the case of language minorities in the U.S., language diversity is seen by those in power as a problem to be solved rather than a right to be protected or resource to be conserved. When majority Anglo members of society learn a second language, their bilingual skills are held in high esteem and often rewarded economically. In contrast, the bilingual skills of immigrant or language minority groups tend to be underappreciated or disparaged outright. Their bilingual skills are often perceived as a sign of divided loyalty between their home countries and the U.S., and as barriers to their full participation in U.S. society.

As an outgrowth of these political attitudes, many of the bilingual programs currently being implemented in the schools are transitional programs wherein the first language is used to teach academic subjects, but an emphasis is placed on transitioning the student into English as quickly as possible. Some schools have Sheltered English classrooms, where an effort is made to teach subject matter using English that is comprehensible to the students. There are many schools that do not have programs for bilingual students at all. Thus, the problem becomes one of determining how to best educate CLD students when the staff and resources needed for instruction in the first language are limited or perhaps nonexistent.

Simultaneous versus Sequential Bilingualism

Researchers have broadly delineated two types of bilingualism: **simultaneous** and **sequential**. Simultaneous acquisition occurs when two languages are acquired simultaneously from infancy (Rowe & Levine, 2006). Simultaneous acquisition has also been defined as the acquisition of two languages before age three (Centeno, 2007; McLaughlin, 2006; Owens, 2005; Patterson & Pearson, 2004). The bilingual development observed in these children closely parallels monolingual development. The children acquire both languages at a rate comparable to that of monolingual children. There is little difference in the diversity and size of the lexicons of bilingual and monolingual toddlers; later reading and syntactic development in both languages appear typical (Jünker & Stockman, 2002; Peña, Bedore, & Rappazo, 2003).

There appear to be three stages that occur in young children who are simultaneous bilingual learners (Long, 2006; McLaughlin, 2006; Owens, 2005). During stage one, the child has two separate lexical systems. These reflect the child's capacity to differentiate between two languages prior to speaking. In the second stage, the child possesses two distinct lexicons but applies the same syntactic rules to both. The child is able to move between the lexicons of the two languages and translate words; this flexibility does not occur at the syntactic level. The nonparallel nature of syntactic learning reflects the linguistic difficulty of specific syntactic structures in the two languages. Usually the child learns structures common to both languages; simpler constructions are learned before more complex ones. In the third stage, the child correctly produces syntactic and lexical structures from both languages. There may be some language transfer, but this occurs mostly at the syntactic level.

Children who acquire two languages simultaneously in naturalistic situations seem to do so with minimal interference (Genesee et al., 2004). If the situation is one of additive bilingualism, children experience cognitive-linguistic and social benefits. Simultaneous acquisition results in equivalent levels of language proficiency in both languages more often than does sequential acquisition (Bliss, 2001).

Students who experience sequential or successive acquisition of the second language show greater diversity in rates and stages of acquisition (Guiberson et al., 2006; Kan & Kohnert, 2005; Kayser, 2002; McLaughlin, 2006). Although some students may acquire the second language with minimal interference, others may experience difficulties. If a student is introduced to a second language before the first language threshold has been reached, the development of the first language may be arrested or may regress while the child is focused on the learning of a second language.

Since, as Cummins (1992b, 2000) has stated, proficiency in the second language is partially a function of competence in the first language, a condition of limited bilingualism may occur in which the student does not fully develop either language. Schiff-Myers (1992) pointed out that for a period of time, these students may obtain low test scores in both languages and consequently appear language-learning disabled. Furthermore, students from low socioeconomic backgrounds who have had little experience with decontextualized language may have difficulty learning a new language readily (Roseberry-McKibbin, 2008).

Thus, when professionals are working with CLD students in the schools, it is necessary when a student appears "low functioning" to find out if language development occurred simultaneously or sequentially. If languages were acquired sequentially, what was the effect of second language acquisition on the development of proficiency in the first language? Did the student develop a high enough level of language proficiency in the primary language to respond to the cognitive demands of the classroom? If the student was "switched" to English before acquiring these cognitive abilities, it is likely that many classroom tasks will be difficult. Moreover, students who have had limited exposure to decontextualized language in the home are often at risk for academic difficulties (Weiner, 2001).

THE IMPORTANCE OF COMPREHENSIBLE INPUT

The extent to which children experience success in learning is influenced by their past experiences. The more experiences that students have had, the more they will learn (see Figure 11.7). It is important to provide second language learners with comprehensible input in the second language (Case, Ndura, & Righettini, 2005; Coltrane, 2003). Krashen (1993) proposed that people acquire language structure by understanding messages and that the learner's focus is the function of the utterance rather than the form. According to Krashen, optimal comprehensible input in the second language includes the following:

1. It includes "*i + 1 input*" that is slightly above the learner's current level but comprehensible enough to be mostly understood.

2. Concrete referents are available (e.g., extra-linguistic aids such as visuals, hands-on materials, etc.)

3. It is interesting, meaningful, and relevant to the learner.

4. It occurs naturally and the learner has practice opportunities in natural, conversational, everyday situations that are communicatively meaningful.

5. It is not grammatically sequenced but, rather, occurs naturally.

6. There are sufficient quantities of this input to ensure optimal learning.

The comprehensible input hypothesis runs counter to the traditional language teaching approach in which language structures are taught first. Krashen (1992) stated that language is best acquired by aiming first for meaning. Language structures develop as the student gains proficiency

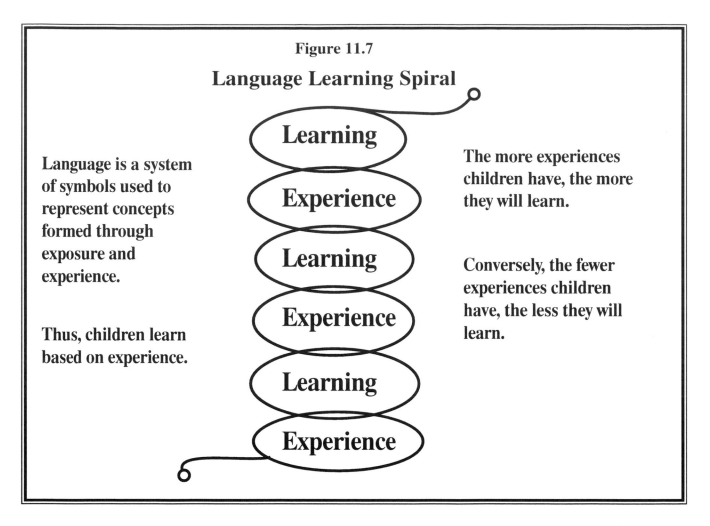

Figure 11.7

Language Learning Spiral

Language is a system of symbols used to represent concepts formed through exposure and experience.

Thus, children learn based on experience.

The more experiences children have, the more they will learn.

Conversely, the fewer experiences children have, the less they will learn.

in using language for specific purposes to communicate meaning. Success in acquiring a second language requires that comprehensible input be provided frequently in situations where language is used for a purpose.

While Krashen's idea regarding comprehensible input makes sense, his claim that comprehensible input alone is sufficient for optimal second language acquisition has been criticized. Swain (1985) stated that while comprehensible input may be essential to second language acquisition, it is not enough to ensure that the outcome will be native-like performance. According to Swain, comprehensible output is a necessary mechanism of successful second language acquisition; she argued that second language learners must engage in interactions in which meaning is negotiated. This interaction gives the learners necessary practice in production of the second language, not just in passive reception of comprehensible input. Second language learners must be active agents in their environment in terms of language output and interaction with others in their environments (Baker, 2000; Coltrane, 2003; Walqui, 2000).

The necessity of comprehensible output can be further explained using the **zone of proximal development (ZPD),** a theory of development proposed by Vygotsky (1962). Vygotsky defined the ZPD as the distance between a child's actual level of development as determined by independent problem solving and the individual's potential level of development through problem solving, either in collaboration with more capable peers or with guidance from an adult. Proponents of this theory maintain that children will show growth when they interact with others and when information is provided for them. This interaction and provision of information helps children learn more and helps them advance to a higher level of learning.

Thus, when a CLD student appears to be having academic and/or linguistic difficulty, professionals can ask if the classroom language input is comprehensible to the student. If not, the student's difficulties may stem directly from a lack of comprehension (Rodríguez & Higgins, 2005). Professionals can also ask if there are adequate comprehensible output situations available to the student. In addition, professionals can ascertain whether or not students are receiving support to advance their levels of learning.

REFLECTION

Define "comprehensible input." Why is comprehensible input so important for CLD students? What happens when they do not receive comprehensible input in the classroom?

CONCLUSION

When professionals evaluate CLD students' linguistic, intellectual, and academic performance, they must take into account factors relating to second language acquisition and bilingual development. In many cases, errors in judgment and the consequent inappropriate placement of students in special education programs can be avoided. The greater the understanding that professionals have of typical second-language learning and bilingualism, the more unbiased and appropriate will be the services provided to CLD students in the schools.

STUDY QUESTIONS

1. Describe three affective variables that are critical in second language acquisition.

2. Define the terms *simultaneous acquisition* and *sequential acquisition*. Will the child who is a simultaneous language learner or the child who is a sequential language learner be more likely to experience difficulty in the classroom? Why?

3. Describe the negative myths about bilingualism in the U.S. How have these negative myths impacted actual practice in U.S. school systems?

TRUE-FALSE

Circle the number beside each statement that is true.

4. Code-switching is generally a sign of linguistic confusion and is thus frequently indicative of a language-learning disability.
5. The younger the child is when first exposed to the second language, the longer the silent period typically lasts.
6. Enclosure refers to the degree to which ethnic groups share the same things in life.
7. Many Americans believe that it is better to be monolingual rather than bilingual.
8. Proficient bilinguals frequently outperform monolinguals on tests of metalinguistic skill.
9. Students with a high affective filter can be described as motivated individuals with a low anxiety level who are readily able to benefit from language input in the second language.
10. The term "interlanguage" refers to a phenomenon in which specific second language "errors" remain firmly entrenched despite good proficiency in the second language.

MULTIPLE CHOICE

Circle the letter beside each choice that is correct.

11. Which term refers to a process in which a communicative behavior or structure from the first language is carried over into the second language?

    A. fossilization
    B. interference/transfer
    C. interlanguage
    D. silent period
    E. enclosure

12. Which of the following statements are TRUE?
    A. Under optimal conditions, the development of BICS to a native-like proficiency level takes approximately two to three years for second language learners.
    B. Under optimal conditions, the development of CALP to a native-like proficiency level takes approximately three to four years.
    C. BICS involves cognitively undemanding, context-embedded forms of communication.
    D. CALP refers to the cognitively demanding, context-reduced forms of communication.
    E. Most English language proficiency tests assess CALP.

13. Which one of the following is NOT a feature of comprehensible input according to Krashen?
    A. The input is slightly below the learner's current level, making it comprehensible enough to be mostly understood.
    B. Concrete referents are available (e.g., visuals).
    C. It is not grammatically sequenced but, rather, occurs naturally.
    D. It is interesting, meaningful, and relevant to the learner.
    E. There are sufficient quantities of this input to ensure optimal learning.

14. For children who are learning two languages, which of the following are true?
    A. It is ideal to learn both languages from infancy.
    B. A strong first language base contributes positively to learning the second language adequately.
    C. Students who do not learn either L1 or L2 adequately often face a state of limited bilingualism which leads to negative cognitive effects.
    D. Bilingualism almost always has detrimental effects when two languages are learned simultaneously.

15. Francisco L., a 5-year-old Spanish-speaking boy, is attending an all-English kindergarten classroom. He has lived his whole life in a trailer with his parents, grandparents, and six siblings. Francisco had never been to preschool. His parents are migrant workers who lack literacy skills in both Spanish and English. Following three months of kindergarten, the teacher referred Francisco for a special education evaluation because of a possible language-learning disability. The student speaks occasionally in class and has friends, but he is having difficulty during writing, spelling, and math activities. What would be the best course of action for the special education team to take?
    A. Use English special education tests because Francisco is in an all-English-speaking school and he will eventually need to perform at the same level as his English-speaking peers.
    B. Test Francisco in both Spanish and English using BICS- and CALP-oriented special education tests.
    C. Assess Francisco's level of proficiency in both English and Spanish, provide him with ESL services in Spanish, assign a Spanish-speaking aide to the classroom to assist him, and re-evaluate him in a year to assess progress.
    D. Do not assess Francisco in any way at this time because his limited language exposure will invalidate any tests that are given.
    E. Place Francisco in special education so that he can receive an individualized program of English language instruction that targets the conceptual skills necessary for success in the general education curriculum.

ANSWERS TO STUDY QUESTIONS
4. False
5. True
6. True
7. True
8. True
9. False
10. False
11. B
12. A, C, D
13. A
14. A, B, C
15. C

Chapter 12

INTRODUCTION TO ASSESSMENT: FOUNDATIONAL PRINCIPLES

Outline

THE DIAGNOSTIC CHALLENGE

When assessment personnel are confronted with CLD students who appear to be struggling in school, the first question that they usually ask is, "Does this student have a language difference or a language-learning disability? Does the student need special education services?" Language differences are behaviors that are commonly observed among second language learners. Differences in sentence structure, speech sound production, vocabulary, and the pragmatic uses of language are to be expected when a child learns a new language. Unfortunately, children with language differences that result from limited experience in using a language are often misidentified as "language-learning disabled." The "language-learning disability" diagnosis is appropriate only for students with disabilities affecting their underlying ability to learn any language (Mattes & García-Easterly, 2007; Roseberry-McKibbin, 2003).

Distinguishing a language difference from a language-learning disability is often a challenge (Oller et al., 2006; Roseberry-McKibbin, 2003; Roseberry-McKibbin et al., 2005). In this chapter and the one that follows, strategies are presented for accurately identifying language-learning disabilities in CLD students.

Bloom and Lahey (1978) defined language as a system of symbols used to represent concepts formed through exposure and experience. Exposure and experience are critical for success in acquiring a language. Children must hear the language and must be provided with experience in using it. Language can be experienced through oral communication and through literacy experiences. Teachers typically assume that students entering school have had opportunities to listen to stories, to explore books, to cut with scissors, to color pictures with crayons, and to use language for a variety of purposes. It is assumed that children have been taken to stores, parks, zoos, libraries, and other places in the community.

Some students come from backgrounds in which they have had all of these experiences. Children who immigrate to the United States may have traveled to a variety of countries and may speak and write in several languages. These students have much to share about their cultural backgrounds and their experiences when they interact with mainstream American students in the school setting.

Other students, however, have had limited experiences with books and limited opportunities for language enrichment. These students and their families may be non-literate for one or more reasons. Perhaps family members have not had the opportunity to attend school or their experience in school is limited. There are some students who come from backgrounds in which there is no written form of the language. In the Netherlands, for example, some students from isolated areas speak Berber languages that do not have a tradition of literacy. These students struggle in school. Some Native American groups and speakers of Haitian Creole have predominantly oral traditions with no formal written language.

When "problems" observed in school result from differences in the student's experiences and the school's expectations, educational professionals might assume that there is something inherently wrong with the student. An emphasis in assessment is often placed on searching for a disability to "explain" the problem. Disabilities are often "created" for students who, in reality, need greater exposure, experience, and support to meet the demands of the classroom curriculum (Montgomery & Moore-Brown, 2006). As Klingner et al. (2006, p. 123) stated:

> We must be mindful that schools are still too focused on finding the "deficit" in the child rather than looking at student performance as the result of strong interactions between the individual and cultural contexts.

If a student's background experiences are different from those of most other children in the school system, he or she may exhibit language behaviors that stand out as being "different." The student may not be learning because of lack of exposure to new experiences or to experiences that are not commensurate with what the school expects. If school professionals do not consider what the student has experienced in the past, misdiagnosis may occur and this misdiagnosis may result in an inappropriate special education placement.

The "diagnostic pie" in Figure 12.1 is a simple conceptual framework that assessment personnel can use to distinguish language differences from language-learning disabilities in bilingual students who are learning English as a second language. Consideration of the child's language experiences is critical in any evaluation.

QUADRANT 1

Students who fall into this quadrant of the pie have no abnormalities in their ability to learn language. They come from backgrounds that may be rich in stimulation and general experiences, but their experiences have not been consistent with expectations in mainstream U.S. schools. These students generally have the conceptual foundation necessary for academic success. The needs of these students can usually be served best in bilingual classrooms that provide opportunities for language development both in English and in the primary language.

If bilingual education is not available, these students can benefit from Sheltered English (academic content taught in English that is comprehensible) or, barring this, a program that teaches English as a second language (ESL). Again, if these students are given time, attention, and support, they will generally succeed in school.

QUADRANT 2

These students have normal language-learning abilities. However, they come from backgrounds where they may have experienced some limitations in environmental stimulation and linguistic exposure. Society may have placed them and their families in an economically disadvantageous situation. The students have the ability to learn, but life circumstances have curtailed their learning opportunities and experiences prior to entering school.

These students often do poorly on standardized tests that are based on mainstream, middle-class expectations. If these students have not had the experiences necessary to perform well on tests, they may appear to be "language-learning disabled."

Students in Quadrant 2 are likely to make adequate progress in school if they receive enough input, exposure, and stimulation. Bilingual education, ESL, and/or Sheltered English programs may be effective because they enhance skills in both the primary language and English. These students often benefit greatly from other non-special education supports such as Response to Intervention (RtI) programs.

For example, at the elementary school where I provide speech and language services, classroom teachers and aides use special reading enhancement programs with students who are struggling with written language skills. These students are not in special education programs but are, rather, in regular education classrooms receiving additional support. Those whose language-learning ability is intact generally respond well to this additional support and do not require special education services.

QUADRANT 3

Students in Quadrant 3 come from backgrounds in which they have had adequate exposure and language stimulation. The life experiences of some of these students are consistent with those expected in mainstream schools. Often parents have given these students as much help as possible in the home, and the students still do not succeed in school. Other students may not have had

Figure 12.1

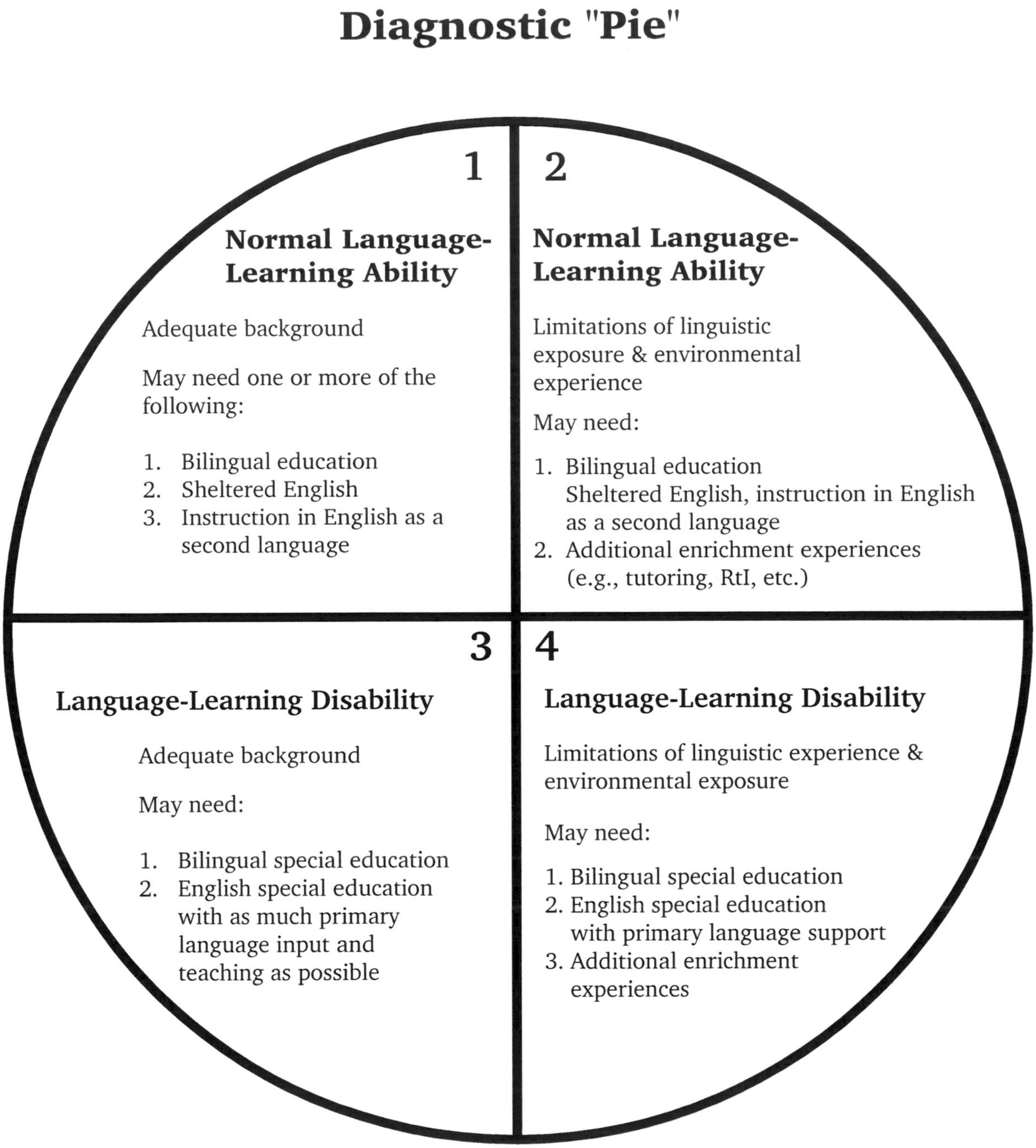

Diagnostic "Pie"

1 **Normal Language-Learning Ability**

Adequate background

May need one or more of the following:

1. Bilingual education
2. Sheltered English
3. Instruction in English as a second language

2 **Normal Language-Learning Ability**

Limitations of linguistic exposure & environmental experience

May need:

1. Bilingual education
   Sheltered English, instruction in English as a second language
2. Additional enrichment experiences (e.g., tutoring, RtI, etc.)

3 **Language-Learning Disability**

Adequate background

May need:

1. Bilingual special education
2. English special education with as much primary language input and teaching as possible

4 **Language-Learning Disability**

Limitations of linguistic experience & environmental exposure

May need:

1. Bilingual special education
2. English special education with primary language support
3. Additional enrichment experiences

life experiences and opportunities that are commensurate with school expectations. However, the school has provided much additional help and support over time to assist these students in developing academic skills (e.g., tutoring, ESL programs). Despite the fact that school personnel have provided supplemental activities within the regular education curriculum in an effort to stimulate academic growth, the students continue to acquire new information more slowly than peers from similar cultural and linguistic backgrounds and continue to manifest learning difficulties.

Students with these characteristics have underlying language-learning disabilities that prevent them from learning and using any language adequately, despite backgrounds that have provided opportunities for appropriate environmental and linguistic stimulation. These students need to receive special education services so that their unique disabilities can be appropriately addressed by personnel with specialized training. Opportunities for instruction in the primary language should be provided, if possible, so that the children can make use of their previously acquired knowledge to learn new information.

Profile

Tanveer D., a sixth-grade speaker of Urdu from a Pakistani family, was referred to me for special education assessment. His teacher was especially concerned about his written language skills. His parents, who did not speak English, were unable to assist Tanveer with his homework. Thus the school provided Tanveer with an Urdu tutor who worked with him weekly on an individual basis for two years. Tanveer had participated in the school's Homework Club, an after-school program for students who needed extra academic support. In addition, Tanveer had attended Reading Clinic (a non-special education program to provide reading support for struggling students) for the last year. Despite this extra support, Tanveer was unable to recite the alphabet and could not identify simple printed words such as "cat" and "the." The other Urdu-speaking students in the school had surpassed Tanveer academically, and the Urdu interpreter confided that Tanveer was "much lower than other Urdu students I have worked with in this district."

Extensive testing revealed evidence of a language-learning disability affecting both Urdu and English, as well as a clinically significant reading disability. Tanveer was placed in special education so that he could receive the necessary services to address the disability that was negatively affecting learning in both languages.

QUADRANT 4

Students in Quadrant 4 come from backgrounds in which there are known limitations in experiences that may be contributing to problems identified in the school setting. These children, however, also have problems learning new language skills. When assessing these students, it is difficult to determine whether the students' low test scores are due to background/environment, an underlying disability, or both. Most professionals wrestle with the issue of whether to place these students into Quadrant 2 or Quadrant 4. Determining why a child is not performing well in the classroom is difficult. Children, however, should not be considered to have a "disability" if their needs can be met by providing a culturally and linguistically appropriate program of instruction in the regular classroom.

Students in Quadrant 4 ideally need bilingual special education with additional enrichment activities to compensate for limited learning opportunities in their environments. Students should be provided with opportunities for support in the primary language to the maximum extent possible.

They can also benefit from participating in whatever additional enrichment experiences are available.

How do assessment personnel know which section of the "diagnostic pie" the student falls into? Examining the child's background is critical. Professionals must also look at the effects of second language acquisition and bilingualism on the student's performance. Understanding the processes of second language acquisition and the nature of bilingualism will help educational professionals assess students in a nonbiased manner.

Then, professionals must understand what constitutes a language-learning disability in a CLD student and must be familiar with laws governing the assessment of these students. If professionals use standardized tests to assess CLD students, they must be familiar with the biases and limitations inherent in these measures. Professionals must also understand the importance of going through a pre-evaluation process that includes the classroom teacher's evaluation, the gathering of a case history, and the determination of the student's primary language, dominant language, and level of proficiency in each language (Brice & Roseberry-McKibbin, 1999; Paradis, 2007).

DEFINITION OF LANGUAGE-LEARNING DISABILITY

Students should not be considered to have language-learning disabilities if "problems" are observed only in English. If the student has a true language-learning disability, problems in communication should be evident in BOTH ENGLISH AND THE PRIMARY LANGUAGE. A language-learning disability is a disability that affects the child's acquisition of any language. Exposure to two languages is not the cause of the disability. Bilingual children with language-learning disabilities will have difficulty learning English, Spanish, or any other language (Gildersleeve-Neumann, 2007; Mattes & Saldaña-Illingworth, 2008; Roseberry-McKibbin & O'Hanlon, 2005).

Students who speak a language other than English should never be diagnosed as language-learning disabled based solely on results obtained from tests administered in English. Information about language functioning in both the primary language and English should be obtained before educational decisions are made.

POSSIBLE INDICATORS OF A LANGUAGE-LEARNING DISABILITY

CLD students with language-learning disabilities demonstrate problems in both the primary language and English. A variety of behaviors commonly observed among students with communication disorders have been described in the literature (see Brice, 2002; Carter et al., 2005; Centeno, 2007; Chamberlain, 2005; González, 2007; Klee, Stokes, Wong, Fletcher, & Gavin, 2004; Mattes & Saldaña-Illingworth, 2008; Paradis, 2007; Roseberry-McKibbin & O'Hanlon, 2005); the list below includes many of the most commonly reported behaviors:

1. Difficulty learning language at a normal rate, even with special assistance in both languages
2. Deficits in vocabulary
3. Short mean length of utterance
4. Communication difficulties at home
5. Communication difficulties when interacting with peers from a similar background
6. Auditory processing problems (e.g., poor memory, poor comprehension)
7. Lack of organization, structure, and sequence in spoken and written language; difficulty conveying thoughts
8. Slow academic achievement despite adequate academic English proficiency
9. Family history of special education/learning difficulties
10. Slower development than siblings (as per parent report)

11. Reliance on gestures rather than speech to communicate

12. Inordinate slowness in responding to questions

13. General disorganization and confusion

14. Difficulty paying attention

15. Need for frequent repetition and prompts during instruction

16. Need for a program of instruction that is more structured than that used with most other students

17. Difficulties affecting grammar and sentence structure

18. Difficulties in the use of precise vocabulary and overuse of words such as *stuff, things, you know*, etc.

19. Inappropriate social use of language (e.g., interrupts frequently, digresses from topic, is insensitive to the needs or communication goals of conversational partners, cannot stay on the topic of discussion, cannot take turns in conversation)

20. Poor sequencing skills. Communication is disorganized, incoherent, and leaves listener confused

21. Overall communication skills that are substantially poorer than those of peers

If a CLD student manifests many of these characteristics, a comprehensive assessment may be necessary. This assessment should examine performance in relation to the specific language experiences that the student has had.

LEGAL CONSIDERATIONS

It is well known that CLD students are overrepresented in special education programs, and this has been a persistent problem in U.S. schools for decades (Chamberlain, 2005; Crowley, 2003; McCardle, Mele-McCarthy, Cutting, Leos & D'Emilio, 2005; Rueda & Windmueller, 2006).

Professionals responsible for conducting special education evaluations need to be aware of legal mandates governing the assessment of CLD children. Recent federal legislation (IDEA, 2004) has emphasized the prevention of inappropriate identification and mislabeling of ethnically and linguistically diverse students. The key mandates of IDEA (2004) and other laws are summarized below (for more detailed information, see Crowley, 2003; Hardman et al., 2006; Moore-Brown & Montgomery, 2001).

❑ *1973 Diana vs. State Board of Education.* Testing must be carried out in the student's primary language. Assessment teams must document the appropriateness of special education placement by collecting extensive supportive data.

❑ *1974 Lau vs. Nichols.* Schools need to provide primary language programs to ensure equal education opportunities for CLD students.

❑ *1974 PL 93-380. Educational Amendments of 1974.* Testing must be conducted in a nondiscriminatory manner.

❑ *1975 PL 94-142. The Education of All Handicapped Children Act* (updated in 1990 to the Individuals with Disabilities Education Act, re-updated in 1997). This law contains the following provisions designed to ensure that nondiscriminatory evaluations are conducted:

1. Personnel must make reasonable accommodations for students with disabilities and may not exclude any school-aged children solely because of the disability.

2. All children, regardless of handicap, are entitled to an appropriate and free education.

3. Informed consent must be obtained in the primary language.

4. Testing and evaluation materials and procedures must be selected and administered in a non-discriminatory manner.

5. Testing and evaluation materials must be provided and administered in the language or other mode of communication in which the child is most proficient.

6. Accommodations may include alternative forms of assessment and evaluation.

7. Tests must be administered to a child with a motor, speech, hearing, visual or other communication disability, or to a bilingual child, so as to reflect accurately the child's ability in the area tested without being influenced by limited exposure to the English language.

8. Personnel must prepare an appropriate individualized education plan that meets the needs of the individual child.

9. Schools must educate children with disabilities in the least restrictive environment (LRE).

10. According to procedural due process, parents must be provided with the opportunity to object or consent to their child's identification, classification, placement, or individualized education plan.

❏ *1986 PL 99-457 - Education of All Handicapped Children's Act Amendment of 1986*

1. Programming for handicapped children down to age three is mandatory.
2. Incentives should be provided for programming beginning at birth.
3. An IFSP (individualized family service plan) is required that describes the services to be provided for children and their families.
4. All services must be provided by qualified personnel.

❏ *2004 Individuals with Disabilities Improvement Act (IDEA, 2004; updated from IDEA, 1997)*

1. There must be procedures to ensure that testing and evaluation materials and methods shall be provided and administered in the child's native language or mode of communication, unless it is clearly not feasible to do so.

2. Those who assess students must use a variety of data-gathering strategies and tools and may not rely upon any single procedure.

3. Evaluation materials should be used for purposes for which the assessments are reliable and valid.

4. In order to qualify students for services under the category of "learning disability," professionals no longer are required to demonstrate a severe discrepancy between intellectual ability and achievement, although individual states may continue to require this if they choose to.

5. Alternative, research-based procedures may be used in evaluating students if standardized tests are not appropriate.

6. States must permit the use of a process based on the child's response to scientific, research-based intervention (also known as RtI, or Response to Intervention). A major goal of RtI is to minimize overidentification and prevent unnecessary referrals to special education.

7. States are required to keep track of how many CLD students are being identified for special education and will be required to provide coordinated, comprehensive, early-intervention programs for children in groups that are determined to be overrepresented. Schools are now allowed to use up to 15% of their annual funds, in combination with other funds, to develop and implement coordinated early intervention services. These services are for students in all grades, with a special focus on students in kindergarten through third grade who have not been identified as needing special education and related services, but who need additional academic and behavioral support to succeed in an academic environment.

8. Additional support may include, but not be limited to the following:

    A. Offering professional development opportunities for teachers and other staff to train them to deliver scientifically-based behavioral and academic interventions

    B. Providing students with behavioral and educational evaluations, services, and supports, including scientifically-based literacy instruction

ASSESSMENT DOCUMENTATION

When conducting assessments, it is important to document, in reports, the procedures used to ensure that legal mandates are being followed. Each state has specific regulations governing the assessment of CLD students. Examples from the California Education Code (CA EC) are presented below with their implications for report writing:

1. *Legislative Requirements*: Identification procedures must be coordinated with school site procedures for referral of pupils with needs that cannot be met with modification of the regular instructional program. (CA EC 56302)

    A pupil shall be referred for special educational instruction and services ONLY AFTER the resources of the regular education program have been considered and, where appropriate, utilized. (CA EC 56303)

    Implications for Assessment: Document what regular education support services, programs, and strategies have already been utilized to help this student. Were they successful or not?

2. *Legislative Requirements:* Testing and assessment materials and procedures used for the purposes of assessment and placement of individuals with exceptional needs are selected and administered so as not to be racially, culturally, or sexually discriminatory. (CA EC 56320.a)

    Implications for Assessment: Document the validity and adequacy of the tests and procedures used in assessment.

3. *Legislative Requirements*: Tests and other assessment materials are provided and administered in the pupil's primary language or other mode of communication, unless the assessment plan indicates reasons why such provision and administration are not clearly feasible. (CA EC 56320.b.1)

Implications for Assessment: Indicate which language was used in assessment. If the student's primary language was not used, explain the reasons why it was not used.

4. *Legislative Requirements*: No single procedure is used as the sole criterion for determining an appropriate education program for an individual with exceptional needs. (CA EC 56320.e)

Implications for Assessment: Do not report the results of just one test or procedure. Use a number of procedures to justify findings.

5. *Legislative Requirements*: The assessment report shall include but not be limited to the following:

...a determination concerning the effects of environmental, cultural, or economic disadvantage, where appropriate. (CA EC 56327.g)

Implications for Assessment: Address any possible effects of the student's socioeconomic status, cultural differences, or lack of environmental opportunities that may be affecting performance.

6. *Legislative Requirements:* A pupil shall be assessed as having a specific learning disability which makes him or her eligible for special education and related services when.... a severe discrepancy exists between intellectual ability and achievements....and the discrepancy is due to a disorder in one or more of the basic psychological processes and is not the result of environmental, cultural, or economic disadvantages. (CA EC 56337.a.c)

Implications for Assessment: If the professional concludes that a CLD student has a learning disability, he or she must document the fact that the learning disability is not caused by any of the above disadvantages.

If school programs are to follow legal mandates, it is important to include a variety of approaches to assessment. Standardized tests are not appropriate measures of performance for many students who come from CLD backgrounds. However, if professionals do use standardized tests, it is important to be aware of the many biases and limitations of these measures.

✐ REFLECTION ✐

Summarize two legal requirements relating to the assessment of CLD students. What are the implications of these requirements for writing reports?

_____

_____

_____

_____

_____

NONBIASED ASSESSMENT AND STANDARDIZED TESTS

In a previously mentioned survey of 1,736 speech-language pathologists across the United States, the number one problem cited by these clinicians was the lack of appropriate nonbiased assessment instruments with which to evaluate the CLD children who were referred for testing (Roseberry-McKibbin et al., 2005). Kritikos (2003) surveyed speech-language pathologists in five different states and found similar results.

Interestingly, in the Roseberry-McKibbin et al. (2005) study, survey respondents with the most coursework in service delivery to CLD children perceived the limited availability of appropriate assessment tools as a problem more often than those with little to no coursework. Possibly individuals who had completed specific coursework were more aware of the difficulties encountered in conducting non-biased assessments. Many respondents indicated that they used standardized English tests to assess CLD students with potential communication disorders.

Many professionals rely almost entirely on the use of standardized tests to evaluate the language abilities of CLD students and to plan intervention/service delivery (Hegde & Maul, 2006). In fact, when speech and language evaluations are conducted, standardized tests are often the primary measure used in determining whether or not students qualify for special education intervention. The procedures commonly used in determining students' eligibility for special education programs are shown in Figure 12.2. Professionals in many school districts are told that they must use standardized measures in determining students' eligibility for special education programs.

Reasons for reliance on standardized testing include *legal considerations* (e.g., percentile ranks and standard deviations used as cut-offs to determine special education eligibility), *time constraints* (standardized tests are perceived as faster to score and administer than informal measures), *caseload constraints* (many schools have large numbers of students who are referred for testing due to academic difficulties), and *convenience* (standardized tests are often more automatic to administer than less structured, informal measures). Many public school professionals believe—incorrectly—that federal law requires the use of standardized tests to determine eligibility for special education services. Because of the heterogeneity of the CLD populations, other approaches are often necessary if these students are to be assessed in a non-biased manner (Mattes & Saldaña-Illingworth, 2008).

Federal law allows for subjective and qualitative measures; norm-referenced tests are not required. However, because many professionals continue to rely heavily on use of standardized tests to assess CLD students, this section addresses considerations in the use of these tests. If professionals continue to use these tests with CLD students, they need to at least be aware of the tests' potential legal, psychometric, cultural, and linguistic limitations in terms of validity and reliability.

As mentioned previously, CLD students who have been classified as "English proficient" based on conversational English language proficiency measures are often not appropriate candidates for the norm-referenced test instruments commonly used to assess students who speak English only. These instruments are often biased in favor of native English-speaking children from middle class backgrounds.

FORMAL TEST ASSUMPTIONS

The development of standardized, formal tests has grown out of a framework that is Western, literate, and "middle class." Kayser (1989, p. 232) stated that "the standardized approach to testing limits the minority student to a stimulus-response set that is considered to be a western European social communication event." For these and many other reasons, formal tests are often highly biased against CLD students (Carter et al., 2005; Roseberry-McKibbin & O'Hanlon, 2005).

It is important for professionals to be aware of the underlying assumptions upon which many formal tests are based. These inherent assumptions are extremely important to consider when working with CLD students (Chamberlain, 2005; Hegde & Maul, 2006). These assumptions hold that test-takers will do the following:

❑ Test-takers will follow the cooperative principle: perform to the best of their ability and try to provide relevant answers.

Figure 12.2

Typical Referral and Assessment Procedures

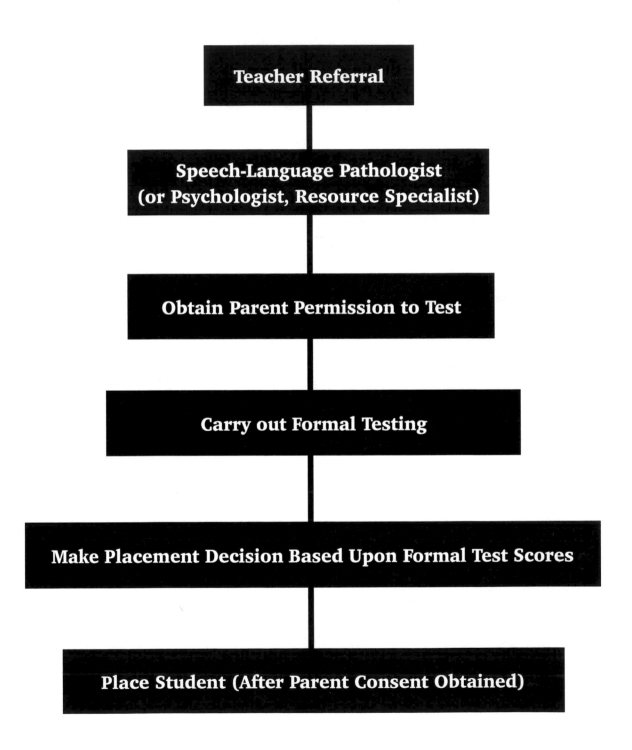

❑ Test-takers will attempt to respond even when test tasks don't make sense.

❑ Test-takers will understand test tasks (e.g., fill in the blank, point to the picture).

❑ Test-takers will have the experience background necessary to perform the assessment tasks.

❑ Test-takers will feel comfortable enough with the examiner in the testing setting to perform optimally, and will be willing to share verbal knowledge when interacting with an unfamiliar adult.

These assumptions do not hold true for many CLD students. In some cultures, individuals are expected to greet unfamiliar events with silence or to be silent in the presence of an adult (Hwa-Froelich & Vigil, 2004). In Kenya, Carter et al. (2005) found that students had no freedom to engage in prolonged dyadic play with adults. It was unusual for Kenyan children to sit and converse with an adult, especially an unfamiliar one; thus, for a child to interact with an adult was an "unfamiliar activity" (p. 390).

Many Native American children are expected to learn by listening and watching, not by verbalizing; they are not encouraged to guess when they are unsure of an answer. Neha, a Native American speech-language pathologist, described her experiences in working with Navajo children (2003, p. 5):

...I noticed that Navajo children observed an activity completely before performing it themselves. After the explanation of activities, many of them refrained from asking questions, even if they did not understand the directions. I found myself having to repeat an entire set of directions and asking them if they understood or requesting them to clarify parts I needed to repeat.

In sum, many students have had no previous experience in a testing situation. Many have had experiences that are not consistent with the experiences assumed within the test design. In addition, some CLD students do not perform optimally when the testing setting and/or examiners are unfamiliar to them and/or from a different ethnic background.

SOURCES OF BIAS IN STANDARDIZED TESTING

The bias in standardized tests can take many forms when these tests are being used with CLD students (Figueroa & Newsome, 2006; Oller et al., 2006). Some of these forms of bias are described below.

Potentially Unfamiliar Items (Cultural and Linguistic Bias)

Cultural and linguistic bias occur when the examiner uses items and activities that do not correspond with the child's experiential base. Certain test items might be unfamiliar to CLD students, especially those who have immigrated to the United States:

1. Various household objects (e.g,. blenders, microwaves)
2. Vehicles (e.g., off-road vehicles, subway trains)
3. Sports, especially those involving snow and cold weather. Sports such as football are not played in some countries.
4. Musical instruments
5. Types of clothing (e.g., suspenders, galoshes, mittens)
6. Professions/occupations (e.g., computer programmer)
7. Historically related events & people (e.g. Thanksgiving, Christmas, Abraham Lincoln)
8. Foods (e.g., apple pie, yogurt, American fruits and vegetables)

9. American nursery rhymes, fairy tales (e.g., Cinderella, Humpty Dumpty)
10. Geography (e.g. New York, Midwest)
11. Games (e.g., tag, hopscotch, Monopoly)
12. Electronic gadgets (e.g., computers, iphones, ipods)

Items Translated from English

Translated versions of English tests are often used with CLD students. There are many problems inherent in the use of translated English tests (Carter et al., 2005; Mattes & Saldaña-Illingworth, 2008).

1. Differences in structure and content between English and the primary language raise questions about the comparability of scores. Many words cannot be directly translated from one language into another. For example, some Asian languages do not have pronouns; translating "she" or "he" or "it" into these languages is impossible. Also, the difficulty level of a specific word may differ in the two languages. For example, German has three different words for "the" that vary depending on the type of word that follows (e.g., *das Buch* = the book; *der Mann* = the man; *die Frau* = the woman). In Spanish, words for "the" vary depending on whether the following noun is singular, plural, masculine, or feminine. English test translations cannot test the student's knowledge of these important distinctions.

2. Information relating to test validity, reliability, and normative data cannot be used if a test is translated.

3. Differences in background and life experiences are not considered when direct translations of tests are used.

Bias in Tests Developed in the Primary Language

Many professionals feel that they can obtain valid assessments of CLD students' language skills if they use tests specifically developed in the primary language. For example, Spanish-speaking students can be given Spanish tests, etc. However, research studies have found that there may be problems even with these tests (Peña & Kester, 2004; Restrepo & Silverman, 2001). One major problem is that much heterogeneity exists among populations that speak a particular language (Wagner, Francis, & Morris, 2005). For example, many dialects of Spanish exist, and Spanish-speaking children may come from such different countries as Cuba, Mexico, Puerto Rico, the Dominican Republic, and Spain (Brice, 2002; Goldstein & Iglesias, 2001; Mattes & Saldaña-Illingworth, 2008; Owens, 2005). Words used frequently by Spanish speakers in one area of the United States may be rarely heard in other parts of the country (Mattes & García-Easterly, 2007). The Philippines has over 100 different mutually unintelligible languages and dialects. Therefore a Filipino student who speaks Odionganon (the local dialect spoken in the town of Odiongan) can be expected to perform poorly on a test written in Tagalog, the national language.

A second difficulty is that developmental data on languages other than English is limited. Some Spanish norms for articulation and language have been developed (e.g., Goldstein & Iglesias, 1996; Jiménez, 1987; Merino, 1992) but few easily-accessible established language development norms exist for languages other than English.

There are also differences in the vocabularies and linguistic knowledge bases of students who are born in the United States and those who immigrate here at a later age. Thus, test norms obtained on students born and raised in Mexico are not valid for many Spanish-speaking students born and raised in the United States (Mattes & Saldaña-Illingworth, 2008).

Examiner Bias

Examiners may show bias in how they administer or interpret assessment instruments (Long, 2006; Roseberry-McKibbin, 2007; Wyatt, 2002). There are several potential forms of examiner bias:

❏ *Overinterpretation bias.* This type of bias occurs when examiners reach conclusions about a student's abilities based on a small sample of a student's behavior. For example, an examiner may show a picture to a child and say "Here is one shoe. Here are two _____." If the child does not say "shoes," the examiner might conclude from this one error that the child does not comprehend or use plural *–s*. This may well be an erroneous conclusion based on a small sample of the child's behavior.

❏ *Examiner sensitivity bias.* Examiners may be unfamiliar with cultural and linguistic issues affecting the student's test performance. For example, if a child is from a culture in which verbal elaboration is not encouraged, an examiner might give the child a lower score on tasks that assess expressive language skills because the examiner is unaware of the child's cultural practices.

❏ *Examiner expectations bias.* Examiners may have low expectations for CLD students and thus not provide them with adequate opportunities to respond. For example, if an examiner believes that a certain child does not know an answer to a test question, she may not give the child adequate time to process an appropriate response.

Leung (1993) stated that the evaluator is the most important instrument in the assessment of CLD students. Thus, it behooves professionals to try to ensure that they are as free from bias as possible when administering assessment instruments and interpreting results.

CONSIDERATIONS IN TEST SELECTION

Variables described as important to consider in selecting assessment instruments (Crowley, 2003; Oller et al., 2006; Roseberry-McKibbin & Hegde, 2006) are the following:

❏ *Purpose of the test.* Is the instrument used for screening or in-depth evaluation?

❏ *Construct validity.* What theory was used in the test's creation? Is one mentioned? Is it appropriate for the student being tested?

❏ *Appropriateness of test content.* Professionals should have native speakers of the student's language review the test whenever possible. Field-testing can be helpful in evaluating the appropriateness of test items.

❏ *Adequacy of norms.* How was the standardization sample selected? Are the students being tested represented in the norming and standardization?

CONSIDERATIONS IN TEST ADMINISTRATION

Professionals must consider formal test assumptions and how these assumptions might negatively impact individual test-takers. There are ways in which professionals can alter the administration of standardized tests so that they are less biased against CLD students and increase these students' chances of performing in ways that reflect their true abilities (Carter et al., 2005; Gopaul-McNichol & Armour-Thomas, 2002; Van Keulen et al., 1998; Wilson, Wilson, & Coleman, 2000). Suggestions for altering test administration procedures include the following:

❑ Provide instructions in both English and L1.

❑ Explain the reason for testing.

❑ Change the pronunciation of test items to reflect the language or dialect of the child.

❑ Rephrase confusing instructions.

❑ Give extra examples, demonstrations, and practice items.

❑ Give the student extra time to respond.

❑ Repeat items when necessary.

❑ If students give "wrong" answers, ask them to explain and write down their explanations. Score items as correct if they are culturally appropriate. RECORD ALL RESPONSES.

❑ Omit biased items that are likely to be difficult for students.

❑ Continue testing even after the ceiling item on the test has been reached.

❑ Devote more than one session to the testing.

❑ Have a parent or other trusted adult administer test items under the professional's supervision.

❑ If giving a timed test, consider how that child's culture views and prioritizes speed. If time factors are not viewed as critical, you may wish to increase the time allotted for the completion of test items.

❑ Use a "dual scoring" system designed to provide two scores: (1) the score the child receives using the scoring procedure specified within the test manual and (2) the score the child receives when responses are scored based on how they would be judged within his culture (or, if the child answers some items in L1 and some items in English, use a combined score that reflects answers in both languages).

Students may demonstrate a higher level of language proficiency for some skills in L1 and a higher level of proficiency for other skills in L2. For example, young children often know "school" vocabulary (e.g., shapes, colors) in English and "home" vocabulary (e.g., body parts, certain foods) in L1. Thus, a dual-scoring or **conceptual scoring** system that uses answers in both languages to compute a total score is more reflective of a child's actual language knowledge than a system that only accounts for answers in one language or the other (Bedore, Peña, García, & Cortez, 2005; Gutiérrez-Clellen, Restrepo, Bedore, Peña, and Anderson, 2000; McCardle, Mele-McCarthy, & Leos, 2005).

CONSIDERATIONS IN TEST INTERPRETATION

When professionals administer standardized tests, there are ways to interpret these tests that can effectively reduce bias:

❑ Do not identify a student as needing special education based on standardized test scores alone. Use informal measures to supplement standardized test scores.

❑ Ascertain whether students' errors are typical of those observed among other students from similar backgrounds.

❏ Review test results with family members and/or other persons from the student's background to gain additional insights that may be helpful in educational decision-making.

❏ Interpret overall test results in a team setting. If professionals review and interpret results without consulting with other team members, errors may occur.

❏ When writing assessment reports, be sure to include cautions and disclaimers about any departures from standard testing procedures. In addition, discuss how the student's background may have influenced testing results.

Profile

Soua L, a shy kindergarten student from a Hmong family, was referred for a special education assessment. At the end of his kindergarten year, Soua was still designated as "Limited English Proficient." However, the special education team used standardized English tests to assess Soua's speech-language, cognitive, and academic skills. Each examiner commented about how Soua was unwilling to speak or make eye contact during testing. Soua's scores on each test were significantly below the norm for the sample tested, and Soua was labeled "disordered in oral and written language." He was then placed in both speech-language and resource services for "remediation."

The next year, a new speech-language pathologist came to the school and reviewed Soua's reports and IEP from the previous year. When it was time for Soua's annual review, the speech-language pathologist carried out a comprehensive pre-evaluation process that included gathering an extensive case history from the student's parents and re-evaluating his language proficiency in English and Hmong.

A home visit was conducted with a Hmong interpreter whom the family knew and trusted. Soua's parents shared that they had been in the U.S. for only two years and that they did not know English. They confided to the interpreter that they did not understand why Soua was receiving "extra help" but that they were grateful that he was "learning more English." Soua's parents said that he learned Hmong rapidly and easily in comparison with his five siblings, and that they had no concerns about his ability to learn or remember in the Hmong language. Soua's first-grade teacher stated that he was progressing well in class, and the interpreter shared that in his five years of experience working with Hmong students in the school district, Soua "looks normal to me when he speaks in Hmong—and he remembers everything I tell him."

Soua was dismissed from special education services but continued to receive support in Hmong from an interpreter who came into his classroom twice a week. Soua was also signed up for the after-school literacy program that allowed him to work in a small group with a tutor who helped CLD students become grade-level proficient in reading. Soua's teacher was given suggestions for use in the classroom.

There are many hazards to using standardized, formal tests with CLD students (Hardman et al., 2006; Zhao, 2007). However, if professionals use these tests, they should be aware of potential forms of bias and try to control for them as much as possible. If professionals are extremely cautious in the way they use standardized tests, and if they administer and interpret them in sensitive and nonbiased ways, the tests' results may help to provide part of the answer to questions regarding the presence or absence of a language-learning disability.

Rather than relying solely on standardized tests to differentiate between a language difference and a language-learning disability, a thorough pre-evaluation process is recommended to determine whether or not a comprehensive assessment is even necessary.

THE PRE-EVALUATION PROCESS

As stated, relying solely on the typical assessment process depicted in Figure 12.2 is inappropriate when CLD students are referred for testing. When assessing these students, a team approach should be implemented, and a variety of strategies should be used to collect the assessment data. When a team approach to assessment is used, the possibilities of a misdiagnosis are greatly diminished.

There are several steps that should be completed before a student undergoes a formal evaluation. The pre-evaluation process consists of the following components:

1. Comprehensive teacher evaluation of the student's classroom performance

2. Ethnographic interviewing and the collection of a case history

3. Language proficiency testing

Again, these components should be completed BEFORE conducting a formal evaluation. When the pre-evaluation process is carried out by a team of professionals, the information gathered will facilitate decision making regarding the student's need for special education intervention. The pre-referral model shown in Figure 12.3 can be used as a guide when collecting information about a student's performance.

Teacher Evaluation of Classroom Performance

It is crucial for teachers to give detailed descriptions of the student's performance in various aspects of classroom life. The Bilingual Classroom Communication Profile (BCCP) (Roseberry-McKibbin, 1993), published by Academic Communication Associates, is an informal tool for collecting information about the student's history, background, and use of language in the classroom environment. The BCCP includes guidelines for administering the instrument and record forms for use in recording responses. The record form includes specific questions that should be explored prior to conducting formal testing. The information reported on the BCCP record form can be helpful in determining whether or not the student is an appropriate candidate for diagnostic testing.

The components and questions contained within the BCCP are described in Table 12.1. The record form includes space for recording responses and comments related to the questions asked. The Bilingual Classroom Communication Profile can be used in conjunction with other informal measures to provide a comprehensive picture of the student's use of language. An informal assessment record form that can be used in evaluating second language-learning is included in Appendix A. This form is divided into three sections:

1. *Normal Processes of Second Language Acquisition.* This form is used to record specific second language processes (e.g., interference) that the student is manifesting.

2. *Affective Second Language Acquisition Variables.* This form is used to record variables relating to motivation, personality, and socioeconomic status that may influence second language-learning.

3. *Second Language-learning Styles and Strategies.* This form is used to record comments relating to learning styles and strategies (e.g., avoidance, use of routines) that are influencing communication in the second language.

Figure 12.3

ASSESSMENT PRE-REFERRAL MODEL

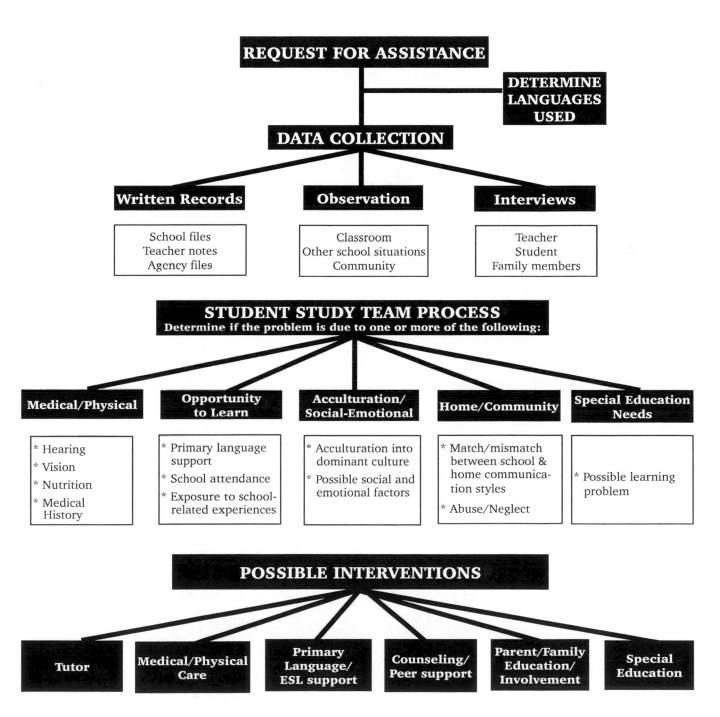

Adapted with permission from Leung (1993)

Table 12.1

Description of the Bilingual Classroom Communication Profile[1]

❏ *Background Information* - The first step in using the BCCP is to collect information about the student's background:

1. Names of individuals residing in the home with the student and their relationship to the student.
2. Countries where student has resided. The time period of residence should be recorded for each country listed.
3. First language or languages learned by the student.
4. Language used most often by the student both at home and at school.
5. Individuals who are responsible for caring for the student. The name, relationship to student, and language(s) spoken by each of these individuals should be recorded.
6. Date and circumstances in which the student was first exposed to English.
7. Previous schools attended, location of these schools, and dates of attendance.

❏ *Health Information* - Specific health concerns and the results of hearing and vision screening tests are recorded.

❏ *Instructional Strategies* - Special programs in the regular classroom that are available to students (e.g., tutors, ESL, etc.) and classroom modifications made to accomodate the student (e.g., preferential seating, special materials used, etc.) are noted.

❏ *Classroom Language Use* - The student's performance in this section of the BCCP is evaluated by asking the teacher to respond "Yes," "No," or "Don't Know" to each item. Performance is evaluated separately in English and in the home language.

   1. *Answers simple questions about everyday activities*
   2. *Communicates basic needs to others*
   3. *Interacts appropriately and successfully with peers*
   4. *Tells a simple story, keeping the sequence and basic facts accurate*
   5. *Communicates ideas and directions in an appropriate sequence*
   6. *Describes familiar objects and events*
   7. *Maintains a conversation appropriately*

❏ *School Social Interaction Problems* - A plus (+) is recorded on the record form for each statement that describes the child accurately, and a minus (–) is recorded for each statement that is false. Responses should be based on observations of the student during interactions with peers from a similar cultural and linguistic background.

   1. *Communicates ineffectively with peers in both English and the home language*
   2. *Often plays alone*
   3. *Is ridiculed or teased by others*
   4. *Is often excluded from activities by peers*
   5. *Does not get along well with peers*

❏ *Language and Learning Problems* - The teacher indicates areas of concern by responding *Yes, No,* or *Don't Know* to each item on the record form.

   Items 1-10 in this section provide an "overall performance summary."
   1. *Appears to have difficulty communicating in English*
   2. *Appears to have difficulty communicating in the primary language*
   3. *Has difficulty learning when instruction is provided in English*
   4. *Has difficulty learning when instruction is provided in the primary language*

(continuation of Table 12.1)

5. *Acquires new skills in English more slowly than peers*
6. *Acquires new skills in the primary language more slowly than peers*
7. *Shows academic achievement significantly below his/her academic English language proficiency, as assessed by an ESL or bilingual professional*
8. *Is not learning as quickly as peers who have had similar language experiences and opportunities for learning*
9. *Has a family history of learning problems or special education concerns*
10. *Parents state that student learns language more slowly than siblings*

Items 11 through 26 are used to pinpoint specific problems observed.
11. *Rarely initiates verbal interaction with peers*
12. *Uses gestures and other nonverbal communication (on a regular basis) rather than speech to communicate*
13. *Is slow to respond to questions and/or classroom instructions*
14. *Is not able to stay on a topic; conversation appears to wander*
15. *Often gives inappropriate responses*
16. *Appears to have difficulty remembering things*
17. *Does not take others' needs or preferences into account*
18. *Has difficulty conveying thoughts in a clear, organized manner*
19. *Appears disorganized much of the time*
20. *Appears confused much of the time*
21. *Has difficulty paying attention even when material is understandable and presented using a variety of modalities*
22. *Has difficulty following basic classroom directions*
23. *Has difficulty following everyday classroom routines*
24. *Requires more prompts and repetition than peers to learn new information*
25. *Requires a more structured program of instruction than peers*
26. *Has gross and/or fine motor problems*

❏ ***Environmental Influences and Language Development*** - The teacher indicates areas of concern by responding "Yes," "No," or "Don't Know" to each item on the record form.
1. *Has the student had frequent exposure to literacy-related materials (e.g., books) in the primary language?*
2. *Has the student had sufficient exposure to the primary language to acquire a well-developed vocabulary in that language?*
3. *Was the student a fluent speaker of the primary language when he/she was first exposed to English?*
4. *Have the student's parents been encouraged to speak and/or read in the primary language at home?*
5. *Has the student's primary language been maintained in school through bilingual education, tutoring, or other language maintenance activities?*
6. *Does the student show an interest in interacting in his/her primary language?*
7. *Has a loss of proficiency in the primary language occurred because of limited opportunities for continued use of that language?*
8. *Doe the student have frequent opportunities to speak English during interactions with peers at school?*
9. *Has the student had frequent opportunities to visit libraries, museums, and other places in the community where opportunities for language enrichment and learning are available?*
10. *Has the student had frequent, long-term opportunities to interact with fluent English speakers outside of the school environment?*

❏ ***Impressions from Classroom Observations*** - The teacher is asked to respond to questions designed to elicit descriptive information about the child's performance.
I. *To what extent does the student have difficulty learning in school because of limited proficiency in English?*
2. *Do you feel that this student requires a different type of instructional program than other students who have had similar cultural and linguistic experiences? Please explain.*
3. *Briefly summarize the communication and learning problems observed in the school setting.*

Table 12.2 is a reproducible assessment tool that can be used to collect information related to the student's conceptual development.

Ethnographic Interviewing

A challenge that confronts many professionals is that of learning about cultural differences and their impact on performance in the school environment. When a student is being considered for a special education assessment, it is crucial for the assessment team to understand that student's culture. When professionals acquire this understanding, they can make informed decisions about the child's performance abilities and instructional needs. One way to gain this cultural information is through the use of **ethnographic interviewing**.

Ethnographic interviewing, a data collection technique originally used by anthropologists, makes it possible to obtain information from the point of view of a cultural informant. In other words, the purpose of the ethnographic interview is to help the interviewer get the perspective of the particular culture that the student is from. In the ethnographic interview, the interviewer asks a cultural informant questions about such issues as cultural values, traditions, and attitudes. Cultural informants can be the student's parents, family members, or they can be persons from the local community who are indirectly involved with the student. Interviews can be general (e.g., about a certain cultural group), or can pertain to a particular student.

Westby (1990, p. 105) gave several suggestions for conducting and developing rapport in an ethnographic interview:

1. Explain the purpose of the interview so that interviewees understand why they are being interviewed (e.g., "You told me on the phone that you were concerned about Juan's stuttering at home; I'd like to find out more about that so we can help him here at school.").

2. Avoid "why" and "what do you mean" questions because they may have a judgmental tone. Questions of this type give the impression that clients know the cause of various problems observed at school. For example, a professional might say, "Tell me more about what happens when Juan starts stuttering" instead of "Why do you think Juan is stuttering?"

3. Restate what informants say to ensure understanding.

An ethnographic interview, conducted with one or more members of the student's culture, can include but should not be limited to the following questions (adapted from Mattes & Omark, 1991):

1. Why has the student's family left the homeland?

2. Why have they settled in the local community?

3. Did the community members come from the same area in the homeland?

4. What is the typical family size and constellation in the community?

5. What is the typical family hierarchy of authority?

6. How are children expected to behave with an adult?

7. What behaviors are expected within the culture to show courtesy (e.g., speaking only when spoken to, avoiding eye contact with authority figures)?

8. What are the family/community concerns (e.g., jobs, food, etc.)?

9. Are the members of the student's cultural group experiencing poverty?

10. How does this cultural group view the role of regular education and the role of special education?

Table 12.2

Linguistic and Conceptual Development Checklist

Student's Name: _____ Date of Birth:_____ Chronological Age:_____

Language Spoken: _____ Person Completing Form:_____

Questions	Yes	No	Don't Know
❏ Has the child been regularly exposed to L1 literacy-related materials?	___	___	___
❏ Is the child's vocabulary in the first language well-developed?	___	___	___
❏ Was the child's L1 fluent and well-developed when s/he began learning English?	___	___	___
❏ Have the child's parents been encouraged to speak and/or read in L1 at home?	___	___	___
❏ Has the child's L1 been maintained in school through bilingual education, L1 tutoring, and/or other L1 maintenance activities?	___	___	___
❏ Does the child show interest in L1 maintenance and interaction?	___	___	___
❏ Is the English classroom input comprehensible to the child?	___	___	___
❏ Does the child have frequent opportunities for negotiating meaning and practicing comprehensible output in English?	___	___	___
❏ Has the child had frequent exposure to enriching experiences such as going to museums, libraries, etc.?	___	___	___
❏ Has the child's school attendance been regular?	___	___	___
❏ Has the child had long-term exposure to standard English models?	___	___	___

The more "yes" answers that are checked, the more likely it is that the child has a good conceptual foundation for language and academic learning. The more "no" answers that are checked, the more likely it is that the child has underdeveloped conceptual and linguistic abilities due to limitations within the school and/or home environment, language loss, limited English practice opportunities, inadequate bilingual services, or a combination of these factors.

11. How does this cultural group view the role of individuals with disabilities?

12. What role does religion play in the cultural group's daily life and decisions?

The Case History

It is crucial to gather a case history for the particular student who is being considered for special education assessment (see Appendix B). Although this can take some time, the information will be helpful in planning for instruction (Centeno, 2007; Gildersleeve-Neumann, 2007). The parent report has been found to be an excellent and valid way to help the professional distinguish a language difference from a language-learning disability (Gutiérrez-Clellen, 1998; Peña, Iglesias, & Lidz, 2000; Restrepo, 1998).

The case history can be obtained from the student's parents or other available relatives who have some knowledge of the student's background. Uncles, aunts, siblings, and grandparents can provide valuable information, especially if they serve as the student's primary caretakers. Professionals can utilize the services of a trained interviewer who is fluent in English and the student's primary language. Experienced professionals find that when parents can speak with someone from their own cultural background, they often feel more comfortable during the interview/case history gathering process.

If an interpreter is used, the interviewer and interpreter need to prepare carefully for the interview in order to ensure its success. The parents/interviewees must understand the purpose of the interview and the questions that are being asked (Wyatt, 2002). Some parents may feel that the case history questions are personal and, therefore, inappropriate. If parents understand why the questions are being asked, however, they will probably feel more comfortable and will be less likely to be offended by the interview questions.

Educational professionals should attempt to develop rapport with parents, create a comfortable atmosphere, and ask open-ended questions that will encourage parents to express themselves freely. I have found that parents often become overwhelmed when confronted with a large team of school professionals in a formal meeting. At times, parents speak most freely when they are in a small, informal setting with only one or two professionals and an interpreter present.

When gathering a case history, professionals must also consider the role that poverty may play in a child's academic and linguistic performance. Although professionals should not ask parents direct questions about their socioeconomic status, answers to questions relating to the home environment often provide this information. Moreover, children's school records may give professionals an idea of whether or not the family is of low-income status.

A thorough coverage of the impact of poverty on academic and linguistic performance is beyond the scope of this book, but generally, it is important to be aware that research from many disciplines indicates that poverty can strongly influence student achievement (Chamberlain, 2005; Payne, 2003; Roseberry-McKibbin, 2008). Students from CLD low-income homes especially may experience disproportionate school failure. These students are often referred inappropriately for special education assessment and tend to be less likely than other students to be referred to programs for the gifted (Coleman & Southern, 2006; Cruzado-Guerrero & Carta, 2006; Hosp & Reschly, 2004; Kitano, 2003; Lohman, 2005; Skiba et al., 2005; Swanson, 2006).

Language Proficiency Variables

Before considering a special education assessment, it is important to deal with language proficiency issues. There are several steps involved in determining language proficiency and dominance:

1. Determine the student's primary language.

2. Determine language dominance.

3. Determine oral and written proficiency level in each of the languages spoken by the child.

Terms commonly used in discussions relating to bilingual students' language abilities are defined below:

- **primary language** - the language the student learned first and used most frequently in the early stages of language development. Information regarding language use in the home is best established through carefully conducted parent interviews and home language surveys.

- **dominant language** - the language spoken most proficiently by the student. The dominant language may change if there are changes in language usage patterns in the child's environment. Moreover, language dominance can vary depending on what aspect of language is assessed (e.g., syntax vs. vocabulary).

- **language proficiency** - the child's level of skill in the use of a particular language.

Whenever special education assessments are conducted, an important preliminary step is to find out the student's relative proficiency in the languages spoken. Schools often make use of individuals who do not have specialized training in language to administer these tests. However, professionals must be sure that language proficiency tests have been administered by trained personnel.

Measurement of a child's language proficiency should consist of three steps:

1. *Request that parents complete a language background questionnaire.* Language background questionnaires provide information about the languages used in the home.

2. *Conduct parent or teacher interviews.* Parent and teacher interviews provide information about the child's language use and proficiency in the home and in classroom situations.

3. *Use information obtained from direct and indirect language measures.* Direct measures of proficiency in a child's two languages yield scores that can be helpful in identifying strengths and weaknesses in each language.

The focus in language proficiency testing is shifting from assessment of knowledge of grammatical forms to the assessment of communication competence. Proficiency testing should provide information about the students' competence in the functional use of language and their effectiveness in using language in all social domains.

Traditionally, language proficiency has been measured using discrete-point tests that yield a proficiency score in each language. It is common practice in public schools for students to be considered "proficient" in a language when they are able to speak and listen to the language with a basic level of conversational fluency. Most language proficiency tests assess speaking and listening skills only. These measures are often highly structured (e.g., *yes-no* and *fill-in-the-blank* questions) and provide little or no information about the child's effectiveness in using language in natural speaking situations.

Researchers in prior years have stated that limiting proficiency testing to the assessment of speaking and listening skills is often appropriate (Hernández-Chavez, Burt, & Dulay, 1978; Ortiz, 1984). Many children attending school in the United States, for example, have no formal education in their first language. These children are likely to perform poorly if tests administered in the first language require reading or writing skills. If proficiency tests that require reading and writing skills are used, they should be used in conjunction with oral communication measures.

The neglect of the academic (reading and writing) side of language competence, however, has negative ramifications. Professionals must keep in mind that the student's level of proficiency in a language can vary depending on the aspect of language being assessed. For example, a student who is proficient in daily conversational English does not necessarily have the cognitive-academic language proficiency skills necessary for success in reading and writing. Children who have learned to answer questions and to share experiences often give the appearance of being fluent in a language. Problems, however, are often observed in situations that require specific and precise responses (Mattes and Saldaña-Illingworth, 2008).

These students may also experience difficulty in situations where contextual information is limited. Skill in reading requires students to construct meaning from textual information based on what they know about language and how it is structured. The cognitive demands placed upon the student in reading and writing activities are much greater than those required for success in an informal conversational setting. As mentioned previously, it takes only about two to three years for a second language learner to acquire basic interpersonal communication skills. The cognitive-academic language skills necessary for success in classroom reading and writing activities generally reach a level commensurate with that of monolingual English speakers in five to seven years, but it may take even longer (Cummins, 2000). Thus, as we have emphasized, a CLD student who is labeled "English proficient" on the basis of a basic conversation skills-oriented language proficiency measure may, in fact, not have the language abilities necessary to function effectively in classroom academic tasks.

Mattes and Saldaña-Illingworth (2008) maintained that formal language proficiency tests often provide a limited picture of the student's language capabilities. Both social communication and the child's competence in using language to perform academic tasks are critical in planning instructional programs for CLD students and in identifying students who may be appropriate candidates for language intervention. These "tests," however, are often of limited value in identifying specific processes that are affecting the acquisition of new language skills or the strategies used by the child in situations where opportunities are available for language learning. Mattes and Saldaña-Illingworth stressed that information about how the student uses language in both social and academic contexts is needed to determine whether or not a language-learning disability is affecting classroom performance.

I have encountered numerous situations in the schools in which students identified as "English proficient" on a conversation-based oral proficiency measure were placed in special education because of reading and writing "problems" in English. The cognitive-academic aspects of language proficiency need to be considered in determining a student's need for special education intervention.

✐*REFLECTION*✐

Discuss the importance of the pre-evaluation process when CLD students are referred for special education testing. What kinds of problems can be prevented by going through this process?

_____

_____

_____

_____

_____

SUMMARY

When CLD students are struggling in school, professionals must decide whether poor school performance can be attributed to language and/or cultural differences or *to* underlying disabilities that affect school performance. Professionals must remember the following:

❑ Behaviors commonly observed among second language learners may be inappropriately labeled as "abnormalities."

❑ Testing must conform to legal requirements and must be non-discriminatory.

❑ Formal language tests do not provide a complete picture of the child's communication skills. Standardized tests have many limitations that need to be recognized and accommodated if these tests are used.

❑ It is important to use a pre-evaluation process to obtain information about the student's background and to determine whether formal special education testing is truly necessary.

❑ This pre-evaluation process should consist of several components, including the classroom teacher's evaluation of classroom performance, a case history, and assessments of the student's primary language, dominant language, and proficiency in L1 and English.

❑ Bilingual students are not language-learning disabled if they demonstrate problems in English only; difficulties must be evident in both the primary language and English.

It is often appropriate for professionals who assess CLD students to avoid using norms from standardized tests altogether because of the bias inherent in these instruments. Remember that there is absolutely NO federal law requiring the use of norm-referenced tests to identify CLD students for special education programs. If the identification of disabilities is based primarily on "percentile scores" from standardized tests, many students will be misdiagnosed and will receive instructional programs that are inappropriate for their needs.

As mentioned previously, professionals should never make educational decisions based solely on scores from norm-referenced measures. The development of "nationally normed tests" for speakers of Spanish or any of the other major languages spoken by students in our schools is not the "solution" for the problems currently being experienced in the identification of students who need speech and language intervention or other special education services (Mattes & Saldaña-Illingworth, 2008). Pre-evaluation procedures and nonstandardized, informal assessment methods, however, provide information about the student's level of language proficiency and about factors that may be contributing to problems observed in the school setting. These methods are described in the next chapter.

STUDY QUESTIONS

1. Discuss the types of bias inherent in norm-referenced tests. Why is the use of test scores from these measures so inappropriate for the majority of CLD students?

2. You are going to conduct an ethnographic interview with a family that just arrived from Romania. What are four things you will keep in mind as you prepare for this interview?

3. List five potential indicators of a language-learning disability in a CLD student.

TRUE-FALSE

Circle the number beside each statement that is true.

4. Most of the language proficiency tests currently in use assess all aspects of language (speaking, listening, reading, writing).

5. Quadrant 3 of the Diagnostic Pie includes students who have had an adequate language-learning background, show no evidence of a language-learning disability, but need more time to learn English.

6. In *overinterpretation bias*, examiners make judgments about a wide range of the student's abilities based on a small sample of a student's linguistic skills.

7. When collecting case history information, the parents should be the only ones interviewed because other relatives often provide inaccurate information in an effort to appear knowledgeable.

8. A student who has a true language-learning disability has an impairment that will affect the acquisition of any language.

9. Professionals who assess CLD students with standardized tests may be able to obtain less biased assessment results on some measures by using a dual-scoring system in which students' answers in both languages are counted in the total score.

10. The development of nationally-normed standardized tests in the primary languages spoken by students in our nation's schools will solve most problems currently being experienced in assessment.

MULTIPLE CHOICE

Circle all choices that are correct.

11. Which of the following statements are TRUE?
    A. The student's primary language is the language the student learned first and used most frequently in the early stages of language development.
    B. The student's dominant language is the language spoken most fluently by the student.
    C. The term "language proficiency" refers to the child's level of skill in the use of a particular language.
    D. If a student is labeled "English proficient," it is then appropriate to administer formal standardized tests in English and use formal scores to determine special education eligibility.
    E. IDEA (2004) mandates that in order for a student to receive intervention for a "learning disability," there must be a severe discrepancy between intelligence and academic performance.

12. Which of the following are TRUE statements about laws governing the assessment of CLD students?
    A. *Lau vs. Nichols* - Testing must be carried out in the student's primary language. Assessment teams must document the appropriateness of special education placement by collecting extensive supportive data.
    B. *Diana vs. State Board of Education* - Schools need to provide language programs in the primary language to ensure equal educational opportunities for CLD students.
    C. *PL 93-380 - Educational Amendments of 1974* - Testing must be conducted in a nondiscriminatory manner.
    D. *The 1975 PL 94-142 - The Education of All Handicapped Children Act (updated in 1990 to the Individuals with Disabilities Education Act, re-updated in 1997)* - All children, regardless of handicap, are entitled to an appropriate and free education.
    E. *The 1975 PL 94-142 - The Education of All Handicapped Children Act (updated in 1990 to the Individuals with Disabilities Education Act, re-updated in 1997)* - Accommodations may include alternative forms of assessment and evaluation.

13. Which question would NOT be part of an ethnographic interview?
    A. How are children expected to behave with an adult?
    B. Why has the student's family left the homeland?
    C. Does the family believe in corporal punishment of children?
    D. What is the typical family size and constellation in the community?
    E. To what extent are members of the student's cultural group living in poverty?

14. When teachers provide information about a student's classroom performance for language assessment purposes, they should include the following:
    A. Information about school social interaction problems
    B. Information about student's classroom language use
    C. Impressions from classroom observations
    D. Information about language and learning problems (in both the primary language and English)
    E. Documentation about the student's personal habits (e.g., eating habits, hygiene, etc.)

15. Indicators of a language-learning disability in an CLD student would include the following:
    A. Family history of special education/learning difficulties
    B. Difficulty in learning language at a normal rate, even with special assistance in both languages
    C. Lack of organization, structure, and sequence in spoken and written language; difficulty conveying thoughts
    D. A low level of proficiency in only one of the languages spoken by the student
    E. A low level of proficiency resulting from limited exposure to English

ANSWERS TO STUDY QUESTIONS
    4. False
    5. False
    6. True
    7. False
    8. True
    9. True
   10. False
   11. A, B, and C
   12. C, D, and E
   13. C
   14. A, B, C, and D
   15. A, B, and C

Chapter 13

ECOLOGICALLY VALID ASSESSMENT: PRACTICAL STRATEGIES

Outline

ALTERNATIVES TO NORM-REFERENCED TESTS

The use of norm-referenced, standardized tests poses many difficulties when professionals assess students from diverse cultural and linguistic backgrounds, as described in the previous chapter. The use of nonstandardized, informal procedures and instruments for the assessment of CLD students has become increasingly common. Many experts recommend the use of these informal methods of evaluation, either alone or in conjunction with the use of standardized, formal tests in evaluating language skills (Brice & Roseberry-McKibbin, 1999; González, 2007; Hegde & Maul, 2006; Horton-Ikard & Ellis Weismer, 2007; McLaughlin, 2006; Oller et al., 2006; Wyatt, 2002). A major advantage of informal testing is that the data obtained can be evaluated in relation to the demands of the classroom curriculum. This curriculum-based approach is consistent with the widely recognized need for outcome-based assessment.

Another major advantage of informal testing is that it allows one to evaluate the student's functioning in real-life contexts. Formal testing seldom taps these students' individualized, functional skills in their own environments. Using informal measures permits ecologically valid assessment, which considers the environment, home, and culture of the child and family (Long, 2006). But most important of all, informal assessment measures and methods that are geared toward the individual student circumvent many of the biases inherent in standardized tests (Mattes & Saldaña-Illingworth, 2008; Roseberry-McKibbin & O'Hanlon, 2005).

In the preceding chapter, it was stated that federal law (IDEA, 2004) does not require the use of formal, standardized measures in the special education assessment and placement of students. Thus, professionals can be assured that federal law allows the use of subjective, qualitative measures in the assessment of CLD students—as long as a team approach is used and the measures are equitable, valid, and nondiscriminatory. It is best to use a combination of formal and informal measures in assessment (see Figure 13.1).

Informal measures often rely on observational data. Developing skill in observing students enables professionals to report information that can be compared to information obtained from language samples and other measures. Combining the information from these data sources provides a broader base for making instructional decisions than the use of any single strategy. Skill in informal assessment enables individuals who are most familiar with the students to collect meaningful, quantifiable data that can be used in developing instructional objectives and in determining the most appropriate educational environment for students.

In this chapter, nonstandardized, informal procedures for assessment are described. General suggestions for use of these measures are the following:

❑ *Use authentic, performance-based assessment.* Evaluate the child's performance within the classroom setting by evaluating portfolios of completed work, essays, stories, and other materials.

❑ *Take advantage of curriculum-based assessment to determine the child's level of functioning and performance in the classroom setting.*

❑ *Use a dynamic approach to assessment.* Evaluate the student's performance over time. This is highly preferable to a static approach in which the student is tested in one or two assessment sessions (Roseberry-McKibbin & Hegde, 2006). Take advantage of the IDEA (2004) concept of Response to Intervention (RtI), described later in this chapter.

Figure 13.1

TEAM APPROACH TO COMPREHENSIVE ASSESSMENT

ASSESSMENT WHEEL FOR MULTICULTURAL STUDENTS

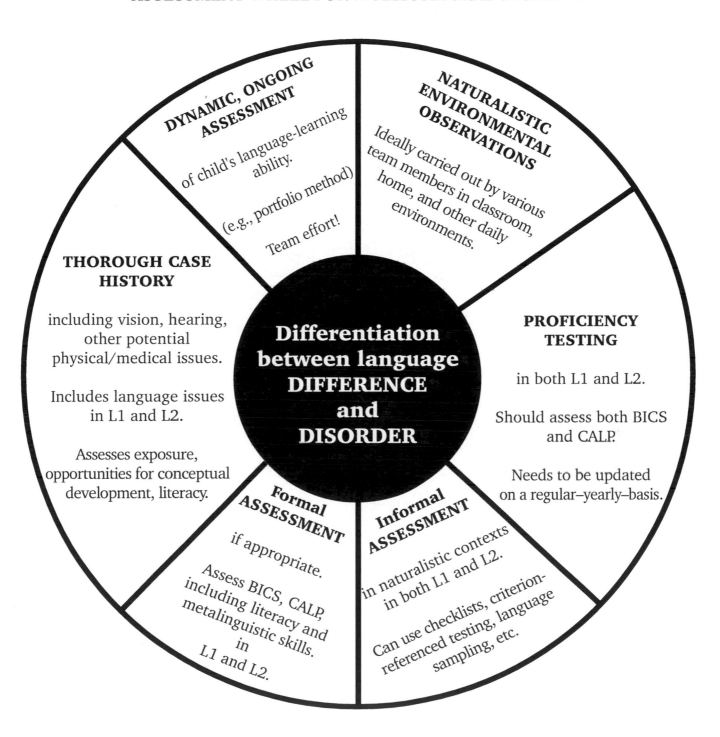

❑ *Evaluate the student's ability to learn language.* Because so many students have had limited exposure to mainstream school concepts and vocabulary, they do poorly in formal testing situations. Thus, professionals should evaluate ability to learn rather than focusing only on identifying the student's current level of functioning. Students who have normal language-learning ability but limited experiences will generally learn new language rules readily, while students with genuine underlying language-learning disabilities will have difficulty learning language rules (Peña et al., 2001). Students with disabilities usually require more repetition in their instructional programs than students who are developing language in the typical manner (Mattes & Saldaña-Illingworth, 2008).

❑ *Evaluate communication holistically.* Focus on the functional aspects of language as the child uses language to communicate meaning and to meet the demands of various communication situations.

❑ *Collect observational data in a variety of naturalistic contexts.* It is important to evaluate the student's ability to interact in everyday situations. The use of multiple observations in naturalistic settings makes it possible to obtain information about the child's overall communication behavior in a variety of situations. Professionals can observe students in the classroom, at recess, at lunch, in the library, in the home, and in other settings.

❑ *Use questionnaires to obtain information from individuals who interact with the student* (Centeno, 2007). The use of questionnaires gives a broad picture of the student's communication functioning in daily contexts.

❑ *Use narratives. Assess the student's ability to construct narratives and to remember stories that have been heard.*

❑ *Use natural language samples.* These samples can be used to evaluate students' communication skills.

❑ *Use school records of students' achievement and performance.* A review of the student's cumulative record file may yield helpful information.

Criterion-referenced measures, parent interview questions, and other informal assessment tools make it possible to examine mastery of specific language structures and the student's effectiveness in using language for specific purposes. Mattes and Saldaña-Illingworth (2008) have created a comprehensive collection of informal assessment measures and observational record forms that can be used to obtain information about the bilingual student's performance in both the structural and functional aspects of communication. Many of these assessment tools were developed specifically for use with individuals from Spanish language backgrounds but can be adapted for use in other languages.

The use of language samples, observational techniques, and informal assessment measures will increase the likelihood that students with communication disorders are accurately identified and that culturally and linguistically appropriate programs of instruction are developed to meet their needs. These measures make it possible to plan intervention programs based on how the student functions in the classroom and in various social contexts.

REFLECTION

You are a new professional in a school district that requires special education personnel to use only standardized measures in the assessment of CLD students. You are told by an administrator in the school district that the law mandates the use of standardized scores and that other types of assessment methods will not be considered in educational decision-making. Summarize what you will share with this administrator.

_____

_____

_____

_____

_____

DYNAMIC ASSESSMENT OF LANGUAGE-LEARNING ABILITY

Program placement decisions are often made based on static assessment procedures in which test scores are obtained during one or two testing sessions. It was stated earlier that this is a less than optimal approach to testing. It was also stated that a major difficulty with static assessment is that the information obtained represents the child's performance at one point in time. If testing is conducted once a year, the child's instructional objectives for an entire year are usually based on these results.

Dynamic, ongoing assessment of students' learning holds much greater promise for obtaining accurate measures of the abilities of CLD students (McCardle et al., 2005). Dynamic assessment determines the child's capacity to learn rather than just assessing the child's knowledge at one point in time. The **dynamic assessment model** is characterized by a *test-teach-retest* format that focuses on the learning process (Peña et al, 2001, 2006). Dynamic assessment allows the examiner to observe how the student learns rather than focusing entirely on what the student already knows.

The Diagnostic Pie was described previously as a graphic representation of the dilemma many professionals face when attempting to determine whether a student manifests a language difference or a language-learning disability. Some students may show typical behavior in acquiring language skills, but limitations of environmental experience and/or linguistic exposure prevent them from developing the skills assessed on standardized tests. Many students come to school with a background that, while adequate for effective functioning within their culture, has not prepared them for demands of the typical classroom in this country. They may be labeled "disabled" because they enter school lacking skills that most of their classmates have already mastered. Other students have a true, underlying disability that has impeded their learning of language. Differentiating these students from those described above is difficult, as both groups do poorly on standardized tests. This is where dynamic assessment can be especially helpful.

Few researchers have empirically addressed the dynamic assessment of language-learning ability in bilingual student populations (Roseberry & Connell, 1991). However, Ukrainetz, Harpell, Walsh, and Coyle (2000) studied two groups of Native American children. Children in one group were from a Shoshone background, and children in the other group were from an Arapahoe background. Based on teacher reports and examiner observation of these children in the classroom setting, the children were labeled as "stronger" or "weaker" language learners. All children were assessed using dynamic assessment procedures.

Findings of the study showed that differences between pre- and post-test performance and modifiability scores were consistently greater in the "stronger" language group. Ukrainetz et al. (2000), suggested that dynamic assessment can be considered as one potentially reliable and valid way to assess the language-learning ability of CLD children. Professionals who wish to evaluate language-learning ability must first understand the theory underlying language-learning assessment.

Theory Underlying Language-Learning Assessment

Reuven Feuerstein, a Romanian philosopher/practitioner/scholar, developed the Theory of Structural Cognitive Modifiability. This theory was based on many years of experience working with low-functioning children from over 70 cultures. He worked with Holocaust survivors, children from concentration camps, and immigrants from Persia, Morocco, and the former Soviet Union, among others. Feuerstein's theory gave birth to the Learning Potential Assessment Device (LPAD). The major tenets of Feuerstein's theory and the LPAD are summarized here:

❏ Conventional tests and most other current methods of assessment are static measures that "passively catalog children's current knowledge and measure their...level of functioning" at one point in time (Cummins, 1984, p. 199). These tests accept a student's current level of functioning as a predictor of how well the student will function in the future.

❏ The LPAD attempts to assess the child's "zone of proximal development" (Vygotsky, 1962) which shows what the child can achieve with active help from a more knowledgeable person such as an adult.

❏ The LPAD focuses on students' ability to profit from learning experiences when presented with instructional activities in which they are able to apply their problem-solving ability and to demonstrate that they can improve their performance. Thus, students may be able to demonstrate problem solving skills that might not even become evident in a formal test situation. This approach makes it possible to observe performance in natural learning contexts and, therefore, provides useful information about the thinking processes being used.

❏ All children are modifiable.

❏ Adults must engage children in mediated learning or purposeful directed activities.

❏ Adults need to use instrumental enrichment (IE) or specific materials and exercises along with guidance and direction in activities.

The LPAD itself can take several days and up to 25 hours to complete with an individual student. This is a very daunting proposition for professionals who must assess many students! However, professionals can utilize the concepts provided by Feuerstein to develop approaches to assessment that examine the student's actual functioning over a period of time.

Practical Implications of Language-Learning Assessment Theory

Learning potential can be informally assessed in classrooms by observing how rapidly students acquire knowledge and skills when instruction is provided in a manner that is context-embedded and culturally relevant. It has also been suggested that professionals compare students' assisted performance with their unassisted performance in order to evaluate their ability to learn when provided with help in a "guided participation" format. Professionals can also use a *pretest-training-*

posttest paradigm that evaluates a student's ability to learn when provided with relevant instruction. However, this can be time-consuming for both professionals and students (Peña et al., 2006). Carter et al. (2005), found, when working with students in Kenya, that using dynamic assessment techniques extended the length of testing time, and many students complained of boredom.

Mattes & Omark (1991, p. 115) presented a helpful list of questions that professionals can ask when assessing a student's underlying language-learning ability. (Professionals should always be sure to compare students with peers who come from similar cultural and linguistic backgrounds):

❏ *How much structure and individual attention is needed for the student to acquire new language skills?* Students with language-learning disabilities usually need more prompts, modeling, and repetition than their peers.

❏ *During instructional activities, to what extent does the student exhibit off-task behaviors or inappropriate responses?* Language-learning disabled students may give responses that are off-topic or inappropriate. Because their problems make learning difficult, they also may show off-task behaviors such as fidgeting, annoying other students, and generally not attending to task.

❏ *To what extent does the student require instructional strategies that differ from those that have been used effectively with peers?* Strategies that have worked effectively with CLD students may not be effective with students who have language-learning disabilities and, therefore, these students require a more "customized" approach to instruction.

Response to Intervention (RtI)

As previously stated, RtI may be used as a form of dynamic assessment of a student's ability to learn when provided with instruction. RtI was mandated in the IDEA (2004) as a way of minimizing misidentification and over-referral of certain groups of students to special education. Today, researchers from many disciplines have recommended the use of RtI with CLD students suspected of having special education needs as an excellent "first step" toward assessing ability to learn when provided with instruction (Barerra, 2006; Chamberlain, 2005; Klingner et al., 2006; Montgomery & Moore-Brown, 2006; Nelson, 2007; Poon-McBrayer & García, 2000; Wagner et al., 2005). The American Speech-Language-Hearing Association (ASHA, 2007) has collaborated with other regular and special education associations to describe RtI and its role in helping students succeed.

Chamberlain (2005, p. 199) described RtI as "pre-referral intervention" designed to help general education teachers appropriately assess the needs of their underachieving students and provide effective instruction for these students. RtI builds on the idea that collaborative, systematic efforts help teachers provide effective intervention for students in the regular education classroom. Chamberlain stated that this places the focus of intervention on helping teachers maintain responsibility for student achievement as opposed to viewing prereferral as a hurdle en route to a special education referral.

This may be especially important in today's high-pressure educational climate, where teachers are forced to focus so heavily on helping students score as high as possible on state standardized tests in response to the No Child Left Behind (2002) regulations. I have found that these teachers sometimes feel so pressured that they refer CLD low achievers to special education, hoping that special education will boost the students' state test achievement scores.

While this concern about raising test scores is certainly understandable, it is definitely not an acceptable answer to the challenges that teachers face in their efforts to improve learning. RtI has a much better chance of actually supporting CLD students who struggle academically because it is specifically geared to increasing these students' access to the curriculum (Montgomery, 2007). And again, it is an excellent form of dynamic assessment; CLD students who do not respond to RtI when their similar peers are responding to it are often appropriate referrals for a special education evaluation (Chamberlain, 2005; Ortiz, 2001).

When observing how students' respond to classroom instruction, Mattes and Saldaña-Illingworth (2008) emphasized the importance of recording information relating to the quality of the responses produced and examining changes in behavior that occur over time. Delays in responding, off-task behaviors, and the need for frequent prompts are among the behaviors that may have relevance in planning appropriate intervention programs. Reproducible assessment forms created by Mattes and Saldaña-Illingworth can be used to record descriptive information about performance during language learning activities in both the home language and English.

Language-learning assessment is a dynamic method for evaluating students' ability to learn language over time when provided with instruction. Before referring students for special education services, professionals need to ensure that these students are given instruction in relevant and comprehensible contexts. If students are given these learning opportunities and continue to exhibit problems, the need for special education services should be examined. Placement in a program for children with communication disorders is warranted only when it is determined that a disability is the cause of the problems observed in the school setting. Problems resulting from limited exposure to English or environmental circumstances are not "disabilities."

ASSESSMENT OF LANGUAGE PROCESSING CAPACITY (INFORMATION PROCESSING SKILLS)

Research has documented that children with specific language impairment (or language-learning disability) have difficulty with information processing (Chiat & Roy, 2007; Conti-Ramsden, 2003; Munson, Kurtz, & Windsor, 2005; Leonard et al., 2007; Roy & Chiat, 2004). Gillam, Cowan, and Day (1995) stated that children with specific language impairment may exhibit a variety of verbal short-term memory deficits and may have difficulty retaining the sequential order of information. Fazio (1998) summarized studies with results supporting the viewpoint that children with language impairments have specific difficulty on tasks that require immediate, verbatim ordered recall. For example, children with specific language impairment have difficulty recalling lists of words and also do poorly on tests of auditory digit span (e.g., repeating a number sequence such as "6-3-5-1").

Difficulty repeating a series of nonsense words, or "non-words," appears to be a measure that is particularly sensitive to memory problems in children with specific language impairment (Chiat & Roy, 2007; Hoffman & Gillam, 2004; Laws & Bishop, 2003; Marton & Schwartz, 2003; Montgomery, 1998). For example, an examiner might say to a child, "I am going to have this puppet say three silly words. I want you to say them back just like he does: *paedish, gothu, humplah*. Now you say those." Estes, Evans, and Else-Quest (2007) presented a meta-analysis of the difference in non-word repetition between children with and children without specific language impairment. They found that in comparison with typically-developing children, children with specific language impairment exhibited major impairments in non-word repetition, even when the non-words were short.

Roy and Chiat (2004) and Chiat and Roy (2007) found that use of non-word repetition tasks was effective in predicting the presence of language impairment in children as young as two years of age. Wagner, Francis, and Morris (2005) agreed that these tasks can be used with children as young as two years of age, and added that a practical advantage of non-word repetition tasks is that they are simple, which makes them easy to explain to children.

Recent research has focused on the assessment of students' information processing skills as a way to circumvent problems associated with the bias in standardized tests that measure acquired knowledge (e.g., knowledge of vocabulary), especially in CLD students (Horton-Ikard & Ellis-Weisner, 2007). Campbell, Dollaghan, Needleman, and Janosky (1997) examined the use of processing-dependent and knowledge-based measures with 156 randomly selected 12-year-old boys. Although English was the primary language in the homes of all the participants, 31% were White, and 69% came from culturally and ethnically diverse homes (Native American, Asian American, and African American). Campbell et al. (1997) administered several processing-dependent measures (e.g., non-word repetition) to the subjects; in addition, they also administered a knowledge-based test that provided information about vocabulary.

Results of the study by Campbell et al. showed that while there were no significant differences between CLD students and White students on processing-dependent measures, CLD students scored significantly lower than White students on the knowledge-based measure that tapped vocabulary. The researchers concluded that knowledge-based measures may be biased against CLD students and suggested that professionals avoid this bias by using processing-dependent measures such as non-word repetition that do not tap prior knowledge and experience.

Dollaghan and Campbell (1998) developed a battery of measures designed to assess information-processing skills. They compared these measures with knowledge-based standardized tests and found that the processing measures were much more valid in assessing CLD children's language ability than the knowledge-based measures. Specifically, the processing-based measures were more accurate in differentiating language delays from language differences in CLD subjects.

A study by Windsor and Kohnert (2004) assessed monolingual English-speaking children and bilingual English- and Spanish-speaking children using processing-dependent measures. Like Dollaghan and Campbell, Windsor and Kohnert concluded that processing-dependent measures have excellent potential for use in nonbiased assessment of CLD students' language skills. Restrepo and Gutiérrez-Clellen (2004) found that processing-dependent measures held good potential for use with Spanish-speaking children.

Hwa-Froelich and Matsuo (2005) showed that processing-dependent measures were also potentially useful with children who speak Vietnamese. Stokes, Wong, Fletcher, and Leonard (2006) used non-word repetition and sentence repetition with Cantonese-speaking children, and found that sentence repetition (but not non-word repetition) reliably differentiated between Cantonese-speaking students who were typically-developing and those who had language impairments. Jacobs and Coufal (2001), in their study with CLD students, also concluded that processing-dependent measures have potential for distinguishing language differences from language-learning disabilities in CLD students.

Professionals must be careful, however, to use only stimuli that are phonologically familiar to the children being tested and that are consistent with their articulatory abilities (Wagner et al., 2005). For example, the use of non-words with consonant clusters might be biased against Asian students whose languages do not contain these clusters (Hwa-Froelich & Matsuo, 2005). Young children might also have difficulty producing consonant clusters, even if those clusters exist in the primary language. In addition, bilingual children may display differences in their processing skills, depending upon their current stage of bilingual development (Gutiérrez-Clellen, Calderon, & Ellis Weismer, 2004). Lastly, non-words should not represent real words (e.g., *ganana* for *banana*) because then children can access their lexical knowledge and thus the validity of the task as a measure of information processing is contaminated (Wagner et al., 2005).

Some recent research has investigated the use of information-processing tasks to assess the presence of reading disabilities in CLD students (Swanson, Saez, & Gerber, 2006). Swanson et al. used tasks such as digit repetition forwards and backwards as well as word memory with Spanish-speaking low-income children. They concluded that "...these measures are particularly well suited to identify children at risk for reading problems in their second language" (p. 262). This research is very preliminary but may hold promise for professionals who must decide if CLD students' lack of progress in reading is due to an underlying disability or to other cultural, linguistic, and/or environmental factors.

More research is needed to assess the efficacy of language-processing tasks in distinguishing language differences from language-learning disabilities in CLD students, but again, the use of these tasks has been shown to be promising (Horton-Ikard & Weismer, 2007; Kohnert, 2004; Meschyan & Hernández, 2004).

Laing and Kahmi (2003, p. 51) emphasized that:

The use of processing-dependent dynamic measures with ELL (English Language Learner) students is appealing for a number of reasons. They are not biased toward life experience, socialization practices, or literacy knowledge, and they are quick and easy to administer...It is very advantageous to use assessment measures that do not rely on a child's prior experience or world knowledge...Performance on non-word repetition and working memory measures has been found to be highly correlated with language impairment and second-language vocabulary acquisition in adults and children. *When children perform poorly on processing-dependent measures, there is a high likelihood that they will have some type of language-learning difficulty* (italics mine).

Profile

Tran, a Vietnamese 14-year-old high-school freshman, was referred for special education assessment. He had a history of learning problems dating back to kindergarten, but school personnel were concerned about mislabeling him. The student spoke Vietnamese as his dominant language and had limited proficiency in English. Thus Tran participated in non-special education support programs such as tutoring and ESL small-group work, but he was never evaluated for special education. His high-school teachers were concerned because Tran had greater difficulty remembering information than his Vietnamese peers. Several teachers confided that "I tell Tran something, and five minutes later he's forgotten it." Tran had few friends and was beginning to show signs of a clinically significant behavior problem. His parents were concerned because he had stated that he wanted to join a gang.

The speech-language pathologist, working with a Vietnamese interpreter, conducted a dynamic assessment screening to evaluate Tran's ability to learn. He found that Tran was slow to learn new information and concepts, even with repeated demonstrations and explanations in both English and Vietnamese. Tran was unable to repeat a sequence of more than four digits (immediate rote memory) in either Vietnamese or English. The interpreter conversed with Tran at length about various topics, and noted that Tran often gave inappropriate responses. Tran also never initiated topics during the conversation. The interpreter said that "When Tran tells me something, I don't know what he's talking about—he makes me confused." The speech-language pathologist scheduled a formal evaluation for Tran because he suspected an underlying language-learning disability.

Assessment of Rapid Automatic Naming (RAN) Skills

Students who have difficulty with written language (e.g., those diagnosed with dyslexia) tend to perform poorly on Rapid Automatic Naming (RAN) tasks (Goldsworthy, 2003; Roth, 2004; Wolf, Bowers, & Biddle, 2000). The Clinical Evaluation of Language Fundamentals:4 (CELF: 4) (Semel, Wiig, & Secord, 2005) has a RAN subtest in which the examiner asks the student to name shapes and colors as rapidly as possible. For example, the student must look at rows of colored shapes and say "Red star, blue circle, green triangle, yellow square." etc. The assessment of RAN has been found to be helpful in identifying naming speed deficits and possible reading disorders in students from several language backgrounds (Wiig, Langdon, & Flores, 2001; Wiig, Zureich, & Chan, 2000).

I have experimented with the use of the RAN subtest of the CELF:4 for the past several years with bilingual students at the school where I work part-time. Anecdotally, I have found this subtest to be useful with the bilingual student population. If these students know shape and color concepts in English, the RAN is a relatively non-biased assessment tool to help in identifying disorders affecting the acquisition of literacy skills. More research is needed to validate the efficacy of using the RAN to assess disabilities affecting reading in CLD students.

Profile

Emilio A., a native speaker of Spanish, was referred for a special education assessment by his second grade teacher, Mrs. X. She noticed that he struggled academically to a much greater degree than other Spanish-speaking students in her class, and was concerned about his progress. Retention was being considered.

I conducted an oral language screening, and found that Emilio's conversational skills in English were excellent. Although identification of written language disabilities is not the job of the speech-language pathologist at my particular school site, I decided to administer the RAN subtest of the CELF:4 to Emilio to see whether or not he might need to be referred for a possible disability affecting written language.

Emilio struggled mightily with the RAN. He skipped shapes, rubbed his eyes, and asked me to please stop administering this subtest. He showed visible signs of distress. He scored lower than would be expected for his age level. I referred Emilio to the site resource specialist and psychologist for further assessment. After a prolonged period of assessment in both English and Spanish, Emilio was diagnosed with a severe reading disorder. He now receives support from the resource specialist for reading and writing.

LANGUAGE SAMPLING

In assessing oral communication, many experts recommend gathering a spontaneous language sample in English and in the child's primary language. Some experts give specific strategies for counting C-units and T-units and utilizing this data (e.g., Goldstein, 2000; Gutiérrez-Clellen et al., 2000; Paul, 2007; Owens, 2004; Washington, Craig, & Kushmaul, 1998). General suggestions for language sampling are presented below.

❑ *Collect language samples in familiar contexts such as the classroom or home.* When a variety of locations are used, assessment yields a more accurate and representative picture of the student's language.

❑ *Use a variety of conversation partners.* Conversational samples are often obtained in situations in which an adult "interviews" a child. Although these samples can be diagnostically useful, the information obtained may be quite different from that obtained when the student interacts with peers. Student interaction with peers is one of the most important sources of information regarding a student's use of language in social contexts. Samples can also be collected while students interact with siblings or parents. Samples of this type provide information about family interaction patterns, social relationships between peers, and so forth.

❏ *Collect the sample in several different settings over a period of time.* It is recommended that three oral samples be obtained in which the communication partners interact for at least 10 minutes. Each sample should be obtained on a different day.

❏ *Tape-record the language sample for analysis.*

❏ *Ask a bilingual speech-language pathologist to evaluate the primary language sample.* If one is not available, knowledgeable professionals who speak the primary language can listen to the sample and give their impressions. Bilingual community members may need to be used if the services of a bilingual professional cannot be obtained. Ideally, at least two native speakers should transcribe the sample. The information obtained should be discussed in detail with the bilingual speech-language pathologist.

❏ *Analyze both content and form.* It is important to examine the student's morphosyntactic (grammatical) usage in both English and the primary language. However, professionals must also evaluate the student's communicative competence in various settings.

❏ *Remember that grammatical errors in English are sometimes a result of interference from the student's primary language.* One should not label a student "language-learning disabled" based only on grammatical errors in English. Grammatical errors are to be expected among second language learners who have had limited exposure to the "rules" of English.

❏ *Ensure that the student is relaxed when a language sample is collected.* The student may verbalize very little if the person conducting the assessment is unfamiliar to him or her. The student may also experience anxiety if the testing is conducted in an unfamiliar environment. It is important to establish rapport with the student and to establish an environment in which the student feels comfortable. Children often verbalize more during interactions with familiar adults.

As a cautionary tale, however, Genesee et al. (2004), described how they tried to gather language samples from Inuit children in northern Canada. Genesee and colleagues set up the language sampling situations in which Inuit-speaking children talked with Inuit-speaking teachers.

Genesee et al. (2004) explained that "...we had made one very significant oversight in setting up this procedure. Inuit children are not accustomed to, nor are they comfortable with, talking to adults. The end result was that the language samples collected by the teachers contained very limited language and were very misleading" (p. 35). Genesee and colleagues recommended that in cases such as these, language samples might be based on children's conversations with other children. In this particular study, Inuit children who talked with other Inuit children used vocabulary and grammatical structures that were much more complex than those used when talking with teachers.

Suggestions for Eliciting Language

It is important to elicit a large quantity of verbal responses as language is used for various speaking purposes. Recommendations for eliciting language samples include the following:

❏ Use interesting, culturally relevant materials such as toys, puppets, and picture books. Older students might enjoy magazines with articles focusing on specific topics such as sports, motorcycles, etc. Make sure that the materials are culturally relevant for students and that the students have prior experience with the materials.

❑ Ask students to talk about the steps required to complete a task such as playing a favorite game, cooking a certain dish, fixing a bike, etc.

❑ Have students tell a story about something they did, or have them talk about a book they have read.

❑ Ask students to describe television shows or movies that they like to watch.

❑ Ask students to describe objects of different shapes, sizes, and textures.

❑ Present pairs of related picture cards. Ask students to choose pictures that go together and to explain how they are related.

❑ Present the student with a group of pictures from a specific category (e.g., several types of food) and with a picture that doesn't fit in that category (e.g., picture of a car). Ask the student to choose the picture that is unrelated and explain why it is unrelated.

❑ Have the student sequence story picture cards and tell the story in both the primary language and English. Recent research has shown that having students generate stories can be more effective for eliciting long utterances than some other methods (Southwood & Russell, 2004).

❑ Present problem situations verbally or in picture form and ask students to resolve the problems. For instance, students might be asked to describe how a child should react if peers do not want him or her to play on their team.

❑ Ask the students to give directions to a location (e.g., home, local grocery store, etc.).

❑ Play barrier games with identical sets of objects. A student is selected to arrange pictures of objects on a board. The other students cannot see the pictures on this board. After arranging the pictures, the student describes the picture arrangement and another student tries to duplicate it based on the verbal information presented. There are other variations of barrier games that can be used (e.g., building a tower with blocks, drawing a picture, etc.).

❑ Present students with pictures or objects and ask them to explain how these items are similar and how they are different.

EVALUATING LANGUAGE USE

It is critical to analyze student interactions in natural communication situations with peers from similar cultural and linguistic backgrounds. Mainstream monolingual English-speaking students may not respond readily to students who are not yet fluent speakers of English (Rice, Sell, & Hadley, 1991). In addition, students should be judged by comparing their performance to that of peers from their own culture and language background.

If a communication disorder is suspected, problems in the functional use of language need to be documented based on observations of the student in natural speaking situations. Some of the behaviors commonly observed in students with communication disorders include the following:

❑ Nonverbal aspects of language are culturally inappropriate.

❑ Student does not express basic needs adequately.

❑ Student rarely initiates verbal interaction with peers.

❑ When peers initiate interactions, student responds sporadically.

❑ Student replaces speech with gestures and communicates nonverbally when talking would be more appropriate.

❑ Peers give indications that they have difficulty understanding the student.

❑ Student often gives inappropriate responses.

❑ Student has difficulty conveying thoughts in an organized, sequential manner that is understandable to listeners.

❑ Student shows poor topic maintenance.

❑ Student has difficulty with presuppositions (providing background information that the listener needs in order to understand the topic of the conversation).

❑ Student has word-finding difficulties that are caused by factors other than the child's limited experience in using the language.

❑ Student fails to provide significant information to the listener.

❑ Student has difficulty taking turns appropriately during communicative interactions.

❑ Student perseverates on conversation topics.

❑ Student fails to ask and answer questions appropriately.

❑ Student needs to have information repeated, even when that information is easy to comprehend and expressed clearly.

❑ Student often echoes what is heard.

In addition to assessing the student's mastery of various language structures, it is important to examine how language is used functionally in various social settings. When a student speaks two languages, language samples should be analyzed in both languages. Performance should always be compared to that of peers from similar backgrounds. Language sampling provides valuable information about students' communication skills that is necessary to differentiate language differences from disorders (Mattes & Saldaña-Illingworth, 2008).

Profile

M. S., a 12-year-old Mien girl, was referred for speech-language testing because she was having academic difficulties. M. S. was born in Thailand, and came to the United States with her family in 1980, as refugees from Laos. M. S. had received a kidney transplant when she was in third grade and missed school frequently due to medical concerns. She had undergone a period of elective mutism during the dialysis. Mr. S. had no concerns about M. S.'s development in Mien. He stated that he and his wife had noticed that M. S. was slower to develop English than her siblings. After the dialysis was completed, however, her English language skills had shown rapid growth.

The speech-language pathologist worked with a Mien interpreter, using informal dynamic measures administered in Mien. M. S. performed well on these measures. She had more difficulty, however, when these measures were administered in English.

Members of the school assessment team argued that M. S. should be placed into a class for students with communication disorders. The speech-language pathologist strongly disagreed with this recommendation, stressing the need for a descriptive analysis of oral communication in natural speaking contexts.

The first time the speech-language pathologist attempted to obtain a spontaneous language sample, M. S. said almost nothing despite repeated attempts to elicit language. M. S. did not know the speech-language pathologist, and the testing room was unfamiliar to her. The speech-language pathologist then talked with M. S. on several different occasions to establish better rapport with her.

Once rapport had been established, a second attempt was made to collect a language sample. In addition to obtaining an informal conversation sample, M. S. was asked to describe pictures.

E = Examiner   M = Student

E: What's the girl doing?

M: Eating breakfast.

E: Can you tell me more about that?

M: The girl is eating breakfast in the morning.

E: What is happening in this picture?

M: Drinking milk.

E: What else is happening?

M: The parent is drinking milk and smiling.

E: What about in this picture?

M: Baking.

E: Can you tell me more?

M: They are having a party and they made turkey and bacon and they had fruits and cake.

The topic then changed to M. S.'s home life. The speech-language pathologist asked about the child's experiences when living in Seattle.

M: In Seattle I did [go to a party]. They make egg roll and they bake some corn muffin . . . and we had turkey and bread stuffing and mashed potato and gravies. I make the mashed potato and they make the turkey . . . we all help. They say if they don't help, they don't get some.

The speech-language pathologist then encouraged M. to talk about her current home life.

M: Yeah, sometime my mommy go to the clinic. . . my mom's go home. And I had to take care of my little baby brother—it's Lim. Sometime I carried him in my back with . . . I don't know how to call it. Sometime my mom tell my daddy. . . my daddy say tell him what to buy . . . like baby diaper, baby's powder, some bread and butter and plants. . . my daddy like plants. So we buy vegetable like broccoli and fruit like strawberry.

Analysis

It was previously mentioned that this young Mien student did not speak to the examiner during the first attempt to gather a language sample. The examiner had seen this behavior when working with other Asian children—they were often very shy initially and due to cultural differences (not disorders!) would not speak willingly with an unfamiliar authority figure. During this second session, however, M. S. seemed much more relaxed because she was no longer interacting with a "stranger."

It was interesting to note that M. S.'s initial descriptions of pictures (a standard technique for eliciting verbalization in children) were quite brief. When asked to elaborate, however, M. S. gave longer, more detailed responses. When topics relevant to her experiences were introduced, M. S. talked enthusiastically and gave detailed responses.

M. S. produced frequent grammatical errors. Plural noun endings, for example, were omitted. This grammatical form, however, is not used in Mien and is commonly omitted by second language learners from Southeast Asia. Problems with verb endings were also commonly observed. M. S.'s level of proficiency in English grammar was felt to be adequate, however, considering her limited experience in using the language.

Assessment Summary

The following points can be made based upon this brief case study:

❑ Although M. S. did manifest some grammatical errors, the errors produced did not seem to be abnormal considering her Mien language background and her limited experience in using the English language. She gave the examiner clear verbal explanations and manifested very appropriate language usage.

❑ M. S.'s language skills in her primary language, Mien, were superior to her English skills (based on comparisons of assessment measures in Mien and English). Her basic interpersonal communication skills were adequate in English, although she had not yet developed the cognitive-academic language proficiency necessary for success in an academic curriculum in which English was used as the language of instruction.

❑ M. S. did not qualify for speech-language intervention or for placement in a self-contained classroom for children with severe communication disorders. A program for teaching English as a second language, however, was appropriate.

USE OF NARRATIVES AND STORY-RETELLING

Many researchers have recommended that language evaluations include an assessment of the students' ability to construct narratives and retell stories (e.g., Fiestas & Peña, 2004; Gutiérrez-Clellen, 2004; Peña et al., 2006; Wong et al., 2004). Professionals must remember that mainstream U.S. culture favors topic-centered narratives characterized by a linear flow of events with a clearly delineated beginning, middle, and end. There is usually a limited number of main characters, a problem that occurs, and a resolution to that problem (Chamberlain, 2005). However, not all cultures utilize this narrative pattern. There are cultural differences in rules for narrative construction and story-telling that must be taken into account when evaluating students' narrative skills (Bliss, McCabe, & Mahecha, 2001).

For example, van Keulen et al. (1998), stated that most standardized tests are scored based on criteria that require use of a **topic-centered style** when telling stories. In this style, as discussed in chapter 4, there is structured discourse on a single topic, elaboration upon the topic, and lack of presupposed shared knowledge. However, among many working-class African Americans, the **topic-associating style** is typically used. Some African American students may show a preference for lengthy narratives and may embellish a story with exaggeration, jokes, slang, and metaphors (Champion & Mainess, 2003). Traditional examiners may view students who use this style as being disorganized because the topic-associating style is characterized by presupposition of shared knowledge, lack of consideration for detail, and structured discourse on several linked topics.

On the other hand, Japanese children may tell stories in a style that is exceptionally succinct in comparison to how children from other cultural and linguistic backgrounds tell stories. This is because many Japanese value discourse that is implicit and relies heavily on the empathy of the listener (Gutiérrez-Clellen & Quinn, 1993). Spanish-speaking children may focus, in their stories, more on descriptive information related to personal relationships and family (Mahecha, 2003; McCabe, 1997). These examples illustrate the great importance of taking children's backgrounds into account when evaluating narrative skills.

During the evaluation, professionals can ask the student to tell a familiar story, to create a story, or to retell a story. When using story retelling, it is important to use culturally appropriate stories that are within the student's realm of experience. When evaluating students' stories, professionals should consider factors such as story organization, effectiveness in making the sequence of story events comprehensible to the listener, and skill in describing important story events.

Story-telling can be used alone or in the context of a spontaneous language sample. Professionals should ask the following questions when evaluating the student's narrative skills:

❑ Does the student organize the story in such a way that it can be easily understood?

❑ Is the information in the story comprehensible to the listener?

❑ Does the student give elaborated comments, opinions, and explanations that are relevant to the story? Or does the student give minimal or even irrelevant comments?

❑ Does the student include all the major details of the story?

❑ If questioned, can the student remember specific details from the story?

THE PORTFOLIO METHOD OF ASSESSMENT

Definition

A portfolio is a box, folder, notebook, or other container that holds materials by and information about a student. Portfolios are a dynamic assessment tool that can be used to obtain performance data in a variety of areas over a period of time (Oller et al., 2006). Portfolios engage teachers and students in a continual process of mediated learning and self-reflection that can be used to develop programs of instruction that are highly individualized (Falk-Ross, 2002).

Characteristics of a Portfolio

❑ A portfolio may contain the following:

1. Student work samples such as writing, art work, science and math projects, social studies reports
2. Video or audiotapes of the student's performance
3. Language samples collected in English and the primary language over time
4. Teacher and parent observation notes
5. Lists of books a student has read

6. Illustrations and pictures drawn by the student

7. Pictures of students' creations (e.g., 3-dimensional art or building projects)

❏ Portfolios are valuable in developing instructional programs for a variety of reasons:

1. They promote student creativity and independence.

2. They help students more fully understand their abilities and strengths so that they can set their own goals.

3. They help students understand learning as a process, not a product.

4. They provide a multidimensional view of students' development.

5. They include information that can be used to track and evaluate students' performance over time.

6. They include information relevant to evaluating the effectiveness of instruction.

7. They can be used to provide parents with samples of the student's achievements.

8. They give professionals a better picture of students' abilities than that revealed by standardized tests.

9. They reflect the student's performance within the classroom curriculum and provide a picture of the types of educational opportunities students have been given.

10. They can be used to generate discussion topics during student-teacher conferences.

11. They help parents understand that the professionals working with their children have specialized knowledge.

12. They engage students in learning and promote an understanding of how learning facilitates the achievement of specific goals.

How to Create and Use Portfolio Assessment

There are many ways that portfolios can be created and used. The following are general suggestions that can be tailored to each student's needs:

1. Teachers and students can make choices together about what goes into the portfolio. Students and teachers can each have separate sections within the portfolio for holding specific items.

2. Portfolios are used to showcase the best examples of students' work.

3. Teachers and students periodically review the portfolio together to assess achievement, effort, etc. Students can also review one another's portfolios in small groups.

4. Students share their portfolios with parents.

5. At the end of the year, students are given their portfolios to take home. Selected portions of the student's work can be maintained by the school as a record of progress.

6. Assessment teams can review students' portfolios to evaluate performance changes over time.

7. Special education personnel can set up portfolios for students at I.E.P. time. They can also use portfolios as part of the pre-referral process.

8. Portfolios are public documents; confidential information should not be included.

✐REFLECTION ✐

List and briefly describe two reasons why the use of portfolio assessment with CLD students is advantageous in obtaining valid assessment data.

_____

_____

_____

_____

_____

USE OF INTERPRETERS

In addition to using the above-described methods of informal, nonstandardized assessment such as portfolios, schools are often using interpreters for assistance in family conferencing, assessment, and intervention (Rojas, 2006). The term "interpreter" is used in this chapter to refer to a bilingual individual who translates written information or who facilitates communication between speakers who do not speak the same language. The role of the interpreter may include translating forms, administering tests, interviewing parents, translating for parents and teachers, and so forth. Finding interpreters is often not an easy task, especially if there are few people in the community who speak the target language.

Family members can be used effectively as interpreters in some situations. It is often difficult to use family members, however, in situations requiring that test items be administered in a predetermined format (Anderson, 2002). Sometimes family members tell the child the answers or show signs of being upset if the child has difficulty performing specific tasks.

Criteria that should be used in selecting and using interpreters have been described (Hegde & Maul, 2006; Langdon & Cheng, 2002; Mattes & Omark, 1991; Murphy & Dillon, 2008). These criteria are explained below, and include (most importantly) the characteristics of interpreters.

Characteristics of Interpreters

1. Interpreters must be trained for their roles.

2. Interpreters must have excellent bilingual communication skills. Interpreters must possess good oral and written proficiency in both English and the primary language.

3. Interpreters must understand their ethical responsibilities. Interpreters must be able to maintain confidentiality at all times. They must also be honest about their abilities and limitations.

4. Interpreters must act in a professional manner. It is important for interpreters to be able to function on professional teams. Interpreters must understand the importance of punctuality, impartiality, responsibility, and professional dress.

5. Interpreters must be able to relate to members of their cultural group. Some interpreters may have grown up in circumstances quite different from those of the students and families with whom they work. Others may speak a different dialect than the students and their families. Interpreters should have the ability to relate to students and families and should be able to establish rapport.

6. Interpreters need good short-term memory skills so that they can record information and report what they learn from contacts with parents and students.

7. Interpreters should help facilitate communication between families and professionals by explaining how cultural differences might be impacting an interaction.

School districts should provide funding so that interpreters can be paid for their services. Interpreters take their jobs more seriously when compensation is provided.

Training Interpreters

When interpreters are being trained, it is optimal for school districts to work together to provide the training. This type of collaboration can reduce costs and promote cooperation between school districts.

The training of interpreters will vary depending on the nature of the interpreters' responsibilities. The following areas are recommended for inclusion in the training of interpreters:

1. Characteristics of speech-language disorders and learning disabilities
2. Information about first and second language acquisition
3. Guidelines for distinguishing language differences from disorders
4. Special education terminology relevant to their roles in working with family members
5. Role of the interpreter on the team
6. Goals of special education testing
7. Procedures for administering tests
8. Cultural differences and their impact on assessment
9. Strategies for interacting with families
10. Use of assessment results in placement decisions
11. Legal requirements and professional ethics

Use of Interpreters in Assessment

The professional who is using the services of an interpreter in assessment has important ethical responsibilities. It is important for the professional to do the following:

1. Recognize the limitations of interpreted tests.
2. Allow the interpreter only to carry out activities for which training has been provided.
3. Involve others in training the interpreter when appropriate.

4. Make sure that the "permission for assessment" form specifies that the services of an interpreter will be used during the assessment.

5. Be sure to specify in the assessment report that the services of an interpreter were used.

6. Provide the interpreter with background information about the student who is to be tested.

7. Prepare the interpreter for each testing session and debrief the interpreter afterwards.

8. Show the interpreter how to use tests and make sure that the interpreter feels comfortable with the testing. Some interpreters come from cultures in which it is not appropriate to admit that something has not been understood. It is imperative that the professional makes certain that the interpreter truly understands the assessment tasks.

9. Allow the interpreter time, before the student arrives, to organize test materials, read instructions, and clarify any areas of concern.

10. Ensure that the interpreter does not protect the student by hiding the extent of the student's limitations/disabilities.

11. Show the interpreter how to use tests.

The professional needs to be sure that the interpreter participates only in activities for which training has been provided. Family members should be informed that an interpreter will be used in assessment. It is important to prepare the interpreter for each testing session and to provide feedback following the assessment. Langdon & Cheng (2002) recommended the process of *B. I. D.*: (1) *briefing*, (2) *interaction*, and (3) *debriefing*. Interpreters should be observed during the testing sessions to prevent the following problems:

1. Recording the assessment data incorrectly

2. Prompting the student or giving clues

3. Using too many words

4. Giving directions that are too brief or too complicated

5. Over- or under-using reinforcement

It is important to remind the interpreter to write down all behaviors observed during testing, even if the behaviors seem extraneous to the immediate task. Interpreters can watch for the following behaviors in students being tested:

1. Response delays (latencies)

2. Use of gestures to replace words

3. False starts, word repetitions

4. Perseveration

5. Confusion

6. Inattention, distractibility

7. Language and articulation errors

I have found it helpful to ask experienced interpreters how the student they just assessed compared with other students from similar cultural and linguistic backgrounds. For example, a question might be, "Based upon your five years of working in Elk Grove Unified School District with 400-500 Tagalog-speaking students, how would you evaluate Cresandro's performance in comparison to these other students? When compared with other Tagalog speakers, does Cresandro stand out to you as having an inordinate amount of difficulty with talking, remembering, or listening?" Anecdotally, I have found that if an experienced interpreter states that the student in question is having difficulties different from those of similar peers, the student almost always turns out to have a language-learning disability based on objective measures. Talking with experienced interpreters has been tremendously helpful.

Use of Interpreters as Interviewers

During meetings, interpreters should be seated as close to family members as possible. It is important to introduce family members to everyone at the meeting. The parents should hear each person's name and understand each person's role as it relates to the student. It is important for family members to understand the purpose of the meeting.

Before the interview, the questions to be asked should be discussed with the interpreter. The interpreter must understand the interview questions completely and know how to record the family's responses.

The educational professional needs to be on hand during the interview to answer questions or resolve problems. It is optimal to tape-record the interview (unless this makes the family nervous or uncomfortable).

I have interviewed interpreters to obtain their viewpoints about common problems encountered in the schools. Interpreters have shared that translating paperwork (e.g., IEPs and reports) was extremely time-consuming, and they were not given enough time for these tasks. Several interpreters stated that during meetings professionals spoke for too long without pausing, and thus the information was difficult to remember and convey. Interpreters also stated that they were frequently called at the last minute and put into meetings or other situations with no preparation at all. Thus, recommendations for optimal utilization of interpreters in meetings include the following:

1. Speak in short units, avoiding slang and professional jargon.

2. Encourage the interpreter to translate the family's words without paraphrasing them.

3. Look at the family rather than the interpreter when speaking.

4. Observe the nonverbal behaviors of the family during the interview.

5. Allow opportunities for family members to ask questions.

6. Provide written information when appropriate.

7. Tape-record the interview if the family is comfortable with the use of a recording device.

It is important that interpreters have the skills necessary to explain the special education process to families. Families who are not familiar with the educational system in the United States may believe that special education is appropriate only for children with severe physical or mental disabilities. As one immigrant put it, "In my country you are either normal, retarded, or crazy. We don't have all these categories like the U.S. does" (E. Rojas, personal communication, December 2001).

The professional should always be present at interviews with family members to ensure that the appropriate information is communicated. The interpreter's responsibility is to facilitate communication between school professionals and family members. If appropriately trained, interpreters can be a valuable resource to school professionals in both assessment and intervention. The material presented in Langdon & Cheng (2002) is excellent for professionals interested in training and using interpreters.

Profile

Jacky C. was referred to me by his first grade teacher. She said that he wasn't learning optimally; that there were attention and behavior issues; and that she wondered if he might have a language-learning disability. I screened Jacky, whose English conversational skills were excellent. In his file, there was no history of language delay in Cantonese. His mother, Tao, came to the school and met with me. She cried for an hour, and I tried in vain to comfort her. She said that her husband gambled away all her earnings, and let Jacky stay up so late that he was always tired at school the next day. Tao had been a computer consultant in Hong Kong, but in the U.S., she was unable to find a computer job due to her limited English skills. She worked in a cookie store, where customers were frequently rude and condescending.

Nothing I said or recommended helped Tao feel better. Fortunately, the Chinese interpreter came in unannounced. Tao lit up and they talked animatedly for several minutes. Tao stopped crying and was all smiles as she left. The Chinese interpreter told me that Tao had agreed to go with her to a local Chinese church, where she could receive some support and advice from other Chinese parents about how to help her son succeed in school.

SUMMARY

The Native American saying below, presented in a previous chapter, has special relevance to professionals who are struggling to meet the needs of CLD students:

When you are riding along on an old horse and it dies, dismount and get a new one.

Most professionals need to dismount the old horse of standardized assessment instead of staying on the horse, kicking it, and hoping that it will be revived, get up, and go again. Instead, we need to realize that the traditional assessment practice of relying on the use of standardized, norm-referenced tests to assess CLD students is fraught with bias and difficulties.

Professionals in today's schools need to get on a new horse and utilize informal, nonstandardized assessment methods and measures that are tailored to the needs and backgrounds of individual students. These methods and measures include dynamic assessment, assessment of information processing skills, language sampling, use of narratives and story-telling, portfolio assessment, and utilization of interpreters to assist in the assessment process. When professionals assess CLD students in an appropriate, individualized, and non-biased manner, the placement of these students into appropriate educational settings will be much more clear-cut and consistent with students' needs.

STUDY QUESTIONS

1. Many professionals use the services of interpreters in the assessment of CLD students. List and describe four characteristics that you would look for in choosing an interpreter to assist in the assessment process.

2. Summarize the research regarding language information processing as it relates to assessment of specific language impairment. How might professionals apply the results of this research to the assessment of CLD students with language-learning disabilities?

3. Describe three informal procedures that the professional can use to obtain valid, non-biased information about the performance of CLD students with suspected language-learning disabilities.

TRUE-FALSE

Circle the number beside each statement that is true.

4. When an interpreter is used during meetings with parents, it is a good idea for the professional to leave the room for a period of time so that the family can confide in the interpreter.
5. IDEA (2004) mandates that standardized tests be used to evaluate the language learning ability of CLD students.
6. During language sampling, it is important to remember that grammatical errors in English are sometimes a result of the influence from the student's primary language.
7. The Theory of Structural Cognitive Modifiability was created by Reuven Feuerstein based primarily upon his work with low-functioning children from many different cultures.
8. When evaluating CLD students with suspected language disorders, it is important to compare their performance with that of monolingual English-speaking peers.
9. A primary goal of dynamic assessment is to look at a student's ability to learn—or how the student learns—rather than to assess knowledge at one point in time.
10. Although portfolio assessment is used in some school districts, norm-referenced tests are preferred because they reflect a student's performance over time on curriculum-based tasks.

MULTIPLE CHOICE

Unless specified otherwise, circle the number beside each statement that is true.

11. When professionals utilize the services of interpreters during meetings, these professionals should do the following:
    A. Look at the interpreter rather than the family when speaking.
    B. Speak in short units, avoid slang, and refrain from using professional jargon.
    C. Encourage the interpreter to paraphrase the family's words for ease of translation.

    D. Allow opportunities for family members to ask questions.

    E. Provide written information when appropriate.

12. Advantages of informal testing include the following:
    A. This type of assessment is generally ecologically valid and considers the environment, home, and culture of the child and family.
    B. Data obtained can be evaluated in relation to the demands of the classroom curriculum.
    C. This type of assessment allows professionals to evaluate the student's functioning in real-life contexts.
    D. Specific standards are specified for scoring each response.
    E. Specialized training is not needed to interpret the results.

13. Which one of the following questions is NOT critical in evaluating a student's ability to produce narratives?
    A. Can the student respond to questions by recalling specific details from the story?
    B. Does the student organize the story in such a way that it can be easily understood?
    C. Is the information in the story comprehensible to the listener?
    D. Does the student conclude the story with a "moral" or main point?
    E. Does the student include all the major details of the story?

14. In the topic-centered style of story-telling, the following elements are observed:
    A. Structured discourse on a single topic
    B. Elaboration upon the topic
    C. Presupposed shared knowledge
    D. Relational ambiguity
    E. Reduced diadokokinetic rate

15. You are evaluating a student from Argentina who may have a language-learning disability. You are conducting the evaluation in both Spanish and English. Which of the following are indicators that the communication problems observed are caused by a language-learning disability?
    A. The student has difficulty conveying thoughts in an organized, sequential manner that is understandable to listeners.
    B. The student fails to provide significant information to the listener.
    C. The student often echoes what is heard.
    D. The student shows poor topic maintenance.
    E. The student fails to ask and answer questions appropriately.

ANSWERS TO STUDY QUESTIONS

4. False
5. False
6. True
7. True
8. False
9. True
10. False
11. B, D, and E
12. A, B, and C
13. D
14. A and B
15. A, B, C, D, and E

Part 3

Intervention for Students with Special Needs

Chapter 14

FOUNDATIONS FOR EFFECTIVE SERVICE DELIVERY

Outline

One of the questions most commonly asked by professionals is, "What are we supposed to do with all these students who don't speak English?" There is no easy answer to this question, especially in a school district like the one in which I work; students from at least 80 language backgrounds are represented. Service to culturally and linguistically diverse (CLD) students is influenced by many factors: (1) availability of various services, (2) current policy and educational trends, (3) needs of students, and (4) legal considerations. Unfortunately, students' needs are often not the primary factor in determining what services they receive. Realistically, service delivery is often driven by the availability of funding; that is, how much money is available to serve the needs of CLD students? The amount of money available is driven primarily by policy trends and laws. In the 21st century, two previously-mentioned key federal laws have had a major impact on service delivery to the increasing number of CLD students in U.S. schools.

LAWS IMPACTING SERVICE DELIVERY TO CLD STUDENTS: FACTS AND RAMIFICATIONS

Most people are keenly aware that federal/state policies and the health of the national economy are key factors in determining resource allocation. Policy makers around the United States are attempting to determine ways to restructure education, especially special education. Many people feel that special education has become so expensive that new strategies for serving these students are a high priority.

There is a trend toward streamlining special education in many school programs, although many special educators are opposed to this trend. The number of students with special education needs increases as the population increases, but limited funding is available for special education programs to help these students. When Congress passed IDEA in 1975, it pledged (under IDEA Part B) to fund up to 40% of the average per-pupil expenditure for each special education student. However, today the federal government only funds 14.8% of that amount. If this funding continues at the current rate, Congress will not meet its promise to fully fund IDEA before the year 2045. Until then, many school districts will have personnel shortages and professionals with large student caseloads.

In an attempt to address this problem, the Individuals with Disabilities Education Act (IDEA, 2004) specifically focuses on prevention and early intervention (pre-referral services) for struggling students in general education classrooms, with the goal being to reduce the number of students who are eventually referred to special education. There is a strong emphasis on providing support to children who are having difficulty developing basic reading skills, especially in the early grades. Schools now may use up to 15% of their funding for early intervention with these students. If too many students from a certain group (e.g., CLD students) are placed into special education, states are asked to account for this and are required to provide comprehensive, coordinated, early intervention programs for these students.

One other major facet of IDEA (2004) that impacts regular and special education is that it allows local education agencies to eliminate the IQ-achievement discrepancy gap that formerly was mandated in order to qualify students for specific types of special education services. For example, previously in my school district, in order to qualify for support from a resource specialist, a student had to have a 20-30 point gap between IQ and achievement as documented by standardized testing. IDEA 2004 has eliminated this requirement, but some states may still choose to continue to mandate this gap for students to qualify for resource or other special education support.

Another law that has greatly impacted education in the U.S. is No Child Left Behind (NCLB, 2002). According to NCLB, students with disabilities must participate in state accountability systems for reading and math in grades 3 through 8 (alternative assessments are permitted; necessary accommodations are allowed). Schools must show adequate yearly progress toward making all students proficient in math and reading by the year 2014, or the schools will face penalties. Progress is measured almost solely by students' performance on challenging standardized tests, which puts school professionals under pressure to improve test scores. Boswell (2004) reported that it is devastating for students with special needs to take standardized tests with grade level subject matter that is inappropriate for their current needs or beyond what can be expected with IEP accommodations. Some of these students put their heads down on their desks and cry because they are so overwhelmed by the complexity of the test content.

The requirements of NCLB are a major source of stress for educational professionals working in schools with large numbers of students who are learning English as a second language (Posnick-Goodwin, 2006). Hale (2004) stated that although NCLB can be commended as an attempt to address students' problems related to school achievement, this reform does not provide the visionary national leadership to show schools specifically how to improve student achievement. Moreover, schools have generally not been given the funds to implement the sweeping curricular changes mandated by NCLB.

In response to NCLB, many school districts have pushed curriculum "down"; they are teaching more sophisticated content at lower grade levels. CLD students, especially those from low-socioeconomic status homes, struggle greatly with this and are often referred to special education because they cannot keep up with abstract curriculum that is far beyond their grasp of English. Referrals to special education are increasing as schools attempt to boost their annual yearly progress scores; in addition, some schools are reluctant to house special education classes (Boswell, 2004). I will always remember how a staff member at my son's former school talked at a parent meeting about the special education kids who "drag everyone else down" in terms of test scores.

In response to the challenges and mandates of NCLB (2002) and IDEA (2004), many schools are implementing a response-to-intervention (RtI) model (mentioned in previous chapters). RtI emphasizes the greater role of the general education teacher in scaffolding instruction for students who are struggling (Nelson, 2007). Teacher Assistance Teams provide peer support and coaching for these teachers, and a referral to special education is made only after a number of alternative teaching strategies and methods have been ineffective in improving academic skills.

EMPHASIS ON MULTICULTURALISM

In addition to implementing RtI, many schools across the United States are making efforts to include multicultural components within their classrooms. As we discussed earlier in the book, historically, the United States was viewed *as a* "melting pot"; people from around the world came to the United States, brought their cultures, and threw them into the American pot. Today, it is common to describe the United States as a tapestry or mosaic. Each thread of the tapestry is distinct and adds to the overall beauty of the object. Differences in ethnicity, religion, gender, and other personal characteristics are acceptable, worthy of being celebrated, and need not be abandoned in order for individuals to have equal opportunities to achieve their life goals (Weaver, 2006).

There are two primary "camps" of multicultural education professionals: those who support **particularism** and those who support **pluralism**. Advocates of particularism emphasize separate ethnic studies courses, separate ethnic clubs, etc. In short, some particularists reject assimilation and unintentionally widen ethnic divisions by encouraging separatism. Pluralists, on the other hand, recommend that information about various cultural groups be woven into traditional curricula. Ideally, pluralism emphasizes interconnection between various cultural and ethnic groups.

There are many reasons for incorporating multiculturalism into regular and special education curricula and activities. Children who are centered in and proud of their cultural heritage tend to be more motivated and show greater academic gains than children whose culture is de-emphasized and suppressed. If schools do not show a respect for cultural differences in learners, interactions may be guided by an expectation of inferiority. Wigginton (1992) stated:

> When students are told by a teacher or a text that they should be proud of their culture, the impact is negligible. A guest speaker at an assembly doesn't remedy the situation, nor do ethnic food festivals or once-a-week 'enlightenment' sessions. Rather, it is sustained exposure that is effective in an environment characterized by independent student research and inquiry, where aspects of a culture are discovered...and brought...to a level of consciousness and examined. (p. 224)

Multiculturalism should be infused throughout class curricula, not merely tagged on or added as a once-a-month feature. If students are in supportive environments that promote multiculturalism and multilingualism, they will be empowered to become valuable and contributing members of mainstream society.

Mainstream "majority" students need to be exposed to a multicultural curriculum for a number of reasons. First, such exposure promotes understanding of other groups and potentially reduces race-related conflict. Being exposed to multiculturalism also prepares students for workplaces in which they will be part of a multi-ethnic workforce and interact with colleagues from a variety of cultural and linguistic backgrounds. Regular and special educators need to be able to reach out to children from a variety of cultural and linguistic backgrounds.

INCORPORATING MULTICULTURALISM INTO THE CURRICULUM

By incorporating multicultural components into general education programs and special education programs, professionals can create a climate that is highly motivating for CLD students. Such components also help mainstream students to develop a better understanding of individuals from other cultural backgrounds. Foundationally, it is critical for professionals to view CLD students not as problems to be solved but rather as rich potential resources of information and experience that can benefit all students (Yeh et al., 2002). Professionals can reach out to CLD students (and enrich the knowledge of mainstream students) in the following ways:

❏ Show interest in students' home language, country, and culture.

❏ Learn a few words of a student's language, and use those words. This can mean a great deal to the student who is learning English.

❏ Use maps of the U.S. and of the world so that all students can see where their families and the families of other students have come from.

❏ Reduce students' anxieties as much as possible. A relaxed learner is an effective learner.

❏ During initial English language instruction, allow a silent period in which students are not required to respond verbally.

❏ Ask parents to come to the classroom in native country dress. Encourage them to talk about their culture and their customs.

❑ Make sure that students know that you are there to help them and that you want them to succeed. Give students special attention when possible.

❑ If nobody in the classroom speaks the student's language, assign a native-born "peer buddy" to assist the student.

❑ Encourage students to use their primary language in various contexts at school and to communicate outside of school. For example, Whitmore and Crowell (2006) found that the use of Spanish for email, restaurant work, and communication with friends in Mexico helped students to maintain their proficiency in Spanish.

❑ Represent languages of the various cultural groups in the school community by having signs in key areas (e.g., front office, auditorium) in these languages.

❑ Display objects and pictures representing various cultures.

❑ Create classroom bulletin boards that display pictures of and information about people from diverse backgrounds and cultures.

❑ Provide and read books written in a variety of languages in which diverse cultural groups are represented (Landt, 2006).

❑ Invite people from various cultural groups to speak to students and to act as resources.

❑ Give students opportunities to study their primary language and culture in required and elective subjects and in extracurricular activities.

❑ Give all students sustained exposure to multicultural activities. Don't just incorporate sporadic, "token" activities into the curriculum.

❑ Take all students on field trips to places such as Native American reservations, Japan Town, Chinatown, and other local community resources.

❑ Develop thematic units that incorporate information about various cultural groups.

❑ Present thematic units in which students learn about a specific country (Jones, 2005). In my son's after-school Discovery Club, the students study one country a month. Bulletin boards, stories, foods, and other items increase students' awareness of cultural differences, and guest speakers from the country being studied share information and answer questions. If a large number of students at the school come from particular countries (e.g., India, Vietnam, Mexico), activities focusing on these countries will be especially valuable.

❑ Use comparative study of folktales. For instance, read the story of Cinderella and ask the librarian for books with parallel stories in other cultures. Read, compare, and discuss the similarities and differences in the stories. The American and Kuwaiti versions of Cinderella, for example, have been used with young children in this country to promote cultural understanding and peace education (Al-Jafar & Buzzelli, 2004).

❑ Teach the entire class words, phrases, and songs in various languages.

❑ Have students read (either silently or aloud) a biographical sketch about a culturally and linguistically diverse leader or role model. For example, students can learn about Greg Louganis (a Samoan American diver and Olympic gold medalist), Connie Chung (a Chinese American journalist), Kristi Yamaguchi (a Japanese American figure-skating Olympic gold medalist), Martin Luther King, and other individuals who are known for their accomplishments.

❑ Celebrate the holidays of various cultures. Food, dance, and music can be included in the celebrations (Hoover & Patton, 2005). Students can even plan and carry out festivals in which families are involved. For example, in one Hawaiian school, there is a luau at the end of eighth grade. Families and community members participate by helping students with this luau (Deering, 2005).

❑ Have students interview their families and explore their family trees, characteristics of their home countries, and the family's reason for coming to the U.S. Students can write a report based upon this.

❑ Have students use the Internet to conduct research about countries in which they are interested. One American child I work with was fascinated with China, so we logged onto the Internet and found information and pictures about China. He enjoyed this activity and asked many questions. Browsers such as Google (http://www.google.com), MSN Search (http://search.msn.com), and Yahoo! (http://www.yahoo.com) can be useful (Parkyn, 2005).

By following the above suggestions, opportunities for CLD students to succeed are maximized. Multicultural activities help mainstream students to experience increased awareness, knowledge, and sensitivity to the needs of others.

One afternoon while working in an elementary school speech and language program, I asked individual students to discuss where their ancestors came from, and used a globe to help the students identify their exact countries of origin. One multiracial girl said proudly, "My ancestors are from China, Korea, and Africa." An African American boy said with great pride, "My ancestors are from Africa!" The White boy in the group paused, thought a minute, and said, "And my family is from....Sacramento!" Much can be learned about how students perceive their world and the world of others by engaging them in conversations about their family history and way of life.

Profile

A university student of mine, Fernan Tolentino, generously gave me permission to share his story. Fernan moved to the U.S. with his family from the Philippines when he was 10 years old. Fernan stressed that he felt like such an outsider coming to an American school and shared that no one showed a personal interest in him. He was under pressure to learn English as fast as possible so that he could translate for his parents in day-to-day situations and help them interact with U.S. agencies and society in general. (To this day, Fernan takes his parents to all their doctors' appointments and translates for them.) Fernan's parents stressed to him that education is the way out of poverty. His parents have a high school education; Fernan is the first person in his family to go to a 4-year college.

He stated that upon beginning to attend an American school as a 10-year old, he noticed how disrespectful American students were; he commented about the relative lack of structure in American classrooms as compared to those in the Philippines. When Fernan read aloud in class, his classmates laughed at his accent—so he stopped talking altogether for a few years. He watched the television show "The Wonder Years" in order to learn English and expose himself to standard models. Friends asked him to play football with them, which is actually kickball/soccer in the Philippines. When the football hit Fernan in the face, he realized that football in the U.S. meant something different!

Fernan stressed that it would have made a world of difference to him if even one person—teacher or fellow student—had cared about him personally and taken a little extra time to talk with him and reach out to him. He said it would have been so great if someone had learned even a few words in Tagalog and expressed interest in his life in the Philippines.

AVOIDING TOKENISM IN EDUCATIONAL PROGRAMS

When general and special educators incorporate multicultural education into their work with students, they need to avoid doing the following (Parkyn, 2005; Whitmore & Crowell, 2006):

Stereotyping

Examples: People from cultures outside the United States are shown only in "traditional" costumes and in rural settings.

The only non-Anglos shown are those who live in poverty.

The same picture is used over and over to represent a group. The diversity that exists within a population is not depicted.

Trivializing

Examples: Activities are based only on the foods commonly eaten and/or the holidays celebrated by members of a cultural group.

Parents and other family members from multicultural backgrounds are invited to school only on "special days."

The classroom has only one book about a particular ethnic group among 15 books about Anglo European Americans.

There is only one "ethnic" bulletin board in the classroom.

Misrepresentation

Examples: Pictures of people participating in an activity commonly associated with Native Americans are shown when discussing a Native American group that does not practice that particular activity.

Pictures from rural Mexico in the 1900s are used to teach students about modern-day Hispanic life in the United States.

Disconnecting

Examples: Books about specific cultural groups are read only on special occasions (e.g., reading about the Mexican culture only on Cinco de Mayo).

An instructional unit is presented about a cultural group without relating the unit to the regular curriculum.

The goal for all professionals is to incorporate multicultural education into the core curriculum as a natural part of teaching and learning. Professionals also need to reduce cultural conflicts within their classrooms.

REDUCING CULTURAL CONFLICTS IN THE CLASSROOM

There are numerous situations within the classroom that can foster cultural conflicts. The extent to which contextual factors are used to communicate meaning varies from culture to culture. In **high-context** cultures, learning often occurs by observing the actions of others, and the role of the individual as a member of a group is emphasized. Situations in which one individual tries to control the actions of an entire group are viewed as something that should be avoided. In **low-context** cultures, an emphasis is placed on the role of the individual, and information is conveyed primarily through verbal interaction. Students from high-context cultures often experience difficulty adjusting to the low-context structure of mainstream American schools (Weiss, 2002). Often, these students do not volunteer information during class, and they may fail to respond when called upon by the teacher.

The manner in which time is used can also be a source of conflict within the classroom. In mainstream American schools, rigid schedules are often followed. If an activity is not completed during the time allotted for the lesson, the teacher often moves on to the next activity. In many cultures, strict adherence to schedules is less important. Thus, a teacher in that culture may continue with a specific activity until it is completed.

Clearly, there is no single strategy that can work effectively with students from every culture. When students from many different cultural backgrounds receive instruction in the same classroom, conflicts sometimes cannot be avoided. Educational professionals must develop an awareness of cultural differences so that they can adapt their instruction to meet the needs of students. Students must also learn to adapt to cultural differences that they observe in the school environment. When professionals attempt to adapt their instruction to meet students' needs, and students learn to adapt to school expectations, cultural conflicts in the classroom are less likely to occur.

SELECTING INSTRUCTIONAL RESOURCES

It has already been stated that the type of service provided for CLD students depends on a variety of factors. One of those key factors is availability of resources or services. In some school districts, there are few, if any, bilingual education classrooms. There may be no teachers with training in bilingual education or ESL instruction. Legislation eliminating bilingual education in California has resulted in major changes in school programs, although many school districts still offer native language support in their classrooms.

Many teachers are desperately in need of services for the students in their classrooms who do not speak English. Often they turn to the speech-language pathologist for help. In the eyes of many classroom teachers, speech-language pathologists teach language skills and therefore should take responsibility for serving English language learners who are struggling with academic content in their classrooms.

Classroom teachers are often overwhelmed by the sheer numbers of students in their class-rooms and feel that they are left "holding the bag" when CLD students are their responsibility. Their concerns are valid because the available support for these students is often limited. In addition, as previously mentioned, teachers today may feel a considerable amount of pressure because of the mandates of No Child Left Behind.

In school districts with bilingual education programs, students are often offered native lan-guage instruction only for a short period of time. They struggle academically in English because they have not acquired the level of proficiency necessary for the cognitive tasks required within the classroom curriculum. Often, these students converse well in informal situations and appear to have adequate English language skills for classroom instruction. However, academically they struggle with context-reduced, cognitively demanding content. Where are teachers to turn when these students fail to learn in the classroom?

As mentioned previously, it is illegal for schools to place limited English proficient students into special education if the purpose of the placement is to teach English language skills. Only a select number of these students are truly eligible for special education services—they must have a disability.

✐REFLECTION ✐

You work as a speech-language pathologist in a school district and speak only English. Approximately 70% of the students on your caseload are from "minority" backgrounds. Describe three strategies you will use to work with these students in a culturally competent manner (either in your therapy room or collaboratively in the students' classrooms).

_____

_____

_____

_____

_____

SERVICE DELIVERY OPTIONS

There are various service delivery options available for serving CLD students. Figure 14.1 shows a continuum of non-special education instructional programs for these students to support their primary language as well as their English development. As illustrated in Figure 14.1, there is a continuum of options to support English-language learners in schools. The availability of each op-tion is often driven by individual states' policies and laws.

❏ *Maintenance bilingual education classrooms:*

1. Instruction is presented in the primary language and English.

2. The activities promote the development of proficiency in both the primary language and English.

3. The goal is to foster English development and simultaneously nurture and develop the pri-mary language.

Figure 14.1

A Continuum of Non-Special Education Options to Support English Language Learners

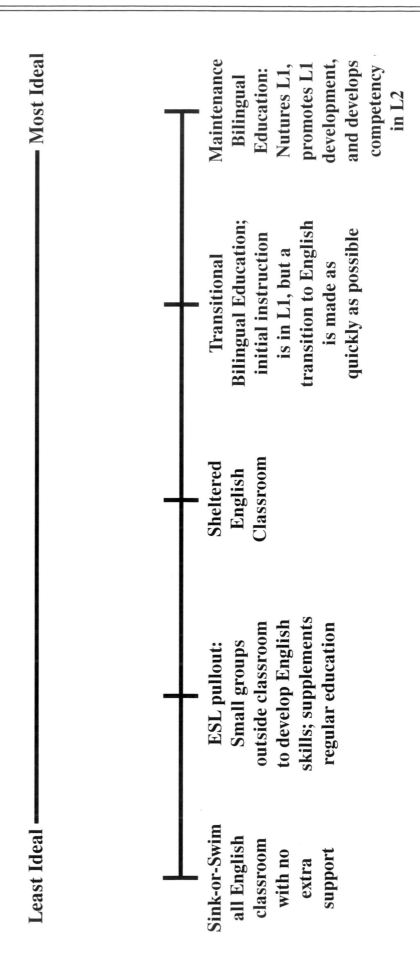

Least Ideal ———————— Most Ideal

Sink-or-Swim all English classroom with no extra support

ESL pullout: Small groups outside classroom to develop English skills; supplements regular education

Sheltered English Classroom

Transitional Bilingual Education; initial instruction is in L1, but a transition to English is made as quickly as possible

Maintenance Bilingual Education: Nutures L1, promotes L1 development, and develops competency in L2

❏ *Transitional bilingual education classrooms:*

1. Initial instruction is in L1.

2. The focus is placed on transitioning students into all-English classrooms as quickly as possible.

❏ *Sheltered English classrooms* (Echevarria & Powers, 2006; ERIC Clearinghouse on Urban Education, 2006):

1. The instructional program emphasizes the importance of making subject-matter instruction in English comprehensible to limited English speakers.

2. Curriculum activities are included to teach academic skills and content, to develop the second language (English), and to promote mastery of academic skills.

3. The instruction aims to develop intrinsic motivation and learner autonomy.

4. The curriculum emphasizes visuals, demonstrations, activities relevant to students' experiences, student-to-student interaction, adaptation of materials, and use of supplementary materials.

❏ *English as a second language (ESL) pull-out:*

1. Students are pulled out of the classroom and brought to a separate room to learn English.

2. ESL instruction is usually presented once or twice a week in a small group for 30-45 minutes.

❏ *"Sink or swim" all-English classrooms:*

1. The student is given no support in L1.

2. No ESL pullout is available.

3. The student must keep up academically with monolingual English-speaking peers with no additional support (least optimal situation).

INSTRUCTIONAL CONTINUUM FOR CLD STUDENTS WITH SPECIAL NEEDS

Around the turn of the century, if CLD students were having difficulties in the classroom, many teachers would automatically refer them for special education testing. Some teachers worked collaboratively with special education personnel to differentiate classroom instruction for these students. Others, feeling relieved that the students were now in "special ed," believed that the students' progress was now a "special education issue" and no longer their responsibility. For those teachers, it was "back to business as usual." The "problem" was handled. This paradigm is illustrated in Figure 14.2.

Sometimes students' disabilities were not severe enough for them to be eligible for special education—especially in the early elementary years. These students needed services and extra support, but they were too high-functioning to merit an IEP and services from special education personnel. Frequently, these students were in a "wait to fail" mode. As they progressed through the primary grades, their performance became so low in comparison to that of their peer group that, technically,

Figure 14.2

Traditional, "Non-Collaborative" Special Education Services

General Education Classroom

Student struggles, unable to keep pace academically

Teacher refers to special education so "experts can handle the problem" outside of the classroom

Special Education

Student receives services outside of classroom

"Expert" such as a speech-language pathologist or resource specialist assumes responsibility for "handling the problem"

IEP created for student

Classroom teacher relieved of responsibility and makes no changes in teaching methods or materials

they ended up qualifying for special education. As Posnick-Goodwin (2007) pointed out, a child could fail several grades before testing revealed a "severe discrepancy" between his academic performance and his intellectual ability.

As illustrated in Figure 14.3, today's emphasis on RtI (Response to Intervention) has made a greater continuum of options available for all students who struggle in the classroom setting—including CLD students. RtI is being implemented nationally, and the goal is to prevent failure and help all students benefit from appropriate instruction (Lloyd-Jones, 2007; Nelson, 2007). In addition, RtI may reduce the stress placed upon special education personnel by reducing the number of inappropriate referrals for testing (Chamberlain, 2005; Ortiz, Wilkinson, & Robertson-Courtney, 2006).

A major tenet of RtI is that students' progress is monitored, and there is increasingly intense and differentiated instruction based on student need (Roberts, 2007). Usually the learning activities occur in the general education classroom and an effort is made to present *scientifically-based* instruction. Ongoing professional development for school professionals is important to help them implement RtI successfully. RtI makes it necessary for teachers in the general education curriculum "to provide high-quality instruction and scientifically-based interventions that make sense for each child who's struggling to keep up" (Posnick-Goodwin, 2007, p. 6).

RtI is now part of a continuum of services for students that is divided into five levels. At Level One, the least ideal level, the teacher does not modify curriculum materials or strategies for any students who are experiencing difficulties in class. They are left to flounder, and frequently do. Fortunately, this is becoming less common as general education teachers must take greater ownership of the progress of *all* students—including CLD students.

At Level Two, the general education teacher incorporates generic modifications to support struggling students. These modifications commonly include such strategies as assigning a peer buddy, having the student in question sit in the front of the class, giving the student extra time to complete assignments, and others. Teachers work by themselves; no other professionals are called in for support. Figure 14.4 illustrates Level Two interventions that we recommend to teachers at my elementary school site.

Level Three constitutes what many experts today are calling RtI. At Level Three, the classroom teacher employs diagnostic or clinical teaching (García & Ortiz, 2006; Ortiz et al., 2006). In clinical teaching, teachers teach concepts, subjects, or skills. If students do not meet expected performance levels, then teachers reteach using significantly different approaches or strategies. They provide explicit, differential instruction designed to eliminate gaps in academic performance. The intervention cycle is repeated as needed.

Frequently, at Level Three, the classroom teacher receives support from other school personnel. This support may come in the form of a Teacher Assistance Team (TAT). TATs differ in composition in every school. Ortiz et al. (2006) stated that having access to a TAT comprised of general education teachers may encourage teachers to seek help for struggling students as soon as possible and not wait until problems are so serious that a special education referral is warranted. TATs help teachers resolve problems; they help teachers design interventions for learners who are struggling.

At TAT meetings, the learners are discussed and the teacher is helped to select relevant strategies for helping these learners. At subsequent meetings, the teacher provides feedback to the TAT about how well these strategies are (or are not) working. García and Ortiz (2006) emphasized that when teachers contact the TAT, they are requesting assistance for themselves. They are not referring students to the TAT. Again, Figure 14.4 illustrates an approach used at the elementary school where I work; this curriculum adaptation plan is used to support classroom teachers as they deal with students who are struggling in the classroom setting. This approach can be used at Level 2 or Level 3.

For teachers, being on a TAT is an excellent professional development opportunity. Oritz et al. (2006, p. 56), stated that support systems such as those provided by TATs "...may also help minimize general education's reliance on special educators...shifting responsibility for struggling learners onto special education may overwhelm the system and limit the resources available to students

Figure 14.3
Instructional Continuum for English Language Learners with Potential Special Education Needs

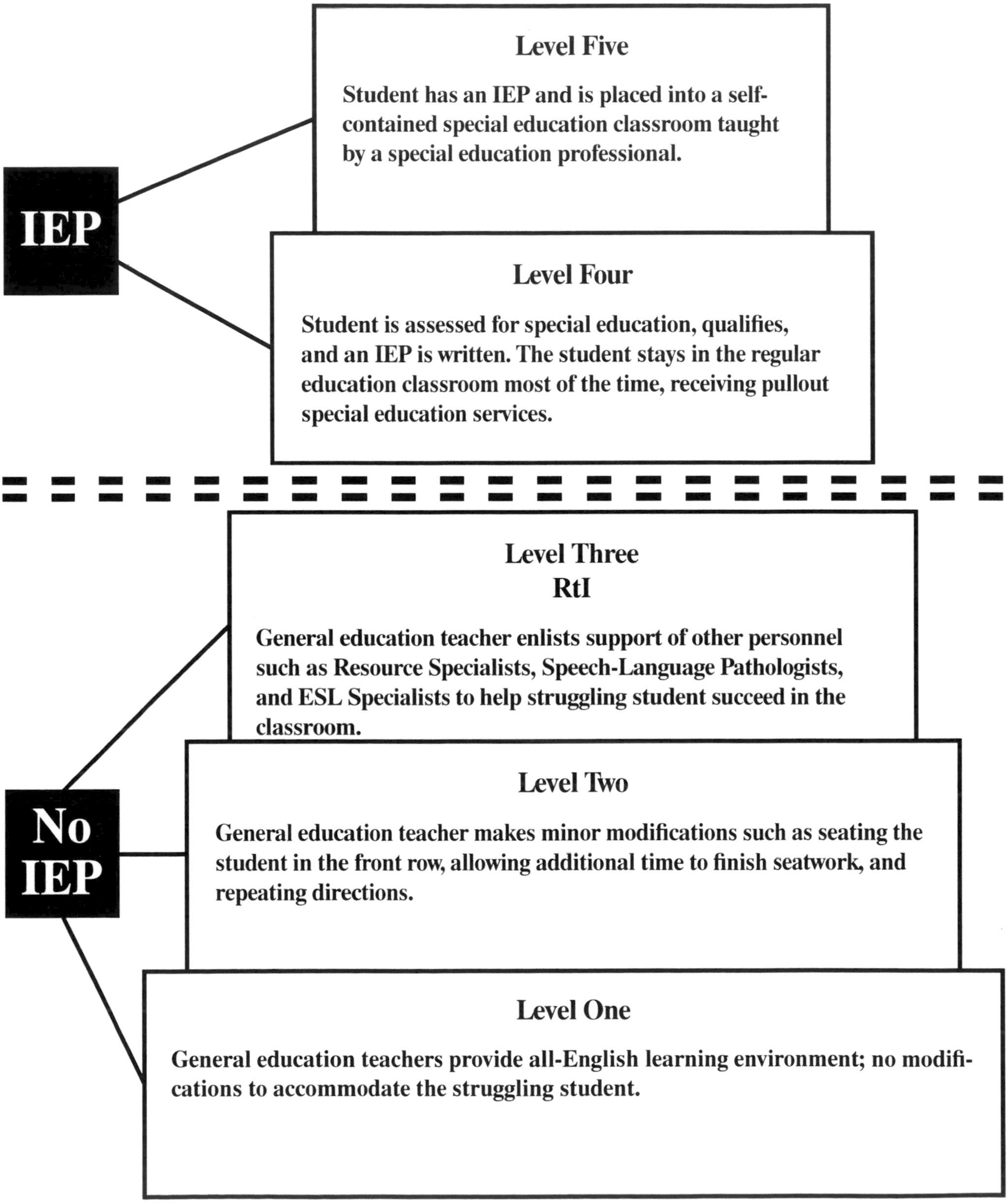

IEP

Level Five

Student has an IEP and is placed into a self-contained special education classroom taught by a special education professional.

Level Four

Student is assessed for special education, qualifies, and an IEP is written. The student stays in the regular education classroom most of the time, receiving pullout special education services.

Level Three
RtI

General education teacher enlists support of other personnel such as Resource Specialists, Speech-Language Pathologists, and ESL Specialists to help struggling student succeed in the classroom.

Level Two

General education teacher makes minor modifications such as seating the student in the front row, allowing additional time to finish seatwork, and repeating directions.

No IEP

Level One

General education teachers provide all-English learning environment; no modifications to accommodate the struggling student.

Figure 14.4

General Education Individual Curriculum/Instruction Adaptation Plan

* =Typically an accommodation   ^ =Typically a modification

*Quantity	***Time**	***Level of Support**
▲ Reduce verbal input to 1-2 instructions. ▲ Check frequently for understanding. ▲ Ask student to paraphrase information.	▲ Provide wait-time. ▲ If student does not respond, repeat, reword, rephrase information and/or question.	* Preferential Seating * Peer buddy * Collaborative learning groups ▲ Individual or small group instruction when possible
*Input	**^Difficulty**	***Output**
Use visual aids such as pictures, objects and manipulatives. Provide multiple models of expected response. Provide multi-modal instruction. State the student's name before asking him/her a question.	Prior to launching a lesson, determine the underlying skills that are required. Probe to determine the student's comprehension of those concepts as a foundation to beginning your approach to the lesson. To improve auditory attention, memory, comprehension, and note-taking abilities, scaffold response using cloze procedure in which student writes in 1 or 2 words to complete a note that has been prepared by the instructor. The teacher then writes the key word in the blank on an overhead as student says it.	Encourage student to reauditorize, visualize and to repeat information silently. Encourage student to ask a question regarding information presented. Encourage student to draw a picture to illustrate a concept or vocabulary word. Increase the number of opportunities during instruction that the student has to respond verbally using academic language.
*Participation	**^Alternate Goals**	**^Substitute Curriculum**
Pre-teach concept individually or in small group prior to large group instruction. Provide opportunities for student to answer questions that he has mastered aloud in class. In order to continually check for understanding, ask for a brief 1-2 word response. The teacher provides 2 possible answers. The last answer offered by the teacher is the correct response.	Narrow instructional focus and expected response to 1 or 2 concepts that are the most dissimilar and that will provide the most auditory and visual contrast. (e.g. The instructor may teach auditory discrimination between words in which the long vowels *ee* and *ou* are present, in order to maximize visual and auditory cues.	Differentiate instruction by teaching underlying weak or missing skills. Provide patterned practice with concepts that have not been mastered.

Developed by Barbara Koski. Adapted with author's permission.

* **Grades based on above Adaptation Plan**
▲ **Rationale/Evidence for Adaptation Plan**

_____

_____

_____

with disabilities." Again, if teachers have access to TATs composed of other teachers, they may become better at team problem-solving and be less reliant on special educators.

Speech-language pathologists are becoming increasingly involved in RtI, especially as part of language/literacy teams that attempt to increase the literacy skills of struggling students (Montgomery & Moore-Brown, 2006). Speech-language pathologists are being encouraged to decrease the amount of time they spend on traditional models of intervention (e.g., pull-out one to two times a week in a small group) and spend more time on classroom-based intervention and consultation with teachers (ASHA, 2007; Ehren, Montgomery, Rudebusch, & Whitmire, 2006; Nelson, 2007). The goal is not to add more tasks to speech-language pathologists' already busy schedules, but to have them reallocate their time to serve more students "up front" and thus decrease the eventual numbers of students who technically qualify for special education. The speech-language pathologist's schedule would reveal that less time is spent on traditional service delivery and more time is spent consulting and collaborating with classroom teachers (Ehren et al., 2006).

One highly positive aspect of using RtI is that it provides an alternative to the use of the aforementioned discrepancy model in assessing students who are underachieving. It is widely believed by experts that if students are provided with high-quality, intensive intervention and still are struggling, then they should qualify for special education (Ehren et al., 2006). The American Speech-Language-Hearing Association (2007) stated that RtI should ultimately use child response data to make educational decisions. Again, the use of RtI to determine who qualifies for special education services is a highly preferable alternative to the discrepancy model, an approach that resulted in a prolonged period of no support for many students who truly had special learning needs. As mentioned in a previous chapter, RtI can be viewed as a form of dynamic assessment—ascertaining a student's ability to learn when provided with instruction.

If a classroom teacher has implemented a variety of strategies at Levels Two and Three, and the student still is struggling when compared to culturally and linguistically similar peers, then a special education referral is made. Personnel such as the school psychologist, resource specialist, and speech-language pathologist are then able to conduct formal assessments using culturally and linguistically appropriate measures. If the student is shown to have a genuine underlying language-learning disability, then he is eligible to receive direct services outside of the classroom. These services must be provided in the least restrictive environment. Therefore, students should be pulled out of the general education classroom only to the extent to which their learning needs cannot be met within that setting.

Options for CLD Students who Qualify for Special Education

There is a range of options for CLD students who qualify for special education after RtI has been found to be insufficient for their specific learning needs. The options include the following:

1. Consultative, collaborative service provision in which CLD students remains in the general education classroom and the teacher receives assistance from special education personnel, ESL teachers, and/or bilingual staff members

2. Pull-out services in English (or, ideally, bilingual intervention) conducted one to two times a week in the specialist's room

3. Placement in regular bilingual education or Sheltered English classroom with support from special education

4. Monolingual English special education classroom (hopefully with primary language support using a bilingual teacher, tutor, etc.)

5. Bilingual special education classroom

Many monolingual English-speaking special educators feel inadequately trained to serve CLD children who have limited proficiency in English. If, however, classroom teachers, parents, special education professionals, and bilingual/ESL specialists work in a collaborative manner, many CLD students with special needs can receive appropriate instructional services.

One way to meet the needs of CLD students is by making use of tutors. Bilingual tutors can, if properly trained, work with CLD students in their primary language. In the absence of bilingual tutors, monolingual English-speaking tutors can be used to give CLD students extra attention, assistance, and social support. If peer tutors are used, a chart such as that illustrated in Figure 14.5 can be helpful in determining their specific roles and in selecting materials for them to use.

The following suggestions may be implemented, as appropriate, to locate both English and primary language tutors who can assist CLD students:

❏ Recruit high school and/or college students from various language backgrounds.

❏ Give these students credit/units for tutoring. For example, a high school Vietnamese student might receive independent study credit for tutoring a younger Vietnamese child.

❏ Seek help from local religious and/or community organizations. Religious organizations are often looking for ways to reach out to their local communities, and their members will often gladly volunteer to tutor students in school settings. Many communities have churches and religious organizations that represent various cultural/linguistic backgrounds. In some communities, for example, there are Samoan churches in which many members speak both Samoan and English. Churches that offer services in Vietnamese, Spanish, or other languages can offer valuable assistance.

❏ Recruit retired bilingual individuals. Many retired persons are active and have children and grandchildren of their own. Some communities have Foster Grandparents, a group devoted to children who need their support.

❏ Seek out community members who may be able to offer helpful suggestions for recruiting tutors.

❏ Contact the Red Cross organization to find out if they have access to multilingual individuals who might be willing to serve as tutors.

❏ Contact various branches of the legal system (police, courts) to locate bilingual interpreters and others who may be able to provide assistance.

❏ Contact businesses that have community service requirements for their employees; bilingual employees can serve as tutors to fulfill their community service requirement.

❏ Use peer tutors from the student's classroom or school. Research has shown that using cross-age tutors can be quite successful. For example, older Spanish-speaking students can assist younger Spanish-speaking students with reading. In a situation such as this, both the older and younger students' reading skills increase (Paterson & Elliott, 2006; Saenz, Fuchs, & Fuchs, 2005).

Remember that tutors need to be trained. They should observe demonstrations of instructional techniques and should be monitored closely by educational professionals. Professionals should meet with tutors regularly to assess students' progress so that appropriate goals and objectives can be carried out.

Figure 14.5

I CAN HELP - YOU CAN HELP

I KNOW

____Big Letters

____Small Letters

____Numbers 1-100

I CAN

____Write all the Big Letters

____Write all the Small Letters

____Write my Name

I CAN

____Add Numbers to ____

____Subtract Numbers to ____

I CAN

____Speak English

____Read my (Book, Story, etc.)

____Do my Worksheet

I CAN HELP YOU LEARN

____Big Letters

____Small Letters

____Count to 100

I CAN HELP YOU

____Write all the Big Letters

____Write all the Small Letters

____Write your Name

I CAN HELP YOU

____Learn to Add

____Learn to Subtract

I CAN HELP YOU

____Learn to speak English

____Read your (Book, Story, etc.)

____Do your Homework

****

YOU CAN

_____

_____

YOU CAN HELP ME

_____

_____

Source: Hearne, D. (2000). *Teaching Second Language Learners with Learning Disabilities.* Oceanside, CA: Academic Communication Associates, Inc. Reprinted with permission.

DETERMINING THE LANGUAGE OF INTERVENTION

When a student does qualify for special education assistance, a major consideration is the extent to which the first and second language will be used in the student's instructional program. Many factors need to be considered in making an appropriate decision (Long, 2006).

1. *What is the student's level of proficiency in the primary language and in English?* These skills can be ascertained by testing language proficiency and observing language usage in functional speaking contexts. If the student is considerably more proficient in the primary language than in English, instruction in the primary language will usually be more effective and efficient (Kayser, 2002; Kiernan & Swisher, 1990; Perozzi & Sánchez, 1992; Goldstein, 2000; Gutiérrez-Clellen, 1999a). Instruction in the primary language is especially beneficial when new concepts are first introduced. Once a concept has been acquired in the primary language, transfer to a second language will be easier. Much current research has emphasized the necessity of bilingual intervention to affect positive changes in language learning disabled students' ability to communicate in both L1 and English (Genesee et al., 2004; Gildersleeve-Neumann, 2007; Kohnert, 2008; Mattes & García-Easterly, 2007; Paradis, Crago, Genesee, & Rice, 2003).

2. *What resources are available for conducting treatment in the primary language?* Ideally, therapy should be conducted by a bilingual speech-language pathologist who speaks English and the child's L1. If no such professional is available, the speech-language pathologist can work in a collaborative manner with an interpreter or bilingual paraprofessional who speaks the child's L1 fluently (Kohnert, Yim, Nett, Kan, & Duran, 2005). A less-desirable alternative, if there are no primary language support personnel and the speech-language pathologist is a monolingual English speaker, is for the speech-language pathologist to collaborate with ESL personnel to develop appropriate goals and strategies for intervention that takes place entirely in English. Parents and family members, however, can often play a key role in facilitating the development of L1 language proficiencies, and their active participation in the intervention program should be encouraged.

3. *What language is used in the home?* If the primary language is not developed or reinforced in the school setting, the student may lose the ability to interact with people in the home who speak only that language. (Mattes & García-Easterly, 2007). As discussed elsewhere in this book, there are many ramifications to this situation. Parents and children who can interact in L1 often report more spontaneous, close, emotionally authentic relationships (Tannenbaum, 2005; Yan, 2003). If students lose their skills in L1 and parents speak little or no English, the quality of the parent-child connection is likely to be negatively affected (Cummins, 2000).

4. *Do the parents wish for the student's primary language to be maintained?* Sometimes parents wish for their children to learn English as quickly as possible, and they may feel that intervention should be provided in English only. Other parents wish for the primary language to be maintained and developed.

5. *Does the student wish to use and maintain the primary language?* The student's attitudes and motivation are of utmost importance.

6. *What attitudes do school professionals have about usage of the primary language at school?* Beaumont (1992, p. 350) stated that ". . . if [school professionals] ignore or merely tolerate the student's primary language, it will be difficult for the student to sustain the motivation to use

that language. On the other hand, if personnel support and develop the primary language, then students will be encouraged to maintain the primary language."

There is no simple formula for determining the language of instruction. Level of proficiency, instructional resources, attitudes of parents and students, and other factors need to be considered. In any instructional situation, it is important to start with the knowledge that the student brings to the learning task. For example, if a student comes to school speaking only Spanish, the use of Spanish in the instructional program can facilitate the learning of basic skills and the acquisition of English. Professionals must always remember that being a proficient bilingual is more advantageous than being a proficient monolingual. Thus, when possible, the development of both English and the primary language should be supported.

WRITING COLLABORATIVE IEP GOALS

Writing goals and objectives for Individual Education Programs (IEPs) is often a challenge, especially if the student speaks two languages. However, there are certain general principles that professionals can follow when writing IEPs for CLD students who need special education services:

❏ In writing objectives, an emphasis should be placed on measurable OUTCOMES (also called "benchmarks").

❏ The special educator may be a monolingual English speaker who is unable to provide direct services to the student (if the student's English is very limited). Thus, the professional may need to work with an interpreter to develop and present the instructional activities. This should be stated specifically in the IEP.

❏ The particular type of service delivery model chosen will dictate, in large part, what IEP goals are written for the student.

❏ Programs must be tailored to the individual needs of the student.

❏ The student's primary language must be taken into account.

❏ Goals related to oral communication need to emphasize overall communicative competence rather than isolated skills.

❏ Goals should focus on teaching both content and strategies for learning.

❏ Special educators should collaborate in developing objectives to avoid fragmentation in service delivery.

❏ Special educators can write several joint, collaborative goals rather than a separate list of goals for each area (e.g., Speech, Resource, etc.).

❏ The current emphasis on collaboration between professionals in general and special education programs makes it imperative to write IEP goals with a collaborative emphasis.

❏ IEP goals and objectives, in many states, must correspond with the school curriculum. In other words, they must be written so that they clearly support classroom content that students are learning (Grimm, 2006).

Ukrainetz (2006) cautioned that although it is important to work on objectives that correspond with grade-level curriculum expectations, it is still important for speech-language pathologists to attend to the underlying processes and skills required for students to become more independent learners.

Developing Collaborative Objectives that Support Classroom Curriculum

As stated, many states require that IEPs include goals and objectives that correspond with the school curriculum. In other words, they must be written so that they clearly support classroom content that the students are learning (Grimm, 2006). Examples are listed below of curriculum-relevant target behaviors that can be used as a basis for the development of IEP objectives. Specific information about the measurement task (e.g., reading a list of 25 one-syllable nonsense syllables) and mastery criteria, however, is necessary before some of these examples can be used as IEP objectives. The goals and objectives included in the IEP must be measurable.

Example 1: Martino will demonstrate the ability to label 50 new vocabulary words selected from the classroom curriculum, as measured by data obtained from teacher-made pretests and posttests, classroom assignments, and a review of progress reports obtained from the classroom teacher and the reading specialist.

Example 2: Jose will count from 1 to 50 and will demonstrate understanding of one-to-one correspondence, as measured by a review of classroom assignments and homework records maintained by the parents.

Example 3: Maria will use oral language to communicate four or more basic needs during observations in 4 mealtime situations, as measured by reports from the speech-language pathologist, classroom teacher, and parent.

Example 4: Jaime will construct a simple, sequenced narrative consisting of 50 or more words when presented with wordless books or picture cards in three or more contexts. Performance will be measured based on reports from the speech-language pathologist, reading specialist, and classroom teacher.

Example 5: Nadia will write at least three journal entries per week and will discuss the contents of each entry with a group of peers, as measured by observational records completed by the teacher and reading specialist over a four-week period.

Example 6: Tran will verbally define the mathematical terms *more than, less than, equals, whole,* and *part*.

Example 7: Jaden will accurately use each of the following fifth grade social studies terms in a sentence that demonstrates understanding of the word's meaning: *citizenship, legislative branch, executive branch*, and *judicial branch*.

Example 8: Javier will decode two-syllable nonsense words when reading a printed list.

Example 9: Katrine will add, delete, or change target sounds within words to create new words (e.g., change *cow* to *how* or *pan* to *tan*).

Example 10: Meuy will label all eight planets in the solar system when presented with a picture of the solar system and will list two descriptors about each one.

Many school professionals are using state curriculum standards to develop IEP goals and objectives. The specific skills included in these "standards", however, are often too general for use as IEP objectives. A review of state standards can be helpful in selecting areas of focus for the instructional program, but IEPs should always include a precise description of the behaviors being taught along with information about the measurement criteria that will be used (Mattes, 2007).

It is not difficult to write collaborative IEP goals when "the right hand knows what the left hand is doing," so to speak. Speech-language pathologists and other special education professionals should consult with classroom teachers so that they can develop instructional objectives relevant to the goals of classroom instruction (Roseberry-McKibbin, 2001b). Professionals should also work with families so that generalization of instructional objectives can occur in the home setting.

WORKING WITH FAMILIES

It is important for professionals to encourage families to participate in their children's educational programs (Barone, 2006; Child Trends Databank, 2003). Families vary greatly in their ability to carry out suggestions from school personnel. Some parents are able to work with their children on a daily basis. Others, however, struggle from day to day to make ends meet and find little time to spend with their children. Some families also struggle to adjust to a new country and culture and may have difficulty understanding what the school expects of them.

Kelley (2001) summarized four keys to working successfully with parents: *information, encouragement, reassurance,* and *support*. If these are provided by professionals, parents will become more involved in their children's school programs and will be receptive to carrying out the school's recommendations. In this section, specific suggestions are provided for enhancing parent and family involvement in students' school experiences.

Profile

Victor G., a third grader from a migrant Mexican family, was placed into speech-language services because he had a language-learning disability as verified by testing conducted by a bilingual Spanish-speaking clinician. The speech-language pathologist spent many hours putting together a comprehensive language stimulation "homework packet" that Victor's family could use to increase his expressive and receptive language skills in Spanish. At the end of a meeting with Mr. and Mrs. G., they expressed appreciation for the clinician's efforts. Mr. G. then said, "We live in our car. Do you have any suggestions for how we might implement these ideas given our current living situation?"

Suggestions for Conducting Home Visits

Professionals should keep the following guidelines in mind when planning and conducting home visits:

❏ Emphasize to parents that being bilingual is a great asset in our society. Many parents, in my experience, believe that schools do not support use of the primary language at home. Parents need to be reassured that bilingualism is a desirable goal. Bilingualism and biliteracy should be promoted because they provide economic, intellectual, and social benefits (Kayser, 2006). Professionals should never suggest that the family needs to speak only English for the student to succeed. To do so derives directly from patterns of coercive power relations in society (Cummins et al., 2006).

❑ Bring some of the student's completed assignments to show parents. If the assignments were completed in the primary language, it may be easier for parents to understand the problems that the student is experiencing. Portfolios with examples of a child's work over time are especially valuable when discussing the student's progress.

❑ Bring pictures showing students participating in school activities. The classroom situations shown in the pictures can be explained to the parents to help them understand what is being taught at school.

✐ REFLECTION ✐

List four general guidelines for involving multicultural families in the education of their children.

_____

_____

_____

_____

_____

ENCOURAGING COMMUNITY, HOME, AND SCHOOL SUPPORT

Support groups can be highly effective for multicultural families. Efforts should be made to recruit multicultural individuals or families who are familiar with the nature of school programs. These individuals can form support groups for families from similar backgrounds.

As has been previously stated, multicultural family members often feel more comfortable if they can interact with others from their own culture when the learning needs of their child are being discussed. If support groups are not available, families may benefit from talking to even one other person from their cultural group. Schools can set up parent information networks to help parents share information with and support one another (Yan & Lin, 2005).

Schools can also sponsor programs to help immigrant parents and their children become accustomed to the "school culture" and its educational practices (Carreon, Drake, & Barton, 2005; Roseberry-McKibbin, 2002). Programs designed to reach out to parents have been described in the literature (see Barone, 2006; Cummins et al., 2006; Tam & Heng, 2005). These programs can help families with basic needs and also provide an introduction to the U.S school system and curriculum.

For example, schools can create a parent center that has social workers and others who help support parents with their basic needs. Interpreters in this center can help parents negotiate the school's expectations. By holding monthly meetings in the evening, many parents who work during the day will be able to participate. Individuals from the parents' culture can attend these meetings to answer questions about U.S. schools and the special education services that are available to students. Topics discussed in parent programs might include the following:

❏ School routines for students that are common within U.S. schools (e.g., standing in line and taking turns)

❏ Role of the parent in helping students with homework

❏ Extracurricular activities

❏ Discussion relating to the emphasis on competition and individual achievement in U.S. school programs

❏ Discussion of the American emphasis on parental involvement

❏ Information about the instructional programs that are available for students with special needs

School professionals should encourage parents to come to the classroom to volunteer for several hours each week. Volunteering helps parents understand how to work with their children at home and increases their overall understanding of what is happening in the classroom.

Profile

Phuong, a Vietnamese kindergarten student, was referred for testing because of a possible stuttering problem. During the evaluation, he was found to stutter frequently in English.

A meeting was set up with the child's father and a Vietnamese interpreter. The father reported that Phuong stuttered in Vietnamese and English, and that his siblings teased him about the problem. Mr. L. said that when this occurred, Phuong was "sad."

The interpreter explained that services were available in the school to remediate the fluency problem. The father was very relieved and expressed gratitude that something was going to be done to improve his son's speech. He had been unaware that the school offered services to help his child.

The program placement meeting ended positively with the speech-language pathologist giving suggestions for home carryover. The father indicated that he was interested in participating in a home program.

SUGGESTIONS FOR PARENTS

When professionals interact with and learn about the student's family background, suggestions can be tailor-made for that family. Among the recommendations often made to parents are the following:

❏ Visit the student's classroom. Again, volunteer if possible. Many parents feel intimidated by their lack of English skills or their modest educational backgrounds (Lee & Bowen, 2006). These parents need to be welcomed and reassured that they have an important role to play (Posnick-Goodwin, 2005).

❏ Share folk tales, home recipes, and cultural experiences with the student.

❑ Continue to develop the student's proficiency in the primary language by presenting a language-rich environment in which the child is exposed to oral and written language.

❑ Show an interest in seeing the child's homework regularly and offer encouragement and support whenever possible.

❑ Stimulate the language of younger children, even infants and toddlers. Research shows that many families do not believe it is important to talk with very small children. Parents should be made aware of how important it is to provide language stimulation beginning early in infancy (Roseberry-McKibbin, 2000b; 2008).

Profile

Ameet S., a kindergarten student from an East Indian family, was first enrolled in a speech and language intervention program in preschool. The family spoke Punjabi at home. Ameet had been placed in a speech and language program because his performance on English language tests was "below the norm for his age." The first speech-language pathologist who worked with Ameet never examined the student's background and, therefore, was unaware that Ameet had spoken only Punjabi until the age of 3 years.

I "inherited" Ameet in my elementary school caseload when he started kindergarten. After learning about his language background, his progress in the classroom was evaluated. The teacher reported that Ameet was making good progress in learning English.

I found that Ameet's progress in English language learning was adequate and that he did not have a language-learning disability. His mother said that Ameet's use of Punjabi had developed quite well. She had never understood why Ameet was in a remedial program and was relieved to learn that these services were being discontinued.

FOSTERING FAMILY LITERACY

It is crucial for professionals to do as much as possible to foster literacy in students' homes. Rather than targeting only the student for literacy development, professionals should include the entire family. It is important to empower both children and parents by fostering literacy for the whole family (Takanishi, 2006). As stated in other chapters, parents from some cultural backgrounds may resist initially; literacy and other "schoolish" type tasks are viewed as the responsibility of the school, and not something that should be taught at home (Lai & Ishiyama, 2004). However, schools still need to take time to welcome and encourage these parents to participate; as stated, utilizing the services of interpreters from the culture can be especially helpful.

Professionals can help foster family literacy by doing the following:

❑ Create classrooms that are examples of print-rich environments with many magazines, books, and posters available to students.

❑ Help parents learn where to find quality reading materials that are inexpensive. Places to find these would include flea markets, used book stores, library sales, garage sales, etc.

❏ Tell parents about the local library and its services, hours of operation, etc. Librarians can be invited to meet parents.

❏ Tell parents about local adult literacy services such as literacy volunteer programs and local adult classes. Some places, such as Burbank, California, have adult literacy classes that include children; parents and children learn together and strengthen parent-child bonds (Peck & Lerner, 2005).

❏ Invite parents to literacy events such as book fairs.

❏ Encourage parents to promote the development of literacy using functional writing tasks such as making lists, composing letters, and discussing print in the environment (Ortiz & Ordoñez-Jasis, 2005).

❏ Encourage students to read to their parents. In this way, literacy is enhanced for both students and parents.

❏ Encourage parents to read to their children as much as possible (Tam & Heng, 2005). It is ideal if parents can read to their children in the primary language of the home. This builds children's L1 literacy skills, which serve as a foundation for eventually becoming biliterate in L1 and English (Kayser, 2004; Miller et al., 2006; Vaughn et al., 2006).

❏ Teach literate parents how to use print-referencing behaviors to enhance their children's literacy skills (e.g., "Show me the longest word on this page" or "Which word begins with the letter 'A'?") (Justice & Ezell, 2000). One school district in Texas used some of its grant money to send a bilingual aide to children's homes during the summer. The aides read with the children, modeled appropriate reading strategies to the parents, and helped parents learn good reading habits with their children. Aides left books for parents to read with their children (Jachman, 2006).

❏ Create a short DVD that can be given to parents to take home and watch. This DVD can model print-referencing behaviors and other literacy strategies for parents to implement during reading activities at home.

❏ Create book bags and give students dual-language books as well as CDs with stories read in both English and the L1 (Cummins et al., 2006).

❏ Let parents know that if they do not read, they can look at books with the children and discuss the stories in the primary language. Wordless books with attractive, relevant pictures are often effective. Parents can use wordless books to help their children become familiar with at least some literacy conventions as turning pages, holding a book right-side up, identifying the front and back of a book, etc. (Roseberry-McKibbin, 2007).

When parents are actively involved in their children's school experiences, students learn the importance of working hard and learning. By communicating with parents on a regular basis, educational professionals can develop programs of instruction that will be meaningful to students and their families.

Profile

Pa X. a 5th-grade student from a Hmong refugee family, was referred to me for testing. Pa's reading skills were at approximately a first- or second-grade level, and she was failing in many 5th grade subjects. She told me that she lived in a small home with 17 relatives and that she slept on the dining room floor with her cousins. At age 11, Pa was thinking of marriage– getting married at age 15 is common in some Hmong families. Our challenge at school was to help the family understand the importance of helping Pa improve her academic performance. The family seemed to be more concerned about Pa's mothering skills. After all, she would be married in a few short years and her life would be spent bearing and raising children, and caring for her husband.

CONCLUSION

When professionals provide intervention and instruction to linguistically and culturally diverse student populations, they need to keep in mind the following foundational principles:

❑ On the national level, No Child Left Behind (2002) and IDEA (2004) have had a major impact on regular and special education. Part of this impact is the development and implementation of Response to Intervention, or RtI, which provides early intervention and support to struggling students. A major goal of RtI is to help students succeed in the regular classroom setting without special education.

❑ As mandated by federal law, the only CLD students who can be placed in special education are those who have been identified as having an underlying language-learning disability or other disabilities based on data obtained from culturally and linguistically appropriate assessment instruments and procedures.

❑ English-language learners who do not qualify for special education can be served using a variety of other options within the regular school program; ideally, bilingual education programs make it possible to maintain and nurture the primary language while English is being learned.

❑ Multicultural activities and materials should be incorporated into the curriculum by professionals in both general and special education programs. The goal is twofold: first, affirm and support CLD students; second, educate mainstream students about CLD issues as they prepare to enter a diverse workforce in adulthood.

❑ IEPs need to be collaborative in nature with goals appropriate for the student's cultural and linguistic background. These IEPs should include goals and benchmarks that align with the curriculum of the student's classroom, and promote the growth of academic skills.

❑ When students are served in special education programs, instruction should be provided using activities that are culturally relevant—the background experiences of the student must be considered.

❑ Professionals must include opportunities for families to participate in planning and implementing programs for students. It is especially important to help foster family literacy.

Finally, it is always important to view each student as a unique individual. Approaches that have been found to be effective with bilingual student populations as a whole, for example, may not always be appropriate for use with a specific child. Some children require more structure than others, and some can be transitioned into another language more easily than others. When planning special education programs for CLD populations, it is important to consider the student's background, interests, and goals, as well as the concerns of the family.

The resources available in the educational environment also need to be considered. The ideal situation is often not possible due to financial constraints, limited materials, and the shortage of appropriately qualified instructional personnel. Through effective collaboration, however, the services currently available for CLD students can be much improved.

STUDY QUESTIONS

1. Summarize the mandates of IDEA (2004) and No Child Left Behind (2002). What has been the impact of these laws on the way that schools serve students?

2. Describe three ways to help families become involved in their children's education (either regular or special education).

3. List four sources for obtaining tutors who can work with CLD students.

TRUE-FALSE

Circle the number beside each statement that is true.

4. Professionals should emphasize the importance of early language stimulation because many families do not believe it is important to talk with infants and young children.
5. Advocates of multicultural pluralism support separate ethnic studies courses for individuals from specific cultural backgrounds, separate ethnic clubs, etc.
6. Response to Intervention (RtI) principles emphasize the importance of referring students immediately for special education if they are struggling in the classroom setting.
7. When providing special education services to students with language-learning disabilities who are more proficient in Spanish than English, a program that includes Spanish language instruction may be more effective than a program that focuses only on language development in English.
8. We need to emphasize to parents that they must discontinue use of the primary language at home and speak only English; this will facilitate their children's academic achievement.

9. In low-context cultures, the role of the individual as a member of a group is emphasized, and observation plays a key role in learning.

10. In writing IEP objectives, an emphasis should be placed on writing outcomes or benchmarks that support the curriculum of the regular education classroom.

MULTIPLE CHOICE

Unless otherwise indicated, circle the letter before all choices that are true.

11. It is very important to avoid specific types of behaviors when working with multicultural students. These behaviors include the following:
    A. Trivializing by always using only one picture from a specific place and time to represent a group. The diversity that exists within a population is not depicted.
    B. Misrepresenting by showing pictures from rural Mexico to teach students about modern-day Hispanic life in the United States
    C. Stereotyping by only showing pictures of non-Anglos in conditions that indicate that they live in poverty
    D. Disconnecting by presenting an instructional unit about a cultural group without relating the unit to the regular curriculum

12. Which one of the following is NOT advisable when working with family members?
    A. Inviting them to come to the school to talk about their language and culture
    B. Helping them find where to purchase or borrow books at little or no cost
    C. Emphasizing to parents that they do a disservice to their child if they speak the primary language at home
    D. Encouraging students to read to their parents
    E. Conducting programs that will help parents understand and adapt to the U.S. school system

13. Response to Intervention involves:

    A. Immediate referral for special education testing if a child is having academic difficulties
    B. The use of Teacher Assistance Teams so that teachers of students who are struggling in the general education curriculum can turn to teams of fellow teachers for support and ideas for classroom interventions
    C. Greater involvement of speech-language pathologists, especially in the area of increasing the literacy skills of struggling students
    D. Ensuring that parents come to the school daily to provide 1:1 help for their struggling children in classroom settings
    E. Re-writing IEPs every 3 months to ensure that intervention programs are successfully building the classroom skills of children who qualify for special education

14. When considering which language to use in intervention programs for children with language-learning disabilities, professionals must think about the following question(s):
    A. Does the student wish to maintain his primary language?
    B. Does the student speak a language that is considered prestigious by the community?
    C. Does the student have a high level of intelligence?
    D. Is the classroom teacher a native speaker of the child's primary language?
    E. Does the child have younger siblings who might be affected by recommended changes?

15. Which of the following are possible options for CLD students who qualify for special education?
    A. Placement in a monolingual English special education classroom with primary language support from a bilingual teacher, tutor, etc.
    B. Pull-out services (speech-language intervention, learning disability program, or both) in the primary language
    C. Bilingual special education classroom
    D. Pull-out services in English with primary language support
    E. Consultative, collaborative program implementation

ANSWERS TO STUDY QUESTIONS

 4. True
 5. False
 6. False
 7. True
 8. False
 9. False
10. True
11. B, C, and D
12. C
13. B and C
14. A
15. A, B, C, D, and E

Chapter 15

PRACTICAL STRATEGIES FOR INTERVENTION

Outline

CLD students may struggle in school for a variety of reasons. Today, the national emphasis on Response to Intervention (RtI) makes it imperative that *all* professionals—in both general education and special-education settings—use specific, well-designed, scientifically-based strategies to help these students succeed in school (Hoover & Patton, 2005; Nelson, 2007). Specific strategies are described in this chapter that can be used in a variety of educational settings. Some may be most useful in a general education classroom setting, while others lend themselves to specific intervention provided by a speech-language pathologist or other special educator.

In this chapter, the holistic-strategies approach to collaborative instruction is defined and suggestions are presented for structuring students' environments for optimal learning. This chapter also includes a description of compensatory strategies for learning, specific suggestions for contextualizing input to make it comprehensible, and practical techniques for building overall language and literacy skills.

A HOLISTIC APPROACH TO COLLABORATIVE INSTRUCTION

Foundational Principles

When regular and special education professionals work with CLD students, they often treat listening, speaking, reading, and writing as areas of language that should be taught separately. Moreover, each of these areas is often broken down into a series of skills that are taught in isolation. This artificial separation of "sub-skills" or "sub-areas" results in instruction that is often reductionistic and skill-specific. Reading programs, for example, often include structured drills designed to teach reading skills one at a time. Often these drills require students to perform tasks very different from those used during the actual activity of reading. These tasks may confuse special needs learners, especially those who lack the academic language proficiency necessary to perform these tasks.

Listening, speaking, reading, and writing can be taught simultaneously, using a holistic-strategies approach to instruction. The holistic-strategies approach was conceived by this author to integrate the best attributes of current, research-based approaches into an eclectic model of teaching and learning. In the holistic-strategies approach, the various components of language are seen as synergistic in that they develop simultaneously as students learn within meaningful contexts. The holistic-strategies approach is a conceptual framework that combines (1) the interactionist theory of language development; (2) constructivist philosophy (see Hearne, 2000; Weiner, 2001); (3) an emphasis on literacy development and academic achievement; (4) the belief that one cannot divorce the teaching of content from the teaching of metalinguistic and metacognitive strategies (Ukrainetz, 2006); (5) the experiential/interactive model of pedagogy; (6) the premise that self-esteem and positive psychosocial adjustment in learners are critical and need to be fostered; (7) Feurstein's Theory of Structural Cognitive Modifiability; and (8) interactive activities to facilitate communicative competence (Echevarria et al., 2006).

Basic assumptions of the holistic-strategies approach include the following:

❑ Students need to develop a strong conceptual knowledge base to be successful in school. Learning relevant vocabulary is especially important (Montgomery, 2007).

❏ Students who have difficulty acquiring new information should be explicitly taught strategies for learning and remembering content.

❏ Students need to learn concepts and strategies in naturalistic, authentic communication situations with a focus on MEANING rather than structure (Oller et al., 2006).

❏ Students with special education needs require more specific guidance and explicit teaching than other learners. Relatedly, these students need frequent review and repetition of information to remember and integrate what they are being taught (Roseberry-McKibbin, 2001b).

❏ Children acquire oral language skills most efficiently when they are immersed in a language-rich environment. A language-rich environment is also important for the acquisition of literacy skills.

❏ Students direct their learning to accomplish personal communication goals.

❏ Adults can facilitate the learning process by following these suggestions:

  1. Provide good communication models.

  2. Listen and respond carefully to children's communication attempts.

  3. Strive to facilitate active participation in the learning process rather than just presenting information.

  4. Mediate learning for students by helping them interpret and make sense of materials. It is important to provide guidance and direction during learning activities.

  5. Help students relate new information to what they already know.

Professionals should use a **whole-parts-whole instructional model**. In this model, the learner is first given the "big picture," and then learns how the component parts relate to the whole. For example, if the professional is going to read a story, the first step is to provide students with a general outline of the entire story (whole). The next step is to read the story and ask questions about individual parts of it (parts). The final step is to present the general outline of the story again (whole). This process is culturally congruent with the way that many CLD students learn. The following suggestions promote effective interaction and active participation during whole-part-whole learning experiences.

❏ Encourage students to interact with one another during learning experiences rather than spending the majority of the day listening to oral presentations of information. Learning requires active participation, not just passive processing.

❏ Allow students to participate in planning the curriculum, choosing activities, and setting goals.

❏ Facilitate the development of cognitive skills that become progressively more difficult rather than emphasizing simple recall (Brice & Montgomery, 1996). Encourage students to explain new information in their own words, summarize information, apply information to new contexts, relate new information to previously learned information, and analyze new information.

❏ Use thematic instructional units. Topics relevant to the interests of students and the goals of the classroom curriculum should be emphasized.

❑ Provide daily opportunities to *TALK—LISTEN—WRITE—READ* (Echevarria & Powers, 2006).

❑ Be sensitive to students' cultural characteristics and learning styles when designing instructional activities. These variables may have a major effect on responses during intervention.

❑ Use materials that are culturally appropriate for students.

❑ Ensure that the environment of the classroom or therapy room is optimally conducive to learning and that the family is given opportunities to participate in the students' educational program.

The holistic-strategies approach is illustrated in Figure 15.1.

STRUCTURING THE ENVIRONMENT FOR CLD LEARNERS WITH SPECIAL NEEDS

Some special needs learners have difficulty structuring their environments for efficient learning. This difficulty can stem from one or more of the following:

1. limited experience in learning situations
2. attention difficulties
3. learning disabilities or language disorders
4. emotional difficulties
5. deficiencies in diet or health care
6. hearing problems

Strategies for Structuring the Environment

Strategies for helping CLD students structure their environment have been described in the literature (Brice & Brice, 2007; Roseberry-McKibbin, 2008):

❑ *Use preparatory sets*. When preparatory sets are used, learners with special needs will know what to expect because their environment has been structured for them. For example, instead of starting an activity with no explanation, the teacher might say, "Today we will share, read a story, and practice our sounds. What will you do?" . . . "That's right - share, read a story, and practice our sounds."

❑ *Limit clutter and excessive visual stimuli in the environment*. Many classrooms and therapy/resource rooms include beautiful collections of student art projects, work centers, pet cages, etc. While these rooms are colorful and quite attractive, they are often distracting to learners with special needs. These students often respond best in an environment that is attractive but very uncluttered and "plain." Because these students have difficulty screening out extraneous stimuli, they are distracted by items and events that do not distract most students.

❑ *Set up an area of the classroom as the "office."* Some classroom teachers in the school district where I work use an area of the classroom called the "office." This area has nothing on the walls; there is a little carrel that blocks off the rest of the classroom. Students who sit in the office to do their work find that visual distractions are removed. If these students are susceptible to auditory distractions, they can wear headphones to block out noise.

❑ *Wait until the room is quiet before presenting important information*. Students who have difficulty concentrating and remembering information will experience even more difficulty if the room is noisy.

Figure 15.1

The Holistic Strategies Tree

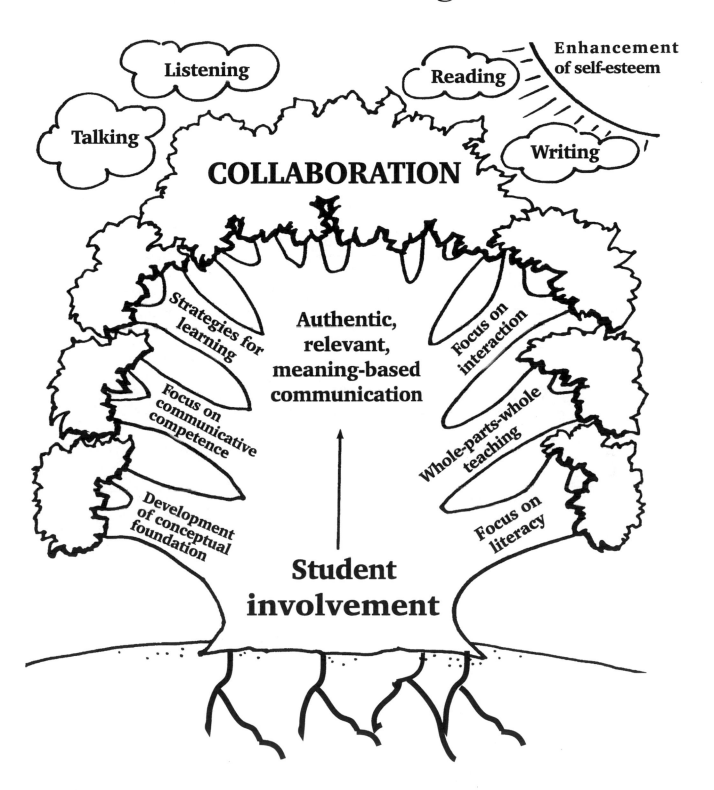

Rooted in constructivism and the interactionist theory

❏ *Reduce auditory distractions.* In many rooms, phones ring, people come in and out, and students talk freely. Learners with special needs can be highly distracted in such situations. Processing information in a second language under less-than-ideal listening conditions is a risk factor for CLD students with language-learning disabilities (Nelson, Kohnert, Sabur, & Shaw, 2005). These students tend to do their best work in quiet, organized environments.

❏ *Speak at an appropriate loudness level.* Research has shown that when teachers speak at a level that is 15-30 decibels above their regular volume level, all children benefit—especially CLD students at risk for struggling in the classroom setting (Eriks-Brophy & Ayakawa, 2000). In some settings, teachers use FM units successfully for the benefit of students (Choi & McPherson, 2005). A teacher's use of an FM unit can improve the signal-to-noise ratio of the classroom, making the teacher's voice stand out better in contrast to background noise.

❏ *Use a multimodal approach to teaching.* Special-needs learners benefit from learning through various channels—visual, auditory, and tactile. Many professionals in American schools present large amounts of information orally during teaching activities. Students are expected to acquire knowledge by listening to the teacher. Students with special learning needs frequently have auditory processing difficulties that make it hard for them to process and remember information that they hear. Activities that incorporate music, bodily movement, and rhythm may facilitate learning and the retention of information (Wolfe, 2001). When an interactive approach involving auditory, visual, and tactile stimuli is used, students will be more likely to learn and remember new information.

❏ *Increase the complexity level of learning activities gradually.* Remember that learners with special needs may become frustrated more easily than normal learners. Consequently, they may have "shorter fuses" and less tolerance for frustration than the "average" learner. Lessons need to be planned carefully so that these learners experience success with simple tasks before more complex tasks are attempted.

❏ *Provide frequent opportunities for the review of information that has been presented.* In this way students will retain more of what they learn.

❏ *Allow additional time for these students to process information.* Learners with special needs often take longer to process information than students who are learning in the typical manner. Thus, professionals need to give these students time to answer, think, etc.

❏ *Seat learners with special needs in the front of the classroom to minimize distractions.*

❏ *Use the learner's name often during teaching to keep the student focused.*

❏ *Break down assignments into small components.* Students with special learning needs take longer to complete assignments and may become overwhelmed if given work that will take a long time to complete.

When professionals follow the above suggestions, students with special learning needs will function more efficiently and will learn more readily. A self-evaluation checklist that can be used during program implementation with multicultural student populations is presented in Table 15.1.

Table 15.1

Working With Linguistically And Culturally Diverse Students: The Interventionist's Self-Evaluation Checklist

Do I	Almost Always	Some-times	Very Rarely	Never
1. Use a multimodal approach to teaching material?				
2. Review previous material?				
3. Make input comprehensible by slowing down, pausing, and speaking clearly?				
4. Rephrase and restate information?				
5. Check frequently for comprehension?				
6. Focus on teaching meaning rather than focusing on teaching correct grammar?				
7. Avoid putting students on the spot by demanding that they talk immediately?				
8. Give extra time for processing information?				
9. Attempt to reduce students' anxieties and give them extra attention when possible?				
10. Encourage students' use and development of their primary language?				
11. Encourage students to interject their own cultural experiences and backgrounds into learning situations?				
12. Expose all my students to multicultural activities and materials on a regular basis?				
13. Include parents and community members from different cultural backgrounds in my teaching?				

Profile

    Mr. J., a fifth-grade teacher, complained that "these bilingual special education kids in my class are driving me nuts. I want to put them somewhere else—just not in my classroom!" The only other fifth-grade teacher in the school was a recent college graduate with no previous teaching experience. The principal, therefore, told Mr. J. that he needed to adapt to the CLD special education students as best he could.

    During lunch one day, Mr. J. asked the speech-language pathologist for suggestions, emphasizing that "these ideas better not take too much time—I'm already busy enough." The speech-language pathologist offered to come and observe Mr. J's class and did so the following day. She noticed that Mr. J. used no visuals and that he spoke rapidly when presenting instructions to the students. He expected students to respond the first time he presented an instruction, and he rarely repeated instructions. The room was noisy and the speech-language pathologist herself found it difficult to focus on what Mr. J. was trying to say.

    The speech-language pathologist offered to do a demonstration lesson, and Mr. J. accepted this offer. The speech-language pathologist asked the students to participate in an experiment in being as quiet as possible. She told the students that a lesson would be presented and that a prize would be given to students at the quietest table. During the lesson, the speech-language pathologist used the overhead projector, whiteboard, and other visuals when presenting the lesson. She also repeated key concepts several times in a slow speaking voice. Mr. J. reported at lunch the next day that the students told him they really enjoyed the lesson.

    Mr. J. tried implementing the strategies demonstrated by the speech-language pathologist. A few weeks later, he reported to the speech-language pathologist that the CLD special education students had "really turned a corner" academically. Mr. J. realized that he could implement changes to meet the needs of these special students.

TEACHING COMPENSATORY STRATEGIES

    A major premise of the holistic-strategies approach is that special learners need to acquire STRATEGIES to learn. These students often have difficulty absorbing information from the environment and organizing it internally by creating schemata. Explicit direction and teaching is needed by these students.

    The following strategies can be taught to CLD students who have language-learning disabilities. Each student must be assessed individually to ascertain which strategy or combination of strategies produces the best results. A sample instructional objective for the teaching of strategies is presented below:

    OBJECTIVE: _____ will use the strategies _____, _____ _____ , and _____ to facilitate word retrieval. She will use these strategies in the speech room, resource room, and the classroom, as reported by teachers and specialists in these settings.

Ten compensatory strategies that can benefit special-needs learners are described below:

Strategy 1: Audio-record lectures and then listen to the recording.

Strategy 2: Write down information and instructions in a notebook. This activity facilitates the development of organizational skills and helps the student to recall information presented during class.

Strategy 3: Focus on key words and write them down. Many students will need explicit direction to help them focus their attention so that they can write down key words.

Sample instructions:

"Listen. I am going to write a sentence. You tell me what the most important words are. Don't worry about listening to all the little words. Just tell me what the most important words are."

Stimulus sentence: I went to the store to buy some milk.

Teacher: Which are the most important words?

Student: I, store, buy, milk.

Teacher: That's right: *I - store - buy - milk.* These are the important or key words that we need to remember.

The educational professional can also ask the student to name the little words in the sentence. After presenting sentences, short paragraphs can be used for this activity. This procedure is especially helpful for older students who need to take notes during lectures and have difficulty separating content (key) words from function (smaller, less important) words.

Strategy 4: Use visualization to help students form mental pictures of information.

Sample instructions:

"We are going to learn how to make pictures in our mind. Think of watching a TV show or a movie. You see a picture on a screen. Who has seen a movie or TV show lately? Tell me what you saw."

"Leo, tell us about your kitchen at home. (Child describes the kitchen). Leo, are you standing in your kitchen right now? No, you are here at school. Then how could you tell us about your kitchen? (pause) You just saw a picture in your brain, didn't you? We are going to learn how to make pictures in our brains to help us remember information."

During instructional activities, students should be encouraged to form mental pictures of what they are learning. For example, encourage students to see color, size, shape, texture, sound, movement, background, and other aspects of their mental pictures (Bell, 1991). Detailed visualization helps children remember new information that they see and hear. The more detail, the better!

Strategy 5: Teach students metacognitive strategies to help them become more efficient learners. Metacognitive strategies include monitoring the success of their current learning efforts, planning ahead so that learning time can be used efficiently, and being aware of one's own learning style and learning strategies.

Strategy 6: Use categorization or grouping to facilitate memory. Discuss categories with students, and explain how categories help us to remember information. Students can be taught categories such as *furniture, fruits,* etc.

Strategy 7: Use or create acrostic sentences. For example, to remember the planets, the student can use the sentence, "My very eager mother just sent us north." (Mercury, Venus, Earth, Mars, Jupiter, Saturn, Uranus, Neptune)

Strategy 8: Use reauditorization/silent rehearsal. The students are told that when they hear something (e.g., directions), they are to repeat what they hear quietly to themselves.

> *Example:*
> Do what I say:
>> Touch your nose, eyes, and ears. I said, *nose - eyes - ears.*
>> I want everyone to repeat after me—*nose - eyes - ears* (Wait for students to respond.)
>
>> Now, what did I say to touch? That's right—nose-eyes-ears. You remembered the words because you said them quietly to yourself. Let's try another one.

Many students profit from this strategy. The professional should encourage students to repeat items out loud at first to ensure that the strategy is working. Then move quickly to silent rehearsal.

Strategy 9: Create a verbal description. If a student cannot retrieve a word, encourage the student to describe it. Ask questions such as, "What does it look like? Sound like? Feel like? What shape is it?" and so on.

Strategy 10: Think of words with a similar meaning. If a student is having difficulty retrieving a word, the professional might say, "Can you think of another word that means the same thing?"

The holistic-strategies approach will be most effective when students receive direct and explicit teaching and opportunities for the rehearsal of appropriate strategies. Professionals should monitor carryover of strategy use into the classroom and other settings. Professionals can work in a collaborative manner with parents, teachers, and other school professionals to ensure that students are being encouraged to use appropriate strategies for learning and remembering information.

MAKING INPUT COMPREHENSIBLE: INCREASING CONTEXTUALIZATION OF INFORMATION

As mentioned previously, students who are English language learners need to hear comprehensible input. This is true regardless of the learning environment—the regular education classroom, speech-language room, resource room, or other setting. When exposed to comprehensible input, most typically-developing CLD learners absorb new information and put that information to use fairly quickly. Special-needs learners, however, must often be presented with new information in small "doses." Frequent modeling and repetition may also be needed for learning to occur. Thus, each step of a task may need to be presented a number of times before these students are able to grasp the information being taught.

To increase comprehensibility of information, students need it to be contextualized (Chamberlain, 2005). A highly challenging situation for many CLD students is that even starting in kindergarten, information is presented in a context-reduced, abstract manner (Weiner, 2001; Roseberry-McKibbin, 2008). Thus, professionals can especially use the following ideas in a response-to-intervention paradigm to ascertain if increasing the contextualization and comprehensibility of input is sufficient to help struggling CLD students make adequate academic gains in the classroom without being placed into special education. If students have already been identified as having special education needs, the strategies can still be helpful.

General Strategies

When working with CLD student populations, it is important to use a multimodal approach to ensure that the input is comprehensible and relevant to the previous learning needs of students. A variety of strategies should be used to meet the diverse needs of students (Brice, 2002; Brice & Brice, 2007; ERIC Clearinghouse on Urban Education, 2006; Gray & Fleischman, 2005; van Broekhuizen, 2006).

❏ Review previously learned material daily.

❏ Check frequently for comprehension. Some students may be embarrassed to admit that they do not know specific information. In some cultures, it is inappropriate to admit not knowing something. Thus if a student indicates that he or she has comprehended something, you should make sure that comprehension has, in fact, occurred.

❏ Use a multimodal instructional approach in which visual and gestural cues are presented frequently. Suggestions for accomplishing are the following:

1. Write assignments on the board.

2. Use pictures, maps, diagrams, and various objects.

3. Accompany oral presentations with gestures and facial expressions.

4. Use visual organizers, clusters, and mental mapping to help organize information for the student.

❏ Teach beginning students the names for common objects in the classroom.

❏ Make input comprehensible to the students by doing the following:

1. Talk slowly enough for them to process the information.

2. Pause frequently to avoid "overloading" students with information.

3. Use students' names to direct and maintain their attention.

4. Use short sentences and phrases.

5. Avoid the frequent use of long words.

6. Explain new slang or idiomatic speech.

7. Enunciate words clearly (e.g., "Did you eat?" instead of "Jueet?").

8. Emphasize key words through increased volume and slightly exaggerated intonation

Example: "**Now** we will **look** at the **calendar**. The **calendar** shows us the **days** of the **week**."

❏ Rephrase and restate information to facilitate comprehension. For example, the teacher might say:

"Today we are going to read a chapter in our math books and do the problems on page 10 of the math workbook. Again, we will take our math books and read a chapter. We will then do the problems on page 10 of the math workbook."

❑ Try to seat students who speak the same language together, especially if one student speaks English with enough proficiency to help others. The advanced student can then explain complicated directions and other information in the primary language.

❑ Focus on the communication of meaning rather than emphasizing the correction of grammatical errors.

❑ Match intervention to the student's stage of second language acquisition. Table 15.2 includes information that professionals can use to plan programs for students who are in various stages of acquiring English.

When intervention strategies such as those described above are adapted to specific situations and used by all professionals who interact with CLD students, the likelihood is increased that the instructional input will be comprehensible to students.

✐REFLECTION ✐

You are giving an in-service to teachers in a school where there has been an influx of students from multicultural backgrounds. The teachers have had limited experience working with multicultural student populations and have asked you to give them some ideas. Describe four ideas you will share with these teachers about working successfully in their classrooms with CLD students who have language-learning disabilities.

_____

_____

_____

_____

Scaffolding

Scaffolding is a technique in which the professional (or peer with a high level of skill) gives a student temporary support that is consistent with the student's current ability level (Weiner, 2001). The professional gradually withdraws support until the student can function independently. Scaffolding increases the comprehensibility of classroom input, making it easier for students to learn. Scaffolding helps contextualize new information. Suggestions for implementation include the following:

❑ Relate the information presented to knowledge that has already been acquired.

Example:

A professional is trying to teach an immigrant Filipino student the concepts _winter,_ _spring, summer,_ and _fall._ The professional starts by discussing the rainy season and the dry season that the student experienced in the Philippines. Following this, the teacher discusses how weather changes during the four seasons in the United States.

By teaching the four seasons in this way, the professional scaffolds the task for the student by relating the new information to the student's previously acquired knowledge.

Table 15.2

MATCHING INTERVENTION TO SECOND LANGUAGE (L2) ACQUISITION STAGES

	Stage I Preproduction (First 3 months of L2 exposure)	Stage II Early Production (3-6 months)	Stage III Speech Emergence (6 months-2 years)	Stage IV Intermediate Fluency (2-3 years)
STUDENT CHARACTERISTICS	• Silent period • Focusing on comprehension	• Focusing on comprehension • Using 1-3 word phrases • May be using routines/formulas (e.g. "gimme five")	• Increased comprehension • Using simple sentences • Expanding vocabulary • Continued grammatical errors	• Improved comprehension • Adequate face-to-face conversational proficiency • More extensive vocabulary • Few grammatical errors
GOALS: ORAL RESPONSES	• *Yes-no* responses in English • One-word answers	• 1-3 word responses • Naming/labeling items • Choral responses • Answering questions: *either/or, who/what/where, sentence completion*	• Recalling • Telling/retelling • Describing/explaining • Comparing • Sequencing • Carrying on dialogues	• Predicting • Narrating • Describing/explaining • Summarizing • Giving opinions • Debating/defending
GOALS: VISUAL/WRITTEN RESPONSES	• Drawing/painting • Graphic designs • Copying	• Drawing/painting, graphic designs • Copying • Grouping and labeling • Simple Rebus responses	• Written responses • Drawing, painting, graphics	• Creative writing (e.g., stories) • Essays, summaries • Drawing, painting, graphics • Comprehensible written tests
GOALS: PHYSICAL RESPONSES	• Pointing • Circling, underlining • Choosing among items • Matching objects/pictures	• Pointing • Selecting • Matching • Constructing • Mime/acting out responses	• Demonstrating • Creating/constructing • Role-playing/acting • Cooperative group tasks	• Demonstrating • Creating/constructing • Role-playing • Cooperative group work • Videotaped presentations

Source: Hearne, D. (2000). *Teaching Second Language Learners with Learning Disabilities*. Oceanside, CA: Academic Communication Associates. Adapted from Table 10-4 with permission.

❏ Gradually let the student take control of the task.

Example:

A student is discovering how to use the dictionary. At first, the professional demonstrates the entire task while the student observes. Next, the professional assists the student in finding a particular word. Finally, the professional tells the student to look up a word independently and to request assistance if problems are encountered.

❏ Use a multimodal approach to teaching in which the student has multiple opportunities to experience concepts.

Example:

A student is learning verbal opposites. First, opposites are demonstrated with objects, pictures, and activities. The student may color pictures, do physical demonstrations, work with objects, etc. Second, the student is asked to complete paper-and-pencil activities with opposites. Third, the professional shows picture cards and asks the student to point to opposites. Fourth, the professional reads a book and asks questions about opposites. Fifth, the student is asked to create a story about opposites. In this way, multiple exemplars or repeated exposures in different situations help the student learn the concept of opposites.

❏ Help the student to learn from mistakes or from conduct that is viewed as inappropriate.

Example:

An Asian student is reprimanded by the school principal during recess. The student smiles because in her culture it is appropriate to smile when reprimanded by a superior. The principal becomes angry and feels that the student is being disrespectful.

In this case, the professional can explain the situation to the principal and talk with the student about social interaction skills that are consistent with expectations for students in the United States. Thus, the student's inappropriate behavior becomes a positive learning situation.

When professionals use the scaffolding strategy, concentrated initial assistance with tasks is provided. This assistance is faded out as the student becomes more independent in the learning situation. Again, many struggling CLD students can become more successful in regular and special education settings if they hear contextualized, comprehensible input and receive scaffolded instruction.

BUILDING RECEPTIVE AND EXPRESSIVE LANGUAGE SKILLS

CLD students with language-learning disabilities need to develop their expressive and receptive language skills. As previously stated, ideally this occurs in a bilingual intervention situation in which the students participate in specific, targeted intervention to build skills in both L1 and English.

The activity suggestions that follow can be implemented in a variety of settings. General education teachers can utilize the suggestions as part of response-to-intervention for individual students or whole classes. Professionals in special education can use the suggestions as they work with students individually and in small groups.

General Activities

❏ When students make grammatical errors, these errors should not be overtly corrected when students are in the early and intermediate stages of learning English (Roseberry-McKibbin, 2001b).

Professionals, however, can recast a student's utterance to model the correct form. For example, if the student says, "I having good day," the professional might respond by saying, "I'm having a good day, too! I'm glad that I'm having a good day and that you're having a good day."

❏ For students who make repeated grammatical errors, professionals can use focused stimulation (Roseberry-McKibbin, 2001b). For example, if a student always omits articles, the professional can model these articles repeatedly in various situations (e.g., "Look, you have **the** book. You have **a** pencil and **a** piece of paper—and **a** box of crayons!").

❏ Use computers if appropriate, especially if the computer programs have pictures/graphics that will aid in comprehension.

❏ Allow students to incorporate their own experiences into learning situations. As previously stated, students learn best when they can relate new learning to their own experiences. For example, when students read texts that are congruent with their background and experience, they understand the text more completely. When they write stories, they will perform more effectively if they can write about their own lives and experiences.

❏ Ask students to listen to stories, read stories, and write their own stories. The use of stories and narratives is a highly successful teaching tool for students from diverse cultural backgrounds.

❏ Encourage students to use a dictionary and to make their own dictionaries using illustrations and pictures to facilitate recall of new vocabulary.

❏ Provide learning experiences in which students work as a team to acquire new information (i.e., cooperative learning). A major goal of cooperative learning is to facilitate and encourage mutual cooperation and interdependence among students. Professionals can use cooperative learning in regular classrooms or in small-group settings.

REFLECTION

You are supervising a student-teacher who has not had previous experience working with CLD students who have language-learning disabilities. List four strategies that she might use to help these students learn and retain new information.

_____

_____

_____

_____

_____

❏ Ask students to write stories in their primary language. Stories can be written by hand or using computers. Students with special needs who have difficulty writing by hand may experience less frustration if they use a computer.

❏ Use a writing program such as *Handwriting without Tears* (Olsen, 2003) with students who have fine-motor problems or other disabilities that make handwriting a difficult and frustrating task. This program is ideal for CLD students because it does not require in-depth knowledge of English for students to benefit from it.

❑ Encourage students to create journals in their primary language and English. Some professionals recommend that students write with pens rather than pencils. When students write with pencils, they may spend more time erasing than writing.

❑ Use "bilingual books" and have one student read in the primary language and another student read in English.

❑ Have students create captions (in English or the primary language) for pictures, photos, or comic strips.

❑ Have students write or dictate letters. Students can become pen-pals with individuals from other areas. Students may use e-mail if computers are available. Encourage students to keep a folder with the letters they receive.

❑ Have students create family trees with descriptions and photos.

❑ Use narratives to enhance learning. Students can listen to stories, read stories, and write their own stories.

❑ Construct narratives using the written or spoken word, paintings and drawings, movement, song, and dramatic play. Story maps such as the one in Figure 15.2 can help students organize their stories.

❑ Have students review newspaper advertisements to find items that they would like to buy. They can describe these items orally or in writing.

❑ Have one student hide an object in the room. The student can write or orally state directions to help the others locate this object. The more precise the directions, the sooner the object will be found.

❑ Have students bring in songs that they like. The songs can be used to help students learn new vocabulary. Students can also play simple instruments and/or use rhythmic objects (e.g., finger cymbals).

❑ Have students prepare a newspaper. They can write stories or poems, draw cartoons with captions, and make illustrations.

❑ Have students write stories about photographs.

❑ Have students engage in drama and role-playing activities that are relevant to their interests and appropriate for their developmental age. The use of puppets can facilitate greater expression in children who are reluctant to speak.

❑ Prepare a multicultural calendar that includes American holidays and holidays celebrated in other countries throughout the world. Be sure that the holidays shown represent the cultures of students in the classroom. All holidays can be discussed and activities can be planned that incorporate these holidays (see Paul, 2007).

Figure 15.2
STORY MAP

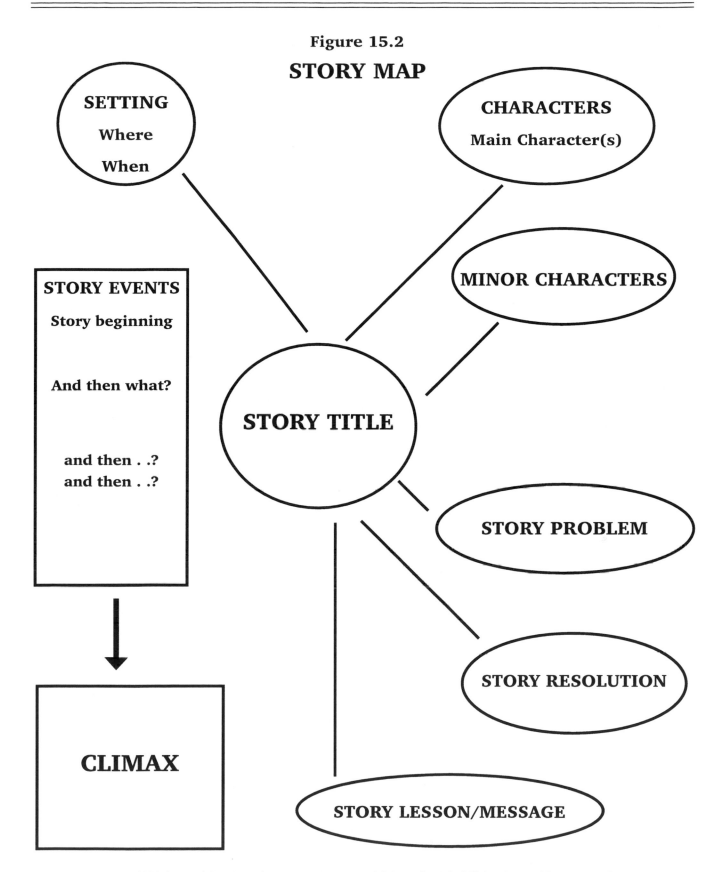

Source: Hearne, D. (2000). *Teaching Second Language Learners with Learning Disabilities*. Oceanside, CA: Academic Communication Associates. Reprinted with permission.

Using Questions to Facilitate Language Development

The effective use of questions increases the student's active participation in learning experiences and facilitates the development of comprehensible output (Brice & Roseberry-McKibbin, 1999b; Grimm, 2006; Woolfolk, 2004). It is important to use a variety of questioning strategies, to include all students in the activities, and to allow enough "wait time"; usually 3-5 seconds is ideal.

Questions are often used to ascertain how much information students comprehend during instructional activities. When asking questions, however, sensitivity to cultural differences is important (Brice & Brice, 2007). Educational professionals need to remember that students from some cultures may not want to be singled out or to appear different from their classmates. Examples of questions that can be used to assess comprehension are presented below.

❑ Ask for a brief summary of what was just said.

❑ Ask students to express opinions about the material.

> *Example:*
> "Manuel, what do you think of that?"
> "What was your favorite thing about this adventure?"
> "What didn't you like about this story?"

❑ Ask students to speculate about and expand on the information that was presented.

> *Example:*
> "Sergio, can you think of another example of ...?"
> "How would you have done things differently than...?"
> "What do you think might happen in the end?"

❑ Check comprehension frequently throughout the session. Don't wait until the end of the lesson to ask if anyone has questions. Use the above comprehension checks frequently to ensure that students are comprehending the material.

❑ Use clarification requests.

> *Example:*
> "When you said nothing happened, did you mean that...?"
> *or*
> "Can you tell me what you mean by that?"

When making requests, the following types of questions should be avoided:

1. **Rhetorical questions.** Some students who are still learning English may have difficulty distinguishing between rhetorical questions and questions that require a response.

2. **Ambiguous or vague questions**. Be as direct and straightforward as possible. If students don't understand the vocabulary and/or intent of the question, they will be much less likely to respond.

3. **Run-on or "machine gun" questions**. Multiple questions often cause confusion, especially among students who are used to hearing only one question at a time. For example, a teacher may say, "What about the main character in the story? What were his motives? What did he hope to accomplish in the end?" It is important to be specific, especially when students are not completely fluent in the language of instruction.

4. **Questions that may clash with the student's cultural style**. Many American professionals ask questions such as:

> "Did everybody understand that?"
> "Are there any questions?"
> "Is that clear?"

Students from some cultural groups have been taught that it is a sign of disrespect to tell a teacher that the information presented has not been understood. Some students feel that they will lose face if they indicate a lack of understanding by asking questions.

Profile

Rosario A. immigrated to the U.S. from the Philippines with his family when he was in 4th grade. The teacher referred Rosario to the special education team because, in her words, "Rosario is SO quiet in class, and I can never get him to raise his hand and answer questions. Also, Rosario copies other students' work and can't seem to complete assignments on his own. I wonder if he needs some special education assistance."

The speech-language pathologist, who had grown up in the Philippines, observed Rosario in class. There were 35 students in the somewhat noisy classroom, and Rosario sat quietly in the back, never volunteering any information. In addition, Rosario was observed trying to get other students to help him with a difficult math assignment. The speech-language pathologist shared with the teacher that being quiet and respectful in class was expected in the Philippines, and that corporal punishment was sometimes used there for students who "got out of line." In addition, she shared that Filipino students frequently help one another with assignments rather than working on classroom tasks independently.

Rather than being evaluated for special education, Rosario was placed into the school's Homework Club, where he received help from older peer tutors who worked individually and in small groups with younger students. A sixth-grade Filipino student was assigned to work with Rosario and three Filipino students from other classrooms in a cooperative, informal, interactive, and friendly situation in the school library. After six months, the teacher reported that Rosario had made excellent gains and that he was even raising his hand occasionally in class to ask questions.

Enhancing Interpersonal Communication Effectiveness (Social Skills)

In the holistic-strategies approach to learning, professionals help students become more effective communicators in their daily environments. Many CLD students in both general and special education programs need to enhance their communicative competence in their daily interactions. They especially need to increase their skills in topic initiation and maintenance (Hegde, 2006). A "Communication Skills Quiz" that students can use to evaluate their own communication is presented in Table 15.3. Students should be asked to respond "yes" or "no" to each question. When presented to a small group, cultural differences can be discussed as they relate to specific items.

The following objectives can be implemented by regular and special-education teachers, tutors, and others who work with the student. It is recommended that professionals work collaboratively to ensure that students practice effective interpersonal communication skills in a variety of communication contexts.

Table 15.3

A COMMUNICATION SKILLS QUIZ FOR STUDENTS

Student's Name:_____   Date:_____

___1.   I greet people when I see them by smiling and saying "hi."

___2.   I listen to people without interrupting.

___3.   I apologize when I have to interrupt.

___4.   I try to be interested in what people say.

___5.   I try to take time to listen when people want to talk to me.

___6.   When people ask me questions, I try to answer as best I can.

___7.   When I talk, I try to talk as clearly as possible so other people will understand me.

___8.   During conversations, I take turns talking.

___9.   During conversations, I try to talk about what other people are talking about instead of bringing up new things in the middle of someone else's sentence.

___10.   If I don't understand what someone says, I ask the person to please repeat what was said.

___11.   If someone doesn't understand me, I repeat what I said more clearly.

___12.   I try to look at people when I talk to them.

Target Behavior: The student will demonstrate effective interpersonal communication skills in daily settings as observed by professionals who work with the student on a regular basis.

Objectives/Benchmarks:

1. The student will greet others by smiling and saying "hello" when appropriate.

2. The student will listen to others without interrupting. If an interruption is necessary, the student will say "excuse me."

3. The student will answer questions appropriately and promptly.

4. The student will take turns during conversation.

5. The student will ask for clarification when he or she does not understand something.

6. If a listener shows confusion, the student will clarify what was said by giving explanations.

7. The student will maintain appropriate eye contact with others during communication.

If students can master these basic social skills, they will be able to make friends more easily and generate many more opportunities for interaction with both adults and peers. Professionals in both general and special education programs can role-model these behaviors and actively teach students how to use them (Pataray-Ching, Kitt-Hinrichs, & Nguyen, 2006; Wong Fillmore & Snow, 2002; Zweirs, 2005).

EVIDENCE-BASED STRATEGIES FOR VOCABULARY DEVELOPMENT

General Principles

The holistic-strategies approach emphasizes the importance of building students' content knowledge or conceptual foundation within meaningful contexts. All activities should be accompanied by adult mediation. In addition to learning social vocabulary, students who are learning English as a second language need to develop their knowledge of vocabulary relevant to the content of the classroom curriculum (Barone, 2006; Lubliner & Smetana, 2005; Montgomery, 2007). As we have said, ideally, students with limited proficiency in English should be taught new concepts in the primary language before these concepts are presented in a second language.

When teaching vocabulary, it is recommended that receptive language activities be presented first. That is, the development of comprehension should be emphasized prior to asking children to produce new concepts verbally. Many students feel uncomfortable in situations that require them to begin speaking immediately. It is ideal for professionals to present receptive vocabulary activities first and follow these by expressive activities that are hierarchically sequenced based on their complexity (Roseberry-McKibbin, 2001b). Indirect language stimulation can be valuable for students who are in the early stages of learning English, and more direct stimulation can follow as students acquire greater proficiency (Paul, 2007).

Vocabulary words should be learned in a variety of meaningful and interesting contexts. Students can be asked to describe pictures and to give word definitions; these activities help students build language skills that are critical for academic success. Wolfe (2001) emphasized that drawing pictures of recently learned words helps students retain their knowledge of these words much better than activities that target the memorization of dictionary meanings.

Formal "drill" activities are often of limited value in developing functional vocabulary skills. It is impossible for a word to have meaning without a context. When students are learning new words, it is ideal if they can have Level 1 or concrete, contextualized experiences (e.g., going to a zoo to actually see zoo animals). If these concrete experiences are not possible, Level 2 experiences—symbols or representations (e.g., pictures, objects) are the next best choice for teaching new concepts (Wolfe, 2001). Finally, at Level 3, students can learn words themselves in the abstract.

For example, a boy walking with his father may see a furry black, barking creature with a collar. His father tells him that this is a *dog*. The boy pets the dog, storing this multisensory experience in his brain in a physiological connection between neurons. In the future, when he encounters other dogs, he will probably remember the word *dog* very easily because he has had a concrete experience (Level 1).

If this boy has never seen an actual dog, he can be exposed to a Level 2 experience. Here, he might play with toy dogs or see pictures of dogs. Although this is not as ideal as a Level 1 experience, the boy is at least exposed to representations that help him learn the word *dog*.

At Level 3, abstract learning, only context-reduced, abstract information is presented. For example, a professional might say to the boy "Look: d-o-g. That word spells *dog*. A dog is a furry household pet that barks." If this Level 3 exposure is all the boy has, he will probably take longer to learn the word *dog* because he has not had contextualized, concrete exposures to this concept.

Specific Activities for Developing Vocabulary Skills

As mentioned previously, graphic organizers can be helpful to students when they are learning new vocabulary. Described as "clustering" by Hearne (2000), the use of graphic organizers is a technique that stimulates divergent thinking as students explore associations relating to a key topic, word, or concept. Graphic organizers help students identify main concepts and assign specific labels to these concepts (Payne, 2003). Graphic organizers not only reduce the language load for CLD students, but they are also much less intimidating for students than activities that require them to read paragraphs of text (Carrier, 2005). In one study of CLD high school students in San Diego, the students reported that use of graphic organizers to supplement classroom lectures was the most helpful strategy employed by teachers (Fisher, Frey, & Williams, 2002). Professionals and students can participate jointly in brainstorming activities and write down all ideas. An example is presented in Figure 15.3.

Lists of common vocabulary words that schools expect students to know are presented in Appendix D. The professional is encouraged to modify the vocabulary lists and to add additional vocabulary from the classroom curriculum. Thematic units can be developed using vocabulary words from the lists. Examples of activities that can be used to build vocabulary skills are presented in Table 15.4.

One highly successful activity for building the vocabulary skills of early English learners in a fun, non-threatening way is Total Physical Response (TPR; Asher, 2007). In TPR, students learn new vocabulary by listening and carrying out bodily movements as instructed by the professional. TPR supports long-term comprehension of material that students are learning. A typical TPR lesson that teaches body parts might run as follows:

Professional: Touch your nose (professional alone touches her nose).

Professional: Touch your nose (professional and students all touch their noses).

Professional: Touch your nose (students alone touch their noses).

Because they are not required to speak, many CLD students in the early stages of learning English enjoy this activity and build their receptive vocabulary skills while they are becoming more

Figure 15.3
Brainstorming Web Sample[1]

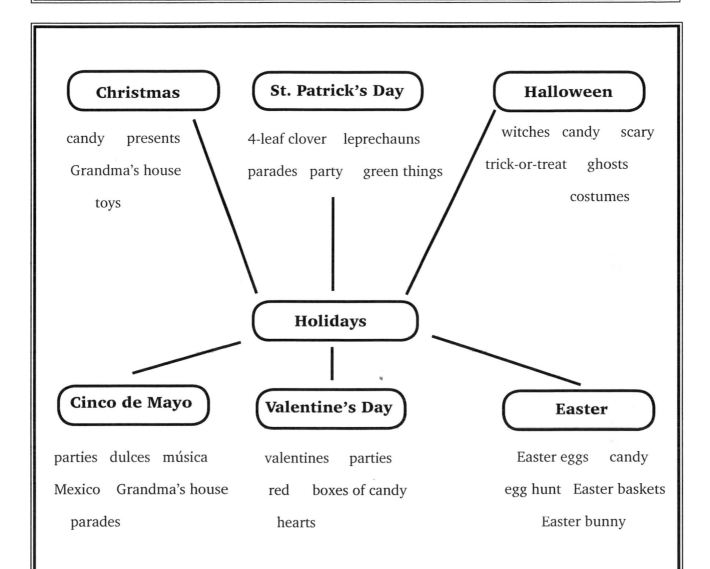

[1]The items listed represent the actual responses of students. Some responses for Cinco de Mayo are in Spanish.

Source: Hearne, D. (2000). *Teaching second language learners with learning disabilities*. Oceanside, CA: Academic Communication Associates. Reprinted with permission.

Table 15.4
Activities For Developing Vocabulary Skills

✦ *Create a Story* - Students use books and pictures of vocabulary words to create stories.

✦ *Category Buckets* - Students put pictures in category "buckets." Each bucket is used for a different word category. Pictures of animals, for example, would be placed in the "animal bucket."

✦ *Guess the Picture* - A student is asked to describe a picture. The other students try to guess which of the pictures on the table is being described.

✦ *Which One Doesn't Belong?* - Five pictures are placed on the table. All but one of the pictures are from the same word category. The student's task is to identify the picture that doesn't belong and to explain why it doesn't belong.

✦ *Memory Games* - Auditory memory games can be created, such as Packing the Suitcase, Grocery Shopping, Catalog Orders, etc. Students are asked to listen to and remember the items named.

✦ *Describe it in Detail* - Students are given points for each attribute mentioned when describing an object or picture of an object. When presented with a picture of an apple, for example, four points would be earned if the student said, "it's shiny, red, juicy, and it's a fruit." Each student receives the same number of turns. The student with the most points at the end of the activity wins.

✦ *Follow the Directions* - Students are asked to manipulate the position of various pictures when presented with verbal directions. (e.g., "Put the pencil on the cup before picking up the chair").

✦ *Rhyming Words* - Students think of words that rhyme with vocabulary words presented in pictures. When presented with the word *hat*, for example, the child might say "cat, mat, and fat." Rhyming should only be used with students whose command of English is strong enough for them to complete this activity without experiencing frustration.

✦ *Word Match* - Students match printed words with pictures of these words.

✦ *Construct a Sentence* - Students construct sentences when presented with a group of words.

✦ *Category Stories* - Students create stories using words from specific categories.

✦ *Drawing Pictures* - Students are asked to draw pictures of new words that they have learned.

✦ *Word Wall* - Students generate the wall list, which contains new words they are learning. Each column can start with a letter, and each list begins with a student's name that starts with that particular letter. For example, the "A" column may start with "Arisbel," the "B" column may start with "Bobby," etc.

✦ *Noun Comparisons* - Students are asked to compare two words/concepts and to discuss what is alike and different about them.

familiar and comfortable with English. Professionals can add more words or commands as students' abilities increase. Students can also give commands for other students to follow (Asher, 2007).

Professionals can boost the learning of new vocabulary by encouraging students to elaborate upon new words they are learning (Grimm, 2006). When students elaborate, they paraphrase the dictionary definition of the word. They can also connect the new word to something they already know. For example, students in one therapy group were trying to learn the new word *booth*. A student finally connected this word to a burrito stand that she was familiar with. Students can further elaborate upon new words by acting them out, drawing pictures, writing sentences or stories using the words, and thinking of other examples of the terms. They can also benefit when professionals elaborate words in storybooks. Collins (2005) showed in her research that bilingual children profited substantially from hearing rich, elaborated explanations of the meanings of vocabulary words in story books.

Justice, Meier, and Walpole (2005) carried out a study in which they used storybooks to foster vocabulary growth for at-risk kindergartners who had low vocabulary knowledge. In this study, adults who read books to children used a vocabulary-elaboration strategy that was shown to be effective. There were three steps: (1) read the word in context, (2) define the word, and (3) use the word in a supportive context. Justice et al. presented the following example:

1. Adult reads text: "They came down to a *marsh* where they saw a muskrat cleaning his house."
2. Adult provides definition: "A *marsh* is a very wet place where there are wetlands covered with grasses."
3. Adult uses word in supportive context: "We took a boat through the *marsh*, and we saw lots of birds and alligators."

It is also important to teach students vocabulary words that are critical for following directions, completing worksheets, and understanding the content of subject matter emphasized within the classroom. For example, students need to understand words such as *before, after,* and *next.* Standardized tests of academic achievement often use words like *compare, contrast, define, describe,* and *enumerate.* Professionals need to ensure that students understand exactly what these words mean and that they are able to answer test questions accurately when these words are used.

Profile

Blanca was a third-grade Spanish-speaking student who had been identified as having a language-learning disability. Cheryl, the speech-language pathologist who worked with her spoke only a little Spanish. Cheryl spoke in Spanish to Blanca when possible but conducted her therapy primarily in English.

One of Cheryl's major goals was to increase Blanca's vocabulary skills so that she would experience greater success in the classroom curriculum. To this end, Blanca brought her third-grade language arts book to each therapy session. Cheryl coordinated with the third-grade teacher so that she knew what story the class was reading. Before Cheryl and Blanca read the actual story, Cheryl conducted a "picture walk" to help Blanca understand the "whole" of the story first. Cheryl and Blanca discussed the pictures in the story and talked about what was happening. Next, they read the story together. When they came across vocabulary words that were unfamiliar to Blanca, Cheryl had her write each word and its definition on a separate index card. She was also asked to draw a picture of the word. Blanca then wrote the word in her journal, using it in a sentence. The vocabulary words were reviewed often in subsequent therapy sessions.

Cheryl found that Blanca's classroom performance was greatly enhanced by this method. Blanca's third-grade teacher commented that Blanca appeared to have less difficulty understanding the stories in the language arts book. Her overall grades were improving. At the end of third grade, Blanca had made such excellent progress that she was able to graduate out of speech-language therapy.

I tried the above technique with students at my own school; it was extremely effective to use curriculum materials that the students were currently being exposed to in the classroom.

BUILDING LITERACY SKILLS

Many speech-language pathologists believe that they should focus only on oral language when working with the students on their caseloads. However, it is crucial for speech-language pathologists to work with other educational professionals to facilitate literacy development in CLD students with language-learning disabilities (Montgomery, 1998; Rosa-Lugo & Fradd, 2000). The acquisition of literacy skills is important for all students who are learning English as a second language.

As students engage in literacy activities, they learn about the world, acquire new vocabulary, and develop a heightened awareness of the structure of language and the ways in which words can be used to communicate information. CLD students with language-learning disabilities often have limited skills in reading, resulting in poor academic performance. These students often face five barriers:

1. Academic materials are usually in English.
2. Academic learning is intrinsically difficult for these students.
3. Phonological awareness may be limited.
4. Environmental experiences may be limited.
5. Problems affecting language interfere with learning.

As shown in Figure 15.5, experiences that provide environmental exposure are critical in helping students build the conceptual foundations that they need for success in learning to read. This exposure will lead to better oral language skills, enhanced phonological awareness, and reasoning skills that are critical for success in acquiring literacy. A major problem in many school programs is that professionals begin instruction at the "top of the ladder"—they try to teach literacy without the prerequisites of environmental experience and exposure. The building of oral language skills and phonological awareness is often underemphasized. The importance of enhancing environmental exposure and building strong oral communication skills cannot be overemphasized.

Language-learning disabled students may also be in need of activities to stimulate the development of phonological awareness. Activities to build phonological awareness help these students perform more successfully in the classroom (Gillon, 2004; Klingner, Artiles, & Mendez Barletta, 2006; Lipka et al., 2005; Vaughn, Mathes, Linan-Thompson, & Francis, 2005).

Strategies for Phonological Awareness Training

Phonological awareness can be defined as the ability to reflect on and manipulate consciously the sound system of a language. Phonological awareness is related to spelling, reading, and writing achievement (Goldsworthy, 2002). Thus, when attempting to develop literacy skills in CLD students, it is important to stimulate the development of phonological awareness (Silliman & Scott, 2006).

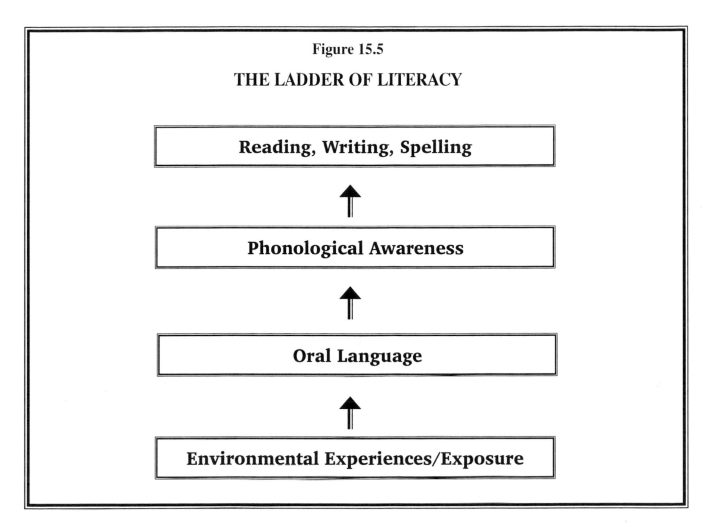

Figure 15.5

THE LADDER OF LITERACY

Reading, Writing, Spelling

↑

Phonological Awareness

↑

Oral Language

↑

Environmental Experiences/Exposure

Hadley, Simmerman, Long, and Luna (2000) found that explicit phonological instruction and vocabulary instruction in the classroom helped monolingual and bilingual children make excellent gains in a number of areas, including beginning sound awareness, letter-sound association, and overall vocabulary skills. Explicit phonological awareness instruction can be especially valuable for second language learners.

Swanson, Hodson, and Schommer-Atkins (2005) conducted a study in which they evaluated the effect of specific phonological awareness intervention conducted in English on reading development in adolescents who were poor readers with histories of low scores in reading. These poor readers, predominantly bilingual, spoke English as well as their first languages. Spanish and a number of Asian languages were spoken by participants in the study. The research was conducted primarily in a low-income, bilingual area.

Regardless of their first languages, the students who received specific phonological awareness intervention (as compared to a control group of students who did not receive this training) showed improvement in their ability to analyze the phonological construct of words. Swanson et al. (2005) concluded that the major clinical implication of their study was that the literacy skills of junior high students who are bilingual—and are also poor readers—can be enhanced by specific, systematic instruction designed to increase phonological awareness.

The phonological awareness activities and suggestions below are based on research reported by Goldsworthy (2002), Hadley et al. (2000), Roseberry-McKibbin (2001, 2002), Swanson et al. (2005), and Vaughn et al. (2005, 2006).

❑ Have students do the following:

A. Count the number of words in a sentence.

B. Count the number of syllables in a word.

C. Count the number of sounds in a word.

D. Identify rhyming words.

E. Use sound-blending skills to form words from individual sounds. (e.g., "c-a-t; what is that?")

F. Identify the first sound in a word.

G. Identify the last sound in a word.

H. Identify medial sounds in words

I. Match words with the same sound (Example: "Which pictures show words that begin with /s/?").

❑ Use rhythm sticks and clapping to emphasize the number of sounds and/or syllables in words.

❑ Ask students to bring items from home that begin or end with target sounds.

❑ Use a grab bag. Ask students to pull out objects, name them, and sort them into piles based on their beginning, middle, or ending sounds.

❑ Use rhymes. Books such as those written by Dr. Seuss work quite well. Children can recite rhymes, act them out, and view pictures that supplement the rhyme. Singing rhymes facilitates the learning of the rhymes.

❑ Use music. For example, the tune to "If you're happy and you know it" may be used by replacing the lyrics with "If your name begins with *b*, raise your hand."

❑ Use stories with Rebus-style pictures, and ask students to "read" the pictures.

❑ Use word play. For example, the professional might say, "This is a story about Prinderella and the Cince. Prinderella lived with her sticked wepmother and two sistee uglers. What am I really talking about?" The infamous "Pig Latin" is also fun. For example, the professional might say, "I'm so glad that Anuelmay is here today. Who am I really talking about? Right! Manuel!"

❑ Read a familiar story or poem and ask the students to fill in missing words as you read.

❑ As you read a rhyme, have students tap the table for each syllable or use a "shaker" for each syllable.

❑ Ask a student to remove a specific segment from a word. For example, "Say *cowboy* without *boy*."

❑ Tell the student that you are going to play a game that involves making up new words for things. For example, you might say that all things in the room now start with "b." So "desk" becomes "besk," "pencil" becomes "bencil," etc.

Professionals often feel that they have to use special programs to help students who have difficulties with reading, writing, and spelling. If students are to learn to function effectively in the classroom, however, it is important that classroom materials be incorporated into the instructional activities. Specialists can work collaboratively with the classroom teacher to develop individualized reading programs. Specialists can also use classroom materials to work on developing phonological awareness as well as overall literacy skills. For example, I recently had several kindergartners bring their decodable books that the classroom teacher was reading with them. We read the books and did phonological awareness activities based on the books.

REFLECTION

You are working in a junior high school where a new group of Hmong students has just arrived from Southeast Asia. These students have not learned to read or write in their primary language, and the teachers are referring them for special education services. The principal gives you some release time to develop a comprehensive summer program for these students. The program needs to help these students gain pre-literacy skills that will make it easier for them to catch up with their grade-level peers. What components will your summer program need to include? What skills will you emphasize and why?

_____

_____

_____

_____

_____

Increasing Reading Fluency and Comprehension: Specific Suggestions

As students get older, reading fluency and comprehension become increasingly more important for academic success. To increase these students' interest in reading, the context of the reading materials and learning activities should be relevant to students' life experiences (Powell & Davidson, 2005). Professionals should strive to be interactive with students when presenting learning activities (Curtin, 2006). For example, many students like talking with peers and teachers about what they are reading rather than just reading silently without any type of interaction.

As mentioned previously, CLD students, especially those with language-learning disabilities, often benefit greatly from vocabulary development activities. Vocabulary development is important for reading comprehension and fluency (Gersten & Geva, 2003; Klingner et al., 2006; McGregor, 2004; Montgomery, 2007; Wasik, Bond, & Hindman, 2006). In one study, researchers used decodable texts with DVDs to build reading vocabulary and fluency. The DVDs were used to preview vocabulary that students would encounter in their texts; these DVDs contained skits that illustrated the vocabulary that appeared in the decodable books. Students who were exposed to these DVDs greatly increased their vocabularies and overall reading comprehension skills (August, Carol, Dressler, & Snow, 2005). Other researchers have successfully used DVDs to enhance students' vocabulary learning (Verhallen, Bus, & de Jong, 2006). Professionals can take advantage of the findings of this research by developing short, interesting, animated DVDs that students can view prior to reading.

As discussed in an earlier chapter, several researchers have put forth the idea of increasing reading comprehension and fluency by teaching content-area cognates if possible (August et al., 2005; Rubenstein-Avila, 2006). For example, many words in Spanish are quite similar to their English counterparts. Professionals can use students' Spanish skills to teach new words in English. Thus, when teaching geometry to Spanish-speaking students, professionals can use cognates such as angle (ángulo), triangle (triángulo), sphere (esfera), and parallel lines (lineas paralelas). A geography teacher can point out such cognates as gulf (golfo), arid (arido), and volcanic (volcanico). English-only learners can also be invited to learn these cognate pairs.

Although this type of learning activity is appropriate for students learning to read in English, it is not appropriate for use in many languages. For example, Wang, Park, and Lee (2006) pointed out that Korean has a unique visual and spatial configuration compared with other orthographic systems in that it has a nonlinear spatial layout. Thus, it may be difficult for Korean speakers to transfer their orthographic skills from Korean to English. Bialystok, Luk, and Kwan (2005) agreed, citing the example of Chinese in Hong Kong; this language requires the memorization of specific characters because there is no phonological coding system. Bialystok et al. (2005), found that in their study, there was no transfer of specific Chinese reading skills to English. Vang (2005) stated that Hmong students cannot transfer Hmong vocabulary cognates to English.

For students from these language backgrounds, especially, the use of cloze activities can facilitate the development of reading fluency and comprehension. In cloze activities, approximately every fifth, seventh, or ninth word is omitted from a reading passage, as shown in the sample story below:

> It was a beautiful day, and the _____ was shining. _____were singing in the trees. Carlita hoped it would not _____, because she wanted to take a walk. She looked up into the sky and saw gray _____ moving in. In Mexico, when it rained, sometimes there was _____ and _____. Everything would be _____ for a long time after it had rained. Carlita decided she had better take an_____ just in case.

Students fill the words in orally, or they can write them in. Cloze activities help students to predict words and to use context to increase their understanding of what they are reading.

Professionals can also provide drill activities to help students learn to quickly identify high-frequency words (Vaughn et al., 2006). CLD students with language-learning disabilities often struggle when reading even simple high-frequency words such as the following:

the	of	and	a
to	in	you	is
that	it	at	he
for	on	are	as
with	his	they	be

Students who have not mastered high frequency words often find reading activities to be frustrating. I generally spend a few minutes every day drilling students on these words by asking them to read the words as quickly as possible. Even students in kindergarten enjoy this activity.

Experts today have emphasized that *Computer-Assisted Instruction* (CAI) can be most helpful for CLD students who are struggling with literacy, especially in the areas of reading fluency and comprehension as well as writing (Black, 2005; Green, 2005; Hallahan et al., 2005). Green (2005) pointed out that CAI increases the interest level of reading for older learners while keeping the text simple and easy to read. In addition, computers offer immediate feedback about performance.

Many computer reading programs have enjoyable graphics and special sound effects. In addition, there is software that can translate information into students' primary languages, thus giving them bilingual support as they learn new concepts (McArdle et al., 2005). This is especially helpful for students when there is no professional available who speaks their primary language. Because research shows that CLD students (especially those who are low-income) use the internet less frequently than their mainstream peers, it is especially important for professionals to encourage the use of computers to support literacy (National Center for Education Statistics, 2005).

One program that has been successful in increasing students' phonological awareness and other reading skills is Earobics (Cognitive Concepts, 2003). Fun, interactive websites for younger learners are www.primarygames.com and www.starfall.com. These lively websites feature music, games, phonological awareness development activities, and curriculum-oriented content in curriculum areas such as science and social studies. The websites include content that is in the public domain. Other highly-recommended websites include Interesting Things for ESL Students (www.manythings.org) and Repeat After Us, Your Online Library and Language Lab (www.repeatafterus.com). The latter is a free resource that provides texts, audio clips, and other information to help CLD students increase their English reading fluency and pronunciation skills.

It is also important to encourage students to engage in sustained silent reading (Trelease, 2006). Points and prizes can be awarded to students who read a specific number of pages or read for a certain number of minutes per month. Students can choose the material they wish to read (Nippold, Duthie, & Larsen, 2005).

The Preview-View-Review Technique

One excellent strategy for increasing students' reading comprehension and overall vocabulary skills is the *Preview-View-Review* technique. The adaptation of the **Preview-View-Review** (PVR) approach described below can be used effectively to help special-needs learners improve their literacy skills. This approach promotes learning within authentic situations in which an emphasis is placed on meaning. As previously stated, the ideal situation is for professionals to utilize books or other curricular materials from the students' regular education classroom settings. For example, students can bring their social studies books to speech-language therapy and clinicians can use these books as treatment materials for teaching the PVR technique.

Sample instructional goals and objectives that can be created when this approach is used are presented below:

IEP Goal: The student will use the preview-view-review technique of reading and studying in the classroom, speech room, and resource room. Performance will be judged by the classroom teacher, Special Education Resource Teacher, and Speech-Language Pathologist during the reading of passages from content area reading materials.

IEP Objectives/Benchmarks:

_____ will summarize and explain the PVR technique verbally upon request.

_____ will demonstrate use of the PVR technique with a chapter from a book selected from the classroom.

_____ will demonstrate use of the PVR technique with notes that have been taken in the classroom.

Professionals can help students use the following PVR strategies when reading chapters in books:

1. *Preview*

❏ Get an overview of the chapter by doing the following:

1. Read the title.

2. Read the introductory paragraph or section.

3. Look at headings, subdivisions, and illustrations.

4. Make a table-of-contents outline from the information and then use it as a study guide.

5. Examine the maps, graphs, charts, and other visuals.

6. Identify words in boldface or italics.

7. Do a "picture walk" by talking about pictures prior to actual reading.

❏ Read the main idea sentence of key paragraphs to understand the chapter's general concepts.

❏ Read the concluding paragraph or summary.

2. *View*

❏ Read the text aloud and have the student follow along.

❏ At natural stopping points, ask the student to explain what has just been read. If the student is working with a primary-language tutor, then the tutor and the student can discuss the printed text in the primary language.

❏ Use the scaffolding technique if the student cannot answer a question. For example, if the student is unable to answer the question "Who was President of the United States during the Civil War?" ask an either/or question, such as "During the Civil War, was Eisenhower or Lincoln the President of the United States?"

❏ Help the student visualize what is being read, especially if there are no pictures accompanying the text. Remind the student to "make pictures in your mind about what we read." For example, if the student is reading about a village in a particular country, you can say, "Tell me what you think the village looks like," or "Make a picture in your mind about that. What does it look like to you?" Students can even draw pictures to illustrate text.

❏ Help students look up definitions of unfamiliar terms. Many students need support in learning how to use a glossary. As mentioned previously, students can write new words and their definitions on index cards and draw pictures of what these terms depict.

❏ Have students highlight key words that will assist in review later on.

❏ Engage students in predicting what might happen next.

3. Review

❑ Look over chapter headings and subdivisions again to keep the big picture in focus.

❑ Review new vocabulary words.

❑ Read over highlights.

❑ Ask questions about the content.

1. general comprehension questions
2. true-false questions
3. either/or questions

❑ Help the student answer the questions at the end of the chapter. Students can respond orally or in writing.

❑ Have the student summarize the chapter orally or in writing. If the student types out the main points of the chapter using the computer, additional information can be inserted easily. The final product can be printed out, and the student can keep it for review.

❑ Ask the student for his/her opinions about what was read by asking questions such as the following:

1. What were the most important things in the chapter?
2. What did you think were the most interesting things in the chapter?
3. Was there anything you disagreed with? Why?

❑ Find out if the student needs questions answered about the chapter.

❑ Help the student create possible test questions and then have that student answer these questions. If there is a small group of students, they can exchange questions for practice.

The preview-view-review technique is illustrated in Figure 15.6. Professionals can use this technique with classroom materials as well as specialized materials. When classroom materials are used, students learn curriculum content as they apply strategies designed to help them learn more efficiently. Ideally, students will learn to use the strategies independently during various learning experiences in the classroom.

When working with students from diverse cultural backgrounds, the use of multi-sensory approaches to reading instruction is highly recommended. Many students with special-learning needs can benefit from the neurological impress method [NIM], a highly successful multisensory approach to reading. In this approach, the professional sits to the right and slightly behind the student so that she can speak clearly into the student's ear. The student reads the passage aloud with the professional, and follows each word by placing a finger underneath it. This approach and various other multi-sensory techniques for teaching reading have been reviewed in *Teaching Second Language Learners with Learning Disabilities* (Hearne, 2000), a practical and helpful resource for professionals who are providing instruction to second language learners who have special learning needs. By offering flexible programs of instruction that integrate oral and written language activities into the curriculum, special educators will be better able to meet the needs of students who come from diverse cultural and linguistic backgrounds.

Figure 15.6

SUPER POWER READING STRATEGIES

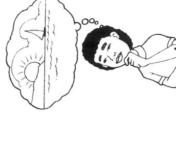

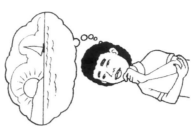

Before I read:

Look at the title, headings, and pictures.
Look at any words in italics or boldface.
Read the introductory and concluding paragraphs.

While I read:

Visualize what I read; make detailed pictures in my brain.
Ask myself questions about what I'm reading.
Predict what will happen next.
Highlight key ideas.
Look up new words that I do not know.

After I have read the whole thing:

Look at the title, headings, and pictures again.
Read over my highlights.
Ask questions about what I have just read.
Summarize what I have just read in my own words.

CONCLUSION

To provide appropriate instructional programs for a student population that is becoming increasingly more diverse, school professionals need to be sensitive to cultural differences and the effects that these differences can have on learning behavior. CLD students with special learning needs often experience difficulty responding appropriately in learning situations that offer instruction in English only. By providing opportunities for instruction in the primary language, the likelihood is increased that these students will experience success.

When developing intervention programs for CLD students, professionals from general education and special education programs should work as a team to ensure that students are provided with learning experiences that are culturally appropriate and relevant to their experiences. By offering collaborative programs of instruction and emphasizing an RtI model, the likelihood is increased that CLD students will develop the oral and written communication skills necessary to reach their full potential.

STUDY QUESTIONS

1. Summarize key components of the holistic-strategies approach.

2. Describe phonological awareness and its relationship to literacy. What are three specific activities professionals can present to increase phonological awareness in students?

3. Many American teachers use questions to help students become involved in the learning process. Discuss two things that professionals should NOT do when using questions with CLD students who have language-learning disabilities.

TRUE-FALSE

Circle the number beside each statement that is true.

4. The holistic-strategies approach emphasizes that professionals should correct students' grammatical errors to help them master English grammar more quickly.

5. Scaffolding is a technique in which the professional (or peer with a high level of skill) gives a student temporary support that is consistent with the student's current ability level. The professional gradually withdraws support until the student can function independently.

6. Phonological awareness can be defined as the ability to consciously reflect on and manipulate the sound system of a language.
7. In the Neurological Impress Technique, the professional uses computer software to help students learn through a multimodal approach.
8. In the strategy of reauditorization/silent rehearsal, students are told to repeat what they hear (e.g., oral directions) quietly to themselves.
9. Rhetorical questions tend to be highly effective with CLD students because questions of this type stimulate critical thinking.
10. Professionals who use the preview-view-review approach need special books with a specific type of focus for use with this strategy.

MULTIPLE CHOICE

Unless specified otherwise, circle the letter beside all choices that are correct.

11. Interpersonal communication goals for language-learning-disabled students may include the following:
    A. The student will maintain appropriate eye contact with others during communication.
    B. The student will request clarification when something is not understood.
    C. The student will listen to others without ever interrupting.
    D. If a listener shows confusion, the student will repeat exactly what she said.
    E. The student will greet others by smiling and saying "hello" when appropriate.

12. Which one of the following is NOT included in the hierarchy for teaching phonological awareness skills?
    A. Count the number of words in a paragraph.
    B. Count the number of words in a sentence.
    C. Count the number of syllables in a word.
    D. Count the number of sounds in a word.
    E. Use sound-blending skills to identify words.

13. To help CLD students with language-learning disabilities, professionals should do the following:
    A. Use preparatory sets.
    B. Limit clutter in the environment.
    C. Use few visuals to reduce distractions, and rely primarily on the auditory mode of teaching to help students focus on the information being presented.
    D. Seat the learner in the front of the classroom.
    E. Avoid saying the student's name so that he or she does not become self-conscious.

14. Which of the following are TRUE statements about graphic organizers?
    A. They can be very helpful when students are learning new vocabulary.
    B. They are used primarily to teach rules of grammar to CLD students with language-learning disabilities.
    C. They stimulate divergent thinking and help students to explore associations related to a key topic, word, or concept.
    D. They are useful for developing oral but not written language skills.
    E. They are used to integrate students' drawings into various language development activities.

15. Which of the following is NOT part of the scaffolding technique?
    A. Relating information presented to knowledge that has already been acquired
    B. Helping students learn from mistakes
    C. Using a multimodal approach with repeated exposure to concepts
    D. Helping and assisting the student until the student is able to work independently
    E. Having the student silently observe a model without talking about the activity

ANSWERS TO STUDY QUESTIONS

4. False	11. A, B, and E
5. True	12. A
6. True	13. A, B, and D
7. False	14. A and C
8. True	15. E
9. False	
10. False	

Chapter 16

WORKING WITH SPECIAL POPULATIONS OF STUDENTS WITH DISABILITIES

Outline

Culturally and linguistically diverse (CLD) students who have exceptional language needs associated with hearing impairment, neurological problems, and other disabilities present unique challenges for professionals who work with special learners. Professionals are also serving increasing numbers of CLD students in early intervention (pre-kindergarten) settings. This chapter addresses the needs of these student populations based on research regarding best practices for service delivery. Current research studies are summarized, and practical implications are described.

The populations of CLD students addressed in this chapter include those with autism, developmental delays, hearing impairments, augmentative communication requirements, and other special learning needs. Some of the information reported in previous chapters is reiterated here because of its relevance to the populations being addressed.

As professionals work with CLD families who have children with various types of severe disabilities, it is important to be aware of the profound stress that these families may be experiencing. (Rossetti, 2001; Shipley & Roseberry-McKibbin, 2006). Families often experience shock as well as confusion, anger, anxiety, and a feeling of being overwhelmed. For most parents, the birth of a child with a severe disability creates a family crisis of considerable magnitude. For parents who are struggling to learn English and survive economically, life can be difficult (Lynch, 2004; Zuniga, 2004).

These families, especially, need to work with professionals who are not only knowledgeable and competent, but who also convey compassion and empathy. They may be especially receptive to professionals who convey an attitude of friendship (Chan & Lee, 2004; Sharifzadeh, 2004). Professionals should show an interest in helping these families by having resources available to share with them. These resources can include free or reduced cost medical care and other "basics" of life (McNeilly & Coleman, 2000).

Professionals also need to bear in mind that children with moderate and severe disabilities often benefit most from exposure to two languages—it is especially important for family members to speak the first language (L1) at home if they have limited proficiency in English. We have already cited evidence that fluent, strong L1 skills support English acquisition and keep family members bonded; this is also the case with students with severe disabilities (Genesee et al., 2004; Harrison-Harris, 2002; Huer & Soto, 2006; Vang & Barrera, 2005). The development of skills in the first language is an appropriate goal even in homes where a child has a language impairment associated with autism, profound hearing loss, or another exceptional need.

EARLY ASSESSMENT AND INTERVENTION FOR YOUNG CLD CHILDREN WITH LANGUAGE-LEARNING DISABILITIES

When working with CLD preschool children who have language-learning disabilities, family participation is important. As mentioned previously, early independence and overall development in language and other areas are not stressed nearly as much as they are in mainstream culture. Thus, one foundational principle germane to serving young CLD children is that their families may not understand the value of services—especially those provided in early intervention settings.

❑ Cultural mediators are often necessary when school professionals are recommending early intervention. It is important to convey a respectful understanding of the families' beliefs and values and the provision of what are frequently much-needed services before the children formally begin kindergarten.

❑ CLD parents need to be provided with information to increase their understanding of how early intervention will positively impact their children's eventual academic performance in elementary school and beyond.

❑ The vast majority of CLD families value education and want their children to succeed in school. If they are shown how early intervention provides the foundation for success in school programs, they will be much more willing to accept early intervention services and to provide requested follow-through at home.

❑ Professionals should be aware that standardized assessment tools are highly inappropriate for many young CLD students who have had limited school experiences. Young children often have difficulty responding to the types of tasks included on norm-referenced measures (Mattes & Saldaña-Illingworth, 2008).

❑ One of the most valid ways for professionals to assess these young children is through parent report (Weitzner-Lin, 2004). This can involve gathering a detailed case history.

❑ Assessment can also include the use of established instruments such as the MacArthur Communicative Development Inventories (Fenson et al., 1992). This instrument has been translated into many languages, including Spanish, and research has shown that it has been successfully used with Spanish-speaking parents to help assess toddlers with potential language impairments (Heilmann, Ellis Weismer, Evans, & Hollar, 2005; Marchman & Martínez-Sussmann, 2002; Thal, Jackson-Maldonado, & Acosta, 2000).

❑ Professionals can also use established communication and symbolic behavior scales such as Wetherby and Prizant's (1992) Communication and Symbolic Behavior Scales, Rescorla's Language Development Survey (Rescorla, 1989; Rescorla & Alley, 2001), and others. Modifications, however, may be necessary to use these instruments effectively.

❑ Rescorla and Achenbach (2002) reported that, based on the results of their research, the Language Development Survey had the potential to be used successfully with CLD children and their families.

❑ Professionals can also conduct play-based assessment. The assessment of toddlers' symbolic play has gained popularity because skills in this area correlate with the development of language skills (Snyder & Scherer, 2004). Play-based assessment can be carried out in a child's home, involve caregivers with whom the child is comfortable, and yield excellent information about the child's developing cognitive-linguistic skills and use of both L1 and English.

More information about current instruments for assessing the language skills of young CLD children is available from the ERIC Clearinghouse on Assessment and Evaluation (available at http://www.ericae.net). Another current, highly comprehensive source for professionals who work with young CLD children is the Early Childhood Research Institute on Culturally and Linguistically Appropriate Services (CLAS). Their website can be accessed at http://clas.uiuc.edu/special/child-find/index.html. Professionals who access this site will find reproducible, informative booklets and brochures in a variety of languages that provide information about the importance of early intervention, general information about child development, guidelines for identifying problems in hearing, vision, and development, and other useful items.

Intervention for young CLD children with language-learning disabilities can take many forms. First, it is ideal if these children are given bilingual intervention by a bilingual speech-language pathologist who emphasizes L1 as well as English development (Rodríguez & Higgins, 2005).

Second, speech-language pathologists and other specialists can train preschool and day-care teachers in specific strategies for promoting these children's language development. Because so many young CLD children attend preschool or day-care programs, the training of their teachers in these settings can facilitate the development of language skills in a variety of areas (de Rivera, Girolametto, Greenberg, & Weitzman, 2005; Dickinson & Tabors, 2001).

Early-childhood professionals can be trained in specific language development techniques (in both L1 and English) such as the use of open-ended questions rather than close-ended questions that discourage further conversation. These professionals can also be trained in specific techniques for facilitating the development of the social interaction skills necessary to interact with CLD peers and mainstream speakers of English.

It is important to help young children develop positive interactions with peers. Researchers have found that even children as young as 3 years of age reject peers whom they perceive as "different"; this includes young CLD children with and without language impairments (Rice, Sell, & Hadley, 1991; Tabors, 1997; Weiss, 2002). Thus, it is extremely important for all professionals to facilitate students' interaction with peers (Genesee et al., 2004). Table 16.1 includes specific, practical strategies that can be used to do this.

Strategies for Facilitating Emergent Literacy

Strategies for facilitating emergent literacy skills in preschool and in other early intervention settings have been described by a number of researchers (Fey, Windsor, & Warren, 1995; Kaderavek & Boucher, 2006; Roseberry-McKibbin, 2008; Tabors, 1997). It is important to target phonological awareness and to facilitate literacy practices at home, as described in other chapters. Common recommendations for early reading instruction include the following:

❏ Keep book-reading time short.

❏ Use predictable books.

❏ Use stories with Rebus-style pictures.

❏ Use books that have highly dramatic or exciting story themes.

❏ Use books that have engaging, colorful pictures, manipulative components such as flaps, buttons that make noise when pressed, and moveable tabs.

CLD preschool children with language-learning disabilities will benefit greatly from early assessment and treatment that promotes oral language development in L1, oral language development in English, and the development of emergent literacy skills. Family participation should be encouraged.

REFLECTION

Describe three specific strategies that professionals can use to support young CLD children with language-learning disabilities and their families.

_____

_____

_____

_____

_____

Table 16.1

Practical Strategies for Increasing Young CLD Children's Successful Peer Interactions

The strategies suggested below are based on a review of the research literature (see Dickenson & Tabors, 2001; Genesee et al., 2004; Girolametto et al., 2005; Nungesser & Watkins, 2005; Rodríguez & Higgins, 2005; Tabors, 1997; Weiss, 2002).

1. If a child has difficulty entering peer groups and initiating play, use picture symbols that visually depict social rules. As suggested by Nungesser & Watkins (2005), for example, stick figures can be used to illustrate appropriate social behaviors:

   Rule 1: "Walk" (Target behavior: "Walk over to your friend.")
   Rule 2: "Watch" (Target behavior: "Watch what your friend is doing.")
   Rule 3: "Get a toy" (Target behavior: "Get a toy like your friend is using.")
   Rule 4: "Do the same thing" (Target behavior: "Do what your friend is doing.")
   Rule 5: "Tell an idea" (Target behavior: "Come up with an idea.")

2. When a CLD child asks an adult for something, direct her to a typically-developing peer and provide information that will facilitate the interaction. For example, the professional might tell José that his friend Mark wants to play in the sandbox. The professional then tells José to say, "Mark, sandbox, please." In this situation Mark is being provided with information about what José will be requesting and José is being helped to provide an appropriate request.

3. Teach the CLD child to use routine phrases to initiate interactions and seek help relating to basic needs. These phrases might include:

   I need help.
   Can I play?
   I'm hungry.
   I want that.
   I need the bathroom, please.
   Hi, how are you?

4. Learn a few key words in the child's first language and use these words frequently, especially during the first few weeks that the child is in a preschool or daycare setting. Hearing words such as *bathroom, eat*, and *listen* in the L1 gives CLD preschoolers a sense of connection and helps them learn preschool routines more quickly.

5. When addressing CLD children, "double the strength of the message" *by* accompanying words with a gesture, action, or directed gaze.

6. Establish simple, consistent, daily routines that can be used by CLD children who speak little or no English. These include snack time, clean up, circle time, and other routines that allow CLD children to immediately act like members of the group.

7. Structure small group activities so that they always include a mix of CLD and monolingual English-speaking children. In this way, CLD children are automatically included in the group and have many more opportunities for interaction.

8. Encourage parents to participate in classroom activities by teaching songs in L1, serving foods from their homeland, and doing general volunteer activities that do not necessarily require fluent English skills. Children frequently "blossom" more when their parents are included.

SERVICE DELIVERY TO CLD DEAF STUDENTS

In this section, the term **hearing impaired** (HI) is used to describe children whose hearing difficulties are moderate to profound and whose hearing impairment impacts daily communication and general life functions. Hearing impairment in children can be mild, creating few problems with communication or academics. It can also be severe to profound, causing major communication problems.

❏ According to the Gallaudet Research Institute (2005), 50% of the U.S. deaf population is White, 25% is Hispanic, 15.3% is African American, and the remaining 9.7% are from an Asian/Pacific Islander or mixed ethnic background.

❏ Prognosis for the improvement of speech and language skills in children with hearing impairment depends on several factors: (1) how early in life these children receive professional help; (2) the scope and quality of the services the children receive; (3) the extent to which parents and other caregivers support these children; and (4) the presence of other disabling conditions (e.g., brain damage, blindness, atypical gross motor development, difficulties with sensory integration) (Wiley & Moeller, 2007).

❏ An important consideration in the educational success of deaf and hearing-impaired children is the age at which the hearing loss is identified (Yoshinaga-Itano, 2003). The later a hearing loss is identified, the more disruptive it is to the process of language development.

❏ White deaf children are typically diagnosed, on the average, at 17 months of age, whereas Hispanic and African American deaf children are often not diagnosed till 19 months of age or later (Stewart & Kluwin, 2001).

❏ CLD families that live in rural areas may not have access to universal newborn screening, which can detect hearing impairment in infancy.

❏ Children of migrant farm workers may be especially vulnerable to childhood-onset moderate-to-severe hearing loss because they work alongside their parents in jobs with high levels of noise exposure. Audiological services for these children are often remote and hard to come by (Smiley & Threats, 2006). For these families, even if their children are identified as having hearing impairment, there are many barriers to receiving services. These barriers include lack of transportation to clinics, and jobs that do not allow parents time off to take their children to medical appointments.

❏ A variety of cultural factors may impact how families react to children with hearing impairment. Many families react with embarrassment and shame, or the belief that God has given the family a deaf child as a cross they must bear. For example, in China, some parents of children with hearing impairment might be embarrassed and feel pity for their children, hiding them from society. These parents have a vital role to play in their children's lives— finding a cure for the hearing impairment. The goal is to fix what is wrong with the child (Lytle, Johnson, & Hui, 2006).

❏ It is important to be sensitive to differences in how families react to hearing impairments. African American families in the U.S. may seek help from their churches and communities; this may be considered more appropriate than seeking help from "strangers" (Stewart & Kluwin, 2001).

❏ Some families believe that a child with a hearing impairment reflects some fault on the part of one or both parents. Part of the difficulty these parents deal with is that in many countries, there are biases against individuals who have hearing impairment. There are very few services and opportunities for them, and their educational and vocational opportunities in life may be limited (Lytle et al., 2006; Mason, 2005; Monreal & Hernández, 2005).

Aarts (2001) described her experiences in providing audiology services at a private clinic in Saudi Arabia. In one particular instance, she (through an interpreter) told a mother that her baby was deaf. In Aarts' words (p. 34):

> The mother's reaction was swift and intense. She swung her chair over to the wall...and began wailing loudly...My interpreter immediately started talking, very fast and very low...Later [when the mother had left] and we had a few free minutes, I asked my interpreter what she had said to this mother. "Well," she said matter-of-factly, "I told her to stop that crying, you know? By her crying she was questioning the will of Allah. I told her 'your son has arms and legs and eyes, you should thank Allah for what he has given you, not wail about what he has not...' Arabic has no word for sadness.

It is possible that in cases such as this, parents may be reluctant to seek out aural rehabilitation or to have these children wear a hearing aid. If a hearing aid is desired, Scott (2002) recommended that professionals pay attention to the color of the hearing aid selected for the child. Hearing aids will be more acceptable if they closely match children's skin tones.

CLD families vary in their beliefs about how to deal with their children's hearing impairment. Some Chinese parents believe that the use of herbs and acupuncture will "heal" the hearing impairment. Some rural U.S. parents believe that a faith healer can restore their child's hearing.

If the family believes that the impairment can be healed by alternative methods, they may postpone seeking intervention and the child may suffer in the classroom. Smiley and Threats (2006) stated that professionals can deal with this problem in either of two ways:

1. Persuade families that the hearing loss is permanent; it cannot be "healed" or improved.

2. Explain that seeking professional services, such as those provided by an audiologist, does not negate the possibility of divine intervention or healing from an alternative means such as acupuncture. As Smiley and Threats (2006, p. 26) stated, "...science is not competing with religion, and they can both co-exist and work together to improve the child's life and possibilities."

Some of the major challenges faced by school professionals in meeting the needs of students with hearing impairment are the following:

❏ For many CLD students with hearing impairment, identity is a major issue. Does a Hispanic child who is deaf identify first with the Hispanic culture or deaf culture? (Berke, 2006).

❏ Multiple sources of prejudice may be experienced by CLD students who are deaf. For example, the African American deaf child must learn to deal with the prejudice associated with deafness and also with her ethnicity. Bagli (2002) pointed out that the deaf African American child in school usually has to deal with teachers who are neither African American nor deaf and thus do not understand the child well. Bagli stated that "The deaf African American child must learn the rules of each culture, abide by them, and also develop his or her own values and self image" (p. 398).

❏ Another challenge experienced by CLD children with hearing impairment is that they are less likely to be placed in appropriate communication situations, less likely to be moved out of restrictive environments, and more likely to be kept in special classes (Stewart & Kluwin, 2001).

❑ The academic underachievement of these children in comparison to their hearing peers is wide- ly documented. Some CLD deaf students start school behind their White peers and fall further behind each year (Parasnis & Fischer, 2005).

❑ Clinically significant oral and written language deficits are common among hearing-impaired speakers of English and other languages. Tur-Kaspa and Dromi (2001), for example, found that deaf speakers of Hebrew had significantly more grammatical deviations in their written and spoken language samples than matched typically-hearing peers.

❑ Regional differences influence the use of sign language by deaf populations. For instance, in China, there are several forms of Chinese sign language (Lytle et al., 2006). Most Spanish-speak- ing countries have their own forms of sign language (e.g., Colombian Sign Language, Mexican sign language) (Berke, 2007). In Spain three major sign languages are used by deaf populations (Mattes & García-Easterly, 2007).

Sign Language and CLD Students

American Sign Language is used widely with deaf and hearing impaired students in the United States. CLD children from other countries, however, may have little or no knowledge of English and may use a sign language system that is considerably different from ASL.

ASL, however, has influenced sign language systems throughout the world. The first schools for the deaf in Peru, for example, were started by immigrants from the United States who brought American Sign Language into the country. Many of these signs have become part of Peruvian Sign Language (Mattes & García-Easterly, 2007).

Immigrant parents of students with hearing impairment may feel that sign language will in- terfere with the development of spoken language skills. Research, however, has shown that deaf children of deaf parents from homes where sign language is used experience greater success in acquiring academic skills than deaf children with parents who do not have impaired hearing and who do not use sign language. Bilingual programs of instruction that promote the development of skills in sign language help students to develop language competencies that facilitate the learning of English (Paul, 2001).

CLD students with severe hearing impairment who immigrate to the United States may have had no exposure to sign language prior to their arrival. Deaf students are often taught to be "oral" so that they can obtain employment and function in society. In Peru, for example, deaf children in school settings are often taught by individuals who have had no specific train- ing related to the education of deaf children or children with other special learning needs. Often students with a variety of types of disabilities are taught in the same classroom (Mattes & García- Easterly, 2007).

School professionals working with hearing-impaired immigrants are faced with many chal- lenges. Students from Mexico may come to school with some level of proficiency in Spanish and may use Mexican Sign Language if they have had any exposure at all to manual forms of com- munication. The teacher, however, may speak only English and may not be familiar with Mexican Sign Language. Placing these students in an English-only classroom with an interpreter who uses American Sign Language is not likely to provide them with the "comprehensible input" that they need to learn academic subjects efficiently.

Hearing Impairment and Sound Amplification

Eriks-Brophy and Ayukawa (2000) investigated the potential benefits of sound field amplifica- tion for Inuit first- and second-language learners. The study was conducted in Kangiqsualujjuaq, a village of approximately 650 Inuit in the Nunavik region of northern Quebec. The primary language in Nunavik is Inuttitut, and students are educated in this language from kindergarten through grade 2 by Inuit teachers. A transition takes place between Inuttitut and second language instruction in either French or English when children enter third grade. At this time, these students are usually taught by non-Inuit teachers, but they continue to have several classes a week in Inuttitut.

One challenge that many Inuit children experience is a high prevalence of otitis media. Sometimes the hearing loss caused by otitis media presents such a challenge to Inuit children that they must be fitted with hearing aids. The replacement of broken hearing aids is often problematic because of Nunavik's isolated geographic location. Consequently, many Inuit students with hearing impairment receive inconsistent amplification in the classroom setting. This places them at risk for academic difficulties because of their reduced levels of hearing.

Accordingly, the purpose of this study was to investigate the usefulness of sound field amplification in the classroom setting using FM systems. FM systems allow teachers to speak into a microphone that transmits sound directly to hearing devices worn by the students. Findings from the study indicated that in classrooms where FM systems were installed, students with and without hearing impairments showed significant improvement on a speech intelligibility task in noise. For some of the students who attended classrooms with FM systems, their overall scores in attending behavior improved significantly.

An analysis of teacher and student comments showed that the students in classrooms that had FM systems learned new words more quickly. In addition, when FM systems were used, students participated more frequently during discussions in L2.

Though only a small number of subjects participated in this pilot study, Brophy and Ayukawa suggested that one might conjecture that sound amplification systems in classroom settings are beneficial to second language learners, especially those who are at increased risk for auditory difficulties. FM systems benefited students with normal hearing and students with behavioral or attentional difficulties.

More research on the efficacy of FM systems in classrooms with CLD students is needed; however, it is interesting to note that second language learners without hearing impairment as well as those with hearing impairment were found to benefit from the use of FM systems in the classroom.

In the United States, individuals with hearing impairment generally have access to technology such as FM systems and text telephones, and this technology enables them to type phone messages over the phone network (National Dissemination Center for Children with Disabilities, 2004). In many countries, access to technology is quite limited (Lylte et al., 2006). Thus, children and families may be uncomfortable using technology that most Americans take for granted. Cultural mediators can help families understand the benefits that technology can offer to children with hearing impairment.

Intervention for CLD Students with Hearing Impairment

Stewart and Kluwin (2001) pointed out that education of deaf children is anchored in two major assumptions: (1) the earlier in life that intervention occurs, the better, and (2) parents are an integral part of the education of their deaf children.

As we have said elsewhere in this book, for some families, early independence for children—and thus early intervention—are not priorities. In addition, families from some cultures believe that it is not appropriate for them to be involved in their children's education. Professionals can offer these families a range of options.

In programs for deaf children, use of sign language as the medium of instruction in content areas is often appropriate in the early school years. Communicative proficiency in ASL, for example, can be used to help students acquire knowledge of classroom subject matter (Paul, 2001). It is important for parents to understand how the use of sign language can facilitate success in learning the classroom curriculum.

Another possible challenge for CLD families is that in some countries, children with hearing impairment are segregated from their hearing peers (Hyde, Ohna, & Hjulstadt, 2006; Mattes & García-Easterly, 2007). In the United States., these children and their families may experience some degree of "culture shock" if the children are integrated into general education classrooms with "normal" children. When CLD children with hearing impairment are integrated into classrooms within the general education curriculum, it is important for teachers to make modifications for these children. Strategies described in the literature (see Lang, 2000; Pagliaro, 2001; Teagle & Moore, 2002) that can be used to accommodate CLD children who have hearing impairment include the following:

1. Seat the student where he can have full visual access to the teacher.

2. Accommodate the student when changes in seating are necessary to maximize visual access.

3. Make sure that teachers and others presenting information have full lighting with no shadows.

4. Face the students when presenting information orally. Try not to speak when writing on the board if you are not facing the student.

5. Use a peer "buddy" to assist the student when problems are experienced understanding information presented orally.

6. Use visual aids as much as possible to supplement what the teacher is saying. For example, when discussing math problems, write the problems on the board or use an overhead projector with transparencies containing the math problems.

7. Ask the student to repeat instructions to verify that the information was heard and understood.

8. Seat the student away from sources of noise such as telephones, pencil sharpeners, and open windows.

It is important to provide the child with appropriate assistive technology. As previously mentioned, FM units can be very helpful. It is important for schools to provide appropriate personnel to maintain these units and ensure that they are working for the child's maximal benefit (Thibodeau & DeConde Johnson, 2005).

The National Dissemination Center for Children with Disabilities has a detailed, informative website about services for children with severe impairments such as hearing loss and blindness. This organization can be reached at *www.nichcy.org*.

Profile

I recently received a speech-language screening referral from a kindergarten teacher. Sven T., a five-year-old child, was referred for "difficulty understanding instructions, expressing thoughts, articulating words clearly, and repeating what he hears." When I talked with Sven on a 1:1 basis in a quiet room, I found that he was a bright, rather shy child who conversed well in English.

Baffled at the reason for the referral, I called Mrs. T. She said that her husband spoke to Sven in English and that she spoke exclusively in Swedish to him at home. Sven had never been to preschool, and he had been in kindergarten for only nine days at the time of the referral. Mrs. T. expressed concern about Sven's hearing. She said that Sven seemed to have difficulty hearing his name after a bad concussion that occurred when he was 1½ years old. Mrs T. thought that sometimes in noisy environments, he was reading her lips. The classroom teacher also noticed that Sven, although well-behaved, spoke quite softly and somewhat unintelligibly. When directions were presented orally during class, he often did not respond.

I referred Mrs. T. to an audiologist for a full evaluation of Sven's hearing, and told his teacher that we needed to take this first step before any special education screening was conducted. If any testing became necessary, information about performance in both Swedish and English would be required.

SERVICE DELIVERY TO CLD STUDENTS ON THE AUTISM SPECTRUM

The rise of autism in children worldwide has been documented by a number of sources (Trembath, Balandin, & Rossi, 2005; Wong et al., 2004). For example, the Australian Education Department reported a 276% rise in students with Autism Spectrum Disorder (ASD) between 2000 and 2005. Japan, the United Kingdom, China, Denmark, and Russia have also reported an increased number of cases (Autism Incidence Encyclopedia, 2007). Thus in the United States, professionals may expect to see an increase in the number of immigrant students with Autism Spectrum Disorder (ASD). Some researchers has reported that there is a higher prevalence of autism among immigrants to the United States than among the general population. However, this research is preliminary; more studies need to be done to confirm this finding (Dyches, Wilder, Sudweek, Obiakor, & Algozzine, 2004). It is important to note that the higher incidence of autism may be due, at least in part, to greater awareness of the problem and improved diagnostic techniques. Further research is needed to identify specific factors that have resulted in the increased incidence of the disorder.

❑ Dyches et al. (2004), pointed out that for any parent of a child diagnosed with ASD, part of the grief is the loss of a previously "normal" child. Parents generally see no evidence of an abnormality when the child is first born.

❑ Identification of ASD in young children is challenging for professionals who work with monolingual English-speaking children and their families. It is often more complex when CLD students are involved.

❑ Wilder, Dyches, Obiakor, and Algozzine (2004) stated that CLD students with autism have a triple-layered challenge: they are culturally diverse, linguistically diverse, and have an exceptionality that often involves highly divergent behavior patterns.

❑ Unfortunately, if young children are not speaking, pediatricians may attribute the observed behaviors to the bilingual situation at home and may tell parents that the children will "grow out of it."

❑ In some cultures, there is a greater tolerance for boys who demonstrate delays in learning to speak. These boys are not viewed with alarm or suspicion; they will eventually speak, and no one is worried about their lack of verbalization.

❑ In many countries, there is little or no recognition of the phenomenon of ASD. If there is recognition of ASD, there may be a stigma attached to it (Cho, Singer, & Brenner, 2003; Magiati, Dockrell, & Logotheti, 2002; Martz, 2005; Rimashevakaia, 2007). For example, the Native American and Native Hawaiian assimilation of individuals with disabilities into mainstream culture is reflected in the absence of native language classifications or labels for disabilities such as

ASD. Descriptors such as "she runs away" or "he gets excited" or "he's in his own world" may be used to describe individuals with specific disabilities (Dyches et al., 2004).

❏ Wilder et al. (2004) reported that South Asian families often fear that females with disabilities will have difficulty finding a marriage partner. In other Asian cultures, even the marriageability of the disabled child's siblings could be affected (Chan & Lee, 2004). Thus, the family may not be willing to accept the label of ASD.

The extent to which families are able to accept having children with disabilities such as ASD varies from culture to culture (Stoll, Tolentino, & Roseberry-McKibbin, 2008). Cho et al. (2003), interviewed immigrant Korean mothers to the United States and mothers living in Korea; all were mothers of children with ASD. Cho et al. found that mothers living in Korea experienced more difficulties than those living in the United States. Mothers in Korea shared more situations of experiencing negative reactions from others, especially involving shame and humiliation in public when their children misbehaved. They reported feeling demoralized much more often than mothers from the United States.

Cho et al. recommended that especially upon initial diagnosis of ASD in children, professionals need to listen carefully to Korean mothers and be sensitive to low morale and suicidal ideation. In traditional Korean families, family suicide may be considered an honorable way to remove shame from the larger extended family. Stress levels for Korean mothers in the United States were greatly mitigated by support groups, the provision of services for children, and professional support.

In some countries, there are few services available for students with ASD—especially early intervention services. Many countries have few professionals who are trained to work with this population (Clark & Zhou, 2005). The available services may come in the form of separate institutions for students with ASD, although efforts are being made to provide other options.

In China, the Ministry acknowledges that there are no public education (including special education) programs for children with ASD. However, there are private programs/institutions in which services are available for these children (Clark & Zhou, 2005).

Denmark researchers Trillingsgaard, Sorensen, Nemec, and Jorgenson (2005) identified specific "red flags" that were indicative of ASD. They stated that professionals in any country can look for these red flags:

1. Child does not respond when others smile.

2. Child does not respond when name is called.

3. Child does not respond when others point.

4. Child does not "read" others' faces for information.

5. Child does not join functional play with an adult.

6. Child does not initiate requests.

It is imperative that educational professionals help educate members of the medical community about early ASD diagnosis in CLD children because research consistently converges upon the fact that early assessment and intervention are critical in helping these children achieve their potential (Trembath et al., 2005; Wong et al., 2004).

❏ Some families of students with suspected or diagnosed ASD view disabilities differently than mainstream professionals and thus may not be comfortable with recommended assessment and intervention protocols. For example, some Navajos believe that a person with a disability is a teacher for the entire tribe. The person with the disability brings special lessons to the tribe; she has a unique gift to offer. If she receives specialized interventions, this could potentially interfere with the delivery of the message to the tribe (Dyches et al., 2004; Rogers-Adkinson, Ochoa, & Delgado, 2003).

❏ Other families, as previously described, may view the child's disability as a punishment for the sins of the parents or even ancestors. Thus, the child is the family's "cross to bear," and intervention to ameliorate aspects of the disability is viewed as inappropriate. Professionals may become frustrated with families who accept their children at a "low" level of functioning. Professionals must not misinterpret this acceptance as families' attempts to resist recommendations.

❏ Families that are in the United States illegally are especially afraid to seek services for their children with ASD because they fear deportation if they become too "visible" (Griffin & de la Vega, 2003).

❏ For some CLD families, seeking services for their children with ASD is difficult because provision of these services may conflict with their cultural values. Also, the teaching strategies used in such programs may not "fit" with the expectations of parents. For example, in many cultures, the use of token economies (a popular strategy for the treatment of students with ASD) is a completely unfamiliar concept (Rogers-Atkinson et al., 2003).

❏ Some special education professionals use a play-based approach to treatment for young children with ASD. Asian parents, however, may prefer highly structured learning that involves repeated and systematic practice of new skills (Fung & Roseberry-McKibbin, 1999; Trembath et al., 2005).

Working with Parents of Students with Autism Spectrum Disorder

School professionals should be open to learning about cultural differences in the treatment of children with ASD. Families may be familiar with alternative treatments not commonly used by school professionals in the United States. In China, for example, treatment for children with ASD can include acupuncture, music therapy, and herbal remedies. Acupuncture for children with ASD is believed to focus on areas thought to be involved with ASD (e.g., the frontal lobe and cerebellum) (Clark & Zhou, 2005). Silva and Cignolini (2005) described several cases of Chinese children with ASD who benefited from Qigong, a highly specialized type of Chinese massage.

It is important to share with parents that instructional approaches used in school can coexist with alternative forms of intervention. For example, if a Chinese family accepts Western intervention for their child with ASD, the use of Qigong massage need not be discontinued at home.

Prelock, Beatson, Bitner, Broder, and Ducker (2003) discussed working with CLD families of students with ASD. They encouraged professionals to work within a "strengths" perspective instead of a "cultural destructiveness" perspective. In the latter perspective, professionals view cultural differences as pathologies and may attempt to discourage access to resources viewed to be important by the family.

In the strengths perspective, the families' pain is acknowledged and the team works to build a trust-based relationship, believing that the families' strengths will ultimately be useful in providing answers to dilemmas faced by themselves and their children.

Callicott (2003) discussed the related and extended concept of person-centered planning (PCP). In PCP, the person with the disability is involved in a meaningful level of planning for his future. A facilitator as well as a team of professionals are involved in jointly addressing issues of vocation, independent or semi-independent living, leisure or recreational choices, and community involvement.

PCP is most appropriate for CLD families of students with ASD because there is an emphasis on discussion, exploring issues (not issuing commands and dictates), and ultimately generating solutions that are mutually agreed upon by everyone. Many mainstream professionals expect that students with ASD and other disabilities will eventually be mainstreamed into the community to function as independently as possible (Wilder et al., 2004). This may not be the goal of some CLD families, who view their job as taking care of the child with ASD for the rest of his life. PCP can address these differing views and help families and students reach decisions that are beneficial to everyone.

Intervention Suggestions for Students with Autism Spectrum Disorder

❏ Use bilingual specialists to provide instruction if at all possible. (Wilder et al., 2004). If bilingual specialists are not available, ESL and special education personnel can collaborate to design appropriate programs.

❏ Reinforce the student for following school rules and conforming to classroom expectations. Students with ASD may have difficulty adapting to changes in routine. Many children with ASD, for example, are sensitive to food textures. Families often want their children to eat ethnic foods as much as possible. Schools, however, may generally not offer these foods in the school cafeteria. Although efforts should be made to offer "ethnic foods," students should also learn to tolerate the more "mainstream" foods that are commonly offered at school (Rogers-Adkinson et al., 2003).

❏ Pair students with peer buddies for increased socialization opportunities. Students with ASD generally need to learn basic social interaction skills (Duran, 2001a, 2001b; Wilder et al., 2004). Specifically, Duran (2001a) recommended teaching these students the following skills:

1. greeting others (e.g., saying "hi")
2. responding to greetings
3. tolerating being touched when greeted by or introduced to someone else (e.g., handshaking)
4. responding to basic questions that co-workers or peers may ask

Duran (2001a, 2001b) found that in her study of older Hispanic students with ASD, working in the community was difficult because Hispanic co-workers misunderstood them. This sometimes resulted in job termination or a decision by the parents to remove the student from vocational training programs.

❏ Provide programs to help classmates and work associates become understanding and supportive of individuals with ASD. Duran (2001b) found that co-workers referred to individuals with ASD as "pobrecito" (poor child) and believed that these students should be at home being cared for by family. Thus, they did not view these individuals as being capable of functioning independently on the job.]

Profile ▬▬▬▬▬▬▬▬▬▬▬▬▬▬▬▬▬▬▬▬▬▬▬▬▬

Abdul S. was referred to me by his kindergarten teacher. The teacher was concerned because after two years of kindergarten, Abdul rarely spoke in the classroom setting. He was from a Pakistani Urdu-speaking family, and the teacher had initially told herself to "give him time" to develop. She did not want to refer him unnecessarily for a special education evaluation. However, after two years of kindergarten and "extra" non-special education services, Abdul's progress was very limited.

When I met with his mother, Mrs. S., she said that prenatal testing during her pregnancy with Abdul revealed that he only had one kidney. The hospital personnel strongly urged Mrs. S. to terminate the pregnancy. Mrs. S., being Muslim, would not terminate her pregnancy. Abdul was born at seven months' gestation and spent much of the first year of his life in the neonatal intensive care unit.

Mrs. S. told me that Abdul spoke his first word in Urdu when he was three years old. She said that his brother spoke much better and earlier than Abdul. Abdul often echoed what his brother said and had difficulty remembering directions that were given to him at home in Urdu.

I evaluated Abdul in both English and Urdu (with the help of an interpreter). He was placed into speech-language therapy. He was also evaluated by the school psychologist, using a battery consisting primarily of nonverbal measures, and was diagnosed with mental retardation and autistic-like behaviors.

Today, Abdul is a handsome, well-behaved fifth grader who receives speech-language therapy and support from the site resource specialist. In junior high school, he will probably participate in a functional life skills class especially designed to support students with similar learning needs.

SERVICE DELIVERY TO CLD STUDENTS WITH DEVELOPMENTAL DELAY (MENTAL RETARDATION)

The identification of children with developmental delay is often difficult in students who use two languages. Students who are identified as being "slow learners," often require help from professionals with specialized training.

❏ Some populations of CLD students may be vulnerable to developmental delay/mental retardation (MR) because of poverty. Pregnant mothers may not be able to access prenatal health care or nutritious food and, therefore, are more likely to have children with disabilities. Professionals need to help these mothers become aware of free prenatal screening services (Roseberry-McKibbin, 2008).

❏ CLD students may also be exposed to lead pre- or post-natally at a higher rate than mainstream students if they are poor or work with their migrant parents in the fields (Cantor, Goldman, Courtney, & Kattan, 2003).

❏ It is well documented that CLD students are overrepresented in the category of "mental retardation," so professionals must be careful to use culturally and linguistically appropriate assessment instruments when determining the presence of developmental delays in CLD students (Green, 2005).

❏ In a study comparing 330 Swedish children with Down Syndrome and 336 typically-developing Swedish children, Berglund, Eriksson, and Johansson (2001) found that vocabulary skills developed slightly ahead of grammar and pragmatics skills in children with Down Syndrome. The researchers emphasized the importance of early intervention and recommended that early language stimulation programs for children with Down Syndrome pay special attention to the development of grammar and pragmatics skills. More research should be conducted to confirm the findings of this study.

❏ Kay-Raining Bird, Trudeau, Thordardottir, Sutton, and Thorpe (2005) compared the language abilities of children with Down syndrome who were being raised bilingually with those of three control groups matched on developmental level. These three groups consisted of (1) monolingual typically-developing children; (2) monolingual children with Down syndrome; and (3) bilingual typically-developing children. The results indicated that exposure to two languages had no detrimental effects on the language development of children with Down Syndrome.

❏ Toppelberg, Snow, and Tager-Flusberg (1999) recommended that bilingual children with mental retardation not experience demands to learn languages that will not be central to their future communication needs (e.g., studying a foreign language in high school).

❏ Valdivia (1999) noted that some CLD families do not view early intervention as something that is critical for children with mental retardation. For example, she stated that in some families, it is acceptable for a child not to learn to use a spoon to feed himself until shortly before kindergarten. Drinking from a cup before three to four years of age is not a priority. Thus, as always, professionals must be especially sensitive to the cultural congruence of early intervention recommendations.

❏ Gronroos (2003) discussed recommendations for interacting with CLD families who have children with mental retardation. She stated that the services of a cultural mediator should be used, and that this mediator should be provided by the school district, not the parents. Parents might not anticipate a diagnosis of mental retardation, and to have someone from their community give them this news might be humiliating for them.

Helping Parents of Students with Developmental Disabilities

In many countries, services for children with mental retardation are limited, and these children are neglected by the system (Wang, Hsieh, Heller, Davidson, & Janicki, 2007). Parents are not able to discuss their children's issues openly. They may feel shame and personal responsibility for their children's circumstances. For example, some Chinese parents who have children with intellectual disabilities experience feelings of humiliation and believe that the mental retardation is a result of sins committed by parents or ancestors (Wang et al., 2007).

School professionals need to be sensitive to cultural differences in beliefs about disabilities and attitudes relating to intervention for students with mental retardation.

❏ Some East Indian parents who practice Hinduism and believe in karma view mental retardation as punishment for actions in a past life (Nichols & Keltner, 2005). Even if these parents live in the United States, they may hide the child and not seek out health or educational services.

❏ Some CLD families believe that they need to take on the entire responsibility for the care of children with mental retardation, even after these children become adults (Rueda et al., 2005). These families should be presented with options for accessing services if they want them. Mothers who spend all of their time caring for children with mental retardation may experience depression (Magana, Seltzer, & Krauss, 2004).

❏ Skinner, Correa, Bailey, and Skinner (2001) conducted interviews with 250 Mexican and Puerto Rican parents of young children with mental retardation who lived in the United States. They found that for the majority of the subjects, faith in God and the church constituted strong foundations of support as they cared for their children.

❏ If CLD parents of children with mental retardation refuse support or services from educational or medical institutions, they might be willing to accept support from their churches. Professionals can create ties with local churches and take advantage of this.

❏ Hispanic parents of children with mental retardation may benefit from support groups, comprised of other Hispanic parents whose children have intellectual deficits (Martorell & Martorell, 2006).

Profile

Alexi, a student in 10th grade, came to an American school as a second grader. His family immigrated from Russia. Alexi had cerebral palsy and was a quadriplegic. He used an augmentative communication device because he was unable to speak. The speech-language pathologist who assessed him in 10th grade found that he had no history of receiving ESL services. No one even knew he was Russian. The speech-language pathologist arranged for Alexi to have ESL support services as well as speech-language therapy to help him become a more successful communicator at school and at home.

STUDENTS WITH AUGMENTATIVE/ALTERNATIVE COMMUNICATION NEEDS

The use of devices for augmentative/alternative communication (AAC) is common in programs for students with disabilities that affect oral expression (Alant, Bornman, & Lloyd, 2006). Huer and Soto (2006) stressed that the purpose of intervention using AAC devices is to provide students with skills that will help them become self-reliant, independent, and productive adults.

Research documents the fact that today, more and more users of AAC devices are from CLD communities (Binger & Light, 2006; Bridges & Midgette 2000; Nakamura, Iwabuchi, & Alm, 2006). It is projected that by the year 2020, the largest non-European American population of AAC consumers will be members of the Hispanic community (Soto, Huer, & Taylor, 1997). When the students are from CLD backgrounds, additional considerations are important:

❏ *What are the socio-pragmatic rules governing interaction in the child's own culture?* We cannot just superimpose Western notions of what comprises successful and appropriate interactions onto clients from various CLD backgrounds. For example, children from traditional African backgrounds are generally not encouraged to question adults or initiate verbal communication with them. However, if an African child uses an AAC device and spends most of her time with an adult caregiver, she will need to learn to do this. Cultural issues are important to consider in determining how AAC devices will be used with students (Alant, Bornman, & Lloyd, 2007). The environmental context in which assistive technology strategies are to be implemented often influences a family's willingness to use these strategies (Parette, Huer, & Peterson-Karlan, 2008).

❏ *To what extent do family members use computers and other "high tech" devices at home?* Some families, especially if they have immigrated from rural areas in developing countries, may be intimidated and overwhelmed by electronic AAC devices and computer-based AAC systems. In cases such as these, professionals may need to introduce low-tech devices or even printed boards that have picture symbols placed on them. Words on communication boards can be arranged alphabetically or grouped into categories.

❏ *Do parents and family members view the use of AAC devices as appropriate for children with disabilities?* If the family views the disability as the "will of God," for example, the use of AAC devices may be considered inappropriate. Families (including members of the extended family) should always be made aware of a range of choices and options with regard to the use of AAC devices by their children (Parette, Huer, & Wyatt, 2003; Vanbiervliet & Parette, 2002).

❏ *Is the development of augmentative communication skills viewed as a high priority by the child's family?* Huer and Soto (2006) stated that for some CLD families, issues of survival might take priority over educational and clinical concerns.

❏ *How should parents be taught to use AAC devices?* Kent-Walsh and Rosa-Lugo (2006) reported that CLD families are not provided with sufficient training in the use of AAC devices. The families in their study valued actual demonstrations of facilitative interaction strategies; they did not want to just be told what to do. It is important to show parents how AAC devices can be used to facilitate effective communication and social interactions in a variety of contexts.

Using Picture Symbols with Bilingual Students

Suggestions are listed below for selecting and using picture symbols with CLD students who have AAC needs:

❏ *Make efforts to set up AAC devices that will make it possible to communicate in both the home and school languages.* (Rogers-Adkinson et al., 2003). Picture communication systems with printed text in L1 and English make it possible for the child to interact with speakers of either language. *The Bilingual Picture Symbol Communication Resource* (Academic Communication Associates, 2007) includes picture communication boards with text in both English and Spanish. These boards can be used to communicate basic needs and share information in either language.

❏ *Make sure that the picture symbols used in AAC devices are relevant to the cultural experiences of the student.* Students from different cultural backgrounds may assign different meanings to identical symbols. Moreover, multiple symbols may be needed even for high frequency words. A picture symbol for the word "eat," that shows a child eating with a fork, for example, may not be a good choice for children who eat with chopsticks at home.

❏ *Consult with families when selecting vocabulary items. Items should be selected that are used frequently at home and in the child's community.* AAC devices need to provide access to vocabulary that will help the student function effectively in his social environment (Grether, 2006).

❏ *Make sure to arrange picture symbols in sequences that are appropriate for the structure of the student's language.* Sentences in Spanish, for example, often include more words than their English translations. Moreover, word order often differs in the two languages. Therefore, boards created for use in English may need to be adapted for use in other languages such as Spanish (Academic Communication Associates, 2007).

❏ *Encourage family members to participate in the actual development of AAC learning materials.* Family members, for example, can record words in the home language for use in AAC devices.

AAC Research with CLD Students

Limited research has been conducted relating to the use of AAC devices with CLD students. In one study that examined the use of AAC devices with CLD students, Huer, Parette, & Saenz (2001) used interview procedures to obtain information from focus groups comprised of Mexican American families of children with disabilities. The results indicated that the families interviewed preferred that their children use speech or sign language over assistive technology. Families were concerned about the cost of AAC equipment, and some family members felt uncomfortable with the responsibility of using expensive equipment. They did not want to be liable in case the equipment broke down or malfunctioned in some way. Huer et al. (2001) conjectured that perhaps some of the AAC devices given to these families were not useful at home because they were programmed in English for use at school.

All of the families in this study wished for devices that would make Spanish communication possible. They also wanted more training in how to operate their children's AAC devices..

Harrison-Harris (2002) reported that bilingual AAC users who are successful in developing biliteracy make great gains in their overall language development. According to Harrison-Harris, it is important to provide strong L1 support for CLD users of AAC devices.

In another study, Parette, Chuang, and Huer (2004) interviewed six Chinese families who had immigrated to the United States from Taiwan and Hong Kong. Each family had been in the United States for at least 10 years. In each family, a child had ASD and used an AAC device. Parette et al., identified some "stereotypical" beliefs about Asian families' acceptance of intervention. Asian families, for example, had negative feelings about accepting professional intervention, believing that the family should care for the child with the disability.

Parette et al. found that Chinese families in their sample differed from stereotypical Asian families in several respects. First, these families did not feel personal shame about their children's ASD. They embraced the mainstream American value of independence for their children. In addition, they actively participated in educational decisions for their children and were happy to be included; they did not abdicate responsibility solely to specialists.

The researchers concluded that the higher degree of income, educational level, and acculturation of these particular families might have impacted their reactions to service providers. Therefore, it may be important to examine families' level of acculturation as a variable affecting whether they will accept services and use AAC devices with their children.

Profile

Lilly came to the United States from Huangzhow to seek help for her son Louie, a student with ASD. When Louie was approaching two years of age, Lilly began to realize that there was something "different" about him. She approached the pediatrician, who told her that everything was fine, emphasizing that children develop on different timelines. After another year had gone by, Lilly knew that Louie wasn't fine. She took him to specialists, who diagnosed him with ASD. After learning about this diagnosis, Lilly's husband divorced her. He disowned Louie and blamed Lilly, saying that it was her fault that Louie had these problems.

Lilly had family in the United States and decided to come here in search of help and support. She brought Louie to a local center that provided speech-language therapy and academic help. Lilly decided to change her name and that of her child because she was afraid for their safety. She knew that she had shamed her husband's family by giving birth to a child with ASD.

Louie responded well to intervention and continues to make progress. Lilly now expresses gratitude for the help provided to Louie since her arrival in the United States and the support that she has received.

PROVIDING SERVICES TO INTERNATIONALLY ADOPTED CHILDREN

International adoptions are becoming increasingly more common in the United States. There are a variety of factors contributing to the increasing numbers of internationally adopted children. Educational professionals need to be aware of issues that may have relevance in the education of these children.

❏ First, many American couples delay having children and find that as they get older, having biological children becomes more difficult. Additionally, some independent single women with careers and secure financial circumstances may choose to adopt children. In other cases, families want to adopt children from other countries to make a contribution to these children's lives and contribute to society from a humanitarian standpoint.

❏ In the last 15 years, over 200,000 children from other countries have been adopted by American parents. In 1995, there were 8,987 children adopted from other countries. In 2005, more than 22,000 children were adopted from outside the U.S. (U.S. Department of State, 2006).

❏ In 7 of the last 10 years, China has been the top source country for internationally adopted children (U.S. State Department, 2005). Figure 16.1 shows the top source countries for the year 2006.

❏ Families in China, India, Vietnam, and other countries tend to prefer male children over female children. As a result, more girls than boys are available for adoption (Selman, 2007).

❏ Children may be placed in orphanages because both parents have passed away or the parents lack the financial resources to care for the child. Children may be also be removed from homes in which abuse or neglect have occurred (Rimashevskaia, 2007).

❏ For many children adopted from Russia, the paperwork documenting their parents' termination of rights refers to alcoholism (Landry, 2007). Many Russian women drink alcohol during pregnancy: they often do not know that this is deleterious to their babies' development (Aronson, 2007).

❏ Conditions in orphanages vary from country to country. In some countries, children are well cared for and nurtured. In other countries, neglect and abuse are rampant. For example, children may be tied to beds or potty chairs so that caregivers can keep track of them (Mason & Narad, 2004).

❏ In many orphanages, infants and toddlers are put into cribs twice a day for three-hour naps. Thus, much time is spent in an isolated, physically restricted space (Glennen, personal communication, November 2001).

❏ Researchers in Europe have stated that some internationally adopted children may exhibit Post-Institutional Autistic Syndrome, a condition in which they have experienced such neglect and trauma that they exhibit autistic-like behaviors such as rocking, hair pulling, and others (Fensbo, 2004; Hoksbergen, ter Laak, Rijk, van Dijkum, & Stoutjesdijk, 2005; Kaland, Moller-Nielsen, Smith, Mortensen, Callesen, & Gottlieb, 2005).

❏ Children who have craniofacial anomalies such as cleft palate may be severely neglected. They may be confined to 'lying down' rooms where they receive no medical care and limited staff attention.

Prospective parents may not be aware of the specific problems that their recently adopted children have experienced or are experiencing. If internationally adopted children demonstrate severe problems, the strain can affect the parents' marriage and overall family dynamics (Fensbo, 2004). Professionals may find it appropriate to refer these parents to support groups or counseling in some cases.

Problems that internationally adopted children may experience are listed in Table 16.2. Whether or not the problems are experienced depends heavily upon the quality of the care they received in their home countries.

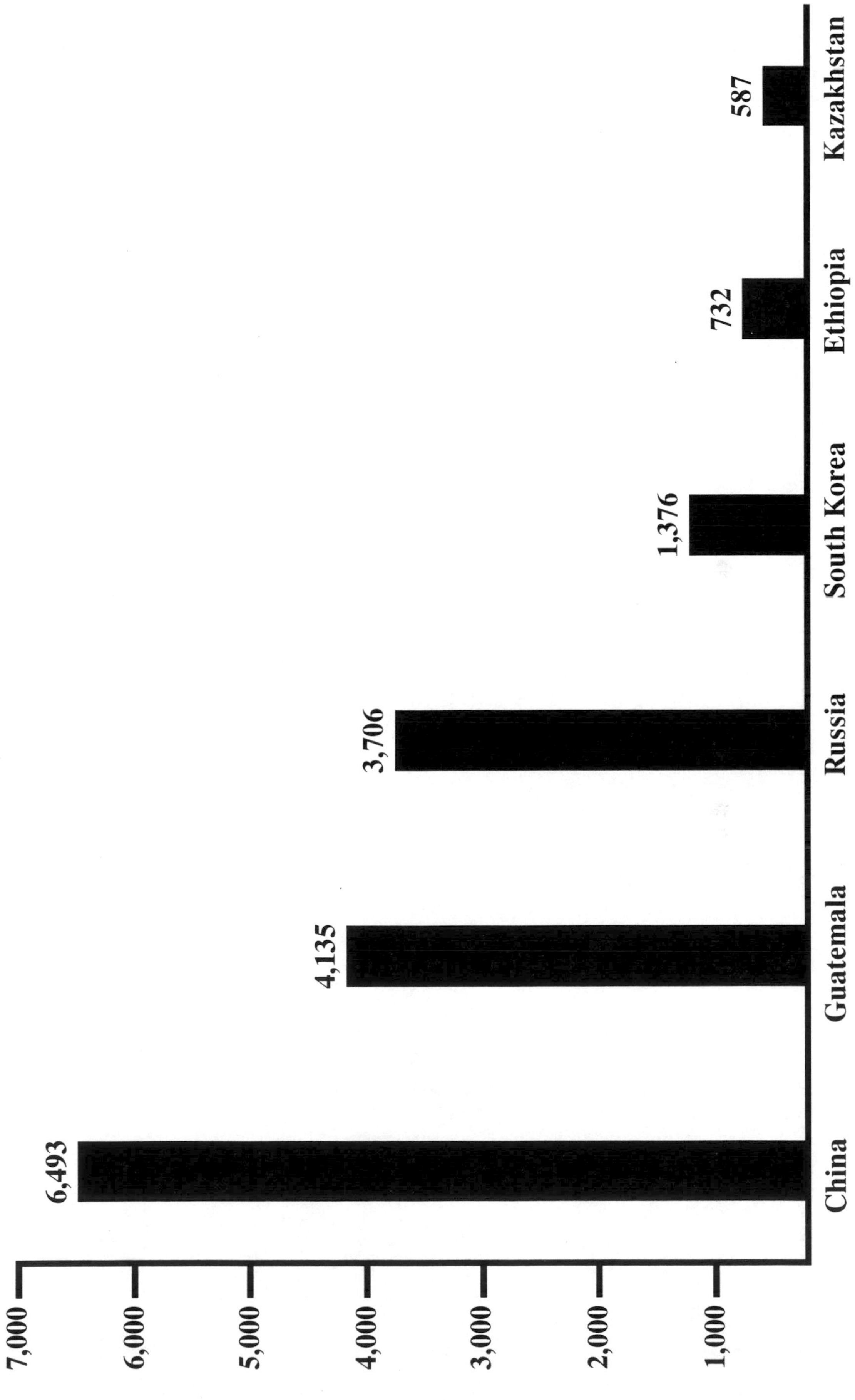

Figure 16.1

Top Six Source Countries for Internationally Adopted Children, 2006
(U.S. Department of State, 2006)

Table 16.2

Possible Challenges Experienced by Children Adopted from Other Countries

This table includes a listing of challenges commonly experienced by internationally adopted children (see Aronson, 2007; Glennen 2007; Glennen & Bright, 2005; Hoksbergen et al., 2005; Hwa-Froelich et al., 2006; Landry, 2007; Pearson, 2001; Rimashevskaia, 2007).

- Malnutrition

- Low birth weight/prematurity

- Conductive or sensorineural hearing loss (chronic otitis media is common)

- Vision problems (e.g., strabismus)

- Lack of language stimulation

- Gross and fine motor delays

- Cognitive impairment

- Emotional disturbance

- Post-traumatic stress syndrome

- Indiscriminately friendly behavior toward all adults

- Attachment disorders

- Sensory processing disorders

- Language and articulation disorders

- Stereotypical, "autistic-like" behavior such as hand flapping, head banging, rocking

- Eating problems, including refusal to chew

- Diagnoses such as mental retardation, fetal alcohol syndrome, cerebral palsy, HIV/AIDS

- Excessive irritability; inconsolability

- Behavior issues such as aggression or withdrawal

- Short- and long-term memory problems

- Attention deficit hyperactivity disorder

Professionals must remember that internationally adopted children often experience culture shock. Within a 24- to 48-hour period, these children have been abruptly removed from their familiar environments and all ties to their cultures and languages have been terminated (Hwa-Froelich, Pettinelli & Jones, 2006; Pearson, 2001; Roseberry-McKibbin, 2007). Thus, these children may need psychological services to help them deal with issues resulting from the change in environment (Gindis, 2005).

Pediatricians sometimes fail to refer internationally adopted children for needed services in a timely fashion. They may take a "wait and see" approach, depriving internationally adopted children of early intervention services that they greatly need (Gindis, 2000; Krakow, Mastriano, & Reese, 2005). Interdisciplinary collaboration is highly recommended for internationally adopted children due to their complex needs (Hwa-Froelich et al., 2006; Pearson, 2001).

Issues relating to the development of language skills in internationally adopted children are summarized below:

❑ In some countries, it is estimated that over 90% of children raised in orphanages have language delays (Glennen, 2007). Most experts believe that the older the child, the longer it will take to "catch up" linguistically with non-adopted peers (Dyer, 2006; Roberts, et. al., 2005).

❑ Adoptive families rarely speak the child's first language. Thus, at the time of adoption, there is arrested development of L1; proficiency in L1 decreases as the child gains proficiency in the L2 of his adoptive family. During this time period, children often demonstrate limited abilities in both languages and thus it is difficult for professionals to determine if the observed "problems" will be overcome without the services of a speech-language pathologist.

❑ Glennen, (2007, p. 530) stated that "...internationally adopted children are at high risk for speech and language disorders because of their orphanage backgrounds. However, many children adopted as infants and toddlers arrive home [to the U.S.] and eventually flourish in their new language-rich environments. The dilemma for speech-language pathologists is determining which internationally adopted children have true language or speech delays versus those who do not."

❑ Children in orphanages often miss the building blocks or precursors to language. They often do not receive adequate modeling, positive feedback, or the reciprocal interaction needed to develop fluent L1 skills.

❑ Some experts believe that time alone cannot remedy this situation and that intensive, focused intervention by an SLP is necessary (Taddonio, 2003; Tan, 2006). Internationally adopted children who are not making adequate progress in learning English vocabulary are appropriate referrals for early intervention (Glennen, 2006).

Glennen and Masters (2002) conducted a longitudinal study of 130 infants and toddlers adopted from Eastern Europe. The children were followed up through the age of 30 to 40 months. Age of adoption was a critical factor in language development. By 36 to 40 months of age, the children who were adopted at younger ages had fully caught up to English language norms. The children who were adopted at older ages lagged behind; the length of their language delay was related to the age at which adoption occurred. The researchers recommended that referrals for speech-language intervention be made if internationally adopted children fail to progress rapidly in oral English acquisition. They also stressed that standardized language tests in English are not valid for assessing the language skills of these children.

Roberts, Pollock, Krakow, Price, Fulmer, and Wang (2005) studied the language development of 55 preschool-aged children adopted from China by American parents. All children had lived in their permanent homes for two or more years. They found that 94.5% of the children were within or above the normal range for native-born monolingual speakers after approximately two or more years of exposure to English.

Slightly over one-fourth of the subjects performed significantly above average on at least two standardized tests of language. Roberts and her colleagues hypothesized that perhaps one important factor that might have contributed to the language outcomes was the age at which the children were adopted (6 to 25 months of age).

On all three language measures in this study, age of adoption was a significant predictor variable. Early adoption was found to be advantageous for success in developing skills in English.

Proficiency in the first language (L1) of internationally adopted children should be assessed as soon as these children arrive in the U.S. if at all possible. This testing is important because these students generally lose proficiency in the L1 if placed in monolingual English-speaking environments (Dyer, 2004; Pearson, 2001; Glennen, 2007).

It is important to note that internationally adopted children are not "bilingual" in the classic sense because of their unique language-learning circumstances (Gindis, 2004, 2005; Glennen, 2002; Hwa-Froelich et al., 2006). Thus, professionals cannot necessarily use practices that research has shown to be valid and reliable for truly bilingual children.

Cognitive Development in Internationally Adopted Children

When they first arrive in the United States, many internationally adopted children make rapid gains in oral language skills. However, over time (especially as they progress through elementary school), linguistic and cognitive deficits may become evident (Hwa-Froelich et al., 2006; Pearson, 2001).

The development of Basic Interpersonal Communication Skills (BICS) and Cognitive Academic Language Proficiency (CALP) was described in the previous chapter. Gindis (2004) reported that internationally adopted children may acquire Basic Interpersonal Communication Skills (BICS) even more quickly than the "typical" English language learner because they are totally immersed in English with no support for the L1. This can lull parents into a false sense of security regarding their children's linguistic abilities. These parents frequently believe that their children will just as easily and automatically acquire the academic language skills necessary for success in the classroom curriculum (i.e., CALP). However, rapid BICS development does not necessarily result in rapid or completely successful CALP development.

As discussed, CALP can take anywhere from 5 to 10 years to develop to a level commensurate with that of native speakers. Often, parents are unpleasantly surprised to learn that their internationally adopted children experience delays in the development of the language skills necessary to function effectively in the classroom. After all, BICS developed within a 6- to 12-month period for many of these children (Gindis, 2005).

Gindis (2005) described the possibility that some internationally adopted children will experience the phenomenon of **cumulative cognitive deficit** (CCD). CCD refers to a downward trend in the measured intelligence and/or scholastic achievement of culturally/socially disadvantaged children relative to age-appropriate expectations.

The theory behind CCD is that children who have been deprived of enriching cognitive and linguistic experiences during their early years are less able to profit from environmental situations as they get older due to a mismatch between their cognitive schemata and the requirements of the new learning situation.

In children with cumulative cognitive deficits, a cognitive language deficiency is thought to exist that blocks information processing, resulting in some level of incompetence in the use of various thinking strategies. The problem can lead to lack of intrinsic motivation to perform cognitively demanding activities, which can in turn exacerbate memory and attention problems. Substantial behavior problems may also occur.

According to Gindis (2005), traditional remediation methods (e.g., intensive individual or small group activities) may fail with internationally adopted children who experience cumulative cognitive deficits. He recommended that these students receive cognitive training that emphasizes skills such as inhibiting impulsive responses, experimenting with several solutions for a problem, and analyzing problems. Basically, these students need to learn how to learn.

Assessing Internationally Adopted Children

In a previous chapter, we referred to metacognitive strategies that professionals can use in intervention. These strategies may be especially appropriate for internationally adopted children who have cumulative cognitive deficits.

Assessment of the language skills of internationally adopted children is most challenging because they often have L1 delays, lose proficiency in the L1 rapidly after coming to the United States, and have not yet had sufficient exposure to English to fully master the language. Dynamic assessment is appropriate for these students (Glennen & Masters, 2002).

Some experts have recommended that professionals develop local norms for internationally adopted children who are in the process of learning English (Glennen, 2007; Roberts et al., 2005). These local norms can be built upon peer-based standards that are developed for specific groups with similar cultural, linguistic, and experiential backgrounds. Children assessed by use of these local norms can then be compared to similar peers rather than to a nationally selected sample of students who, for the most part, have little in common with them.

Prelinguistic measures that assess the presence of joint attention, prespeech vocalization, symbolic play, object permanence, social interaction skills, and other language precursors may be helpful in identifying internationally adopted children with possible language disorders. Language disorders are often found among children who have problems in these areas (Glennen, 2007).

Two measures that Glennen found to be highly predictive of language delays in internationally adopted children were the Communication and Symbolic Behavior Skills—Developmental Profile (CSBS-DP; Wetherby & Prizant, 2002) and the MacArthur Communicative Development Inventory—Words and Gestures (MCDI-WG; Fenson et al., 1993). She emphasized that standard measures of prelinguistic abilities that are not language- or culture-specific are a good method of predicting eventual language outcomes in newly-arrived internationally adopted infants and toddlers. Glennen cautioned that linguistic assessments should only be used with internationally adopted children when local norms are available to compare these children against their internationally adopted peers.

One might speculate that for older internationally adopted children who are experiencing L1 attrition and still gaining English skills, professionals such as psychologists can use nonverbal measures to obtain useful diagnostic information. In addition, professionals might attempt to use information-processing measures, described in a previous chapter, that are not knowledge-based (e.g., repetition of digits and nonwords). Research, however, is needed to determine if these measures can be used to obtain useful diagnostic information with internationally adopted children.

Because internationally adopted children appear to be vulnerable to speech and language delays, early speech and language intervention is highly recommended (Dyer, 2004). Professionals can provide assistance to parents in a variety of ways:

❏ Provide parents with information about local services and support groups that may be of help to them. Parents of internationally adopted children can especially benefit from support groups that allow them to interact with others who have shared similar experiences (Stein, 2004).

❏ Help parents establish a bond with their children by recommending activities such as playing games, reading, and doing turn-taking activities. Encouraging parents to hug the child and to provide frequent social reinforcement may also be appropriate.

❏ Encourage the use of games that promote mobility and action to help children with sensory processing problems and motor delays (e.g., playing Simon Says with instructions that require students to follow simple classroom directions).

❏ Present sensory stimulation activities using a box of sand and small toys. Ask children to feel the toys inside the box, draw out a toy, and label it.

❏ Demonstrate appropriate ways of expressing both positive and negative feelings. Parents and professionals can model acceptable outlets for anger or aggressive impulses.

❏ Provide a well-structured learning environment with daily routines. Overstimulating environments need to be avoided because some children have difficulty with sensory integration. New stimuli should be introduced gradually.

❏ Consider using sign language when working with internationally adopted children who have significant language delays. Sign language can facilitate the learning of critical language skills (Dyer, 2004).

❏ Make it easy for students to watch lip movements when speaking to them. Mason and Narad (2004) stated that parents should get down to children's eye level so that the children can watch the movement of their lips. They also reported that the use of games involving singing and other vocalizations is helpful when working with children who are not talking.

Internationally adopted children are in particular need of intervention in a variety of areas. Communication, motor skills, social interaction skills, behavior, and other areas may be affected. Despite the numerous challenges experienced by internationally adopted children, many develop satisfactorily and are able to live full lives (Glennen & Masters, 2002; Hwa-Froelich et al., 2006; Tan, 2006). Professionals must always bear this in mind and not stereotype these children as being doomed to lifetimes of hardship and disability.

✐REFLECTION ✐

A dilemma for many parents of internationally adopted children is that Basic Interpersonal Communication Skills (BICS) develop more quickly than Cognitive/Academic Language Proficiency (CALP) and thus eventual difficulties with CALP come as an unwelcome surprise. How can professionals support parents and children in this situation?

_____

_____

_____

_____

_____

Profile

At an outpatient rehabilitation center, I met Sharon, who brought her 7-year-old son Gregor for his weekly physical therapy session. Sharon and Gregor were in tears; clearly they had a rough day. After Gregor went in for his physical therapy appointment, I asked Sharon if she would like to talk. She poured out her story.

Gregor was residing in an Eastern European orphanage when he was adopted by Sharon and her husband at three years old. When they arrived at the orphanage to bring him to their home in California, he was living in conditions of filth and squalor. Gregor had been beaten, sexually abused, kicked in the head, and locked in small closets. There were scars on his head from the abuse.

When Gregor arrived in the United States, he would not let Sharon out of his sight. She could not let him hear the sound of a door shutting; if he heard this, he would scream and cry inconsolably. She could not even spend a few minutes a day away from the child; Gregor had to have her within his range of vision at all times.

Gregor was diagnosed as having significant emotional and behavioral problems, gross and fine motor delays, mental retardation, and significant post-traumatic stress syndrome. He also had a profound language delay.

Gregor's speech was highly unintelligible, and he only spoke in 3-4 word utterances. I wanted to recommend speech-language therapy, but Sharon was exhausted, depleted, and depressed. Her financial resources were stretched to the breaking point because she was paying for so many services for Gregor.

USING COMPUTER SOFTWARE WITH CLD SPECIAL NEEDS POPULATIONS

Children with hearing impairment, autism spectrum disorder, augmentative communication needs and other special needs often require intensive programs of intervention. In the absence of school professionals who speak the child's language, parents, bilingual assistants, and others can help. Finding native speakers of the child's language to help with program implementation on a daily basis, however, is often difficult. When schools are unable to find native speakers of the child's language or appropriate learning materials, students with severe disorders who truly need L1 instruction may not receive it.

Advances in software technology are making it possible for school professionals to meet the needs of a greater number CLD students with disabilities. These programs allow students to progress at their own pace and facilitate collaborative efforts between speech-language pathologists, parents, classroom teachers, and other school personnel (Mattes & García-Easterly, 2007).

A major problem with many software programs is that they cannot be easily modified for students who require a highly individualized approach to instruction. Moreover, most of the available programs include content only in English. For this reason, many professionals who work with special needs populations continue to use traditional approaches to instruction with most of their students.

To meet the diverse needs of students in special education programs, software programs are becoming available that can be modified easily for use with individual children. One program that holds much promise for CLD students with severe communication disorders or AAC needs is Picture Master Language Software (Assistive Technology Engineering Lab, 2005). This comprehensive program allows users to create customized communication boards, worksheet pages, and other visual displays with text and speech in a variety of languages. The initial release of Picture

Master Language Software in the United States, published by Academic Communication Associates, features digital speech files created by native speakers of English, French, German, and Spanish. Databases for this program have also been created in Mandarin, Japanese, Vietnamese, Italian, and other languages, although some languages are not yet available commercially.

Picture Master Language Software includes thousands of simple line-art picture symbols, realistic-style picture symbols, animated illustrations, photographs, and background scenes that can be combined in various ways to create communication boards and learning resources that will be especially useful to students with communication disorders. The speech and text for individual pictures can be changed quickly from English to other languages, using the digital speech files contained within the software. By allowing users to make changes to the speech and text files, the program content can be adapted for use with students who speak different dialects of a language. Changes can be made to speech and text files without permanently replacing the speech and text files that came with the program.

Another software tool that can be easily adapted for use with speakers of languages other than English is the ItemWriter Language Software Series (Pickett, 2003). This series includes programs that target synonyms and antonyms, drawing conclusions, analogies, completing familiar phrases, and answering *yes/no* questions. Although the program content is provided in English, the software allows users to create their own items. Both text and speech can be modified, making it possible to create task items in other languages.

The development of software that allows users to modify the speech and/or text contained within the program will make it possible for schools to improve special education services for CLD students with a variety of special learning needs. Software can be used in numerous ways to facilitate the development of communication skills and academic proficiencies that are critical for success in school:

❑ Software programs that allow users to modify text and speech make it possible to create materials in more than one language, to modify items for effective use with speakers of the local dialect, and to create customized learning experiences.

❑ Software programs provide opportunities for students to interact, take turns, make decisions, and solve problems using activities that are interesting and relevant to their experiences.

❑ Students with severe disabilities often have difficulty responding to tasks in which static pictures are used as stimuli for their responses. Software programs that include animated illustrations (e.g., Picture Master Language Software) make it possible to demonstrate actions such as eating and drinking and, therefore, may be more effective in facilitating learning than the use of picture cards and other printed materials.

Clearly, a major problem experienced by special education professionals in our schools is that there are not enough published resources available to meet the needs of MOST students who speak a language other than English. Software that allows users to modify the language content of individual items will make it possible to create linguistically appropriate learning resources for speakers of a variety of languages. Parents, paraprofessionals, and community members who speak languages other than English can help create speech and text databases for use in these programs. By working with the international community, software resources can be developed that will benefit individuals with special learning needs throughout the world.

Technological advances offer much promise for school professionals who are struggling to provide appropriate services for CLD special needs populations. Moreover, customizable programs will make it possible to create instructional resources that can be used internationally to help students who have special learning needs. These programs will be especially useful in countries that have limited services available for individuals with various types of disabilities.

CONCLUSION

CLD students who have language learning problems associated with exceptional needs can present a particular challenge to professionals. Some research has been conducted to address best service delivery practices for these students, but much more research needs to be done. In the meantime, professionals can work as part of multidisciplinary teams to support students and their families, using the services of cultural mediators to bridge the gap between the families and the professionals who serve them.

STUDY QUESTIONS

1. Many CLD parents of children with special needs do not believe that early intervention is necessary or desirable. How can professionals deal with these parents in a manner that is culturally sensitive but that encourages parents to seek out this intervention?

2. What are some practical strategies that can be used in the classroom to support the success of CLD children with hearing impairment?

3. What types of skills do CLD children need to learn if they are on the autism spectrum?

TRUE-FALSE

Circle the number beside each statement that is true.

4. When assessing CLD preschool children, professionals should not use parent reports because these reports are too biased and inaccurate.
5. Children of migrant farm workers may be especially vulnerable to hearing loss because they work alongside their parents in jobs where there is a great deal of noise exposure.
6. If CLD families want to try alternative methods to "heal" their children's hearing impairments, professionals must try to dissuade them because this will only delay appropriate assessment and intervention.
7. An advantage in working with CLD families whose children are on the autism spectrum is that, thankfully, many parents come from countries where autism spectrum disorder is widely recognized and accepted.

8. Research has shown that CLD children with Down syndrome can be successfully raised in a bilingual environment; families do not have to limit themselves to just one language.

9. Many CLD families appreciate the opportunity to use high-tech AAC devices with their children, especially if these devices are used in English to facilitate classroom learning.

10. One valid way to evaluate very young internationally adopted children is to use prelinguistic measures to assess the presence of such skills as symbolic play, object permanence, joint attention, and others.

MULTIPLE CHOICE

Circle the letter beside each of the choices that is correct.

11. Challenges experienced by some internationally adopted children may include:
    A. Attention deficit disorder with hyperactivity

    B. Indiscriminate attachment to strangers

    C. Hearing loss

    D. Refusal to chew

    E. Aggression and tantrums

12. Research with some CLD families of children who used AAC devices showed that:
    A. Parents' reactions can be influenced by factors such as a higher degree of acculturation and educational level.

    B. Virtually all CLD parents believed that their children should be institutionalized.

    C. Some families felt uncomfortable with "high tech" devices, preferring that their children use speech or sign language.

    D. Most families did not want AAC devices that were "bilingual"; they desired devices that were only programmed in English.

    E. It is best not to provide L1 support for children who use AAC devices; restricting them to just English will better support their academic development in American schools.

13. In terms of providing support for CLD children with mental retardation and their families, professionals should remember that:
    A. CLD students are underrepresented in the category of "mental retardation," so professionals must be especially careful not to miss these students in screenings and assessments.

    B. Children with mental retardation should probably not be asked to learn languages that are not central to their communication needs in daily life (e.g., learning a foreign language in high school).

    C. Some CLD mothers of children with mental retardation experience depression because they spent all their time caring for these children.

    D. CLD parents of children with MR may accept support from their churches, even if they do not want help from schools or medical institutions.

14. Lia X. is a Chinese immigrant mother whose 3-year old son, Fong, has ASD. The speech-language pathologist must remember which of the following when working with Mrs. X and Fong?

   A. Mrs. X. will probably appreciate a play-based approach to treatment.

   B. Use of a token economy, so popular in the treatment of children with ASD, will probably be highly successful.

   C. Mrs. X. may believe that acupuncture and herbal remedies will be helpful in treating Fong's ASD.

   D. It is important to stress to her that these are unscientific remedies that will not be helpful; Fong needs traditional, research-based intervention.

   E. It would be ideal to find a bilingual specialist to provide intervention for Fong.

15. You are a speech-language pathologist who is consulting with a local preschool that has several CLD children with documented language-learning disabilities. The preschool teachers are trying to promote emergent literacy skills in these children to better prepare them for kindergarten. Which of the following suggestions would you make to these teachers?

   A. Don't use books with too many pictures or the children will not learn to decode print.

   B. Keep book-reading time short.

   C. Avoid stories that have Rebus-style pictures so that students don't get confused.

   D. Use books that have manipulative parts like flaps and moveable tabs.

   E. Do not reinforce the children's use of their first languages so that they will learn to become fluent in English quickly and without difficulty.

ANSWERS TO STUDY QUESTIONS

   4. False
   5. True
   6. False
   7. False
   8. True
   9. False
   10. True
   11. All of the above
   12. A, C
   13. B, C, D
   14. C, E
   15. B, D

Appendices

Appendix A

ASSESSING PROCESSES IN SECOND LANGUAGE ACQUISITION

Student's Name:_____Date of Birth:_____

Chronological Age:_____   Assessment Date:_____

Language Background:_____

_____

A. MAJOR SECOND LANGUAGE ACQUISITION PROCESSES

Please put a check mark beside the second language acquisition (SLA) processes you and/or other professionals believe the student is manifesting at this time. Record any comments that are relevant in this situation.

_____**Interference**
            Comments:

_____**Interlanguage**
            Comments:

_____**Silent period**
            Comments:

_____**Code-switching**
            Comments:

_____**Language loss**
            Comments:

B. AFFECTIVE SECOND LANGUAGE ACQUISITION VARIABLES

Please put a check mark beside any variables you and/or other professionals believe are influencing the child's acquisition of English:

_____**Motivation**

___Acculturation (student and family's ability to adapt to the dominant culture)
___Enclosure with American culture (shared activities with Americans)
___Attitudes of child's ethnic group and dominant group toward one another
___Family plans to stay in/leave this country (circle one)
___Possibility that learning English is a threat to the student's identity
___Student's efforts to learn English are successful/unsuccessful (circle one)
___Student appears enthusiastic/unenthusiastic about learning (circle one)

Comments:

_____**Personality**

___Self-esteem
___Extroverted/introverted (circle predominant pattern)
___Assertive/non-assertive (circle predominant pattern)

Comments:

_____**Socioeconomic status** (Compare to that of other children in school.)

Comments:

C. SECOND LANGUAGE LEARNING STYLES AND STRATEGIES

Please comment on any second language learning styles and strategies that may characterize or be utilized by this student:

Avoidance (of situation, persons, topics, etc.)

Use of routines and formulas (e.g., "How are you?" or "Have a good day!")

Practice opportunities (quantity and quality; Who does the student interact with in English? In what settings? School? Neighborhood?)

Modeling (Who are the student's primary speech and language models? What languages do these models speak? If they speak English, what is the quality of their English? How much time does the student spend with them?)

Additional Comments/Recommendations:

Appendix B
Sample Background Information Questionnaire

Instructions: We are going to ask you some questions about your child's medical history, educational history, and related areas. Please be as thorough as you can in your remarks. If I am not clear, please stop me and ask me to say it again. If you don't feel comfortable in answering the question, please let me know. All we want to do here is to obtain as much background information as possible, and, since you are the child's parent, we feel that you have much to contribute.

1. When was your child born?

2. Was this a hospital?

3. How was the pregnancy?

4. How was your health during pregnancy?

4. How was the delivery?

5. Were any instruments used?

6. Were there any postnatal complications?

7. How was your child's physical development? Were there any handicapping conditions? If yes, who made the diagnosis? When? How did you feel about it?

8. Was your child ever hospitalized? If yes, where? When? Why? How long? Who was the physician?

9. Were there problems in feeding?

10. Were there any prolonged illnesses? High fever? Accidents?

11. Has his/her hearing been checked?

12. Has his/her vision been checked?

13. Has he/she seen a dentist? What is the condition of his/her teeth?

14. What is his/her diet history?

15. How is his/her diet now?

16. Does he/she have a pediatrician? Who? Has your child seen any other medical specialist? If yes, Who? When? Where? Why?

17. When did you come to the United States? Why did you come?

    For refugees: Was he/she ever in a refugee camp? How long? Tell us about it.

18. Was he/she ever on a boat? How long? Tell us about it.

19. How many brothers and sisters does he/she have? Are they all here?

20. Are there any family members who had or have difficulty in speaking or hearing, or problems such as mental retardation, cerebral palsy, cleft palate, or stuttering? If yes, please explain.

21. Was your child ever in school? Where? How long?

22. How was his/her performance in school? Grade?

23. Do you have a report from the school? Any comments from the teacher?

Source: Cheng., L. L. (1991). *Assessing Asian Language Performance: Guidelines for Evaluating Limited-English Proficient students. (Second edition)* Oceanside, CA. Academic Communication Associates. Reprinted with permission.

24. Was he/she involved in special programs? How did he/she do?

25. Was he/she in a day-care or child care program? If yes, how did he/she do?

26. Did he/she repeat a grade? If yes, why?

27. How was the program similar to his/her program now? How was the program different from his/her program now?

28. How many are living in your home?

29. Who takes care of your child after school?

30. Who makes the decisions at home?

31. Does your child have his/her own room? If no, who does your child share the room with? Where does he/she study?

32. Does your child mostly play inside the house? Outside? By himself/herself? With a sibling?

33. Who does he/she play with? Are they older or younger? How does he/she play?

34. What does he/she like to play? What toys do you have? Does he/she read? What books and magazines do you have?

35. Do you work? If yes, what do you do? When are you home?

36. Does your spouse work? If yes, what does he/she do? When is he/she home?

37. What is your educational background? Your spouse's educational background?

38. What language(s) is used at home?

39. When did your child say his/her first word? How do you feel about his/her speech now?

40. Do you feel that your child understands everything you say? Explain.

41. What language does he/she speak when he/she responds to you?

42. Does your child speak your native language with his siblings? Friends?

43. Do your children speak your native language or English among themselves?

44. Do you help your child with homework?

45. How do you feel about his/her maintenance of your native language? Do you send him/her to language school during the weekend?

46. What do you expect the school to do for your child?

47. Do you attend any social function? Where? With whom? What are your leisure activities?

48. Do you have difficulty disciplining your child? His/her siblings?

49. What responsibilities are placed on your child? On his/her siblings?

50. Does he/she dress himself/herself?

51. Does he/she know your telephone number and address?

52. Do you read to him/her? What are his/her favorite stories? Can he/she tell the story back to you?

53. Does he/she watch TV? What is his/her favorite program?

54. Do you think your child is a hard worker? If so, why? Do you think your child is lazy? Why?

Appendix C

INTERNET SITES

This listing of websites will be helpful in obtaining information relevant to the education of students from multicultural backgrounds. Sources of websites are included in a variety of resources (see Brice & Roseberry-McKibbin, 1999; Goldstein, 2000; Kuster, 2000). These sites may change without notice, and the reader is advised to check each source online.

Many of the websites below are also listed online, along with other useful multicultural resources at www.acadcom.com/multicultural.asp.

General Information/Demographic Data
Census Bureau - http://www.census.gov

Center for Immigration Studies - http://www.cis.org

ERIC Clearinghouse on Assessment and Evaluation - http://ericae.net

Multicultural/Bilingual Issues
Bilingual Families Web Page - http://www.nethelp.no/cindy/biling-fam.html

Center for Multilingual Multicultural Research - http://www-bcf.usc.edu/~cmmr/BEResources.html

National Association for Bilingual Education - http://www.nabe.org

National Clearinghouse for Bilingual Education - http://www.ncbe.gwu.edu

U.S. Department of Education - http://www.ed.gov/index.html

African American English Websites
Center for Applied Linguistics - http://www.cal.org/ebonics

Summer Institute of Linguistics - http://www.sil.org

Asian Languages
Hmong Language Users Group - http://www.geocities.com/tokyo/4908

Native American Cultures/Languages
American Indian Institute - http://aii.asu.edu

American Indian Studies - http://www.csulb.edu/projects/ais

American Indian Information - http://indiannet.indian.com/americaninfo.html

Spanish
Directorio Online de Español - http://donde.uji.es/Donde

CiberCentro - http://www.cibercentro.com

Yahoo! en Español - http://espanol.yahoo.com

Information About Specific Countries

http://www.wtgonline.com/data/(name of country)

http://home.about.com/travel

http://www.iranian.com

Miscellaneous Bilingual and ESL Websites

http://web1.toefl.org (Teachers of English as a Foreign Language general website)

http://www.comenius.com (free online activities including Fluency Through Fables, short tales created to improve English reading comprehension, and a collection of idioms)

http://www.mhhe.com/socscience/education/multi_new (Multicultural Supersite is a valuable source of information and resources)

http://www.wordsmith.org

http://www.wordfocus.com/index.html (Focusing on Words site is dedicated to enhancing vocabulary skills through looking at the Latin and Greek elements of words)

http://www.enchantedlearning.com (online picture dictionaries and resources in a variety of languages)

http://www.pdictionary.com (online picture dictionaries in English, Spanish, French, German. and Italian)

http://www.stonesoup.com (Stone Soup; contains stories by young writers, links, resources, and children's art from around the world)

Miscellaneous Contacts

http://www.hhs.csus.edu/homepages/SPA/Roseberry (Information from Celeste Roseberry-McKibbin)

http://www.bilingualtherapies.com (Bilingual Therapies recruits bilingual speech-language pathologists and is a source that school districts and other organizations can use to obtain the services of bilingual professionals.

Publishers and Organizations with Bilingual/Multicultural Speech and Language Research Focus

Academic Communication Associates, Inc. - http://www.acadcom.com. A listing of websites, online resources, and other useful tools relating specifically to the bilingual/multicultural issues in special education can be found at the following web address: http://www.acadcom.com/multicultural.asp ACA has been actively involved in the development of assessment tools and learning resources for CLD students with special learning needs.

American Speech-Language-Hearing Association - http://www.asha.org. ASHA plays an active role in research and professional issues relating to the needs of CLD students with communication disorders. The professional journals published by ASHA include research studies and informational articles relating to assessment and intervention with CLD students.

Appendix D

BASIC VOCABULARY RECORD FORMS

The reproducible record forms in this section can be used to assess progress in learning basic vocabulary in English and other languages. Some languages, however, may not have a word that is an exact equivalent for the English word listed. Therefore, modifications may be necessary in some cases. When assessing students in languages other than English, consult with native speakers of the student's dialect to ensure that the vocabulary selected is appropriate.

The *Bilingual Speech and Language Intervention Resource* (Mattes & García-Easterly (2007) includes a comprehensive collection of English and Spanish word lists organized by word category. This resource also includes bilingual lists of spatial concepts, synonyms/antonyms, idiomatic expressions, words that vary across dialects, and other items that can be used in program implementation.

SCHOOL ITEMS

Student's Name: _____ **Date:** _____ **Language:** _____

Goal

The student will demonstrate receptive and expressive knowledge of school items.

Mark a **plus** or **minus** to indicate correct and incorrect responses.

Words	Comp.	Expr.		Words	Comp.	Expr.
1. Desk	____	____		15. Eraser	____	____
2. Chair	____	____		16. Paper	____	____
3. Classroom	____	____		17. Scissors	____	____
4. Restroom	____	____		18. Paste	____	____
5. Library	____	____		19. Book	____	____
6. Office	____	____		20. Notebook	____	____
7. Playground	____	____		21. Ruler	____	____
8. Bus	____	____		22. Crayons	____	____
9. Teacher	____	____		23. Paint	____	____
10. Principal	____	____		24. Computer	____	____
11. Blackboard	____	____		25. Flag	____	____
12. Chalk	____	____		26. Calendar	____	____
13. Pencil	____	____		27. Student	____	____
14. Pen	____	____		28. Map	____	____

SAFETY AND SURVIVAL

Student's Name:_____**Date:**_____ **Language:**_____

Goal

The student will be able to identify and explain the meaning of safety and survival words when presented with pictures.

Record a **plus** or **minus** to indicate correct and incorrect responses.

Words	Comp.	Expr.	Words	Comp.	Expr.
1. Police	____	____	26. Ambulance	____	____
2. Fire	____	____	27. Open	____	____
3. Poison	____	____	28. Closed	____	____
4. Railroad crossing	____	____	29. Detour	____	____
5. Stop	____	____	30. Gasoline	____	____
6. Emergency	____	____	31. No trespassing	____	____
7. Danger	____	____	32. Condemned	____	____
8. Caution	____	____	33. Wanted	____	____
9. Hot	____	____	34. One way	____	____
10. Out of order	____	____	35. Caution	____	____
11. Entrance	____	____	36. Cigarettes	____	____
12. Exit	____	____	37. Alcohol	____	____
13. Warning	____	____	38. No smoking	____	____
14. Men	____	____	39. Emergency exit	____	____
15. Women	____	____	40. No parking	____	____
16. Help	____	____			
17. Doctor	____	____			
18. On	____	____			
19. Off	____	____			
20. Explosives	____	____			
21. Flammable	____	____			
22. Drugs	____	____			
23. Telephone	____	____			
24. Dynamite	____	____			
25. Private	____	____			

BODY PARTS

Student's Name: _____ **Date:** _____ **Language:** _____

Goal

The student will be able to identify and label body parts.

Record a **plus** or **minus** to indicate correct and incorrect responses.

Words	Comp.	Expr.
1. Eyes	_____	_____
2. Nose	_____	_____
3. Hair	_____	_____
4. Ears	_____	_____
5. Mouth	_____	_____
6. Legs	_____	_____
7. Arms	_____	_____
8. Feet	_____	_____
9. Hands	_____	_____
10. Stomach	_____	_____
11. Back	_____	_____
12. Knees	_____	_____
13. Toes	_____	_____
14. Fingers	_____	_____

FAMILY RELATIONSHIPS

Student's Name:_____ **Date:**_____ **Language:**_____

Goal

The student will be able to identify and use words relating to family relationships.

Record a **plus** or **minus** to indicate correct and incorrect responses.

Words	Comp.	Expr.
1. Mother	_____	_____
2. Father	_____	_____
3. Sister	_____	_____
4. Brother	_____	_____
5. Grandmother	_____	_____
6. Grandfather	_____	_____
7. Baby	_____	_____
8. Cousin	_____	_____
9. Aunt	_____	_____
10. Uncle	_____	_____
11. Relative	_____	_____
12. Niece	_____	_____
13. Nephew	_____	_____

COMMUNITY WORKERS/CAREERS

Student's Name: _____ **Date:** _____ **Language:** _____

Goal

The student will be able to identify community workers when presented with pictures and will be able to describe their activities.

Record a **plus** or **minus** to indicate correct and incorrect responses.

Words	Comp.	Expr.	Words	Comp.	Expr.
1. Teacher	____	____	16. Truck driver	____	____
2. Lawyer	____	____	17. Waiter	____	____
3. Nurse	____	____	18. Plumber	____	____
4. Pilot	____	____	19. Librarian	____	____
5. Doctor	____	____	20. Actor	____	____
6. Secretary	____	____	21. Custodian	____	____
7. Dancer	____	____	22. Mail carrier	____	____
8. Beautician	____	____	23. Teacher	____	____
9. Bus driver	____	____	24. Firefighter	____	____
10. Judge	____	____	25. Police officer	____	____
11. Carpenter	____	____	26. Musician	____	____
12. Mechanic	____	____	27. Artist	____	____
13. Cashier	____	____	28. Dancer	____	____
14. Dentist	____	____	29. Soldier	____	____
15. Farmer	____	____	30. Cook	____	____

ANIMALS

Student's Name: _____   **Date:** _____   **Language:** _____

Goal

The student will demonstrate receptive and expressive knowledge of animal names.

Record a **plus** or **minus** to indicate correct and incorrect responses.

Words	Comp.	Expr.		Words	Comp.	Expr.
1. Cat	_____	_____		16. Sheep	_____	_____
2. Dog	_____	_____		17. Rabbit	_____	_____
3. Bird	_____	_____		18. Lion	_____	_____
4. Fish	_____	_____		19. Zebra	_____	_____
5. Kitten	_____	_____		20. Snake	_____	_____
6. Puppy	_____	_____		21. Seal	_____	_____
7. Lamb	_____	_____		22. Bear	_____	_____
8. Goat	_____	_____		23. Elephant	_____	_____
9. Chicken	_____	_____		24. Alligator	_____	_____
10. Rooster	_____	_____		25. Tiger	_____	_____
11. Pig	_____	_____		26. Butterfly	_____	_____
12. Cow	_____	_____		27. Frog	_____	_____
13. Horse	_____	_____		28. Mouse	_____	_____
14. Duck	_____	_____		29. Spider	_____	_____
15. Goat	_____	_____		30. Fly	_____	_____

TIME, SEASONS, AND WEATHER

Student's Name: _____ **Date:** _____ **Language:** _____

Goal

The student will demonstrate receptive and expressive knowledge of concepts relating to time, seasons, and weather.

Record a **plus** or **minus** to indicate correct and incorrect responses.

Words	Comp.	Expr.	Words	Comp.	Expr.
1. Spring	____	____	16. Christmas	____	____
2. Summer	____	____	17. Valentine's Day	____	____
3. Fall	____	____	18. New Year's Day	____	____
4. Winter	____	____	19. Cinco de Mayo	____	____
5. Night	____	____	20. Easter	____	____
6. Day	____	____	21. Independence Day	____	____
7. Month	____	____	22. Halloween	____	____
8. Week	____	____	23. Thanksgiving	____	____
9. Year	____	____	24. Season	____	____
10. Hour	____	____	25. Windy	____	____
11. Minute	____	____	26. Cold	____	____
12. Second	____	____	27. Sunny	____	____
13. Morning	____	____	28. Rainy	____	____
14. Afternoon	____	____	29. Cloudy	____	____
15. Evening	____	____	30. Snowy	____	____

CLOTHING

Student's Name:_____ **Date:**_____ **Language:**_____

Goal

The student will demonstrate receptive and expressive knowledge of articles of clothing.

Record a **plus** or **minus** to indicate correct and incorrect responses.

Words	Comp.	Expr.		Words	Comp.	Expr.
1. Shoes	____	____		16. Bathrobe	____	____
2. Socks	____	____		17. Shorts	____	____
3. Pants	____	____		18. T-shirt	____	____
4. Dress	____	____		19. Cap	____	____
5. Blouse	____	____		20. Mittens	____	____
6. Shirt	____	____		21. Gloves	____	____
7. Skirt	____	____		22. Nightgown	____	____
8. Tie	____	____		23. Belt	____	____
9. Hat	____	____		24. Vest	____	____
10. Boots	____	____		25. Helmet	____	____
11. Sweater	____	____		26. Pajamas	____	____
12. Coat	____	____		27. Bra	____	____
13. Jacket	____	____		28. Underwear	____	____
14. Scarf	____	____		29. Raincoat	____	____
15. Glasses	____	____		30. Undershirt	____	____

TRANSPORTATION

Student's Name:_____ **Date:**_____ **Language:**_____

Goal

The student will demonstrate receptive and expressive knowledge of transportation items.

Record a **plus** or **minus** to indicate correct and incorrect responses.

Words	Comp.	Expr.
1. Airplane	_____	_____
2. Helicopter	_____	_____
3. Parachute	_____	_____
4. Hot air balloon	_____	_____
5. Rocket	_____	_____
6. Bus	_____	_____
7. Truck	_____	_____
8. Car	_____	_____
9. Bicycle	_____	_____
10. Motorcycle	_____	_____
11. Wagon	_____	_____
12. Roller skates	_____	_____
13. Train	_____	_____
14. Subway	_____	_____
15. Boat	_____	_____

HEALTH AND SELF-CARE

Student's Name:_____ **Date:**_____ **Language:**_____

Goal

Goal:

The student will demonstrate receptive and expressive knowledge of words relating to health and self-care.

Record a **plus** or **minus** to indicate correct and incorrect responses.

Words	Comp.	Expr.
1. Comb	____	____
2. Brush	____	____
3. Toothbrush	____	____
4. Toothpaste	____	____
5. Soap	____	____
6. Towel	____	____
7. Washcloth	____	____
8. Shampoo	____	____
9. Tissue	____	____
10. Deodorant	____	____
11. Hair dryer	____	____
12. Perfume	____	____
13. Makeup	____	____
14. Thermometer	____	____
15. Medicine	____	____

References

Aarts, N. (2001). Audiology overseas: A Saudi experience. *Hearsay: Journal of the Ohio Speech-Language-Hearing Association, 14*, 28-39.

Abbott, P., & Sapsford, R. (2006). Life satisfaction in post-Soviet Russia and Ukraine. *Journal of Happiness Studies, 7*, 251-287.

Abboud, S.K., & Kim, J. (2007). *How do Asian students get to the top of the class?* Retrieved 4/5/07 from http://www.greatschools.net/cgi-bin/showarticle/ca/933?cpn=20070404pa1.

Abedi, J. (2004). No Child Left Behind Act and English language learners: Assessment and accountability issues. In O. García & C. Baker (Eds.), *Bilingual education: An introductory reader* (pp. 286-301). Clevedon, England: Multilingual Matters Ltd.

Abu Baker, K. (2003). Marital problems among Arab families: Between cultural and family therapy interventions. *Arab Studies Quarterly, 24*, 53-62.

Academic Communication Associates (2007). *Bilingual picture symbol communication resource.* Oceanside, CA: Author.

Acevedo, M.A. (1991). *Spanish consonant acquisition among two groups of Head Start children.* Paper presented at annual convention of the American Speech-Language-Hearing Association, Atlanta, GA.

Afsaruddin, A. (2006). The "Islamic state": genealogy, facts, and myths. *Journal of Church and State, 48*, 153-174.

Ahmad, N.M. (2004). *Arab-American culture and health care.* Available at http://www.case.edu/med/epidbio/mphp439/Arab-Americans.htm.

Alant, E., Bornman, J., & Lloyd, L.L. (2006). Issues in AAC research: How much do we really understand? *Disability and Rehabilitation, 28*, 143-150.

Al-Hazza, T., & Lucking, B. (2005). The minority of suspicion: Arab Americans. *Multicultural Review, 14*, 32-38.

Ali, S.R., Liu, W.L., & Humedian, M. (2004). Islam 101: Understanding the religion and therapy implications. *Professional Psychology: Research and Practice, 35*, 635-642.

Al-Jafar, A., & Buzzelli, C.A. (2004). The art of storytelling for cross cultural understanding. *International Journal of Early Childhood, 36*, 35-48.

Allison, S. R., & Begay Vining, C. (1999). Native American culture and language: Considerations in service delivery. *Bilingual Review, 24*, 193-205.

Alvarez McHatton, P., & Correa, V. (2005). Stigma and discrimination: Perspectives from Mexican and Puerto Rican mothers of children with special needs. *Topics in Early Childhood Special Education, 25*, 131-139.

American Community Survey (2007). *Asian/Pacific American Heritage Month: May, 2007.* U.S. Census Bureau, American CS Office. Retrieved 6/21/07 from *http://www.prnewswire.com.*

American Speech-Language Hearing Association (2001). Focused initiative: Culturally/Linguistically diverse populations. *Asha Supplement #21, 9.*

American Speech-Language-Hearing Association (2003). *Highlights and trends: ASHA counts for 2003.* Retrieved June 6, 2004 from www.asha.org/about/membership-certification/member-counts.htm.

American Speech-Language-Hearing Association (2005). *Introduction to evidence-based practice: What it is (and what it isn't).* Retrieved 7/28/05 from www.asha.org/members/ebp/default.

American Speech-Language-Hearing Association (2006). *Highlights and trends: ASHA member counts. Constituents—How many are there? How have numbers changed?* Retrieved May 25, 2006, from www.asha.org/about/membership-certification/member-counts.htm.

American Speech-Language-Hearing Association (2007). Responsiveness to intervention (RTI). Retrieved 6/28/07 from http://www.asha.org/members/slp/schools/prof-consult/RtoI.htm.

Anderson, I., Crengle, S., Kamaka, M., Chen, T., Palafox, N., & Jackson-Pulver, L. (2006). Indigenous health in Australia, New Zealand and the Pacific. *Lancet, 367*, 1775-1785.

Anderson, R.T. (1998). The development of grammatical case distinctions in the use of personal pronouns by Spanish-speaking preschoolers. *Journal of Speech-Language-Hearing Research, 41(2)*, 394-406.

Anderson, R.T (1999). Impact of first language loss on grammar in a bilingual child. *Communication Disorders Quarterly, 21(1)*, 4-16.

Anderson, R. (2002). Practical assessment strategies with Hispanic students. In A.E. Brice (Ed.), *The Hispanic child: Speech, language, culture and education (pp. 143-184).* Boston, MA: Allyn & Bacon.

Anderson, R. (2004). Children: Patterns of loss and implications for clinical practice. Influences, contexts, and processes. In B.A. Goldstein (Ed.), *Bilingual language development and disorders in Spanish-English speakers* (pp. 187-211). Baltimore, MD: Paul H. Brookes Publishing Co.

Andrade, N. N., Hishinuma, E. S., McDermott, J. F., Jr., Johnson, R. C., Goebert, D. A., Makini, G. K., Jr., et al. (2006). The National Center on Indigenous Hawaiian Behavioral Health study of prevalence of psychiatric disorders in Native Hawaiian adolescents. *Journal of the American Academy of Child and Adolescent Psychiatry, 45*, 26-36.

Andreev, A.L. (2003). Society and education: A sociocultural profile of Russia. *Russian Education and Society, 45,* 5-22.

Annett, M.M. (2001). More federal funds could reduce caseloads. *The ASHA Leader, 6(7),* 1.

Arida, H. (2006). Teaching the Middle East: The perspectives method. *Teaching History: A Journal of Methods, 31,* 74-84.

Arizona Department of Health Services (2005). *Differences in the health status among ethnic groups: Arizona 2003.* Phoenix: Author.

Arond, D.E. (2006). Eye on religion: Buddhism and medicine. *Southern Medical Journal, 99,* 1450-1451.

Aronson, J. (2007*).* FAS and FAE issues in Russia. Retrieved 3/5/07 from http://www.russianadoption.org/fas.htm.

Asher, J.J. (2007). *TPR: After 40 years, still a very good idea.* Retrieved March 28, 2007, from http://www.tpr-world.com/JapanArticle.pdf.

Asia Foundation (2007). Pacific Island overview. Retrieved 6/21/07 from http://www.asiafoundation.org/Locations/pacificisland.html.

Asian and Pacific Islander American Health Forum (2006). Samoans in the United States. Available at http://www.apiahf.org/resources/index.htm.

Assistive Technology Engineering Lab (2005). *Picture Master Language Software.* Oceanside, CA: Academic Communication Associates.

August, D., Carlo, M., Dressler, C., & Snow, C. (2005). The critical role of vocabulary development for English language learners. *Learning Disabilities Research & Practice, 20,* 50-57.

Australian Centre for International and Tropical Health (2003). Community Health Profile: Samoa and Tonga. Retrieved 3/5/07 from http://www.health.qld.gov.au/multicultural/cultdiv/samoa_tonga.asp.

Autism Incidence Encyclopedia (2007). Available at http://en.allexperts.com/e/a/au/autism_(incidence).htm.

Autism Society of America (2007). *Facts and statistics: Based on prevalence statistics from the Centers for Disease Control and Prevention.* Retrieved 2/21/07 from http://www.autism-society.org.

Ayoob, M. (2004). Political Islam: Image and reality. *World Policy Journal, 21,* 1-14.

Bagli, A. (2002). Multicultural aspects of deafness. In D.E. Battle (Ed.), *Communication disorders in multicultural populations* (3rd ed.) (pp. 361-414). Woburn, MA: Butterworth-Heinemann.

Baker, C. (2000). *A parents' and teachers' guide to bilingualism.* London: Anness Publishing.

Balderas, J.B. (2001, August 12). American Indians' enemy: Diabetes, lifestyle, diets blamed as 50% of Native Americans over 45 are affected. *The Washington Post,* p. A2.

Banks, J.A. (2002). *An introduction to multicultural education (*3rd ed.). Boston: Allyn & Bacon.

Barker, A.M. (1999). *Consuming Russia.* London: Duke University Press.

Barnett, W.S., & Camili, G. (2002). Compensatory preschool education, cognitive development, and "race." In J.M. Fish (Ed*.), Race and intelligence: Separating science from myth* (pp. 369-406). Mahwah, NJ: Lawrence Erlbaum.

Barone, D.M. (2006). *Narrowing the literacy gap: What works in high-poverty schools.* New York: The Guilford Press.

Barrera, M. (2006). Roles of definitional and assessment models in the identification of new or second language learners of English for special education. *Journal of Learning Disabilities, 39,* 142-156.

Barrow, D. (2004). Networked collaboration transforms curricula: The case of Arab culture and civilization. *Liberal Education, 90,* 48-55.

Battle, D.E. (Ed.) (2002a). *Communication disorders in multicultural populations* (3rd ed.). Woburn, MA: Butterworth-Heinemann.

Battle, D.E. (2002b). Middle Eastern and Arab American cultures. In D.E. Battle (Ed.), *Communication disorders in multicultural populations* (3rd ed.) (pp. 113-134). Woburn, MA: Butterworth-Heinemann.

Beane, M. (2006). *An adventure in American cultures and values: International student guide to the United States of America.* Retrieved 12/27/06 from http://www.internationalstudentguidetotheusa.com/articles/american_culture/culture.htm.

Beardsmore, H.B. (1993). European models of bilingual education: Practice, theory and development. *Journal of Multilingual and Multicultural Development, 14 (1,2),* 103-120.

Beaumont, C. (1992). Service delivery issues. In H. Langdon and L. Cheng (Eds.), *Hispanic children and adults with communication disorders.* Gaithersburg, MD: Aspen Publishers, Inc.

Bebout, L., & Arthur, B. (1992). Cross-cultural attitudes about speech disorders. *Journal of Speech and Hearing Research, 35(2),* 45-52.

Bedore, L.M., & Leonard, L.B. (2000). The effects of inflectional variation on fast mapping of verbs in English and Spanish. *Journal of Speech-Language-Hearing Research, 43(1),* 21-33.

Bedore, L.M., Peña, E.D., García, M., & Cortez, C. (2005). Conceptual versus monolingual scoring: When does it make a difference? *Language, Speech, and Hearing Services in Schools, 36,* 188-200.

Begay Vining, C. (1999, November). Navajo perspectives on developmental disabilities. Paper presented at the annual meeting of the American Speech-Language-Hearing Association, San Francisco, CA.

Bell, N. (1991). *Visualizing and verbalizing for language comprehension and thinking*: Paso Robles, CA: Academy of Reading Publications.

Bellafante, G. (2004, December). An immigrant group in a rush to marry young. *The New York Times,* Section A, Column 1, Metropolitan Desk, p. 1.

Bengston, D., & Baldwin, C. (1993). *The international student: Female circumcision issues. Journal of Multicultural Counseling and Development, 21 (3),* 168-173.

Bennett, C.I. (2003). Comprehensive multicultural education: Theory and practice (4th ed.). Boston: Allyn & Bacon.

Berglund, E., Eriksson, M., & Johansson, I. (2001). Parental reports of spoken language skills in children with Down syndrome. *Journal of Speech, Language, and Hearing Research, 44,* 179-191.

Berke, J. (2007). Sign language—Spanish sign language. Your Guide to Deafness. Available at www.deafness.about.com.

Bernstein, D.K., & Tiegerman-Farber, E. (2002). *Language and communication disorders in children* (5th ed.). Boston, MA: Allyn & Bacon.

Bialystok, E., Luk, G., & Kwan, E. (2005). Bilingualism, biliteracy, and learning to read: Interactions among languages and writing systems. *Scientific Studies of Reading, 9*, 43.

Bialystok, E., McBride-Chang, C., & Luk, G. (2005). Bilingualism, language proficiency, and learning to read in two writing systems. *Journal of Educational Psychology, 97*, 580-590.

Bianchi, S.M., & Caspter, L.M. (2005). Explanations of family change: A family demographic perspective. In V.L. Bengsten, A.C. Acock, K.R. Allen, P. Dilworth-Anderson, & D.M. Klein (Eds.), *Sourcebook of family theory and research.* Thousand Oaks, CA: Sage.

Bilici, M. (2005). American jihad: Representations of Islam in the United States after 9/11. *American Journal of Social Sciences, 22*, 50-69.

Binger, C., & Light, J. (2006). Demographics of preschoolers who require AAC. *Language, Speech, and Hearing Services in Schools, 37*, 200-208.

Black, R.W. (2005). Access and affiliation: The literacy and composition practices of English-language learners in an online fanfiction community. *Journal of Adolescent and Adult Literacy, 49*, 118-128.

Blair, S.L., & Qian, Z. (1998). Family and Asian students' educational performance. *Journal of Family Issues, 19*, 355-374.

Bland-Stewart, L.M. (2005). Difference or deficit in speakers of African American English: What every clinician should know...and do. *The ASHA Leader, 10*, 6-31.

Bliss, L.S. (2002). *Discourse impairments: Assessment and intervention applications.* Boston, MA: Allyn & Bacon.

Bliss, L.S., McCabe, K., & Mahecha, N. (2001). Analyses of narratives from Spanish-speaking bilingual children. *Contemporary Issues in Communication Sciences and Disorders, 28*, 733-739.

Bloom, L., & Lahey, M. (1978). *Language development and language disorders.* New York: John Wiley & Sons.

Boswell, S. (2004). An overview of No Child Left Behind. *The ASHA Leader, 9*, 8-9.

Bowen, D. E. (2005). Honoring the elders: Interviews with two Lakota men. *Journal of Sociology and Social Welfare, 32*, 125-134.

Bozorgmehr, M. (2001). Information available from www.iranian.com/Opinion/2001/May/Iranians.

Brice, A.E. (2000a). Code switching and code mixing in the ESL classroom: A study of pragmatic and syntactic features. Advances in speech language pathology. *Journal of the Speech Pathology Association of Australia, 20(1)*, 19-28.

Brice, A.E. (2000b). Which language for bilingual speakers? Factors to consider. Special Interest Division 14, *Communication Disorders and Sciences in Culturally and Linguistically Diverse Populations, 6(1)*. Rockville Pike, MD: American Speech-Language-Hearing Association.

Brice, A.E. (2002). *The Hispanic child: Speech, language, culture and education.* Boston, MA: Allyn & Bacon.

Brice, A.E, & Anderson, R. (1999). Code mixing in a young bilingual child. *Communication Disorders Quarterly, 21(1)*, 17-22.

Brice, A.E., & Brice, R.G. (2007). School language and classroom programs for children with language impairments: Collaborating with parents and school personnel. In C. Roseberry-McKibbin, *Language disorders in children: A multicultural and case perspective* (pp. 441-464). Boston: Allyn & Bacon.

Brice, A.E., & Miller, K.J. (2000). Case studies in inclusion: What works, what doesn't. *Communication Disorders Quarterly, 21(4)*, 237-241.

Brice, A.E., Miller, K.J., & Brice, R.G. (2006). Language in the English as a second language and general education classrooms: A tutorial. *Communication Disorders Quarterly, 27*, 240-247.

Brice, A.E., & Montgomery, J. (1996). Adolescent pragmatic skills: A comparison of Latino students in English as a second language and speech and language programs. *Language, Speech, and Hearing Services in Schools, 27(1)*, 68-81.

Brice, A.E., & Roseberry-McKibbin, C. (1999a). *A case example of a bilingual evaluation: A tutorial. Florida Journal of Communication Disorders, 19*, 25-31.

Brice, A.E., & Roseberry-McKibbin, C. (1999b). Turning frustration into success for English language learners. *Educational Leadership, 56(7)*, 53-55.

Bridges, S.J., & Midgette, T.E. (2000). Augmentative/alternative communication and assistive technology. In T. Coleman (Ed.), *Clinical management of communication disorders in culturally diverse children* (pp. 295-333). Needham Heights, MA: Allyn & Bacon.

Brito, L., Pérez, X., Bliss, L., & McCabe, A. (1999, November). The narratives of school-aged Spanish speaking children. Paper presented at the annual convention of the American Speech-Language-Hearing Association, San Francisco, CA.

Britto, P., Brooks-Gunn, J., & Griffin, T. M. (2006). Maternal reading and teaching patterns: Associations with school readiness in low-income African American families. *Reading Research Quarterly, 41*, 68-89.

Burnett, B. (2000). *Close-up. The ASHA Leader, 5(10)*, 26.

Burt, H., & Dulay, H. (1978). Some guidelines for the assessment of oral language proficiency and dominance. *TESOL Quarterly, 12*, 177-192.

Cadge, W. (2005). *Heartwood: The first generation of Theravada Buddhism in America.* Chicago: University of Chicago.

Caesar, L. G., & Kohler, P. D. (2007). The state of school-based bilingual assessment: Actual practice versus recommended guidelines. *Language, Speech, and Hearing Services in Schools, 38*, 190-200.

Cahnmann, M., & Varghese, M. M. (2005). Critical advocacy and bilingual education in the United States. *Linguistics and Education, 16*, 59-73.

California Department of Education (1999). *Language census summary statistics, 1998-1999.* Sacramento, CA: California Department of Education.

California Education Code (1991). *California Education Code, 1991 Compact Edition.* St. Paul, MN: West Publishing Company.

Callicott, K. J. (2003). Culturally sensitive collaboration within person-centered planning. *Focus on Autism and Other Developmental Disabilities, 18*, 60-68.

Campbell, D. (2001). Multicultural competency. *ADVANCE for Speech-Language Pathologists and Audiologists, 11(9)*, 7-8.

Campbell, L.R. (1993). Maintaining the integrity of home linguistic varieties: Black English Vernacular. *American Journal of Speech-Language Pathology, 2*, 85.

Campbell, L.R. (1996). Issues in service delivery to African American children. In Kamhi, A.G., Pollock, K.E., & Harris, J.L. (Eds.), *Communication development and disorders in African American children* (pp. 73-94). Baltimore: Paul H. Brookes Publishing Co.

Campbell, T., Dollaghan, C., Needleman, H., & Janosky, J. (1997). Reducing bias in language assessment: Processing-dependent measures. *Journal of Speech, Language, and Hearing Research, 40*, 519-525.

Cantor, A.G., Goldman, L., Courtney, J.G., & Kattan, D. (2003). *Differences in sources of lead exposure for Hispanic and non-Hispanic childhood lead poisoning cases in California.* Paper presented at the 131st annual meeting of the APHA, November 17, 2003.

Cárdenas-Hagan, E., Carlson, C. D., & Pollard-Durodola, S. D. (2007). The cross-linguistic transfer of early literacy skills: The role of initial L1 and L2 skills and language of instruction. *Language, Speech, and Hearing Services in Schools, 38*, 249-259.

Carreon, G.P., Drake, C., & Barton, A.C. (2005). The importance of presence: Immigrant parents' school engagement experiences. *American Education Research Journal, 42*, 465-500.

Carrier, K. A. (2005). Key issues for teaching language learners in academic classrooms. *Middle School Journal, 37*, 4-9.

Carta, J.J., & Atwater, J.B. (2003, September). The impact of an early intervention program on parent-child interactions and children's developmental trajectories. In J. Carta (Chair), *Panel on parent-child interactions.* Panel presented at the meeting of the International Society of Early Intervention, Rome, Italy.

Carter, J. A., Lees, J. A., Murira, G. M., Gona, J., Neville, B. G.R., & Newton, C. R. J. C. (2005). Issues in the development of cross-cultural assessments of speech and language for children. *International Journal of Language & Communication Disorders, 40*, 385-401.

Case, R.E., Ndura, E., & Righettini, M. (2005). Balancing linguistic and social needs: Evaluating texts using a critical language awareness approach. *Journal of Adolescent and Adult Literacy, 48*, 374-391.

Cashman, H.R. (2006). Who wins in research on bilingualism in an anti-bilingual state? *Journal of Multilingual and Multicultural Development, 27*, 42-60.

Centeno, J.G. (2007). From theory to realistic praxis: Service-Learning as a teaching method to enhance speech-language services with minority populations. In A.J. Wurr & J. Hellenbrandt (Eds.), *Learning the language of global citizenship: Service-learning in applied linguistics* (pp. 190-218). Boston: Anker Publishing Company, Inc.

Center for International Rehabilitation (2004). Russia. Retrieved June 30, 2004 from www.cirnetwork.org/idrm/reports/russia.cfm.

Chadwick, D. (2000). The Samoan way. *National Geographic, 198*, 72.

Chamberlain, A., & Roseberry-McKibbin, C. (2008, April). *American Indians and mainstream SLPs: The merging of two worlds.* Paper presented at the annual meeting of the California Speech, Language, and Hearing Association, Monterey, CA.

Chamberlain, S.P. (2005). Recognizing and responding to cultural differences in the education of culturally and linguistically diverse learners. *Intervention in School and Clinic, 40*, 195-211.

Champion, T., & Mainess, K. (2003). Typical and disordered narration in African American children. In A. McCabe & L.S. Bliss, *Patterns of narrative discourse: A multicultural lifespan approach* (pp. 55-70). Boston: Allyn & Bacon.

Champion, T.B., Hyter, Y.D., McCabe, A., & Bland-Stewart, L.M. (2003). "A matter of vocabulary": Performances of low-income African American Head Start children on the Peabody Picture Vocabulary Test-III. *Communication Disorders Quarterly, 24*, 121-128.

Chen, C. (2006). From filial piety to religious piety: Evangelical Christianity reconstructing Taiwanese immigrant families in the United States. *IMR, 40*, 573-602.

Chen, E., Martin, A.D., & Matthews, K.A. (2006). Understanding health disparities: The role of race and socioeconomic status in children's health. *American Journal of Public Health, 96*, 702-708.

Chan, S., & Lee, E. (2004). Families with Asian roots. In E.W. Lynch & M.J. Hanson (Eds.), *Developing cross-cultural competence: A guide to working with young children and their families* (3rd ed.) (pp. 219-298). Baltimore: Paul H. Brookes Publishing Co.

Chen, Y. (2001). Chinese values, health and nursing. *Journal of Advanced Nursing, 36*, 270-273.

Cheng, L.L. (1987). *Assessment and remediation of Asian language populations.* Rockville Pike, MD: Aspen.

Cheng, L.L. (1991). *Assessing Asian language performance* (2nd ed.). Oceanside, CA: Academic Communication Associates.

Cheng, L.L. (1999). Struggling to be heard: The unmet needs of Asian Pacific Americans. *Asha, 41(6)*, 10-13.

Cheng, L.L. (2002). *Asian and Pacific American cultures.* In D.E. Battle (Ed.), *Communication disorders in multicultural populations* (3rd ed.) (pp. 71-111). Boston: Butterworth Heinemann.

Cheng, L.L. (2007). Codes and contexts: Exploring linguistic, cultural, and social intelligence. *The ASHA Leader, 12*, 8-33.

Cheng, L.L. (2002). Asian and Pacific American cultures. In D.E. Battle (Ed.), *Communication disorders in multicultural populations* (3rd ed.) (pp. 71-112). Woburn, MA: Butterworth-Heinemann.

Cheng, L.L., Nakasato, J., & Wallace, G.J. (1995). The Pacific Islander population and the challenges they face. In L.L. Cheng (Ed.), *Integrating language and learning for inclusion: An Asian-Pacific focus* (pp. 63-106). San Diego: Singular Publishing Group, Inc.

Chiat, S., & Roy, P. (2007). The preschool repetition test: An evaluation of performance in typically developing and clinically referred children. *Journal of Speech, Language, and Hearing Research, 50*, 429-443.

Child Trends Data Bank (2003). *School communication in parents' native language.* Retrieved 8/7/06 from http://www.childtrendsdatabank.org/indicators/104CommunicateNativeLang.cfm.

Cho, S.J., Singer, G.H.S., & Brenner, M.B. (2003). A comparison of adaptation to childhood disability in Korean immigrants and Korean mothers. *Focus on Autism and other Developmental Disabilities, 18*, 9-19.

Choi, C., & McPherson, B. (2005). Noise levels in Hong Kong primary schools: Implications for classroom listening. *International Journal of Disability, Development and Education, 52*, 345-360.

Chung, C. (2006). Between principle and situation: Contrasting styles in the Japanese and Korean traditions of moral culture. *Philosophy East & West, 56*, 253-280.

Clark, E., & Zhou, Z. (2005). Autism in China: From acupuncture to applied behavioral analysis. *Psychology in the Schools, 42*, 285-295.

Clark, R. L., & Mendoza, R. H. (2002). Assessing cultural lifestyles of urban American Indians. *American Indian Culture and Research Journal, 26*, 1-13.

Clark, S., & Kelley, S.D.M. (1992). Traditional Native American values: *Conflict or concordance in rehabilitation? Journal of Rehabilitation, 58 (2)*, 23-27.

Cognitive Concepts (2003). *Earobics: Sound foundations for reading and spelling*. Evanston, IL: Author.

Coleman, L. J., & Southern, W. T. (2006). Bringing the potential of underserved children to the threshold of talent development. *Gifted Child Today, 39*, 35-45.

Coleman, T.J., & McCabe-Smith, L. (2000). Key terms and concepts. In T.J. Coleman, *Clinical management of communication disorders in culturally diverse children* (pp. 3-12). Needham Heights, MA: Allyn & Bacon.

Coles-White, D. (2004). Negative concord in child African American English: Implications for specific language impairment. *Journal of Speech, Language, and Hearing Research, 47*, 212-222.

Collins, M.F. (2005). ESL preschoolers' English vocabulary acquisition from storybook reading. *Reading Research Quarterly, 40*, 406-408.

Connor, C.M., & Craig, H.K. (2006). African American preschoolers' language, emergent literacy skills, and use of African American English: A complex relation. *Journal of Speech, Language, and Hearing Research, 49*, 771-792.

Coltrane, B. (2003). Working with young English language learners: Some considerations. *ERIC Digest*; retrieved 7/17/03 from http://www.cal.org/ericcll/digest/0301coltrane.html.

Conti-Ramsden, G. (2003). Processing and linguistic markers in young children with specific language impairment (SLI). *Journal of Speech, Language, and Hearing Research, 46*, 1029-1037.

Cox, P. (2006). Samoan Americans. Retrieved 3/5/07 from http://www.everyculture.com/multi/Pa-Sp/Samoan-Americans.html.

Craig, H.K., Thompson, C.A., Washington, J.A., & Potter, S.L. (2003). Phonological features of child African American English. *Journal of Speech-Language-Hearing Research, 46*, 623-635.

Craig, H.K., & Washington, J.A. (2000). An assessment battery for identifying language impairments in African American children. *Journal of Speech-Language-Hearing Research, 43(2)*, 366-379.

Craig, H.K., & Washington, J.A. (2004a). Grade-related changes in the production of African American English. *Journal of Speech, Language, and Hearing Research, 47*, 450-463.

Craig, H.K., Washington, J.A., & Thompson-Porter, C. (1998). Average C-unit lengths in the discourse of African American children from low-income, urban homes. *Journal of Speech-Language-Hearing Research, 41(2)*, 433-444.

Craig, H.K., & Washington, J.A. (2004b). Language variation and literacy learning. In C.A. Stone, E.R. Silliman, B.J. Ehren, & K. Apel (Eds.), *Handbook of language and literacy: Development and disorders* (pp. 228-243). New York: The Guilford Press.

Crawford, J. (2003). Hard sell: Why is bilingual education so unpopular with the American public? In O. García & C. Baker (Eds.), *Bilingual education: An introductory reader* (pp. 145-164). Clevedon, England: Multilingual Matters Ltd.

Crowley, C.J. (2003). Diagnosing communication disorders in culturally and linguistically diverse students. *ERIC Digest E650*, October, 2003.

Cruzado-Guerrero, J.R., & Carta, J.J. (2006). Assessing vocabulary and the bilingual environment in young Latino children. *Perspectives on Communication Disorders and Sciences in Culturally and Linguistically Diverse Populations, ASHA SID 14 Newsletter, 13*, 9-13.

Culatta, B., Reese, M., & Setzer, L. A. (2006). Early literacy instruction in a dual language (Spanish-English) kindergarten. *Communication Disorders Quarterly, 27*, 67-42.

Cullen, T. (2006). HIV/AIDS in Papua New Guinea: A reality check. *Pacific Journalism Review, 12*, 153-164.

Cummins, J. (1990, January). *Empowerment and critical pedagogy in bilingual teacher training programs*. San Francisco: California Association of Bilingual Education.

Cummins, J. (1991a). Empowering culturally and linguistically diverse students with learning problems. *ERIC Digest, EDO-EC-91-5*, 9-10.

Cummins, J. (1991b). Interdependence of first- and second-language proficiency in bilingual children. In E. Bialystok (Ed.), *Language processing in bilingual children* (pp. 70-89). New York: Cambridge University Press.

Cummins, J. (1992a). Bilingual education and English immersion: The Ramírez report in theoretical perspective. *Bilingual Research Journal, 16 (1,2)*, 91-104.

Cummins, J. (1992b). Empowerment through biliteracy. In J.R. Tinajero & A.F. Ada (Eds.), *The power of two languages: Literacy and biliteracy for Spanish-speaking students*. New York: MacMillan/McGraw Hill.

Cummins, J. (1992c). The role of primary language development in promoting educational success for language minority students. In C. Leyba (Ed.)., *Schooling and language minority students: A theoretical framework*. Calif. State University, Los Angeles, CA.

Cummins, J. (2000). *Language, power and pedagogy: Bilingual children in the cross-fire*. Clevedon, England: Multilingual Matters.

Cummins, J., Chow, P., & Schecter, S.R. (2006). Community as curriculum. *Language Arts, 83*, 297-307.

Curenton, S.M., & Justice, L.M. (2004). African American and Caucasian preschoolers' use of decontextualized language: Literate language features in oral narratives. *Language, Speech, and Hearing Services in Schools, 35*, 240-253.

Curtin, E. M. (2006). Lessons on effective teaching from middle school ESL students. *Middle School Journal, 37*, 38-45.

Dabars, Z. (1995). *The Russian way*. Chicago: Passport Books.

Daley, K.A., Pirie, P.L., Rhodes, K.L., Hunter, L.I., & Davey, C.S. (2007). Early otitis media among Minnesota American Indians: The Little Ears study. *American Journal of Public Health, 97,* 317-322.

Daneshpour, M. (1998). Muslim families and family therapy. *Journal of Marital and Family Therapy, 24,* 355-390.

Dapice, A.N. (2006). The medicine wheel. *Journal of Transcultural Nursing, 17,* 251-260.

Darling, C.A. (2005). Changes and challenges: *Families in a diverse culture. Journal of Family and Consumer Sciences, 97,* 8-13.

de Jesus, M.L. (2005). *Pinay power.* New York: Routledge Taylor and Francis Group.

de Rivera, C., Girolametto, L., Greenberg, J., & Weitzman, E. (2005). Children's responses to educators' questions in day care play groups. *American Journal of Speech-Language Pathology, 14,* 14-26.

Deering, P.D. (2005). It takes an 'ohana to educate young adolescents in a multilingual, multicultural society. *Middle School Journal, 37,* 15-21.

Delgado, E.A., & Canabal, M.E. (2004). Work and family balance among Latinos in the U.S.: Barriers and facilitators. *Journal of Family and Consumer Sciences, 96,* 26-31.

Demine, A.K. (2000). Public health in eastern Europe. *The Lancet Perspectives, 356,* 49.

Demmert, W.G. (2005). The influences of culture on learning and assessment among Native American students. *Learning Disabilities Research and Practice, 20,* 16-23.

Dickinson, D., & Tabors, P.O. (2001). *Beginning literacy with language: Young children learning at home and school.* Baltimore, MD: Brookes Publishing Co.

Diken, I. H., & Rutherford, R. B. (2005). First step to success early intervention program: A study of effectiveness with Native American children. *Education and Treatment of Children, 28,* 444-465.

Dillon, B.C., & Murphy, C. (2008). *Interviewing in action in a multicultural world* (3rd ed.). Belmont, CA: Thomson Higher Education.

Dilworth-Bart, J.E., & Moore, C. F. (2006). Mercy mercy me: Social injustice and the prevention of environmental pollutant exposures among ethnic minority and poor children. *Child Development, 77,* 247-265.

Dingle Swanson, J. (2006). Breaking through assumptions about low-income, minority gifted students. *Gifted Child Quarterly, 50,* 11-25.

Doan, D. (2005). Moral education or political education in the Vietnamese educational system? *Journal of Moral Education, 34,* 451-463.

Dodge, E.P. (2000). Communication and collaboration. In Dodge, E.P. (Ed.), *The survival guide for school-based speech-language pathologists* (pp. 57-97). San Diego, CA: Singular Publishing /Thomson Learning.

Dollaghan, C.A., & Campbell, T.F. (1998). Nonword repetition and child language impairment. *Journal of Speech, Language, and Hearing Research, 41,* 1136-1146.

Domyancic, L. (2000). Service delivery to Russian immigrants: An ethnographic survey. Unpublished master's thesis, California State University, Sacramento.

Drabick, D. A. G., Beauchaine, T. P., Gadow, K. D., Carlson, G. A., & Bromet, E. J. (2006). Risk factors for conduct problems and depressive symptoms in a cohort of Ukrainian children. *Journal of Clinical Child and Adolescent Psychology, 35,* 244-252.

Dragga, S. (1999). Ethical intercultural technical communication: Looking through the lens of Confucian ethics. *Technical Communication Quarterly, 8,* 365-381.

Draper Rodríguez, C., & Higgins, K. (2005). Preschool children with developmental delays and limited English proficiency. *Intervention in School and Clinic, 40,* 236-242.

Duran, E. (2006). *Teaching English learners in inclusive classrooms* (3rd ed.). Springfield, IL: Charles C. Thomas.

Dyches, T.T., Wilder, L.K., Sudweeks, R.R., Obiakor, F.E., & Algozzine, B. (2004). Multicultural issues in autism. *Journal of Autism and Developmental Disabilities, 34,* 211-222.

Dyer, L. (2006). *Language development and internationally adopted children.* Retrieved 12/27/06 from http://www.adoptvietnam.org/adoption/health-language.htm.

Education Week Research Center (2007). English-language learners. Edweek.org. Retrieved 6/27/07 from http:www2.edweek.org/rc/issues/engilsh-language-learners/?levelId=1000&.

Education World (2007). Celebrating Asian and Pacific-Island heritage. Retrieved 6/21/07 from http://www.education-world.com/a_lesson/lesson/lesson340.shtml.

Ehren, B.J., Montgomery, J., Rudebusch, J., & Whitmire, K. (2006). *Responsiveness to intervention: New roles for speech-language pathologists.* American Speech-Language-Hearing Association; retrieved 12/29/06 from http://www.asha.org/members/slp/schools/prof--consult/NewRolesSLP.htm.

Englebret, E., Bear Eagle, D., & CHiXapKaid, D.M. P. (2007). American Indian stories enrich intervention. *The ASHA Leader, 12,* 26-27.

ERIC Clearinghouse on Urban Education (2006). *Facilitating transition to the mainstream: Sheltered English vocabulary development.* Retrieved 10/24/06 from http://www.ncela.gwu.edu/pubs/classics/pig/06sheltered.htm.

Eriks-Brophy, a., & Ayukawa, H. (2000). The benefits of sound-field amplification in classrooms of Inuit students of Nunavik: A pilot project. *Language, Speech, and Hearing Services in Schools, 31,* 234-33.

Eschevarria, J., Short, D., & Powers, K. (2006). School reform and standards-based education: A model for English-language learners. *The Journal of Educational Research, 99,* 195-211.

Estes, K.G., Evans, J.L., & Else-Quest, N.M. (2007). Differences in the nonword repetition performance of children with and without specific language impairment: A meta-analysis. *Journal of Speech, Language, and Hearing Research, 50,* 177-195.

Evans, E., Spear, S.E., Huang, Y-C., & Hser, Y-I. (2006). Outcomes of drug and alcohol treatment among American Indians in California. *American Journal of Public Health, 96,* 889-396.

Fadiman, A. (1997). *The spirit catches you and you fall down: A Hmong child, her American doctors, and the collision of two cultures.* New York: Farrar, Straus, and Giroux.

Falk-Ross, F.C. (2002). *Classroom-based language and literacy intervention: A programs and case studies approach.* Boston, MA: Allyn & Bacon.

Faumuina, M. (2001). Being Samoan, through a child's eyes. *Christian Science Monitor, 93,* 16.

Fan, R. (2002). Reconstructionist Confucianism and health care: An Asian moral account of health care resource allocation. *Journal of Medicine and Philosophy, 27,* 675-682.

Fan, R., & Li, B. (2004). Truth telling in medicine: The Confucian view. *Journal of Medicine and Philosophy, 29,* 179-193.

Fang, X., & Ping-an, H. (1992). Articulation disorders among speakers of Mandarin Chinese. *American Journal of Speech Language Pathology, 1 (4),* 15-16.

Fazio, B.B. (1998). Serial memory in children with specific language impairment: Examining specific content areas for assessment and intervention. In R.B. Gillam (Ed.), *Memory and language impairment in children and adults: New perspectives* (pp. 64-82). Gaithersburg, MD: Aspen Publishers, Inc.

Fensbo, C. (2004). Mental and behavioural outcome of inter-ethnic adoptees: A review of the literature. *European Child and Adolescent Psychiatry, 13,* 55-63.

Fenson, L., Dale, P., Reznick, J., Bates, E., Thal, D.J., & Pethick, S.J. (1993). *McArthur Communicative Developmental Inventories: User's guide and technical manual.* San Diego, CA: Singular.

Feuerstein, R., Rand, Y., Jensen, M.R., Kaniel, S., & Turzel, D. (1987). Prerequisites for assessment of learning potential: The LPAD model. In C.S. Lidz (Ed.), *Dynamic assessment: An interactional approach to evaluating learning potential* (pp. 35-51). New York: The Guilford Press.

Fey, M., Windsor, J., & Warren, S.F. (1995). *Language intervention: Preschool through elementary years.* (Vol. 5 in Communication and Language Intervention Series). Baltimore, MD: Paul H. Brookes Publishing Co.

Fiestas, C.E., & Peña, E.D. (2004). Narrative discourse in bilingual children: Language and task effects. *Language, Speech, and Hearing Services in Schools, 35,* 155-168.

Figueroa, R.A., & Newsome, P. (2006). The diagnosis of learning disability in English learners. *Journal of Learning Disabilities, 39,* 206-214.

Fisher, D., Frey, N., & Williams, D. (2002). Seven literacy strategies that work. *Educational Leadership, 60,* 70-73.

Fleming, W.C. (2006). Myths and stereotypes about Native Americans. *Phi Delta Kappan, 88,* 213-234.

Fontes, L.A. (2005). *Child abuse and culture: Working with diverse families.* New York: Guilford.

Forum on Child and Family Statistics (2006). *America's children in brief: Key National Indicators of well-being, 2006.* Retrieved 8/28/06 from http://www.childstats.gov/americaschildren/eco.asp.

Freeman, D.E., & Freeman, Y.W. (2004). *Essential linguistics: What you need to know to teach reading, ESL, spelling, phonics, and grammar.* Portsmouth, NH: Heinemann.

Freeman, R. (2004). Reviewing the research on language education programs. In O. García & C. Baker (Eds.), *Bilingual education: An introductory reader* (pp. 3-18). Clevedon, England: Multilingual Matters Ltd.

Friedlander, R. (1993). BHSM comes to the Flathead Indian Reservation. *Asha, 35(5),* 28-29.

Frisbie, W.P., Cho, Y., & Hummer, R.A. (2006). Immigration and the health of Asian and Pacific Islander adults in the United States. *American Journal of Epidemiology, 153,* 372-380.

Fukuyama, S., Inaoka, T., Matsumura, Y., Yamauchi, T., Natsuhara, K., Kimura, R., & Ohtsuka, R. (2005). Anthropometry of 5-19 year old Tongan children with special interest in the high prevalence of obesity among adolescent girls. *Annals of Human Biology, 32,* 714-723.

Fung, F., & Roseberry-McKibbin, C. (1999). Service delivery considerations in working with clients from Cantonese-speaking backgrounds. *American Journal of Speech-Language Pathology, 8(4),* 309-318.

Galanti, G. (2004). *Cultural diversity in health care.* Retrieved 12/27/06 from http://www.ggalanti.com/concepts.html.

Gallaudet Research Institute (December, 2005). *Regional and National Summary Report of Data from the 2004-2005 Annual Survey of Deaf and Hard of Hearing Children and Youth.* Washington, DC: GRI, Gallaudet University.

Gandara, P. (2004). Building bridges to college. *Educational Leadership, 62,* 56-60.

Gandhi, R.S. (2003). Family and feminism: Women, their position, rights and obligations in cross-cultural perspective. *Journal of Comparative Family Studies, 34,* 605-611.

García, B., Mendez Pérez, A., & Ortiz, A.A. (2000). Mexican American mothers' beliefs about disabilities: Implications for early childhood intervention. *Remedial and Special Education, 21,* 90-102.

García, S.B., & Ortiz, A.A. (2006). New directions in research: Cultural considerations with respect to international models. *Reading Research Quarterly,* Jan/Feb/March 2006 issue.

Garrett, M.T., Garrett, J.T., Torres-Rivera, M.W., & Roberts-Wilbur, J. (2005). Laughing it up: Native American humor as spiritual tradition. *Journal of Multicultural Counseling and Development, 33,* 194-204.

Garrett, M., & Pichette, E.F. (2000). Red as an apple: Native American acculturation and counseling with or without reservation. *Journal of Counseling & Development, 78,* 3-13.

Geaves, R. (2005). *Aspects of Islam.* Washington, DC: Georgetown University Press.

Genesee, F., Paradis, J., & Crago, M.B. (2004). *Dual language development and disorders: A handbook on bilingualism and second language learners.* Baltimore, MD: Brookes Publishing Co.

Gersten, R., & Geva, E. (2003). Teaching reading to early language learners. *Educational Leadership, 60,* 44-49.

Ghali, J.K., Cooper, R.S., Kowatly, I., & Liao, Y. (1993). Delay between onset of chest pain and arrival to the coronary care unit among minority and disadvantaged patients. *Journal of the National Medical Association, 85 (3),* 180-184.

Gibbons, P. (2002). *Scaffolding language, scaffolding learning: Teaching second language learners in the mainstream classroom.* Portsmouth, NH: Heinemann.

Gildersleeve-Neumann, C. (2007, May). *Valid assessment and treatment of clients from diverse backgrounds: A workshop for SLPs.* Workshop presented in Sacramento, CA.

Gillam, R.B., Cowan, N., & Day, L. (1995). Sequential memory in children with and without language impairment. *Journal of Speech and Hearing Research, 38,* 393-402.

Gillam, R.B., & van Kleeck, A. (1998). Phonological awareness training and short-term working memory: Clinical implications. In R.B. Gillam (Ed.), *Memory and language impairment in children and adults: New perspectives* (pp. 83-96). Gaithersburg, MD: Aspen Publishers, Inc.

Gillon, G.T. (2004). *Phonological awareness: From research to practice.* New York: Guilford Publications, Inc.

Gindis, B. (2000). Language-related issues for international adoptees and adoptive families. In T. Tepper, L. Hannon, & D. Sandstrom (Eds.), *International adoption: Challenges and opportunities* (pp. 98-108). Meadow Lands, PA: Center for Cognitive-Developmental Assessment and Remediation.

Gindis, B. (2004). Language development in internationally adopted children. *China Connection, 10,* 34-37.

Gindis, B. (2005). Cognitive, language, and educational issues of children adopted from overseas orphanages. *Journal of Cognitive Education and Psychology, 4,* 291-311.

Glennen, S. (2006, April). *Language development and disorders in internationally adopted infants and toddlers.* Seminar presented at the annual meeting of the California Speech-Language-Hearing Association, San Francisco, CA.

Glennen, S. (2007). Predicting language outcomes for internationally adopted children. *Journal of Speech, Language, and Hearing Research, 50,* 529-548.

Glennen, S., & Bright, B.J. (2005). Five years later in school-age internationally adopted children. *Seminars in Speech and Language, 26,* 86-201.

Glennen, S., & Masters, M.G. (1999, November). Language development and delay in children adopted internationally. Paper presented at the annual convention of the American Speech-Language-Hearing Association, San Francisco, CA.

Goehner, D. (2005). *Russian/American cultural contrasts.* Retrieved 12/27/07 from http://www.goehner.com/russinfo.htm.

Goldstein, B.A. (2000). *Cultural and linguistic diversity resource guide for speech-language pathologists.* San Diego, CA: Singular Publishing Group/Thomson Learning.

Goldstein, B.A. (2004). Bilingual language development and disorders: Introduction and overview. In B.A. Goldstein (Ed.), *Bilingual language development and disorders in Spanish-English speakers* (pp. 3-20). Baltimore, MD: Paul H. Brookes Publishing Co.

Goldstein, B.A., Fabiano, L., & Washington, P.S. (2005). Phonological skills in predominantly English-speaking, predominantly Spanish-speaking, and Spanish-English bilingual children. *Language, Speech, and Hearing Services in Schools, 36,* 201-218.

Goldstein, B.A., & Iglesias, A. (1996). Phonological patterns in normally developing Spanish-speaking 3- and 4-year olds. *Language, Speech, and Hearing Services in Schools, 27(1),* 82-90.

Goldsworthy, C. (2003). *Developmental reading disabilities: A language-based treatment approach* (2nd ed.). San Diego, CA: Singular Publishing/Thomson Learning.

Gollnick, D.M., & Chinn, P.C. (2002). *Multicultural education in a pluralistic society* (6th ed.). Columbus, OH: Merrill.

Gonzales, D. (2007). *Evaluating bilingual students for eligibility as speech/language impaired: A handbook for evidence-based decision-making.* Houston, TX: Region 4 Education Service Center.

Gonzales, M.D., Ezell, H.K., & Randolph, E. (1999, November). *Home literacy environments of migrant Mexican-American families.* Paper presented at the annual convention of the American Speech-Language-Hearing Association, San Francisco, CA.

GoPaul-McNichol, S., & Armour-Thomas, E. (2002). *Assessment and culture: Psychological tests with minority populations.* San Diego: Academic Press.

Graham, L.O. (2000). *Our kind of people: Inside America's Black upper middle class.* New York: HarperCollins Publishers.

Gray, T., & Fleischman, S. (2005). Successful strategies for English language learners. *Educational Leadership, 62,* 84-85.

Green, T. (2005). Using technology to help English Language Learner students develop language skills: A home and school connection. *Multicultural Education, 13,* 56-59.

Green, T.D. (2005). Promising prevention and early intervention strategies to reduce overrepresentaion of African American students in special education. *Preventing School Failure, 49,* 33-41.

Grether, S.M. (2006). Augmentative and alternative communication (AAC) and literacy: Strategies for building skills. HEARSAY Focuses on Literacy, *Journal of the Ohio Speech-Language-Hearing Association, 18,* 21-25.

Griffin, A., & de la Vega, N. (2003). Overwhelmed and underequipped: Latino immigrants whose children have autism struggle to find care and support. *LD online,* available at http://www.ldonline.org/xarbb/printtopic/9764?theme=print (WETA, 2006).

Grimm, D. (2006, March). *Curriculum-relevant therapy: From design to delivery.* Paper presented at the annual meeting of the California Speech-Language-Hearing Association, San Francisco, CA.

Gronroos, N. (2003). Cultural considerations in discussing mental retardation. Retrieved 7/14/03 from http://www.naspcenter.org/teachers/culture_conferencing.html.

Guiberson, M.M., Barrett, K.C., Jancosek, E.G., & Yoshinaga Itano, C. (2006). Language maintenance and loss in preschool-age children of Mexican immigrants: Longitudinal study. *Communication Disorders Quarterly, 28,* 4-17.

Gutiérrez-Clellen, V.F. (1998). Syntactic skills of Spanish-speaking children with low school achievement. *Language, Speech, and Hearing Services in Schools, 29(4),* 207-315.

Gutiérrez-Clellen, V.F. (1999a). Language choice in intervention with bilingual children. *American Journal of Speech-Language Pathology, 8(4),* 291-302.

Gutiérrez-Clellen, V.F. (1999b). Mediating literacy skills in Spanish-speaking children with special needs. *Language, Speech, and Hearing Services in Schools, 30(3),* 285-292.

Gutiérrez-Clellen, V.F., Calderon, J., & Ellis Weismer, S. (2004). Verbal working memory in bilingual children. *Journal of Speech, Language, and Hearing Research, 47,* 863-877.

Gutiérrez-Clellen, V.F., & DeCurtis, L. (1999). Word definition skills in Spanish-speaking children with language impairment. *Communication Disorders Quarterly, 21(1),* 23-31.

Gutiérrez-Clellen, V.F., & Quinn, R. (1993). Assessing narratives of children from diverse cultural/linguistic groups. *Language, Speech, and Hearing Services in Schools, 24 (1),* 2-9.

Gutiérrez-Clellen, V.F., Restrepo, M.A., Bedore, L., Peña, E., & Anderson, R. (2000). Language sample analysis in Spanish-speaking children: Methodological considerations. *Language, Speech, and Hearing Services in Schools, 31(1),* 88-98.

Gutiérrez-Clellen, V.F., Restrepo, M.A., & Simon-Cereijido, G. (2006). Evaluating the discriminant accuracy of a grammatical measure with Spanish-speaking children. *Journal of Speech, Language, and Hearing Research, 49,* 1209-1223.

Hadley, P.A., Simmerman, A., Long, M., & Luna, M. (2000). Facilitating language development for inner city children: Experimental evaluation of a collaborative, classroom-based intervention. *Language, Speech, and Hearing Services in Schools, 31(3),* 280-295.

Hai, T., & Chuong, T. (1999). Vietnam and activities of community-based rehabilitation. *Disability and Rehabilitation, 21,* 474-478.

Hakuta, K., Butler, Y.G., & Witt, D. (2000). *How long does it take English learners to attain proficiency?* Santa Barbara, CA: University of California Linguistic Minority Research Institute.

Hale, J. E. (2004). How schools shortchange African American children. *Educational Leadership, 62*(3), 34-38.

Haleem, A.(Ed.) (2004). *The Qu'ran.* Oxford: New York.

Hall, R.E., & Livingston, J.N. (2006). Mental health practice with Arab families: The implications of spirituality vis-a-vis Islam. *The American Journal of Family Therapy, 34,* 139-150.

Hallahan, D.P., Lloyd, J.W., Kauffman, J.M., Weiss, M.P., & Martínez, E.A. (2005). *Learning disabilities: Foundations, characteristics, and effective teaching* (3rd.). Boston: Allyn & Bacon.

Hammer, C.S. (1994). Working with families of Chamorro and Carolinian cultures. *American Journal of Speech-Language Pathology, 3,* 5-12.

Hammer, C.S, Lawrence, F.R., & Miccio, A.W. (2007). Bilingual children's language abilities and early reading outcomes in Head Start and kindergarten. *Language, Speech, and Hearing Services in Schools, 38,* 237-248.

Hammer, C.S., & Miccio, A.W. (2001). Bilingual preschoolers. *The ASHA Leader, 6(21),* 6.

Hammer, C.S., Miccio, A.W., & Rodríguez, B. (2004). Bilingual language acquisition and the child socialization process. In B.A. Goldstein (Ed.), *Bilingual language development and disorders in Spanish-English speakers* (pp. 21-50). Baltimore, MD: Paul H. Brookes Publishing Co.

Hammer, C.S., Miccio, A.W., & Wagstaff, D. (2003). Home literacy experiences and their relationship to bilingual preschoolers' developing English literacy abilities: an initial investigation. *Language, Speech, and Hearing Services in Schools, 34,* 20-30.

Hammer, C.S., Rodríguez, B. L., Lawrence, F. R., & Miccio, A. W. (2007). Puerto Rican mothers' beliefs and home literacy practices. *Language, Speech, and Hearing Services in Schools, 38,* 216-224.

Hammer, C.S., & Weiss, A.L. (1999). Guiding language development: How African American mothers and their infants structure play interactions. *Journal of Speech-Language-Hearing Research, 42(5),* 1219-1233.

Hammer, C.S., & Weiss, A.L. (2000). African American mothers' views of their infants' language development and language-learning environment. *American Journal of Speech-Language Pathology, 9(2),* 126-140.

Han, M. (2005). Relationship among perceived parental trauma, parental attachment, and sense of coherence in Southeast Asian American college students. *Journal of Family Social Work, 9,* 25-46.

Hanna, F.J., & Green, A. (2004). Asian shades of spirituality: Implications for multicultural school counseling. *Professional School Counseling, 7.*

Hanson, M.J. (2004a). Ethnic, cultural, and language diversity in service settings. In E.W. Lynch & M.J. Hanson, *Developing cross-cultural competence: A guide for working with young children and their families* (pp. 3-18). Baltimore: Paul H. Brookes Publishing Co.

Hanson, M.J. (2004b). Families with Anglo-European roots. In E.W. Lynch & M.J. Hanson (Eds.), *Developing cross-cultural competence: A guide for working with young children and their families* (3rd ed.) (pp. 81-108). Baltimore: Paul H. Brookes Publishing Co.

Hardman, M.L., Drew, C.J., & Egan, M.W. (2006). *Human exceptionality: School, community, and family* (8th ed.). Boston: Allyn & Bacon.

Harris, G. (1998). American Indian cultures: A lesson in diversity. In D. Battle (Ed.), *Communication disorders in multicultural populations* (2nd ed.) (pp. 117-156). Stoneham, MA: Butterworth-Heinemann.

Harris, K.L., & Moran, M.J. (2006). Phonological features exhibited by children speaking African American English at three grade levels. *Communication Disorders Quarterly, 27*, 195-205.

Hayden, T. (2004). A modern life. *U.S. News and World Report*, Wednesday, 9/26/04.

Health and Environment Alliance (2006). *Environment and health policy*. Available at http://www.env.health.org/m/173.

Hearne, D. (2000). *Teaching second language learners with learning disabilities: Strategies for effective practice*. Oceanside, CA: Academic Communication Associates.

Heath, S.B. (1983). *Ways with words: Language, life, and work in communities and classrooms*. New York: Cambridge University Press.

Heath, S.B. (1986). *Sociocultural contexts of language development*. In Leyba, C.F. (Ed.), *Beyond language: Social and cultural factors in schooling language minority students* (pp. 143-186). Los Angeles: Evaluation, Dissemination, and Assessment Center, Calif. State Univ., Los Angeles.

Hedayat, K.M., & Pirzadeh, R. (2001). Issues in Islamic biomedical ethics: A primer for the pediatrician. *Pediatrics, 108*, 965-971.

Hegde, M.N. (2006). *Treatment protocols for language disorders in children: Volume II, social communication*. San Diego: Plural Publishing.

Hegde, M.N., & Maul, C.A. (2006). *Language disorders in children: An evidence-based approach to assessment and treatment*. Boston: Allyn & Bacon.

Heilman, J., Ellis Weismer, S., Evans, J., & Hollar, C. (2005). Utility of the MacArtuhur-Bates Communicative Development Inventory in identifying language abilities of late-talking and typically developing toddlers. *American Journal of Speech-Language Pathology, 14*, 40-51.

Heine, S., & Prebish, C.S. (2003). *Buddhism in the modern world: Adaptations of an ancient tradition*. Oxford: Oxford University Press.

Helfman, U. (1999). Survey portrays new immigrants as political force: 52% of Russians identify as Jews. *Forward, 1-2*.

Hernández-Chavez, E., Burt, M., & Dulay, H. (1978). Language dominance and proficiency testing: some general considerations. *NABE Journal, 3*, 41-60.

Herr, R. (2003). Is Confucianism compatible with care ethics? A critique. *Philosophy East & West, 53*, 471-489.

Hightower, J.M., O'Hare, A., & Hernández, G.T. (2006). Blood mercury reporting in NHANES: Identifying Asian, Pacific Islander, Native American, and multiracial groups. *Environmental Health Perspective, 114*, 173.

Hinshaw, L. (2005). The Albuquerque area Indian Health Board. *The ASHA Leader, 10*, 11-13.

Hodge, D.R. (2005). Social work and the House of Islam: Orienting practitioners to the belief and values of Muslims in the United States. *Social Work, 50*, 162-173.

Hoffman, L.M., & Gillam, R. (2004). Verbal and spatial information processing constraints in children with specific language impairment. *Journal of Speech, Language, and Hearing Research, 47*, 114-125.

Hoksbergen, R., ter Laak, J., Kijk, K., van Dijikum, C., & Stoutsjesdijk, F. (2005). *Journal of Autism and Developmental Disorders, 35*, 615-623.

Holden, G. (2004). *Karma kids: Answering everyday parenting questions with Buddhist wisdom*. Berkeley: Ulysses Press.

Holliday, P.A.C. (2001). Demand may exceed supply in future job market. *The ASHA Leader, 6(8)*, 18.

Holt, J.K., & Cecil Smith, M. (2005). Literacy practices among different ethnic groups: The role of socioeconomic and cultural factors. *Reading Research Instruction, 44*, 1-21.

Hoover, J.J., & Patton, J.R. (2005). Differentiating curriculum and instruction for English-language learners with special needs. *Intervention in School and Clinic, 40*, 231-235.

Hornberger, N.H. (2002). Multilingual language policies and the continua of biliteracy: An ecological approach. In O. García & C. Baker (Eds.), *Bilingual education: An introductory reader* (pp. 177-194). Clevedon, England: Multilingual Matters Ltd.

Hornblower, M. (1998). No habla Espanol. *TIME* (January 26), 44.

Horton-Ikard, R., & Weismer, S.E. (2007). A preliminary examination of vocabulary and word learning in African American toddlers from middle and low socioeconomic status homes. *Language, Speech, and Hearing Services in Schools, 16*, 381-392.

Hosp, J.L., & Reschly, D.J. (2004). Disproportionate representation of minority students in special education: Academic, demographic, and economic predictors. *Exceptional Children, 70*, 185-199.

Hsin-Chen Hsin, D., & Macer, D. (2006). Comparisons of life images and end-of-life attitudes between the elderly in Taiwan and New Zealand. *Journal of Nursing Research, 14*, 198-207.

Huang, Z.J., Yu, V., & Ledsky, A. (2006). Health status and health service access and use among children in U.S. immigrant families. *American Journal of Public Health, 96*, 634-640.

Hubenthal, W. (2004). Older Russian immigrants' experiences in learning English: Motivation, methods, and barriers. *Adult Basic Education, 14*, 104-126.

Huer, M.B., Parette, H.P., & Saenz, T.I. (2001). Conversations with Mexican Americans regarding children with disabilities and augmentative and alternative communication devices. *Communication Disorders Quarterly, 22*, 197-206.

Huer, M.B., & Saenz, T.I. (2003). Challenges and strategies for conducting survey and focus group research with culturally diverse groups. *American Journal of Speech-Language Pathology, 12*, 209-220.

Huer, M.B., Saenz, T.I., & Doan, J.H.D. (2001). Understanding the Vietnamese American community: Implications for training education personnel providing services to children with disabilities. *Communication Disorders Quarterly, 23(1)*, 27-39.

Huer, M.B., & Soto, G. (2006, November). *Cultural issues in the practice of augmentative and alternative communication*. Paper presented at the annual meeting of the American Speech, Language, and Hearing Association, Miami, FL.

Hume, S.E., & Hardwick, S.W. (2005). African, Russian, and Ukrainian refugee resettlement in Portland, Oregon. *Geographical Review, 95*, 189-209.

Hunter, D., & Sawyer, C. (2006). Blending Native American spirituality with individual psychology in work with children. *The Journal of Individual Psychology, 62*, 234-250.

Hunter, R.C., & Bartee, R. (2003). The achievement gap: Issues of competition, class, and race. *Education and Urban Society, 35*, 151-160.

Hwa-Froelich, D.A., Hodson, B., & Edwards, H. (2002). Characteristics of Vietnamese phonology. *American Journal of Speech-Language Pathology, 11*, 264-273.

Hwa-Froelich, D.A., Pettinelli, J.D., & Jones, S. (2006). Interdisciplinary collaboration with internationally adopted children. *Perspectives on Communication Disorders and Sciences in Culturally and Linguistically Diverse Populations, ASHA SID 14 Newsletter, 13*, 8-16.

Hwa-Froelich, D.A., & Matsuo, H. (2005). Vietnamese children and language-based processing tasks. *Language, Speech, and Hearing Services in Schools, 36*, 230-243.

Hwa-Froelich, D.A., & Vigil, D. C. (2004). Three aspects of cultural influence on communication: A literature review. *Communication Disorders Quarterly, 25*, 107-118.

Hwa-Froelich, D.A., & Westby, C.E. (2003). Frameworks of education: Perspectives of Southeast Asian parents and Head Start staff. *Language, Speech, and Hearing Services in Schools, 34*, 299-319.

Hyde, M., Ohna, S.E., & Hjulstadt, O. (2006). Education of the deaf in Australia and Norway: A comparative study of the interpretations and applications of inclusion. *American Annals of the Deaf, 150*, 415-424.

Iglesias, A. (2002). Latino culture. In D.E. Battle (Ed.), *Communication disorders in multicultural populations* (3rd ed.) (pp. 179-202). Woburn, MA: Butterworth-Heinemann.

Indian Health Service (IHS). (2000). *Trends in Indian health*. Rockville, MD: Author.

Individuals with Disabilities Education Act (IDEA; 1997). *Federal Register, Volume 62, No. 204. Part V,* Department of Education, 34 CFR parts 300, 303.

Individuals with Disabilities Education Improvement Act of 2004 (IDEA, 2004). Public Law 108-446, 108th Congress.

Inglebret, E., Bear Eagle, D., & CHiXapKaid, D.M. (2007). American Indian stories enrich intervention. *The ASHA Leader, 12*, 1-27.

Ingram, L. (2005). Understanding American worldview: Part II. Extracted from *Life in the USA*, copyright Elliot Essman 2005. Retrieved 12/27/06 from http://www.lifeintheusa.com/culture/worldview2.htm.

Isaac, K.M. (2001). What about linguistic diversity? A different look at multicultural health care. *Communication Disorders Quarterly, 22(2)*, 110-113.

Isaacs, G.J. (1996). Persistence of non-standard dialect in school-age children. *Journal of Speech and Hearing Research, 39(2)*, 434-441.

Ispa, J.M., Thornburg, K.R., & Fine, M.A. (2006). *Keepin' on: The everyday struggles of young families in poverty*. Baltimore: Paul H. Brookes Publishing Company.

Ja Hyun, K. (2001). Sociocultural change and traditional values: Confucian values among Koreans and Korean Americans. *International Journal of Public Relations, 25*.

Jachman, A. (2006). Reading and the migrant student. Retrieved 8/15/06 from http://www.sedl.org.

Jackson, S.C., & Roberts, J.E. (2001). Complex syntax production of African American preschoolers. *Journal of Speech, Language, and Hearing Research, 44*, 1083-1096.

Jackson-Maldonado, D. (2004). Verbal morphology and vocabulary in monolinguals and emergent bilinguals. In B.A. Goldstein (Ed.), *Bilingual language development and disorders in Spanish-English speakers* (pp. 131-161). Baltimore, MD: Paul H. Brookes Publishing Co.

Jackson-Maldonado, D., Bates, E., & Thal, D. (1992). *Fundación MacArthur: Inventario del desarrollo de habilidades comunicativas*. San Diego, CA: San Diego State University.

Jacobs, E.L., & Coufal, K.L. (2001). A computerized screening instrument of language learnability. *Communication Disorders Quarterly, 22*, 67-76.

Jacobson, P.R., & Schwartz, R.G. (2005). English past tense use in bilingual children with language impairment. *American Journal of Speech-Language Pathology, 14*, 313-323.

James, C. (2007). *Climbing off dead horses: Changing to a life of balance*. Retrieved 6/25/07 from www.cheewa.com.

James, R. (1999). Human rights conference. The Professional, Spring, 1999. *The Elk Grove Education Association Publication* (p. 1).

Jia, G. (2003). The acquisition of the English plural morpheme by native Mandarin Chinese-speaking children. *Journal of Speech, Language, and Hearing Research, 46*, 1297-1323.

Jia, G., & Aaronson, D. (2003). A longitudinal study of Chinese children and adolescents learning English in the United States. *Applied Psycholinguistics, 24*, 131-161.

Jiménez, B. (1987). Acquisition of Spanish consonants in children aged 3-5 years, 7 months. *Language, Speech, and Hearing Services in the Schools, 18*, 357-363.

Joe, J.R., & Malach, R.S. (2004). Families with American Indian roots. In E.W. Lynch & M.J. Hanson (Eds.), *Developing cross-cultural competence: A guide to working with young children and their families* (3rd ed.) (pp. 109-140). Baltimore: Paul H. Brookes Publishing Co.

Johnson, C.E., & Viramontez Anguiano, R. P. (2004). Latino parents in the rural Southeast: A study of family and school partnerships. *Journal of Family and Consumer Sciences, 96*, 29-46.

Johnson, V.E. (2005). Comprehension of third person singular /s/ in AAE-speaking children. *Language, Speech, and Hearing Services in Schools, 36*, 116-124.

Johnston, R.C. (2001). Who is 'Asian'? Cultural differences defy simple categories. Available from *Education Week* at http://www.edweek. org.

Johnston, L., & Wong, A.M. (2002). Cultural differences in beliefs and practices concerning talk to children. *Journal of Speech, Language, and Hearing Research, 45*, 916-926.

Johnstone, R. (2002). Characteristics of immersion programmes. In O. García & C. Baker (Eds.), *Bilingual education: An introductory reader* (pp. 19-32). Clevedon, England: Multilingual Matters Ltd.

Jones, T. S. (2005). 20 ways to incorporate diversity into your classroom. *Intervention in School and Clinic, 41*, 9-12.

Jordan Institute for Families (2002). *Children's services practice notes: Latinos in North Carolina.* Retrieved 12/28/06 from http://ssw.unc. edu/fcrp/Cspn/vol17_no3/Latinos%20in%20NC.htm.

Juffer, E., & Van Ijzendoorn, M.H. (2005). Behavior problems and mental health referrals of international adoptees: A meta-analysis. *Journal of the American Medical Association, 293*, 2501-2515.

Jünker, D.A., & Stockman, I.J. (2002). Expressive vocabulary of German-English bilingual toddlers. *American Journal of Speech-Language Pathology, 11*, 381-394.

Juntunen, C.L., Barraclough, D.J., Broneck, C.L., Seibel, G.A., Winrow, S.A., & Morin, P.M. (2001). American Indian perspectives on the career journey. *Journal of Counseling Psychology, 48*, 274-285.

Justice, L.M., & Ezell, H.K. (2000). Enhancing children's print and word awareness through home-based parent intervention. *American Journal of Speech-Language Pathology, 9(3)*, 257-268.

Justice, L.M., Meier, J., & Walpole, S. (2005). Learning new words from storybooks: An efficacy study with at-risk kindergarteners. *Language, Speech, and Hearing Services in Schools, 36*, 17-32.

Kaderavek, J., & Boucher, D.M. (2006). Temperament profiles in children: Implications for academic performance and literacy learning. Hearsay: *Journal of the Ohio Speech-Language-Hearing Association, 18*, 14-20.

Kaderavek, J., & Justice, L.M. (2002). Shared storybook reading as an intervention context: Practices and potential pitfalls. *American Journal of Speech-Language Pathology, 11*, 395-406.

Kaland, M., Moller-Nielsen, A., Smith, L., Mortensen, E.L., Callesen, K., & Gottlieb, D. (2005). The Strange Stories Test: A replication study of children and adolescents with Asperger syndrome. *European Child and Adolescent Psychiatry, 14*, 73-82.

Kamalipour, Y.R. (2001). Information available from www.iranian.com/Opinion/2001/May/Iranians.

Kamhi, A.G. (2006). Combining research and reason to make treatment decisions. *Language, Speech, and Hearing Services in Schools, 37*, 255-256.

Kan, P.F., & Kohnert, K. (2005). Preschoolers learning Hmong and English: Lexical-semantic skills in L1 and L2. *Journal of Speech, Language, and Hearing Research, 48*, 372-383.

Karamustafa, A. (2003). Islam: A civilizational project in progress. In O. Safi (Ed.), *Progressive Muslims: On justice, gender and pluralism* (pp. 98-110). Oxford: One World Press.

Katz-Stone, A. (2000). Russia to the suburbs. *Baltimore Jewish Times*, 58-62.

Kaufman, A., & Kaufman, N. (1983). *Kaufman Assessment Battery for Children: Interpretive Manual.* Circle Pines, MN: American Guidance Service.

Kay-Raining Bird, E., Cleave, P., Trudeau, N., Thordardottir, E., Sutton, A., & Thorpe, A. (2005). The language abilities of bilingual children with Down Syndrome. *American Journal of Speech-Language Pathology, 4*, 187-199.

Kay-Raining Bird, E., & Vetter, R.S. (1994). Storytelling in Chippewa-Cree children. *Journal of Speech and Hearing Research, 37(6)*, 1354-1368.

Kayser, H. (1998). *Assessment and intervention resource for Hispanic children.* San Diego: Singular Publishing Group.

Kayser, H. (1995). Assessment of speech and language impairments in bilingual children. In H. Kayser (Ed.), *Bilingual speech-language pathology: An Hispanic focus* (pp. 243-264). San Diego: Singular Publishing Group.

Kayser, H.R. (2002). Bilingual language development and language disorders. In D.E. Battle (Ed.), *Communication disorders in multicultural populations* (3rd ed.) (pp. 205-232). Woburn, MA: Butterworth-Heinemann.

Kayser, H.R. (2006). Parent programs in literacy: Differences for Latinos. *The ASHA Leader, 11*, 8-9, 22-28.

Kaza, S. (2005). Paying attention to food. *Tikkun, 20*, 55.

Kelley, E. (2001). *Everything they didn't teach you: Guide to a successful school year for the caseload-challenged.* Youngtown, AZ: ECL Publications.

Kent, M., & Lalasz, R. (2006). *In the news: Speaking English in the United States.* Retrieved 3/5/07 from http://www.prb.org/ Articles/2006/IntheNewsSpeaking.

Kent-Walsh, J., & Rosa-Lugo, L. (2006). Communication partner interventions for children who use AAC: Storybook reading across culture and language. *The ASHA Leader, 11*, 28-29.

Kessler, C. (1984). Language acquisition in bilingual children. In N. Miller (Ed.), *Bilingualism and language disability: Assessment and remediation* (pp. 26-54). San Diego, CA: College Hill Press.

Khan, Z., Roseberry-McKibbin, C., O'Hanlon, L., Roberts, K., Weger, L., & Roy, M. (2005). *A survey of ethnic Pashtuns from Pakistan and Afghanistan.* Paper presented at the annual convention of the American Speech-Language-Hearing Association, San Diego, CA.

Kiernan, B., & Swisher, L. (1990). The initial learning of novel English words: Two single-subject experiments with minority-language children. *Journal of Speech and Hearing Research , 33*, 707-716.

King, S.H. (1993). The limited presence of African-American teachers. *Review of Educational Research, 63*, 115-149.

King, K., & Fogle, L. (2006). Raising bilingual children: Common parental concerns and current research. *CAL Digest*, April, 2006.

Kitano, M.K. (2003). Gifted potential and poverty: A call for extraordinary action. *Journal for the Association of the Gifted, 26*, 292-303.

Klee, T., Stokes, S.F., Wong, A. M-Y, Fletcher, P., & Gavin, W.J. (2004). Utterance length and lexical diversity in Cantonese-speaking children with and without specific language impairment. *Journal of Speech, Language, and Hearing Research, 47*, 1396-1410.

Klingner, J.K., Artiles, A.J., & Barletta, L.M. (2006). English language learners who struggle with reading: Language acquisition or LD? *Journal of Learning Disabilities, 39*, 108-128.

Kliucharev, G.A., Kofanova, E.N. (2005). On the dynamics of the educational behavior of well-off and low-income Russians. *Russian Education and Society, 47*, 22-36.

Kobeisy, A. (2004). *Counseling American Muslims: Understanding the faith and helping the people.* Westport, CT: Greenwood Publishing Group, Inc.

Kohler, C.T., Bahr, R.H., Silliman, E.R., Bryant, J.B., Apel, K., & Wilkinson, L.C. (2007). African English dialect and performance on non-word spelling and phonemic awareness tasks. *American Journal of Speech-Language Pathology, 16*, 157-168.

Kohnert, K. (2004). Processing skills in early sequential bilinguals. In B.A. Goldstein (Ed.), *Bilingual language development and disorders in Spanish-English speakers* (pp. 53-76). Baltimore: Paul H. Brookes Publishing Co.

Kohnert, K. (2008). *Language disorders in bilingual children and adults.* San Diego: Plural Publishing.

Kohnert, K.J., Bates, E., & Hernández, E. (1999). Balancing bilinguals: Lexical-semantic production and cognitive processing in children. *Journal of Speech-Language-Hearing Research, 42(6)*, 1400-1413.

Kohnert, K., & Derr, A. (2004). Language intervention with bilingual children. In B.A. Goldstein (Ed.), *Bilingual language development and disorders in Spanish-English speakers* (pp. 311-338). Baltimore, MD: Paul H. Brookes Publishing Co.

Kohnert, K., Windsor, J., & Miller, R. (2004). Crossing borders: Recognition of Spanish words by English speaking children with and without language impairment. *Journal of Applied Psycholinguistics, 25*, 543-564.

Kohnert, K., Yim, D., Nett, K., Kan, P.F., & Duran, L. (2005). Intervention with linguistically diverse preschool children: A focus on developing home languages. *Language, Speech, and Hearing Services in Schools, 36*, 251-264.

Kolchevska, N. (2005). Angels in the home and at work: Russian women in the Khrushchev years. *Women's Studies Quarterly, 33*, 114-137.

Kopp, H. (2002). Dress and diversity: Muslim women and Islamic dress in an immigrant/minority context. *The Muslim World, 92*, 59-78.

Korkunov, V. V., Nigayev, A. S., Reynolds, L. D., & Lerner, J. W. (1998). Special education in Russia: History, reality, and prospects. *Journal of Learning Disabilities, 31*, 186-192.

Kornblatt, J.D. (1999) Christianity, antisemitism, nationalism: Russian orthodoxy in a reborn Orthodox Russia. In A.M. Barker (Ed.), *Consuming Russia* (pp. 414-436). London: Duke University Press.

Koss, M.P., Yuan, N.P., Dightman, D., Prince, R.J., Polacca, M., Sanderson, B., & Goldman, D. (2003). Adverse childhood exposures and alcohol dependence among seven Native American tribes. *American Journal of Preventative Medicine, 25*, 238-244.

Krakow, R., Mastriano, B., & Reese, L. (2005). *Early intervention and international adoption.* Paper presented at the annual convention of the American Speech-Language-Hearing Association, San Diego, CA.

Krashen, S.D. (1992). Bilingual education and second language acquisition theory. In C. Leyba (Ed.), *Schooling and language minority students: A theoretical framework.* Calif. State University, Los Angeles, CA.

Krashen, S.D. (1993). *Beyond the basics of language education.* Sacramento, CA: California Elementary Education Association.

Kratcoski, A. (1998). Guidelines for using portfolios in assessment and evaluation. *Language, Speech, and Hearing Services in Schools, 29(1)*, 3-10.

Kritikos, E.P. (2003). Speech-language pathologists' beliefs about language assessment of bilingual/bicultural individuals. *American Journal of Speech-Language Pathology, 12*, 73-91.

Kruassioukov, O. (1996). Russian attitudes: Fear, ignorance, misunderstanding, and silence. Disability International. Retrieved June 30, 2004, from www.dpa.org.sg/DPA/publication/dpipub/spsring96/dpi7.htm.

Kummerer, S.E., & López-Reyna, N.A. (2006). The role of Mexican immigrant mothers' beliefs on parental involvement in speech-language therapy. *Communication Disorders Quarterly, 27*, 83-94.

Kummerer, S.E., López-Reyna, N.A., & Hughes, M. (2007). Mexican immigrant mothers' perceptions of their children's communication disabilities, emergent literacy development, and speech-language therapy program. *American Journal of Speech Language Pathology, 16*, 271-282.

Kuster, J.M. (2000). English as a second language: Web sites. *ASHA Leader, 5(12)*, 6.

Ladson-Billings, G. (1994). *The dreamkeepers: Successful teachers of African American children.* San Francisco, CA: Jossey-Bass/John Wiley & Sons, Inc.

Lai, A., (2006). Eye on religion: Cultural signs and caring for Chinese patients. *Southern Medical Journal, 99*, 688-689.

Lai, Y., & Ishiyama, F. (2004). Involvement of immigrant Chinese Canadian mothers of children with disabilities. *Exceptional Children, 71*, 97-108.

Laing, S.P., & Kamhi, A. (2003). Alternative assessment of language and literacy in culturally and linguistically diverse populations. *Language, Speech, and Hearing Services in Schools, 34*, 44-55.

Lambert, W., & Tucker, G. (1972). *Bilingual education of children: The St. Lambert experiment.* Rowley, MA: Newbury House.

Landt, S.M. (2006). Multicultural literature and young adolescents: A kaleidoscope of opportunity. *Journal of Adolescent and Adult Literacy, 49*, 690-697.

Landry, D.A. (2007). Alcoholism—from Russia to you and here in the USA. *Adoption Week*, available at http://e-magazine.adoption. com/articles (Adoption Media, LLC 1995-2007).

Lane, H. (2005). Ethnicity, ethics, and the deaf world. *The Journal of Deaf Studies and Deaf Education, 10*, 291-310.

Lang, J.S. (2000). Hearing impairment. In E.P. Dodge (Ed.), *The survival guide for school-based speech-language pathologists* (pp. 241-262). San Diego: Singular Publishing Group/Thomson Learning.

Langdon, H.W. (2000). Diversity. In E.P. Dodge (Ed.), *The survival guide for school-based speech-language pathologists* (pp. 367-398). San Diego: Singular Publishing Group/Thomson Learning.

Langdon, H.W. (2007). *Assessment and intervention for communication disorders in culturally and linguistically diverse populations*. New York: Thomson/Delmar.

Langdon, H.W. and Cheng, L. (Eds.) (1992). *Hispanic children and adults with communication disorders: Assessment and intervention*. Gaithersburg, MD: Aspen Publishers, Inc.

Langdon, H.W., & Cheng, L.L. (2002). *Collaborating with interpreters and translators: A guide for communication disorders professionals*. Eau Claire, WI: Thinking Publications.

Langdon, H.W., & Saenz, T.I. (1996). *Language assessment and intervention with multicultural students: A guide for speech-language-hearing professionals*. Oceanside, CA: Academic Communication Associates.

Lapin, N.I. (2004). How the citizens of Russia feel and what they are striving for. *Russian Social Sciences Review, 45*, 4-21.

Laws, G., & Bishop, D.V.M. (2003). A comparison of language abilities in adolescents with Down Syndrome and children with specific language impairment. *Journal of Speech, Language, and Hearing Research, 46*, 1324-1339.

Leap, W. (1993). *American Indian English*. Salt Lake City, UT: University of Utah Press.

Lebedko, M. (2003). Axiosphere: The linguistic representation of value concepts in American and Russian cultures. *American Studies International, 44*, 38-58.

Lee, J.S., & Bowen, N.K. (2006). Parent involvement, cultural capital, and the achievement gap among elementary school children. *American Educational Research Journal, 43*, 193-218.

Leipzig, C. (2006). When Russians come to therapy. *The American Journal of Family Therapy, 34*, 219-242.

LeMoine, N. (1993). Serving the language needs of African American students: Strategies for success. Presentation, at the Annual Conference of the California Speech-Language-Hearing Association, Palm Springs, CA.

Leonard, L.B., Ellis Weismer, S., Miller, C.A., Francis, D.J., Tomblin, J.B., & Kail, R.V. (2007). Speed of processing, working memory, and language impairment in children. *Journal of Speech, Language, and Hearing Research, 50*, 408-428.

Leung, B. (1993). Assessment considerations with culturally and linguistically diverse students. Paper presented at National Association for Multicultural Education, Los Angeles, CA.

Li, S.C. (2003). Bicultural orchestration of developmental plasticity across levels: The interplay of biology and culture in shaping the mind and behavior across the life span. *Psychological Bulletin, 129*, 171-194.

Liam, C.H.T., & Abdullah (2001). The education and practice of speech-language pathologists in Malaysia. *American Journal of Speech-Language Pathology, 10(1)*, 3-9.

Libby, A.M., Orton, H.D., Barth, R.P., Webb, M.B., Burns, B.J., Wood, P., & Spicer, P. (2006). Alcohol, drug, and mental health specialty treatment services and race/ethnicity: A national study of children and families involved with child welfare. *American Journal of Public Health, 96*, 628-630.

Lillie-Blanton, M., & Robideaux, Y. (2005). Understanding and addressing the health care needs of American Indians and Alaska Natives. *American Journal of Public Health, 95*, 259-261.

Lindeman, B. (2001). Reaching out to immigrant parents. *Educational Leadership, 58(6)*, 62-67.

Linz, S.J. (2003). Motivation and reward: A case study of Russian workers. *Problems of Post-Communism, 50*, 44-55.

Lipka, O., Siegel, L.S., & Vukovic, R. (2005). The literacy skills of English language learners in Canada. *Learning Disabilities Research and Practice, 20*, 39-49.

Liu, C. J., & Regehr, C. (2006). Cross-cultural application of self-in-relation theory: The case of Taiwanese young women. *International Social Work, 49*, 459-470.

Lloyd-Jones, A., (2007, June*). Response to intervention* (RtI). Paper presented at the NCLB/IDEA Symposium, Sacramento, CA.

Locke, D. (1998). *Increasing multicultural understanding: A comprehensive model* (Multicultural aspects of counseling, Series 1: 2nd ed.). Thousand Oaks, CA: Sage.

Lohman, D.F. (2005). An aptitude perspective on talent: Implications for identification of academically gifted minority students. *Journal for the Education of the Gifted, 28*, 333-360.

Long, S.H. (2006). Language and linguistically-culturally diverse children. In V.A. Reed, *An introduction to children with language disorders* (3rd ed.) (pp. 301-334). Boston: Allyn & Bacon.

Love, A., & Kruger, A. (2005). Teacher beliefs and student achievement in urban schools serving African American students. *The Journal of Educational Research, 99*, 87-98.

Lu, L. (2002). A preliminary study on the concept of health among the Chinese. *Counseling Psychology Quarterly, 15*, 179-189.

Lubliner, S., & Smetana, L. (2005). The effects of comprehensive vocabulary instruction on Title I students' metacognitive word-learning skills and reading comprehension. *Journal of Literacy Research, 37*, 163-200.

Lum, D. (2004*). Social work practice and people of color: A process-stage approach* (5th ed.). Belmont, CA: Thomson-Brooks/Cole.

Lund, N.J., & Duchan, J.F. (1993). *Assessing children's language in naturalistic contexts* (3rd ed.). Englewood Cliffs, NJ: Prentice Hall.

Lynch, E.W. (2004). Conceptual framework: From culture shock to cultural learning. In E.W. Lynch & M.J. Hanson (Eds.), *Developing cross-cultural competence: A guide for working with young children and their families* (3rd ed.) (pp. 19-40). Baltimore, MD: Paul H. Brookes Publishing Co.

Lytle, R.R., Johnson, K.E., & Jun Hui, Y. (2005). Deaf education in China: History, current issues, and emerging Deaf voices. *American Annals of the Deaf, 150*, 457-469.

Madding, C.C. (1999, April). Mama e hijo: The Latino mother-infant dyad. Conference proceedings from the fourth annual communicative disorders multicultural conference, California State University, Fullerton. *The Multicultural Electronic Journal of Communication Disorders, 2(1)*, 1-4.

Madding, C.C. (2000). Maintaining focus on cultural competence in early intervention services to linguistically and culturally diverse families. *Infant-Toddler Intervention: The Transdisciplinary Journal, 10(1)*, 9-18.

Madding, C.C. (2002). Socialization practices of Latinos. In A.E. Brice (Ed.), *The Hispanic child: Speech, language, culture and education* (pp. 68-84). Boston, MA: Allyn & Bacon.

Maestas, A.G., & Erickson, J.G. (1992). Mexican immigrant mothers' beliefs about disabilities. *American Journal of Speech-Language Pathology, 1 (4)*, 5-10.

Magana, S., Seltzer, M.M., & Krauss, M.W. (2004). Cultural context of caregiving: Differences in depression between Puerto Rican and Non-Latina White mothers of adults with mental retardation. *American Association on Mental Retardation, 42*, 1-9.

Magiati, I., Dockrell, J.E., & Logotheti, A. (2002). Young children's understanding of disabilities: The influence of development, context, and cognition. *Applied Developmental Psychology, 23*, 409-430.

Mahecha, N.R. (1991, November). Perception of pre-switch cues by Spanish-English individuals. Paper presented at the annual meeting of the American Speech-Language-Hearing Association, Atlanta, GA.

Mahecha, N. (2003). Typical and disordered child narration in Spanish-speaking children. In A. McCabe & L.S. Bliss, *Patterns of narrative discourse: A multicultural, lifespan approach* (pp. 73-90). Boston: Allyn & Bacon.

Mahmood, S.S. (2004). A word about ourselves. *Journal of Muslim Minority Affairs, 24*, 5-7.

Malach, R.R., Segel, N., & Thomas, R. (1989). *Overcoming obstacles and improving outcomes: Early intervention service for Indian children with special needs*. Bernalillo, NM: Southwest Communication Resources.

Mannes, M. (1993). Seeking the balance between child protection and family preservation in Indian child welfare. *Child Welfare, 72 (2)*, 141-152.

Manning, M.L., & Lee, G.L. (2001). Working with parents—cultural and linguistic considerations. *Kappa Delta Pi Record, 37(4)*, 160-163.

Marchman, V.A., & Martínez-Sussman, C. (2002). Concurrent validity of caregiver/parent report measures of language for children who are learning both English and Spanish. *Journal of Speech, Language, and Hearing Research, 45*, 983-997.

Marshall, C.A., & Hawk Largo, H. (1999). Disability and rehabilitation: A context for understanding the American Indian experience. *Lancet, 354*: 758-760.

Marton, K., & Schwartz, R.G. (2003). Working memory capacity and language processes in children with specific language impairment. *Journal of Speech, Language, and Hearing Research, 46*, 1138-1153.

Martorell, S., & Martorell, G. (2006). Bridging uncharted waters in Georgia: Down Syndrome Association of Atlanta outreach to Latino/a families. *American Journal of Psychology, 37*, 219-225.

Martz, E. (2005). Rehabilitation in Russia. *Rehabilitation Counseling, 48*, 118-123.

Mason, P.W., & Narad, C. (2004). International adoptions: Myths and realities. *Pediatric Nursing, 30*, 483-487.

Mason, P., & Narad, C. (2005). International adoption: A health and developmental perspective. *Seminars in Speech and Language, 26*, 1-9.

Mason, T.C. (2005). Cross-cultural instrument translation: Assessment, translation, and statistical applications. *American Annals of the Deaf, 150*, 67-72.

Mathes, P.G., Pollard-Durodola, S.D., Cárdenas-Hagan, E., Linan-Thompson, S., & Vaughn, S. (2007). Teaching struggling readers who are native Spanish speakers: What do we know? *Language, Speech, and Hearing Services in Schools, 38*, 260-271.

Matsuda, M., & O'Connor, L. (1990, November). Paper presented at the annual convention of the American Speech-Language-Hearing Association, Seattle, WA.

Matsuda, M., & O'Connor, L. (March, 1993). Creating an effective partnership: Training bilingual communication aides. Paper presented at the annual conference of the California Speech-Language-Hearing Association, Palm Springs, CA.

Matsuo, H., Pryor, C., & Sessions, L. (2006). *Assessment protocol for internationally adopted children*. International Adoption Clinic, Saint Louis University, Saint Louis, MO.

Mattes, L.J. (2008). *Guidebook of objectives and activities for language skills (GOALS)*. Oceanside, CA: Academic Communication Associates.

Mattes, L.J., & García-Easterly, I. (2007). *Bilingual speech and language intervention resource*. Oceanside, CA: Academic Communication Associates.

Mattes, L.J., & Omark, D. (1991). *Speech and language assessment for the bilingual handicapped*. (2nd ed.). Oceanside, CA: Academic Communication Associates.

Mattes, L.J., & Saldaña-Illingworth, C. (2008). *Bilingual communication assessment resource. Tools for assessing speech, language, and learning*. Oceanside, CA: Academic Communication Associates.

McAvoy, J., & Sidles, C. (1991). The effects of language preference and multitrial presentation on the free recall of Navajo children. *Journal of American Indian Education, 30 (3),* 33-42.

McCabe, A. (1997). Developmental and cross-cultural aspects of children's narration. In M. Bamberg (Ed.), *Narrative development: Six approaches* (pp. 137-174). Mahwah, NJ: Erlbaum.

McCardle, P., Mele-McCarthy, J., Cutting, L., Leos, K., & D'Emilio, T. (2005). Learning disabilities in English language learners: Identifying the issues. *Learning Disabilities Research & Practice, 20,* 1-5.

McCardle, P., Mele-McCarthy, J., & Leos, K. (2005). English language learners and learning disabilities: Research agenda and implications for practice. *Learning Disabilities Research & Practice, 20,* 68-78.

McCarty, T. (2003). Revitalising indigenous languages in homogenising times. In O. García & C. Baker (Eds.), *Bilingual education: An introductory reader* (pp. 33-49). Clevedon, England: Multilingual Matters Ltd.

McCollin, M., & O'Shea, D. (2005). Increasing reading achievement of students from culturally and linguistically diverse backgrounds. *Preventing School Failure, 50,* 41-44.

McGregor, K.K. (2004). Developmental dependencies between lexical semantics and reading. In C.A. Stone, E.R. Silliman, B.J. Ehren, & K. Apel (Eds.), *Handbook of language and literacy: Development and disorders* (pp. 302-307). New York: The Guilford Press.

McGregor, K.K., Williams, D., Hearst, S., & Johnson, A.C. (1997). The use of contrastive analysis in distinguishing difference from disorder: A tutorial. *American Journal of Speech-Language Pathology, 6(3),* 45-56.

McHatton, P.S., & Correa, V. (2005). Stigma and discrimination: Perspectives from Mexican and Puerto Rican mothers of children with special needs. *Topics in Early Childhood Special Education, 25,* 131-142.

McKinnon, J. (2003). *The black population in the United States:* March 2002 U.S. Census Bureau, U.S. Department of Commerce, 520-541.

McLaughlin, B. (1984). Second language acquisition in childhood. *Volume 1: Preschool children* (2nd ed.). New Jersey: Lawrence Erlbaum and Associates.

McLaughlin, S. (2006*). Introduction to language development* (2nd ed.). Clifton Park, NY: Thomson Delmar Learning.

McNeilly, L., & Coleman, T.J. (2000). Language disorders in culturally diverse populations: Intervention issues and strategies. In T. J. Coleman, *Clinical management of communication disorders in culturally diverse children* (pp. 157-196). Needham Heights, MA: Allyn & Bacon.

Mendez Pérez, A. (2000). Mexican-American mothers' perceptions and beliefs about language acquisition in infants and toddlers with disabilities. *Bilingual Research Journal, 24,* 277-294.

Merino, B., & Spencer, M. (1983). The comparability of English and Spanish versions of oral language proficiency instruments. *NABE Journal, 7,* 1-31.

Merino, B. (1992). Acquisition of syntactic and phonological features in Spanish. In H.W. Langdon & L. Cheng, *Hispanic children and adults with communication disorders: Assessment and intervention.* Gaithersburg, MD: Aspen Publishers, Inc.

Meschyan, G., & Hernández, A.E. (2004). Cognitive factors in second-language acquisition and literacy learning: A theoretical proposal and a call for research. In C.A. Stone, E.R. Silliman, B.J. Ehren, & K. Apel (Eds.), *Handbook of language and literacy: Development and disorders* (pp. 73-81). New York: The Guilford Press.

Miller, J.F., Heilmann, J., Nockerts, A., Iglesias, A., Fabiano, L., & Francis, D.J. (2006). Oral language and reading in bilingual children. *Learning Disabilities Research & Practice, 21,* 30-43.

Minochin, S. (1999). Russian immigrants squeezing social services groups. *Forward,* 5-7.

Mohammed, S.A. (2006). Moving beyond the "exotic:" Applying postcolonial theory in health research. *Advances in Nursing Sciences, 29,* 98-110.

Mohtasham-Nouri, N. (1994). *Iranians in America.* San Francisco: Many Cultures Publishing.

Mokuau, N., & Tauili'ili, P. (2004). Families with Native Hawaiian and Pacific Island roots. In E.W. Lynch & M.J. Hanson (Eds.), *Developing cross-cultural competence: A guide for working with young children and their families* (3rd ed.) (pp. 345-372). Baltimore, MD: Paul H. Brookes Publishing Co.

Monreal, S., & Hernández, R. (2005). Reading levels of Spanish Deaf students. *American Annals of the Deaf, 150,* 379-381.

Montgomery, J.K. (1998). Reading and the SLP: Using discourse, narratives and expository text. *CSHA Magazine, 27(3),* 8-9.

Montgomery, J.K. (2006). *Responsiveness to intervention (RtI): New tools for SLPs.* Paper presented at the annual meeting of the California Speech-Language-Hearing Association, San Francisco, CA.

Montgomery, J.K. (2007). *The bridge of vocabulary: Evidence-based activities for academic success.* Minneapolis: NCS Pearson, Inc.

Montgomery, J.K., & Moore-Brown, B. (2006). *Response to intervention: An alternative to special education.* Audio CD and manual produced by the American Speech-Language-Hearing Association, Rockville Pike, Maryland.

Montgomery, J.W. (1998). Sentence comprehension and working memory in children with specific language impairment. In R.B. Gillam (Ed.), *Memory and language impairment in children and adults: New perspectives (pp. 28-46).* Gaithersburg, MD: Aspen Publishers.

Moore, C.L., Giesen, J.M., & Cavenaugh, B.S. (2005). Latino VR access rates by disability type and proportions in the general population with disabilities. *Journal of Applied Rehabilitation Counseling, 36,* 25-32.

Moore, K.A. (2001). Time to take a closer look at Hispanic children and families. *Policy & Public Human Services, 59,* 8-9.

Moore-Brown, B., & Montgomery, J.K. (2008). *Making a difference for America's children: Speech-language pathologists in public schools* (2nd ed.). Eau Claire, WI: Thinking Publications.

Moskovkina, A. G., Pakhomova, E. V., & Abramova, A. V. (2001). Studying stereotypes of teachers' and parents' attitudes toward the mentally retarded child. *Russian Education and Society, 43,* 61-69.

Munson, B., Kurtz, B.A., & Windsor, J. (2005). The influence of vocabulary size, phonotactic probability, and wordlikeness on nonword repetitions of children with and without specific language impairment. *Journal of Speech, Language, and Hearing Research, 48,* 1033-1047.

Muñoz, M.L., Gillam, R., Peña, E.D., & Gulley-Faehnle, A. (2003). Measures of language development in fictional narratives of Latino children. *Language, Speech, and Hearing Services in Schools, 34,* 332-342.

Murphy, B.C., & Dillon, C. (2008). *Interviewing in action in a multicultural world* (3rd ed.). Belmont, CA: Thomson Higher Education.

Murphy, J. (2001). http://nativeamculture.about.com/culture/nativeamculture/library/weekly/aa052301a.htm.

Nakamura, K., Iwabuchi, M., & Alm, N. (2006). A cross-cultural study on the interpretation of picture-based sentences. *International Journal of Computer Processing of Oriental Languages, 19,* 239-248.

National Center for Children in Poverty (2006). *Basic facts about low-income children.* Retrieved 8/15/06 from http://nccp.org/public06.html.

National Center for Education Statistics (1997). *The condition of education, 1997.* Washington, DC: U.S. Department of Education.

National Center for Education Statistics (1999). *Teacher quality: A report on the preparation and qualifications of public school teachers.* Washington, DC: U.S. Department of Education.

National Center for Education Statistics (2001). Digest of education statistics. Washington, DC: U.S. Department of Education.

National Center for Education Statistics (2005). *Rates of computer and internet use by children in nursery school and students in kindergarten through twelfth grade: 2003.* Jessup, MD: U.S. Department of Education.

National Center for Health Statistics (2004). Selected demographic and health characteristics of birth by race of mother, 2004. *National Vital Statistics Reports, 53*(9), Nov. 23, 2004. Retrieved 9/5/06 from http://www.infoplease.com.

National Council on Disability (2003). *Understanding disabilities in American Indian and Alaska Native communities: ToolKit guide.* Washington, DC: Publisher.

National Dissemination Center for Children with Disabilities (2004). *Deafness and hearing loss.* Retrieved 3/4/07 from http://www.nichcy.org/pubs/factshe/fs3txt.htm.

National Literacy Trust (2006). *Ethnic minority issues and poverty.* Retrieved 11/2/06 from http://www.literacytrust.org.uk/Database/EAL/poverty.html.

N.C. Division of Social Services and the Family and Children's Resource Program (2002). *Latinos in North Carolina, Children's Services Practice Notes, 7*(3). Retrieved 12/27/06 from http:ssw.unc.edu/fcrp/Cspn/vol17_no3/Latinos%20NC.htm.

Neha, V.K. (2003). Home again: A Native American SLP's experiences teaching in a Navajo reservation school. *The ASHA Leader, 14,* 62-65.

Nellum-Davis, P., Gentry, B., & Hubbard-Wiley, P. (2002). Clinical practice issues. In D. Battle (Ed.), *Communication disorders in multicultural populations* (3nd ed.) (pp. 461-482). Stoneham, MA: Butterworth-Heinemann.

Nelson, N.W. (2007) "Be-attitudes" for managing change in school-based practice. *The ASHA Leader, 12,* 20-21.

Nelson, P., Kohnert, K., Sabur, S., & Shaw, D. (2005). Classroom noise and children learning through a second language: Double jeopardy? *Language, Speech, and Hearing Services in Schools, 36,* 219-229.

Nguyen, A. T. (2007). Confucian ethics and "the age of biological control." *Philosophy East & West, 57,* 83-96.

Nichols, A., & Keltner, B. (2005). Indian family adjustment to children with disabilities. *American Indian and Alaska Native Mental Health Research (online), 12,* 22-49.

Nippold, M.A., Duthie, J.K., & Larson, J. (2005). Literacy as leisure activity: Free-time preferences of older children and adolescents. *Language, Speech, and Hearing Services in Schools, 36,* 93-102.

Nixon, S.M., McCardle, P., & Leos, K. (2007). Implications of research on English language learners for classroom and clinical practice. *Language, Speech, and Hearing Services in Schools, 38,* 272-277.

NOAA Pacific Island Services Center (2006). *Pacific Islands context.* Retrieved 12/27/06 from http://www.csc.noaa.gov/psc/picpeople.html.

No Child Left Behind Act (NCLB), 20 U.S.C. (2001 & Supp. 2002). Available at http://www.ed.gov/policy/elsec/leg/esea02/107-110.pdf.

Nungesser, N.R., & Watkins, R.V. (2005). Preschool teachers; perceptions and reactions to challenging classroom behavior: Implications for speech-language pathologists. *Language, Speech, and Hearing Services in Schools, 36,* 139-151.

Obama, B. (2006). *The audacity of hope: Thoughts on reclaiming the American dream.* New York: Crown.

Office of Minority Health (2007). *American Indian and Alaska Native (AI/AN) Populations.* Retrieved 3/3/07 from http://www.cc.gov/omh/Populations/AIAN/AIAN.htm.

Ogakaki, L., & Frensch, P.A. (1998). Parenting and children's school achievement: A multiethnic approach. *American Educational Research Journal, 35(1),* 123-144.

Ogbu, J. (1992). Understanding cultural diversity and learning. *Educational Researcher, 21 (8),* 5-14.

Ogbu, J. (1995). Literacy and Black Americans: Comparative perspectives. In V.L. Gladsen & D.A. Wagner (Eds.), *Literacy among African-American youth: Issues in learning, teaching, and schooling* (pp. 83-100). Creskill, NJ: Hampton Press.

Ogbu, J., & Matute-Bianchi, M. (1990). Understanding sociocultural factors: Knowledge, identity, and school adjustment. In Leyba, C.F. (Ed.), *Beyond language: Social and cultural factors in schooling language minority students* (pp. 73-142). Los Angeles: Evaluation, Dissemination, and Assessment Center, California State University., Los Angeles.

Oller, J.W., Oller, S.D., & Badon, L.C. (2006). *Milestones: Normal speech and language development across the life span.* San Diego: Plural Publishing Inc.

Olsen, J.Z. (2003). *Handwriting without tears.* Cabin John, MD: Handwriting Without Tears, Inc.

Omar Nydell, M. (2006). *Understanding Arabs: A guide for modern times (4th ed).* Yarmouth, ME: Intercultural Press, Inc.

Ontario Consultants on Religious Tolerance (2004). *Religions of the world.* Retrieved 12/28/07 from http://www.religioustolerance.org/var_rel.htm.

Ortiz, A.A. (2001). English language learners with special needs: Effective instructional strategies. In O. García & C. Baker (Eds.), *Bilingual education: An introductory reader* (pp. 281-285). Clevedon, England: Multilingual Matters Ltd.

Ortiz, A.A., Wilkinson, C.Y., Robertson-Courtney, P., & Kushner, M.I. (2006). Considerations in implementing intervention assistance teams to support English language learners. *Remedial and Special Education, 27,* 53-63.

Ortiz, R.W., & Ordoñez-Jasis, R. (2005). Leyendo juntos (reading together): New directions for Latino parents' early literary involvement. *The Reading Teacher, 59,* 110-121.

Ortiz, R.W., & Ordoñez-Jasis, R. (2005). Leyendo juntos (reading together): New directions for Latino parents' early literary involvement. *The Reading Teacher, 59,* 110-121.

Ott, B.B., Al-Khadhuri, J., & Al-Junaibi, S. (2003). Preventing ethical dilemmas: Understanding Islamic health care practices. *Pediatric Nursing, 29,* 227-230.

Owens, R.E. (2004). *Language disorders: A functional approach to assessment and intervention* (4th ed.). Boston: Allyn & Bacon.

Owens, R.E. (2005). *Language development: An introduction* (6th ed.). Boston, MA: Alllyn & Bacon.

Pacifica Mental Health (2006). *Pacific Island approach to mental health.* Retrieved 12/27/06 from http://www.headspace.org.nz/pacifica-mental-health.htm.

Padilla, A.M. (1992). Reflections on testing: Emerging trends and new possibilities. In K.F. Geisinger (Ed.), *Psychological testing of Hispanics* (pp. 271-284). Washington, DC: American Psychological Press.

Paglario, C. (2001). Addressing deaf culture in the classroom. *Kappa Delta Pi Record, 37,* 173-179.

Pajewski, A., & Enriquez, L. (1996). *Teaching from a Hispanic perspective: A handbook for non-Hispanic adult educators.* Retrieved 12/2/02 from http://literacynet.org/lp/hperspectives.

Palcich, W.J. (1992). Native American bilingualism: A hidden challenge for speech-language pathologists. *ADVANCE for Speech-Language Pathologists and Audiologists, 2 (22),* 10-11.

Pang-Ching, G., Robb, M., Heath, R., & Takumi, M. (1995). Middle ear disorders and hearing loss in Native Hawaiian preschoolers. *Language, Speech, and Hearing Services in Schools, 26(1),* 33-38.

Paradis, J. (2005). Grammatical morphology in children learning English as a second language: Implications of similarities with specific language impairment. *Language, Speech, and Hearing Services in Schools, 36,* 172-187.

Paradis, J. (2007). Second language acquisition in childhood. In E. Hoff & M. Shatz (Eds.), *Handbook of language development* (pp. 387-406). Oxford: Blackwell.

Paradis, J., Crago, M., Genesee, F., & Rice, M. (2003). French-English bilingual children with SLI: How do they compare with their monolingual peers? *Journal of Speech, Language, and Hearing Research, 46,* 113-127.

Parasnis, I., & Fischer, S.D. (2005). Perceptions of diverse educators regarding ethnic-minority Deaf college students, role models, and diversity. *American Annals of the Deaf, 150,* 343-348.

Parette, P., Chuang, S. L., & Huer, M.B. (2004). First-generation Chinese American families' attitudes regarding disabilities and educational interventions. *Focus on Autism and Other Developmental Disabilities, 19,* 114-123.

Parette, H.P., Huer, M.B., & Peterson-Karlan, G.R. (2008). Meeting the needs of persons with developmental disabilities across cultures. In. H.P. Parette & G.R. Peterson-Karlan (Eds.). *Research-based practices in developmental disabilities.* (2nd Edition) (pp. 143-167). Austin, TX: Pro-Ed.

Parette, H.P., Huer, M.B., & Wyatt, T.A. (2003/4). Young African American children with disabilities and augmentative and alternative communication issues. In K.L. Freiburg (Ed.), *Annual editions: Educating exceptional children* (15th ed.) (pp. 76-81). Guilford, CT: Dushkin Publishing Group.

Parkyn, L.K. (2005). Cultural authenticity in a few clicks. *Essential Teacher, 2,* 42-47.

Pataray-Ching, J., Kitt-Hinrichs, B., & Nguyen, V. (2006). Inquiring into a second language and the culture of school. *Language Arts, 83,* 248-257.

Patterson, J.L. (1999). What bilingual toddlers hear and say: Language input and word combinations. *Communication Disorders Quarterly, 21(1),* 32-38.

Paterson, P.O., & Elliott, L.N. (2006). Struggling reader to struggling reader: High school students' response to a cross-age tutoring program. *Journal of Adolescent and Adult Literacy, 49,* 378-389.

Patterson, J.L. (2000). Observed and reported expressive vocabulary and word combinations in bilingual toddlers. *Journal of Speech-Language-Hearing Research, 43(1),* 121-128.

Patterson, J.L., & Pearson, B.Z. (2004) Influences, contexts, and processes. In B.A. Goldstein (Ed.), *Bilingual language development and disorders in Spanish-English speakers* (pp. 77-104). Baltimore, MD: Paul H. Brookes Publishing Co.

Paul, P. (2001). *Language and deafness.* (3rd edition) San Diego: Singular/Thompson Learning.

Paul, R. (2007). *Language disorders from infancy through adolescence* (3rd ed.). St. Louis, MO: Mosby, Inc.

Payne, K. (1986). Cultural and linguistic groups in the United States. In O. Taylor (Ed.), *Nature of communication disorders in culturally and linguistically diverse populations.* San Diego: College-Hill Press.

Payne, R.K. (2003). *A framework for understanding poverty.* Highland, TX: aha! Process, Inc.

Peal, E., & Lambert, W. (1962). The relation of bilingualism to intelligence. *Psychological Monograph, 72,* 1-23.

Pearce, R.R., & Lin, Z. (2005). Cultural capital and postsecondary educational attainment among White and Chinese Americans: An analysis of NELS 1988-2000. *Asian American Policy Review, 14*, 19-38.

Pearson, C.M. (2001, October). Internationally adopted children: Issues and challenges. *The ASHA Leader*, 4-13.

Peck, S., & Lerner, L. (2005). Parent and child activities in a community-based English tutoring program. *The CATESOL Journal, 17*, 120-124.

Pelczarski, Y., & Kemp, S.P. (2006). Patterns of child maltreatment referrals among Asian and Pacific Islander families. *Child Welfare, 85*, 5-32.

Pell, G. (2006). Islam and us. *First Things: A Monthly Journal of Religion and Public Life, 33*, 164-169.

Peña, E.D. (2006). Dynamic assessment of school-age children's narrative ability: An experimental investigation of classification accuracy. *Journal of Speech, Language, and Hearing Research, 49*, 1037-1057.

Peña, E.D., Bedore, L.M., & Rapazzo, D. (2003). Comparison of Spanish, English, and bilingual children's performance across semantic tasks. *Language, Speech, and Hearing Services in Schools, 34*, 5-16.

Peña, E.D., Gillam, R.B., Malek, M., Ruiz-Felter, R., Resendiz, M., Fiestas, C., & Sabel, T. (2006). Dynamic assessment of school-age children's narrative ability: An experimental investigation of classification accuracy. *Journal of Speech, Language, and Hearing Research, 49*, 1037-1057.

Peña, E.D., Iglesias, A., & Lidz, C.S. (2001). Reducing test bias through dynamic assessment of children's word learning ability. *American Journal of Speech-Language Pathology, 10(2)*, 138-154.

Peña, E.D., & Kester, E.S. (2004). Semantic development in Spanish-English bilinguals: Theory, assessment, and intervention. In B.A. Goldstein (Ed.), *Bilingual language development and disorders in Spanish-English speakers* (pp. 105-130). Baltimore, MD: Paul H. Brookes Publishing Co.

Peña, E.D., & Quinn, R. (1997). Task familiarity: Effects on the test performance of Puerto Rican and African American children. *Language, Speech, and Hearing Services in Schools, 28(4)*, 323-332.

Peña-Brooks, A., & Hegde, M.N. (2007). *Assessment and treatment of articulation and phonological disorders in children* (2nd ed.). Austin, TX: Pro-Ed.

Perozzi, J., & Sánchez, M.L.C. (1992). The effect of instruction in L1 on receptive acquisition of L2 for bilingual children with language delay. *Language, Speech, and Hearing Services in the Schools, 23 (4)*, 358-352.

Peter, L., & Hirata-Edds, T.E. (2006). Using assessment to inform instruction in Cherokee language revitalisation. *The International Journal of Bilingual Education and Bilingualism, 9*, 643-650.

Pickett, L. (2003). *ItemWriter Language Software Series*. Oceanside, CA: Academic Communication Associates.

Pierce, L.V. (2006). *Facilitating transition to the mainstream: Sheltered English vocabulary development*. Retrieved 10/24/06 from http://www.ncela.gwu.edu/pubs/classics/pig/06sheltered.htm.

Pieretti, R.A., & Goldsworthy, C.L. (2001). Language-based reading disorders: A bottom-up perspective. *CSHA Magazine, 31(1)*, 8-9.

Politzer, R., & Ramírez, A. (1974). An error analysis of the spoken English of Mexican-American pupils in a bilingual school and a monolingual school. *Language Learning, 23 (1)*, 39-51.

Poon-McBrayer, K. F., & García, S. B. (2000). Profiles of Asian American students with LD at initial referral, assessment, and placement in special education. *Journal of Learning Disabilities, 33*, 61-71.

Posnick-Goodwin, S. (2005). Low-income, minority families have the most to gain. *California Educator, 10*, 12-115.

Posnick-Goodwin, S. (2006). Immersion requires patience. *California Educator, 11*, 11.

Posnick-Goodwin, S. (2007). Response to intervention. *California Educator, 12*, 6-12.

Poupart, L.M. (2003). The familiar face of genocide: internalized oppression among American Indians. *Hypatia, 18*, 86-102.

Powell, R., & Davidson, N. (2005). The donut house: Real world literacy in an urban kindergarten classroom. *Language Arts, 82, 248-256.*

Powers, K. (2005). Promoting school achievement among American Indian students throughout the school years. *Childhood Education, 338.5.*

Prelock, P.A., Beatson, J., Bitner, B., Broder, C., & Ducker, A. (2003). Interdisciplinary assessment of young children with Autism Spectrum Disorder. *Language, Speech, and Hearing Services in Schools, 34*, 194-202.

Price, J.R., Roberts, J.E., & Jackson, S.C. (2006). Structural development of the fictional narratives of African American preschoolers. *Language, Speech, and Hearing Services in Schools, 37*, 178-199.

Pridmore, S., & Pasha, M.I. (2004). Psychiatry and Islam. *American Psychiatry, 12*, 380-385.

Qi, C.H. (2006). Beyond assessment: Issues of assessing language and behavior of African American children from low income backgrounds. *ASHA Special Interest Division 14 Newsletter, 13*, 14-18.

Qi, C.H., & Kaiser, A.P. (2004). Problem behaviors of low-income children with language delays: An observation study. *Journal of Speech, Language, and Hearing Research, 47*, 595-609.

Ramírez, J.D., Yuen, S., & Ramey, D. (1991). *Executive summary final report: Longitudinal study of structured English immersion strategy, early-exit and late-exit transitional bilingual education programs for language-minority children*, Washington, DC: U.S. Department of Education.

Rasheed, A.S., Liu, M.W., & Humedian, M. (2004). Islam 101: Understanding the religion and therapy implications. *Professional Psychology: Research and Practice, 35*, 635-642.

Rayle, A.D., Chee, C., & Sand, J.K. (2006). Honoring their way: Counseling American Indian women. *Journal of Multicultural Counseling and Development, 34*, 66-79.

Reese, D. (2007). Proceed with caution: Using Native American folktales in the classroom. *Language Arts, 84*, 245-255.

Reid, R., Casta, C.D., Norton, H.J., Anastopolous, A.D., & Temple, E.P. (2001). Using behavior rating scales for ADHD across ethnic groups: The IOWA Conners. *Journal of Emotional and Behavioral Disorders, 9,* 210-218.

Reid, R., Riccio, C.A., Kessler, R.H., DuPaul, G.J., Power, T.J., Anastopolous, A.D., Rogers-Adkinson, D., & Noll, M. (2000). Gender and ethnic differences in ADHD assessed by behavior ratings. *Journal of Emotional and Behavioral Disorders, 8,* 38-48.

Renfrew, C. (1991). *The Bus Story Language Test: A Test of Continuous Speech.* Oxford, England: Author.

Rescorla, L. (1989). The Language Development Survey: A screening tool for delayed language in toddlers. *Journal of Speech and Hearing Disorders, 54,* 587-599.

Rescorla, L., & Achenbach, T.M. (2002). Use of the Language Development Survey (LDS) in a national probability sample of children 18 to 35 months old. *Journal of Speech, Language, and Hearing Research, 44,* 733-743.

Rescorla, L., & Alley, A. (2001). Validation of the Language Development Survey (LDS): A parent report tool for identifying language delay in toddlers. *Journal of Speech, Language, and Hearing Research, 44,* 434-445.

Restrepo, M.A. (1998). Identifiers of predominantly Spanish-speaking children with language impairment. *Journal of Speech-Language-Hearing Research, 41,* 1398-1411.

Restrepo, M.A., & Gutiérrez-Clellen, V.F. (2004). Grammatical impairments in Spanish-English bilingual children. In B.A. Goldstein (Ed.), *Bilingual language development and disorders in Spanish-English speakers* (pp. 213-234). Baltimore, MD: Paul H. Brookes Publishing Co.

Restrepo, M.A., & Kruth, K. (2000). Grammatical characteristics of a Spanish-English child with specific language impairment. *Communication Disorders Quarterly, 21(2),* 66-76.

Rice, M., Sell, M.A., & Hadley, P.A. (1991). Social interactions of speech- and language-impaired children. *Journal of Speech and Hearing Research, 3),* 1299-1307.

Richmond, Y. (1995). *From da to yes: Understanding the East Europeans.* Yarmouth, ME: Intercultural Press, Inc.

Richmond, Y. (2003). *From nyet to da: Understanding the Russians* (3rd ed.). London: Intercultural Press/Nicholas Brealey Publishing.

Riquelme, L. (1994, July). Hispanic American cultures. Paper presented at the conference for Competent Assessment and Intervention with Hispanic and Asian/Pacific Islander Populations, Maui, Hawaii.

Rimashevskaia, N. M. (2007). Children and young people are the future of Russia. *Russian Education and Society, 49,* 70-86.

Ritzman, M.J., Sanger, D., & Coufal, K.L. (2006). A case study of a collaborative speech-language pathologist. *Communication Disorders Quarterly, 27,* 221-231.

Rivera, H.H., & Tharp, R.G. (2006). A Native American community's involvement and empowerment to guide their children's development in the school setting. *Journal of Community Psychology, 34,* 435-451.

Roberts, G. (2007, June). *Response to intervention: A national perspective.* Paper presented at the NCLB/IDEA Symposium, Sacramento, CA.

Roberts, J.E., Medley, L.P., Swartzfager, J.L., & Neebe, E.C. (1997). Assessing the communication of African American one-year-olds using the Communication and Symbolic Behavior Scales. *American Journal of Speech-Language Pathology, 6(2),* 59-65.

Roberts, J.E., Pollock, K.E., Krakow, R., Price, J., Fulmer, K.C., & Wang, P.P. (2005). Language development in preschool-age children adopted from China. *Journal of Speech, Language, and Hearing Research, 48,* 93-107.

Robertson, B., & Liu, M. (2006, March). China: Can Confucianism quell dissent? *Newsweek International, March 20, 2006 issue,* p. 2.

Robinson, F., Sandoval, N., Baldwin, J., & Sanderson, P. R. (2005). Breast cancer education for Native American women: Creating culturally relevant communications. *Clinical Journal of Oncology Nursing, 9,* 689-692.

Robinson, T.L., & Crowe, T.A. (1998). Culture-based considerations in programming for stuttering intervention with African American clients and their families. *American Journal of Speech-Language Pathology, 29(3),* 172-179.

Robinson-Zañartu, C. (1996). Serving Native American children and families: *Considering cultural variables. Language, Speech, and Hearing Services in Schools, 27(4),* 373-384.

Rodríguez, B.L., & Olswang, L.B. (2003). Mexican-American and Anglo-American mothers' beliefs and values about child-rearing, education, and language impairment. *American Journal of Speech-Language Pathology, 12,* 452-462.

Rogers-Adkinson, D. L., Ochoa, T. A., & Delgado, B. (2003). Developing crosscultural competence: Serving families of children with significant developmental needs. *Focus on Autism and Other Developmental Disabilities, 18,* 4-8.

Rojas, R. (2006). School-based assessment of bilingual speakers in 2006: Clinical practice and federal law. *CSHA Magazine, 36(2),* 8-10.

Romanovich, N.A. (2005). Democratic values and freedom "Russian style." *Russian Social Science Review, 45,* 42-48.

Rosa-Lugo, L.I., & Fradd, S. (2000). Preparing professionals to serve English-language learners with communication disorders. *Communication Disorders Quarterly, 22(1),* 29-42.

Roseberry, C.A., & Connell, P. J. (1991). The use of an invented language rule in the differentiation of normal and language-impaired Spanish-speaking children. *Journal of Speech and Hearing Research, 34,* 596-603.

Roseberry-McKibbin, C.A. (1993). Bilingual Classroom Communication Profile. Oceanside, CA: Academic Communication Associates.

Roseberry-McKibbin, C.A. (1994). Assessment and intervention for children with limited English proficiency and language disorders. *American Journal of Speech-Language Pathology, 3(3),* 77-88.

Roseberry-McKibbin, C. (1995). Distinguishing language differences from language disorders in linguistically and culturally diverse students. *The Magazine of the National Association for Multicultural Education, 2(4),* 12-16.

Roseberry-McKibbin, C. (1997). Understanding Filipino families: A foundation for effective service delivery. *American Journal of Speech-Language Pathology, 6(3),* 5-14.

Roseberry-McKibbin, C. (2000a). Mirror, mirror on the wall: Reflections of a third culture American. *Communication Disorders Quarterly, 21(4)*, 242-245.

Roseberry-McKibbin, C. (2000b). Multicultural matters: The culture of poverty. *Communication Disorders Quarterly, 21(4)*, 242-245.

Roseberry-McKibbin, C. (2001a). Serving children from the culture of poverty: Practical strategies for speech-language pathologists. *The ASHA Leader, 6(20)*, 4-5, 16.

Roseberry-McKibbin, C. (2001b). *The source for bilingual students with language disorders.* East Moline, IL: LinguiSystems, Inc.

Roseberry-McKibbin, C. (2002). Principles and strategies in intervention. In A.E. Brice (Ed.), *The Hispanic child: Speech, language, culture and education* (pp. 199-233). Boston, MA: Allyn & Bacon.

Roseberry-Mckibbin, C. (2003). *Assessment of bilingual learners: Language difference or language disorder?* Video published by the American Speech-Language-Hearing Association, Rockville, MD.

Roseberry-McKibbin, C. (2007). *Language disorders in children: A multicultural and case perspective.* Boston: Allyn & Bacon.

Roseberry-McKibbin, C. (2008*). Increasing the language and academic achievement of children in poverty.* San Diego: Plural Publishing, Inc.

Roseberry-McKibbin, C., & Brice, A. (1999). The perception of vocal cues of emotion by Spanish-speaking limited English proficient children. *Journal of Children's Communication Development, 20(2)*, 19-25.

Roseberry-McKibbin, C.A., & Eicholtz, G.E. (1994). Serving limited English proficient children in schools: A national survey. *Language Speech and Hearing Services in Schools, 25(3)*, 156-164.

Roseberry-McKibbin, C., & Hegde, M.N. (2006). *An advanced review of speech-language pathology: Preparation for PRAXIS and comprehensive examination* (2nd ed.). Austin, TX: Pro-Ed.

Roseberry-McKibbin, C., & O'Hanlon, L. (2005). Nonbiased assessment of English language learners: A tutorial. *Communication Disorders Quarterly, 26*, 178-185.

Roseberry-McKibbin, C., Peña, A., Hall, M., & Smith-Stubblefield, S. (1996, November). Health care considerations in serving children from migrant Hispanic families. Paper presented at the annual convention of the American Speech-Language-Hearing Association, Seattle, WA.

Rosenberg, L. (2000). *Living in the light of death: On the art of being truly alive.* Boston: Shambhala Publications.

Rossetti, L.M. (2001). *Communication intervention birth to three* (2nd ed.). Boston: Allyn & Bacon.

Roth, F.P. (2004). Word recognition assessment frameworks. In C.A. Stone, E.R. Silliman, B.J. Ehren, & K. Apel (Eds.), *Handbook of language and literacy: Development and disorders* (pp. 461-480). New York: The Guilford Press.

Rowe, B.M., & Levine, D.P. (2006). *A concise introduction to linguistics.* Boston: Pearson Education, Inc.

Roy, P., & Chiat, S. (2004). A prosodically controlled word and nonword repetition task for 2- to 4-year olds: Evidence from typically-developing children. *Journal of Speech-Language-Hearing Research, 47*, 223-234.

Rubinstein-Ávila, E. (2006). Connecting with Latino learners. *Educational Leadership, 63*, 38-43.

Rueda, R., Monzo, L., Blacher, J., Shapiro, J., & González, J. (2005). Cultural models and practices regarding transition: A view from Latina mothers of young adults with developmental disabilities. *Exceptional Children, 71*, 401-414.

Rueda, R., & Windmueller, M.P. (2006). English language learners, LD, and overrepresentation: A multiple-level analysis. *Journal of Learning Disabilities, 39*, 99-107.

Rybak, C.J., Eastin, C.L., & Robbins, I. (2004). Native American healing practices and counseling. *Journal of Humanistic Counseling, Education and Development, 43*, 25-32.

Sáenz, L. M., Fuchs, L. S., & Fuchs, D. (2005). Peer-assisted learning strategies for English language learners with learning disabilities. *Exceptional Children, 71*, 231-247.

Saenz, T.I. (1996). An overview of second language acquisition. In H.W. Langdon & T.I. Saenz (Eds.), *Language assessment and intervention with multicultural students: A guide for speech-language-hearing professionals (pp. 51-60).* Oceanside, CA: Academic Communication Associates.

Salas-Provance, M.B., Erickson, J.G., & Reed, J. (2002). Disabilities as viewed by four generations of one Hispanic family. *American Journal of Speech-Language Pathology, 11*, 151-162.

Salas-Provance, M.B., & Oprandy, R. (2006). Collaboration between teachers and speech-language pathologists: A university model to benefit Hispanic children in schools. *Perspectives on Communication Disorders and Sciences in Culturally and Linguistically Diverse Populations, ASHA Special Interest Division 14 Newsletter, 13*, 17-22.

Saldaña-Illingworth, C. *Language activities for young Hispanic children.* Oceanside, CA: Academic Communication Associates.

Salend, S.J., & Duhaney, M.G. (2005). Understanding and addressing the disproportionate representation of students of color in special education. *Intervention in School and Clinic, 40*, 213-221.

Savin, D., Garry, M.T., Zuccaro, P., & Novins, D. (2006). Telepsychiatry for treating rural American Indian youth. *Journal of the American Academy of Adolescent Psychiatry, 45*, 484-488.

Schiff-Myers, N. (1992). Considering arrested language development and language loss in the assessment of second language learners. *Language, Speech, and Hearing Services in the Schools, 23*, 28-33.

Schmit, K. (2005). Nursing implications for treating "kanser" in Filipino patients. *Journal of Hospice and Palliative Nursing, 7*, 345-353.

Schvaneveldt, P.L., Kerpelman, J.L., & Schvaneveldt, J.D. (2005). Generational and cultural changes in family life in the United Arab Emirates: A comparison of mothers and daughters. *Journal of Comparative Family Studies, 36*, 77-92.

Scott, D.M. (1998). Multicultural aspects of hearing disorders and audiology. In D.E. Battle (Ed.), *Communication disorders in multicultural populations* (2nd ed.) (pp. 335-354). Newton, MA: Butterworth-Heinemann.

Seals, L.M., Pollard-Durodola, S.D., Foorman, B.R., & Bradley, A.M. (2007). *Vocabulary power: Lessons for students who use African American English Vernacular*. Baltimore: Brookes Publishing Co.

Selman, P. (2007). The diaper diaspora. *Foreign Policy, 32*, 1-6.

Semel, E., Wiig, E.H., & Secord, W. (2005). *Clinical Evaluation of Language Fundamentals-4 (Spanish)*. San Antonio, TX: The Psychological Corporation.

Senices, J. (2005). The complexity behind the Hispanic identity. *Journal of Applied Rehabilitative Counseling, 36*, 20-24.

Seymour, H.N., Bland-Stewart, L., & Green, L.J. (1998). Difference versus deficit in child African American English. *Language, Speech, and Hearing Services in Schools, 29(2)*, 96-108.

Seymour, H.S., Roeper, T.W., & deVilliers, J. (2004). *Diagnostic Evaluation of Language Variation*. San Antonio, TX: Psychological Corporation.

Shaikh, M. (2005). *What teachers need to know about Islam*. Bloomington, IN: Phi Delta Kappa Educational Foundation.

Sharifzadeh, V.S. (2004). Families with Middle Eastern roots. In E.W. Lynch & M.J. Hanson (Eds.), *Developing cross-cultural competence: A guide for working with young children and their families* (3rd ed.) (pp. 373-414). Baltimore, MD: Paul H. Brookes Publishing Company.

Shekar, C., & Hegde, M.N. (1995). India: Its people, culture, and languages. In L.L. Cheng (Ed.), *Integrating language and learning for inclusion: An Asian-Pacific focus* (pp. 125-148). San Diego: Singular Publishing Group, Inc.

Sheng, L., McGregor, K.K., & Marian, V. (2006). Lexical-semantic organization in bilingual children: Evidence from a repeated word task. *Journal of Speech, Language, and Hearing Research, 49*, 572-587.

Shohamy, E. (1999). *Unity and diversity in language policy*. Paper presented at the AILA conference, Tokyo, August.

Shukshin, A. (2004). Ailing Russian health-care system in urgent need of reform. *Bulletin of the World Health Organization, 82*, 391.

Sileo, T. W., & Prater, M. A. (1998). Creating classroom environments that address the linguistic and cultural backgrounds of students with disabilities. *Remedial and Special Education, 19*, 323-337.

Silliman, E.R., & Diehl, S.F. (2002). Assessing children with language learning disabilities. In D.K. Bernstein., & E. Tiegerman-Farber (Eds.), *Language and communication disorders in children* (5th ed.) (pp. 184-255). Boston, MA: Allyn & Bacon.

Silliman, E.R., & Scott, C.M. (2006). Language impairment and reading disability: Connections and complexities—Introduction to the special issue. *Learning Disabilities Research and Practice, 21*, 1-7.

Silva, L.M.T., & Cignolini, A. (2005). A medical Qigong methodology for early intervention in autism spectrum disorder: A case series. *The American Journal of Chinese Medicine, 33*, 315-327.

Singh, S. (2001). Information available from: http://www.aapi.gov/info.aapi_factsheet.htm.

Skiba, R. J., Poloni-Staudinger, L., Simmons, A. B., Feggins-Azziz, L. R., & Chung, C.-G. (2005). Unproven links: Can poverty explain ethnic disproportionality in special education? *The Journal of Special Education, 39*, 130-144.

Skinner, D.G., Correa, V., Skinner, M., & Bailey, D. (2001). Role of religion in the lives of Latino families of young children with developmental delays. *American Journal on Mental Retardation, 106*, 297-313.

Skutnabb-Kangas, T. (2000). Linguistic rights in human education? In O. García & C. Baker (Eds.), *Bilingual education: An introductory reader* (pp. 137-144). Clevedon, England: Multilingual Matters Ltd.

Sleeter, C. (1994). White racism. *National Association for Multicultural Education, 1(4)*, 5-8.

Smiley, D.F., & Threats, T. (2006). Audiologists and speech-language pathologists working together to serve children in rural communities who are deaf and hard of hearing. *Perspectives on Communication disorders and Sciences in Culturally and Linguistically Diverse Populations (Special Interest Division 14 Newsletter), 13*, 22-28.

Smith, T.T., Lee, E., & McDade, H.L. (2001). An investigation of T-units in African-American English-speaking and Standard American English-speaking fourth-grade children. *Communication Disorders Quarterly, 22(3)*, 148-157.

Smith-Stoner, M. (2003). How Buddhism influences pain control choices. *Nursing, 33*, 17.

Snow, C.E., Porche, M.V., Tabors, P.O., & Harris, S.R. (2007). *Is literacy enough? Pathways to academic success for adolescents*. Baltimore: Brookes Publishing Co.

Snyder, L.E., & Scherer, N. (2004). The development of symbolic play and language in toddlers with cleft palate. *American Journal of Speech-Language Pathology, 13*, 66-80.

Soto, G., Huer, M.B., & Taylor, C. (1997). Multicultural issues. In L.I. Lloyd, D.H. Fuller, & H.H. Arvidson (Eds.), *Augmentative and alternative communication* (pp. 406-413). Boston: Allyn & Bacon.

Southwood, S., & Russell, A.F. (2004). Comparison of conversation, freeplay, and story generation as methods of language sample elicitation. *Journal of Speech, Language, and Hearing Research, 47*, 366-376.

Sparks, S. (2000). Classroom and curriculum accommodations for Native American students. *Intervention in School and Clinic, 35*, 259-263.

Spencer, G., & Hollmann, F.W. (1998). In *Population profile of the United States, 1997*, pp. 8-9. U.S. Bureau of the Census, Current Population Reports, Series P23-194. Washington, DC: U.S. Government Printing Office.

Sperling, V. (1999). *Organizing women in contemporary Russia: Engendering transition*. New York: Cambridge University Press.

Starnes, B.A. (2006). What we don't know *can* hurt them: White teachers, Indian children. *Phi Delta Kappan*, 384-392.

Stein, M.T. (2004). International adoption: A 4-year old child with unusual behaviors adopted at 6 months of age. *Pediatrics, 114*, 1425-1431.

Stewart, D.A., & Kluwin, T.N. (2001). Diversity in deaf education. In S. Dragin (Ed.), *Teaching deaf and hard of hearing students: Content, strategies and curriculum* (pp. 272-288). Needham Heights, MA: Allyn & Bacon.

Stewart, J.L. (1986). Hearing disorders among the indigenous peoples of North America and the Pacific Basin. In O. Taylor (Ed.), *Nature of communication disorders in culturally and linguistically diverse populations.* San Diego: College-Hill Press.

Stockman, I.J. (1996). The promises and pitfalls of language sample analysis as an assessment tool for linguistic minority children. *Language, Speech, and Hearing Services in Schools, 27(4),* 355-366.

Stockman, I.J. (2000). The new Peabody Picture Vocabulary Test-III: An illusion of unbiased assessment? *Language, Speech, and Hearing Services in Schools, 31(4),* 340-253.

Stockman, I.J. (2006). Alveolar bias in the final consonant deletion patterns of African American children. *Language, Speech, and Hearing Services in Schools, 37,* 85-95.

Stodolska, M., & Livengood, J.S. (2006). The influence of religion on the leisure behavior of immigrant Muslims in the United States. *Journal of Leisure Research, 38,* 293-320.

Stokes, S.F., Wong, A.M.-Y., Fletcher, & Leonard, L.B. (2006). Nonword repetition and sentence repetition as clinical markers of specific language impairment: The case of Cantonese. *Journal of Speech, Language, and Hearing Research, 49,* 219-236.

Sue, D.W., & Sue, D. (2008). *Counseling the culturally diverse: Theory and practice* (5th ed.). New York: John Wiley & Sons.

Suico, J.L. (2005). Pentecostalism and social change. *Asian Journal of Pentecostal Studies, 13,* 195-213.

Susan, H.E., & Susan, H.W. (2005). African, Russian, and Ukrainian refugee resettlement in Portland, Oregon. *Geographical Review, 95,* 189-209.

Swain, M. (1985). Communicative competence: Some roles of comprehensible input and conprehensible output in its development. In S. Gass, & C. Madden (Eds.), *Input in second language acquisition.* Boston: Newbury House.

Swanson, T.J., Hodson, B.W., & Schommer-Aikins, M. (2005). An examination of phonological awareness treatment outcomes for seventh-grade poor readers from a bilingual community. *Language, Speech, and Hearing Services in Schools, 36,* 336-345.

Szlemko, W.J., Wood, J.W., & Thurman, P.J. (2006). Native Americans and alcohol: Past, present, and future. *The Journal of General Psychology, 13,* 435-451.

Tabors, P.O. (1997). *One child, two languages.* Baltimore, MD: Paul H. Brookes Publishing Co.

Taddonio, R. (2003). *International adoption and language development.* Retrieved 7/4/06 from http://www.adopting.org/adoptions/adoptive-parenting-international-adoption-and-language-development.html.

Takanishi, R. (2006). Leveling the playing field: Supporting immigrant children from birth to eight. *The Future of Children: Children of Immigrant Families, 14,* 62-79.

Talbert-Johnson, C. (2004). Structural inequities and the achievement gap in urban schools. *Education and Urban Society, 37,* 22-36.

Tam, K. Y. B., & Heng, M. A. (2005). A case involving culturally and linguistically diverse parents in prereferral intervention. *Intervention in School and Clinic, 40,* 222-230.

Tan, G.T. (2006). Diverse issues: Providing services to internationally adopted children. *CSHA Magazine, 36*(2), 11-12.

Tannen, D. (1994). *Talking from 9 to 5: Women and men in conversation.* William Morrow.

Tannenbaum, M. (2005). Viewing family relations through a linguistic lens: Symbolic aspects of language maintenance in immigrant families. *The Journal of Family Communication, 5,* 229-252.

Teagle, H.F.B., & Moore, J.A. (2002). School-based services for children with cochlear implants. *Language, Speech, and Hearing Services in Schools, 33,* 162-171.

Terrell, S.L., Arensburg, K., & Rosa, R. (1992). Parent-child comparative analysis: A criterion-referenced method for the nondiscriminatory assessment of a child who spoke a relatively uncommon dialect of English. *Language, Speech, and Hearing Services in the Schools, 23 (1),* 34-42.

Terrell, S.L., Battle, D.E., & Grantham, R.B. (1998). African-American cultures. In D.E. Battle (Ed.), Communication disorders in multicultural populations (2nd ed.) (pp. 31-72). Stoneham, MA: Butterworth-Heinemann.

Terrell, B., & Hale, J. (1992). Serving a multicultural population: Different learning styles. *American Journal of Speech-Language Pathology, 1 (2),* 5-8.

Terrell, S.L., & Jackson, R.S. (2002). African Americans in the Americas. In D.E. Battle (Ed.), *Communication disorders in multicultural populations* (3rd ed.) (pp. 33-70). Woburn, MA: Butterworth-Heinemann.

Terrell, S.L., & Terrell, F. (1996). The importance of psychological and sociocultural factors for providing clinical services to African American children. In A.G. Kamhi, S.E. Pollock, & J.L. Harris (Eds.), *Communication development and disorders in African American children* (pp. 55-72). Baltimore: Paul H. Brookes Publishing Co.

Thal, D., Jackson-Maldonado, D., & Acosta, D. (2000). Validity of a parent-report measure of vocabulary and grammar for Spanish-speaking toddlers. *Journal of Speech-Language-Hearing Research, 43(5),* 1087-1100.

Thibodeau, L. M., Johnson, C. (2005, Sept. 27). Serving children with hearing loss in public school settings. *The ASHA Leader,* 6-7, 36-38.

Thomas, W.P., & Collier, V.P. (1998). Two languages are better than one. *Educational Leadership, 12/97-1/98,* 23-26.

Thomas-Tate, S., Washington, J., Craig, H., & Packard, M. (2006). Performance of African American preschool and kindergarten students on the Expressive Vocabulary Test. *Language, Speech, and Hearing Services in Schools, 37,* 143-149.

Thomas-Tate, S., Washington, J., & Edwards, J. (2004). Standardized assessment of phonological awareness skills in low-income African American first graders. *American Journal of Speech-Language Pathology, 13,* 182-190.

Thompson, C.A., Craig, H.K., & Washington, J.A. (2004). Variable production of African American English across oralcy and literacy contexts. *Language, Speech, and Hearing Services in Schools, 35,* 269-282.

Thordardottir, E. (2006, Aug. 15). Language intervention from a bilingual mindset. *ASHA Leader, 11*, 6-7, 20-21.

Tiegerman-Farber, E. (2002). Interactive teaming: The changing role of the speech-language pathologist. In D.K. Bernstein., & E. Tiegerman-Farber (Ed.), *Language and communication disorders in children* (5th ed.) (pp. 96-125). Boston, MA: Allyn & Bacon.

Topmiller, R. (2000). Vietnamese Buddhism in the 1990s. *Cross Currents, Spring/Summer 2000*, 232-239.

Torres-Guzman, M.E. (2002). Dual language programs: Key features and results. In O. García & C. Baker (Eds.), *Bilingual education: An introductory reader* (pp. 50-63). Clevedon, England: Multilingual Matters Ltd.

Trelease, J. (2006). *The read-aloud handbook*. Retrieved 8/15/06 from http://www.trelease-on-reading.com.

Trembath, D., Balandin, S., & Rossi, C. (2005). Cross-cultural practices and autism. *Journal of Intellectual & Developmental Disability, 30*, 240-242.

Trillingsgaard, A., Sorensen, E.U., Nemec, G., & Jorgensen, M. (2005). What distinguishes autism spectrum disorders from other developmental disorders before the age of four years? *European Child & Adolescent Psychiatry, 14*, 65-72.

Tsai, D. (2006). Confucianism, autonomy and patient care. *Southern Medical Journal, 99*, 685-687.

Tsai, G., & Alanis, L. (2004). The Native American culture: A historical and reflective perspective. *NASP Communique, 32*, #8.

Tur-Kaspa, H., & Dromi, E. (2001). Grammatical deviations in the spoken and written language of Hebrew-speaking children with hearing impairments. *Language, Speech, and Hearing Services in Schools, 32*, 79-89.

Uccelli, P., & Pez, M. M. (2007). Narrative and vocabulary development of bilingual children from kindergarten to first grade: Developmental changes and associations among English and Spanish skills. *Language, Speech, and Hearing Services in Schools, 38*, 225-236.

Uffen, E. (1998). Where the jobs are: Keeping an eye on the future. *Asha, 40*, 24-28.

Ukrainetz, T.A. (Ed.) (2006). *Contextualized language intervention: Scaffolding PreK-12 literacy achievement*. Eau Claire, WI: Thinking Publications.

Ukrainetz, T.A., Harpell, S., Walsh, C., & Coyle, C. (2000). A preliminary investigation of dynamic assessment with Native American kindergarteners. *Language, Speech, and Hearing Services in Schools, 31*, 142-154.

Unger, J. B., Shakib, S., Boley Cruz, T., Hoffman, B. R., Howard Pitney, B., & Pohrbach, L. A. (2003). Smoking behavior among urban and rural Native American adolescents in California. *American Journal of Preventive Medicine, 25*, 251-254.

United Nations Economic and Social Commission for Asia and the Pacific (2002). Focus on ability, celebrate diversity: Highlights of the Asian and Pacific Decade of Disabled Persons, 1993-2002. Special needs education survey project in Samoa. Retrieved 6/21/07 from http://www.unescap.org/esid/psis/publicaitons/spps/13/chap9.htm.

University of Michigan Health System (2007). *Program for multicultural health*. Retrieved 3/3/07 from http://www.med.umich.edu/multicultural/ccp%20/nativeamerican.htm.

Updegraff, K.A., McHale, S.M., Whiteman, S.D., Thayer, S.M., & Delgado, M.Y. (2005). Adolescent sibling relationships in Mexican American families: Exploring the role of familism. *Journal of Family Psychology, 19*, 512-522.

Urban Institute (2006). *Young children of immigrants in two-parent families have triple poverty rate of children with U.S.-born parents*. Retrieved 8/15/06 from http://www.urban.org/publications/900779.html.

U.S. Bureau of the Census (1986). *Statistical abstract of the United States, 1987* (107th ed.). Washington, DC: U.S. Government Printing Office.

U.S. Bureau of the Census (1987). *Statistical abstract of the United States, 1988* (108th ed.). Washington, DC: U.S. Department of Commerce.

U.S. Bureau of the Census (1990). *Statistical abstract of the United States, 1990* (110th ed.). Washington, DC: U.S. Department of Commerce.

U.S. Bureau of the Census (1992). *Statistical abstract of the United States, 1992* (112th ed.). Washington, DC: U.S. Government Printing Office.

U.S. Bureau of the Census (1999). *Statistical abstract of the United States, 1999* (119th ed.). Washington, DC: U.S. Department of Commerce.

U.S. Bureau of the Census (2000). *Statistical abstract of the United States, 2000* (120th ed.). Washington, DC: U.S. Department of Commerce.

U.S. Bureau of the Census (2005). *Statistical abstract of the United States, 2005* (125th ed.). Washington, DC: U.S. Department of Commerce.

U.S. Bureau of the Census (2006). *Black History Month: February 2007*. Retrieved 2/7/07 from htp://www.census.gov/Press-Release/www/releases/archives/facts_for_features_special_edi.

U.S. Bureau of the Census (2007). *Statistical abstract of the United States, 2007* (127th ed.). Washington, DC: U.S. Department of Commerce.

U.S. Center for Immigration Studies (2001). Information available from http://www.cis.org/articles/2001/back101.html.

U.S. Center for Immigration Studies (2003). Immigration in a time of recession: An examination of trends since 2000 (as summarized by Steven A. Camarota). Retrieved 7/4/04 from http://www.cis.org/articles/2003/back1603.html.

U.S. Central Intelligence Agency (2004). *The world factbook: Russia*. Retrieved July 1, 2004, from www.cia.gov/cia/publications/factbook/geos/rs.html.

U.S. Department of Agriculture (2007). *Rural income, poverty, and welfare: High-poverty counties*. Retrieved 2/28/07 from http://www.ers.usda.gov/Briefing/IncomePovertyWelfare/HighPoverty/Analysis.htm.

U.S. Department of Health and Human Services (1985). Health status of minorities and low income groups *(DHHD Publication No. [HRSA] HRS-P-DV 85-1)*. Washington, DC: U.S. Government Printing Office.

U.S. Department of State (2004). *Background note: Russia*. Retrieved July 1, 2004 from www.state.gov/r/pa/ei/bgn/3183.htm.

U.S. Department of State (2006). *Countries and numbers of U.S. adoptions in 2006*. Available at http://travel.state.gov/family/adoption/adoption_485.html.

U.S. Environmental Protection Agency (2007). *Protect your child from lead poisoning*. Retrieved 2/24/07 from http://search.netscape.com.

U.S. State Department (2007). *Immigrant Visas Issued to Orphans Coming to the U.S.* Available at http://travel.state.gov/orphan_numbers_html.

Valdivia, R. (1999). The implications of culture on developmental delay. *ERIC Digest*; ERIC Clearinghouse on Disabilities and Gifted Education.

vanBiervliet, A., & Parette, H.P. (2002). Development and evaluation of the families, cultures and augmentative and alternative communication (AAC) multimedia program. *Disability and Rehabililtation, 24*, 131-143.

Van Broekhuizen, L.D. (2006). *Sheltered English: Techniques for ensuring comprehension*. Retrieved 10/24/06 from http://prel.org/products/paced/oct04/re_sheltered.htm.

Van Hook, J., Brown, S.L., & Kwenda, M.N. (2003). One step forward, two steps back: The increase in immigrant child poverty from 1970 to 2000. Paper presented at the Population Association of America 2003 Annual Meeting, Minneapolis, MN. Retrieved 8/15/06 from http://paa2003.princeton.edu/abstractViewer.asp?submissionId=63346.

van Keulen, J.E., Weddington, G.T., & DeBose, C.E. (1998). *Speech, language, learning and the African American child*. Needham Heights, MA: Allyn & Bacon.

van Kleeck, A. (1994). Potential cultural bias in training parents as conversational partners with their children who have delays in language development. *American Journal of Speech-Language Pathology, 3(1)*, 67-78.

Vang, C. T. (2005). Hmong-American students still face multiple challenges in public schools. *Multicultural Education, 13*, 27-35.

Vang, H., & Barrera, M.T. (2005). Hmong parents' perceptions on instructional strategies for educating their children with disabilities. *Hmong Studies Journal, 5*, 1-20.

Vansteenkiste, M., Zhou, M., Lens, W., & Soenens, B . (2005). Experiences of autonomy and control among Chinese learners: Vitalizing or immobilizing? *Journal of Educational Psychology, 97*, 468-483.

Vaughn, S., Linan-Thompson, S., Mathes, P.G., Cirino, P.T., Carlson, C.D., Pollard-Durodola, S.D., Cardenas-Hagan, E., & Francis, D.J. (2006). Effectiveness of Spanish intervention for first-grade English language learners at risk for reading difficulties. *Journal of Learning Disabilities, 39*, 56-73.

Vaughn, S., Mathes, P.G., Linan-Thompson, S., & Francis, D. (2005). Teaching English language learners at risk for reading disabilities to read: Putting research into practice. *Learning Disabilities Research and Practice, 20*, 58-67.

Verhallen, M.J.A.J., Bus, A.G., & de Jong, M.T. (2006). The promise of multimedia stories for kindergarten children at risk. *Journal of Educational Psychology, 98*, 410-419.

Visscher, C. (2006). Understanding the cultural/religious mélange in treating Chinese patients. *Southern Medical Journal, 99*, 683-684.

Vygotsky, L.S. (1962). *Thought and language*. Cambridge, MA.: MIT Press.

Wagner, R. K., Francis, D. J., & Morris, R. D. (2005). Identifying English language learners with learning disabilities: Key challenges and possible approaches. *Learning Disabilities Research & Practice, 20*, 6-15.

Wallace, I.F., Roberts, J.E., & Lodder, D.E. (1998). Interactions of African American infants and their mothers: Relations with development at 1 year of age. *Journal of Speech-Language-Hearing Research, 41(4)*, 900-912.

Wallach, G.P., & Madding, C.C. (2001, November). *Language-based literacy intervention: From language disorders to language differences*. Short course presented at the annual convention of the American Speech-Language-Hearing Association, New Orleans, Louisiana.

Walqui, A. (2006). Scaffolding instruction for English language learners: A conceptual framework. *International Journal of Bilingual Education and Bilingualism, 9*, 159-180.

Wang, K., Hsieh, K., Heller, T., Davidson, P., & Janicki, M. (2007). Carer reports of health status among adults with intellectual/developmental disabilities in Taiwan living at home and in institutions. *Journal of Intellectual Disability Research, 51*, 173-183.

Wang, M., Park, Y., & Lee, K.R. (2006). Korean-English biliteracy acquisition: Cross-language phonological and orthographic transfer. *Journal of Educational Psychology, 98*, 148-158.

Warne, D. (2006). Research and educational approaches to reducing health disparities among American Indians and Alaska Natives. *Journal of Transcultural Nursing, 17*, 266-271.

Washington, J.A. (2001). Early literacy skills in African American children: Research considerations. *Learning Disabilities Research and Practice, 16*, 213-219.

Washington, J.A., & Craig, H.K. (1994). Dialectal forms during discourse of poor, urban, African American preschoolers. *Journal of Speech and Hearing Research, 37(4)*, 816-823.

Washington, J.A., & Craig, H.K. (2004). A language screening protocol for use with young African American children in urban settings. *American Journal of Speech-Language Pathology, 13*, 329-340.

Washington, J.A., Craig, H.K., & Kushmaul, A.J. (1998). Variable use of African American English across two language sampling contexts. *Journal of Speech-Language-Hearing Research, 41(5)*, 1115-1124.

Wasik, B.A., Bond, M.A., & Hindman, A. (2006). The effects of a language and literacy intervention on Head Start children and teachers. *Journal of Educational Psychology, 98*, 63-74.

Weaver, G. (2006). *The American cultural tapestry.* Retrieved 12/27/06 from http://usinfo.state.gov/journals/itsv/0606/ijse/weaver.htm

Weiner, C. (2001). *Preparing for success: Meeting the language and learning needs of young children from poverty homes.* Youngtown, AZ: ECL Publications.

Weiss, A.L. (2002). Planning language intervention for young children. In D.K. Bernstein., & E. Tiegerman-Farber (Eds.), *Language and communication disorders in children* (5th ed.) (pp. 256-314). Boston, MA: Allyn & Bacon.

Westby, C.E. (1990). Ethnographic interviewing: Asking the right questions to the right people in the right ways. *Journal of Childhood Communication Disorders, 13 (1)*, 101-111.

Westby, C.E. (1997). There's more to passing than knowing the answers. *Language, Speech, and Hearing Services in Schools, 28(3)*, 274-287.

Westby, C.E. (2007). Child maltreatment: A global issue. *Language, Speech, and Hearing Services in Schools, 38,* 140-148.

Westby, C.E., Dezale, J., Fradd, S.F., & Lee, O. (1999). Learning to do science: Influences of culture and language. *Communication Disorders Quarterly, 21(1)*, 50-63.

Westby, C., & Vining, C.B. (2002). Living in harmony: Providing services to Native American children and families. In D.E. Battle (Ed.), *Communication disorders in multicultural populations* (3rd ed.) (pp. 135-178). Woburn, MA: Butterworth-Heinemann.

Western, B., & Petit, B. (2005). Black-White wage inequality, employment rates, and incarceration. *American Journal of Sociology, 111,* 553-578.

Wetherby, A., & Prizant, B. (1993). Communication and Symbolic Behavior Scales. Chicago: Riverside Publishing.

White-Kaulaity, M. (2007). Reflections on Native American reading: A seed, a tool, and a weapon. *Journal of Adolescent & Adult Literacy, 50,* 560-566.

Whitmore, K.F., & Crowell, C.G. (2006). Bilingual education students reflect on their language education: Reinventing a classroom 10 years later. *Journal of Adolescent and Adult Literacy, 49,* 270-285.

Wigginton, E. (1992). Culture begins at home. *Educational Leadership, 49 (4)*, 60-64.

Wiig, E.H., Langdon, H.W., & Flores, N. (2001). Nominación rápida y automatica en niños hispano hablantes bilingües y monolingües. *Revista de Logopedia y Foniatria, 21,* 106-117.

Wiig, E.H., Zureich, P., & Chan, H.W. (2000). A clinical rationale for assessing rapid naming abilities in children with language disorders. *Journal of Learning Disabilities, 33,* 359-374.

Wilder, L.K., Dyches, T.T., Obiakor, F.E., & Algozzine, B. (2004). Multicultural perspectives on teaching students with autism. *Focus on Autism and Other Developmental Disabilities, 19,* 105-113.

Wiley, T.G. (2002). Accessing language rights in education: A brief history of the U.S. Context. In O. García & C. Baker (Eds.), *Bilingual education: An introductory reader* (pp. 89-107). Clevedon, England: Multilingual Matters Ltd.

Williams, K. (1997). *Expressive Vocabulary Test.* Circle Pines, MN: American Guidance Service.

Willis, W. (2004). Families with African American roots. In E.W. Lynch and M.J. Hanson (Eds.), *Developing cross-cultural competence: A guide for working with young children and their families* (3rd ed.) (pp. 141-178). Baltimore: Paul H. Brookes Publishing Co.

Wilson, F. (1998). Delivering speech, language, and hearing services in the Arab world: Some cultural considerations: In D.E. Battle (Ed.). Communication disorders in multicultural populations (2nd ed.) (pp.197-202). Newton, MA: Butterworth-Heinemann.

Wilson, F., Wilson, J.R., & Coleman, T.J. (2000). Culturally appropriate assessment: Issues and strategies. In T.J. Coleman, *Clinical management of communication disorders in culturally diverse children* (pp. 202-238) Needham Heights, MA: Allyn & Bacon.

Windsor, J., & Kohnert, K. (2004). The search for common ground: Part I. Lexical performance by linguistically diverse learners. *Journal of Speech, Language, and Hearing Research, 47,* 877-890.

Wiseman, A. W. (2000). Navajo transition to higher education: Knowledge systems, cultural values, and educational policies. *International Journal of Educational Research, 33,* 621-629.

Wolf, M., Bowers, P., & Biddle, K. (2000). Naming-speed processes, timing, and reading: A conceptual review. *Journal of Learning Disabilities, 33,* 387-407.

Wolfe, P. (2001). *Brain matters: Translating research into classroom practice.* Alexandria, VA: Association for Supervision and Curriculum Development.

Wong, A.M.-Y., Au, C.W.-S. & Stokes, S.F. (2004). Three measures of language production for Cantonese-speaking school-age children in a story-retelling task. *Journal of Speech, Language, and Hearing Research, 43,* 1322-1336.

Wong, A. M., Leonard, L.B., Fletcher, P. & Stokes, S.F. (2004). Questions without movement: A study of Cantonese-speaking children without specific language impairment. *Journal of Speech, Language, and Hearing Research, 47,* 1440-1453.

Wong, F., & Halgin, R. (2006). The "model minority": Bane or blessing for Asian Americans? *Journal of Multicultural Counseling and Development, 34,* 38-49.

Wong, V., Hui, L., Lee, W., Leung, L.S.J, Ho, P.P, Lau, W.C., Fung, C.W., & Chung, B. (2004). A modified screening tool for autism (Checklist for Autism in Toddlers [CHAT-23]) for Chinese children. *Pediatrics, 114,* 176.

Wong Fillmore, L. (1976). The second time around: Cognitive and social strategies in second language acquisition. Unpublished doctoral dissertation, Stanford University.

Wong Fillmore, L. (2000). Loss of family languages: Should educators be concerned? *Theory into Practice, 39,* 203-210.

Woolfolk, A. (2004). *Educational psychology* (9th ed.). Boston: Allyn & Bacon.

World Health Organization (2004). Health statistics. Available at http://www.who.int/en/.

Wyatt, T. (1997). Developing a culturally sensitive preschool screening tool. *Asha, 39(2)*, 50-51.

Wyatt, T. (1998). Children's language development. In C.M. Seymour & E. H. Nober, *Introduction to communication disorders: A multicultural approach* (pp. 59-86). Newton, MA: Butterworth-Heinemann.

Yamey, G., & Greenwood, R. (2004). Religious views of the 'medical' rehabilitation model: a pilot qualitative study. *Disability and Rehabilitation, 26*, 455-462.

Yan, R. (2003). Parental perceptions on maintaining heritage languages of CLD students. *Bilingual Review, 27*, 99-113.

Yan, W., & Lin, Q. (2005). Parent involvement and mathematics achievement: Contrast across racial and ethnic groups. The Journal of Educational Research, 99, 116-127.

Yeh, C.J., Chen, J., Kwong, A., Chiang, L., Wang, Y., & Pu-Folkes, F. (2002). Educators of Asian bilingual students: Pedagogical techniques, strategies and challenges. *Journal of Multilingual and Multicultural Development, 23*, 296-315.

Yoshinaga-Itano, C. (2003). From screening to early identification and intervention: Discovering predictors to successful outcomes for children with hearing loss. *Journal of Deaf Studies and Deaf Education, 8*, 11-30.

Yunus, S.M. (2005). Childcare practices in three Asian countries. *International Journal of Early Childhood, 37*, 39-56.

Zecker, L.B. (2004). Learning to read and write in two languages: The development of early biliteracy abilities. In C.A. Stone, E.R. Silliman, B.J. Ehren, & K. Apel (Eds.), *Handbook of language and literacy: Development and disorders* (pp. 248-265). New York: The Guilford Press.

Zelensky, E.K. (1999). Popular children's culture in post-perestroika Russia: Songs of innocence and experience revisited. In A.M. Barker (Ed.), *Consuming Russia (pp. 138-160)*. London: Duke University Press.

Zhao, G. (2007). The making of the modern subject: A cross-cultural analysis. *Educational Theory, 57*, 75-88.

Zorkaia, N., & Diuk, N.M. (2005). The values and attitudes of Russia's young people. *Russian Education and Society, 47*, 6-33.

Zuniga, M.E. (2004). Families with Latino roots. In E.W. Lynch & M.J. Hanson (Eds.), *Developing cross-cultural competence: A guide to working with young children and their families* (3rd ed.) (pp. 179-218). Baltimore: Paul H. Brookes Publishing Co.

Zwiers, J. (2005). The third language of academic English. *Educational Leadership, 62*, 60-63.

Index